THE ACHILLES TRAP

ALSO BY STEVE COLL

Directorate S

Private Empire

The Bin Ladens

Ghost Wars

On the Grand Trunk Road

Eagle on the Street (with David A. Vise)

The Taking of Getty Oil

The Deal of the Century

THE ACHILLES TRAP

SADDAM HUSSEIN, THE C.I.A.,
AND THE ORIGINS OF
AMERICA'S INVASION OF IRAQ

Steve Coll

PENGUIN PRESS
NEW YORK
2024

PENGUIN PRESS
An imprint of Penguin Random House LLC
penguinrandomhouse.com

Photo credit: p. iv, Chip HIRES/Gamma-Rapho via Getty Images

LIBRARY OF CONGRESS CATALOGING-IN-PUBLICATION DATA
Names: Coll, Steve, author.
Title: The Achilles trap : Saddam Hussein, the C.I.A., and
the origins of America's invasion of Iraq / Steve Coll.
Description: New York : Penguin Press, 2024. |
Includes bibliographical references and index.
Identifiers: LCCN 2023022034 (print) | LCCN 2023022035 (ebook) |
ISBN 9780525562269 (hardcover) | ISBN 9780525562276 (ebook)
Subjects: LCSH: Iraq War, 2003–2011. | Hussein, Saddam,
1937–2006. | United States. Central Intelligence Agency. |
United States—Politics and government—2001–2009. |
Iraq—Politics and government—2003– | United States—
Foreign relations—Iraq. | Iraq—Foreign relations—United States.
Classification: LCC DS79.76 .C654 2024 (print) | LCC DS79.76 (ebook) |
DDC 956.7044/3—dc23/eng/20231117
LC record available at https://lccn.loc.gov/2023022034
LC ebook record available at https://lccn.loc.gov/2023022035

Printed in the United States of America
1 3 5 7 9 10 8 6 4 2

Designed by Amanda Dewey
Maps by Jeffrey L. Ward

For Eliza

Author's Note

Sarah Moawad, who earned a master's degree in Middle Eastern studies from Harvard and another in journalism from Columbia, made vitally important contributions to this book. She tracked down sources, helped conduct interviews, traveled to Jordan, and translated archival Arabic-language material with exceptional clarity. Her passion for the subject matter and her engagement with our sources inspired me throughout, and I owe her an immeasurable debt. Amel Brahmi, an experienced French journalist who is now a doctoral student at Columbia, also made invaluable contributions. She tracked down important Iraqi, French, and photographic sources, adding to the book's detail and authority. Finally, on this five-year project's last lap, David Kortava, a writer and fact-checker at *The New Yorker*, recontacted interviewees and rechecked documentary sources, adding nuance and clarity while also rescuing me from embarrassing errors. I am also indebted to many others, as described in the acknowledgments.

CONTENTS

List of Maps

Cast of Characters

Saddam Hussein and His Closest Family

Saddam Hussein, born on April 28, 1937

Subha Tulfah al-Musallat, his mother, died in 1983

Hussein al-Majid, his natural father, died before Saddam's birth

Ibrahim al-Hassan, his stepfather

Khairallah Tulfah, his uncle and mentor

Sajida Khairallah Tulfah, Saddam's wife, married in 1963

Uday, son, born in 1964

Qusay, son, born in 1966

Raghad, daughter, born in 1968

Rana, daughter, born in 1969

Hala, daughter, born in 1972

Hussein Kamel al-Majid, son-in-law married to Raghad, born in 1954

Saddam Kamel al-Majid, son-in-law married to Rana, born in 1960

Sabawi al-Tikriti, half brother, born to his mother and stepfather
    in 1947

Barzan Ibrahim al-Tikriti, half brother, born in 1951

Watban al-Tikriti, half brother, born in 1952

Samira Shahbandar, Saddam's paramour and rumored second wife

In Saddam's Government

Tariq Aziz, Saddam's principal external envoy

Izzat Ibrahim al-Douri, Revolutionary Command Council

Nizar Hamdoon, ambassador in Washington and at the U.N.

Jafar Dhia Jafar, physicist and nuclear program leader

Abid Hamid Mahmud, Saddam's personal secretary

Ali Hassan al-Majid ("Chemical Ali"), Baath Party commander, minister, and governor

Taha Yassin Ramadan, Revolutionary Command Council

In the Iraqi Opposition

Ayad Allawi, medical doctor and leader of the Iraqi National Accord

Ahmad Chalabi, banker and leader of the Iraqi National Congress

Masoud Barzani, leader of the Kurdistan Democratic Party

Wafiq al-Samarrai, former general in military intelligence and C.I.A. liaison

Hussain Al-Shahristani, physicist and humanitarian activist

Mohammed Abdullah Shawani, former Iraqi special forces commander

Jalal Talabani, leader of the Patriotic Union of Kurdistan

At the C.I.A.

Frank Anderson, head of Middle East operations under George H. W. Bush and Bill Clinton

Robert Baer, operations officer specializing in the Middle East

William Casey, director under Ronald Reagan

John Deutch, director under Bill Clinton

John Maguire, case officer in Amman under Bill Clinton, deputy head of the Iraq Operations Group under George W. Bush

David Manners, Amman station chief

Bruce Riedel, Middle East analyst and White House policy adviser

Luis Rueda, head of the Iraq Operations Group under George W. Bush

Charles "Charlie" Seidel, Baghdad station chief

George Tenet, director under Bill Clinton and George W. Bush

Thomas "Tom" Twetten, Amman station chief, later head of Middle East operations and deputy director of operations

At the State Department

William Eagleton, ambassador to Iraq for Ronald Reagan

April Glaspie, ambassador to Iraq for George H. W. Bush

David Mack, senior diplomat in Iraq and Washington

David George Newton, ambassador to Iraq for Ronald Reagan

Joseph Wilson, deputy chief of mission in Iraq under George H. W. Bush

At the Pentagon

Colin Powell, chairman of the Joint Chiefs of Staff under George H. W. Bush and Bill Clinton, secretary of state under George W. Bush

Rick Francona, Defense Intelligence Agency liaison to Baghdad

W. Patrick "Pat" Lang, Middle East analyst and Defense Intelligence Agency liaison to Baghdad

At the White House

Samuel "Sandy" Berger, national security adviser to Bill Clinton

Richard Haass, Middle East adviser to George H. W. Bush

Martin Indyk, Middle East adviser to Bill Clinton

Anthony "Tony" Lake, national security adviser to Bill Clinton

Robert "Bud" McFarlane, national security adviser to Ronald Reagan

Condoleezza Rice, national security adviser to George W. Bush

At the United Nations

Rolf Ekéus, director of the U.N. Special Commission to disarm Iraq

Hans Blix, director general of the International Atomic Energy Agency

Charles Duelfer, deputy director of the U.N. Special Commission

Scott Ritter, inspector at the U.N. Special Commission

THE ACHILLES TRAP

Introduction

n October 2003, seven months after the American-led invasion of Iraq, I traveled to Baghdad on assignment for *The Washington Post*. Saddam Hussein was by then a fugitive in hiding. Occasional car bombs rattled the capital, a prelude of much worse to come. One afternoon, at a fortified compound near the Republican Palace, I met Hamish Killip, a British investigator with the Iraq Survey Group, a C.I.A.-sponsored multinational task force dispatched at the onset of the invasion to find Saddam's hidden stocks of nuclear, biological, and chemical weapons. By now it was apparent that Iraq possessed no such weapons. The shock of this revelation had already touched off investigations into the profound failures of U.S. intelligence and White House decision-making. In Iraq, the Survey Group's mission had unexpectedly changed from hunting for weapons to sorting truth from lies in the history of the Saddam Hussein regime.

One set of questions involved Saddam's motivations. Why had he seemingly sacrificed his long reign in power by giving the impression that he had dangerous weapons when, in fact, he had none? Or as Killip put it that afternoon, addressing Saddam: "What was so damned important that you were willing to go through all of this?"

Across town, I met David Kay, the Survey Group's leader. He was exploring a theory that Saddam had been bluffing—pretending that he might have WMD in order to deter the radical ayatollahs of Iran from attacking Iraq. And yet the matter seemed uncertain, Kay told me, since Saddam did not appear to have been particularly afraid of Iran. When one of his ministers had worried aloud that Iran might pursue its own nuclear or chemical arsenal, Saddam had reportedly replied, "Don't worry about the Iranians. If they ever get WMD, the Americans and the Israelis will destroy them."

This was vintage Saddam, I now recognize—half joking, capable of striking prescience, reliably fixated on American and Israeli power, and, above all, impossible to reduce to a simple explanation. Successive American presidents misjudged him. They often dismissed him as a cartoon autocrat, akin to the faux Adolf Hitler played for laughs by Charlie Chaplin in *The Great Dictator*. Certainly, Saddam Hussein was as unsubtle as a shotgun blast. He was a cruel tyrant directly responsible for the deaths of hundreds of thousands of Iraqis, as well as for the torture or imprisonment of many tens of thousands more. Without serious provocation, he invaded two of his neighbors, Iran and Kuwait. During the Iran-Iraq War, he gassed Iranian troops and his own rebellious Kurdish population. During the Gulf War, he lobbed terrifying Scud missiles at Saudi Arabia and Israel. He plastered Iraq with his image to promote his cult of personality. His speeches were often bombastic and alarming. Against such a record, it seems more than a little odd to argue that Saddam's enemies failed to grasp important nuances of the man and his rule through the Baath Party. Yet as America's tragic invasion to eliminate a nonexistent WMD arsenal amply demonstrated, there was more to Saddam than Washington's politicians and spies could grasp—even when the stakes were very high.

The Achilles Trap is an investigation into how this failure of comprehension unfolded. It seeks to enlarge the story of the 2003 invasion's origins by elevating Saddam's side of the conflict and by adding substantial new information. Saddam left an extraordinary and still mostly secret trove of about two thousand hours of tape recordings of his leadership meetings—private discussions he recorded as assiduously as Richard Nixon—as well as meeting minutes, intelligence files, and other materials. They document what the Iraqi leader was saying privately at turning points of his struggle against the United States. The Saddam tapes have a complicated, problematic history. They were captured by invading U.S. forces and repatriated to Iraq in 2013, but most have never been released, and virtually all are currently unavailable to researchers (see "A Note on Sources"). During the more than four years I worked on *The Achilles Trap*, I obtained several hundred transcripts, audio files, and document sets, including those of Saddam's internal discussions. With support from Adam Marshall and the Reporters Committee for Freedom of the Press, I sued the Pentagon under the Freedom of Information Act and acquired a cache of 145 transcripts and files, including materials never before published. The scholar Michael Brill generously shared his sizable private archive assembled from previously open sources since closed. By connecting these and additional parts of the captured files with other sources, including interviews with surviving participants, it became possible to see in new ways what drove Saddam in his struggle with Washington, and to understand how and why American thinking about him was often wrong, distorted, or incomplete.

Starting with Saddam's rise to unchecked power in 1979 and the birth of Iraq's secret nuclear-weapons program soon afterward, it is a story that encompasses diverse episodes and crises: Saddam's furtive collaboration with the C.I.A. during the 1980s; the Gulf War of 1991; the struggle over Iraqi disarmament that followed; and the climactic confrontation after 9/11. One recurring theme is the trouble American decision-makers had in assessing Saddam's resentments and managing his inconsistencies. It is a theme that resonates in our present age of authoritarian rulers, when the world's stressed democracies seek to grasp the often unpredictable decision-making of cloistered rulers, such as Vladimir Putin, or to influence other closed dictatorships, such as North Korea's. Saddam believed—not without reason—that he was besieged by would-be assassins and international conspirators. He was very keen to remain in power. About this, he was exceptionally cunning. In discussions with comrades—he usually did most of the talking—he

regularly steered the conversation around to the subject of conspiracies. In his worldview, nothing was ever quite what it seemed. Great
Powers like America and regional powers like Iraq were ceaselessly
plotting in the shadows against one another. In one memorable meeting, he mused aloud about the relative strengths of the spy services
out to get him. (He gave high marks to the Israelis and the British.)
And, of course, they *were* out to get him.

One after another, three American presidents—George H. W. Bush,
Bill Clinton, and George W. Bush—signed Top Secret "findings" directing the C.I.A. to overthrow Saddam. This campaign to foster a
coup d'état in Baghdad, which lasted from May 1991 until the 2003
invasion, proved to be spectacularly unsuccessful. As recently available
records show, Saddam was well aware of the C.I.A.'s not-so-covert actions, which he regarded, in any event, as nothing new or unexpected—
just another day at the office. Saddam entered politics as a Baath Party
assassin. He and his comrades had grappled as young revolutionaries
with the C.I.A.'s prior involvement in Iraqi affairs, dating to 1963,
when the C.I.A. supported a Cold War–driven coup that briefly
brought the Baath Party to power.

Like many people in the Middle East and elsewhere, Saddam thought
of the C.I.A. as all-knowing. This contributed to his own misunderstandings of America, which were at least as profound as America's misunderstandings of him. For instance, after 1991, Saddam assumed that
the C.I.A. *knew* that he had no WMD, and so he interpreted American
and British accusations about his supposed arsenal of nukes and germ
bombs as merely propaganda lines in a long-running conspiracy to get
rid of him. He resisted the disarmament inspections demanded by
Washington and London as a possible alternative to war partly because
he saw the camera-wielding, walkie-talkie-toting inspectors as spies
with a hidden agenda—again, not without reason. A C.I.A. capable of
making a gigantic analytical mistake on the scale of its error about Iraqi
WMD was not part of Saddam's worldview.

For its part, the C.I.A.—assigned a central role in America's dramas with Saddam from the early 1980s onward—suffered from White Houses and agency leaders who often halfheartedly deployed their spies as if they were wizards with magic wands, conjurers who might solve the otherwise unsolvable Saddam problem. This was a prescription for failure, history showed, but the C.I.A. has been no better at learning from its own history than the nation it serves. Although marked by episodes of daring, success, and shrewd judgment—and populated by a remarkable cast of committed American operatives— the C.I.A.'s record in Iraq after 1991 was mostly one of operational and analytical calamities. This is not just an outsider's hindsight verdict. Inside the C.I.A. during the late 1990s, the Iraq Operations Group was known sardonically as "the House of Broken Toys."

In addition to the stories of Saddam and his flamboyantly brutal ruling family, I have chronicled the sometimes astonishing experiences of other Iraqis who lived on the front lines of the conflict with Washington, such as Jafar Dhia Jafar, the British-educated physicist who was the intellectual leader of Iraq's atomic-bomb program, and Tariq Aziz, Saddam's longtime envoy. No dictatorship is a monolith, and I hope the complicated lives of talented Iraqi patriots who accommodated Saddam may add dimension to our understanding of what the regime was and how it so confounded America. Equally, I have tried to humanize some of Saddam's victims and opponents (also Iraqi patriots), such as Hussain Al-Shahristani, the Canadian-educated physicist who worked with Jafar on the nuclear program but was tortured and then imprisoned after refusing Saddam's entreaties to help build a bomb.

Much of America's self-examination since 2003 has concentrated on the post-9/11 run-up to the invasion—the false claims about Iraqi WMD, the media's complicity, neoconservative hubris, and George W. Bush's choices. Investigative journalists have produced a remarkable shelf of book-length work on the C.I.A.'s covert-action campaigns before and after 9/11, the Bush administration's selling of the war, and the intrigues of specific episodes, such as that involving the infamous intelligence source known as Curveball. In addition, there have been significant studies of the conflict that go back to its origins. In September 2004, the Survey Group, under its second leader, Charles Duelfer, published a multivolume study of the history of the Saddam Hussein regime's internal dynamics and weapons programs. In recent years, scholars have dug into the available regime files and offered groundbreaking insights or brought forward other new information. I have relied gratefully on all of this documentary record, journalism, and scholarship.

America's conflict with Saddam Hussein is saturated in the primary colors of political history—the corruptions of power, the follies of war, the lies of diplomacy, the price of dissent, the absurdity of vanity. It is a story of avoidable errors of statecraft that exacted an immeasurable toll in human life and suffering. Some of these errors resulted from blindness about the enemy, others from "mirroring," the human habit of assuming that adversaries will analyze a situation as you would and act accordingly. Saddam was right that nothing in this long struggle was quite what it seemed. Much of what mattered lay hidden from public view. It is in these shadows, as Saddam Hussein reaches a fateful decision to inaugurate a secret atomic-bomb program, that *The Achilles Trap* begins.

BAGHDAD IN THE SADDAM HUSSEIN ERA

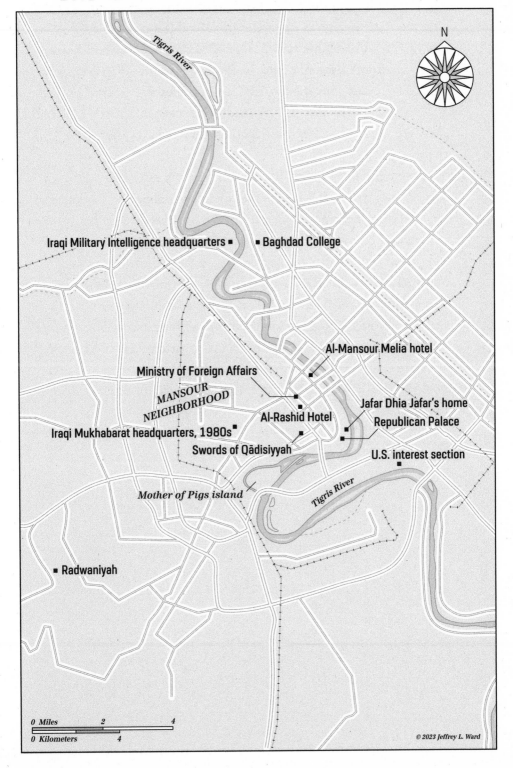

Tigris River

N

Iraqi Military Intelligence headquarters ■   ■ Baghdad College

Al-Mansour Melia hotel

Ministry of Foreign Affairs

MANSOUR
NEIGHBORHOOD

Jafar Dhia Jafar's home
Republican Palace

Iraqi Mukhabarat headquarters, 1980s ■   Al-Rashid Hotel

Swords of Qādisiyyah

U.S. interest section

Mother of Pigs island

Tigris River

■ Radwaniyah

0 Miles   2   4
0 Kilometers   4

© 2023 Jeffrey L. Ward

PART ONE

THE ENEMY OF MY ENEMY

December 1979 to August 1990

ONE

The Physicist and
the Dictator

Jafar Dhia Jafar downed a last glass of sugared tea and slid into a chauffeured Toyota Crown Saloon for his morning commute to the Tuwaitha Nuclear Research Center, a drive of about twelve miles from his home in Baghdad, where he resided in a neighborhood of former palaces and ministerial residences. It was December 4, 1979, and Jafar, a senior scientific adviser in Iraq's nuclear program, expected a typical day of meetings and consultations. He was thirty-seven years old, tall and evenly featured, reserved in manner and deliberate in speech. In addition to Arabic, he spoke English fluently, in a refined British accent acquired during years of study at the University of Birmingham, where he had earned a doctorate in nuclear physics and met a British woman, Phyllis, who became his wife. His Iraqi colleagues thought of him as aristocratic. Jafar's maternal grandfather had served as a provincial governor, and his father had been a minister in Iraq's last royal government until it was overthrown in a bloody 1958 revolution. Successive coups had overtaken the Jafars' world of elegant privilege, yet his family had adapted and persevered. Their Baghdad properties included a traditional riverside home with latticed windows near the British embassy. Jafar had a new house under construction nearby, as well as a flat in London.[1]

The Nuclear Research Center was an industrial-looking complex of about five dozen buildings surrounded by irrigated wheat fields, set beside a meander in the Tigris River. Jafar passed through its heavily guarded gates. To one side was the pride of Iraq's program, a five-megawatt IRT-5000 research reactor purchased from the Soviet Union during the 1960s. Jafar's office was in a low-slung headquarters building, near a library.[2]

That morning, he visited the center's director general, Humam Abdul Khaliq, a longtime member of President Saddam Hussein's ruling Baath Party—formally, the Baath Arab Socialist Party. Khaliq was an amiable man with a graduate degree in physics, also earned in Britain. They were discussing administrative matters when Khaliq's phone rang. Jafar listened as the director spoke curtly, seeming to take orders.

After he hung up, the director said the secret police were coming.

They wanted to speak with Hussain Al-Shahristani, a senior scientist at Tuwaitha and a good friend of Jafar's. The two mid-career physicists were the same age. They had recently traveled together to France, where they had worked on Iraq's acquisition of two new French-made nuclear research reactors that were to be installed at the research center, with the goal of greatly expanding Iraq's work in fields such as power generation and medicine. Shahristani had earned his doctorate at the University of Toronto, where he had met his Canadian wife, Berniece, a convert to Islam. He belonged to a well-known family of Islamic scholars in the Shia tradition of Islam, one of the faith's two major branches.

Jafar feared he knew why Shahristani might now be in difficulty. Jafar, whose family was also Shia, was not especially religious, but his friend was devout. Shahristani prayed five times every day; at Tuwaitha, in lieu of a prayer rug, he sometimes unfurled computer paper on the floor and bowed toward Mecca. For many years, his devotion had seemed of little consequence to Jafar and other colleagues, but the climate in Iraq around politics and Islam was shifting.[3]

In neighboring Iran, Ayatollah Khomeini had announced a militant revolution in the name of Shia Islam. Khomeini despised Saddam Hussein. (Saddam and many Baath Party leaders were Sunni, the most prevalent branch of Islam worldwide but a minority within Iraq.) Khomeini predicted "that pig" in Baghdad would fall within six months because of a "revolution like ours." An underground Shiite movement in Iraq, the Islamic Dawa Party, energized by Khomeini, had opened an office in Tehran and was planning assassination attempts against Baath Party leaders. Saddam's intelligence services were on high alert for spies and terrorists inspired by Khomeini. Shahristani was not a Dawa Party member, but he had met Khomeini years earlier and sympathized with the Iranian Revolution. He had contact with Iraqi Shiite activists. By attending meetings and helping out here and there, Shahristani hadn't done anything so seditious that it would be illegal in, say, Canada, but he was aware that Iraqi intelligence operated bluntly and that he was at risk. That autumn, he had told his wife to be ready to leave Iraq at any time.[4]

Jafar found Shahristani in his office. Soon, a captain in charge of security at Tuwaitha joined them. He gave a military salute.

"I have a question for Dr. Hussain," he said.

"Please ask," Shahristani replied.

"No, not here. Come with me outside."

The officer placed Shahristani under arrest. The reality of what had happened hit Jafar "like a thunderbolt." Iraq's police state operated through a vast web of overlapping forces. It outraged Jafar that the secret police could just walk into Tuwaitha and grab a scientist who served as a high-ranking adviser to the national nuclear program.

Shahristani turned to Jafar as he departed. "Please tell my family if I am late," he said.

From a window, Jafar watched the police bundle his friend into the back seat of an unmarked car with civilian plates. The vehicle sped away from Tuwaitha.[5]

The security men brought Shahristani to an interrogation room in the headquarters of a secret police force known informally as the Amn. It quickly became apparent that Jafar had been right—Shahristani had been arrested because of his contacts with the Dawa Party.

Yes, Shahristani explained, he had been involved in various religious activities while studying in Canada and England, but he had no "organizational relationship with any Islamic party."

His interrogators took him to another room and hung him on a hook attached to the ceiling. They administered electric shocks and beat him with whips and cables, demanding confessions. Shahristani lost all feeling in his arms and legs.

The police seemed fixated on a mysterious incident that had taken place earlier that year in France. On the night of April 6, 1979, in La Seyne-sur-Mer, on the French Mediterranean coast, saboteurs had broken into a warehouse and blown up sections of the new nuclear reactors that were to be installed at Tuwaitha. Shahristani had looked into the case and had concluded (correctly, as it turned out) that Israel's Mossad intelligence service had mounted the attack to set back Iraq's nuclear capabilities. His interrogators, however, offered another hypothesis: "We have confirmed information that Dr. Jafar was complicit, because his father was a minister during the royal era and he grew up and studied in England, so he is the party that was in contact with Western intelligence," they said, suggesting that he had colluded with the West to arrange the sabotage in France.

They offered to release Shahristani if he would name Jafar as a traitor.

"I cannot make such an accusation against Dr. Jafar," Shahristani said, as he recalled. In fact, neither he nor Jafar had anything to do with the sabotage in France.

The beatings and electric shocks resumed. Shahristani counted twenty-two consecutive days and nights of torture.[6]

Jafar visited Shahristani's home in Baghdad a couple of days after his colleague's arrest to check on Berniece and the family. He felt a duty to his friend. Two civilian security officers answered the door and aimed their pistols at him. Inside, nobody but the officers appeared to be present. The house had been ransacked; books and files lay on the floor. Jafar waited. Berniece soon returned with her children, understandably confused about what was happening. Jafar assured her that her husband "must be acquitted and he will return to his family safely, God willing."

In the days following, Jafar discussed Shahristani's detention with Khaliq and other bureaucrats at Tuwaitha, but they answered his concerns with a "terrible silence," stating only that they were instructed by the Baath Party not to interfere in the affairs of the secret police.

Jafar had once met Saddam, during a brief ceremonial visit. He decided to write to the Iraqi president. He thought he could appeal to Saddam's passionate support for Iraq's atomic-energy program. In a short letter, Jafar attested to Shahristani's reliability and warned that his colleague's imprisonment would damage Iraq's nuclear ambitions.[7]

He heard nothing. Jafar's relationship with Saddam's regime was delicate, if not precarious. He had declined to join the Baath Party; he did not wish to affiliate directly with the party's ideology and rule. His social background and prestigious education abroad cut both ways—it might protect him, since Saddam needed and promoted talented scientists, but it also might endanger him, since the secret police, like their president, were automatically suspicious of Iraqis with Western ties.

That December, Jafar decided to move his family out of harm's way. His wife, Phyllis, was away in England. Their two sons, Sadiq, fourteen, and Ameen, thirteen, were living with Jafar in Baghdad. He telephoned his old boarding school, Seaford College, in West Sussex, England, and asked to enroll his boys quickly. The headmaster agreed, and Jafar put his sons on a flight to London before Christmas.[8]

Late in December, Jafar again wrote to Saddam, repeating his earlier pleadings on Shahristani's behalf. On January 16, he received a telephone call from an official at the Iraqi Atomic Energy Commission, the political body that oversaw Iraq's nuclear activities. The caller asked Jafar to stay late after work at Tuwaitha that day for a meeting. When he arrived, he found a man from the General Intelligence Directorate, known as the Mukhabarat, waiting to arrest him.

The officer drove him to a former synagogue now occupied by the secret police. Guards handed Jafar pajamas and bedding and placed him in a windowless room holding four other detainees. One identified himself as Saddam's barber; he had been jailed after turning up late for a morning shift. Jafar was comforted to hear that none of the men had yet been physically assaulted. That night, however, he could hear prisoners wailing in nearby interrogation rooms.

He remained in this cell for two months, but his interrogators did not beat him or question him. Why had he been arrested? The distorted, ever-shifting suspicions of Iraq's police state could be difficult to parse, but it seemed very likely that Jafar's impertinence in writing to Saddam on Shahristani's behalf was the reason. By speaking up for his colleague, Jafar had violated Iraq's unwritten rules demanding silence about such matters.

In March 1980, Jafar's wardens transferred him to a larger cell with thick bars and a window looking out on a corridor. Here he was alone. The room contained a bed, a wardrobe, and a table with paper and pen. There was a note: "You can write to whomever you want, whenever you want." Soon he was dining on take-out kebabs from nearby restaurants. Yet he had no indication of how his detention might be resolved.

In June, they moved him again, this time to a cell with a window that looked out on a courtyard. After a few days, the prison's director met Jafar and escorted him to a government car. The director explained that Jafar was to meet the leader of the Mukhabarat—Barzan Ibrahim al-Tikriti, a half brother of Saddam's.[9]

On July 17, 1968, Saddam had ridden with Baath comrades into the Republican Palace on tanks and trucks to seize control of the Iraqi government. It was a landmark day in the "revolution"—in reality, more of a coup d'état—that would catapult Saddam to power. At Saddam's side was Barzan, a skinny bodyguard with a pistol and a readiness to use it. He had come of age "like a shadow" to Saddam, a constant presence during the 1960s, Iraq's tumultuous decade of conspiracies and coups. Saddam was fourteen years older than his half brother. They were bound not only by family but by murder. As a teenager, Saddam had shot dead a man over an employment dispute involving their extended families. The matter escalated, and Barzan, by his later account, subsequently killed four other men connected to the feud.[10]

After the July 17 takeover, Saddam became Iraq's vice president. He dispatched Barzan to Cairo to be trained in intelligence and security by the hard men of Egypt's police. When he returned, Saddam placed him in charge of security in his office. Barzan's receding hairline added years to his appearance—usefully so, given that he was still in his early twenties as he took command of powerful security services. He had dark eyes, kept a neat black mustache, and wore fashionable Western suits, in keeping with the Baath Party's urban, secular look. He exuded the callow hubris that can accompany the acquisition of vast authority in youth. He was unsubtle and easily offended. He struck some who encountered him as "a nitwit," as a scientist at Tuwaitha put it. In later years, Saddam came to think of him as "an asshole." Yet Saddam needed fiercely loyal henchmen.[11]

In 1977, over breakfast, Saddam asked Barzan to become the second-in-command at the Mukhabarat. "Barzan, you need to know something," Saddam told him. "We went down the road we did, and reached a point of no return. Therefore, we must continue to the end." This was typical of Saddam's aphoristic instructions to subordinates—menacing and vague.[12]

Barzan soon took full charge of an intelligence service that had officers and gunmen across Iraq and spies placed under diplomatic cover in embassies around the world. In 1979, Saddam became president and tightened his grip on Iraq. Barzan relished his mission: "Not even an Iraqi sitting in a café in a remote part of Japan would feel safe if he spoke disparagingly of Saddam and our regime," he recalled.[13]

On the day in June 1980 when Jafar met Barzan in his spacious office, he found the intelligence chief in a solicitous mood. Jafar's recollection of the discussion is consistent with other conversations Barzan had around this time, and with Barzan's later writings to Saddam.

"Have you been abused?" Barzan asked initially.

"I have not been mistreated," Jafar said, "but I do not know the reason for my arrest."

Barzan came to the point: "The president wants you to work toward producing a nuclear weapon for Iraq."

Jafar demurred. "I am a physicist, and I have no experience in this field," he said.

"We know you can do it," Barzan replied.

Of course, Jafar understood that the nuclear facilities and scientists at Tuwaitha might theoretically be employed in an attempt to build an atomic bomb. But such an effort would be very difficult, and it had never been seriously explored. After the Baath Party came to power in 1968, Iraq had signed the Nuclear Nonproliferation Treaty, which required the country to forswear nuclear weapons and accept international inspections at Tuwaitha. The French reactors sold to Iraq would be supervised by the International Atomic Energy Agency (I.A.E.A.), a watchdog assigned to prevent the spread of nuclear arms. If they tried to build a bomb, they would have to evade the international inspectors.

Barzan pressed Jafar. Saddam, he insisted, "is confident that you can work on this mission."

Jafar said little, by his account, but he decided to cooperate. A few days later, security officers transferred him to a spacious house with a

large garden by the Tigris River. It contained a telephone and two televisions. Five guards watched the physicist day and night. He was under
house arrest and still had no idea how long he would be detained.

An intelligence officer brought Jafar some clothes from home, as
well as books from the library at Tuwaitha. One volume was titled *The
Theory of Isotope Separation as Applied to the Large-Scale Production of
U-235*, referring to a uranium isotope that can provide the explosive
material in atomic weapons. The book was published in 1951. It summarized theoretical work undertaken at a Columbia University lab
with ties to the Manhattan Project, America's secret World War II–era
bomb program, led by the physicist J. Robert Oppenheimer. This was
the first book Jafar selected. As summer heat suffocated Baghdad, he
began to read.[14]

Following his three weeks of torture, Shahristani was hauled before a
Baath Party court. He was placed in a cage with three other defendants, all of them charged with crimes against the state. "These are
agents of imperialism and Zionism, and enemies of the party and the
revolution," the prosecutor declared.

The judge cursed Shahristani. The scientist's appointed defense
lawyer rose to speak. "These are traitors, foreign agents and enemies of
the party and the revolution," he affirmed.[15]

Shahristani was sentenced to life in prison at hard labor. He was
taken to Abu Ghraib, the notorious maximum-security facility about
twenty miles west of Baghdad, where many hundreds of political prisoners were held. Torture and executions were commonplace there.
Shahristani was placed in a closed section that housed prisoners judged
to be threats to national security. The inmates were allowed no visitors
and had no information about the outside world. Desperate for meaning, they reported their nightly dreams, Shahristani discovered—
stories that were interpreted as factual "news" of Iraq and the world
beyond, and that spread quickly from cell to cell. Shahristani relied on
prayer to keep his mind and spirit intact.

About seven months after his initial arrest, at around the time Jafar was transferred to comfortable house arrest, Shahristani was also moved to a separate home in Baghdad's upscale Mansour neighborhood. Neither man knew about the fate of the other. Shahristani was permitted no calls or visitors, but a cook arrived to prepare his meals. He still suffered numbness from his torture and had difficulty walking. He often lay down on the floor to be comfortable.

He was lying prone in his bedroom one day when Barzan arrived.

"Dr. Hussain, we know all about you," the intelligence chief said. "You are a good scientist."

Barzan cursed the security services for having arrested and abused Shahristani. "Sayyid Rais Saddam," he continued, referring to the president with a double honorific, "was very upset when he learned that these people had arrested you."

Soon he got to the reason for his visit. "We need to develop a nuclear weapon. That will give us a long arm to reshape the map of the Middle East." He made a sweeping gesture with his hand.

"I know nothing about making atomic bombs," Shahristani protested. His scientific specializations had little direct relevance.

"We know of your capabilities," Barzan insisted. He made the choice explicit: "A person who is not willing to serve his country does not deserve to be alive."

"I agree with you," Shahristani said, looking up from the floor. "It's a person's duty to serve his country. But what you are asking may not be a service to my country."

Shahristani's mind was made up. After what he had seen in the torture rooms, he thought to himself, *Any weapon in Saddam's hand would be used against the Iraqi people before it was used on anybody else.*[16]

When Jafar Dhia Jafar was thirteen, in 1956, he met Sir John Douglas Cockcroft, a British physicist who had shared a Nobel Prize for work on atomic particles, and who was visiting Baghdad. Jafar was then a precocious student at Baghdad College, an elite boys' prep school founded by Jesuits from Boston. Jafar's father was the minister for development and construction in the Iraqi government led by King Faisal II. He held a reception for Cockcroft at his home near the Tigris.

"What do you want to be when you grow up, Jafar?" Cockcroft asked playfully when he was introduced to the minister's son.

"I want to build an atomic bomb," Jafar replied.

Cockcroft raised his eyebrows and turned to other guests.

The Bomb was in the news, and Jafar had spoken with "childlike innocence," as he recalled, to please his family's honored guest. Yet he proved to be attracted to nuclear physics as he came of age. He was a conceptual thinker. After leaving Baghdad College to enroll at an English boarding school, he matriculated at seventeen at Birmingham, a university known for advanced research in nuclear physics. The university housed a particle accelerator—an elaborate device that uses electromagnetic fields to accelerate atomic particles to nearly the speed of light, with the aim of facilitating experiments that can provide insights into the building blocks of the physical universe. After three years of undergraduate work, Jafar gained entry to Birmingham's doctoral program; while there, he wrote a thesis concerning elementary atomic particles. At twenty-eight, through a research appointment at London's Imperial College, Jafar found himself in a particle physicist's dream job—working at the European Organization for Nuclear Research, or CERN, in Geneva, the site of some of the world's most prodigious particle accelerators.[17]

Jafar stayed at CERN for four years until, in late 1974, Iraq's consul general in Geneva paid him a visit. Vice President Saddam Hussein was already seen as Iraq's man of the future, pouring money into literacy drives, health care, industrialization, weaponry, and technology—including nuclear science.

The Iraqi diplomat told Jafar that he had a message for him from Saddam: it was time for the physicist to come home, to take up a senior position at Tuwaitha and work for the benefit of his country. Jafar understood the request as "an offer I shouldn't—I cannot—refuse."[18]

In the polarizing Cold War, Saddam sought to minimize Iraq's dependence on both the United States and the Soviet Union. Yet he wanted the world's most advanced technologies to speed the development of Iraq's economy and society. During the 1970s, he embraced France, and France embraced him. When Iraq nationalized its oil industry alongside other Arab states, Saddam cut a side deal that allowed France to continue buying almost a quarter of Iraq's output. He visited Paris in 1972. Charles de Gaulle had recently died, but Gaullism's independent streak lived on in French policy toward the Arab world. French politicians and diplomats played a long game in Arab capitals and courted leaders of even the most brutal governments. The grandiose, secular-leaning Arab nationalism promoted by Saddam's Baath Party echoed aspects of French nationalism and attracted the open admiration of some Gaullists. Saddam's envoys shuttled to and from Paris, where Iraq owned four diplomatic properties in the posh Sixteenth Arrondissement. High-ranking Baathists traveled to France for medical treatment or recruited French surgeons to perform difficult surgeries in Baghdad. Iraq's oil revenues had skyrocketed, soaring on their way from $476 million in 1968 to $26 billion by 1980. During the 1970s, Saddam drew up an extraordinary shopping list in France: dozens of Mirage fighter jets for the Iraqi Air Force, a petrochemical plant, two cement factories, a military hospital, the modernization of Baghdad's airport, and the two nuclear reactors destined for Tuwaitha.[19]

On Friday, September 5, 1975, Saddam landed at Orly Airport in Paris, where Jacques Chirac, then forty-two and France's prime minister, received him. Chirac had cultivated a friendship with Saddam, whom he found "intelligent, not devoid of humor, even rather nice." Saddam traveled to Les Baux-de-Provence, a picturesque village in the South of France. He lodged at the Baumanière hotel, home to a three-Michelin-star restaurant. At dinner, his taste for house specialties, such as poulet de bresse à l'estragon, proved to be limited; on his third evening, he asked for comfort food: lentil soup, grilled fish, and stuffed lamb with cinnamon. Saddam was wary; one bodyguard stood vigil inside his hotel room door, and another slept at his feet. Yet he was generous to his hosts. There were about five dozen hotel and restaurant staff working around the clock during his visit. Typically, guests left an envelope with a cash tip to be shared. Saddam's aides left nothing but asked for a list of each French worker by name. A year later, a representative returned with a suitcase containing one thousand French francs for each staff member, or just over $1,000 in 2021 dollars.[20]

Saddam attended a festival of games in Les Baux displaying feats on horseback and in a bullring. In one match, young men on foot, dressed in white, tried to grab a red cloth tied to the horns of a wild bull. Saddam warmed to these Mediterranean relics of peasant prowess. Normally only the winners received prize money, but Saddam showered every competing horseman and raseteur with fifteen thousand francs.[21]

His hosts arranged for Saddam to visit the nearby French nuclear research center at Cadarache, spread over nearly four thousand acres. Saddam sported a burnt-orange, double-breasted, wide-striped business suit that was loud even by the garish styles of the time. He pulled on a white lab coat for his walking tour and beamed with apparent curiosity. France had tested its first nuclear bomb in 1960 and had been legitimized as a nuclear weapons power by the Nonproliferation Treaty. De Gaulle had exported nuclear reactors to Israel, which enabled that country to secretly build its own, undeclared atomic bombs in defiance of the accord. Even though the French reactors destined for Iraq would be subject to international inspections, it seemed plain that Saddam was keen on the possibility that Iraq might someday develop its own nuclear bomb option. The fuel in the research reactors France planned to install at Tuwaitha would be highly enriched uranium—of such a type that if Saddam decided to misuse the material to make a bomb, Iraqi scientists might be able, eventually, to extract enough plutonium from the reactors' spent fuel to make at least a single weapon.

After his visit to Cadarache, Saddam declared in public that the Arab world needed nuclear weapons to defend itself against Israel. Iraq's Baath Party rejected Israel's right to exist and supported armed Palestinian liberation movements and terrorist splinter groups. Saddam foresaw a conventional war between Iraq and Israel and said that mutual nuclear deterrence would prevent escalation. He also suggested that nuclear war might be survivable. If Israel "said, 'We will hit you with the atom,'" he explained in 1978, "we would say, 'We will hit you with the atom too.' The Arab atom will finish them off, but the Israeli atom will not finish the Arabs."[22]

Such talk chilled the Israeli defense establishment. Its leaders were for the most part united in a belief that Saddam must not have access to an atomic bomb, and that the two reactors France planned to export would put him too close. Mossad authorized sabotage, such as the April 1979 attack on the warehouse near Marseille. (This was the strike that had fueled the secret police's baseless suspicion of Jafar.) The Israelis also carried out assassinations. In June 1980, Mossad operatives tracked Yahya al-Mashad, an Egyptian scientist working for Iraq's nuclear program, to Paris. Two Israelis bludgeoned him to death with a large ashtray inside his room at the Méridien Etoile hotel. Two other Iraqi nuclear scientists died mysteriously in Europe in the subsequent months. Yet Israeli spy chiefs concluded that their dirty work could at best only delay the installation of France's reactors at Tuwaitha. A few months after Meshad's murder, Yitzhak Hofi, the Mossad chief, advised Menachem Begin, Israel's prime minister, "We will not be able to stop it. The only way still open is bombing from the air."[23]

In the spring and summer of 1980, as Jafar settled into his reading about the Manhattan Project, Saddam, by now Iraq's president, became preoccupied with Iran. Khomeini's incitement of uprisings against Baghdad provoked him. That summer, Saddam concluded that revolutionary Iran's instability—the country was roiling in political and social conflicts—offered an opportunity to overthrow Khomeini. That is, Saddam would do to Khomeini what Khomeini sought to do to him. Publicly, Saddam called the ayatollah a "mummy" and a "rotten man." Privately, he reviewed military options.[24]

Iran—historically Persia—interacted with Arab nations across a complex landscape of history, language, ethnicity, and religion. Saddam believed he would enhance his prestige in Arab capitals by punishing Khomeini and checking his arrogant revolution. He dismissed Iran's smaller Sunni Arab neighbors and rivals—the oil-rich and thinly populated kingdoms of Saudi Arabia, Kuwait, and the United Arab Emirates—as "the Arabs of corruption, the Arabs of shame" who could not stand up to the ayatollahs. Iran's smaller neighbors feared that Khomeini's revolution might stir their own Shia populations. These were oppressed minorities in nearly all of the emirates, except in Bahrain, where the Shia were also oppressed by Sunni rulers but constituted a majority, as in Iraq. Saddam would knock off the new neighborhood bully in Tehran, and the rich weaklings around him would owe him fealty, his thinking went. He also sought to regain a vital waterway, the Shatt al-Arab, which Iraq had ceded to Iran in a 1975 agreement. On September 16, 1980, he told his defense minister: "We will force their heads into the mud to enforce our political will on them, which can only happen militarily."[25]

Six days later, Iraqi warplanes launched a lightning strike designed to knock out Iranian warplanes on the ground. It was a disaster; Iraq lost almost its entire attacking force because commanders miscalculated how much fuel the planes would need to reach their targets and return. Six Iraqi tank columns rolled across the Iranian border into Khuzestan, an oil-rich province where the population spoke Arabic, leading Saddam to believe they might be ripe for revolt. But the Iraqis were not welcomed, and the invasion soon bogged down. The initial failures forecasted the Iran-Iraq War to come, a fiasco of command incompetence and martyrs' blood that would claim about one million casualties in Iraq and Iran over the next eight years.

In his home near the Tigris, Jafar listened at night to the pulsing rattle of Iraqi antiaircraft guns as they lit up the Baghdad sky with tracers, in search of Iranian jets. He watched war propaganda on television. The Baath-run channels—there was nothing else to watch—resounded with songs and poems glorifying Saddam.

Barzan dropped by Jafar's place now and then. Jafar indicated that he was doing the work the secret police chief had requested. Yet Barzan offered no indication about when he might be freed. Autumn turned to winter, and winter to spring, and still Jafar had armed guards as housemates.

He worked out mathematical calculations to deepen his understanding of the science that had led to the creation of the first atomic bomb. Many of the books he consulted had been donated to Iraq by the Eisenhower administration as part of America's worldwide "Atoms for Peace" initiative during the 1950s.[26]

In May 1981, Saddam bestowed automobiles as gifts to the top twenty or so scientists at Tuwaitha. Such outbursts of presidential appreciation were a perk of service in Iraq's nuclear program. (Another was exemption from conscription into the war against Iran.) By now, the final components of the first of two French-made reactors had reached Tuwaitha. A new building, domed and cylindrical, loomed over the complex grounds. The French called the reactor Osirak, and the Iraqis referred to it as Tammuz-1, after the month in the Islamic calendar when the Baath revolution had occurred. One hundred and fifty French specialists worked at Tuwaitha to complete the installation while about two hundred Iraqi technicians trained at a nuclear research center in Saclay, outside Paris.

Prime Minister Begin concluded that he could wait no longer. The French reactor was not yet loaded with fuel, but once it was, bombing it could disperse radiation and create an environmental disaster. On June 7, Rafael Eitan, the Israel Defense Forces' chief of staff, briefed elite pilots assigned to Operation Opera, a surprise air attack against Tuwaitha. "The alternative is our destruction," Eitan told them.[27]

Fourteen F-15 and F-16 fighter jets sold to Israel by the United

States roared low over the deserts of Jordan and Saudi Arabia and then veered toward Baghdad. Begin did not provide advance warning or seek permission from any foreign government, not even the U.S., Israel's closest ally. The jets reached Tuwaitha unopposed and dropped a dozen bombs in less than two minutes. One blew a hole in the French reactor's roof, and a second exploded inside, destroying the control room and causing the dome and an upper floor to collapse into the reactor's core. The damage was severe. Ten Iraqi soldiers died, as did a twenty-five-year-old French technician.

Saddam had been humiliated. During a long monologue at a closed meeting with top advisers, he spun the attack as evidence of Israel's fear of Iraq's revival under his leadership: "What scares Begin is the scientific, cultural, humanitarian, political, economic, sociological, and educational development" in Iraq under the Baath, Saddam said.

The lesson, he continued, was that if world powers wanted peace, they must give nuclear weapons to Arab states such as Iraq so that they could "face the Zionist threat of the atomic bombs." Perhaps he was half joking, but this, of course, was a complete misreading of international attitudes. Saddam went on to say, less ludicrously, that nuclear parity between Israel and its Arab foes might hold "the same logic that the U.S.S.R. uses to deal with the U.S. and the U.S. uses to deal with the U.S.S.R." He said he did "not believe that any of the Americans or the Soviets would use the atomic bomb against each other." Yet they always try "to better develop their weapons, so that they can prevent war." Such balance was now required between Israel and its Arab rivals. Otherwise, Israel's aggression would only expand.

He offered a clear statement of Iraq's strategic purpose in acquiring nukes: "The deterrent capability is not a provocative, hostile action," but it provides "Iraqi protection as well as Arab protection."[28]

Saddam grasped nuclear science only in broad strokes. He did seem to understand that acquiring fissionable material—plutonium or highly enriched uranium—was the most difficult part of building a bomb. He certainly knew that he would need expertise of a high order. The most likely candidate to become "the Oppenheimer of Iraq," as one scientist at the Iraqi Atomic Energy Commission put it, was Jafar. Shahristani's knowledge of nuclear reactors could also be helpful.

That summer, Barzan met separately with the two scientists, both still under house arrest.

Shahristani followed Iraq's propaganda about the faltering war with Iran on his television, and he also knew of Israel's attack. He had not seen Barzan or anyone else high up in the regime for about a year.

"You may be upset that we arrested you," Barzan acknowledged when he arrived, as Shahristani recalled. "Believe me, this has been for your own safety. If you had been outside, the Israelis would have gotten you."

They discussed the strike on Tuwaitha. "Is it repairable or not?" Barzan asked. A few days later, the intelligence chief's deputy returned with photos of the damage. Shahristani looked them over. But the scientist had made clear more than once that he had no interest in working on a bomb program. Eventually, Barzan gave up on him. Guards arrived to transport Shahristani back to Abu Ghraib, to serve out his life sentence in solitary confinement.[29]

Jafar was animated and outraged by the Israeli strike, which had "destroyed all my scientific hopes and aspirations," he recalled. Although he was at ease in Britain and Europe, his sense of self and his pride in his family's history was rooted in Iraqi nationalism. He promised himself that he would help create a new nuclear program, one that would restore "the glories of Iraq's history."[30]

Many of his colleagues in the nuclear program felt similarly. One then training at Saclay recalled "a feeling of having a child murdered or taken away from you." In the days following, as cleanup crews hauled away debris that included unexploded bombs, "our vengeance was way up," remembered Imad Khadduri, a Tuwaitha scientist who had earned his master's in physics from the University of Michigan. The attack created "a strong conviction" among scientists and technicians in the program that Iraq "had to adopt a new policy of pursuing an independent course based on self-reliance," as an official Iraqi history put it.[31]

Jafar believed that it had been a mistake for Iraq to have signed the Nuclear Nonproliferation Treaty. Why should the country have voluntarily given up its nuclear rights and options when Israel held weapons outside international law, as did India, which had successfully tested a "peaceful nuclear device" in 1974? Jafar thought Iraq should follow the examples set by India and Pakistan: those countries had accepted international safeguards for some nuclear reactor imports, akin to the French reactor deal, while running other nuclear programs without oversight.[32]

Saddam dropped whatever doubts he may have once harbored about Jafar's loyalty. Over the summer, Jafar indicated that he would be willing to go back to work.

In September, Barzan escorted the physicist to Saddam's second-floor office in the Republican Palace, the seat of Iraq's government, a turquoise-domed edifice from the royal era. The room Saddam occupied hadn't been renovated in years; marble floors and chandeliers endowed it with a tired dignity. The president rose from his chair and shook Jafar's hand. He motioned him and Barzan to chairs facing his desk. Orderlies served fresh orange juice and tea.

Saddam said that he had been concerned about Jafar's safety, which was all the explanation he would offer about the scientist's twenty-one months in detention. The president delivered a bitter monologue about Israel's strike and then said, "We must build with the arms and minds of Iraqis an alternative nuclear program. . . . We must possess a nuclear weapon to be a deterrent to the attacks of Israel and to those who protect the State of Israel and provide continuous support to it." It was an obvious reference to the United States.

Saddam instructed Barzan, "Give this man all he asks, for Iraq and Iraq's future."

"I'll try my best, sir," Jafar said.[33]

TWO

A Spy Bearing Gifts

I n the early afternoon of July 27, 1982, a private jet belonging to the Kingdom of Jordan touched down in Baghdad. It carried a single American passenger: Thomas "Tom" Twetten, a C.I.A. operations officer. He had spent most of his career under diplomatic cover, for which he was a natural. He had grown up in small-town Iowa and held a master's degree in international affairs from Columbia University. His interests included antique books, such as travelogues by nineteenth-century voyagers. By the time he reached his forties, his hair and full eyebrows had whitened, but his face was unlined; he looked like a bank officer with abstemious habits. Twetten had served tours posing as a diplomat in Benghazi, Accra, and New Delhi before becoming the C.I.A.'s chief of station in Amman, Jordan. This position brought him into close contact with the country's ruler, King Hussein, a neighbor and ally of Saddam Hussein, as well as a friend of the Reagan administration and the C.I.A. The Jordanian monarch was a charming adventurer and political survivor—a pilot, motorcyclist, and amateur radio enthusiast who seemed to regard running secret backchannels in the Middle East as a fun perk of being king. Twetten's trip to Baghdad was just such an operation, and King Hussein had readily lent the C.I.A. his jet.

Twetten's mission, conceived at the White House, was to persuade Saddam's regime to accept C.I.A. assistance in Iraq's war against Iran. If Saddam was willing, the agency would secretly provide highly classified imagery from U.S. spy satellites that showed recent Iranian battle positions on crucial war fronts, to advantage Iraqi forces. The National Security Council had given Twetten clear instructions: stay in Iraq as long as it takes to set up a channel to share this intelligence, and "do not ask for *anything* in return; this was an American *gift*."[1]

The generosity reflected panic inside the Reagan administration. America hewed publicly to a policy of neutrality in the Iran-Iraq War. But this no longer seemed viable. "Iraq has essentially lost the war with Iran," the C.I.A. concluded in a Special National Intelligence Estimate circulated six weeks before Twetten arrived in Baghdad. Satellite imagery showed about a hundred thousand Iranian troops mustered near the Iraqi border for an attack on Basra, Iraq's second-largest city—a blitzkrieg that Iraq could not fully see coming, agency analysts believed. If it succeeded, Iranian forces might capture Basra and drive on Baghdad to achieve Ayatollah Khomeini's goal of replacing Saddam's regime with a "fundamentalist Islamic one," as a classified paper from the National Intelligence Council warned. President Reagan signed a Top Secret National Security Decision Directive authorizing the United States to do "whatever was necessary and legal," as one of the drafters put it, to prevent Khomeini from toppling Saddam. A radical Tehran-backed Shiite government in Baghdad would expand the Iranian revolution, threatening America's oil-pumping allies in the conservative Sunni royal families of Kuwait, Bahrain, Saudi Arabia, and the United Arab Emirates.[2]

Saddam had never expected to fight a long war against Iran, never mind a losing one. Initially, Iraqi forces seized almost ten thousand square miles of Iranian territory, but rather than driving on toward Tehran, Saddam's invading soldiers hunkered down in positions that were difficult to defend. Their commander in chief was a liability:

Saddam traveled frequently to the front lines to provide detailed orders about matters such as how to dig trenches. As the Iranians counterattacked, thousands of battlefield deaths decimated Iraq's infantry; by the summer of 1982, the size of Iraq's army had shrunk from 210,000 to 150,000. Iran's military atrophied, too, from casualties and purges of senior officers carried out during Khomeini's revolution. But the ayatollahs could draw on a larger population, and they supplemented their professional forces with tens of thousands of Pasdaran conscripts and volunteers, many of them teenagers who heedlessly charged Iraqi lines—sometimes to clear land mines—in a religiously inspired form of suicide-by-combat. These martyrdom seekers who charged forward when other soldiers would not—"insects," as one Iraqi general dismissed them—influenced Saddam's embrace of chemical and biological weapons. On his orders, Iraqi forces would increasingly turn to gas attacks, draping the battlefield with clouds of sickly and debilitating poison. Saddam soon stopped speaking about Khomeini's defeat. He would settle for a peace that "keeps our sovereignty and our dignity intact," he told advisers privately. But Khomeini vowed to fight on until Saddam was deposed and tried as a war criminal.[3]

Reagan's aides met repeatedly in the White House Situation Room during the spring of 1982 to debate what support for Baghdad might actually work. Weapons supplies did not seem to be the answer. In comparison to Iran, Iraq did not suffer from a lack of quality tanks or planes. Its bigger problem was poor generalship caused by Saddam's sacking of professional commanders in favor of Baathist political hacks—a problem Washington could not fix. In the end, the National Security Council settled on secret action by the C.I.A. "Baghdad's most basic need is for accurate and timely intelligence" on Iran's troop layout and war plans, as a National Security Council options paper put it. The decision would tilt U.S. policy toward Iraq and against Iran, which the administration was not willing to acknowledge openly. There was a risk that the Reagan administration would get caught slipping satellite maps to Iraq, which would further anger Iran, but sharing intelligence with

Baghdad "could have an immediate impact on the war and it maintains at least some degree of deniability."[4]

An Iraqi colonel in an army uniform received Twetten at Baghdad's airport. The colonel worked for the General Military Intelligence Directorate, a spy service that was part of the Ministry of Defense. He escorted Twetten to the Mansour, a new eleven-story hotel on the Tigris boasting swimming pools and casinos. The hotel was designed like a ship, with its prow pointed toward the river. The Iraqis checked Twetten in as "Mr. Hussein." He explained that he had C.I.A. colleagues standing by in Amman, about a ninety-minute flight away. These officers had intelligence maps of the current war front, and if Iraq agreed to accept the agency's assistance, he would order the C.I.A. men to fly to Baghdad immediately.

After consultations, the colonel said they were willing. King Hussein's jet flew back to Baghdad that evening. On board were an operations officer and the C.I.A.'s top analyst following the Iran-Iraq War.[5]

That night, the Americans unfurled their maps in a secure room, and their hosts pored over them. By morning, however, it emerged that Barzan Ibrahim al-Tikriti, Saddam's half brother at the Mukhabarat, objected to cooperating with the C.I.A. He wanted to abort the meetings and send the Americans home.

The Mukhabarat and military intelligence struggled over authority. The main job of military intelligence was to collect information to support warfighting and national defense. Barzan's secret police and overseas spies collected foreign and "strategic" intelligence, such as information about Saddam's political opposition. During the war with Iran—a conventional conflict in which the enemy also fomented revolution inside Iraq—the two spy agencies were bound to knock heads.

Barzan demanded to meet Twetten. The army colonel brought Twetten to the Mukhabarat's headquarters. Barzan's large, gaudy office was decorated with green wallpaper and portraits of Saddam. (Saddam

made a habit of checking where his portraits were hung when he visited people's homes. He once told Barzan that you "can know how loyal
people are" by eavesdropping on their children's unfiltered chatter and
by "whether or not they have my pictures up in their houses.") The Iraqi
spy chief sat behind an ornate desk. He "looked like hell," Twetten
thought.

Still in his midtwenties, lightly traveled, Barzan's sense of world affairs was informed by the grievances that filled every Baath Party newspaper: that America was the power behind Zionism; that Zionism was
a blight upon the Arab world; that Israel was likely the secret driving
force behind Ayatollah Khomeini's revolution and his war against Iraq;
and that the C.I.A. was an enabler of all these conspiracies. Barzan
uncorked what Twetten later described as a "loud, seething forty-five-
minute lecture about why I wasn't welcome" in Baghdad. As for the
C.I.A.'s Top Secret battle maps, he was emphatic, as Twetten recalled:
"We don't need it. We don't want it—and you can leave."

Twetten pleaded his case. "We're talking about Iraqi lives, and we're
talking about the president of the United States wanting to help you."
Barzan was unyielding.[6]

After this dressing-down, Twetten spoke to the military intelligence
officers who had received him: "It's really not a good idea to tell the
president of the United States that the information he has authorized
me to give you is unwelcome," he said. There was more battlefield intelligence to share if the Iraqis could bring themselves to accept it.

His appeal worked, or seemed to. His hosts received permission,
presumably from Saddam himself, to spend more time with the C.I.A.
delegation in order to further examine what the maps showed. Twetten
judged that his hosts found the information "*very* significant."[7]

The Iraqis soon moved the C.I.A. team from the Mansour to a
guesthouse near military intelligence headquarters, a gated campus on
a thumb-shaped peninsula jutting into the Tigris. Wafiq al-Samarrai, a
military intelligence officer then in his midthirties, joined the meetings.

The White House was ready to build a longer-term intelligence-
sharing relationship with Iraq, through the C.I.A., to aid Iraq in the

war, Twetten explained as he prepared to leave. "You've got to talk your political side into doing this," he said.[8]

P olitics in Iraq turned on the outlook of just one man, of course. Barzan's secret police provided a formidable defense against Khomeini's incitements of popular revolution within Iraq, yet Saddam looked vulnerable. In July 1982, the same month when Twetten turned up, the president traveled to Dujail, a Shiite-populated town about thirty-five miles north of Baghdad, to speak about recruitment for the war. A would-be assassin fired twelve rounds at him from an AK-47 assault rifle. It was a glancing threat, but Saddam had at least 1,400 Dujail villagers rounded up. Baathist tribunals ordered the execution of more than one hundred of them.

Across the Arab world, newspapers carried speculation that Saddam might—or should—relinquish power to a Baath Party successor, to make a settlement with Khomeini easier. A story went around that Saddam's minister for health, Riyadh Ibrahim Hussein, had suggested during a cabinet meeting that Saddam temporarily step down. Supposedly, Saddam had calmly asked Riyadh to step outside for consultations, then shot him dead within earshot of his comrades. The story became a widely circulated anecdote of Saddam's management style. The truth was more prosaic, if also an example of arbitrary Baath justice. Riyadh was dismissed from his ministry in June 1982 and arrested two months later, accused of being a "traitor" and importing a medicine that killed people. He was tortured and then executed by firing squad that autumn, according to his daughter.[9]

In this season of insecurity, the C.I.A.'s "gift" of satellite-derived maps of Iran's troops triggered Saddam's deep-seated suspicions about the United States. He feared, among other things, that the U.S. and the Soviet Union wanted Iraq and Iran to debilitate themselves in a long, costly war. He was justified in this anxiety: the year before, former secretary of state Henry Kissinger had remarked that the "ultimate American interest" in the conflict would be met if "both sides lose."

During the summer of Twetten's visit, Saddam commented publicly, "If the two superpowers wanted to stop the war, they could have."[10]

Saddam did not trust that the C.I.A.'s satellite intelligence was reliable. What if the imagery was being doctored to promote a military stalemate? He feared, too, that the U.S. was already helping Iran in the war—playing both sides. "I mean, America has two faces, one face that it displays in front of us" but another that "does not want the Iranians to be defeated," he once explained to his advisers.

Prior to Khomeini's revolution, the shah of Iran, Mohammad Reza Pahlavi, had been among Washington's closest allies in the Middle East. Iran's military still flew American warplanes and fired American guns left from the shah's arsenal. Washington had firmly broken off relations with Iran after the 1979 revolution, and the Reagan administration maintained an official arms embargo against both Iran and Iraq. Yet somehow Iran continued to obtain American-made spare parts. How? There was a commercial black market, but Saddam suspected that Israel might be covertly sending American parts to Khomeini. Iraqi intelligence picked up traces of this apparent Israeli trade and reported the evidence to Saddam. (The reporting was accurate, as the world would learn years later; Israeli leaders had secretly agreed to provide Iran with supplies in exchange for liberating Iranian Jews so that they could migrate to Israel.) Saddam assumed, reasonably, that any covert Israeli arms deals with Iran must be known to the C.I.A.

He also believed—it is not clear why—that Iran was receiving satellite photos of Iraqi battlefield positions from somewhere. He was clearly worried that the C.I.A. might be feeding satellite intelligence to both Iraq and Iran. "You tell me how Iran gets satellite pictures?" Saddam asked visitors in the summer of 1982. He wasn't prepared to accuse the United States openly, but the matter nagged him. He could also see that American AWACS radar aircraft and intelligence planes based in Saudi Arabia flew close to the Iran-Iraq war zone to monitor the fighting. "We are afraid that the collected information will go to the Iranians in one way or another," he told his aides.[11]

Saddam cast himself as the Fidel Castro of the Middle East, the one

Arab leader bold enough to stand up to Washington's oil-driven neocolonialism in the Persian Gulf. "We talk about the American occupation," he told his comrades. "The Americans came, the Americans went. . . . They wanted to embarrass the Iraqi position." Yet he recognized that having hostile relations with a superpower was "unnatural" and that better ties with Washington might strengthen his rule, if he managed things carefully. That July, Saddam told *Time* magazine, "I have nothing personal against the U.S."[12]

Saddam soon accepted regular deliveries of maps and satellite pictures from the C.I.A. The intelligence proved its worth on the battlefield, or so the C.I.A. deduced from Iraq's willingness to normalize a highly secret intelligence relationship. The agency now had to build a formal "liaison" relationship with Iraqi intelligence in order to analyze and ship over satellite imagery from week to week. The C.I.A. had a playbook for such partnerships. They were typically built on reciprocal exchanges of visits by spy leaders and as many alcohol-soaked get-to-know-you dinners as the partnering foreign service would tolerate. There was an inherent edginess in this relationship-building, since the C.I.A. officers involved were often tasked with identifying foreign spies they might pitch to become agents for the United States—and sometimes, depending on the country, vice versa.

There was but a single C.I.A. officer posted in Baghdad at the time Saddam agreed to work with the agency. Gene "Kim" McGill was a well-regarded Arabist, and during his tour in the Iraqi capital, he was "undeclared," meaning he was posted in the guise of a U.S. diplomat, and the C.I.A. did not inform Iraq that he was really one of theirs. After Twetten's breakthrough, the agency needed a "declared" officer in Baghdad—that is, one who would maintain diplomatic cover but whose true employer would be disclosed to the Mukhabarat to facilitate cooperation. After McGill rotated out, the C.I.A. posted a declared officer named Bruce Johnson—whom the Iraqis came to call "Abu Eric," or Father of Eric (his son)—to run the satellite intelligence exchanges.

The C.I.A. passed its maps to the Mukhabarat, which passed them to military intelligence. The Mukhabarat's access to the material seemed to resolve the earlier conflict caused by Barzan.[13]

The C.I.A.'s Baghdad station was situated on the second floor of one of America's more decrepit outposts in the Middle East: the "United States Interests Section of the Embassy of Belgium." In 1967, an Iraqi government preceding the Baath Party's had broken diplomatic relations with Washington over the Six-Day War, a brief conflict between Israel and its Arab enemies. Thereafter, Belgium represented the U.S. For several years, the State Department posted no diplomats to Iraq. In 1972, the Nixon administration sent out some Americans to serve in Baghdad under the Belgian flag, but the Belgians didn't have enough office space. The U.S. ended up occupying a former embassy of Romania.

This was a three-story beige concrete building in the Masbah district of Baghdad. A Belgian tricolor flew over the chancery door, and portraits of a young, bespectacled King Baudouin adorned the walls. American diplomats were provided stationery in French and Flemish, as well as business cards advertising their affiliation with Belgium. The Masbah compound was "a huge dump," as Deborah Jones, who worked there, put it. Some rooms had red velvet wallpaper. The staff numbered about a dozen by the early 1980s. They were crammed together amidst a mélange of unsightly furniture. There was but a single phone line that required a switchboard operator to direct calls to extensions. To run the intelligence program with the Mukhabarat, the C.I.A. installed a secure communications system that could transmit satellite imagery. (C.I.A. officers also couriered materials to Baghdad.) In the small classified area, someone mounted a sign: "Remember, this is a former Romanian embassy." In other words, it was likely riddled with listening devices. State Department diplomats (the real ones) recalled that some classified messages required the use of onetime code pads of midcentury vintage; the messages could then be dispatched by weekly courier to Kuwait. There were no U.S. Marine guards, yet the main building was less than ten feet from the street, an unnerving situation given the voluminous incoming intelligence that described "how the

Iranians had plans to blow us to kingdom come," as one diplomat recalled.[14]

Foreign diplomats in Baghdad were reluctant to speak Saddam's name out loud, given the ubiquitous presence of informers, so they developed various tongue-in-cheek codes to discuss the president. One technique was to refer to Saddam silently by placing an index finger above one's lip, indicating a mustache. Traveling out of Baghdad entailed an epic project of obtaining permission forms and photocopied checkpoint passes. For those diplomats tasked with reporting to their capitals about Iraqi affairs, often the best they could do was monitor Saddam's propaganda on state television; read the official press; walk around markets to track prices or scan for small insights about ordinary life; talk to other diplomats about their readings of Baath Party intrigues; and exchange messages with mid-level counterparts at the Iraqi Ministry of Foreign Affairs.[15]

William Eagleton, a career foreign service officer in his fifties, was the senior diplomat at the U.S. interests section. Eagleton became enamored of Kurdistan, traveled there regularly, and eventually wrote a book about Kurdish rugs—perhaps not the most urgent matter in U.S.-Iraqi relations—and another about Kurdish political history. The analysis he transmitted to Washington promoted a then-common theme among Arabists in the Reagan administration: Saddam was obviously a brutal ruler, but he had some merit as a "paternalistic national leader" whose modernization drives during the 1970s had led him to a "progressively more pragmatic foreign policy."

Such reporting lifted the hopes of those Reagan administration strategists who believed that Iraq under Saddam—with its vast oil wealth—could be not only saved from defeat by Ayatollah Khomeini but also coaxed closer to America's "moderate" Arab allies, led by Egypt, Jordan, and Saudi Arabia. The Reagan team hoped Saddam might cease threatening Israel and end aid to Palestinian terrorists.

There was, however, the problem of Saddam's "dark side," as Eagleton put it in a cable to Washington on March 23, 1983. "The two sides of life in Iraq reflect the two basic aspects of President Saddam

Hussein's own personality," he wrote. The Iraqi president's "extensive social/economic welfare system" reflected his plan to "forge 'a new Iraqi man (and woman)' capable of leading Iraq into its rightful place on the Arab and world stage." But "there is another side to Saddam," Eagleton went on, one visible in the Mukhabarat's secret police. With a workforce of about forty thousand, "the Mukhabarat operates as a separate and distinct entity," Eagleton reported. Its powers encompassed "summary arrests, including disappearance; torture, mistreatment and degrading treatment of prisoners; arbitrary arrests and detention without trial. . . . These and other Gestapo-like tactics . . . are well-known to all who live in Iraq."[16]

Early in 1983, Saddam asked Said K. Aburish, an American-educated Palestinian journalist and Arab nationalist, to travel to Washington. He was to buy two hundred American-made M-16 rifles for Iraq's elite presidential guard. It was a test of Saddam's nascent secret alliance with the Reagan administration. Such a small batch of M-16s was of no great military significance, but Saddam's motivation, Aburish concluded, was to have his crack bodyguard "be photographed parading with them." The Iranians would then see the rifles and "surmise that he and the Americans were close enough for the U.S.A. to equip his personal guard." But the U.S. turned down his request. When Aburish visited the Iraq desk at the State Department, an official read him a statement about America's neutrality in the Iran-Iraq War, and its refusal to sell arms to either side.[17]

This was one in a chronic series of misunderstandings between Reagan's strategists and Saddam's inner circle over what the Iraqis thought of as "courtesy" gun purchases when their officials visited the U.S. When the Iraqi president and his top aides considered the attractions of America, they thought of gun stores. The Iraqis maintained their own small interests section in Washington, and the State Department discovered that Iraqi diplomats were buying up guns at D.C.-area marts and shipping them home in diplomatic pouches. When David Mack took a posting at State headquarters, a superior told him, "Well, you won't have much to do with Iraq, but all they want to do is buy guns! Guns!" Mack came to understand the Iraqis' dismay about refusals such as the one endured by Aburish: they could not fathom "this strange country" where you could buy guns as easily as chewing gum but must not ship them abroad.[18]

As part of its relationship-building, the C.I.A. invited a Mukhabarat delegation to secretly visit its Langley headquarters. The trip became a fiasco because members of Saddam's family who had hitched a ride to America skipped formal meetings to go shopping for pistols with silencers. Twetten, who had by now taken a senior position in the C.I.A.'s Near East Division, received a call from an F.B.I. agent assigned to monitor the Iraqi visitors. One member of the delegation, the agent reported, had claimed that Twetten was his sponsor and that "you will approve it," meaning the purchase of handguns and silencers.

Ah, the joys of intelligence work, Twetten thought. No, he would not approve it. But now he had to explain to a senior Mukhabarat officer leading the Iraqi delegation that the C.I.A. couldn't allow his companions to carry home these guns. The purchases violated the Reagan administration's arms embargo, and it hardly needed mentioning that, in Iraqi hands, the silencers might be used in assassinations.

The Mukhabarat officer dismissed Twetten's scruples. He made his point with an anecdote: "A couple of years ago, we had a Russian intelligence officer in Baghdad who ran over and killed somebody on the street. We took care of him. He didn't have to go home—we just covered it up, paid a little money to the family, and that was that. That's what intelligence services do for each other. Now, why can't I have some pistols?"[19]

Early in May 1983, Eagleton rode to Mukhabarat headquarters. Barzan received him. The C.I.A.'s intelligence operation had been running for nearly a year. Saddam's fears of American trickery seemed to be easing. The number of sensitive subjects that could be discussed between U.S. and Iraqi officials had expanded. For Iraq, the main priorities were obtaining more high-quality arms and ensuring that the U.S. was truly committed to choking off Iran's supplies. For the U.S., a major goal was ending Iraq's support for terrorists.

Eagleton used his meeting to challenge Barzan about Iraq's relationship with the Abu Nidal Organization, a violent Palestinian group that would eventually carry out attacks in twenty countries, claiming hundreds of lives. Sabri al-Banna, a.k.a. Abu Nidal, had broken from Yasser Arafat's Palestine Liberation Organization (P.L.O.) in 1974; he had an office in Baghdad. Eagleton told Barzan that "a major barrier to better U.S.-Iraqi relations was the presence of Abu Nidal in Iraq and operations he has conducted, particularly during the last year."

This seemed to be a reference to an assassination attempt in which Barzan was directly implicated. In June 1982, in London, an Abu Nidal operative shot and gravely wounded Shlomo Argov, Israel's ambassador to Great Britain, as Argov left the Dorchester hotel. Nawaf al-Rosan, among the attacking party, turned out to be an Iraqi intelligence colonel. (Israel inaccurately blamed the P.L.O. for the attack and cited it as a justification to invade Lebanon.)

Barzan insisted that "it was a mistake" to view Abu Nidal as "a tool of the Iraqi government" and that Iraq "could not completely control" the Palestinian. Still, he conceded that he could "exert some influence on him through dialogue." For example, Barzan continued, with apparent pride, Abu Nidal had been planning attacks "against Jews in Europe and we convinced him there was no benefit in this."

Eagleton suggested that Iraq should expel Abu Nidal.

"This would be dangerous," Barzan countered, and the U.S. "would regret it if it happened," because Washington would lose Iraq's moderating influence.

Since they were trading complaints, Barzan had one to share: He noted that an Iraqi visiting America had recently "bought presentation pistols," meaning guns intended as gifts back home. These pistols had then been "confiscated at the airport." Was this really necessary?

Yet they ended their discussions cordially, with "mutual expressions of interest in maintaining high-level dialogue," as Eagleton reported to Washington.[20]

A week later, in Paris, Secretary of State George Shultz welcomed Tariq Aziz, Saddam's deputy prime minister, to his hotel suite for a forty-five-minute discussion. Aziz conveyed the "personal" desire of Saddam "for better relations with the U.S." The secretary wrote that the U.S. and Iraq had reached "a new stage in the development of better understanding of our very important common interests."[21]

The Reagan administration had marked its course: by mid-1983, it had shifted from a panicked effort to stave off an Iranian takeover of Iraq to an acceptance of Saddam as a prospective partner in America's strategy for the Middle East. It was a decision that would have deep and unforeseen consequences for the U.S., Iraq, and Iran. Washington had now lashed itself to a dictator whose economic ambitions and ruthless "dark side" were easy enough to grasp. Yet Saddam was much more than his development plans or his secret police.

Saddam would prove to be a leader of immense energy, self-confidence, restless suspicion, and unpredictability. He was a dogmatic revolutionary who had imbibed the sweeping idealism of 1960s pan-Arabism. He could lose himself in long monologues about postcolonial revolutionary politics in countries from Algeria to Cuba to Ethiopia to Yemen. He was capable of both cunning insights about his adversaries and dumbfounding blindness about global affairs—sometimes in the same conversation. He harbored ambitions as a writer and a patron of the arts. And he was the continually beleaguered patriarch of an extended family that was becoming Iraq's next royal family, whose members chronically abused their privileges. From one day to the next, the president was not always easy for even his nearest relatives or Baath Party comrades to understand. In distant Washington, it was less the man than the chess piece that attracted interest—in the Cold War's struggle, and in the face of the Iranian Revolution, Saddam looked like a weighty piece that might be shifted to advantage. He appeared to be manageable.

THREE

A Man and a City

He who is not alert, even with a long stick,
the dogs will cover him and bite him.

—SADDAM HUSSEIN, from his third novel,
Men and a City

On July 23, 1983, at the end of Saddam Hussein's fourth year as president of Iraq, his mother, Subha Tulfah al-Musallat, died of natural causes. She had lived into her sixties. Like other women in the countryside, she draped herself in black robes, at times accented by a decorative length of flowered cloth. In photographs, she gazes out with relaxed confidence. By some accounts, Subha dabbled as a clairvoyant in the poverty-stricken area north of Baghdad, near the town of Tikrit, where she lived for the great majority of her years. She was clearly an influential force within her family as Saddam acquired power, and if she foretold the future, it was probably to shape family alliances. On her deathbed, according to her son Barzan Ibrahim al-Tikriti, she was still issuing edicts about her grandchildren's arranged marriages. Her passing may have liberated Saddam to reorganize the family, however, and to anoint new princes that his mother may not have favored. In any event, Saddam's decisions in the months following Subha's death would have serious consequences for his rule, and for America's struggles with his regime.[1]

Saddam was his mother's second son by her first husband, Hussein al-Majid. Their village was a jumble of one-story mud-brick houses near the Tigris, a redoubt of poor tenant farmers working irrigated fields and hustlers who traded or thieved or both. The area had no running water, electricity, or paved roads. Anwar, Subha's first son, died before his first birthday, a fate that awaited perhaps one out of three babies born in the region at the time. Loss followed loss: Subha became pregnant again, but her husband died several months before she was due. She moved into her father's house and gave birth to Saddam. They remained there for about two years until her father died, too. One of her late husband's brothers, Ibrahim al-Hassan, who already had one wife, proposed to marry her, following a custom in which surviving brothers assured the care of widows. Saddam was barely a toddler.[2]

His new stepfather was a formidable-looking tribal peasant with a black Vandyke beard; in one photograph, he wears pin-striped robes and poses with a shotgun, while in another, he seems to have a dagger tucked against his thigh. Saddam described him as "tall, strong, good-looking . . . with yellow-green eyes."

Rural Tikrit was a hard place, steeped in violence and death, where corporal punishment and even murder were common, and this milieu clearly shaped Saddam's character. In an autobiographical novel, he recounts how he intimidated other children by brandishing a gun, and how he once pistol-whipped someone on a bus who did not move over to make room. Some biographers have placed emphasis on Ibrahim's supposed beatings and cruel treatment of Saddam as a formative influence on the future man. It is hard to judge what degree of harshness would have seemed exceptionally cruel to Saddam. In his novel, he describes the rural life he knew as a boy as worse "than the life of dogs." In one episode, his mother makes him wear earrings, to appear as a young girl, because she is afraid of losing him to violence among local men. (Predictably, the fictional Saddam insists that he must fight, come what may: "Mother, Iraq is burning!") He suggests in the book that he witnessed domestic conflicts when he was a child, yet as the scholar Hawraa Al-Hassan has noted, he deflects these observations with a repetitive phrase: "But we were a happy family." He may have suppressed difficult truths, yet as an older adult, Saddam spoke of his stepfather with only warmth and admiration.[3]

As he later constructed his own myth, Saddam identified as a peasant, firmly located on the rural and tribal sides of Iraq's rural-urban, tribal-cosmopolitan divides. This was clever populist politics but also a true reflection of his persona. He bore the tattoo of his father and stepfather's tribe: the inked symbols of the al-Bu Nasir clan marked his right hand, an arrangement of geometrical shapes that served, in effect, as a birth certificate and an identity card. His paternal tribe offered solidarity and protection. His childhood of deprivation in an area where land was wealth provided him with an authentic grounding in social and political struggle more important than the ideologies of Arab nationalism that he would adopt in adulthood.[4]

After Subha remarried, Saddam had to adjust to his mother's expanding family, which came to include a half sister, Siham, and three half brothers a decade or more younger than him—Barzan, Sabawi, and Watban. These three attached themselves to Saddam after he migrated to Baghdad and rose within the Baath Party during the 1960s. All of them held positions in Saddam's administration at the time of his mother's death. Barzan still ran the Mukhabarat; Sabawi worked on Syrian affairs; and Watban served as governor of Tikrit.

Barzan easily had the most powerful job. Their relations could hardly have been more intimate. They had married sisters. They had apparently collaborated on murders against enemies of their family in Tikrit. But this familiarity had not worn well, and Barzan had failed to navigate the redline that Saddam laid down for everyone: *Do nothing to undermine my authority or visibility.* Gradually, during the early 1980s, Saddam grew suspicious of his half brother.

A great source of tension arose from marriage compacts. For some time, the family had discussed the engagement of Saddam's eldest daughter, Raghad, who was fourteen, to a son of either Barzan or Sabawi. By mid-1983, however, Saddam seemed reluctant to proceed. This grated on Barzan. Such a marriage would cement him as a privi-

leged prince at the apex of the Baathist regime. But the president appeared to now prefer to pledge Raghad's hand to Hussein Kamel
al-Majid, a relative of Saddam's father and stepfather.

Hussein Kamel, a peer and rival of Barzan's, was about twice
Raghad's age. Raghad had met him when she was a middle schooler
and he was serving as her father's driver and bodyguard. With his thick
brush mustache, he looked like a wax figure of a young Saddam. The
dashing soldier joined the family for meals. He struck young Raghad as
"bold and brave." She flirted with him across the table, she recalled,
and soon agreed to a match. Hussein Kamel had clearly caught the
president's eye as a potentially more desirable henchman and political
partner than the temperamental, grudge-prone Barzan. Saddam appointed him as head of Iraq's Republican Guard, the country's elite
warfighting troops, despite his brief and insignificant military career.

As Hussein Kamel ascended, his Majid clan, promoting its interests, fed Saddam's suspicions by whispering that Barzan was plotting to
seize power in Iraq, or so Barzan came to believe. For months during
1983, Saddam avoided meeting Barzan. Then, in August, following the
death of his mother, the president invited his three half brothers to
lunch.

After a meal, they adjourned to the living room for tea, according
to Barzan's account. He is the only source of his exchanges with Saddam, but the essence of what took place is confirmed by other sources.

The president announced that relatives from the Majid side would
be joining them to ask for permission for Hussein Kamel to marry
Raghad.

Saddam asked Barzan his opinion. "We think that boy is not good
enough," he recalled saying.

"Why?" Saddam asked.

"Because he does not care about us and always tries to cause trouble, and attempts to separate us."

"Do you know me as a person who could be influenced by others?"
Saddam asked.

"At the end of the day, you are a human being, and when Hussein

[Kamel] gets married with your daughter, his sitting place will be on one of these chairs that we sit on," Barzan replied. "You will begin to listen to what he says."[5]

Saddam relied on his family to secure his dictatorship, yet their abuses of power often aggravated him. He advised his closest relatives not to become dependent on his government: "Don't deal with the state on a permanent basis," he said. "Don't become a neighbor of the state." He regularly transferred or dismissed his half brothers from high offices, at times because their performances disappointed him, but also to unsettle them and prevent them from consolidating independent power. All along, nonetheless, family members lined their pockets through contracting, import-export deals, intimidation, and other schemes, of which Saddam was sometimes unaware, or claimed to be.

His closest relatives felt free to rough up civil servants or shopkeepers who displeased them. At times, Saddam meted out punishment. When one of his brothers-in-law beat up and broke the arm of a Baghdad University professor who had failed him in a class, Saddam ordered his bodyguards to break his relative's arm in the same place. Watban, the youngest of the three half brothers, was a repeat offender. He was a "trivial person . . . illiterate," complained one of Saddam's ministers. Once, Saddam removed Watban from a government post after he shot out a traffic light, apparently because it didn't turn green fast enough. Another time, Watban reportedly beat up and kidnapped two traffic cops when they didn't let his Mercedes through an intersection promptly. Saddam put out stories about how he punished transgressors like Watban in order to shore up his reputation and assuage comrades in the Baath Party, which theoretically opposed family-based rule. Still, Saddam very rarely ordered relatives to be executed or imprisoned for long terms.[6]

The president's kin presented him with just one management challenge among many. Saddam shouldered a monumental workload and actively presided over a nation almost continuously at war (thanks largely to his own miscalculations). He advanced huge state-building projects, such as the Iraqi nuclear program and campaigns to construct hospitals and highways. He oversaw budgets, propaganda, foreign policy, and domestic politics, including the internal affairs of the Baath Party, which numbered about one and a half million members by 1984. He worried daily about threats to his life, real and imagined. Yet he met his public responsibilities with vigor and a resilient attitude. He called staff meetings in the middle of the night, six or seven days a week. He kept this pace up, year after year, well into his sixties.

As evidenced by his oversight of the Iranian battlefront, Saddam micromanaged. A typical day's file excavated by the scholar Aaron Faust saw Saddam checking off on such matters as a request from a Baathist comrade for use of a house when he was in Baghdad and another from a woman seeking permission to receive medical treatment in France and then to visit her brother in the United Arab Emirates. (Saddam wrote "approved" in the margin.) On other days, Faust found, Saddam "got involved in minor law enforcement and corruption cases . . . and even local neighborly and domestic disputes, usually after hearing about them via petition."[7]

He typically rose at about 5:00 a.m. A valet served him tea and laid out his clothing. He varied his office wardrobe between the green fatigues de rigueur among anti-colonial revolutionaries of his era and tailored business suits, often Italian, with a pocket behind the waistband to hide a small pistol. He smoked about four cigars a day; after a visit to Havana in 1978, he favored Cubans. Part of his charisma with colleagues arose from his embrace of small pleasures. At a dull cabinet meeting called to review the 1982 budget, Saddam passed out Cuban cigars, joking, "Whoever wants to smoke, go ahead and feel free. . . . We are going to give you something bourgeois, but it is from a socialist country."

In theory, Baath Party members were to model moral conduct and eschew gambling, drinking, and carousing. In practice, Saddam often tolerated these vices among his subordinates as long as they did not embarrass him. Owning a satellite dish to pick up international entertainment and news was against the law, but many of Saddam's colleagues mounted them on the roofs of their homes anyway. Gambling could be punished with fines or jail time, but one of Saddam's translators ran a lively poker game at his home for years; it made him nervous, but he believed, correctly, that if he gambled with trusted friends and kept the stakes low, he would be left alone.[8]

Saddam drank whiskey, but there is no evidence that he used alcohol heavily. After he married, he became involved with other women, which exacerbated the tensions within his family. When he got away to the countryside or retreated to one of his palaces, he relaxed by fishing, swimming, reading, and playing chess, at which he was very good. He had a self-made man's taste for luxury—Italian marble, Mercedes sedans—but also a self-identified peasant's readiness to travel or sleep rough, for security or nostalgic pleasure. Although he loved to hear himself talk, he could also be a calm and a capable listener. "He does not interrupt, and he never gets irritated or bothered by your suggestions," recalled a scientist who worked with him. "On a personal level, he did not make you feel anxious." The extent to which he intimidated individuals seems to have depended in part on how they reacted to his intense gaze. "He looked you straight in the eye, as if to control you," a military officer remembered. "In general, he was an intelligent person and an amazingly thorough listener. Not knowing what was on his mind was scary."[9]

Saddam was an active reader bent on self-improvement. His information office sent him uncensored daily translations of the international press: *Figaro* and *Le Monde*, the major American and British papers, and Arab dailies such as *Al-Quds* and *Al-Hayat*. He was drawn to memoirs and biographies of historical leaders. It became common in the West to take pointed note of Saddam's evident fascination with Joseph Stalin, the ironfisted Soviet ruler who presided over show trials and about a million political executions. Yet Saddam was also interested in Nelson Mandela, Jawaharlal Nehru, Josip Tito, Mao Zedong, George Washington, and Charles de Gaulle. He read fiction, including

the novels of Naguib Mahfouz. In his late twenties, he read and admired Ernest Hemingway's novella *The Old Man and the Sea*; he was
attracted to the heroic—in literature, in the history of other nations,
and in the story of Iraq, whose ancient and modern glories he celebrated with great verve. Yet there was one heroic story Saddam Hussein adored above all others: his own.[10]

In 1979, the Iraqi novelist Abd al-Amir Muallah published a trilogy
entitled *The Long Days*, which narrated the Baath revolution and the
valor of Saddam Hussein. It became an anchor of Saddam's relentlessly
celebrated biography, a tale told so often in diverse media that it would
be difficult for any sentient Iraqi to avoid. The president regarded
novels—his own and those of other Iraqi authors hired out by the
state—as prestigious propaganda.

He also had an instinct for cinematic spectacle: soon after he became president, in 1979, he became a film producer. He first bankrolled *Clash of Loyalties*, about the emergence of an independent Iraq
from the British Empire in the early twentieth century. The British
actor Oliver Reed starred as an imperial colonel, and Helen Ryan played
Gertrude Bell. Saddam flew the actors in from London; Reed traveled
with his seventeen-year-old girlfriend and spent much of the production
drinking himself into oblivion beside the Mansour Hotel's swimming
pool. Next, Saddam commissioned a six-hour television adaptation of
The Long Days, to bring to Iraqi audiences the story of his own indispensable place in their country's history. He cast a lookalike relative
as himself and paid Terence Young, the British director of the first
two James Bond movies, to provide a final edit. The import of all this
storytelling was consistent if banal: Iraq was a glorious, revolutionary
nation of scientists, artists, and warriors led by a brave visionary—an
"eagle," as Saddam has his mother describe him in his autobiographical
novel.[11]

The story of Saddam's political life—the self-mythologized one and the factual one—begins with his decision to run away from home at about age ten to attend school for the first time. In doing so, he defied his stepfather, who had told him to "forget about school" and "live like our fathers," meaning as peasant farmers, as Saddam recalled. The basic story appears to be reliable: Saddam snuck away one night, determined to learn to read and write. Due to "more than one obstacle," he enrolled at Salahuddin Elementary School "at a late age," as a Baath Party archive puts it delicately. The school had six classrooms and a fenced garden containing a mulberry tree. Saddam then moved to the nearby First Elementary School for Boys, where he passed into middle school with an exam score of 468 out of 600, or 78 percent. Records indicate he struggled because of absences and may eventually have been expelled.

Saddam moved to Baghdad, where he was taken in by Khairallah Tulfah, a brother of his mother. From then on, his shotgun-toting stepfather faded from Saddam's life, while Khairallah became singularly responsible for the boy's passage from countryside to city. Under his uncle's tutelage, he enrolled in high school. He lived in a terraced three-story house in Baghdad's Karkh district. Two of Khairallah's children—a son, Adnan, and a daughter, Sajida—lived there at times, too.

In an early photograph, Khairallah sports a thin, trimmed mustache and wears a coat and tie. He was perhaps the best-educated and most accomplished individual in Saddam's extended family. He had graduated from the Baghdad Military Academy as an officer but was arrested and imprisoned by the royal government of King Faisal II on charges of fomenting revolt. He was an Arab nationalist whose thinking was influenced by antisemitic blood libels, such as those derived from *The Protocols of the Elders of Zion*, an early twentieth-century fabrication of czarist Russia that circulated widely in the Arab world. Khairallah's teachings were later collected in a Baath Party book titled *Three Whom God Should Not Have Created: Persians, Jews, and Flies*. When released from prison, he returned to the Tikrit area and became a schoolteacher. To the family, he was an anti-imperialist notable. Khairallah retained connections with army officers who continued to plot in Baghdad against the royal family. One of these people was Ahmed Hassan al-Bakr, Khairallah's cousin and the future president of Iraq, whom Saddam would later serve for eleven years as vice president.[12]

Saddam fell in love with Sajida, his first cousin, and the two made plans to marry, eventually. In 1957, while he was still attending high school, Saddam joined the Baath Party. It was a time of revolutionary fervor and ideological conflict in Iraq, and the next several years would alter Saddam Hussein's life irrevocably.

On July 14, 1958, army units calling themselves the "Free Officers" invaded the royal palace, surrounded King Faisal II and members of his family—women and children among them—and shot them all dead. Brigadier Abd al-Karim Qasim emerged from the massacre as Iraq's new leader. The Baathists, initially, welcomed his rule.

Saddam was distracted during these events by a killing of a different genre. At some point during 1958, he traveled to the Tikrit area, where he ambushed and shot dead a distant relative who had offended his uncle Khairallah. The matter seems to have had as much to do with personal grievance as with politics. Saddam and Khairallah were both imprisoned for several months over the affair, but they escaped prosecution for murder. When Saddam returned to Baghdad, the capital was again beset by factional violence, and the Baath Party's leaders had lost faith in Qasim. They plotted to do away with him and take power themselves. The party's high command recruited Saddam, now twenty-one and recently credentialed as an assassin, to be a gunman in the hit team that would attempt to take Qasim out.

On October 7, 1959, Saddam and a handful of comrades crouched with pistols and machine guns near Rasheed Street, a bustling Baghdad commercial street where, they had learned, Qasim's convoy would pass. Saddam was supposed to hold his fire initially, but he was "unable to restrain himself," as an authorized biographer put it, and "immediately opened fire" when Qasim drove by. In the made-for-TV version of *The Long Days*, the attack erupted as in a tommy-gun gangster film, all

muzzle flashes and deafening fusillades. Qasim survived; Saddam took
a bullet in his thigh but evaded arrest.[13]

He embarked on a dramatic escape that he would tell and retell for
the rest of his days. The basic facts are well established, even if truth
and exaggeration are not easy to parse. In a Baghdad safe house, comrades pulled the bullet out of Saddam's thigh as, supposedly, he sat
stone-faced. He then donned traditional robes, bought a horse, and
rode for several days and nights toward Tikrit, hungry and hunted. He
swam across the Tigris—"on such a cold night and with a painful
wound. . . . his little knife between his teeth," as a biographer described
it—and reached safety among his rural clansmen. He mounted a motorcycle, rode on toward the Syrian border, found a smuggler's route,
saddled up a horse again, and crossed out of Iraq and into exile.[14]

In Damascus, Saddam was "a minor figure," other Iraqis recalled,
and after three months, he moved to Cairo, arriving in early 1960. He
took a room on the second floor of a two-story building in an old quarter of the city, on the east bank of the Nile. He joined the Iraqi Student
Association and soaked up Egyptian president Gamal Abdel Nasser's
fire-breathing rhetoric of Arab nationalism. Saddam enrolled in high
school, earning a diploma in May 1961, and he later studied law at
Cairo University, where he debated politics with other would-be revolutionaries. Saddam admired Nasser but was most heavily influenced by
the ideas of Michel 'Aflaq, a Sorbonne-educated Christian and co-
founder of the Baathist movement. They developed a cordial personal
relationship. 'Aflaq emphasized the necessity of pan-Arab conscious-
ness and unity in defeating Zionism and Western colonialism. He
advocated a form of secular socialism but opposed Soviet-backed international communism. The agenda of the Baathist "revolution" included
land reform, literacy drives, and industrialization. Yet party leaders focused heavily on the decidedly nonideological, bare-knuckled project
of seizing and consolidating power. The rise and success of a gunman
like Saddam among the Iraqi Baathists of the 1960s epitomized the importance of hard men over philosophers.

From Egypt, Saddam formalized his marriage engagement to his

cousin Sajida. In a photograph of this celebration, organized by the Association of Iraqis in Cairo, Saddam is smiling widely, dressed in a dark
business suit, with a pocket square accenting his tie. A dozen likewise
sharply dressed young men and a handful of uncovered women surround him. "Cairo for us was an open society," a friend from this period
remembered, "like someone moving from Basra to Paris." Yet Saddam
was still a provincial young man influenced by the conservative mores
of the Iraqi countryside. He told comrades privately in later years that
he had been offended by "this kind of liberal social behavior that we
saw in Egypt and the women in the streets and all the stories that went
with them."[15]

In February 1963, Iraqi Baath Party conspirators finally ousted and
executed General Qasim, the strongman they had tried earlier to assassinate. There were questions then and later about what role the C.I.A.
might have played in the Baath Party's successful coup against Qasim.
Eisenhower-era Washington was divided over whether Qasim was an
acceptable strongman-reformer or a proto-communist. The Kennedy
administration had embraced regime change in Iraq. The U.S. embassy
in Baghdad had been in close contact with the Baathist conspirators at
the time of their February coup. The extent of C.I.A. aid to the plotters and the agency's involvement in the Baathists' subsequent house-
by-house murder of hundreds of suspected Iraqi communists—by now
blood rivals of the Baath Party—is unknown. The C.I.A. has kept its
records classified for more than half a century.

Saddam, still exiled in Cairo, was not involved in these events in
Baghdad, but he would have heard details from insiders. It was an inau-
gural episode in Saddam's fevered, confusing experience of the C.I.A.
as an ally, enemy, and manipulative force in the Middle East. He soon
returned home to join the shaky new Baathist regime. He married Sajida, and they moved into a modest house in Baghdad to start a family.
In November, however, a military-backed junta pushed the Baath Party
out of power again, just nine months after it had taken charge.

By now, Saddam's cousin, Ahmed Hassan al-Bakr, who was more
than two decades older, had become a leading figure among the

Baathists. The authorities soon imprisoned both Saddam and Bakr on conspiracy charges, although the conditions were not oppressive. Saddam tried to make the most of his latest downtime. Some of his fellow prisoners "played backgammon, some played dominos," he recalled, but "I was always following a reading program."[16]

One day, while he was still imprisoned, Saddam was escorted by two armed men on a trip to court. They stopped for lunch. He excused himself to use the bathroom, climbed out a window, and returned to hiding. On July 17, 1968, when the Baathists at last took over Iraq decisively, Saddam's participation in the revolution—joyriding on a tank with his younger brother Barzan—proved to be of minor consequence, but he did play a significant part by cleaning up a personnel problem soon after the coup. The revolution had been made possible by the defection of the deputy head of Iraqi military intelligence, General Abdul Razzak al-Naif. The Baath Party had promised Naif the position of prime minister in exchange for his cooperation. Yet the general's loyalties were uncertain, and the Baath leadership didn't want to take chances. They instructed Saddam, their in-house intimidator, to handle the matter.

On July 30, Saddam confronted the general at the Republican Palace.

"I pulled a gun on him," Saddam recalled. "He carried a gun, too. It was like a movie." Naif backed down and pleaded for mercy, mentioning his four children.

"You forced your way into the revolution," Saddam told him. But he offered to send Naif into exile as an Iraqi ambassador.[17]

Naif suggested Lebanon and Algiers, but Saddam thought these were places for international troublemakers, so they settled on Morocco. Saddam walked the general out of the Republican Palace while pointing a pistol at his back, rode with him to the airport, and put him on a plane to Rabat.

As Iraq's vice president, Saddam traveled more widely during the 1970s than during any other period of his life. In addition to his trips to

France, he visited Moscow twice and signed an expansive Treaty of Friendship and Cooperation with the Soviet Union in 1972, alarming Washington's Cold Warriors. He met Josip Tito in Belgrade and Fidel Castro in Havana. Like Tito, Saddam was wary of Soviet expansionism and control. The Soviets will "not be satisfied until the whole world is communist," he complained.[18]

On July 17, 1979, the eleventh anniversary of the revolution, Bakr resigned. On that day, Saddam Hussein, at the age of forty-two, became Iraq's president, the unchallenged ruler of a nation possessed of vast oil riches and a large, well-equipped standing army. It was widely assumed that Saddam had strong-armed Bakr into retirement. Some form of putsch clearly occurred, but exactly what happened remains opaque. Bakr was an aging leader and had health problems. For years, Saddam treated Bakr courteously, even deferentially, but he "tightened control over all the security services and intelligence" while making no secret of his impatient ambition, recalled Fakhri Kaddouri, a minister and Central Bank governor during this period.[19]

When he seized full power, Saddam moved immediately against a faction of the Baath Party that he believed opposed him. On July 22, six days into his presidency, he summoned more than two hundred senior Baath members to the Khuld Hall, an auditorium near the Republican Palace. As cameras whirred, Saddam staged a ghoulish purge worthy of Stalin. The president sat at a table onstage, puffing a big cigar. A trusted comrade, Taha Yassin Ramadan, took the podium and announced that a "painful and atrocious plot" against Saddam had been discovered. He revealed—as if on a twisted episode of reality television—that all the criminal plotters were at this very moment in the hall, unaware of why they had been invited to the meeting.

The accused ringleader of the supposed conspiracy—a man named Muhie Abd al-Hussein Mashhadi—stepped onto the stage. He delivered a long, convoluted confession. "His appearance was that of a broken person, reconciled to his imminent death," as the historians Efraim Karsh and Inari Rautsi described his performance.[20]

Saddam then rose to speak. He unfolded a piece of paper and slowly read out the names of about five dozen conspirators. He had loved and trusted some of them, he emoted. One by one, guards escorted the accused from the room. Saddam wept and dabbed his eyes with a handkerchief.

A Baath Party court hastily tried the men and sentenced about twenty of them to death. In early August, firing squads made up of "volunteer" civilian Baath Party comrades gunned them down in "democratic executions," a grotesque form of capital punishment Saddam used repeatedly to bind party members to his rule. Saddam distributed copies of the filmed purge at Khuld Hall to Baath Party leaders, Iraqi schoolteachers, and Arab officials beyond Iraq; the tapes made for an indelible announcement of Saddam's arrival to the Middle East's game of thrones.

By instinct, the new president was most suspicious about the very security institutions that protected him from threats—his spy services, his secret police, his armed forces. He built a layered defense of overlapping intelligence agencies that spied on one another and the armed forces. The Mukhabarat and the General Military Intelligence Directorate focused largely on external threats. The General Security Service, or the Amn, was the biggest force of internal secret police. In the early 1980s, Saddam created the secretive Special Security Organization partly to spy on the other spies. His spies routinely tapped the telephones of his generals and planted informers throughout the army, which meant that some of his relatives were always spying on other relatives of his. He "always conspired against the closest people to him," recalled Brigadier General Raad Majid al-Hamdani. In the case of the army, this was for the practical reason that the institution was "the only force capable of conspiring against me," as Saddam once remarked. The army, he said, was like "a pet tiger," but as Hamdani noted, Saddam managed to pull out "its eyes, teeth, and claws."[21]

Saddam learned to control Iraq through generous patronage as well as cruelty. His giveaways attracted less publicity in the West than his atrocities, yet the codified entitlements available to compliant citizens meant that if they followed the rules and adjusted to the vicissitudes of Saddam's arbitrary justice, they had a shot at a tolerable life. The Ministry of Interior handed out "Friend of the President" identification cards with benefits listed on the back. These included at least one meeting with "His Eminence" each year, as well as two summer suits and two winter suits annually. Eventually, Saddam gave a Friend of the President card, plus a monthly pension, to anyone disabled or wounded at war. The regime doled out pensions, too, to the families of "martyrs" who died during military service or other work for the party or the government. Medals for civilians and soldiers conferred benefits such as life insurance, privileged school admissions for children, free medical treatment, free airline tickets, invitations to national events, and land. In time, Saddam favored artists alike, establishing three levels of monthly salaries doled out by the Ministry of Culture.[22]

Annual bonuses for those who worked most closely with Saddam could range as high as what a senior civil servant might earn from salary over five years. He also doled out cash tips spontaneously when he inspected some industrial project that had passed a milestone or just put him in a good mood. The president had a particular penchant for gifting cars—Toyotas and Volkswagens, typically—as his nuclear scientists at Tuwaitha had discovered. He cemented relations with foreign visitors by the same method. During the 1980s, Hissène Habré, the ruthless dictator of Chad, visited Baghdad. During a meeting, Saddam put a hand on the shoulder of an Iraqi aide and declared, "This man will give you one million dollars tonight." A courier soon carried a suitcase groaning with cash to Habré's hotel. The next day, when Saddam drove Chad's leader to the airport, Habré thanked him warmly. "It's nothing," Saddam answered. "You will receive one million dollars every year for you and your family." [23]

His protocol office kept a store of luxury European watches to present to guests and their spouses; the most prestigious visitors received Rolexes, while others had to settle for Piagets. He seemed to bestow such favors partly because it made him feel powerful and virtuous. The cartoonish aspects of Saddam's cult of personality may distract from the fact that he truly enjoyed being president. A portfolio of his propaganda pictures contains familiar poses of the modernizing leader: the technocrat in a business suit inspecting factories and farms; the patron of hospitals comforting patients at their bedsides; the father of the nation smiling amidst a gaggle of well-dressed children. Other staples include Saddam in a general's uniform, commanding troops near the front lines of the Iran-Iraq War, or in Kurdish dress, which was meant to signal that while he might have acted harshly against Kurdish rebels, he regarded Kurds as part of Iraq. Saddam is beaming uncontrollably in some of these pictures, or hugging people who appear slightly stunned at his presumption of intimacy. Outbursts of his laughter regularly interrupted his meetings with advisers and ministers.[24]

Saddam's enmity toward Israel was grounded in the geopolitical conflicts between Arab nationalists and the Jewish state after 1948, as well as in the Palestinian drive for justice and statehood. His antisemitism may not have been unusual among Arab elites, yet it was profound, and it distorted his understanding of the Middle East. He did not distinguish between the challenge of Israel and what he imagined to be the innate perfidy of the Jewish people. He accepted the authenticity of the forged *Protocols of the Elders of Zion* and relied on that libel to explain Israel's motivations. "The Zionists are greedy—I mean, the Jews are greedy," he told comrades privately. "We should reflect on all that we were able to learn from the Protocols. . . . I do not believe there was any falsification with regard to those Zionist objectives, specifically with regard to the Zionist desire to usurp—usurping the economies of people." In his privately recorded conversations, he only occasionally generalized about "Jews," but when he did, he voiced the ugliest calumnies, and he repeated these in his fiction, where he tried to sketch Iraq's place in the moral and political universe. He continually obsessed over Jewish power in the form of the State of Israel and the influence of Israeli lobbying in Washington.

Saddam had little, if any, personal experience of Iraq's centuries-old, once-thriving Jewish civilization. By the time he came of political age, Iraq's Jewish population had been reduced by decades of pogroms and discrimination to no more than several thousand people. The Baath Party advanced this oppression after seizing power. In 1970, the secret police also confiscated religious texts and artifacts and apparently added them to an archive of thousands of sacred and secular items later discovered in the basement of the Mukhabarat's headquarters.[25]

Saddam's displays of generosity could be followed by darker moods. "One moment he would be extremely affectionate, the next moment he would be extremely hostile and cruel," an Iraqi general recalled. "One minute he could be overly generous, the next he could be extremely stingy." Ali Hassan al-Majid, the cousin who would become a powerful and murderous figure in the regime, described "two faces to Saddam." He freely shared his wealth with people in need and sometimes wept while reading the Quran, Majid recalled. Yet he was "so cruel you could not imagine."[26]

Saddam routinely imprisoned generals and civil servants, and allowed them to be tortured and sentenced to death. Then, sometimes, out of the blue, he pardoned them. The parolee might then undergo a period of informal house arrest until one day Saddam called him in and appointed him to a new, high-ranking position. There is no convincing record of Saddam personally killing anyone after he took power, but he "would tell the security services to take care of things, and they would take care of it," said Tariq Aziz, his longtime cabinet member. The president "issued many pardons and executions at the same time," Aziz noted. He had an uncanny instinct for keeping those closest to him—indeed, the whole nation—fixated on his moods and expectations, a well-worn method of authoritarian control.[27]

In September 1983, after the family luncheon at which Saddam and Barzan had argued over the marriage of the president's daughter, the spy chief learned that the wedding he had opposed had taken place.

Neither Barzan nor Saddam's other two half brothers were invited. Furious, the three men sent Saddam a letter. "We are in this administration because you are the president," they wrote. Now, however, since Saddam had decided to marry Raghad to Hussein Kamel, the president should "consider us as having resigned from our positions."

Saddam flew into a rage. The president blamed his half brothers for uniting against him because they resented him as a stepbrother, according to what the head of Saddam's presidential office told Barzan. "Just wait and you will see," Saddam reportedly threatened.[28]

A few days later, Saddam wrote an angry letter to Barzan, blaming him for leading his brothers "to hell." The dispute over his daughter's marriage, Saddam insisted, was nothing but a "Trojan horse": Barzan's true objective was power.

It was the end of their alliance. Security forces impounded Barzan's cars and stripped him of his privileges until Saddam calmed down and they established an uncomfortable truce. The two were bound together— not only through Barzan's marriage to a sister of Saddam's wife but also through other marriages in the clan. For the next several years, Barzan and his family lived in an area of the capital controlled by Saddam's security forces. He and his relatives suffered small humiliations "almost daily." Barzan came to think that his enemies within the president's extended family, particularly on the Majid side, used "surveillance and forgery methods" to make sure that he remained discredited in Saddam's eyes.[29]

Barzan's sudden resignation from the Mukhabarat shocked Baghdad and set embassies and intelligence services scrambling to assess what it meant for the stability of Saddam's rule. The C.I.A. would conclude that Saddam had fired his half brother because he "was suspected by the President of building a political power base within the service and in part because he abused his position by alienating too many high personages."[30]

Barzan was right about one thing: the next prince, Hussein Kamel, the son-in-law Saddam had chosen for the hand of his eldest daughter, was destined to wield great power, ultimately establishing far greater influence in Iraq than Barzan ever had. In his memoir, Barzan recounts a "final word" of warning that he gave to Saddam. In light of future events, Barzan's recollection may be too foresightful to be believed, although he "swears" that it is exactly what he told Saddam "at the time," in 1983.

"Hussein Kamel is just like a time bomb in your pocket," Barzan recalled saying. "You do not know where and when it will explode."[31]

FOUR

Ambassadors
of Cynicism

On December 19, 1983, a United States military jet carrying Donald Rumsfeld on a mission for President Ronald Reagan landed at Saddam International Airport, a recently inaugurated monument to Baathist modernization dreams by the French architect and designer Jean-Louis Berthet. Metallic art by the sculptor Pierre Sabatier, whose work graced office buildings in Paris and Brussels, decorated the airport's terminal halls. Rumsfeld had come to "initiate a dialogue and establish personal rapport" with Saddam, as a State Department memo put it.

Seventeen months had passed since Tom Twetten of the C.I.A. had pitched up in the Iraqi capital. Since then, the agency's continual supply of satellite-derived battlefield intelligence had helped Iraq stave off defeat by Iran. Yet the U.S. and Iraq still had no formal diplomatic relations. Rumsfeld, who carried the title of "Personal Representative of the President of the United States in the Middle East," had been assigned to strengthen the tentative alliance, and to move toward the restoration of full relations, whenever Saddam was ready. The Iraqi president had never before met an emissary from the White House. To make an impression, Rumsfeld carried a letter from Reagan, as well as a gift chosen with the two presidents' love of horses in mind—a pair of golden spurs.[1]

Rumsfeld's mission had resulted from a shocking catastrophe in Lebanon. The country was being ripped apart by an eight-year-old civil war. On October 23, a suicide bomber driving a truck loaded with explosives had barreled into a four-story barracks at Beirut International Airport. The building housed a battalion of United States Marines originally deployed to help stabilize Lebanon's conflict. The detonation killed 241 servicemen—the largest loss of Marines in a single episode since the Second World War. As flag-draped coffins of dead servicemen came home, Ronald Reagan and his advisers felt an urgent need to respond but lacked clarity about what to do. Reagan felt that the U.S. could not back down in the face of a "despicable act" that had claimed so many American lives, yet some of his aides also believed that the mission in Lebanon was hopeless, and that the U.S. should withdraw its forces. The war was exceedingly complex, worsened by invasions by Syria and, more recently, by Israel, as well as by the covert involvement of Iranian radicals seeking to spread their revolutionary doctrine among Lebanon's Shiite minority.

Secretary of State George Shultz called Rumsfeld, then the chief executive of a pharmaceutical company in Chicago. Shultz said that the president needed a new envoy to "work on the Lebanon crisis and help with the American response to the terrorist attacks." Rumsfeld readily agreed.[2]

He was fifty-one years old, a Princetonian and former naval aviator who had been elected to Congress as a Republican during the early 1960s and then served in the Nixon and Ford administrations. In 1975, Ford had appointed him secretary of defense, making Rumsfeld the youngest-ever leader of the Pentagon, a distinction that seemed to top off his already ample self-confidence. In government, even back then, Rumsfeld's habit of writing pointed messages to subordinates—"snowflakes," as the missives would come to be known—grated on many. Usefully, however, at interagency meetings he was willing to buck conventional wisdom, since he held such a firm belief in his own opinions.

Rumsfeld consulted a map of the Middle East and considered the Lebanon problem in light of political geography. Iraq's significance seemed obvious to him. The Lebanon crisis suggested a new rationale for tilting toward Saddam Hussein, beyond helping him avoid losing his war. The Reagan administration wanted Syrian occupation forces in Lebanon to withdraw as part of a broader peace effort that would also include Israel's departure. Syria's president, Hafez al-Assad, espoused the same Baath Party ideology as Saddam Hussein, but Assad and Saddam had become rivals. They had grown to despise one another at least as much—perhaps more than—they each hated Israel. The White House hoped that since Syria was a common enemy of America and Iraq, closer American ties with Saddam might squeeze Assad. Rumsfeld insisted later that no one in the administration "harbored illusions" about the Iraqi dictator, yet he believed a fuller embrace made sense in a region where "America often had to deal with rulers who were deemed 'less bad' than the others."[3]

An Iraqi reception party welcomed Rumsfeld, loaded the envoy and his aides into an armed convoy, and rolled to the Ministry of Foreign Affairs, which was housed in an unattractive building of about a dozen stories, its windows recessed within concrete arches. Inside, striplights cast a dim, unhealthy glow over meeting rooms the size of basketball courts. Rumsfeld rode an elevator to an upper floor.

Unexpectedly, two armed Iraqi guards separated him from his aides and led him down a dark hallway. He entered a windowless room whose walls were padded in "what looked to be white leather." A gray-haired man with owlish, thick-lensed glasses, wearing belted green fatigues and a pistol on his hip, extended his hand.

"Welcome, Ambassador Rumsfeld," he said in perfect English. "I am Tariq Aziz." Now Saddam's foreign minister and deputy prime minister, Aziz was "among the four most powerful men in Iraq," as a State Department memo would soon describe him, and "second only to Saddam in formulating foreign policy." This assessment probably overstated Aziz's power, but the minister was certainly influential. Now forty-seven, he had risen to the top because he had language and analytical skills Saddam needed. Not incidentally, as a member of Iraq's tiny Chaldean Christian community in an overwhelmingly Muslim country, he posed no political threat to the president.[4]

Aziz had grown up in Baghdad and earned a degree in English literature from Baghdad University. He joined the Baath Party and worked as an English interpreter and as an Arabic-language writer and party propagandist. He first met Saddam at a Baath Party conference in Syria, in 1963. They were close to the same age, and he found his comrade to be "a smart young man with a good intellect" who had "worked on improving himself . . . He read a lot." Aziz came to think of Saddam as "a leader and very intellectual, but violent and strict, too." When the Baathists took power, Aziz edited party newspapers, served three years as minister of information, and then, toward the end of Saddam's vice presidency, became a member of the supreme Revolutionary Command Council.[5]

He shared his mentor's fondness for Cuban cigars. By the time he became Iraq's leading international diplomat, he smoked Cohibas continuously, and he seemed to deploy thick clouds of aromatic smoke as a cloaking device. His bulky glasses could give him a slightly bug-eyed appearance; one interlocutor thought of him as the hookah-puffing caterpillar in *Alice in Wonderland*. When at home in Baghdad, he lived in a walled compound of comfortable houses across from the Baath Party's headquarters; a ramp conveyed cars up to an entrance on his residence's second floor. Within Saddam's inner circle, he mastered the art of accommodating his boss's moods, rambling soliloquies, and insecurities while providing Saddam with enough reliable advice that he became a fixture in meetings about international matters. Saddam was wary of allowing close aides to travel abroad, where they might connect with foreign spy agencies and enter into conspiracies against him. Yet he trusted Aziz and permitted him to travel to Arab capitals, China, the Soviet Union, and Europe. Aziz was the main architect of Saddam's special relationship with France; he seemed to particularly enjoy his sojourns in Paris. Like Saddam, Aziz occasionally conducted the kind of diplomacy in which the exchange of gifts between friends—bribes, as puritanical lawyers might describe them—could play a role. Mainly, though, he served as a professional negotiator and communicator, providing Baathist Iraq with competent representation in global capitals. In meetings, Aziz could be skillfully recessive. He would sometimes open a session by asking his counterpart, without preamble, "What do you have?" and then sit back and wait for his flat-footed visitor to start talking. Yet he could also be candid, forthright, and humorous, and his English fluency allowed him to engage in the subtleties often required in high-stakes diplomatic exchanges. One of his half-joking practices was to outright refuse to carry a foreigner's proposal to Saddam if he was certain his boss would reject it. "I'm not going to bring this to the president, because I'll be executed for proposing it," Aziz would say. The quip was just plausible enough to stop a counterpart cold.[6]

On the evening of December 19, Aziz lit up a Cohiba, while Rumsfeld smoked Chesterfield cigarettes. They spoke for two and a half hours. They agreed that it was in both of their interests "that there be limits on Syria's ambitions," according to a record of the session. They touched on Iraq's strained relations with Egypt following the 1978 Camp David Accords; the Israeli-Palestinian conflict; and Iraq's oil exports.

"The building we are sitting in," Aziz said, "could not have been built as well or as quickly as it was without the help of Americans, French, Germans, or Japanese. If a country is truly interested in modernization, as Iraq is, the only way is to have ties with Western nations."

Rumsfeld said it was "unnatural" for a generation of Americans and Iraqis to grow up with no knowledge of one another. He peppered Aziz with questions about the Iran-Iraq War. Aziz said he felt the "war was over in the strategic sense, in that Iraq will not lose." He did not know when it would end, however—"one, two, three, four years from now."

"The U.S. has no interest in an Iranian victory," Rumsfeld said at one point, reiterating the rationale for America's tilt toward Saddam. "To the contrary, we would not want Iran's influence expanded at the expense of Iraq." It was a declaration Aziz might have quoted back to Rumsfeld two decades later, if he had recalled it.

Rumsfeld said the U.S. could use its influence to mediate a settlement of the Iran-Iraq War, but there were "certain things that make it difficult for us," such as "the use of chemical weapons, possible escalation in the Gulf, and human rights." This passing, indirect comment was the only time Rumsfeld raised Iraq's use of chemical arms during his visit, notes of the meetings indicate. The signal was clear: Iraq's gassing of Iranian troops was not an obstacle to a deepening alliance with Washington.[7]

The next morning, outside the entrance to Saddam Hussein's office at the Republican Palace, Rumsfeld shook hands with the Iraqi president. Rumsfeld wore a suit, Saddam his fatigues and pistol. The Iraqi president stood several inches taller than the envoy, and his ink-black hair and mustache made Rumsfeld wonder privately if the dictator used a dye. Rumsfeld formally presented the letter he carried from Ronald Reagan. They stepped into the president's large, ornate office and took up places at opposite ends of a gold-and-burgundy sofa.

The presence of interpreters and aides ensured that their ninety-minute discussion would be stiffer than Rumsfeld's bull session with Tariq Aziz the night before. Saddam said Reagan's letter indicated "deep and serious understanding" of Iraq's war with Iran and its "dangers." He was pleased that the U.S. was ready to resume full diplomatic ties, although he did not commit to a timetable. To Rumsfeld's lasting satisfaction, Saddam played back a line Rumsfeld had used with Aziz the night before. "Having a whole generation of Iraqis and Americans grow up without understanding each other . . . could lead to mix-ups," Saddam remarked.

He spoke at length about the United States. It was "incorrect and unbalanced" for Iraq to have ties with Moscow but not with Washington. He did not wish for the Middle East to "fall under Soviet influence," yet the Arab world did not want to fall under the "influence of either superpower." Once Saddam got started on geopolitics, it could be difficult to stop him. He went on to muse about the Cold War, and how the West could lure impoverished countries like North Yemen and Mauritania away from Soviet influence. He gave Rumsfeld a dose of anti-colonial, anti-Israel rhetoric. He also said that the United States had initially "acted with indifference" during the Iran-Iraq War, but that Iraq had come to the rescue of America and its weak Arab allies by fighting Khomeini's expansionism, at great cost to itself. What would have happened to the likes of Saudi Arabia and Kuwait if Iraq had not "stood fast" against the Iranian Revolution?

"No one would have been able to put out the fire," Saddam said, answering his own question.

When his turn came at last, Rumsfeld delivered his main points: The U.S. and Iraq had "shared interests in preventing Iranian and Syrian expansion." The Reagan administration was moving to shut down arms exports to Iran.

At one point, Saddam summoned Rumsfeld to join him at a window. "See that building?" he asked, pointing at the Baghdad skyline. "When an elevator breaks in that building, where do we look to have it repaired?" The nations of Europe and the United States, Saddam continued. The message seemed plain: Iraq had constructed an alliance with France through lucrative, oil-financed business deals, and Saddam could do the same for American companies.[8]

Before Rumsfeld parted, Saddam offered him a gift. It was not the typical bauble favored by diplomatic protocol officers. It was a videotape made by one of his propaganda offices. The tape showed several minutes of "amateurish footage," as Rumsfeld recalled, in which Syrian president Hafez al-Assad inspected troops and applauded. Then it depicted "people purported to be Syrians strangling puppies" followed by a "line of young women biting the heads off of snakes." The tape was edited to suggest that Assad was present and applauding. The gift understandably struck Rumsfeld as bizarre. It reflected an ocean-sized gulf between Saddam's ideas about how to influence America and the realities of what might work.[9]

Many of Reagan's advisers judged Rumsfeld's visit to Baghdad a success. Early in 1984, they planned to dispatch him on a second trip to Baghdad to deepen the "rapport." But the White House—not for the first or last time—had failed to think through the contradictions inherent in its embrace of Saddam Hussein.

In the early 1960s, Iraq had begun researching chemical weapons. One reason was defensive: to understand the effects of chemical arms in case they were ever used against Iraq. Officers appointed to a new Iraqi Chemical Corps went abroad to train. In 1971, when Saddam was vice president, Iraq had tried to synthesize small amounts of agents historically used in chemical warfare—including the compound used in mustard gas—but these efforts were unsuccessful. After Saddam ordered the invasion of Iran, his interest in chemical weapons revived.[10]

In March 1981, during a discussion with military commanders, an Iraqi officer asked him for permission to use six short-range missiles in an upcoming battle.

Saddam asked if the missiles "could be used tactically" in a "chemical war."

"And bacterial war also," a colleague replied.

"Yes, it can be used in bacterial and chemical war. . . . Let's start the implementation of this program."[11]

It isn't clear what immediately followed this seeming order, but on June 8, 1981—the day following Israel's surprise attack on Iraq's nuclear reactors at Tuwaitha—Iraq's Ministry of Defense launched Project 922, a crash research and manufacturing program to produce mustard gas and, eventually, the even deadlier agents tabun, sarin, and VX, as well as chemical-ready bombs and artillery shells. Under the cover of pesticide production, West German corporations quickly built for Iraq what was "at the time the world's most modern and best-planned [chemical-weapons] facility" about forty miles northwest of Baghdad, as investigators later described.[12]

Iraqi forces most likely first gassed Iranian troops in July 1982, near

Basra, but the effectiveness of the weapons "was not established" at first, an Iraqi intelligence assessment found. Interrogations of Iranian prisoners in another case showed that they had suffered from only "light dizziness." It became apparent to Saddam, nonetheless, that gas had one notable advantage: it frightened people.

The first successful documented use of mustard gas by Iraq took place in July 1983. The country was "armed with new weapons," Baghdad's high command warned Iran two months later. "These modern weapons . . . were not used in previous attacks for humanitarian and ethical reasons." Such qualms had now been set aside. "This time we will use a weapon that will destroy any moving creature."[13]

In early 1984, Iranian forces threatened an invasion of Iraq. On February 21, Iraqi major general Maher Abd al-Rashid spoke publicly: "The invaders should know that for every harmful insect there is an insecticide capable of annihilating it, whatever their number, and Iraq possesses this annihilation insecticide." The next day, Iranian units that included young volunteers and conscripts launched human-wave attacks, trying to cut a Basra–Baghdad highway. An Iraqi armored corps hit them with "a crude sulfur-mustard, similar to that used by Germany in 1917 on the Western Front," as one account described it, and inflicted an estimated 2,500 casualties. The battle also involved the first-ever recorded attack using a nerve agent: tabun. The Iranian charge faltered as the soldiers' skin blistered and burned, their lungs seared, and they temporarily lost sight.[14]

Ayatollah Khomeini's government protested Iraq's use of gas publicly. Credible reports reached international journalists. Iqbal Riza, a U.N. official, visited a Tehran hospital in March. He met a badly mutilated victim who made a victory sign from his bed before dying of his wounds a few hours later. Iran would soon transport chemical victims for medical treatment to Europe, where bedraggled men with chronic coughs and grotesque burns staggered off airplanes as barely-living evidence of Iraqi war crimes.

General Rashid's "insecticide" remark was too much for the Reagan administration to ignore. For decades, the U.S. had worked to prevent the spread and use of chemical arms. His grotesque metaphor gave the Reagan administration "a peg" to clarify its position, as Francis Ricciardone, then on the State Department's Iraq desk, put it. On March 4, State acknowledged publicly for the first time that "the available evidence substantiates . . . that Iraq has used chemical weapons." Its statement went on: "The United States strongly condemns the prohibited use of chemical weapons wherever it occurs. There can be no justification for their use by any country." The message qualified this criticism by denouncing Iran's unwavering war aim of "eliminating the legitimate government" in Baghdad. Yet the next day's front-page headline in *The New York Times* captured the main news as it played around the world: "U.S. Says Iraqis Used Poison Gas against Iranians in Latest Battles."[15]

The Iraqis had assumed that their reception of Rumsfeld would immunize them from such embarrassing denouncements. How could Saddam trust the Americans? One minute they came bearing gifts, the next—and without warning—they discredited him before the world. "Iraq is confused by our means of pursuing our stated objectives in the region," a State Department memo reported in late March. After the Reagan administration's scolding, "their temptation is to give up rational analysis and retreat to the line that U.S. policies are basically anti-Arab and hostage to the desires of Israel."[16]

The administration immediately walked back its criticism, at least in private. On March 15, Ismat Kittani, a deputy of Tariq Aziz, visited Washington to meet Lawrence Eagleburger, an undersecretary of state. In a preplanned move known in diplomacy as the "drop by," in which a high-ranking official drops in on a foreign visitor to convey an important message, Secretary of State George Shultz entered Eagleburger's office. He told Kittani that America's public criticism of Iraq's use of mustard gas reflected "strong U.S. commitment to long standing policy" but should not be misunderstood as an "anti-Iraqi gesture." The key message for Baghdad was that "our desires and our actions to prevent an Iranian victory and to continue the progress of our bilateral relations remain undiminished."[17]

This repudiation of the Reagan administration's own headline-making statement of eleven days earlier inaugurated a dark and cynical chapter in American policymaking. Between 1984 and 1988, the United States not only accepted but also effectively collaborated with Saddam Hussein's use of chemical weapons against Iran by sharing intelligence about Iranian positions. All the while, Washington continued to insist, in public, that it condemned chemical-weapon use by any and all. Of course, the Reagan administration would have preferred that Saddam not gas Iranian forces, but there was no practical way for the C.I.A. to prevent Iraqi commanders from using U.S. satellite intelligence to plan chemical-weapon attacks. Nor was the Reagan White House willing to withdraw the intelligence for this reason.

Nonetheless, the Iraqis remained confused about U.S. policy. Rumsfeld's planned return to Baghdad now seemed urgent—to pick up where Shultz's "drop by" had left off. He would encounter a "worsened" atmosphere, State Department analysts warned him. On April 26, 1984, Donald Rumsfeld arrived back in the Iraqi capital carrying instructions to soft-pedal the chemical-weapons problem: America's public condemnation of reported Iraqi chemical use "was made strictly out of our strong opposition" to gassing soldiers "wherever it occurs," as a trip memo put it. The Reagan administration's interest in "(1) preventing an Iranian victory and (2) continuing to improve bilateral relations with Iraq . . . remain[ed] undiminished."[18]

Saddam refused to see Rumsfeld. The envoy had to settle for another smoke-filled-room session with Tariq Aziz before convoying back to the airport.

Aziz dispatched a new representative, Nizar Hamdoon, to advocate for Saddam in Washington. In the absence of formal diplomatic relations, Hamdoon would initially run Iraq's "interests section" in the capital. As a practical matter, this meant he worked in the old ambassador's office in Iraq's former embassy building near Dupont Circle. He resided in a grand ambassador's residence on Woodlawn Drive N.W., nestled near Rock Creek Park. Nizar Hamdoon would become a prominent figure in the conflict between the U.S. and Iraq in years to come, but there was little on his résumé when he arrived to suggest this future. He had joined the Baath Party as a teenager during the late 1950s, in that bloody era of factional street battles. "You got beaten. You could be imprisoned," he recalled of his introduction to Iraqi politics. When he first turned up in Washington, he chain-smoked Marlboros and dressed in white suits, black shirts, and white ties. His favorite Scotch was Johnnie Walker Black. The State Department's David Mack, who had served in Baghdad, thought he "looked like a Baath Party thug." His English "wasn't very good, and even his Arabic seemed closer to the Iraqi street than to the foreign ministry."[19]

Yet Hamdoon was smarter than he appeared. He had attended the same Jesuit day school in Baghdad as Jafar Dhia Jafar, the distinguished physicist, and had studied architecture at university. Enthusiastic about his assignment in America, he improved his English rapidly while watching popular TV police procedurals of the early 1980s, such as *Cagney & Lacey*. (Hamdoon enjoyed American shows in which the police "control the cities" and "control the gangs," he explained.) He was not conventionally charismatic—he rarely laughed and had a brooding demeanor—but he was candid and straightforward, a listener eager to understand and connect. He took advice well and soon replaced his Al Capone attire with the standard Washington uniform of dark suits, white shirts, and inoffensive ties. He adopted local Christmas rituals and sent around gift boxes of Cuban cigars and bottles of Veuve Clicquot to his growing list of contacts.[20]

America's capital city had entered an era of prosperity and hubris. A new space-age international airport with moon lander–inspired passenger shuttles had recently opened in the far Virginia suburbs. Cranes dotted the downtown skyline from the U.S. Capitol to Georgetown as developers built gleaming new glass-and-granite office buildings for lobbyists, think tanks, law firms, defense contractors, newsrooms, and trade associations—a bipartisan class of elite beneficiaries of the Cold War's economic and defense-spending dividends.

Hamdoon had no formal training as an agent of influence, but he infiltrated this political aristocracy by perseverance and uncanny instinct. Soon after he arrived, Judith Kipper, a Middle East specialist at the American Enterprise Institute, a center-right think tank, hosted Hamdoon at a luncheon. He was introduced to Odeh Aburdene, an American of Palestinian origin who was then vice president for the Middle East at Occidental Petroleum. The two men developed a friendship, and Aburdene schooled Hamdoon on how the more effective ambassadors cultivated newspaper columnists and reporters, as well as congressional aides and fellow diplomats.[21]

Hamdoon also met Mary King, a minister's daughter who had joined the Student Nonviolent Coordinating Committee as a civil rights organizer and later worked in the Carter administration on anti-poverty programs. She found Hamdoon "honest in his ability to ask questions," with "no fear of appearing ignorant," unlike other cautious, status-conscious Arab diplomats she had met. She tutored Hamdoon about "the division of powers in the U.S. political system so that he would understand that it was planned and intentional." King would carry a pocket Constitution to dinner with him and whip it out as they talked to explain the Bill of Rights and other features of the American governmental design. They discussed creating a new forum for U.S. oil companies, manufacturers, and construction firms interested in doing business in Iraq, to take advantage of the opening between the Reagan administration and Saddam's regime.[22]

Hamdoon enjoyed an unusual, candid relationship with Saddam. Hamdoon recalled that he wrote critically to the boss, and that Saddam took it in stride. "I conveyed some bad—bad from his perspective—unacceptable ideas to him. . . . All about policy," Hamdoon recalled later. Yet Saddam "let me off." Mary King believed that Saddam trusted Hamdoon "because he was so forthright, because he was so deadpan, because he was so straight."

"Are there people around Saddam who think like you?" Aburdene once asked him, after Hamdoon had candidly discussed his ideas about political reform at home.

"No," Hamdoon admitted, as Aburdene recalled. "There are a lot of blind followers and crude thinkers."[23]

The envoy's residence was a sizable Georgian brick house with bay windows and a carriage driveway. There he hosted dinner parties where George McGovern, the former presidential candidate, and William Colby, the former C.I.A. director, might share a table with Middle East watchers in the Washington press corps. "He played the media," recalled David Mack. "There was nobody that he would not try to cultivate." Daniel Pipes, publisher of the Middle East Quarterly, recalled Hamdoon as "probably the most skilled diplomat I ever encountered." Less than two years after he arrived, The Washington Post put Hamdoon on the cover of its Sunday magazine, posed with his arms folded across his chest. The profile's headline was "The Artful Ambassador."[24]

Hamdoon promoted a narrative of common interests between Washington and Baghdad that went beyond shared enmity toward Iran and Syria. In conversation with Middle East hands, he "implicitly accepted the virtues of democracy, the existence of Israel, and the horrors of nuclear weapons," recalled Pipes. "He then argued that to achieve these goals meant working with Baghdad, not against it." During increasingly frequent public appearances, Hamdoon argued that "the model of Khomeinism," or radical and expansionist Islamism, threatened not just the Middle East but "everybody else in the world." He deflected criticism of Saddam's human rights record and use of poison gas. As reports of Iraq's chemical attacks on Iranian troops became all but irrefutable, he maintained official denials in public while subtly justifying Iraq's actions. The Iranians "have very little problem in sending thousands of brainwashed boys and young men to the front lines to meet a certain death," he said. Iraq merely sought to "minimize casualties" among its own troops in the face of this inhuman onslaught. "We don't believe in a 'clean' war," Hamdoon continued. "All wars are ugly."[25]

During 1984, Hamdoon's first full year in Washington, the Reagan administration offered enlarged support to Baghdad. It increased credits and promoted business investments by U.S. corporations in Iraq while continuing the C.I.A.'s covert supply of intelligence. By summer,

Saddam had paused his acid public denouncements of the United States. He returned to the logic that had first led him to embrace the C.I.A.'s assistance: if he moved closer to Washington, it might help him salvage the war with Iran, balance his ties with Moscow, and provide access to advanced technologies.

O n August 28, 1984, the C.I.A. reported in a classified intelligence assessment that it was now "unlikely" that Iraq would lose the war. As a result of arms sales by France and the Soviet Union, as well as U.S.-led efforts to stop arms smuggling to Iran, "the military balance has shifted overwhelmingly in favor of Iraq during the past year." Baghdad enjoyed a four-to-one advantage in armor and an eight-to-one advantage in combat aircraft. Moreover, "Iraq's development of chemical weapons also provides its armed forces with an advantage in destructive power that the Iranians cannot match."[26]

A few weeks later, Tariq Aziz told American diplomats that Iraq was at last ready to restore formal diplomatic relations with the United States—to upgrade the two interests sections to embassies and appoint ambassadors. The Reagan administration pounced on the invitation and invited Aziz to Washington in late November. He would meet ranking members of Congress in both parties, appear on national news shows, and sit down privately with the defense secretary, the C.I.A. director, the secretary of state, the vice president, and Ronald Reagan himself.

National Security Adviser Robert McFarlane prepared Reagan with a nuanced briefing memo and a handful of talking points printed on index cards that the president could consult during the meeting. McFarlane conveyed the optimism and illusions that had come to saturate American thinking about Saddam by late 1984. Iraq "has moved away from radical anti-Western domestic and foreign policies," he wrote. "As the chief barrier to the spread of Iranian-supported Islamic fundamentalism, Iraq is promoting regional stability in the course of securing its own defense."[27]

On November 26, Reagan greeted Aziz in the Oval Office and posed smiling with him for photographs before ushering his guests to chairs and couches. McFarlane, Secretary of State Shultz, and three other aides joined the president. Nizar Hamdoon was in the small Iraqi delegation.

Aziz conveyed Saddam Hussein's thanks to President Reagan "for agreeing to establish relations. This visit represents a very good beginning."

The only awkward moment came when Reagan appeared to deviate from his index cards to ask a question about the Israeli-Palestinian conflict. The United States had concluded that the bulk of the Palestinians were moderate in their outlook, Reagan said. "What motivates the radicals?" he asked. "Is it a power play?"

"The Middle East is very complicated," Aziz answered gingerly. "It is suffering from crises. Some states—such as Syria—benefit politically, financially, and militarily from crises," such as the Israeli-Palestinian conflict and the Lebanese civil war. "There are many contradictory elements," Aziz concluded. "The U.S. must understand why these elements are causing trouble."[28]

Ronald Reagan, by habit of mind, was optimistic. "Tariq Aziz came in," he wrote briefly in his diary that evening. "Today we re-established diplomatic relations which Iraq had broken off 17 yrs. ago. We maybe helped in our peace efforts because Iraq is pretty cool toward Syria— the bad boy of the Middle East." It was a tag that Saddam Hussein's Iraq had finally managed to shed.[29]

FIVE

Department 3000

O n an April morning in 1985, a convoy of chauffeured cars bearing the brain trust of Iraq's secret nuclear program snaked toward Radwaniyah, a presidential estate on requisitioned farmland near Baghdad's airport. Jafar Dhia Jafar, now the program's director of research and development, joined the procession. They were on their way to meet Saddam Hussein.[1]

The cars halted before a Wanderlodge recreational vehicle. The Wanderlodge was a forty-foot luxury motor home manufactured by Blue Bird, an American company headquartered in Georgia. The vehicle was an icon of 1980s-era faux outdoors indulgence; Johnny Cash, Tom Cruise, and King Hussein of Jordan were all owners. Customized, tricked-out models could command $350,000. Standard amenities included two TVs, a bathtub, a bedroom, a central vacuuming system, and a horn that could play five dozen songs. There were also optional features; King Fahd of Saudi Arabia installed a throne. Saddam had imported a dozen of the vehicles and kept them garaged at Radwaniyah. Some had large meeting rooms; others, bedrooms and high-end entertainment systems. When Saddam flew to cities around Iraq, his aides sometimes drove a Wanderlodge or two to meet him.[2]

His taste in offices mirrored his approach to Radwaniyah, his Xanadu-under-construction—when finished, the estate would contain roaming wild game, a dozen artificial lakes stocked with carp, and many palaces. Saddam wanted a refuge where he could escape people he didn't want to see, where he could fish, work, and take meetings on his own schedule. Radwaniyah seemed to be a perpetual work in progress, dotted with cranes and bulldozers. The president often roamed the grounds, ordered changes, and chose materials. His vision was typical of the luxury styles of oil-boom Arabia, except that Saddam's obsession with security required features more familiar in James Bond movies—secret tunnels, camouflaged entrances, and control rooms blinking with screens tied to surveillance cameras.[3]

Jafar filed into the Wanderlodge with five other members of Iraq's Atomic Energy Commission. The scientists were there to brief the president about Department 3000, as Iraq's clandestine nuclear program had been named. The program now employed about two hundred scientists, engineers, and support workers. Their goal was to enrich uranium to bomb-grade levels.

Humam Abdul Khaliq, the commission's vice-chairman, provided Saddam with a formal update. At length, he walked through the major tracks of the program. One effort being overseen by Jafar planned to enrich uranium through techniques of electromagnetic isotope separation, or EMIS, commonly referred to acronymically as "ee-miss." Jafar had succeeded with lab-scale enrichment, far below bomb level, but he had demonstrated that Iraq could separate U-235, the essential isotope of a uranium-fueled bomb. Department 3000 had already started to design production-scale EMIS facilities.

Saddam listened attentively. The president was—or could convincingly pretend to be—fascinated by even the lengthiest Department 3000 presentations. He not only showed "great interest," as Jafar recalled, but also gave the impression "that he [was] aware of all that was presented to him."[4]

That morning, Khaliq made a fateful forecast. He told Saddam that the nuclear program would reach its "fruitful objectives" in five years, or in 1990, according to an atomic energy commissioner who was present. Jafar thought Khaliq was talking about achieving only production-scale uranium enrichment—a finished bomb would require additional work. In any event, when Saddam heard the forecast, his eyes welled with emotion.

"If you produce the nuclear bomb," the president told Jafar, "I will make a golden statue of you."

After the meeting, the commissioner recalled, the president rewarded his nuclear team with another round of Mercedes-Benz cars, and in a more novel gesture, he handed out recreational vehicles, too.[5]

Jafar had by now grown accustomed to Iraq's idiosyncratic leader. Saddam had elevated him to membership on the Iraqi Atomic Energy Commission. The commission supervised all of the country's nuclear programs—the research reactor and science programs openly declared to international watchdogs, as well as the secret bomb effort. Jafar was the commission's most qualified scientist by far. The body's chairman at the time, Izzat Ibrahim al-Douri, a former ice salesman and longtime Baath Party apparatchik, didn't know an isotope from a socket wrench.

Jafar was widely respected, but some of his colleagues felt that he could be haughty and controlling, and that he was too enamored of basic science. This critique held that he was not moving fast enough to build a nuclear-weapons device—an actual bomb that could reliably explode. Indeed, although Jafar had made notable progress on uranium enrichment, he had yet to start work on "weaponization," meaning the design and testing of a bomb shell and a conventional explosives package that would cause uranium fuel to detonate. In fact, Jafar was reluctant to get personally involved with weaponization, although it would eventually come under his supervision. It was more of a military engineering project than a matter for a particle physicist. As of the

Wanderlodge session in the spring of 1985, he thought there was still more work to do on enrichment before it would make sense to turn to bomb-building.

Exactly what was promised to Saddam in the motor home would become a matter of dispute among Iraqi scientists, but some of those who heard about the "fruitful objectives" pledge became terrified that a 1990 timeline for a finished bomb had been promised, and that they might be held personally accountable by Saddam if they disappointed him. Jafar was surprised to hear about these anxieties; according to him, any such fears were groundless. He had spoken privately with Saddam, and he wasn't worried about disappointing the president. In all their conversations, Saddam had "never asked for a deadline, and we never gave a deadline," Jafar recalled. The president treated his chief physicist carefully and did not pressure him. His questions were personal, and he always asked if his scientist needed anything. Jafar always demurred, he recalled. "God bless your efforts" was Saddam's typical refrain.[6]

Whether 1990 was a hard deadline or not, the question was if they were on the right path to a bomb—and the main responsibility lay with Jafar. When he was not on-site at EMIS or other secret facilities, he still worked day-to-day in the same prefabricated administrative building at the Tuwaitha Nuclear Research Center where he had been based when he was detained and held incommunicado. He had resumed his chauffeured daily commute from Baghdad. Early in 1982, after his release, Jafar had moved into the new house he had been building when he was arrested—a flat-roofed two-story home of about 6,500 square feet with four bedrooms, a study, and a large garden.

He was an orderly decision-maker, the sort of person who listed options with their advantages and disadvantages. This was the method he had applied to Department 3000's critical choices. Acquiring bomb fuel, or fissionable material, was the most difficult part of building a nuclear device. The first choice was between uranium and plutonium.

Jafar considered how Iraq might acquire enough plutonium to make a few atomic bombs, but this looked problematic. It would be impossible to hide a plutonium-production reactor from satellite reconnaissance. The fuel in Iraq's Soviet-supplied research reactor could theoretically be reprocessed to make plutonium, but only a small amount, and the reactor was under international monitoring. Trying to buy additional nuclear reactors that might provide an option to extract a lot of plutonium would be difficult—Israel's raid on Tuwaitha was an indicator of Saddam's dubious reputation in the global nuclear marketplace.

That left uranium. Before and during Jafar's house arrest, Iraq had imported partially refined uranium ore, known as yellowcake, from Niger and Brazil. It had also acquired five tons of lightly enriched uranium from Italy. Some of the imports were open, others undeclared. (The International Atomic Energy Agency did not require reporting of yellowcake purchases.) The country now had plenty of stock; the question was how to enrich the uranium. There were several proven methods. Saddam impressed upon Jafar, as the physicist recalled, that he wanted Iraq's nuclear program to be as indigenous as possible; he did not want to cross "redlines" by seeking to purchase equipment abroad that was on restricted lists because it could be used in the building of nuclear bombs. Saddam's reasoning wasn't always clear, but Iraq was in the middle of a war with Iran, and its fate in that conflict depended on support from France, the Soviet Union, and the United States. All of these countries opposed the spread of nuclear weapons to countries like Iraq. If Jafar got caught smuggling nuclear-related materials, it might jeopardize Iraq's war effort and Saddam's own survival in power.[7]

Because of Saddam's edict, Jafar had ruled out building centrifuges, an increasingly popular technology for creating highly enriched uranium. This method lay at the heart of Pakistan's secret bomb program, for example. A. Q. Khan, the metallurgist who led Pakistan's effort, had worked for a subcontractor of a uranium enrichment consortium in Europe, where he obtained access to advanced West German centrifuge designs and apparently stole them. Centrifuges are precise conical devices that can separate the U-235 isotope by spinning uranium at supersonic speeds. Pakistan had built many centrifuges from Khan's pilfered designs. Yet its bomb program had also been detected by international governments. For Iraq to build centrifuges without shopping abroad for materials and designs, Jafar felt, someone on his team would have "to invent something," and yet, you "cannot put a timescale" on a project like that.[8]

EMIS attracted Jafar the most. This was the method Manhattan Project scientists had employed to enrich the uranium fuel used in Little Boy, the atomic bomb dropped on Hiroshima in 1945. Essentially, large magnets separate U-235 to create a highly enriched blend that can go critical and detonate. The list of advantages in Jafar's initial study was lengthy. The technology was "open and reasonably well documented in the literature," and although there would be much trial and error, there was "no basic scientific or technical problem" that necessitated a breakthrough invention by Iraqi scientists. Much of the software and manufacturing equipment required was "not on the trigger list" of restricted nuclear trade items and "therefore [could] be procured relatively easily." The disadvantages mainly had to do with scale. To separate enough U-235 to make a bomb would require very large, heavy magnets. The manufacturing and production project would be labor-intensive and expensive.

A third option was called "gaseous diffusion," in which uranium fuel feed is filtered through a complex barrier designed to separate U-235. This was a proven technology, and Jafar judged indigenous development to be possible. He authorized a program in Department 3000, partly because he wanted to invest in more than one pathway to avoid a single point of failure.

During the next several years, Jafar devoted his own time to the EMIS project. When it got underway, the goal was to run successful experiments, then scale up production to fifteen kilograms of highly enriched uranium per year at an enrichment of 93 percent—a pace, roughly, that would yield at least enough fissionable material for one basic atomic bomb every fifteen to eighteen months. If they used Iraq's stocks of Italian uranium fuel, they could move much faster.

Jafar oversaw an initial hiring spree and divided the enrichment work into three overlapping phases: first, the design and manufacture of an experimental forty-centimeter magnetic separator; second, the development of larger "demonstration" magnet units; and third and finally, the construction of two large production plants. The experimental and demonstration work took place at Tuwaitha; the larger plants would be built elsewhere.[9]

The work progressed slowly. By 1985, after three years and the expenditure of large sums from Iraq's war-stressed treasury, Department 3000 had made considerable progress, but it was only just proving that it could separate U-235 isotopes successfully, and it was still working with tiny quantities. And yet Saddam was happy. The president was not known for his relaxed forbearance. What explained his patience? If he did not feel an urgent need to possess a workable nuclear weapon, then why did he want a bomb program at all?

The sheer arbitrariness of Saddam's rule was an aspect of its cruelty. Four years after the birth of the clandestine bomb program, Hussain Shahristani still languished in solitary confinement at Abu Ghraib. His unstated crime—the real cause of his continuing imprisonment—seemed to be his refusal to accept a lucrative role in the bomb effort.

At Abu Ghraib, the scientist's life had become a dark ordeal, a test of his faith. He was held in solitary confinement in a section of the prison supervised by the Mukhabarat. An intelligence officer brought him soup and bread once a day but would not speak to him. "The hardest part of solitary confinement was the torturing silence," Shahristani recalled. "We don't appreciate such simple blessings as background noises until we miss them." He passed his time praying and reciting verses of the Quran that he had memorized. He was not allowed newspapers or books.

Gradually, the conditions of his confinement improved somewhat. He was permitted monthly visits with Berniece, his wife, and their two daughters and son. They were allowed to bring him food. They transported their supplies in a cooler. One time, Zahra, Shahristani's oldest girl, then eight, hugged him and whispered, "Dad, open the lid of the box."

Back in his cell, he removed the cover and found a pencil and a small piece of paper. It was a letter containing family news. He began to correspond monthly with his family—mostly through his brother, to protect Berniece in case they were caught. Later his relatives managed to smuggle him a circuit board that he could use as a radio, as well as an earpiece attachment. Shahristani could only tune in to state-run broadcasts but at least he could follow the regime's propaganda about the Iran-Iraq War, guessing at the war's ups and downs. But his main preoccupation was his family's morale. He knew that his daughters would be stigmatized as children of a traitor. He wrote to assure them that he had not betrayed his country, that he had made his choices "to please my God, and to serve my people and save lives."

During the mid-1980s, Shahristani made a new acquaintance. The intelligence officers who brought him his food grew tired of this duty, which was beneath their station. They handed the job to Ali Aryan, a prisoner from Nasiriyah, in Iraq's Shia heartland. He bent the rules and chatted with Shahristani. Ali had trained with Fatah, a militant wing of the Palestine Liberation Organization. He had been imprisoned during a period when Saddam's regime persecuted the P.L.O. because its leader, Yasser Arafat, had supported the Iranian Revolution. Arafat's followers—Ali among them—had been rounded up and jailed. Later, Saddam and Arafat reconciled, yet Ali's sentence was not commuted. His Mukhabarat jailors had recruited him as their orderly—to prepare meals for them, launder their uniforms, and wash their vehicles.

Eventually, they entrusted Ali with the key to Shahristani's cell door. One day, he showed the key to the scientist, who traced it on a piece of paper. Shahristani then smuggled the drawing to his brother, who cut a rough copy and sent it back. Shahristani filed the key until he could open his own cell door. He and Ali now discussed the possibility of escape.

Ali had seemed to prove his bona fides by helping with the key, yet

Shahristani still worried that he might be a spy sent to entrap him. He asked his brother to investigate Ali's family. His brother reported back that they seemed to be desperately poor, and that he saw no reason to be concerned. Shahristani and Ali now discussed various escape plans inspired by Ali's access to the Mukhabarat vehicles. The risks would be high, and neither thought the time was yet right to try. But in his imagination, at least, Shahristani had found a hopeful glimmer of the future.[10]

The questions facing Jafar about whether to accelerate bomb-building depended to some extent on Saddam's thinking about nuclear-weapons doctrine. From their discussions, Jafar believed he understood that Saddam wanted a bomb to deter additional preemptive Israeli attacks on his regime. The president clearly feared Israel, and he took a pragmatic, long-term view. By 1985, Saddam believed, like the C.I.A., that he was no longer in danger of losing his war with Iran, and that its conclusion was only a matter of time. If it required five or more years to clandestinely develop a nuclear bomb that would surprise Israel after Iran accepted a cease-fire and political settlement, Saddam was willing to be patient, or so it seemed to Jafar.

For all his heedless talk in public and private about weapons of mass destruction, Saddam understood the rationality—if it can be called that—of the Cold War deterrence equation of "mutually assured destruction." His pattern of behavior showed that he sought to deter his enemies from striking Iraq. He also sought to avoid provoking adversaries when he felt the risk of escalation might be too great. Yet Saddam rarely followed a strategic line cogently. He was by temperament a rash improviser and opportunist. This created a kind of structural incoherence in his comments and actions.

As Iraq's chemical arsenal grew after 1983 and his forces gassed Iranian positions almost routinely, for example, Saddam thought aloud in private meetings about developing a "heavy chemical blow that will be the equivalent of an atomic weapon . . . to annihilate [Iranian cities] totally, that no living soul will survive." Yet he would then pull back from his own dark thoughts: "We should be very careful in our timing. . . . The current situation does not call for the use of this weapon now."[11]

Inside Department 3000, the idea that deterrence against Israel was the core purpose of the covert bomb program was an article of faith among leading scientists and engineers. Basil al-Saati, an engineer educated at the University College of Swansea (now called Swansea University) in Wales, compared Iraq's position against Israel to Pakistan's position against India. "We have to balance it out," he said, just as Pakistan had moved to acquire a bomb to deter and balance India.

"It was not only the scientists" who believed Iraq had "a right to have a bomb if Israel did," said Fadhil al-Janabi, who had earned a doctorate in Germany before working on the program. So did the great majority of Iraqis and Arab peoples. After China, India, and Israel all acquired nuclear weapons, and as Pakistan now pursued one, the scientists understood Iraq's program as part of "a domino effect," Janabi recalled.[12]

C.I.A. analysts assumed that Iraq could not build a bomb without foreign help. They lacked intelligence about—or respect for—the brain trust led by Jafar. Dismissive attitudes toward Arab societies, or outright racism, no doubt skewered the judgments of at least some American analysts. In any event, the C.I.A. concluded that because of the complexity of enrichment technologies, unless a foreign nation provided Iraq with highly enriched bomb fuel or nuclear reactors that would allow Iraq to extract or reprocess such fuel, Saddam Hussein's regime "will not be able to produce the material for a nuclear weapon before the 1990s. Attaining that capability, even then, depends critically on the foreign supply of a nuclear reactor—preferably a power reactor—of substantial size fairly soon." The C.I.A.'s analysis did not credit the possibility that Iraq's own physicists and engineers might manage to enrich uranium using techniques pioneered during the Manhattan Project.[13]

By the mid-1980s, the agency continued to assure the Reagan cabinet that "Iraq will have to depend on extensive foreign assistance and technology to master virtually all aspects of the nuclear cycle." Its analysts extended further the predicted time Iraq would need to acquire atomic bombs: Iraq was "still at least a decade away from having nuclear facilities with the potential to support nuclear weapons development," the C.I.A. reported.[14]

At the end of 1986, Jafar and Khaliq finally started talking about work on a bomb device. Jafar suggested the following year that the work commence outside Tuwaitha: "It's time to start thinking about a weapon, because that takes time." He said that Khaliq should plan to build a high-explosives package for an implosion bomb. The best experts within Iraq worked in the country's military industrialization complex, Jafar advised. They would try to create a prototype of a basic Fat Man–inspired device. (In such an "implosion" bomb, symmetrically arrayed conventional explosives compress highly enriched uranium, leading to a detonation.) The project would also require advanced diagnostic testing equipment, which, if imported, might risk getting caught. Iraq's military industries had the most experience with such smuggling. Jafar thought the whole project might take another five years or longer.[15]

Khaliq sent a long letter to Saddam, informing him that the time had arrived to start work toward building a nuclear bomb. Saddam passed the letter to Hussein Kamel al-Majid, his son-in-law, for evaluation and advice.

Hussein Kamel was by now on the verge of consolidating power—with Saddam's enthusiastic approval—over all Iraqi ministries and state enterprises responsible for war manufacture, industry, oil, and atomic energy. There seemed to be no limit to his ambition or to his father-in-law's support for him. The proposal to build a nuclear bomb for the glory of Iraq was "a gift from heaven" and a "golden opportunity" for Hussein Kamel to "get on the nuclear program's train," as Jafar put it. In any event, Hussein Kamel soon persuaded Saddam that there was an urgent need to restructure Department 3000—and he put himself in charge.[16]

Hussein Kamel was thirty-two when he usurped Jafar as the most influential leader in the atomic-bomb program. Like many Tikriti relatives of Saddam, he had become a member of the president's security detail. He was a mere second lieutenant when he first caught his future father-in-law's eye. "Lieutenant Hussein is smart . . . If we had more like him . . . he is smart!" Saddam exclaimed to comrades during a meeting in 1980. "He studies and works hard to improve himself!"[17]

This was Saddam's self-image, of course. Hussein Kamel also presented a marked contrast to the president's eldest son, Uday, who was ten years younger and already exhibiting the self-indulgence and criminal indiscipline for which he would become notorious. Saddam's son-in-law, on the other hand, seemed to be an industrious doppelgänger of the president and a potential heir—a fact that Uday noticed.

Barzan Ibrahim al-Tikriti recalled a family gathering, with Saddam present, where Hussein Kamel and Uday got into a heated argument over whether Hussein Kamel could finish rebuilding a Baghdad bridge over the Tigris as fast as he had promised. The back-and-forth escalated until Hussein Kamel angrily declared that if he did not meet his deadline, "I will behead myself!" Saddam laughed; it was, however, the sort of attitude toward duty that he preferred among his subordinates.[18]

Nevertheless, Hussein Kamel was an unlikely leader of a nuclear bomb program. He had no background in science or engineering and lacked much of a formal education, "even less than high school," according to Jafar. Yet he had "a very good memory." Dhafir Selbi, Jafar's colleague at Tuwaitha, described Hussein Kamel as "a clever person" who lacked "any database to process his intelligence." Yet nobody "could control him, and everyone feared him," as one of his subordinates recalled.[19]

As his authority grew during the mid-1980s, Hussein Kamel moved into lucrative import and smuggling businesses. He groomed himself in the image of his father-in-law and favored Saddam's fatigues-and-pistol look. He worked around the clock, racing from office to office and meeting to meeting. He sometimes summoned subordinates to conferences in the small hours of the night. His management philosophy seemed to have only one tenet: more, more, faster, faster.

His pressure and impatience would rapidly transform Iraq's bomb program—accelerating its potential while raising the risks of international exposure. Hussein Kamel's takeover touched off a succession of crisis meetings and restructurings across 1987. His first move was to pull the new project to design and test a nuclear explosive device under his direct control. He next set his sights on the uranium enrichment effort.

One night in July, he telephoned Mahdi Obeidi, a materials engineer with an undergraduate degree from the Colorado School of Mines and a doctorate from the University College of Swansea. Obeidi had worked on the French research reactor project and then transferred to the clandestine uranium enrichment program. Hussein Kamel identified him as a qualified scientist and experienced administrator.

Around midnight, they met in a hospital parking lot in Baghdad's fancy Mansour neighborhood. Hussein Kamel "strode toward me through the long shadows," Obeidi recalled. He was not tall, but "he walked with an air of authority, pushing his chest forward in the same way that some animals inflate themselves to warn off predators."[20]

They moved to a conference room. Hussein Kamel announced that he was interested in leading "a method for enriching uranium that Iraq has not yet explored," as he put it. He was referring to the pathway to a bomb that Jafar had set aside as impractical and too risky: building fast-spinning centrifuges. Hussein Kamel assured Obeidi that his plan to build centrifuges was "not only my decision. This is a direct order of Saddam Hussein." He wanted Obeidi to take charge. Without confronting the prestigious Jafar head-on, Hussein Kamel had decided to prove to his father-in-law that he could complete a bomb faster than Jafar would.

Obeidi mentioned that Brazil had experimented with using centrifuges to enrich bomb-grade uranium and that Pakistan was said to be working on a centrifuge program.

"The Pakistanis!" Hussein Kamel exclaimed. "Surely, if the Pakistanis can develop such a thing, then so can we. Iraq is at least as advanced as Pakistan!"

He leaned forward in his chair. By Monday, he said, he wanted a list of all the materials needed. A new and frightening chapter in the global history of nuclear weapons had opened.[21]

SIX

A Conspiracy Foretold

ven as the C.I.A. continually shared Top Secret satellite-derived intelligence about Iranian military vulnerabilities after 1982, Saddam persisted in his belief that the spy agency was playing a dirty game. He continued to believe the C.I.A. had a hidden hand in geopolitical conspiracies against him—conspiracies in which the United States cooperated with Iran and Israel. Yes, American diplomats repeatedly assured Iraq that the U.S. was trying hard to block Iran from obtaining weapons. Yet Saddam still suspected that Washington was allowing Israel to supply arms to Ayatollah Khomeini's regime. The evidence about this remained fragmentary, but Saddam mainly seemed to think that the Americans were congenital double-dealers and that, in this case, they were parceling out secret aid to both Baghdad and Tehran as part of a scheme to keep the war going. Saddam's thinking reflected a common belief in salons, coffee shops, and ministries across the Arab world: that America must have installed Ayatollah Khomeini in power to gain leverage over oil kingdoms such as Saudi Arabia and Kuwait or to sow instability in a region that the U.S. could exploit.

Saddam was right to sense a secret conspiracy—far more so than he could have possibly known. In early November 1986, a Lebanese magazine published a jaw-dropping story reporting that the Reagan administration had been secretly selling weapons to Khomeini's Iran, in collaboration with Israel, apparently to secure the release of American hostages held by Iranian proxies in Lebanon. Then, on the evening of November 25, in Washington, D.C., Attorney General Edwin Meese delivered the shocking admission that not only was the magazine story essentially true, but in a bizarre twist, the White House had also used profits from arms sales to Khomeini's regime to funnel money to antigovernment Nicaraguan rebels known as the Contras, in apparent violation of U.S. law.

Speaking at a press conference in the White House briefing room, Meese gripped the podium with both hands and narrated a summary of the matter in the passive voice, as if the misdeeds had been orchestrated by spectral beings. "Certain monies . . . were taken and made available to the forces in Central America, which are opposing the Sandinista government there," Meese said.

"How much money, sir?"

"We don't know the exact amount yet. Our estimate is that it is somewhere between ten and thirty million dollars."

"How did it come to your attention?"

"In the course of a thorough review of a number of intercepts and other materials . . . the hint of a possibility that there was some monies being made available for some other purpose . . . came to our attention."

The scandal soon to be known as Iran-Contra—a covert initiative run from the Reagan White House that would result in criminal convictions of eleven administration officials—had been born. The two-line banner across the top of *The New York Times'* front page on the morning after Meese's announcement—"Iran Payment Found Diverted to Contras; Reagan Security Adviser and Aide Are Out"—reflected the political thunderbolt that had just hit Washington. Iran-Contra would consume journalists and congressional investigators for years. In

Baghdad, as he absorbed the early headlines about America's secret partnership with Israel to deliver weapons to Tehran, Saddam Hussein was perhaps the world's least surprised leader.[1]

The decision to provide arms to Khomeini had originated around 1984, when some of Reagan's National Security Council aides began to think that the U.S. could not afford to be entirely estranged from Iran, a key ally prior to Khomeini's revolution. In late 1984, two years into the C.I.A.'s secret intelligence-sharing relationship with Saddam, an interagency review concluded that the Reagan administration had "no influential contacts" in Iran whatsoever. The review's authors worried this might create an opening for Soviet influence. This was arguably an irrational anxiety, but it was typical of the Cold War's zero-sum calculations. Moreover, during 1984 and 1985, Iranian allies in Lebanon had kidnapped C.I.A. station chief William Buckley, Presbyterian minister Benjamin Weir, and Associated Press correspondent Terry Anderson, among others; the White House had no credible channel to negotiate with Tehran to pursue their release.

Israel, meanwhile, for its own reasons, supplied arms to Iran and maintained contacts in Tehran. Iran was hostile to some of Israel's Arab enemies, including Iraq. Iran also had a sizable Jewish population that Israel sought to protect. Jews had settled in what was now Isfahan at least fifteen centuries before. By the time of the 1979 revolution, about eighty thousand to one hundred thousand Jews remained in the country. Khomeini's hostility ignited an exodus of about two-thirds of that population—between thirty thousand and forty thousand to the U.S., twenty thousand to Israel, and another ten thousand to, mostly, Europe. Tel Aviv sought to ease the plight of those fleeing by buying favor with Khomeini's regime. At the same time, some in the Israeli establishment hoped that pragmatists in Tehran might yet see the benefits of renewed collaboration, as the last shah of Iran had.

In August 1985, David Kimche, a longtime Mossad officer then at the Ministry of Foreign Affairs, proposed that the Reagan administration bless Israel's transfer of one hundred American-made TOW anti-tank missiles to Iran, a gesture that "would establish good faith and result in the release of all the hostages" held by Iranian allies in Lebanon. TOW—short for "tube-launched, optically tracked, wire-guided"— missiles were high-quality weapons that could accurately strike Iraqi tanks on the battlefield.

Reagan agreed, telling an aide that he would take "all the heat for that." The initial transfer was followed by a second air shipment of 408 TOWs to Iran on September 14, 1985. The next day, Benjamin Weir's captors in Lebanon released him. The seductive idea that the Reagan administration could free American kidnapping victims by secretly supplying arms to Khomeini had now been established.[2]

Tom Twetten was by now head of the C.I.A.'s Near East Division, supervising espionage and covert-action operations across the Middle East. In January 1986, he accompanied Clair George, the C.I.A.'s deputy director of operations, to the White House to meet Reagan's national security adviser, John Poindexter, and an aide, Lieutenant Colonel Oliver North. The president's men showed the C.I.A. men a draft "finding," the legal document that presidents must sign to authorize the agency to carry out a covert action, such as arming guerrillas or trying to fix an overseas election. This finding would instruct the C.I.A. to locate and transfer to Iran four thousand more TOW missiles, with Israel's help. Twetten and his colleagues were not to tell anyone in Congress or in other parts of the administration about the arms deal.

"This is not going to end well," Twetten told George when he returned to Langley. It got worse. Some months later, the White House instructed the C.I.A. to provide Iran with a package of intelligence about Iraqi battlefield positions. North asked for "a map depicting the order of battle on the Iran/Iraq border" and showing the "units, troops, tanks, electronic installations" of Saddam Hussein's forces, according to a contemporaneous memo. This would fulfill Saddam's worst suspicions— that the C.I.A. also supplied to Tehran the kind of "exclusive" intelligence it provided to Baghdad. Twetten was not sentimental about Saddam, and no professional spy could afford to be too squeamish about such a rank betrayal, since C.I.A. officers routinely asked the foreign agents they recruited to commit treason. Still, it seemed to Twetten and his colleagues that this was a terrible proposal.

"Everyone here at headquarters advises against this operation," John McMahon, the deputy director of the entire C.I.A., wrote to William Casey, Reagan's spy chief, on January 25. "We would be aiding and abetting the wrong people," he argued, meaning the Iranians. But the C.I.A. director was largely impervious to the cautions of career intelligence officers. At seventy-two, jowly and prone to mumbling, William Casey was an Irish saloonkeeper's son and a devout Catholic who had made a fortune on Wall Street and then helped elect Ronald Reagan. He was an ardent anti-communist who had never paid much attention to rulebooks. Twetten and McMahon were especially exercised in providing satellite intelligence to Ayatollah Khomeini's military, which "could cause the Iranians to have a successful offense against the Iraqis with cataclysmic results. . . . We are giving the Iranians the wherewithal for offensive action." The C.I.A. had shared intelligence with Saddam precisely to prevent Ayatollah Khomeini from deposing him. Now they were risking that very outcome.

McMahon told Casey that he had raised these objections directly with the White House but had been overruled. "In spite of our counsel to the contrary, we are proceeding to follow out orders," McMahon wrote forlornly.[3]

Twetten continued to work with Iraq during 1986 as if the betrayal were not taking place. In February, Casey established the DCI Counterterrorist Center at the C.I.A. and put Duane "Dewey" Clarridge, a legendary adventurer in the clandestine service, in charge. Clarridge thought the C.I.A. should be getting more out of Iraq in return for the satellite intelligence the agency provided. On March 30, 1986, a Palestinian splinter group detonated a bomb on a Trans World Airlines flight as it approached Athens, killing four Americans. A week later, a bomb planted by Libyan agents exploded in a Berlin nightclub, killing two U.S. soldiers and wounding more than six dozen others. What was the point of propping up Saddam Hussein in his war with Iran if Saddam's spy services—deeply connected with Palestinian extremist networks—would not help the U.S. solve and prevent such heinous crimes? Twetten flew back to Baghdad to accompany Clarridge on a secret mission to persuade the Iraqis to do more to crack down on terrorists with ties to Baghdad, and to provide better information to the C.I.A. The visit didn't yield much, but Twetten kept the channel open.[4]

The TOW missiles that the C.I.A. supplied to Iran under White House orders were valuable to Iran, but they did not have a decisive impact on the war. In February, Iranian forces invaded and occupied the Faw peninsula, a sliver of muddy tidal flats southeast of Basra that provided Iraq with its only direct access to international waters. The TOW missiles helped Iran defeat Iraqi tanks and achieve a major victory. Yet the Iranians received many more anti-tank missiles from suppliers such as China and North Korea. And the TOWs did not change the fact that Iran could still only field a quarter of the number of tanks that Iraq possessed, or that its air force remained inferior.[5]

C.I.A. satellite intelligence showing Iraqi positions, by comparison, could be of greater importance. It could help Iranian forces map the best way to break out of Faw and drive on Baghdad to win the war. In fact, the Iraqis came to believe, after the Iran-Contra scandal broke, that C.I.A.-supplied intelligence—doctored intelligence given to Iraq, to confuse Saddam's generals, and accurate intelligence given to Iran—had allowed Iran to win the battle for Faw.[6]

How much intelligence about Iraq's battlefield positions and vulnerabilities did the United States actually provide to Iran? The documentary evidence remains classified more than three decades after the events. There appear to have been three separate transfers to Tehran during 1986. Twetten recalled that C.I.A. leaders made sure to provide only the most basic topographical maps covering unimportant areas of the

battlefield, undermining the White House orders and giving the Iranians little of value. The C.I.A.'s leading specialist on Iran, George Cave,
who participated in some of the secret contacts with Tehran, has made
similar statements, as have other senior C.I.A. officers aware of the
intelligence sharing with Iran at the time. But according to W. Patrick
"Pat" Lang, then the chief Middle East analyst at the Defense Intelligence Agency, North's team at the White House worked around the
C.I.A. by independently accessing classified computers. Lang said that,
according to C.I.A. inspector general reports he read, the take North
shared with Iran included all of the records of the C.I.A.'s four-year liaison with Baghdad after Twetten's initial visit, plus all of the Defense
Intelligence Agency's "order of battle" material on Iraq, meaning files
describing Iraqi military organization, command, weaponry, bases,
doctrines, and logistics. The intelligence was "extensive and encyclopedic," according to Lang.[7]

One glimpse of the operation is available in a message North wrote
on October 2, 1986. North inventoried the "intelligence assistance"
Iran sought from the United States. Tehran's wish list included one-to-
fifty-thousand-scale maps of Iraqi battlefield positions—maps of the
precision sometimes used by the U.S. military. Khomeini's regime also
sought the locations of Iraqi division and corps headquarters; locations
of logistics depots and supply routes; and information "on Iraqi troop
movements, reserve units and tank concentrations."

North noted in his message, as if it really needed spelling out by
now: "We DO NOT have to tell the truth about all of this."[8]

After the scandal broke, Ronald Reagan hoped to quell the "irresponsible press bilge" about his dealings with Ayatollah Khomeini's
regime. The president told the American people that his main motives
had been to renew relations with Iran, help end the Iran-Iraq War,
"eliminate state-sponsored terrorism," and "effect the safe return of all
hostages." He admitted that he had "authorized the transfer of small

amounts of defensive weapons and spare parts for defensive systems to Iran." Yet the president insisted: "The United States has not swapped boatloads or planeloads of American weapons for the return of American hostages."

Except that no boats were involved, this last declaration was false, and the entirety of his initial speech on the matter that November was incomplete and misleading. Reagan's advisers had certainly discussed the potential benefits of discovering and engaging with Iranian moderates to better manage the geopolitical earthquake of the Iranian Revolution. Still, the record would eventually make clear that the release of American hostages in exchange for weapons shipments had been Reagan's own prime motivation. The arms transfers were, at their heart, a harebrained ransom operation, even if Reagan and his advisers persuaded themselves that it was something else.

Reagan made no mention in public of the C.I.A. intelligence about Iraqi military positions provided to Iran. As the White House moved into cover-up mode, aides circulated a Top Secret inventory of "information that must remain classified." The list included "intelligence support to the operation."[9]

In Baghdad, Saddam Hussein, Tariq Aziz, and members of the Revolutionary Command Council met to discuss a response to the revelations. Saddam asked "Comrade Tariq" to take notes and help craft a letter to Ronald Reagan in Saddam's name.

Taha Yassin Ramadan, an old Baath Party warhorse, noted that from what they now understood, America's secret contact with Iran had started soon after the Reagan administration restored diplomatic relations with Iraq in late 1984, which, he said, "indicates this is an intentional goal for this conspiracy," to lull Iraq into complacency and then bolster Iran.

Saddam thought "the weapons issue" was the key to America's devious plan to get "close to the new regime" in Tehran. "We have the right to be suspicious of the U.S. call to stop the war," he said, now that the United States had been exposed arming Iran.

"You want this in the statement?" Aziz asked.

"Well, I want these details in the message—that now, we are suspicious of the U.S. calls" for peace. He continued, "Reagan said that we are getting closer to Iran through weapons. A nation like Iran needs weapons more when it is at war. So therefore, how many more years does Reagan need the war to continue?"

The Americans had been telling Saddam for years that Operation Staunch, their public initiative to stop arms sales to Iran, was intended to increase Iraq's military advantage and hasten the conflict's end. Operation Staunch had just been revealed as a fraud. How could this be explained? Saddam tutored his comrades: Staunch was designed all along "to isolate Iran" from the international arms market so that the Iranians would become desperate and then "agree upon an American deal" for weapons—a deal that would, in turn, advance Washington's conniving schemes for controlling the Middle East.[10]

It was a pattern that would recur between Washington and Baghdad: what many Americans understood as staggering incompetence in their nation's foreign policy, Saddam interpreted as manipulative genius.

"I swear, I am not surprised" by Iran-Contra, Saddam told his advisers at another meeting soon after Reagan's initial speech. Even so, "this level of bad and immoral behavior is a new thing." The scandal affirmed Saddam's bedrock convictions: Israel and Iran were in cahoots, and the C.I.A. was their silent partner. "Zionism is taking the Iranians by the hand and introducing them to each party, one by one, channel by channel," Saddam declared. "I mean, Zionism—come on, comrades—do I have to repeat that every time?"

For Saddam, the disclosures merely surfaced what had always been there to understand: "the real American conspiracy—the real American-Israeli-Iranian conspiracy . . . a conspiracy against us." He could "not imagine" that the U.S. would ever stop, "even if the Democrats won" in the next elections.[11]

Saddam Hussein was hardly the only Arab leader taken aback by Iran-Contra. King Hussein of Jordan headed a list of Arab allies of the United States angered by the revelations. "I had, out of conviction, done much to remove Iraqi suspicions" that the C.I.A. was deliberately supplying false intelligence to Saddam in order to prolong the war, the king wrote to Reagan. "Will not the Iraqis now feel that they were misled, not only by the United States but also by anyone who tries to explain, justify or defend American actions," such as the king himself?[12]

National Security Council aides drafted letters from Reagan to bruised Arab friends, essentially repeating the misleading points in the president's speech to the American people. David George Newton, the American ambassador in Baghdad, received a letter from Reagan intended for Saddam.

Newton had succeeded William Eagleton at the ramshackle American embassy compound. He was a talented Arabic speaker who had joined the diplomatic service after graduating from Harvard and serving in the U.S. Army. Before Baghdad, he had put in tours in Yemen, Saudi Arabia, and Syria. During 1985 and 1986, Newton had become devoted to the improvement of U.S.-Iraqi understanding. Like other State Department diplomats who had been kept in the dark about the weapons sales to Iran, Newton was shocked and disappointed.

He carried Reagan's bland letter to Aziz, who read it and dismissed it as nothing new. Newton found Aziz "very quiet, very reasoned and very angry." Iraq judged the Reagan administration's explanations to be "absolutely unconvincing." American actions had "rendered unreliable" three years of assurances by Washington.

Aziz added that "he personally feels betrayed," Newton cabled to Washington. Aziz "commented bitterly" that high-ranking American officials, including C.I.A. director William Casey, had "knowingly deceived him" by encouraging Iraqi air attacks against Iran "while aware that their own government was providing Iran with the means to shoot down Iraqi aircraft."[13]

The exposure of American double-dealing damaged Aziz's standing in Saddam's inner circle. But the scandal was particularly crushing
for Nizar Hamdoon. He was the face of Saddam's campaign to win favor with America, down to his portrait on the cover of *The Washington
Post*'s Sunday magazine. For two years, Hamdoon had been speaking to
think tanks, reporters—anyone who would listen—about the opportunity to construct a U.S.-Iraqi alliance. Iran-Contra hit him as if "somebody took my only son," he told a colleague. In Baghdad, old-school
Baathists close to Saddam discovered that their views "about the U.S.
being an imperialist pro-Israeli power now were reconfirmed," as Newton recalled. They came after Hamdoon and blamed him for getting
too close to Israel while cavorting around Washington. "People were
out to get him," Odeh Aburdene, Hamdoon's friend, remembered.[14]

Aziz shepherded a nearly two-thousand-word reply from Saddam
to Reagan's letter. It calmly enumerated Iraqi grievances. It also drifted
into Saddam's hypotheses about Zionism's grip on America. Reagan
had not even mentioned an "important issue" during his speech to the
American people or in his letter, Saddam wrote. The Israelis saw it in
their interests to prolong the Iran-Iraq War indefinitely, and so "this
has naturally deepened our suspicions about the entire issue."[15]

Aziz avoided attacking President Reagan directly or publicly. He
argued nonetheless that America's actions would prolong the war; that
its example would encourage other countries to sell arms to Iran; and
that the Reagan administration's search for moderates to talk to in Iran
was delusional, since there were no moderates in Tehran with any
power. As to the future of U.S.-Iraqi relations, the recent revelations
constituted a stab in the back and the burden now fell to Washington
to repair the damage.

In the spring of 1987, as Saddam's fiftieth birthday approached, Barzan Ibrahim al-Tikriti sent his estranged half brother a letter. He
noted the significance of a golden jubilee birthday. The president was
getting to his "second half of life," a time when "one would have

special thoughts and feelings. This comes from being at the summit of his wisdom."

That was certainly how Saddam viewed his station. His publishing machine would soon bring out *The Political Dictionary of Saddam Hussein*, containing five hundred examples of his sayings, each interpreted by an Iraqi poet. *The Complete Writings of Saddam Hussein* would require eighteen volumes. Newspapers carried his maxims across the tops of their front pages.

Barzan had in mind a family reconciliation. He hoped that Saddam would "turn this ugly page of our relationship and start a new one." He was rewarded, to an extent. On April 27, 1987, the day before Saddam's birthday, Barzan received a message that Saddam had invited all three of his half brothers—Barzan, Sabawi, and Watban—to his party the next day. "We will meet, but we have nothing in common but honor," Saddam wrote. He warned his half brothers not to "bother my relatives," meaning Hussein Kamel and his kin.

When Barzan arrived, he found the atmosphere "very heavy and strained," but after about two hours, Saddam turned up, and "we greeted him and hugged him."

Saddam wore a tailored suit and beamed as children chanted "Father Saddam." Some guests were in military uniform, others in tuxedos. Smiling widely, the patriarch lit candles and cut a large cake.[16]

As the initial shock of the Iran-Contra revelations wore off, Saddam groped again for a sustainable relationship with Washington. The fact that he had suspected all along that the Americans were double-dealing liars actually made it easier for him to reconnect—he had been proved right. And Iraqi interests hadn't changed: Saddam wanted balanced relationships with both Cold War superpowers; he wanted his war with Iran to end as soon as possible; and he was willing to accept American aid and exports to bolster his cash-strapped war economy. Nor had American goals changed. The Reagan administration did not want Ayatollah Khomeini to conquer Baghdad.

Reagan's aides worked assiduously during the winter and spring of 1987 to bring Saddam back onside. They revived Operation Staunch as well as economic aid and bank credits for Iraq. Assistant Secretary of State for Near Eastern and South Asian Affairs Richard Murphy, a gaunt-faced Arabic speaker and seasoned Middle East hand, traveled to Baghdad. He delivered a letter to Saddam noting the administration had been "very active" in seeking to deny Iran weapons and force Khomeini to withdraw his troops from Iraqi territory and enter negotiations.[17]

Saddam received Murphy in person, signaling his openness to a restored if more cold-eyed relationship. Just over three years earlier, when he met Donald Rumsfeld, Saddam had walked his guest to a window to look out at the Baghdad skyline, suggesting the expansive business opportunities available in a new American-Iraqi partnership. His attitude with Murphy was more acerbic.

"Your relationships with the Third World are like an Iraqi peasant's relationship with his new wife," Saddam told the diplomat.

"Oh?"

"Yes, absolutely—three days of tea and honey, and then off to the fields for life."[18]

SEVEN

Druid Leader

On the hazy morning of May 17, 1987, three weeks after Saddam's fiftieth birthday, the U.S.S. *Stark*, a Navy missile frigate, sailed from Manama, Bahrain, on a routine patrol mission in the Persian Gulf to monitor the shipping lane that slaked the world's thirst for oil. Through the Strait of Hormuz flowed millions of barrels, daily pumped by Saudi Arabia, Kuwait, Iraq, Iran, Qatar, and the United Arab Emirates. The United States had declared protection of free shipping there of vital national interest. The Iran-Iraq War had lately given this mission a dangerous edge, as Iranian and Iraqi aircraft and fast boats battled in the northern Gulf. The *Stark* and other U.S. ships policed the region to protect commercial vessels, tracking and warning off any aircraft or ship that looked threatening.

At about 8:00 p.m., the *Stark* detected an Iraqi warplane flying a "ship attack profile." Iraqi jets often flew south over the Gulf, sometimes into international waters, to search for Iranian maritime targets. The *Stark* had watched two similar flights that morning, without incident. The Iraqis had never attacked an American vessel. The U.S. Navy did not operate as if Iraqi Air Force planes were presumed to be hostile. An American AWACS surveillance plane marked this latest Iraqi jet as "track 2202."

At 8:30 p.m., the *Stark*'s commanding officer, Captain Glenn Brindel, a youthful-looking Penn State graduate who was then forty-three, stepped onto the bridge. For the next half hour, "2202"—identified as an Iraqi French-made Mirage F1, typically armed with Exocet air-to-ship missiles—flew in the *Stark*'s general direction. Brindel ordered no warnings or defensive measures. At 9:05 p.m., the Mirage was just over thirty nautical miles away. It suddenly turned directly toward the U.S. Navy frigate. No one on the ship initially noticed.

"Missile inbound! Missile inbound!" lookouts soon called out over the ship's JL communications circuit.

"We have been locked on twice—"

The transmission of the *Stark*'s urgent broadcast broke as one Exocet slammed into the frigate's port side, followed by a second missile that detonated and ripped a hole the size of a garage door in the ship's skin. Fires erupted, and the *Stark* listed portside. A heavy plume of smoke rose into the darkened sky as sailors fell or leapt into the sea.[1]

W hen news of the *Stark* attack reached Washington, Reagan's military and diplomatic advisers assumed the strike had been an accident. On May 18, as the American death toll rose toward thirty-seven, President Reagan made a statement that included no criticism of Iraq. Saddam hastily signed a letter to Reagan: "I would like to express to you my deepest regret for the painful incident," he wrote. Iraqi warplanes "had no intention whatsoever to strike against a target belonging to your country or any country other than Iran." The incident was a "tragic accident." Saddam asked Reagan to "kindly convey to the families of the victims my personal condolences and sympathy."[2]

Tariq Aziz soon issued a public apology and pledged to pay compensation to the families of the victims. On May 21, Saddam sent a second, even more emotive letter to Reagan, expressing his "heartfelt condolences to the families of the victims. . . . Rest assured that the grief which you feel as a result of the loss of your sons is our grief too."[3]

Saddam also agreed to receive American investigators to jointly review the cause of the incident and to prevent such confusion in the future. A Pentagon team met Iraqi counterparts in Baghdad in late May. The Iraqis insisted that the *Stark* had drifted into Iraqi territorial waters—an assertion contradicted by America's radar and surveillance evidence. Still, Richard Murphy reported to Secretary of State George Shultz that "the Iraqis were reasonably forthcoming." The U.S. side concluded that the "only plausible explanation" was "a navigational error by the pilot" that had led him to misidentify his target, Murphy wrote.[4]

The Iraqi side refused to allow the Americans to interview the pilot, however. They asked pointedly if the Americans would allow such an interview if the circumstances were reversed. The Americans accepted Iraq's refusal. They focused on strengthening protections for neutral shipping in the Gulf, looking ahead.

The attack was probably an accident, yet the eagerness of the Reagan administration to absolve Saddam reflected a certain desperation in Washington about restoring ties with Baghdad after Iran-Contra. And not everything about the *Stark* incident was as it had first seemed. It turned out that the attacking plane was not a Mirage fighter jet, as the U.S. Navy reported in a published investigation later that year. It was a French-made Dassault Falcon 50 business jet modified to fire anti-ship Exocet missiles. Saddam had purchased a pair of these executive jets from France. He used one for presidential trips and modified the other as a warplane that could fly stealthily with civilian markings on reconnaissance missions.[5]

W. Patrick "Pat" Lang, a U.S. Army colonel and the chief Middle East analyst at the Defense Intelligence Agency, was part of the U.S. investigative team that traveled to Baghdad that May. He was a sergeant's son who had earned an English degree from the Virginia

Military Institute before taking a commission. Lang had landed in Saigon as an intelligence officer and commanded a clandestine defense spying unit on the Cambodian border. After a second tour in Vietnam, he studied Arabic and took up postings as a defense attaché in Saudi Arabia and what was then North Yemen before rotating to D.I.A. headquarters. By the mid-1980s, he had grown into a balding, square-jawed man—irascible and sharp-tongued but well-informed.

In 1986, before Iran-Contra broke, Leonard Perroots, the three-star U.S. Air Force general who led the D.I.A., had asked Lang to draw up a plan to provide even more battlefield intelligence to the Iraqis than the C.I.A. was already providing. There were times when the D.I.A. and the C.I.A. each found it difficult to concede that the other might be doing something constructive. In this case, Perroots, as an Air Force man, concluded that the C.I.A. intelligence could be improved upon by providing more precise target packages to the Iraqis—including flight paths to and from Iranian targets, suggestions about what bombs to drop, and after-action damage assessments. Later that year, the National Security Council discussed the plan, code-named Elephant Grass, but it was not adopted.[6]

In mid-1987, after Lang returned from Baghdad, Perroots suggested they revisit the proposal. The context had shifted. Iran-Contra had all but destroyed the fragile relationship between the C.I.A. and Saddam Hussein's regime. There was an opportunity for the D.I.A. to step in. The Pentagon already maintained a small defense attaché's office, led by a colonel, in the U.S. embassy in Baghdad. That summer, Perroots gave permission to provide intelligence to the Iraqis.

For his part, Pat Lang, taking note of the many C.I.A. officers forced to lawyer up as Iran-Contra investigations went on, sought written instruction to proceed. Perroots eventually delivered a one-page authority letter on a blank piece of paper bearing "what purported to be" the signature of then defense secretary Frank Carlucci, as Lang recalled it. He decided the letter was good enough.[7]

By late 1987, Rick Francona, a U.S. Air Force captain and intelligence officer, had joined the incipient Iraq operation at the D.I.A. Then

in his midthirties, Francona had served as a Vietnamese-language interpreter before he also shifted to study Arabic. He was a smooth briefer,
dashing in a dress uniform, and comfortable on the D.C. embassy
cocktail circuit—a presentable deputy to the less diplomatic Lang.

Sometime before Christmas 1987, the D.I.A. circulated an intelligence report about the Iran-Iraq War. It presented a worrying forecast
about the year ahead, predicting that if Iranian troops broke Iraqi lines
during a spring offensive, they could yet roll into Baghdad, overthrow
Saddam, and win the war. Once more, "an Iraqi defeat seemed all too
possible," recalled Haywood Rankin, then a State Department political
officer in the Baghdad embassy. And, once again, the Reagan administration concluded "that Iraq must not be defeated, must not be overrun
by Khomeini."[8]

The White House directed the D.I.A. to move forward. Francona
and Lang soon had a new code name for their project: Druid Leader.

America's Arab allies smoothed the D.I.A.'s way with Saddam and
Iraqi military intelligence. After Lang and Francona briefed King
Hussein in Amman, the king called Saddam and urged him to take the
D.I.A.'s intelligence seriously. The D.I.A. officers also traipsed over to
the Virginia home of Prince Bandar bin Sultan Al Saud, the Saudi ambassador and an inveterate operator. They unpacked a display of satellite photographs on the living-room floor. The goal, Francona recalled,
was for Bandar and other Arab allies "to tell the Iraqis" that they needed
to accept the Pentagon's assistance. Iran-Contra had only deepened
Saddam's distrust of American intentions, but he seems to have decided that if the D.I.A. satellite photographs depicting Iranian positions were accurate (which his generals could determine for themselves),
then even if Washington's game was to provide help to both sides of the
war, he should take advantage of the stratagem as best he could.[9]

In February 1988, Lang and Francona traveled to Baghdad. The
Iraqis chauffeured them in Mercedes sedans and lodged them at the
Rashid, a new hotel built by India's Oberoi chain to four-star standards.

The hotel housed a bar frequented by Saddam Hussein's louche young adult sons, as well as sports facilities, a helipad, and an underground bomb shelter. Francona assumed the guest rooms were wired for video and audio surveillance.

The D.I.A. men rode out to the sprawling General Military Intelligence Directorate headquarters complex in Khadimiya, along the Tigris, where C.I.A. officers had taken many meetings after 1982. Francona met his Iraqi liaison, a major who had studied English at Baghdad University.

"Is your counterpart in Tehran right now?" the major asked. He and his colleagues assumed that for every D.I.A. delegation bringing intelligence to Baghdad, there was probably another on the same mission in Tehran.

"No, he's not," Francona sputtered.[10]

The D.I.A. officers' instructions were to provide battlefield information on Iranian forces that would help the Iraqi Air Force bomb Iranian military formations and infrastructure behind the front lines. The targets would include large-scale troop concentrations, groups of ships moored near one another, railroad trestles, and important bridges. The goal was to disrupt Iranian preparations for the presumed spring offensive. Yet the Americans were instructed not to provide any intelligence of "direct, immediate tactical value" to Iraq.[11]

It was a prohibition that could be difficult to interpret. Francona's take was that if U.S. satellite imagery showed an Iranian logistics buildup underway to support an upcoming military offensive, they could share intelligence to encourage the Iraqi Air Force to strike. Yet if the U.S. imagery showed an Iranian tank battalion moving down a particular road to mount an imminent attack against an Iraqi brigade headquarters, the Americans could *not* share that information. These rules—and their dubious logic—reflected the Reagan administration's continuing ambivalence. The White House did not want to be seen as joining Saddam Hussein's generals in fighting day-to-day—taking on an advisory role so close to the action that America would effectively be a combatant in the war. It was a fine line, if it existed at all.

At the initial meeting at General Military Intelligence Directorate headquarters, Lang explained why the Pentagon had concluded that Iraq was potentially vulnerable to an Iranian breakthrough.

General Wafiq al-Samarrai, the deputy director of General Military Intelligence, led the Iraqi delegation. He was a full-faced man with a thick head of black hair and the look of a Baath Party loyalist. He reacted defensively: "We're very capable of assessing the threat."

This was not just pride speaking. By the war's seventh year, General Military Intelligence ran an all-source operation to support its fighting generals. The department received war intelligence from the Soviets, Yugoslavs, and French, among others, and it ran its own eavesdropping and reconnaissance flight operations against the Iranians—to good effect, Lang would come to believe. Yet the latest American satellite maps from the D.I.A. provided over-the-horizon insights about Iranian logistics that the Iraqis did not possess.

"What do we have to give you to get this?" Samarrai asked the Americans. "What do you want from us?"

"We don't want anything," Lang answered. "We do not want the Iranians to win."[12]

From Washington that winter and spring, Francona and D.I.A. colleagues sent textual analytical reports about Iranian activity to the defense attaché's office in Baghdad to be passed on to General Military Intelligence. During periods of intense fighting, the D.I.A. might transmit a report to the Iraqis once a day or every other day. In quieter periods, the frequency might be once a month. By Lang's count, in addition to this flow of updates, the D.I.A. supplied about two dozen fully developed descriptions of potential targets. The Americans conducted bomb-damage assessments after Iraqi strikes and sometimes counseled the Iraqis to hit certain targets again. In addition, Francona made five trips to Baghdad during 1988, often with Lang, carrying satellite photos and line drawings that could not be easily transmitted over the embassy's secure communications link.

When the D.I.A. teams traveled to Iraq, they typically flew to Kuwait, where the Baghdad-based U.S. defense attaché, along with an

Iraqi minder, would meet them. At a time when city-busting missiles rocketed in both directions between Baghdad and Tehran, it was safer to drive into Baghdad than to fly, and the ride up from Kuwait City allowed Lang and Francona to see the battlefield up close. On a typical visit, they might spend five or so nights at the Rashid. As they got to know their military intelligence counterparts, they went out in the evenings to Baghdad's thriving nightclubs, such as the Khan Marjan, a former rest stop on ancient caravan routes converted to a domed nitery that could seat at least five hundred people, serving up meals, alcohol, and dancers. To amuse themselves, the D.I.A. and Iraqi officers revisited a century-old shaggy-dog story based on the idea that William Shakespeare was in fact a stranded-in-England Yemeni sailor known as Sheikh Zubair. After enough rounds, it seemed very funny.[13]

It was hard to judge the strategic importance of the satellite-derived imagery and photographs that Druid Leader delivered. Francona's assessment was that they enabled the Iraqis to go on the offensive during 1988. There were other factors in the Iraqi successes of that year—their use of chemical arms and the intimidating effects on Iran's leadership of Iraq's newly modified Scud missile, al-Hussein, which smashed into Tehran indiscriminately. Iraqi broadcasts aimed at Iran claimed that al-Hussein missiles could carry chemical arms (they did not), and the propaganda exacerbated panic in the Iranian capital, where the authorities carried out partial evacuations. "The combination of having chemical weapons, the ability to incite terror in the population of Tehran, and the intelligence provided by the United States—those three things" influenced Iran's calculations about continuing the war, Francona believed. The C.I.A.'s assessment that year was similar; by its judgment, the Iraqis were starting to win notable victories but remained "chemically dependent," as an agency analyst put it. The Iraqi Army had rebounded from its initial problems of recruitment and retention, and it had grown from 190,000 soldiers in 1980 to nearly a million men under arms by 1988, almost twice the size of Iran's ground forces.[14]

That spring, Iraqi forces retook the Faw peninsula and other territories lost the previous year. For the first time, it seemed possible to imagine that Iraqi victories could force Iran to accept the war's end—not an outright Iranian defeat but an armistice that restored prewar borders and left both Saddam Hussein and Ayatollah Khomeini in power. For Saddam, battlefield momentum seemed to breed greater aggression. More than ever before, he now embraced gas as a winning weapon. According to Iraq's accounting, its military fired 54,000 chemically armed artillery shells, launched 27,000 short-range rockets, and dropped 19,500 aerial gas bombs during the war. Nearly two-thirds of these chemical weapons were used during 1987 and 1988, when the D.I.A.'s intelligence sharing under Druid Leader was taking place.[15]

There was certainly no confusion inside the D.I.A. about the extent to which Iraqis gassed Iranian soldiers and volunteers. At one point, Francona flew by helicopter to Faw to see the front firsthand. He met the intelligence director of Iraq's Seventh Corps and walked across the battlefield for a day. At abandoned Iranian positions, Francona noticed scores of atropine injectors lying around—the detritus of Dutch-made injectable antidotes to nerve gas, similar to what NATO issued in preparation for chemical warfare.

"Oh, this is atropine," Francona noted to his Iraqi host.

"We used a lot of smoke rounds. They must have thought it was gas," the Iraqi officer explained.

"I don't know," Francona replied. "I've been in this situation. Unless I know there's gas, I'm not sticking that thing in my thigh." Surreptitiously, he and a colleague traveling with him collected a few empty injectors. They smuggled them back to Washington and sent them to the F.B.I. for analysis.[16]

There was no practical way to prevent the Iraqis from using Druid Leader intelligence to plan chemical attacks against Iranian forces.

(The same could be said of C.I.A. intelligence provided to Iraq earlier in the 1980s.) "We didn't know when the Iraqis would use chemical weapons," Lang said. "Plus, we didn't really want to know."

"The D.I.A. was not telling the Iraqis, 'Put sarin here,'" recalled Bruce Riedel, a C.I.A. analyst who traveled to Baghdad as part of his agency's intelligence liaison during the 1980s. "But did they know that that's what the Iraqis would do? Of course."[17]

EIGHT

"Who Is Going to Say Anything?"

n March 1987, Saddam Hussein had appointed his cousin Ali Hassan al-Majid to lead the Baath Party's Northern Bureau, encompassing Iraqi Kurdistan, the region inhabited primarily by ethnic Kurds who spilled across Iraq's north, as well as swaths of Iran, Turkey, and Syria. Saddam granted Majid authority over all Iraqi security forces in the area. His cousin was then forty-five years old, just a few years younger than Saddam. In Tikrit's pinched world of tribal peasants that he and Saddam had shared as boys, Majid had claims to prestige. One of his grandfathers had been a governor of Tikrit. Majid considered himself a sheikh of a branch of the Albu Nasr tribe to which Saddam also belonged. After Saddam attained power, Majid served him in a succession of administration and security jobs. He was rougher and more traditional than Saddam's three half brothers—an intimidating man steeped in Tikrit's social codes who saw himself as Saddam's peer. Yet he also lived in fear of his cousin. "I was afraid that if I disobeyed him, he would tell our tribe that I was a coward," Majid explained years later.

He exhibited some of Saddam's diligent work habits and ruthlessness but little of his cousin's charisma.[1]

Saddam had handed Majid one of the knottiest problems in the Iran-Iraq War. The region's rough mountains made it difficult for either Iraq or Iran to maneuver forces in large numbers. (Most of the war's major artillery and tank battles took place across flatter borderlands and deserts to the south.) Iraqi Kurdish rebel groups opposed to Saddam sometimes collaborated with Khomeini's Iran. The rebels were a political and military wild card—an independent but fractious Iraqi movement fighting for autonomy and the possibility of a new Kurdish nation.

The Kurdish insurgents were also a fixture of Saddam's conspiratorial thinking about Iran, Israel, and America—thinking rooted in recent history. After the Baath takeover in 1968, Saddam, as vice president, had negotiated an autonomy agreement with Mustafa Barzani, the leader of the Kurdistan Democratic Party and a lion of the Kurdish opposition. The deal soon foundered. Barzani secretly received arms and money from Israel, the shah of Iran, and, later, the Nixon administration's C.I.A. Henry Kissinger, Nixon's national security adviser, wary of the Baath Party's ideology and ties to Moscow, sought to destabilize Iraq by aiding the Kurdish rebels. Yet Kissinger cynically hoped the Kurds "would not prevail" and would merely weaken Iraq, as a congressional investigation concluded.

In 1975, Saddam helped his regime wriggle out of this scheme by negotiating the Algiers Agreement, which settled several border disputes between Iraq and Iran. The shah pulled support for the Kurds, and the C.I.A. followed, betraying Barzani. "Complete destruction hanging over our head," the Kurdish leader wrote to his C.I.A. liaison. "No explanation for this." He died in bitter exile in suburban Virginia four years later. For the Kurds, the 1970s taught that America could not be trusted. For Saddam, the era provided concrete proof that the C.I.A., Iran, and Israel would not hesitate to collaborate against the Baath Party.[2]

Barzani's son Masoud succeeded him, and the Kurdistan Democratic Party revived itself during the 1980s. For Saddam, the ongoing rebellion by Iraqi Kurds, in the midst of an existential war against Ayatollah Khomeini, offered a glaring sign that his grip on the nation was weak, at least in the north. He regarded Kurdish rebels who collaborated with Iran as traitors and insurrectionists who had crossed the Rubicon. Kurdish guerrillas relentlessly attacked Baath Party outposts in the region. Between 1980 and 1986, of the approximately 1,700 Baathists assigned to Kurdish provinces, just over 500 were killed by local rebels. By the late 1980s, Saddam had decided to unleash fury on Kurdistan. He told comrades: "The Kurds we have are traitors and agents of Israel, and Iran has been playing them for tens of years. . . . This is our opportunity to remove the traitors and never bring them back. If they come back, they'll come back according to our law, not theirs."[3]

For what followed, Ali Hassan al-Majid would earn the immortal nickname Chemical Ali.

On March 15, 1988, Kurdish rebels entered Halabja, a Kurdish mountain city near the Iranian border that was then home to about eighty thousand people and was tenuously under Baath Party control. Some Iranian forces accompanied the rebels into the city. Seemingly liberated, Halabja's Kurds sacked the local party headquarters and offices of the secret police.

The next day, the Iraqi Air Force counterattacked with chemical bombs. Low-flying Soviet-made Sukhoi bombers spread sickly gas clouds across the region's fields and villages. A Kurdish witness with a video camera recalled that gas "had killed all natural life, animals and trees. I saw thousands of goats and sheep, all dead." An acquaintance he met, a survivor, led him to the cellar of her home, where he saw her family, unmarked by violence, lying dead in a heap. In another basement, a dead woman lay with her arm outstretched, holding her son.[4]

The gas attacks unfolded over several days and claimed about three thousand to five thousand lives, according to contemporaneous Iraqi intelligence assessments. Iran's government—long frustrated in its efforts to discredit Saddam Hussein on the world stage over his use of chemical arms—ferried journalists to Halabja by helicopter on March 20. David Hirst, a veteran Middle East correspondent with *The Guardian*, described what he found: "No wounds, no blood, no traces of explosions can be found on the bodies. . . . The skin of the bodies is strangely discolored, with their eyes open and staring where they have not disappeared into their sockets, a grayish slime oozing from their mouths and their fingers still grotesquely twisted. Death seemingly caught them almost unawares."[5]

Within days, Halabja had become a famous place around the globe, the site of one of the most visible instances of Iraq's gas attacks during the war, all the more outrageous for the high and indiscriminate civilian toll. The Reagan administration could not ignore it, but it did not want to break with Saddam over the event, either.

The administration embraced flawed intelligence reports from both the D.I.A. and the C.I.A. that both Iraq and Iran had resorted to gas. On March 23, State Department spokesman Charles Redman said that while Iraq had committed a "grave violation" of the Geneva Protocol at Halabja, Iran "may also have used chemical artillery shells in this fighting."[6]

This was misleading at best. The question of whether Iran had used chemical weapons against Iraq at any point in the war—apart from smoke or tear gas—would remain controversial. It is clear, however, that the impression publicized by the Reagan administration after Halabja—that the use of gas by Iraq and Iran in that atrocity might be militarily and morally equivalent—was false. This line was supported by Pat Lang, the Middle East analyst at the D.I.A. who was deeply involved in the intelligence liaison with Baghdad and who "insisted" that Iran share blame for Halabja. "Who defended the Iraqis?" Lang recalled. "I did." The "both sides do it" narrative settled like fog over a war the world mainly ignored.[7]

There is no public evidence that any of the D.I.A.'s Druid Leader target packages were used to support the Halabja attacks or other gassing campaigns carried out against Kurdish civilians during 1988. According to Lang, the D.I.A. told the Iraqis that it would not provide satellite-derived intelligence to support strikes in Kurdistan. Still, the Reagan administration would largely evade accountability for the support it provided to the chemical war machine Iraq deployed elsewhere against Iran.

Later, referring to Halabja, Rick Francona asked an Iraqi pilot, "Why did you drop chemical weapons on your own people?"

"They're not my own people," he answered. "They're Kurds."

In the late spring of 1988, Francona recalled, a series of interagency meetings at the White House reviewed whether to terminate the intelligence sharing program with Iraq because of the fallout over Halabja. But the word soon came down to the D.I.A.: Druid Leader would continue.[8]

The gassing of Halabja had been opportunistic, a ruthless attempt by Majid to punish the enemy and regain local control after an unexpected success by Kurdish rebels and Iranian allies. But the atrocities there coincided with a more systematic campaign to remove large numbers of Kurdish villagers from militarily sensitive regions near Iran—a campaign that also involved chemical weapons. Its goal was to deprive Iraqi Kurdish rebels of their population base and to relieve the Iraqi Army of fighting the rebels in hostile and mountainous terrain.

During a speech to Baath Party loyalists, Majid explained his strategy. He recounted how he had recently threatened a Kurdish audience to encourage voluntary evacuations: "I cannot let your village stay. I will attack it with chemical weapons. Then you and your family will die. You must leave right now." He made a promise to his Baathist comrades: "I will kill them all with chemical weapons! Who is going to say anything? The international community? Fuck them!"[9]

He issued orders banning Kurds from remaining in villages that fell within designated security zones and gave permission to raze villages and exterminate all life if the Kurds did not comply. "The presence of human beings and animals is completely prohibited in these areas," one of Majid's directives read. His order used a common code for chemical strikes ("special bombardments") and made explicit that the goal of the campaign was mass killing of Kurds:

> The Corps Commands shall carry out random special bombardments using artillery, helicopters and aircraft at all times of day or night in order to kill the largest number of persons present in those prohibited areas. . . . All persons captured in those villages shall be detained because of their presence there, and they shall be interrogated by the security services, and those between the ages of 15 and 70 must be executed.[10]

In early 1988, embracing this methodology, the authorities in Baghdad announced the start of a military operation they called "the Anfal," or "Spoils of War"—officially, a counterinsurgency campaign. It would become notorious years later as one of Saddam Hussein's greatest crimes against humanity.

In the weeks following the gas attacks on Halabja, rumors circulated from village to village in the Garmian region of Kurdistan, about fifty miles to the southeast. Entire families in Halabja had apparently suffered gruesome deaths. Wahid Kochani, twenty-three, a farmer and occasional armed scout for Kurdish rebels, who were called peshmerga, or "those who confront death," knew he and his family were living on borrowed time. The previous October, the Baghdad administration had formally designated his village as part of a "prohibited zone." The Kochanis had ignored their evacuation order, as had the great majority of their neighbors. But on April 10, 1988, government jets dropped gas bombs on a village close to the Kochanis' home. Iraqi ground forces then moved in and bulldozed that village to the ground. They plowed under every home and shed until a mud-brick enclave where hundreds of families had lived for centuries became a pile of debris.[11]

The Iraqi Army was moving freely across the region, destroying one village after another. Kochani and other auxiliary fighters grabbed their assault rifles, gathered their families, and hiked into the mountains to take shelter in a network of caves. Kochani's wife, Selma, and their two young sons accompanied him. With scores of others, Kochani and his family slept in the mountains for five or six nights. At nighttime, they looked down at the plain below and saw fires burning. There was not enough food or milk at the caves to feed everyone, so the men snuck back to their villages during the day to make bread and to milk their cows and goats. At one point, from a distance, Kochani watched bulldozers crush his village—and, as it turned out, his home—into a jumble of broken bricks.[12]

Kochani was uncertain about what to do. Local Kurdish paramilitaries on the regime's payroll—known derisively as jash, or baby donkeys—rode around in trucks, attempting to coax the locals out of hiding, promising men of military age that they could join the Iraqi Army. "You are going to be safe!" they called out. "Just come to the city." Kochani was a draft dodger, but as long as fugitives like him were not guerrillas named on government lists as "saboteurs," they might be conscripted, earn salaries, and return to their families after a tour of military duty. They would be resettled in slums near urban areas, where the regime hoped closer surveillance would prevent Kurdish guerrillas from reorganizing. These were the rumors, at least.

Kochani knew that his family could not hold out in the caves for very long. A few days before he and Selma had left their home, they had lost an infant son to illness; they had not even had time to put a marker on the boy's grave before they fled. They were hardened to difficulties, but there was only so much grief and fear anyone could endure.

Days passed and Kochani managed to dispatch Selma and their two boys to the home of a relative. He returned to the caves with a friend, Luqman. Some neighbors approached them.

"What are you guys doing up here?" they asked. "Go surrender. If they catch you, they're going to slaughter you."

The next morning, they woke up to the raspy sound of megaphones. The jash were back, urging surrender and making promises. The two men gave in to fate and packed up their belongings. They both carried loaded AK-47 assault rifles as they walked to the road. They climbed into the back of a vehicle filled with pro-regime paramilitaries and rode about a mile to a leveled village. They found hundreds of men like themselves milling about under the eye of Iraqi soldiers and Kurdish allies.

They lined up to register. When it was their turn, they handed over their rifles, accepted receipts, and submitted to interrogation. "Are you peshmerga? Did you dodge the draft?" Kochani admitted the truth: he was an auxiliary fighter, and yes, he had evaded military conscription.

A Kurdish paramilitary officer picked up a microphone tethered to a loudspeaker. "I welcome you all! You are going to become soldiers."

He explained that the men would board buses and ride to a nearby military base, where they would be issued army identification. Kochani and Luqman crammed their way onto one of the buses. When they reached a military base, they were kept aboard for many hours, without food or access to a bathroom. The heat and stench from human waste became unbearable.

An Iraqi soldier boarded the bus and asked them more basic questions. Daylight faded and they rolled out again. They reached a base called Topzawa, near Kirkuk. The bus stopped and new soldiers ordered the passengers out, motioning them to the ground, where they sat cross-legged in a mass. "No more jash," Kochani recalled. They had been comfortable with their Kurdish captors, traitors though they were. Now they confronted unhinged-looking Iraqi soldiers, "like the movies, evil-looking people." Kochani and his comrades felt trapped.[13]

The Anfal campaign unfolded in eight stages between late February and early September of 1988. Each of the eight Anfals, as they came to be known, opened with gassing attacks—to kill and demoralize villagers and to smoke them out of their homes so that they would move onto roads where Iraqi forces could round them up. The Third

Anfal, between April 7 and April 20, targeted the Garmian region where Wahid Kochani lived. Because of the area's relatively level topography, it was the stage of the Anfal in which the Iraqi forces used the least gas. Yet it was perhaps the cruelest.

Ali Hassan al-Majid exercised overall command. "I'm going to evacuate it," he told colleagues on April 15, speaking of Garmian. He made his remarks shortly after Wahid Kochani had surrendered to government forces.

"For five years, I won't allow any human existence there," Majid continued. "I don't want their agriculture. I don't want tomatoes. I don't want their okra and cucumbers. If we don't act in this way, the saboteurs' activities will never end—not for a million years."[14]

The Topzawa military base contained filthy warehouses crammed with people—hundreds of men, women, and children in each building. A newcomer could barely fit in standing up. The soldiers threw bread to the crowds, setting off melees; to eat, you had to be fierce or lucky. Kochani's warehouse contained only men. The soldiers locked the doors on the outside but sometimes allowed groups of ten to walk to latrines, passing through a gauntlet of armed guards. That night, cheek by jowl with hundreds of other young men, Kochani napped by crossing his legs and tucking his head into folded arms.

Early in the morning, Iraqi soldiers appeared with lists and read out names. Each detainee was assigned a bus. Kochani was on the last one to be loaded. The vehicle's windows had been painted over in white. The front door folded open like a typical bus door, but a metal barrier separated the driver's cabin from the passenger seats. The barrier had a small window that allowed some passengers to look forward through the windshield at the world outside. Kochani took a seat on the left in the second row, behind the driver. Three dozen or so detainees boarded— all from Kochani's home district. The barrier door slid shut. In addition to the driver, there was a single armed guard stationed in the front cab.

The bus roared off at about 9:00 a.m. Kochani recognized one other detainee, Anwar Tayyar. He was an older, locally well-known pesh-merga fighter of stalwart reputation. Like Kochani, Tayyar was sitting up front, and he could peer through the small window at the road ahead. He had worked as a taxi driver in the region and would point out landmarks he recognized. He narrated for the men the possibilities that awaited them. He spoke in Kurdish dialect; it was evident that the Arab soldier and driver up front could not understand him. He shared rumors of recent mass executions of captured peshmergas.[15]

Every so often, the driver pulled over for a food and bathroom break. He and the armed guard would eat, rehydrate, and smoke while their prisoners remained locked inside with no food or water. Tayyar told the men that back in 1975, after he had been arrested, he and an-other prisoner had attacked and killed a driver and guard taking them to prison. "I hope that we are going to do the same as we did then," Tayyar said. He counted the passengers. "There's thirty-four of us."

As evening fell, the bus turned off asphalt roads onto tracks leading into the desert. The area was flat and sandy. The sun set, and in the darkness they could no longer see through their small window. After a time, the bus halted. Now they could see other buses parked nearby. Headlights flickered, and they heard the sounds of bulldozers or other heavy equipment rumbling.

Then they heard gunshots. Through their narrow prism, they could see men being dragged to the edge of a pit—some blindfolded, some not—where firing squads shot them. Some of the executioners had as-sault rifles; others, pistols. Some sprayed bullets but aimed badly. The bus driver and the armed guard left the bus. It seemed as if the passen-gers on the bus parked next to them were being executed now, and they would be next.

Kochani and the men around him prayed. They embraced and of-fered forgiveness, one to another, for any transgressions in this life. Ko-chani pictured his oldest son, Hemin, who was barely a toddler. He thought about what it would be like for the boy to grow up without him. He wondered what it would feel like to have a bullet go through his head or his body.

Tayyar spoke up again. "My dear brothers!" he said. "We are a group of men able to do something. We should keep calm and collected until we all get off, and then we attack them." His idea was to try to grab the soldiers' guns and open fire on their captors. As they waited, another former peshmerga offered an amendment to the plan: as soon as an armed guard came onto the bus, they should jump him and try to take his gun.

After about fifteen minutes, three new armed guards approached their bus. Two stood outside and the third entered. He unlocked a sliding door to the passenger area and pulled out the first prisoner in front of him—a beardless teenager who Kochani reckoned was no more than fourteen. The guard put a white blindfold on him. Tayyar leapt forward and tried to punch the guard and seize his gun. Other men tried to join the attack. They fell into a chaotic scrum, powered by adrenaline and terror.

The two soldiers outside opened fire at the side of the bus, unleashing a wild fusillade through the skin of the vehicle. Bullets struck Tayyar, but he kept fighting. He wrested the first guard's gun away, shot him dead, and then shot one of the two soldiers outside.

Kochani took a bullet in his back and fell to the floor. He reached around to feel his wound—a flesh wound but deep. Dead and dying comrades fell on top of him. He forced himself to stand up, lurched toward the bus door, punched one of the guards, and stepped outside. On one side he saw the shadowy outlines of what appeared to be construction equipment. He ran in the opposite direction, into the darkness.[16]

He was dressed in Kurdish robes and wore rubber shoes. As he ran, his shoes slipped off, and he kept going in bare feet. He could feel his back bleeding. He saw some bushes, sat down, and rested. He prayed to God: "Why is this happening to us?"

He pulled himself up and started moving randomly forward, sometimes walking, sometimes jogging. The pain in his back faded; he felt another surge of adrenaline. He stumbled ahead in the dark. Finally, he saw lights in the distance. It was a cluster of family homes. He approached and stared at the houses, uncertain which door to knock on. He prayed again, this time for guidance to make the right choice. He selected a one-story house, walked to the front door, and knocked.

A girl of about fourteen or fifteen answered. She summoned her father, mother, a brother, and two sisters. "Tfadal," they said, speaking Arabic. *Welcome, come in.* They led him to a living room with pillows and cushions on the floor and against the walls. Kochani sat on his knees to minimize his back pain. They saw that he was dripping blood onto their cushions.

"Sir, what happened to you?" the father asked in Arabic. Kochani knew just enough Arabic to explain the very basics. He said the Iraqi Army was taking women, children, and men into the desert. He tried to explain that they were carrying out executions. Not too far from you, he said. They are killing everyone.

The father exclaimed, "Why are they doing this?!" Family members soon carried in bread, sweets, water, and tea for Kochani.[16]

The family led him to another room, peeled off his bloody clothes, and had him lie down on his belly. They washed his back, daubed his wound with alcohol, and covered it with gauze. Then they brought him a clean robe to wear. He slept. The next morning, the women served him breakfast—meat, chicken, and bread. The girls brought in a cassette player and played some Arabic music to cheer him up. They apologized for not having Kurdish songs.

He stayed with the family that day. The next morning, two women—nurses—arrived at the house. They washed his wound again and rebandaged it.

Kochani's host also brought home a Kurdish acquaintance, a man named Amin who lived in a nearby camp for Kurdish refugees from Iran. Amin spoke fluent Kurdish and Arabic. Now Kochani was able to tell the story in full as Amin translated.

He learned that he had stumbled onto the outskirts of Ramadi, an Arab-majority city in Anbar Province, not far from Baghdad. It was a place where Saddam's secret police would be all around. Who knew what the government was doing to track down stragglers who escaped from the execution sites? On his third night with the family, Kochani talked with the father about his unease. He said he needed to find his way to a city with a large Kurdish population, such as Kirkuk. "I have cousins there. They can hide me."

The father agreed. The next day he provided Kochani with traditional Arab robes, sandals, and a headdress so that Kochani would not stand out in Ramadi. He asked how much money Kochani had with him.

"Seven dinars," Kochani answered, then worth about twenty dollars. The family gave him five more dinars. But the journey would be risky. Kochani had no official identification or documents of the sort necessary to travel between cities.

He embraced his host family, expressed his thanks emotionally, and left with his host's son. It turned out that the young man was a serving Iraqi soldier. He drove Kochani in a pickup truck to a taxi stand in Ramadi and escorted him to a particular vehicle. "This will take you to Baghdad," he said, and from there Kochani could find cars going to Kirkuk.[17]

There were two senior Iraqi Army officers in the taxi—men in uniform with stars on their shoulders. They made way for Kochani to sit between them in the back seat so that they could have the window seats. The taxi left for Baghdad. At numerous checkpoints, soldiers looked into the back seat, saw the uniformed officers, and waved the vehicle through without asking for any documents. Kochani would long wonder if the family had arranged this privileged escort for him or if he had just enjoyed God's protection.

In Baghdad, he found a bus for Kirkuk, but before it had gone very far, soldiers boarded and asked everyone for identification. They scoffed at the papers Kochani presented. They arrested him and about a dozen other young men on the bus whom they judged to be draft dodgers or soldiers absent without leave. His captors took him to a military prison. But they didn't question him closely, and he kept his wound a secret. Over the next weeks, Kochani endured beatings in several prisons, but he also managed to get in touch with some cousins from home. They posted bond for him in exchange for his commitment to serve in the army. He was released with a military identification card that allowed him to travel freely.

He made his way home. Selma and his boys were safe. Kochani's only brother and his friend Luqman had both disappeared, along with almost everyone else who had surrendered themselves in the days when Kochani had walked down from the caves.

Eventually, Kochani and his family visited the remains of their village and their home. Their saddest task was their search for the grave of Awara, Kochani and Selma's baby, whom they'd had to bury in haste. They could not find him. After the destruction of their village, wild dogs had scavenged in the ruins. Their neighbors speculated that the dogs must have dug up the baby's corpse and dragged it away.

Wahid Kochani was among six Kurdish men and one boy who survived the desert executions and later provided testimony to human-rights researchers and Iraqi courts. Scholars and researchers estimate that Saddam Hussein's regime killed at least 50,000 people during the Anfal, between February and September; Kurdish authorities place the death toll at 182,000. Most of the victims were military-age men, but many women, children, and older civilians were also executed and buried in mass graves, as the Kurdish researcher Choman Hardi has documented. The Iraqi Army destroyed more than 2,600 villages. At least one bulldozer driver who participated in digging mass graves during desert executions has provided a vivid account of the killings; he described how he and other drivers at the pits were ordered to keep their engines running to cover up the sounds of shootings and screaming.[18]

Records from the campaign described the bureaucratization of mass detention and killing. Medals went to lists of "heroic and brave" Iraqi officers battling "saboteurs," "traitors," and "Iranian agents." The correspondence includes light chiding of comrades who acted too hastily, as in a letter from the Northern Bureau of the party to an Iraqi Army

Corps commander, quoting Ali Hassan al-Majid: "We have no objection to beheading the traitors. However, it would have been preferable to send them to security for interrogation before executing them."[19]

While Iraq's gassing of Kurdish civilians at Halabja in March 1988 caused a global sensation, the expulsions and exterminations of the Anfal were less visible. The Reagan administration had a weak grasp of the campaign's dimensions during the time it unfolded. "We did know that villages were being razed and that people were being taken to the desert," David George Newton, the U.S. ambassador in Baghdad during the first half of 1988, recalled. "We had the impression they were being executed. . . . What nobody realized at the time was the scale of the campaign."[20]

Yet the Anfal was announced by name in Iraqi official media, although it was described as a military campaign, not a mass killing of unarmed prisoners. Thousands of Kurdish refugees poured into Iran and Turkey during 1988, testifying to the terror they had endured, but they did not know what had become of the many men and families detained. In any event, the alliance between the Reagan administration and Saddam Hussein against Iran—especially as Iraq at last won battles that winter and spring and brought a long war to the brink of closure—remained the White House's priority. In the summer of 1988, Peter Galbraith, a staff member on the Senate Foreign Relations Committee, took a fact-finding trip to Kurdistan to look into reports of atrocities after Halabja. When he got back, he spurred the committee's chairman, Claiborne Pell, a Democrat from Rhode Island, to introduce the Prevention of Genocide Act, which would have sanctioned Iraq for its gassings and devastation of Kurdistan. The Reagan administration lobbied successfully against the bill.[21]

As the Anfal wound down, Saddam met with Tariq Aziz and other foreign-policy advisers to discuss the pressure they were under because of international publicity about their gassing attacks. They continued to deny publicly that Iraq had ever used chemical weapons.

Aziz read out a draft public statement for Saddam's approval: "Iraq respects and abides by all international laws and treaties . . . including the Geneva Protocol of the year 1925, which forbids the use of chemical weapons, poison gas, and biological weapons in warfare, and all other treaties within the frame of international humanitarian law."

"All right," Saddam said.

"Can I send it, sir?"

"Yes."

"So we gain time," Aziz noted.

Saddam went on to speak about the future of negotiations with Iraqi Kurds. He laughed when he said, "Autonomy? Let's discuss autonomy. Kurdish state? Let's discuss a Kurdish state!"[22]

He was not jesting. In private, Saddam periodically expressed openness to a future of Kurdish political autonomy and even independence—a taboo subject for Turkey and Iran, each with large, restive Kurdish populations. Often, Saddam seemed to want to promote his openness to Kurdish autonomy in order to irritate his neighbors. Yet he had enough experience of the intractable problem of Kurdish separatism to think that some sort of negotiated autonomy would be required. He laid out a long-term policy that summer. He would cut off the heads of "those who oppose the nation," he said, pointing to his neck to emphasize the point. Yet he would also construct a new politics between Baghdad and Kurdistan to provide Kurds with "peaceful and prosperous circumstances with autonomy and real governance."[23]

To Saddam, the summer of 1988 seemed a season of great victory. On July 20, Ayatollah Khomeini, who was nearing his eighty-sixth birthday and in failing health, at last capitulated and announced a cease-fire, a decision that effectively ended the Iran-Iraq War. It was the outcome Saddam had long sought—an armistice and a return to prewar borders. "Taking this decision was more deadly than poison," Khomeini admitted. By September, Saddam had terminated cooperation with the D.I.A. and no longer welcomed American spies to Baghdad.[24]

The Iraqi leader had needlessly started one of the most costly and aimless wars in recent world history and, after eight terrible years, had ended up where he started. His nation had suffered hundreds of thousands of casualties, inflicted a comparable number on Iran, and spent more than $500 billion. When the war began, Iraq had at least $35 billion in foreign exchange reserves; when it ended, the country owed more than $80 billion—about twice the size of its economy— to various lenders, including Japan, France, West Germany, America, and the Soviet Union. Its two largest creditors were Saudi Arabia and Kuwait. Iraq owed them as much as $35 billion and $10 billion, respectively. Yet Saddam had no choice but to declare this fiasco another win in his series of glorious triumphs; to do otherwise would be to admit weakness and invite more attempts to overthrow him. To the United States, he would soon insist: "Victory in the war against Iran made a historic difference to the Arab world and the West."

In Washington, Saddam sounded delusional. It seemed to many White House and State Department experts that he couldn't possibly believe what he said, that he was just speaking for political and diplomatic effect, as many politicians do. As it turned out, the end of the Iran-Iraq War touched off a new cascade of misunderstandings between Washington and Baghdad, a chain of events that would soon shatter their fragile alliance and wreak yet more devastating violence and disruption.[25]

NINE

The Prodigal Son

On the evening of Tuesday, October 18, 1988, Kamel Hana Gegeo threw a party on "Mother of Pigs," an island in the Tigris River that jutted from an oxbow a few hundred yards from the Republican Palace. Once covered by date palms, the island had caught the eye of Frank Lloyd Wright, who, during the 1950s, considered using it as the fulcrum of his "Plan for Greater Baghdad," a passion project that was ultimately tabled by Iraq's king and ignored by the strongmen who followed. Guesthouses, some with swimming pools, now flanked the island's tree-shaded lawns. The houses could be rented out for weddings and parties. Some were reserved for connected officials of Saddam Hussein's regime.

Gegeo was an intimate of Saddam Hussein—his chief servant or valet, a full-faced man ready with a smile or a struck match for Saddam's cigar. He also helped manage the president's personal staff and schedule. He was a Christian and a rare non-Tikriti who enjoyed Saddam's trust. In the jealous opinion of some of the president's close relatives, he reaped outsize financial rewards for his loyalty. In any event, he was privileged enough to book a place on Mother of Pigs, and that night he threw a party for about fifty people, replete with raucous music, dancing, and free-flowing hard liquor.

There are two available eyewitness accounts of what ensued—they align on the main points but diverge on some details. The most reliable account appears to be that of Zafer Muhammad Jaber, who was a contemporary and close aide to Uday Hussein, the president's eldest son. Uday was then twenty-four. He was up late at his official home in the government quarter, within earshot of the party, according to Zafer. The two were drinking vodka and watching TV when the sound of shooting disturbed them. Uday dispatched a bodyguard to see what was happening. The man returned to report that Gegeo's party was "out of control." The guests were drinking heavily, and some were firing off assault rifles, he reported.

"Go over there and tell them to stop," Uday ordered.[1]

The bodyguard did so, but the shooting went on. Uday decided to handle it himself. He, Zafer, and two bodyguards rode across a bridge to the island. Uday wore a black dishdasha, an ankle-length robe, and carried a bamboo walking stick with an ivory handle carved into the head of a snake baring its fangs. It was one among a collection of about 150 walking sticks of "varying quality and design" possessed by Uday, according to Ala Bashir, one of Saddam's physicians. "The art of restraint was unknown to him," he noted of the president's son.

On the island, they found Gegeo so drunk he could barely stand. "You should be ashamed of yourself," Uday told him, according to the account attributed to Zafer. Gegeo spoke back to him, and Uday called the valet "a dog." He struck Gegeo on the head with his stick and watched the man crumple to the ground.

Uday and his companions left, believing that Gegeo had fallen because he was drunk and that he was not seriously hurt. As it turned out, Uday's blow caused internal bleeding in the valet's brain. He died before dawn. The killing was a prologue to a drama in Saddam's family worthy of the most over-the-top Middle Eastern telenovelas, a crisis that would produce perhaps the most serious assassination threat Saddam Hussein had yet confronted—this time, from his eldest son.[2]

U day Hussein was just four years old when his father became vice president of Iraq. As a boy, he barely knew the striving, modestly comfortable years of his parents' early marriage. He came of age amidst rising ostentation and privilege, colored by his father's harsh rule. Notwithstanding the Baath Party's democratic-revolutionary rhetoric, given the record of succession in the Arab world, as Saddam's eldest son, Uday was his heir apparent. Other of Saddam's close and highly privileged relatives abused power, but as Uday reached high school, he took this to baroque extremes. He lived out a prolonged arrested adolescence that lasted well into midlife. He was "like a child," one of his government interpreters remembered. "His ideas were not clear. . . . He was not really mature." Tariq Aziz dismissed the adult Uday as "just a kid" whose conduct admittedly "went beyond what is acceptable."[3]

By the late 1980s, Uday had grown physically into a tall man— taller than his father—with large brown eyes and perpetual black stubble. His default look was menacing insouciance. He was reportedly less than a success in school, but he received high marks from terrified teachers and earned multiple degrees from Iraqi universities, including, eventually, a doctorate. He did acquire excellent English. He had wanted to pursue his education in the United States, at the Massachusetts Institute of Technology, he recalled: "I did my SATs, everything. I did very well. Passed with high marks." The Iran-Iraq War prevented him from pursuing his dream of "nuclear studies."[4]

He settled for racketeering and rapidly enriched himself by smuggling scarce and coveted goods, such as cigarettes and alcohol. In 1987, having reached the same age at which some of Saddam's half brothers had taken on significant responsibilities, Uday was appointed by his father to run the National Olympic Committee of Iraq; it was an indication that Saddam grasped his son's limitations.

He was a feared man about town, a wildly self-indulgent collector of "watches, jewels and rings, money, women and luxury cars," as Bashir put it. He kept dozens of imported Mercedes-Benzes, Ferraris, BMWs, Rolls-Royces, and the like in a garage near the Republican Palace. He prowled the capital at night in his ostentatious rides, turning up with an armed entourage at nightclubs and five-star hotels, where he and his mates held court at tables shrouded in the fog of cigar smoke. Some young women volunteered for his privileged company, but Uday was indifferent to consent and could threaten the safety of any girl or woman who strayed into his sight.[5]

You have killed him," Saddam told Uday icily the morning after Gegeo's death, according to Ala Bashir. "Give yourself up to the police and accept your punishment."

Devastated, Uday swallowed a bottle of Valium and soon collapsed. His bodyguards transported him to Ibn Sina Hospital, a two-story, white-walled facility flanked by palm trees. The hospital had been opened in 1964 and soon gained a reputation as the best in Baghdad; in 1974, Saddam took it over and turned it into a private twenty-bed facility for his family and senior Baath Party officials and their families. Ala Bashir, a plastic surgeon, was on staff. By 1988, he recalled, the hospital "had a large staff of highly qualified doctors and nurses on call at any time for the President, his family and the regime's top echelon."[6]

Doctors pumped Uday's stomach, revived him, and kept him overnight for observation. Saddam telephoned his half brother Barzan Ibrahim al-Tikriti, who joined family members at the hospital the next day. Hussein Kamel was there. Barzan sized up the family dynamics: Hussein Kamel, as a contender for succession to power, "was pleased" by Uday's disgrace because it would now "take a long time to restore the relationship between the father and son."[7]

As soon as he was able, Uday checked out of the hospital. He dismissed his bodyguards, grabbed a Kalashnikov rifle, and shot at his own security men when they tried to approach him. The bodyguards

informed Saddam that "his son's mental state was still slightly precarious," as Bashir put it.[8]

That evening, the president called Barzan and asked him to come
immediately to Radwaniyah. Barzan found the president dressed in
"sports attire" at one of the compound's palaces. We have only Barzan's
record of what followed, but it is consistent with the general run of
events described in private later by Saddam, as well as with accounts
from Ala Bashir and other sources.

Saddam told Barzan that Uday had driven out to Radwaniyah to
confront his father. He had tried to shame Saddam over a long-term
affair the president was having with Samira Shahbandar, who was from
a prestigious family and had been married to an executive at Iraqi Air-
ways. She was spending more and more time with Saddam—she was
his undeclared second wife, in the eyes of some. The couple reportedly
had a young child—a son named Ali.[9]

"Go back to your wife!" Uday had demanded, referring to his
mother, Sajida, as Saddam explained to Barzan. The president added,
"Fortunately, I did not have a handgun on me. Otherwise, I would have
killed him."

He was still steaming a short time later when his second son, Qusay, burst into the palace, screaming, "He is here! . . . Uday!"

"Tell him to come in so that we can put an end to this nonsense,"
Barzan advised, as he recalled it.

"No, he has a rifle in his hands and wants to kill Dad," Qusay
warned.

Barzan went outside, where his brother Watban joined him. They
found Uday gripping an assault rifle. They stepped toward him to take
it away, but Uday shuffled back and fired off a burst around their feet.
Eventually, Uday began to cry and dropped his gun. They escorted him
to meet his father, but when they reentered the palace, Qusay drew a
pistol on his older brother, "in an attempt to shoot his brother," as Barzan judged it.

To Barzan, as ever, family relations were a zero-sum struggle for

Saddam's favor. He reprimanded Qusay, calling him "a hypocrite and an opportunist who was trying to take advantage of the situation" by murdering Uday at a moment when this might be justified so as to eliminate a rival and move up the line of succession. Whatever his thinking, Qusay stood down.

They gathered before Saddam in the living room. Uday apologized and kissed his father. "The atmosphere was very miserable, the women were crying," and Saddam remained distraught and quiet for about ten minutes, Barzan recalled.

"After what has happened, I do not consider Uday my son," the president finally said. He told Uday "that he was a killer and must prepare to go to the police station and give himself up."[10]

Uday retreated to his rooms in the palace. Later that evening, Hussein Kamel arrived, handcuffed Uday, and removed him to a guesthouse on the Radwaniyah compound, where he was placed under a kind of house arrest. It emerged, according to Barzan, that shortly after Saddam had renounced his son before the family, Uday had secretly telephoned the American embassy to ask for asylum. Hussein Kamel or his men had been monitoring Uday's line and moved in to detain him.

Rumors spread. The killing "is becoming known to people—maybe not all people, but to some Iraqis," Saddam told his advisers about two weeks later. He could repress the truth, but it would be "much better," he said, to put out the facts himself and control the narrative. He settled on a public resolution: he disclosed the killing and called for an official investigation while also saying that Uday had acted unintentionally and had felt so much remorse that he had tried to take his own life.[11]

Saddam released Uday from his Radwaniyah quarters after a few weeks, but Uday promptly beat up a telephone operator who had irritated him. Days after that, he pistol-whipped a security guard and fractured the man's skull.

Saddam again summoned Barzan. The president lamented that if Uday remained in Baghdad and continued to behave this way, he was

going to "force me to kill him." Saddam had an idea: he could appoint
Barzan as an ambassador in an overseas embassy, and Barzan could take
Uday with him, to settle him down.

Barzan readily agreed; he had been yearning for years to leave Iraq.
He told Saddam that England would be his first choice, Switzerland his
second.

"Honestly, I do not trust Uday, and England is full of enemies," Saddam said, as Barzan recalled. They settled on Geneva. Saddam's office
ordered the Ministry of Foreign Affairs to make the arrangements immediately.[12]

On December 18, Barzan flew to Switzerland with Uday in a government Boeing 737. Uday brought along two heavy suitcases full of
cash; more than fifty suits; and at least a dozen fur coats and hats. As
they settled into Geneva that winter, Uday insisted on wearing his fur
ensembles when he went out. When Barzan tried to explain that Gene-
vans were staring at him because of his outlandish outfits, Uday replied,
"Yes, of course—they could not buy such clothes."

Predictably, he caused trouble. He pulled a gun on a nightclub patron. He racked up traffic tickets and was cited for illegally importing a
vehicle. At first, the Swiss authorities "uncharacteristically" did not
press for his prosecution or expulsion, because of "the status of Iraq at
that time," as Barzan put it. One day in January, however, at the Iraqi
embassy, Uday shot an Iraqi guard in the chest. Barzan bundled the
screaming employee into a car and rushed him to the hospital, hoping
that neighbors or guards at the German embassy across the street
hadn't heard the gunfire and wouldn't call the police.

The guard survived. Barzan fed the Swiss police a story that the
man had accidentally shot himself while cleaning his gun. It was obvious that Uday had to leave the country before he ended up in a Swiss
prison. On January 19, just a month after his arrival, Uday left to visit
Paris. He passed through Bonn and Istanbul before returning to Baghdad later that winter. Saddam never imprisoned his son, and Uday
gradually reestablished himself in Baghdad. Saddam allowed Barzan to
remain in Geneva with his wife and children. His half brother was not

exactly restored to favor; their relations remained strained. But he could again meet the president and write to him about sensitive family and political matters.[13]

The year following the end of his war with Iran might have been an opportunity for Saddam Hussein to reset and rebuild. The eastern and southern borders of Iraq were at last calm. Ports and trade reopened. Iraq's budget was pinched by war debts and falling oil prices, but Saddam had emerged as by far the strongest military leader in the Gulf region—a heavily armed giant among the flaccid royal families nearby. The United States, Britain, and France were greatly relieved that the Iran-Iraq War was over, and that oil shipping through the Persian Gulf was no longer under daily threat. Those countries continued to see Saddam's Iraq as a bulwark against revolutionary Iran and as a potential market for lucrative exports. It would have been a natural time for Saddam to return to the sort of leadership he had exercised during the 1970s—to travel back to Europe, perhaps, and negotiate deals for advanced technology; to shrink and restructure his military; and to refocus Iraq's emphasis on industry and science. For its part, during its tilt toward Baghdad, the United States had approved the export of more than $1 billion in military equipment to Saddam's regime after 1985, and trade between the two nations had grown sevenfold, from $500 million to $3.5 billion annually. The White House hoped to continue this business-friendly partnership.[14]

Yet Saddam seemed to have emerged from the war in an angry, paranoid, inward-looking state of mind. In matters where he might have earlier perceived complexity or irony, he now seemed to see only the dark side. His nearly mortal struggle with his eldest son had surely unsettled him. In foreign affairs, he referred regularly to the Iran-Contra revelations of 1986 and their seeming proof of an ongoing conspiracy against him by the United States, Israel, and Iran. The C.I.A. reported to American policymakers on plots against Saddam uncovered by the regime in November 1988 and again in January 1989;

the latter case led to "the purging of dozens, possibly hundreds, of officers from the army and air force," according to Richard Pollack, then a C.I.A. analyst studying Iraq. Assassination threats had long been background noise in Saddam's experience of power. Now they seemed to be a preoccupation.[15]

At some point during the spring of 1989, Saddam received an intelligence report that Israel planned to assassinate him by launching an armada of about thirty fighter jets to bomb a family home in Tikrit when the president was visiting. The planes would race low over the desert floor to evade radar, as they had during the Osirak strike of 1981. To prepare, the president ordered his air force to stage an exercise simulating such an attack so that he could learn how to defeat it. On July 2, Saddam traveled to Tikrit to observe the maneuvers. Nine Soviet-made Sukhoi Su-25 fighter jets swooped in low from the west, as if flying from Israel. On approach, one plane's engine failed, and the pilot ejected. His jet crashed near enough to Saddam's observation post that the president concluded the pilot was trying to kill him.[16]

When not dodging assassins, real or imagined, Saddam devoted himself during 1989 to self-glorification before the Iraqi people. He promoted his place in the pantheon of great leaders to have emerged from Mesopotamia dating back to ancient Babylon. If modern Egypt's claims to leadership of the Arab world owed something to the longevity of its civilization, Saddam was not about to be outdone. His government reburied Babylonian kings in new tombs and knocked down Babylonian ruins to build fresh walls using yellow bricks that contained an inscription reporting that the reconstruction had taken place "in the era of the leader President Saddam Hussein."[17]

He also commissioned monuments to Iraq's "victory" in its war with Iran. In August, Saddam dedicated the Swords of Qādisiyyah, named for a seventh-century battle in which an Arab Muslim army had defeated Persian enemies. Fashioned out of steel and bronze and held by arms modeled from plaster casts of Saddam's own, two bending crossed swords towered forty feet above a plaza in central Baghdad. The Iraqi artist Khalid al-Rahal designed the monument in collaboration with

Saddam; following Rahal's death in 1986, Mohammed Ghani Hikmat, one of Iraq's best-known sculptors, completed the project. At the dedication, Saddam donned a white jacket and a white helmet sporting an ostrich feather as he rode beneath the swords on a white horse, an appropriation of a Shia tradition commemorating Imam Hussain, the revered grandson of Prophet Muhammad.[18]

The mishmashed cult of personality Saddam cultivated was a far cry from the collectivist pretensions of the early Baath Party years. His costume wardrobe for propaganda messaging had grown dizzyingly diverse—Kurdish peasant one day, Sunni Arab sheikh the next. He regularly donned his green fatigues and pistol belt to reprise his revolutionary heritage. The catastrophic war with Iran was in fact a triumph, his propaganda machine trumpeted.

On September 4, 1989, Barzan wrote to Saddam from Geneva. He did nothing to assuage his half brother's sense that he was besieged and insufficiently celebrated. In protesting Iraq's gas attacks and human-rights abuses, America was waging "psychological warfare" against Iraq, Barzan asserted. Washington's themes were "Human Rights issues, Kurdish rights, sectarian divide, and other allegations that are designed solely for one aim, which is to defame Iraq and dilute the efficacy of our victory" over Iran.

He accused Washington of trying to "invade us from the inside out" by fomenting rebellion within Iraq. Saddam should be wary of an American-authored assassination attempt, he concluded. If an assassin is willing to kill himself in the act, "there isn't any security procedure that could be taken to prevent him from achieving his objective." He worried about Iraqi prisoners of war held in Iran who might have been indoctrinated with revolutionary zeal and venomous hatred of Saddam.[19]

Barzan offered a prescription for long-term regime survival: a nuclear-weapons deterrent. "We have to hurry," he wrote. "We are in a constant race with Iran and Israel." A nuclear deterrent would "enable us to defend our sovereignty and independence . . . before being attacked or becom[ing] subjected to a conspiracy."[20]

Barzan's writings were in sync with Saddam's thinking. The gap between what Saddam Hussein believed about the United States in the autumn of 1989 and what Washington's foreign-policy elite assumed about him had grown wider than at any time since the Reagan administration had first come to his rescue seven years before. In Washington, it would take time for this reality to begin sinking in.

On November 8, 1988, George H. W. Bush had been elected president of the United States. He was arguably the best-prepared foreign-policy president since Dwight Eisenhower. A former C.I.A. director and U.N. ambassador, he had spent eight years as vice president watching Ronald Reagan's foreign policy up close. As he moved into the Oval Office, Bush assembled a team of foreign-policy pragmatists led by National Security Adviser Brent Scowcroft, a retired U.S. Air Force general. Bush and Scowcroft were both inclined to continue the Reagan administration's support of Iraq. Saddam's influential Arab allies, King Hussein of Jordan and President Hosni Mubarak in Egypt, continued to argue for American engagement with Baghdad. The prospect that Saddam might start arresting terrorists or quietly back the Israeli-Palestinian peace process tantalized the American foreign-policy establishment. Whatever the likelihood of such breakthroughs, the C.I.A. and other intelligence agencies reported that Iraq was war-weary and debt-burdened and posed no near-term threat.

In September 1989, Bush attended a National Security Council meeting in which Richard Kerr, a bespectacled analyst who served as acting director of the C.I.A., gave a briefing about Iraq to inform a White House policy draft on Saddam's regime for distribution across the national security bureaucracy.

Is it possible that Saddam Hussein could really change? Bush asked.

"The leopard does not change his spots," Kerr said. And yet the consensus at the meeting, as Scowcroft summarized it, was that there was nothing to lose by trying to strengthen ties with Baghdad. Bush agreed. The president sought to "encourage acceptably moderate behavior on the part of Saddam Hussein" while aiding American businesses by winning them access to "what was assumed would be a substantial Iraqi reconstruction effort" after the war with Iran.[21]

On October 2, Bush signed National Security Directive 26, which essentially extended the Reagan-era tilt toward Saddam. "Normal relations between the United States and Iraq would serve our longer-term interests and promote stability in both the Gulf and the Middle East," it said. "The United States Government should propose economic and political incentives for Iraq to moderate its behavior and to increase our influence." The main incentive Bush had in mind was the extension of U.S. credits to allow Iraq to import American wheat, a policy that had support from farm-state politicians, such as Senator Bob Dole, the influential Republican from Kansas. Bush's willingness to advance trade with Iraq also had backing from corporate America. The U.S.-Iraq Business Forum boasted blue-chip members such as AT&T, Bechtel, Bell Helicopter Textron, and oil giant Exxon. Saddam had warmly received American corporate executives in Baghdad. ("I look forward to having a Westinghouse refrigerator," Tariq Aziz quipped.) The Forum's corporate members sometimes carried Iraq's case to Congress. The White House assured the Forum that its goals were "consistent with U.S. policy," recalled Richard Fairbanks, a Forum board member and registered lobbyist for Iraq. "The administration wanted closer diplomatic and commercial ties to Iraq."

In Baghdad, the ascendant Hussein Kamel was, in return, bullish on America. The weapons programs he oversaw drew on more than $4 billion in unauthorized loans from the Atlanta, Georgia, branch of an Italian bank, Banca Nazionale del Lavoro. The bank's Atlanta manager had leveraged the program of credit guarantees to Iraq and had provided large off-the-books loans to Kamel's military industrialization ministry—a scandal that broke just before Bush signed National Security Directive 26 and that would plague his administration for the next three years.

Congress members outraged by Saddam's recent mass killings of Kurds and his use of chemical arms continued to press for economic sanctions against Iraq. The White House lobbied to defeat these pro-posals, all part of what Bush and Scowcroft later described as "a good-faith effort toward better relations."[22]

Amidst this official optimism, on October 6, Tariq Aziz traveled to Washington to meet Secretary of State James Baker, a shrewd Texas lawyer and political fixer. Aziz shocked Baker by reporting that Saddam had concluded that the United States was secretly working against him. He even feared he could be marked out for assassination.[23]

Baker tried to disabuse Aziz of this thinking. The State Department soon cabled the Baghdad embassy to instruct diplomats there to assure their Iraqi counterparts that Washington was not conspiring against Saddam. Yet those diplomats had no way to influence Saddam or his inner circle. The C.I.A. had no sources among Saddam's confidants. The D.I.A. no longer had the ties to Iraqi military intelligence that it had enjoyed in the days of Druid Leader. The plan to coax Saddam toward moderation suffered from a void of access and understanding. This was about to become clear to all the world.

TEN

Project 17

n November 1989, the Berlin Wall fell, and as the Soviet Union tee-
tered and the Cold War expired, Saddam Hussein saw trouble. He
concluded that the Soviets were "finished as a world power" and that
the United States now had a "free hand" to assert itself, as he told Assistant Secretary of State John Kelly in Baghdad on February 12, 1990.
Saddam did not generally receive mid-level envoys such as Kelly at the
Republican Palace, but a few weeks before, President Bush had set
aside objections in Congress and signed another expansion of American credit guarantees for U.S. trade with Iraq. Saddam reciprocated
with courtesy to Kelly: during a two-and-a-half-hour conversation, he
refrained from hostile rants about America. He reviewed for Kelly the
implications of Washington's coming post–Cold War imperial moment.
During the next five years, he said, the Arab world would learn whether
the U.S. would use its unrestrained power for "constructive purposes"
or blindly support Israel.[1]

The Cold War's end—a destabilizing inflection point in many parts
of the world—would provide a backdrop during the next nine months
for Saddam's stunning transformation from tenuous American ally to

mortal enemy. The sweep of political events during 1989 and 1990 encouraged grand thinking about the future. It also created opportunities for profound miscalculation.

Eleven days after his meeting with Kelly, Saddam took a rare trip outside Iraq to attend a two-day summit of Arab leaders in Amman. He arrived in a smart double-breasted overcoat and Russian-style hat. In his keynote address, he offered one of his long reviews of colonial history in the Arab region—the decline of British and French influence after the Second World War, the battle for power between the United States and the Soviet Union. The Americans had backed Israel; the Soviets had backed some Arab states. Now, with the eclipse of Moscow, "it has become clear to everyone that the United States has emerged in a superior position in international politics."

Over time, Saddam predicted, new powers would emerge to "fill the vacuum" and challenge America, to check its influence. He hoped independent Arab nations like Iraq would do this. In the meantime, Washington would act without restraint: "We believe that the U.S. will continue to depart from the restrictions that govern the rest of the world . . . until new forces of balance are formed." And what would America's priority be during this period of hegemony? Controlling oil and helping Israel, Saddam said.

If Iraq, Jordan, Egypt, and the Gulf kingdoms united, they could defeat Washington's designs. The Arab people would then "see how Satan will grow weaker." Even as a superpower, the U.S. "has displayed signs of fatigue, frustration, and hesitation," he said, and gave an example. "We saw that the U.S. as a superpower departed Lebanon immediately when some Marines were killed" by a terrorist truck bomb in 1983.

"All strong men have their Achilles' heel," Saddam assured his audience.[2]

Saddam was in a broadly defiant mood. He had imprisoned a thirty-one-year-old British resident named Farzad Bazoft, a boyish-looking freelance journalist of Iranian origin who wrote for *The Observer*. His favorite film was *The Killing Fields*, about a heroic foreign correspondent covering genocide in Cambodia. The Iraqi regime invited him to visit, to cover Kurdish elections the regime was staging, but after he arrived, he traveled to the site of an Iraqi munitions dump to the south of Baghdad that had reportedly blown up the previous autumn. He collected soil samples, which he hoped to return to Britain for analysis that could detect evidence of chemical weapons. The Iraqis arrested him and forced him to confess on television to being a spy. "He had lost much weight and seemed to be exhausted, drugged or suffering from the effects of torture, or possibly all of these," recalled his editor, Donald Trelford. The regime tried Bazoft in secret and sentenced him to death.

British prime minister Margaret Thatcher's policy toward Baghdad was strongly influenced by her Tory cabinet's desire to promote exports. When Harold Walker arrived as the U.K.'s ambassador in February, his brief was, as he recalled: "Saddam is recovering from this eight-year war with Iran. . . . Iraqi-U.K. relations have always been tricky, choppy, but your job is to keep them smooth enough so that we can do good business."[3]

Thatcher's government nonetheless pressed Iraq about releasing Bazoft. Saddam was belligerent: "He is an Israeli spy working for the British," he assured Tariq Aziz and other advisers privately in the winter of 1990.

Saddam turned to a colleague, using only his first name. "Ahmad, how long does it take a person to be executed?" He was speaking of the technical arrangements, now that Bazoft had been sentenced.

"One month, sir."

"A whole month?"

"Yes."

"To be executed?"

Ahmad wisely backpedaled. "I mean, one month is the maximum."

"We will execute him . . . as punishment for Margaret Thatcher."[4]

When London learned of this decision, Robin Kealy of the British embassy visited Abu Ghraib to tell the young reporter that he would die by hanging. In the visiting room, they smoked Silk Cut cigarettes. Bazoft "took it bravely, with sort of resignation, really," Kealy remembered. He ventured a question.

"Is there a chance you were a spy, or weren't you a spy?"

"No," Bazoft said. "Investigative journalist after a scoop."[5]

The Abu Ghraib authorities delivered his corpse to the British embassy in mid-March. "Thatcher wanted him alive," announced Latif Jassim, Saddam's minister of culture and information. "We sent him in a box."

The hanging provoked international denunciations, but Britain's foreign secretary, Douglas Hurd, advised that it was not in the government's interest to respond by cutting off trade. "Our competitors would happily step in to take up our share of the market," Hurd wrote five days after Bazoft's execution.[6]

In Saddam's attempt to achieve parity with Israel—or at least some form of deterrence against an Israeli attack—his greatest challenge was to find a way to plausibly threaten Tel Aviv, which lay 570 miles from Baghdad. Iraq's Mirage fighter jets were no match for Israeli air defenses. Saddam had acquired heavy Soviet Scud ballistic missiles during his war with Iran. His son-in-law Hussein Kamel oversaw modifications that extended the missiles' range, allowing them to reach Israel if they were fired from Iraq's western deserts. In the spring of 1990, Saddam ordered a test firing of one of these longer-range Scuds with a chemical agent in the warhead—an experiment that went undetected by the C.I.A. and all other Western intelligence agencies at the time. Yet Scuds were difficult to aim and harder still to successfully equip with chemical weapons. The intense heat created by the warhead's explosive impact tended to incinerate a chemical payload before it could be dispersed. Firing a Scud laden only with conventional explosives would be like throwing an expensive bomb at Israel—unnerving and deadly but not a threat likely to deter Tel Aviv from attacking Iraq.

To explore another option, starting in 1988, Saddam had constructed a giant experimental artillery gun on Jabal Hamrin, a low mountain ridge along an ancient caravan route in northeastern Iraq. He called the project Babylon. The mastermind was Gerald Bull, a talented Canadian rocket scientist who, during a long career working on American and Canadian defense projects, had tinkered with "superguns"—massive artillery pieces that might fire satellites into space. Saddam invested $25 million to hire Bull to adapt the idea so that an Iraqi weapon might fire chemical shells on Israel—shells that dispersed poison gas lethally, as Iraqi artillery shells had during the war with Iran. The work went far enough—and seemed plausible enough—that Mossad sent warnings to Bull, informing him what would happen if he didn't abandon Project Babylon: "We will have to take harsh action against you, your companies, and the people involved with you." Bull persisted. At Jabal Hamrin, his team initiated construction of the world's largest-ever artillery gun, fitted with a steel barrel 170 yards long.

On March 22, 1990, in Brussels, where Bull kept an apartment, a squad of Mossad assassins armed with Makarov pistols waylaid the engineer and shot him dead. For Saddam, it was one more aggravating loss in a shadow war with Israel that only he and the spymasters of Tel Aviv seemed to regard as urgent and serious. "We are dealing with a country that considers the war between us not to be over," Saddam reminded his advisers privately. "We do not have a truce with Israel."[7]

Saddam remained convinced that some sort of Israeli attack loomed. Iraqi diplomats told American and British counterparts that they had reliable information about an imminent preemptive Israeli strike on Iraq's chemical-weapons facilities. Bull's murder tended to confirm these fears. Saddam concluded that the United States was a party to the Israeli conspiracy against him. From February onward, the Iraqi media "literally every day was full of these accusations," recalled April Glaspie, the American ambassador in Baghdad. An experienced Arabist, Glaspie had succeeded David George Newton at the embassy. She thought Iraq's allegations were "genuinely believed by Saddam."[8]

In early April, Saddam apparently concluded that he should deter

Israel by threatening catastrophic retaliation if Tel Aviv struck first. He chose a televised speech to the General Command of the Iraqi Armed Forces. Saddam admitted that Iraq possessed chemical arms. "I swear to God, we will let our fire eat half of Israel if it tries anything against Iraq," he declared. He qualified his warning by emphasizing that he would not strike first: "Everyone must know his limits. Thanks be to God, we know our limits and will not attack anyone." Saddam may have thought that his speech expressed a doctrine of deterrence derived from the Cold War. Yet headlines about his threat to devour half of Israel by fire predictably drowned out any subtler reading of his speech.[9]

During the first months of 1990, recalled Brent Scowcroft, Bush's national security adviser, "it gradually became apparent to me that Saddam had made an abrupt change" in his thinking. He had apparently decided that getting along with Washington was no longer a priority, and that he would stand with what Scowcroft called the "rejectionists" of the Arab world—those states opposed to peace with Israel or even Israel's existence.[10]

Scowcroft was busy. That winter, Soviet leader Mikhail Gorbachev presided over the dissolution of Moscow's sphere of influence in Europe. Germany moved toward reunification. At this turning point in world history, the White House had little time to parse Saddam Hussein's rambling speeches. The Iraqi president's "combination of bellicosity and tractability," as the scholar Jerry Long has described it, as well as his habit of saying quite different things to visitors he received only days apart, was confounding even to those diplomats and intelligence analysts who watched him closely.[11]

Nonetheless, after Saddam's "devour with fire" speech, Scowcroft and his aides decided to send an "unambiguous message" to Baghdad. The State Department instructed April Glaspie to raise concerns about Iraq's construction of Scud missile launchers within range of Israel. Yet she was also told to give the Iraqis an assurance: "As concerned as we are about Iraq's chemical, nuclear, and missile programs, we are not in any sense preparing the way for a preemptive military unilateral effort to eliminate these programs."[12]

In that case and over the next several months, the Bush administration would prove little better than Saddam Hussein at communicating its intentions clearly. President Bush still clung to the core assumption of his National Security Directive of the previous October: namely, that the potential benefits of improved ties with Saddam—greater regional stability and expanding U.S. trade—warranted more effort. The administration did, however, pause its expansion of export credits for Iraq that spring to signal its displeasure with Saddam's provocations. Yet the White House hadn't worked out how it might respond if Saddam acted on any of his more extreme threats.

In early April, five senior United States senators led by Republican Robert Dole of Kansas embarked on a fact-finding tour of the Middle East, and Bush encouraged the group to make a stop in Iraq to meet Saddam. Secretary of State James Baker cabled Dole: "Bob, the Iraqis are less sophisticated about the U.S. than many other Arabs and tend to exaggerate or misread [American politics]." Saddam's evident fears about America conspiring to attack or depose him were an example. "There is no conspiracy on our part to isolate or threaten Iraq," Baker wrote. Also: "There is no green light from the U.S. to Israel."

Glaspie sent the delegation a note describing Saddam as "shrewd, smart, well-read (in Arabic)" but also "deeply provincial and ignorant of cultures other than his own, which is why he often blunders badly in international affairs. His assumptions are often wrong."

On April 12, Saddam welcomed the senators to a modern, glass-walled salon in one of his palaces in Mosul, north of Baghdad. Saddam wore a double-breasted suit; Dole, as guest of honor, took a chair beside him. Around them sat the four other senators—Republicans Frank Murkowski of Alaska, James McClure of Idaho, and Alan Simpson of Wyoming, as well as Ohio's Howard Metzenbaum, the lone Democrat.

Tariq Aziz also joined, with a notetaker, as did April Glaspie, with a notetaker of her own. Translators squeezed in, too. With so many people present, the meeting would inevitably have an air of performance, and yet with Saddam in the chair, the unexpected could be expected.

The senators handed over to Saddam a letter that they had reviewed with the Bush White House. It expressed a desire for improved relations but also cited "very deep concerns about certain policies and activities of your Government." Iraq's "efforts to develop a nuclear, chemical and biological capability seriously jeopardize—rather than enhance—your security," the letter read.

Saddam welcomed them, spoke at some length about the importance of frankness and mutual understanding, and then got to the point: "We know that an all-out campaign is being waged against us in America and in the countries of Europe."

"Not by President Bush," Dole said.

"This is sufficient for me," Saddam replied, seeming to wave off his previous statement. Still, he went on to say, press reporting about Iraq's human-rights record and gassing of enemies had effectively created "psychological propaganda and political cover for Israel to attack us, as it did in 1981."[13]

"Once again, I assure you that the U.S. government is not the cause of this campaign," Dole said.

Saddam explained his recent remarks about Israel—they were intended only for deterrence. "I said that if Israel uses atomic bombs, we will strike it with binary chemical weapons," meaning nerve agents such as sarin. "I repeat, if this is done, we will do that."

He anticipated objections: "I know that chemical weapons have been banned," Saddam said, referring to the treaty-based prohibition on their use in international armed conflict. "However, are chemical weapons more dangerous to mankind than are nuclear bombs?"

Saddam made other remarks that hinted at secrets the Americans did not know. He said he considered it "the right of the Arabs to possess any weapon that their enemy possesses. Iraq does not possess atomic bombs. If we did, we would announce that, to preserve peace and to prevent Israel from using their atomic bombs." Saddam all but admitted that he was pursuing such weapons, but the senators did not appear to notice.[14]

Saddam was savvy enough, with the advice of Aziz, to adopt the technocratic language of American nuclear deterrence doctrine. Yet his genuine belief that Israel might preemptively attack Iraq with nuclear bombs struck his American listeners as entirely irrational, and his loose talk about gassing Israeli civilians appalled them.

Dole pressed Saddam forcefully about his embrace of weapons of mass destruction, yet from what the senators said, it would have been hard for Saddam to perceive that he was at risk of losing American aid.

Metzenbaum, who introduced himself as "a Jew and one of the staunch supporters of Israel," said that while he was "not the right person to be your public-relations man," he believed that Iraq's president could become "a very influential force for peace in the Middle East." Metzenbaum said, "I am now aware that you are a strong and intelligent man, and that you want peace."

Simpson assured Saddam that the conspiracy he imagined the U.S. had organized was really just the product of irresponsible American journalism, and that the Bush administration and Congress had nothing to do with it. "I believe that your problems lie with the Western media. . . . It is a haughty and pampered press—they all consider themselves political geniuses," Simpson said. "They are very cynical."[15]

After he heard Senator Dole's account of the meeting, Bush telephoned some of his Arab allies, still trying to get his message to Saddam. "There is no conspiracy against Iraq," the president told King Hussein on April 23.[16]

Saddam believed that he needed "at a minimum a correct relationship" with Washington because of his "own political theorizing" that the U.S. was now the world's sole superpower, as April Glaspie had noted in a cable. Yet Saddam's aspiration was to unite the Arab world and fill some of the geopolitical space vacated by the Soviet Union.[17]

Soon after his meeting with the U.S. senators, he received Yasser Arafat, the chairman of the Palestine Liberation Organization. Saddam

arranged a video recording of the discussion, presumably for selective
distribution in the Arab world. He declared that he was ready for war
with America. "We will fight America, and with God's help we will
defeat it and kick it out of the whole region," he pledged. "If America
strikes us, we will hit back. . . . Maybe we cannot reach Washington,
but we can send someone who has an explosive belt."[18]

Saddam was contemptuous of Kuwait, his small and wealthy neighbor. His feelings were inseparable from his loathing of the rich Gulf
Arabs generally—those trust-fund royals with the "billions" they had
earned from oil "without sweat," as he once said privately. He insisted
that he was holding off Tehran's expansive theocracy on behalf of all
Arabs—and especially his timid neighbors. "They are afraid."[19]

The Gulf kingdoms had indeed been fearful of what an Iranian victory over Saddam might mean for their security. Saudi Arabia, Kuwait,
and the United Arab Emirates were then the wealthiest among them.
They had bankrolled Saddam's war. The $35 billion to $40 billion Iraq
owed its neighbors after the conflict was more than half the size of
Iraq's economy. Saddam demanded that his royal creditors convert the
loans to gifts, in recognition of his sacrifices keeping Ayatollah Khomeini at bay. King Fahd of Saudi Arabia decided to avoid trouble, and
in March 1989, Saudi Arabia signed a military nonaggression and aid
pact with Baghdad; the kingdom converted a significant portion of its
loans to gifts.

But Kuwait, to whom Saddam owed between $10 billion and $15 billion, held out. Its emir, Jaber al-Ahmad al-Sabah, was then sixty-three
years old. Lean and stern-looking, he was a quiet, withdrawn, often
indifferent-seeming ruler who had fathered at least seventy children by
about forty wives, marrying and divorcing serially to maintain four
wives at any one time, as permitted by Islamic law. He presided over
an extended family of about 1,200 Sabahs who enjoyed the lion's share
of the emirate's vast oil wealth. Brothers and cousins notionally ran
Kuwait's ministries, but technical operations—electricity generation,

shipping, airlines—often depended on the talents of Lebanese, Palestinian, Indian, Pakistani, European, Australian, and American expatriates. The emirate's service economy relied on Filipino and Sri Lankan maids and shop clerks, as well as tens of thousands of Pakistani, Indian, and Bangladeshi drivers, construction workers, and bellhops. There were roughly twice as many non-Kuwaitis living in Kuwait as there were enfranchised subjects of the emir. "I know the Kuwaiti society, and I know what type of corruption and luxury this society lives in," Saddam once told his advisers. "Who do they think they are? They think they are better than any other Arab country, and they look down at everybody else. They think that anyone who tries to get close to them and be friends with them is after their money."[20]

The contempt was mutual. Many native Kuwaitis regarded Saddam Hussein as a buffoon, even if a dangerous one. On sofas in the diwaniyas, or parlors where Kuwaiti men socialized, they watched Iraqi television for "comic relief," as one visitor put it, guffawing as Saddam bored his audiences with lectures "about everything from animal husbandry to military tactics."[21]

Saddam fixated opportunistically on the disputed history of Kuwait's borders and independence. During the nineteenth century, before the age of oil, the emirate was poor and of little interest to world powers; it occupied a fragile place between the British and Ottoman Empires. It had not been administered by the Ottomans and eventually became a British protectorate. After oil was found, successive Iraqi leaders laid claims to Kuwaiti territory near their shared border, and they occasionally declared with scant historical backing that all of Kuwait belonged to Iraq. In 1961, Britain granted independence to Kuwait. The Iraqi strongman Abd al-Karim Qasim threatened a takeover, but he backed off after Britain deployed warships and marines. Iraq's claims about Kuwait had festered ever since.

Late in 1989, Saddam had received the Kuwaiti emir in Baghdad on a state visit. Their private dialogue is not recorded, but Sabah rarely gave much away in meetings. His brother Sabah al-Ahmad al-Sabah, who served as foreign minister, was the face of Kuwaiti diplomacy. The

Sabahs had a stubborn streak and were "methodical bankers," as Richard Murphy, the American Arabist, put it. They argued, in essence: "He's got debts, and even if we don't collect what he owes us now, it's got to stay on the books." They knew they were almost certainly not going to be repaid, but they refused to wipe Saddam's ledger clean. Why should they? "Kuwaitis regarded the Iraqi debt as the one card it held in relations with a much more powerful" neighbor, recalled W. Nathaniel Howell, then the U.S. ambassador to Kuwait. Loan forgiveness was "Kuwait's ace, to be played, if at all, only in return for the country's overriding objective," which was for Iraq to recognize Kuwait's borders and sovereignty.[22]

Iraq and Kuwait possessed similarly prodigious amounts of oil—each country's holdings were estimated at the time at about one hundred billion barrels. Yet Iraq's population was eighteen million, while Kuwait's native subjects numbered only about seven hundred thousand, so the Kuwaitis enjoyed much greater wealth per person. By 1990 they inhabited a gleaming emirate dotted with construction cranes and shopping centers displaying the latest in consumer electronics. Futuristic water towers rose beside shimmering minarets on Kuwait City's skyline; souks stocked Snickers and Kit Kat bars beside traditional sweets. The emirate's wealth and qualified liberties meant that many of its subjects could vacation in Europe during the Gulf's stultifying summers and send their children to study in Britain or the United States. Most Iraqis could only dream of such privileges.

In early 1990, Saddam declared that the Sabah family was conspiring with Washington and Tel Aviv to undermine his rule. He speculated with cabinet ministers about seizing and looting the emirate by allowing Iraqi tribes to invade Kuwait and reap their own spoils, "like buildings and stores."[23]

The heart of the matter was money—Iraq's desperate need for more and Kuwait's refusal to hand some over. During the first six months of 1990, world oil prices fell by about a quarter, from twenty-two dollars a barrel to less than seventeen dollars, crippling all of the Middle East's oil-dependent governments. Kuwait and other producers pumped out more oil to make up for the lost revenue per barrel, but this additional supply put further downward pressure on prices. In public, Saddam now regularly accused both Kuwait and the United Arab Emirates of conspiring against Iraq through their overproduction of oil.

In late May 1990, Saddam hastily called an "emergency" summit of Arab leaders in Baghdad. Kings, princes, presidents, and foreign ministers arrived at a manicured conference center and took their places in high-backed chairs at a table laden with soft drinks.

"You know, brothers," Saddam told them, "some of our Arab brothers . . . flooded the world market with more oil than it needed." He did not name names, but everyone knew who he meant.

He was losing billions, Saddam continued, and he made himself plain: "War is fought with soldiers and much harm is done by explosions, killing, and coup attempts—but it is also done by economic means. . . . We have reached a point where we can no longer withstand pressure."[24]

The Sabah family was on notice, but Kuwait's leaders remained unmoved. Sabah al-Sabah, the foreign minister, believed that Saddam's bravado was akin to "summer clouds" passing in the sky. It was just a bluff to strong-arm them into debt concessions.[25]

During May and June, in strict secrecy, Saddam planned for a surprise attack against Kuwait. He initially ordered intelligence reports about the emirate and possible invasion routes. Then he met clandestinely with top commanders of his elite Republican Guard armored forces, leaving the rest of his military and many of his closest civilian advisers in the dark. The Iraqi president had come of age as an assassin and as a coupmaker. He still knew how to organize an ambush.

During the last week of June or the first days of July—the date is uncertain—Saddam ordered Lieutenant General Ayad al-Rawi, the chief of staff of the Republican Guard, to "write up a detailed plan to accomplish the task of retrieving Kuwait" for Iraqi rule, according to the military historian Kevin Woods, who reviewed unpublished records of the covert planning. On Wednesday, July 11, Iraq's Directorate of Air Intelligence flew surveillance missions and photographed 110 Kuwaiti targets, including oil installations, military camps, radar installations, and seaports. By the following day, Saddam had issued what his General Military Intelligence Directorate described as "verbal orders" and "Top Secret and personal correspondence" to individual commanders to prepare for an invasion. Kuwait had little practical way to stop an Iraqi invasion. The flat, sandy, 150-mile border was open and barely defended. Kuwait's military forces numbered twenty thousand, while Iraq's approached one million.

Later, there would be speculation that Saddam planned at first to seize only oil fields and disputed territories along the Kuwaiti border, not to occupy the entire country. His secret planning in July indicates that he had decided by then on a full takeover—occupation of the capital and the seizure of Kuwait's ruling family. The operation acquired a code name: Project 17.[26]

On Sunday, July 15, Tariq Aziz dispatched one of his forceful, lawyerly letters to Chedli Klibi, the secretary general of the Arab League, a coalition of governments. The letter indicted Kuwait for its supposed economic crimes against Iraq: The emirate had "encroached on Iraq and systematically, deliberately, and continuously harmed it," Aziz wrote. Kuwait had specifically stolen Iraqi oil by slant-drilling under their border, he alleged. This theft alone had cost Iraq $24 billion. "Such behavior amounts to a military aggression."[27]

The Bush administration still knew nothing of Iraq's preparations. C.I.A. satellites detected no movement of Iraqi forces toward Kuwait during June. (Iraqi records show that Saddam did send a single missile battalion south that month, but no other significant forces.) The lack of observable military preparation was consistent with the hypothesis Arab leaders regularly transmitted to the Bush administration—that Saddam was just putting the arm on his creditors, looking to be paid.

George H. W. Bush had been preoccupied during June, busy with selecting a nominee for the Supreme Court (David Souter) and negotiating fiscal issues with Congress. In mid-July, his National Security Council staff drafted—and Bush signed—a routine congratulatory letter to Saddam on the occasion of Revolution Day, July 17, the anniversary of the Baath Party's ascendence to power. The message reiterated America's desire to improve relations.

In Baghdad, Saddam used the holiday to reprise his threats against the Sabahs: Iraqis would "not forget the proper saying that cutting necks is better than cutting the means of living," he said, referring to the Kuwaitis. He insisted this was not just talk: "Raising our voice against evil is not the final resort."

That day, C.I.A. spy satellites detected the first units of the Hammurabi Division of the Republican Guard, named for an ancient Babylonian king, arriving near the Kuwaiti border. Reports about the troop movement filtered to the White House. Still, as then secretary of defense Dick Cheney recalled: "We heard from many quarters that he was bluffing."[28]

On Wednesday morning, July 18, David Mack arrived at his office at State Department headquarters to find translated texts of Tariq Aziz's threatening letter to the Arab League of three days before, which the Iraqis had now decided to publicize. Foreign service officers on State's Iraq desk had drafted talking points for the department's noon press briefing. The talking points would spell out American policy in light of the Iraqi threats. Mack reviewed the document and passed it upstairs for clearance at higher levels at State and the White House. He received no edits and heard no concerns.

"We remain determined to ensure the free flow of oil," the final statement said. "We also remain strongly committed to supporting the individual and collective self-defense of our friends in the Gulf with whom we have deep and longstanding ties." The reference to unnamed "friends" was intended to include Kuwait, even though the U.S. had no formal defense pact with the kingdom.

"The United States takes no position on the substance of the bilateral issues concerning Iraq and Kuwait," the document stated. This had been the default U.S. position for decades. Still, Washington was "committed" to the "sovereignty and integrity of the Gulf states." With some effort, this phrasing could be read as a threat to use force if the Gulf states were attacked. Yet it was all deliberately vague—a plain vanilla flavor of professional diplomacy-speak.[29]

Mack had a previously scheduled lunch in the State Department's eighth-floor private dining room with Iraq's new ambassador in Washington, Mohammed al-Mashat, a Baath Party hand with a doctorate in sociology. Mashat had succeeded Nizar Hamdoon, who had rotated to the Americas desk at the foreign ministry in Baghdad.

Mack was just senior enough to qualify for a private table in the dining room, near the cavernous and ornate Benjamin Franklin Room. There was only a self-service buffet on offer, but the room offered a veneer of formality and discretion. Mack carried a copy of the policy statements drafted that morning. He handed it to the ambassador for onward transmission to Baghdad.

"You're overreacting," Mashat told him after he had read it. Iraq would never harm U.S. economic interests in the region. The border with Kuwait was no longer in dispute.[30]

The next day, to be sure that the Iraqis had absorbed the American declarations, State dispatched a cable under the signature of Secretary of State James Baker to U.S. embassies in Baghdad and elsewhere in the region, transmitting the language Mack had shepherded. These words now had the force of official instructions. April Glaspie passed the statements to the Iraqi Ministry of Foreign Affairs.[31]

The Bush administration had plainly stated America's general commitment to the defense of Kuwait, but without naming the emirate or specifying what such a commitment would entail. The language certainly did not attempt to grab Saddam's attention, lay out redlines, or explicitly threaten him with military retaliation if he dared to follow through with his threats to wage war on his neighbor. Those sorts of threats were well above David Mack's pay grade. In reality, the State

Department's indirect warnings and Bush's friendly Revolution Day letter meant that Washington's messages had provided only the barest indication to Saddam that America might confront him with armed force if he invaded Kuwait.

On July 20, Brigadier General Raad Majid al-Hamdani, who commanded a section of the Hammurabi Division of the Republican Guard, was summoned by his commanding general, who worked out of a recreational vehicle. When Hamdani entered, he "saw a Quran on his table in a very prominent position, which was very unusual," as he recalled. He took a seat. His superior described the division's military preparations—to seize Kuwait entirely.

Hamdani was stunned. His commander asked him to stand up and swear an oath on the Quran that he would keep Project 17 secret.

"We are going to occupy Kuwait . . . our neighboring country?" Hamdani asked.

They were. The next day, Saddam ordered another thirty thousand troops toward the border.[32]

The maneuvers were just an exercise, Saddam stated publicly. In Washington, among the relatively small number of officials paying close attention, the bluff hypothesis still seemed quite plausible. "The Iraqis camped right on the main road from Basra to Kuwait in plain sight," John Kelly, at State, recalled. "The road was still open to general traffic; our military attachés from Baghdad and Kuwait were driving up and down the road, counting the troops as they drove along, confirming all that we could see from our satellites." That Iraq made no effort to hide its preparations suggested that it was seeking to exert pressure, not necessarily planning to act.[33]

Zayed bin Sultan al-Nahyan, the ruler of Abu Dhabi and the preeminent decision-maker in the United Arab Emirates, had started to worry that Saddam might mean what he had been saying. Iraq had also threatened the U.A.E., demanding financial relief. Yet the U.A.E. had no land border with Iraq, and the nearest point of its frontier was some nine hundred miles away; if Saddam attacked, he would have to strike by air. Sheikh Zayed decided to accept U.S. military support. On July 24, the U.S. dispatched two KC-135 Stratotankers to help the U.A.E.'s French-equipped air force set up a defensive air patrol, with assistance from U.S. Navy radars aboard ships in the Gulf. Still, Sheikh Zayed demanded that there be no publicity, for fear of further aggravating Saddam.[34]

The Sabahs remained confident that they knew how to manage Saddam. They did not invite the Pentagon to help them signal military preparedness. They lowered Kuwait's military alert level. They declined to receive W. Nathaniel Howell, the U.S. ambassador, at Kuwait's Ministry of Foreign Affairs, where Howell's comings and goings might be noticed. (Instead, a Kuwaiti undersecretary visited the ambassador at his residence, at night.) The message from Kuwait was "to play down the Iraqi actions, and that we should not further provoke the Iraqis," Kelly remembered.[35]

The Sabahs still refused to grant Saddam relief: "The sons of Kuwait, in good as well as bad times, are people of principle and integrity," the foreign ministry wrote to the Arab League. "By no means will they yield to threat and extortion."

The Kuwaitis' apparent plan was to let Saddam huff and puff while other Arab leaders—King Hussein of Jordan, Hosni Mubarak of Egypt—mediated a solution. Kelly was among those who thought that a peaceful resolution of the crisis was near, and that money would change hands: "I believed the Kuwaitis would resolve the issue by making a major financial contribution—in the neighborhood of ten billion."[36]

When the United States sent U.S. Air Force tankers to help the U.A.E., the Pentagon made no public announcement, but April Glaspie did notify Saddam's regime. After the disastrous strike against the U.S.S. *Stark*, the U.S. and Iraq had pledged to exchange more data about their forces to avoid another incident. When the news reached

Saddam, he demanded a meeting with the U.S. ambassador. On the morning of July 25, the Ministry of Foreign Affairs summoned Glaspie. She had no specific indication that she would meet Saddam. As she noted in a cable to Washington later that day, "In the memory of the current diplomatic corps, Saddam has never summoned an ambassador."[37]

When she arrived, she was put in a car and shuttled to the presidential palace. Why was Saddam breaking protocol?

Glaspie had been serving in Iraq for two years and in the Arab world for nearly two decades. She was respected at State for her knowledge of the Middle East and her professionalism. When she realized she would see Saddam, she had no way to call back to Washington to consult. She did have with her Secretary of State Baker's written instructions about U.S. policy cabled out just a week earlier, however. A second cable from Baker the day before had reiterated those points and added slightly tougher language: "Iraqi statements suggest an intention to resolve outstanding disagreements by the use of force, an approach which is contrary to U.N. charter principles. The implications of having oil production and pricing policy in the Gulf determined and enforced by Iraqi guns are disturbing." As Glaspie well understood, her role in circumstances like this was not to invent U.S. policy but to transmit it. She would also record and report on what Saddam had to say, and use her judgment in responding to him spontaneously. This was the essence of ambassadorial tradecraft, and Glaspie had practiced it for many years.[38]

The meeting that followed at noon in the presidential palace would become one of the most notorious and second-guessed diplomatic encounters in postwar American history. Glaspie arrived with Nancy Johnson, a political officer at the U.S. embassy, who would take notes. Tariq Aziz was there for the Iraqis, along with his own notetaker and an Iraqi interpreter for Saddam. Glaspie found the Iraqi president "cordial, reasonable and even warm."

The two records of the meeting—one originating from notes taken by Johnson, the other from notes taken under Aziz's supervision—show that Saddam launched into an initial monologue that lasted perhaps an hour. While he spoke, Glaspie had no opportunity to say anything of substance. It was the kind of extemporaneous speech familiar to Saddam's comrades and visitors—alternatingly blunt and obscure, complicated by digressions, and open to interpretation.[39]

Saddam said that he wished to send "a message" to President Bush. Yet instead of stating any message succinctly, he wandered off into the history of U.S.-Iraq diplomatic relations during his presidency—his decision in 1984 to reestablish formal ties with the Reagan administration, followed by the disappointments of "Irangate," as he called Iran-Contra. "We accepted the apology . . . we wiped the slate clean," Saddam said of that dark time. Yet it turned out that America was still secretly cooperating with his enemies, he continued. He offered an aphoristic appraisal: "We shouldn't unearth the past except when new events remind us that old mistakes were not just a matter of coincidence." He meant that the betrayal of Iraq exposed by Iran-Contra had never stopped.

He was not blaming George H. W. Bush or James Baker, he quickly added. He had in mind the American deep state. "Some circles," including within the C.I.A. and the State Department, had undermined the U.S.-Iraqi relationship. He had learned that "some circles" were gathering information on "who might be Saddam Hussein's successor." Moreover, he had "evidence" that "some parties" were also pressing the Gulf oil kingdoms to refuse Iraq's request for financial relief.

He listed other grievances, including the "assault on Iraq and its President" by the American media. And yet, despite being "somewhat annoyed," he had retained hope. Now, however, Washington seemed to be joining Kuwait and the U.A.E. in "economic warfare." This was too much. "Iraq cannot accept such a trespass on its dignity and prosperity."[40]

Saddam then came to what Glaspie recognized as "one of his main points," and the apparent reason he had invited her to meet. He probed the meaning of America's joint military maneuvers with the U.A.E., as well as the language in the recent State Department messages, which had referred to America's "commitment" to the "defense of its friends" in the Gulf region, "individually and collectively." Any country may choose its friends, Saddam acknowledged, but in this case, he said, the Bush administration was forgetting that Iraq had protected Kuwait and the U.A.E. from Iran.

"So what can it mean when America says it will now protect its friends?" Saddam asked. It was a highly pertinent question. A wiser Iraqi president might have paused there and let the question hang in the air. Could Glaspie say what America would do if he attacked Kuwait? Did she have any brief on the matter?[41]

But Saddam did not stop to listen. Instead, he answered his own question: America's support for Kuwait and the U.A.E. "can only mean prejudice against Iraq." He acknowledged that the U.S. could "send planes and rockets and hurt Iraq deeply," but he warned Washington not to "force Iraq to the point of humiliation," when "logic must be disregarded."

At last, following a further digression by Saddam into Iraqi diplomatic history during the 1970s, Glaspie had a chance to speak. In polite reference to Saddam's monologue, she noted that he had raised "many issues" but that she would comment on two.

First, she wished to express President Bush's "desire for friendship." She mentioned Bush's letters to Saddam. The Iraqi leader interrupted her to say that he had been "touched" by the president's sentiments.

Glaspie turned to Iraq's threatening display of force against Kuwait. "Is it not reasonable for us to be concerned when the president and the foreign minister [of Iraq] both say publicly that Kuwaiti actions are the equivalent of military aggression, and then we learn that many units of the Republican Guard have been sent to the border? Is it not reasonable for us to ask—in the spirit of friendship, not confrontation—what are your intentions?"

Saddam said this was indeed a reasonable question. Rather than answering it, however, he asked how Iraq could make the royal families of Kuwait and the U.A.E. "understand how deeply we are suffering." Iraq's financial crisis, exacerbated by its war debts, was such that pensions for "widows and orphans will have to be cut."

As if on cue, the Iraqi interpreter and notetaker in the meeting "broke down and wept," as Glaspie would describe it.

Glaspie enunciated the policy she had been instructed on from Washington: "We have no opinion on the Arab-Arab conflicts, like your border disagreement with Kuwait. . . . I was in the American embassy in Kuwait during the late '60s. The instruction we had during this period was that we should express no opinion on this issue and that the issue is not associated with America. James Baker has directed our official spokesmen to emphasize this instruction. We hope you can solve this problem using any suitable methods," such as mediation by the Arab League or Egypt. "All that we hope is that these issues are solved quickly." Glaspie's comments would later be cited as a subtle "green light" to Saddam to invade. The truth was more prosaic: she was repeating, almost to the letter and with attribution to her boss, a formulation that had been sent to her from Washington and that she recognized as a decades-old, almost rote talking point.

An aide interrupted to report that Hosni Mubarak, the president of Egypt, was on the line. Saddam excused himself. When he returned, he reported that he had just learned from Mubarak that the Kuwaitis had "agreed to negotiate" and that a meeting was being set in Saudi Arabia for the upcoming weekend. After this session, the Kuwaitis would come to Baghdad, presumably to finalize a deal, no later than Monday, July 30.

Glaspie said she was "delighted to hear this good news."

Saddam said that he had told Mubarak to give the Kuwaitis "our word that we are not going to do anything until we meet with them. When we meet and when we see that there is hope, then nothing will happen." According to the Iraqi transcript, but not the American one, Saddam added, "But if we are unable to find a solution, then it will be natural that Iraq will not accept death." According to Glaspie, this line was fabricated by the Iraqis later on.

The meeting broke up. Saddam asked Glaspie to "convey his warm greetings to President Bush and to convey his message to him."

Overall, Glaspie found Saddam's posturing to be puzzling. She was struck by the uncharacteristic weakness the Iraqi leader seemed to convey. He was allowing Mubarak, his disdained rival, to mediate for him. He had accepted that Iraq's deployment of troops near the Kuwaiti border was a legitimate matter of interest for the United States, and he had conceded that Washington could choose its friends in the region. He was accepting delays and more negotiation sessions. Glaspie didn't know what to make of these departures from Saddam's typical belligerent form.[42]

Because of her occasional soft-sounding remarks, Glaspie would be blamed by pundits, members of Congress, and some of her own colleagues for failing to prevent a costly and disruptive war that would lead, in its aftermath, to cascading disasters for Iraq and the United States. She missed opportunities, but the blame heaped upon her was grossly unjustified. Her polite language reflected the routine vernacular of diplomacy, and her expressions of friendship on behalf of President Bush only transmitted clearly established policy reflected in the U.S. president's own recent letters. Glaspie did fail to discern from Saddam's deceptive and opaque remarks that he had a secret operation underway to invade Kuwait; that the die was cast; and that his pretensions of diplomacy were merely an annex to Project 17, not the main event. Saddam's repeated public threats to act drastically if negotiations with the Kuwaitis failed, and his marked anxiety about America's defense commitments to Kuwait, offered clues that might have been recognized or probed. Saddam's hints, if perceived, might have conceivably caused the Bush White House to hastily consider issuing a sharp deterrence warning to Saddam, threatening military action, to try to prevent an invasion. This would have required a sudden reversal of policy and judgment, and even then, the administration likely would have had to threaten retaliation on its own, as Kuwait had already made plain its reluctance to join in such warnings. In any event, in missing Saddam's signals, Glaspie did no worse than anyone else in the senior ranks of the Bush administration.

The ambassador would nonetheless become, in just a week's time, a convenient scapegoat for the sudden, unanticipated failure and collapse of American policy toward Saddam's Iraq from the C.I.A.'s secret opening in the summer of 1982 until the summer of 1990. Glaspie was a rare female ambassador and Arabist of her generation, and embedded sexism at the State Department and in political Washington surely contributed to her scapegoating. She became a convenient distraction from the fact that her boss, President Bush, wrote several ingratiating letters to Saddam during 1990. Glaspie was in no position to threaten Saddam with America's military might, absent instructions; Bush was commander in chief. For his part, Saddam said years later that he had already decided to invade by the time he met Glaspie, and the more recently available evidence of his secret planning supports this claim. Tariq Aziz recalled in 2013 that Glaspie "didn't say anything that can be interpreted as encouraging the invasion, to be fair." The problem was not that Glaspie failed to warn Saddam when she had the chance. It was that the Bush administration failed to recognize what Saddam had decided upon until it was too late.[43]

When Glaspie returned to the U.S. embassy in Baghdad, it was still morning in Washington. With aides, she composed a cable to the State Department about her meeting with Saddam. "Saddam's Message of Friendship to President Bush" was the unfortunate headline. In her first paragraph, Glaspie reported that Saddam had promised Hosni Mubarak, Egypt's president, that "nothing will happen" before upcoming talks with the Kuwaitis. The crisis had paused, or so a quick reading of her key points would have suggested.

Yet C.I.A. director William Webster, guided primarily by satellite images of Iraqi troop deployments, warned President Bush later that day that an Iraqi attack was now about a fifty-fifty possibility. The D.I.A. also increased its threat assessment to Watch Condition 2, or WATCHCON 2, meaning that there were signs of imminent danger. D.I.A. sources reported that about three hundred buff-looking, newly arrived Iraqi "diplomats" had joined the Iraqi embassy in Kuwait City and were "extremely active in moving around the city." They seemed to be "conducting last-minute pre-attack reconnaissance of the city," recalled Rick Francona, the D.I.A. officer.[44]

Inundated with mixed messages, President Bush again sought advice from King Hussein of Jordan. The king was the closest thing to an "access agent"—C.I.A.-speak for an agent who is close to a target but not fully on the inside—that the president could rely on. They spoke by telephone on July 28.

"I certainly hope that the situation doesn't get out of hand," Bush said. "We are very worried about possible escalation."

"Really, sir, there is no possibility of that happening," the king assured him. "It will not come to that."[45]

Bush sent a three-paragraph letter to Saddam that day. "I was pleased to learn of the agreement between Iraq and Kuwait to begin negotiations," he wrote. "We believe that differences are best resolved by peaceful means and not by threats involving military force or conflict." He went on to "reassure" Saddam "that my Administration continues to desire better relations with Iraq. We will also continue to support our other friends in the region with whom we have had long-standing ties. We see no necessary inconsistency between these two objectives."

The letter contained not a hint of warning or a threat of retaliation if Iraq attacked. It gave no indication that Bush actually feared Saddam might invade Kuwait. If American messaging ever had a chance to seize Saddam's attention and make him reconsider his plans, Bush's letter of July 28—not Glaspie's conversation three days earlier—was the biggest missed opportunity.[46]

Saddam sent a delegation to negotiate with the Kuwaitis, as he had promised Mubarak. But rather than Tariq Aziz, he chose Izzat Ibrahim al-Douri, the Baath Party diehard, to handle the talks. At the meeting, Kuwait's crown prince again refused to forgive Saddam's debts.

The next morning, at the White House, Charles Allen, the C.I.A.'s national intelligence officer for warning, passed an upgraded "Warning of Attack" to Richard Haass, the leading Middle East specialist on the National Security Council. This level of warning meant that the C.I.A. now judged an attack by Saddam on Kuwait to be imminent.[47]

"I think they're going to attack," General H. Norman Schwarzkopf, the commander of all U.S. military forces in the Middle East, told Defense Secretary Dick Cheney that day. But he predicted that the Iraqis would only seize two disputed oil fields on the Kuwait-Iraq border and stop. If that happened, Schwarzkopf went on, the United States would do nothing. "The world will not care."[48]

That evening, Haass approached National Security Adviser Brent Scowcroft to discuss whether President Bush should now send a stronger message to Saddam. They decided to speak with the president.

President Bush had hit a bucket of golf balls earlier in the day, and his shoulders were flaring up. Scowcroft and Haass found him sitting on an exam table in the White House medical office, taking a heat treatment.

"Mr. President, it looks very bad," Scowcroft said. "Iraq may be about to invade Kuwait."

There was no time left for a letter; Haass suggested that the president call Saddam.

As they talked, Scowcroft took a call from the State Department. Shooting had broken out in Kuwait City.

"So much for calling Saddam," Bush said.[49]

In the cascade of errors that led to the U.S. invasion of Iraq in 2003, the Bush administration's failure to deter Saddam Hussein from invading Kuwait—as well as Saddam's failure to grasp what would happen after he acted—stand out. Saddam's invasion drew the U.S. into a major war to liberate Kuwait, followed by a succession of limited wars and C.I.A. covert actions against Saddam, ultimately culminating with George W. Bush's fateful decision to invade. Counterfactual history is speculative and unreliable. There is no way to know how events would have unfolded if the United States had prevented Saddam from invading Kuwait. Yet the question invites reflection partly because deterrence—credible threats of military retaliation aimed at stopping Saddam before he acted—might have worked. Iraq had a large army but was no match for the United States, and Saddam knew this, even if he harbored doubts about America's ability to absorb casualties. Irrational, rageful, and blind though he could be, Saddam was clearly deterrable—on more than one occasion, he refrained from using chemical weapons because he feared massive retaliation from Israel or the United States. So why did the Bush administration fail to signal harsh consequences to Saddam if he tried to take Kuwait, and why did Saddam fail to anticipate the American-led war of liberation that would follow?

In Washington, the main problem was that the Bush administration remained committed to improving relations with Baghdad, hoping against hope. In pursuit of this policy, Presidents Reagan and Bush pulled their punches when Saddam gassed his enemies. Saddam saw what he could get away with, and this surely influenced his calculations about Kuwait in 1990. "If we had taken strong action against the Iraqis for what they had done in Halabja, and in their later offensives against both the Kurds and the Iranians . . . I mean *really* strong action . . . would Saddam Hussein, under these circumstances, have believed he could get away with invading Kuwait in August 1990?" asked Charles Cogan, the head of the C.I.A.'s Middle East operations during the early 1980s. "Maybe he would" have invaded anyway, since "the grandiosity of the man's thinking was immense. But I am not so sure." Thomas Pickering, a respected career ambassador who served at the United Nations and in Moscow, also concluded "that Saddam was encouraged in his Kuwait adventure by our tolerance for just about everything he did, including his use of chemical weapons."[50]

Arab rulers repeatedly advised Bush that Saddam was bluffing. "It was important that we listen closely to, and take seriously, their advice and not act unilaterally in the face of it," recalled Scowcroft. But the larger problem was woefully familiar: "Governments have a hard time coming to terms with failed policies," recalled David George Newton, the former U.S. ambassador to Baghdad, referring to the long Reagan-Bush tilt toward Saddam. "They will do almost anything to convince themselves that by tinkering with the old policy, they will be just fine. I think this comes from not wanting to admit you've been wrong."[51]

For his part, Saddam misunderstood Washington. He also badly underestimated his own self-inflicted global isolation, his unpopularity even among leaders generally sympathetic to developing nations opposed to America and Israel. Yet some of Saddam's miscalculations seem understandable. George H. W. Bush did not know what he would be prepared to do if Iraq invaded Kuwait until it happened, as the president's diary and record of decision-making clearly show. The global response that he orchestrated would have been very difficult for Saddam to foresee. Nearly forty countries would join the U.S.-led effort to oust Iraq from Kuwait. Such a coalition might never have formed but for the Cold War's expiry, coupled with Soviet leader Mikhail Gorbachev's willingness to experiment with a "new world order."

Moreover, Saddam tended to think that the C.I.A. was omniscient, that it knew Iraq's important secrets. Surely, therefore, the U.S. knew about his clandestine plan to occupy Kuwait. In any event, by mid-July, Saddam was no longer hiding his preparations. Yet Bush still wrote him friendly notes, and the president's envoys delivered no direct or forceful warning against an attack. In Saddam's way of thinking, this meant that Bush might *want* him to take Kuwait. Years later, in captivity, Saddam asked U.S. investigators: "If you didn't want me to go in, why didn't you tell me?"[52]

PART TWO

THE LIAR'S TRUTHS

"You overlook many truths from a liar."

—Amir al-Saadi,
citing an Arabic proverb

August 1990 to September 2001

ELEVEN

Crash Programs

S addam's invasion of Kuwait did not begin well. In the early hours of August 2, more than one hundred Iraqi helicopters carrying special forces lifted off to assault Kuwaiti bases and strike in downtown Kuwait City, to kill or capture the Sabah royal family. But Iraqi helicopter pilots had no night-vision equipment and scant experience flying in the dark. By one account, Hussein Kamel, Saddam's son-in-law, ordered the pilots to "fly as low as possible," to evade antiaircraft missiles and achieve surprise. Someone, in any event, gave that catastrophic order, and more than forty of the helicopters crashed. Some collided with one another after churning up clouds of sand from the desert floor. Others flew over the highway to Kuwait, to avoid getting lost, but hit power lines or electricity towers.[1]

Jaber al-Ahmad al-Sabah, the Kuwaiti emir, was at his main residence, Dasman Palace, on the northern tip of Kuwait City's peninsula. A light royal guard protected him. Crown Prince Saad al-Abdullah al-Sabah gathered hastily with ministers at the capital's international airport. By radio, they had learned of the helicopter crashes and other sightings of the Iraqi invasion force. Soon they heard gunshots and heavy vehicles rumbling on Kuwait City's streets. Before dawn, they decided to flee. Saad led a snaking convoy of luxury cars to Dasman Palace. He got on his car phone to persuade Jaber to jump aboard. The vehicles sped south toward Saudi Arabia less than thirty minutes before Iraqi special forces turned up at Dasman. The Iraqis shot dead a younger brother of the emir, Fahad al-Ahmad al-Sabah, who had arrived at the palace too late to join the convoy. But the rest of the royal leadership escaped into exile, providing the Bush administration with an intact Kuwaiti government it could seek to restore to power, if Bush chose to challenge Saddam.[2]

It wasn't initially clear that Bush would. Just after 8:00 a.m. in Washington on August 2, his national security team gathered at the White House to discuss the crisis. The meeting that followed was unhelpful. Brent Scowcroft, the national security adviser, called it "a bit chaotic," informed by an "undertone" of resignation about Saddam's invasion. Dick Cheney said that "the rest of the world badly needs oil" and has "little interest in poor Kuwait." There was extensive discussion about the invasion's impact on oil markets and very little about the restoration of Kuwait's independence.[3]

Bush's most important Arab allies were no less flummoxed. King Hussein tried repeatedly to get through to Baghdad, but Saddam would not take his calls. The king then flew to Alexandria, Egypt, where, sitting on a veranda, he and Hosni Mubarak telephoned Bush. The president was by now on Air Force One, flying from Washington to Aspen, Colorado, where he would meet Margaret Thatcher.

"I really implore you, sir, to keep calm," Hussein said. "We want to deal with this in an Arab context."

Bush said the invasion was unacceptable to the United States and Hussein could relay that to Saddam "from me."[4]

Bush convened with Thatcher at the Woody Creek ranch of Henry E. Catto Jr., the U.S. ambassador to London.

"If Iraq wins, no small state is safe," Thatcher told the president. "This is no time to go wobbly, George," she added. The prime minister also said that King Hussein was "not helpful." Even after this outrageous invasion, the king had said the Kuwaitis "had it coming."

Bush said he feared that Israel might strike Iraq with atomic weapons. Of all the Middle Eastern governments he had consulted during July, only Tel Aviv's had predicted that Saddam would take Kuwait. "Israel was right and we were wrong," Bush admitted.

As Bush and Thatcher prepared to face the press, someone noted that there might be a question about whether the U.S. administration's "approach to Iraq has been a failure."

"At this point, I wouldn't say it's been an outstanding success," Bush quipped.[5]

That evening, the president called King Fahd of Saudi Arabia from one of Catto's bedrooms. Fahd had spoken with Saddam earlier in the day, he reported, and he now diagnosed him: "He is conceited. He doesn't realize the implications of his actions. . . . He seems to think only of himself. He is following Hitler in creating world problems, with one difference—one was conceited, and one is both conceited and crazy.

"I believe nothing will work with Saddam but use of force," Fahd continued. "He is a liar. . . . Saddam must be taught a lesson he will not forget the rest of his life—if he remains alive."

Yet at the end of their conversation, when Bush offered to immediately send a squadron of American F-15 warplanes to Saudi Arabia, to strengthen the kingdom's defenses, Fahd demurred.[6]

On August 5, Bush arrived back at the White House and addressed reporters on the South Lawn. "This will not stand, this aggression against Kuwait," he said. It was his most forceful pronouncement yet, but it was still unclear what America or America's Arab allies would do to back it up.

Cheney flew to Jeddah to meet King Fahd and persuade him to join the United States in a military response. "He will grow stronger—especially if he has all that Kuwaiti wealth," Cheney warned. "He will

dominate the Gulf. . . . He will acquire more, deadlier armaments."
Fahd finally agreed to accept American military forces on Saudi soil,
even though it would be provocative to his subjects and Islamic clergy.
Thousands of American, British, and French soldiers poured into the
kingdom. Ultimately, thirty-nine countries would come to the defense
of Saudi Arabia and Kuwait, mustering a total force of more than eight
hundred thousand.

In modern times, the Saudis and their small neighboring emirates
had never been involved in a destructive war. They seemed uncertain
about what such a conflict might entail.

Cheney stopped in Qatar to meet that emirate's royal leadership.
Afterward, he rode back to the airport with the minister of defense.

"So, are you going to nuke Saddam?" the minister asked.

No, Cheney answered. That was not the plan.[7]

Saddam, like Bush, regarded nuclear war as a realistic possibility.
Soon after the invasion, he received the president of Yemen, Ali
Abdullah Saleh, a fellow strongman, and told him that the United
States and Israel "may attack us by the atomic bombs. . . . We are ready
for that." He assured Saleh that Iraq could also manage any American
"blockade" or other military retaliation. He would attack American
"fleets in the Gulf" with "Kamikaze" air strikes.[8]

The Iraqi Ministry of Foreign Affairs summoned Joseph Wilson,
the senior U.S. diplomat then in Baghdad, to a morning meeting on the
day after Bush's "this will not stand" comment made headlines. After
her late July session with Saddam, April Glaspie had left the country to
arrange for her ailing mother's care in London.

Wilson and Nancy Johnson, the political officer, arrived at the ministry's concrete headquarters at about 10:00 a.m. Tariq Aziz ushered
them to see Saddam. Wearing military fatigues and his signature pistol
belt, he greeted them in a curtained meeting room and again began his
messaging to the Bush administration with a monologue that lasted
forty-five minutes to an hour.

His main argument was: Why fight? If the U.S. would allow him to have his way in Kuwait, he could supply cheap oil to America for years to come. He also pledged that he would not attack Saudi Arabia, as long as King Fahd did not allow his kingdom to be used to attack or destabilize Iraq. But if the U.S. sent its armed forces to confront Iraq, Saddam continued, America would face the "spilling of the blood of ten thousand soldiers in the Arabian desert. . . . You are a superpower and I know you can hurt us, but you will lose the whole area. You will never bring us to our knees."

Overall, Saddam offered "the carrot of cheap oil coupled with the stick of dead American soldiers," as Wilson summarized it. The Iraqi leader dismissed Kuwait's royal family as a thing of the past. The interpreter had trouble with Saddam's meaning, so Aziz jumped in, using the popular phrase in English: "The Sabah family is history."[9]

To make good on that forecast, Saddam appointed his cousin Ali Hassan al-Majid, the mass killer behind the Anfal, to govern the "Nineteenth Province," as Iraq's propagandists soon called Kuwait. Majid swiftly established a regime of official looting, widespread arrests, and the erasure of Kuwaiti national identity. At an early meeting with Saddam and other Iraqi leaders, he announced that the province "must become less developed" and reported that Kuwaitis "only care about money and not moral values." Some were already taking up arms against Iraq.

Saddam ordered that looting be managed as an official "spoils of war" operation to transfer Kuwaiti machinery, medical equipment, and luxury cars to Iraq. He asked his longtime comrade Taha Yassin Ramadan to include the appropriation of camel herds in the plundering program. Iraqis stole 3,216 gold bars from government stores, worth at least $390 million. Ultimately, the occupying forces would ransack or vandalize about 170,000 Kuwaiti homes; a U.N. commission would later approve $52 billion in compensation payments.[10]

The occupation authorities changed the names of schools, streets, public buildings, and residential areas, removing any reference to the Sabah family and honoring Saddam Hussein or well-known dates and figures in Iraqi history. In a letter headed "Erasing Kuwaiti Identity, Absorbing Kuwait," the Ministry of Education banned textbooks that depicted Kuwait "as an independent state or anything related to the old regime and their family."[11]

Hussein Kamel al-Majid, rarely sluggish, sprang into hyperdrive after the invasion. He seemed to work without sleep. On August 18, he met with Jafar Dhia Jafar and three other high-level scientists. Jafar now served as one of Hussein Kamel's deputies. Their collective work—to enrich uranium to bomb grade using electromagnetic and gas centrifuge technologies—had made substantial progress during the last several years. But despite what they had once forecasted to Saddam, they still appeared to be several years away from producing enough fissile material for a single bomb.

Hussein Kamel announced that he had a new plan. In light of the imminent threat of war with America, he proposed to quickly make a crude atomic bomb by grabbing highly enriched uranium that Iraq held at its Tuwaitha Nuclear Research Center, stored under international safeguards. One cache of this fuel had been supplied for the French reactor at Tuwaitha that had never operated because of Israel's air strike in 1981. It had been kept on-site, inspected periodically by the watchdog International Atomic Energy Agency to be sure it wasn't misused for weapons. A second batch of enriched uranium, also under safeguards, had been received to fuel the 1960s-era Soviet research reactor. The two batches would need alterations in order to be most suitable for a bomb, but this might be done in a matter of months, if they got cracking. Should their modifications work, they would be able to produce about twenty-five kilograms of highly enriched uranium bomb fuel—enough for a single, highly destructive device.

"You must do this," Hussein Kamel said.

Jafar was stunned. It was a desperate plan, one that was almost certainly unworkable on Hussein Kamel's timeline and sure to be discovered by international nuclear inspectors, who visited Iraq once every two or three months. If they got caught, the outcry would be immediate, and they might risk exposing the secret enrichment work they had been doing for almost a decade.[12]

Days later, Jafar wrote to Hussein Kamel, pointing out that what he was proposing would violate not only Iraq's obligations as a signatory of the Nuclear Nonproliferation Treaty but also related promises it had made to France. If Jafar was to supervise the work, he wanted "direct presidential approval."

Hussein Kamel wrote back the same day. Approval had "been obtained and signed" from Saddam, he asserted. Jafar had no way of knowing whether this was true, but he now had written orders, and defying Saddam's son-in-law meant a return to prison or worse. So he began work. Hussein Kamel directed that they finish an atomic bomb within six months—by February 1991. This became known as Project 601.

There were several tasks. One was making preparations to "reprocess" the highly enriched French fuel, which was already radioactive, so that it would be better suited for a bomb. This would require constructing a facility to safely apply chemical treatments. Jafar appointed a group to work on that. They also had to modify the fuel from the Soviet reactor. This uranium was enriched to about 80 percent, not as fissionable as the French fuel, at 93 percent. So they discussed using gas centrifuges they had built in their secret program to enrich some of the Soviet fuel to a grade of 93 percent, matching that of the French.[13]

The centrifuge program had advanced impressively since 1988. This was largely because Hussein Kamel had secretly enlisted West German technical specialists. He had handed out multimillion-dollar deals to secure the services of German engineers who had access to classified European designs. They had made so much progress by the fall of 1990 that they were building a new facility for a thousand or so centrifuges.

In late September or early October, A. Q. Khan, the metallurgist who had fathered Pakistan's bomb, secretly wrote to Iraq to offer

"project designs for a nuclear bomb," as well as European-made equipment. Khan was becoming the world's leading smuggler of atomic-
bomb technology, and he saw a sales opportunity in Iraq's effort to
fend off war with America. Jafar rejected the entreaty, noting that it
was standing policy to avoid such proposals "because of the technique
of entrapment which is still used by hostile parties."

Jafar visited Mahdi Obeidi to explain the plan to remove enriched
uranium from safeguarded stores. This meant that "Saddam was desperate for a nuclear weapon as soon as possible," Obeidi thought.[14]

Even if the reprocessing and enrichment of uranium worked on the
timeline Hussein Kamel had demanded, there remained the problem
of manufacturing a reliable bomb. As part of the reorganization of
1988, Iraq had created a team, known as Group Four, to design a workable bomb device. The team examined the open literature about Little
Boy, the uranium-fueled bomb that had devastated Hiroshima, and Fat
Man, the plutonium implosion device that leveled Nagasaki. They settled on a more challenging design that would require less highly enriched uranium but might produce an explosion of twenty kilotons, or
about the same yield as that of the bombs dropped on Japan.

Obeidi asked himself what Saddam's calculation might be. Even if
Iraq could come up with "a crude bomb," where would it explode the
device? In Israel, which had "a vast nuclear arsenal of its own" and was
likely to respond with an "annihilating counterattack"? Acquiring a single bomb in order to deter the United States and its allies from launching a war over Kuwait made more sense. But in that case, the smart
move would be to delay any war until the bomb could be completed
and revealed, and Saddam showed no sign of such strategic patience.
"Iraq was in the grip of a delusional leader," the scientist concluded.[15]

Saddam's conduct in the aftermath of his invasion of Kuwait altered
his place in world politics. He had not just mistimed his gambit by
invading when the Cold War's sudden end had created new possibilities
for alliances against him; he had also acted at a moment when cable

and satellite television created new networks and audiences for cross-border TV news coverage, bringing world audiences directly into the lurid visual theater of Saddam's propaganda. CNN, the BBC, and Arabic-language satellite networks beamed out Saddam's speeches, interviews, and glad-handing strolls. He decided to hold hostages—diplomats and civilians from the United States, Britain, and other countries—and called them "guests." He visited them before the cameras, all hospitality and solicitude. In one viral moment, Saddam walked among British hostages and met a five-year-old boy named Stuart Lockwood. He patted him on the head and asked, "Did Stuart have his milk today?" The image of Stuart shrinking away became fodder for countless outraged editorials. Yet Saddam seemed oblivious to how his hostage-taking shredded his threadbare credibility and narrowed—rather than enlarged—his room to maneuver.

He continued to perform, too, for the Arab audiences he imagined he would rally to his side in a decisive conflict against the United States. He seemed particularly offended that Bush had called him a liar. "President of the superpower," he wrote in an open letter to Bush, "you have lied to the people and public opinion, because you accused Saddam Hussein of being a liar." After Bush compared the danger of Iraqi expansionism to the threat Hitler posed, Saddam responded in another open letter: "He forgets that all these descriptions apply to him."[16]

Bush had served as a naval aviator during the Second World War, and he continually invoked comparisons of Saddam to Hitler after the Kuwait invasion. "It has been personalized," he wrote in his diary. "He is the epitome of evil." The analogy seemed to influence Bush's decisions—he should stop Saddam militarily while he had the means to do so, before the Iraqi leader could engorge himself on Kuwaiti oil and expand his warmaking potential. Yet like all analogies comparing geopolitical problems in different eras and regions, this one suffered from simplification. After a decade of helping to manage Saddam subtly, Bush had abruptly adopted a Manichaean outlook. His uncompromising policy was perhaps the best available, given American and European interests in the free flow of oil, and in light of Israel's security, yet it also closed down the president's curiosity and ability to listen. Arguably, he had stumbled into this mess by taking too much counsel from Arab friends; he now seemed determined to use the Hitler analogy to close off further arguments.[17]

Weeks after the invasion, Bush met Soviet leader Mikhail Gorbachev at a summit in Helsinki, Finland. Gorbachev had already gone to unprecedented lengths to cooperate with Bush. Yet he sought to maintain Soviet influence even as his multinational country crumbled. At a morning session in the Finnish presidential palace, Gorbachev unveiled a plan by which Saddam would withdraw and the U.S. would agree to participate in a conference on the Middle East to address Saddam's grievances.

"We need to give him some daylight," Gorbachev said. "Let's give the impression that he is not on his knees."

"If we had offered Hitler some way out, would it have succeeded?" Bush countered.

"Not the same situation."

"Only in personality," Bush insisted.[18]

Weeks after the invasion of Kuwait, Bush signed a Top Secret order authorizing the C.I.A. to work with Iraqi exiles and dissidents to remove Saddam from office. This was a long shot, given Saddam's octopus-like security regime and the paucity of American contacts with Iraqis in a position to stage a coup d'état. As a practical matter, during the months ahead, the agency's most significant work would be collecting intelligence to aid an eventual U.S.-led war to strike Iraq and liberate Kuwait, if Bush ordered one.

The C.I.A.'s station chief in Baghdad at the time of the invasion was Charles "Charlie" Seidel, who was in his early thirties. He was a "legacy" officer, meaning that he had followed his father into the spy business. His family line, colloquial Arabic, and willingness to take initiative marked him as a rising star in the Near East Division. Seidel had had no better luck than his predecessors at recruiting agents inside Saddam's inner circle. But after the invasion, he embraced an emergency mission in which he could act directly: rescuing American diplomats and other citizens stranded in Kuwait City.

W. Nathaniel Howell, the U.S. ambassador, lived on a five-acre embassy compound in the capital. His deputy, Barbara Bodine, and the C.I.A. station chief, J. Hunter Downes, lived nearby. But other diplomats and military officers were scattered around Kuwait City. Howell invited all Americans inside the compound, and many joined him there.

Saddam initially set August 24 as a deadline for all embassies in Kuwait to close or withdraw—since it was no longer an independent state, the emirate no longer required foreign embassies, Iraq explained. Howell and the White House decided to defy that order, but they wanted to evacuate as many people as possible—all but a core staff— before the deadline arrived.

Seidel drove down to Kuwait City. On August 22, at about 3:00 a.m., after much chaos, arm-waving, and shouting, Howell's flag-flying Cadillac led a convoy full of American children and government colleagues toward the Iraqi border. Nervous drivers speeding in darkness crashed into one another, and two injured Americans had to be rerouted to a Kuwaiti hospital. Howell got out at a border post and waved his comrades on to Baghdad. They made it to the U.S. embassy, where they found temporary cots and sleeping areas. Seidel soon led a second convoy through Kurdistan and across the Turkish border.[19]

The Iraqis tightened their occupation of Kuwait as summer turned to autumn. They established more than two dozen interrogation and torture centers in Kuwait City. They arrested anyone who spoke ill of Saddam, and they bulldozed and burned the homes of suspected members of the Kuwaiti resistance. Warned of an upcoming public protest by Kuwaitis, Bariq Abdullah al-Haj Hinta, the local commander of special forces, sent orders to his 65th Brigade about how to respond:

> You need to walk to the demonstration area, without vehicles and quietly, quietly, quietly get close to the demonstrators

from behind and close their alternative routes of escape. Then
open fire at the same time with everything you have, including
rifles, automatic weapons, light cannons, and flamethrowers
for the objective of killing all the demonstrators so to serve as
an example to all others.

Iraqi soldiers raped Western, Asian, and Arab women in Kuwait,
although the extent of these crimes is unknown. The Iraqis arrested
nearly four thousand Kuwaitis during the first seven weeks of the occupation, according to regime records. Kuwait later compiled a list of
2,242 civilians and military personnel who went missing; many almost
certainly died or were executed in Iraqi prisons.[20]

I n mid-September, Bush addressed Congress. "Iraq will not be permitted to annex Kuwait," he said. "That's not a threat, that's not a boast,
that's just the way it's going to be."

"It looks like the old man Bush is beginning to warn us," Saddam
told Tariq Aziz in a private meeting soon after. "He must be crazy."
The public rhetoric between Bush and Saddam—you're a liar; no, *you're*
a liar—narrowed the potential for international diplomacy to stave off
war. The more the Bush administration pushed through tougher sanctions at the U.N., "the more unbending we become," Saddam told Aziz
privately. He found it "disgusting" the way the U.S. was leading the
U.N. "under its whip. . . . This is an organization that belongs to Bush."[21]

Saddam had long deftly parlayed with Washington, Moscow, and
Paris while often defying their rules for international conduct. Now
that he was under direct threat, he seemed to regress to his revolutionary youth, extending his middle finger to the world's great powers.
Saddam had always spoken radically in private to his comrades, as if he
felt a continual need to renew his credentials as a revolutionary before
them. But then he often acted to avoid confrontation. Now he spoke
rashly in private and seemed to mean what he said.

On October 6, Yevgeny Primakov, an envoy of Gorbachev, met with Saddam in Baghdad. Primakov and Saddam had known one another since the former's days as a Middle East correspondent for *Pravda*. The Russian brought a letter from Gorbachev, who was still trying to find a way to resolve the Kuwait crisis by launching a new effort to resolve the Arab-Israel conflict.

Saddam dismissed the possibility that America would bargain seriously over Palestine. In any event, if he backed down now, he intimated, he might lose his grip on power. He needed to save face. He suggested that a compromise might be possible, such as a partial withdrawal from Kuwait, if Bush allowed him to "preserve his authority in Iraq."

Two weeks later, Primakov flew to Washington and met Bush in the Oval Office. Saddam "was not being well informed by his inner circle and was hearing more about his support than about his political isolation," Primakov reported.

Bush asked if Saddam would survive the crisis. Primakov predicted that he would. Economic and trade sanctions alone "would not force Saddam out and could be counterproductive, encouraging him to strike at Israel." If Saddam believed that his choice was withdrawal or war, Primakov reported, his attitude was: "I'm prepared to die."

The envoy outlined Gorbachev's ideas for diplomacy, which struck Bush as "face-savers" for Saddam that would be seen as a "reward" for Iraqi aggression. The president remained firmly committed to "unconditional withdrawal." The discussion left Bush pessimistic about "finding any solution to the crisis short of the use of force."[22]

Bush ordered preparations for a war to liberate Kuwait. General H. Norman Schwarzkopf, commanding from Saudi Arabia, and Colin Powell, who advised the White House as the chairman of the Joint Chiefs, led the planning. They possessed sharply contrasting temperaments. Six foot three and 240 pounds, Schwarzkopf was an egoist at press-conference podiums who could inspire troops with his energy and audacity. He was also a short-tempered screamer behind closed doors. Powell, with whom Schwarzkopf spoke several times a day, screened the general from the White House. A son of Jamaican-born parents, Powell had grown up in Harlem and the South Bronx and had attended City College of New York before rising through the U.S. Army to become his country's first Black chairman of the Joint Chiefs. He was a classic staff officer—part diplomat, part strategist, and part facilitator of military decisions. He often reflected on the connection between America's armed forces and public opinion. He had served two tours in Vietnam, an experience that gave rise to what came to be known as the "Powell Doctrine," which held that the United States should only fight wars with overwhelming force, clear goals, and a decisive exit plan. As a practical matter, this meant fewer wars, which Powell favored: "Of all manifestations of power, restraint impresses men most," read an aphorism he kept on his desk.[23]

Week by week that autumn, the United States, Britain, and France deployed to Saudi Arabia and neighboring emirates a massive armada of tanks, ships, aircraft, and soldiers. Bush and his national security adviser, Brent Scowcroft, came to conceive of the war to liberate Kuwait as an exemplar of the Powell Doctrine: they would apply overwhelming force to achieve in the shortest time possible a clear and finite goal—namely, the expulsion of Iraqi forces and the restoration of Kuwait's independence. Powell believed the war would ultimately have to be won on the ground, by armor and infantry. The president and his top generals were not nearly as deterred by the prospect of U.S. casualties as Saddam Hussein believed. Yet they worried nonetheless about American losses. The Joint Chiefs predicted that the U.S. might endure twenty thousand to thirty thousand dead and wounded, while some independent military specialists forecasted up to one hundred thousand.[24]

Bush had built his formidable alliance around a war aim derived from United Nations resolutions: Iraq must withdraw unconditionally from Kuwait. That fall, however, Bush also asked his National Security Council staff to review other war aims the United States might pursue.

They recommended destroying as much of Iraq's elite armored force, the Republican Guard, as possible. The loss of these divisions would diminish Saddam's potential to threaten neighbors in the future, and "since these troops were also the backbone of the regime, their destruction would further undermine Saddam's grip on power," as Scowcroft recalled.

The president's closest Arab allies—the same kings and strongmen who had failed to predict the invasion of Kuwait—now advised Bush that if Saddam were crushed in war against the U.S.-led coalition, this would "shatter what support he had within the military, which probably would then topple him." This prediction appealed to Bush, a former C.I.A. director. The White House review "raised the question of making Saddam's removal an objective" of the military campaign to liberate Kuwait, but neither Bush nor Scowcroft believed this was wise or easily achievable. "The best solution was to do as much damage as we could to his military, and wait for the Baath regime to collapse," Scowcroft concluded.[25]

In Washington, opposition to going to war over Kuwait grew among Democrats and some Republicans in Congress. Watching from Baghdad, Saddam struggled to understand. If Bush "can't reach an agreement with the opposing party, would the president be able to make a dangerous decision" to go to war on his own authority? "What we have here is a complicated country," Saddam remarked at one point.

He told his advisers that he was prepared to use Iraq's chemical and biological weapons, if necessary. "If we wanted to use chemicals, we will beat them down," he said at a meeting in November. "We have biological weapons that can kill, even if you step on it forty years later." The latter claim was, of course, absurd.[26]

Saddam's comrades assured him that he had tied the Americans in knots. "Bush is losing his mind, he is going crazy," Izzat Ibrahim al-Douri told him around this time. "He is wondering: Are they mentally stable? Are they bluffing? Will they really fight or not? The United

States is stunned . . . stunned!" Saddam continued to describe the looming conflict as the inevitable result of the American-Israeli-Iranian conspiracy against Iraq dating back years. "The war was launched on us long before all this . . . and was exposed under the title 'Irangate,'" he told his comrades.[27]

He remained fixated on the prospect that Iraq would be struck pre-emptively with nuclear weapons, most likely by Israel. After the inva-sion, he had ordered preparations for the evacuation of Baghdad. The capital's two million or so residents were instructed to find compan-ions in the countryside who might shelter them. A civil-defense cam-paign educated Baghdadis about the effects of atomic war. At a meeting late in 1990, Ali Hassan al-Majid questioned the need for "all this hoopla about the effects of nuclear and atomic attack. . . . It frightens children, it frightens parents, it frightens fighters."

Saddam reacted with an angry rant: "What are we, a bunch of kids?" He excoriated Izzat for his work on the preparations—"I swear on your mustache . . . pay attention to civil defense!"—before agreeing that the campaign "should not explain to the citizen what the atomic bomb will do."[28]

O n November 29, the United Nations adopted a deadline for Iraq's withdrawal from Kuwait. If Saddam did not retreat by January 15, 1991, the United States and its allies could use force to liberate the emirate. The Security Council's unity would have been all but impos-sible to imagine before Gorbachev—Saddam had misjudged this aspect of the Cold War's end. Bush had accepted by now that January 15 would all but certainly mark the start of war. In Baghdad, Tariq Aziz assured Saddam that war would at least not begin before the announced deadline: the intervening Christmas holidays, he explained, were a time for "family gatherings," and any American president "who brings corpses to his country" during that season "will be skinned alive."[29]

The White House authorized one last try at diplomacy. Secretary of State James Baker sought a meeting with Saddam in Baghdad, but the Iraqis refused. They settled on a conference between Baker and Aziz in Geneva on January 9, 1991.

Aziz flew from Baghdad to Switzerland. They convened late the next morning at the Intercontinental Hotel, on a rise above Lake Geneva. Baker led a delegation that also included Cheney. Barzan Ibrahim al-Tikriti, still posted as a diplomat in Geneva, joined Aziz. The Americans saw Barzan as an "enforcer" of Saddam's, there to keep Aziz in line—an assessment of Barzan's influence that was years out of date.[30]

Baker had met Aziz before and found him "urbane and sort of cosmopolitan," a strong English speaker with "an excellent command of his brief." The two delegations faced off across a conference table laden with water bottles and vinyl ice buckets. Baker handed across a sealed envelope containing a three-page letter from Bush to Saddam, as well as a copy translated into Arabic for Aziz. "Unless you withdraw from Kuwait completely and without condition, you will lose more than Kuwait. What is at issue here is not the future of Kuwait . . . but rather the future of Iraq. The choice is yours to make."

Aziz read Bush's letter and then set it back on the table. He called the document insulting and said he would not accept it or carry it to Saddam. He suggested that the Americans hand it out to the media.

The Baker-Aziz meeting proved to be mainly rehearsed theater on both sides, except in one respect: at the urging of Dick Cheney and Colin Powell, Baker issued a stark warning about what the U.S. would do if Saddam used chemical or biological weapons. "The American people will demand vengeance," Baker said. "And we have the means to exact it. Let me say with regard to this part of my presentation, this is not a threat; it is a promise. If there is any use of weapons like that, our objective won't just be the liberation of Kuwait, but the elimination of the current Iraqi regime." The retaliation Iraq would face in that case would leave the country "weak and backward."

Although the secretary of state did not mention nuclear weapons, he wanted to impress on Aziz that the U.S. might go nuclear if it were hit with Iraqi chemical or biological arms. Whether Baker knew it or not, his threat reinforced Saddam's belief that America and Israel would not hesitate to strike Iraq with atomic bombs.[31]

The meeting ended, and Baker and Aziz told the world's press that there had been no breakthrough. Six days remained until the war deadline.

Around the time of the summit in Geneva, Saddam met with senior advisers, including his son-in-law Hussein Kamel. The president sought assurance that he had an option to use chemical and biological arms. "I want to make sure that—close the door, please—the germ and chemical warheads, as well as the chemical and germ bombs, are available to the 'concerned people,' so that in case we ordered an attack, they can do it without missing any of their targets," Saddam said.

The demand put Hussein Kamel in an awkward position. In reality, as he now sought to delicately explain, Iraqi forces were prepared to wage chemical war against the American-led coalition, if so ordered, but the biological and nuclear programs were less ready.

"Sir, if you'll allow me," he began, "some of the chemicals now are distributed. . . . Chemical warheads are stored and ready at air bases," he said. As he started to wander into details—mentioning phosphorous, ethyl alcohol, methyl alcohol—Saddam interrupted.

"This is not important to me. . . . The missiles, by tomorrow, will be ready on the fifteenth."

"Sir, we don't have the germs," Hussein Kamel now admitted.

"Then, where are they?"

"It's with us," he said, meaning the ministries he ran.

"What is it doing with you? I need these germs to be fixed on the missiles. . . . Starting the fifteenth, everyone should be ready for the action to happen at any time, and I consider Riyadh as a target." They went on to discuss other targets: Jeddah, Saudi Arabia's sprawling city on the Red Sea, and "all the Israeli cities."[32]

Such was Hussein Kamel's work, dancing to his father-in-law's demands. Only Saddam's son-in-law could offer a truth like "Sir, we don't have the germs" and expect to live a free man.

Saddam did make extensive preparations to use chemical weapons on American and coalition troops. Documents show Iraqi forces preparing to field 1,232 chemical aircraft bombs, 13,000 artillery shells loaded with mustard, and 8,320 Soviet-made Grad rockets loaded with nerve agents. Hussein Kamel also managed to prepare 166 bombs and 25 missiles loaded with biological weapons, although the chance that these weapons would work if fired was much smaller than with Iraq's battle-tested chemical arsenal.[33]

Yet for all his bold talk, Saddam reserved judgment on whether he would ever use "special weapons" against the United States and its allies. He made clear that the decision rested solely with him. He indicated ambiguously that he would permit use "only in case we are obliged and there is a great necessity." He added, "We will never lower our heads as long as we are alive, even if we have to destroy everybody."[34]

Predictably, the nuclear-weapons program had also missed Hussein Kamel's deadlines. Work on a usable bomb device remained particularly far behind. The bottom line was that Iraq was in no position to finish or launch an atomic bomb that winter.

How far had the secret bomb program first conceived in 1980 actually come toward success, after roughly a decade of effort and enormous expenditure? The answer depends on many hypotheticals and so cannot be given with precision. If Saddam had not invaded Kuwait, the bomb program's prospects probably would have depended on how quickly the electromagnetic and centrifuge teams could produce enough highly enriched uranium, and on how quickly a workable device could be completed and tested. Fadhil al-Janabi, who served as chair of the Iraqi Atomic Energy Commission, estimated that the program was still six or seven years away from a finished bomb. That seems a conservative estimate. Garry Dillon, who spent years examining Iraq's nuclear program during the 1990s as a senior inspector at the watchdog International Atomic Energy Agency, judged that the effort "had been close to the threshold of success" in such important areas as the production of highly enriched uranium and the development of an explosives package for a bomb. He noted, however, that by early 1991, Iraq had yet to produce more than a few grams of bomb-grade material indigenously. Late in 1991, the C.I.A. concluded that Iraq "probably" had the technical competence to build a bomb by the end of the 1990s with its own talent and resources. It might have been able to do so "within a few months" in the "much less likely" scenario of a crash program to misuse Iraq's reactor fuel—at the time it produced its 1991 report, the C.I.A. did not know Iraq had taken steps to do just that as the Gulf War loomed.

Whether Saddam was months or seven years away, in Washington, Tehran, and Tel Aviv, *any* chance that he might have acquired an atomic bomb before he could be stopped was terrifying.[35]

The qualities that had led George H. W. Bush to miss the chance to deter Saddam Hussein from invading Kuwait—his reliance on personal diplomacy, his openness to the advice of allies, and his innate optimism—served him better as he prepared for war. To expel Iraq from Kuwait, Bush constructed a formidable warfighting coalition. He secured Gorbachev's cooperation without succumbing to Soviet interference. He allowed Congress to debate the war and won its approval. The underlying Western interests driving Bush toward war—the free flow of oil, above all—were less noble than the president believed. Yet Bush's performance was impressive. So was his prescience about the decisions he would soon have to make.

"I have trouble with how this ends," he dictated to his diary on the morning of January 15, as the war loomed inescapably. He planned a prolonged aerial bombardment of Iraq that would destroy much of its infrastructure and—he hoped—might make American casualties in a ground war unnecessary. "Say the air attack is devastating and Saddam gets done in by his own people," he speculated. "How do they stop? How do we keep from having overkill? Most people don't see that as a scenario because they are convinced it will be long and drawn out, with numerous body bags on the U.S. side. But I want to be sure we are not in there pounding people. I think we need to watch and see when our military objectives are taken care of in Baghdad and Iraq."[36]

Even before the first shot was fired, Bush was reminding himself to stop the fighting before "pounding people" undermined the common cause of the coalition he had assembled. After months of councils with his generals, Bush understood his war plan well. America's virtual monopoly on air power would set conditions for the ground war to liberate Kuwait. America's superior armor would then speed across desert terrain, out of Saudi Arabia, to flank Iraqi forces and encircle the Republican Guard while U.S. Marines punched into Kuwait City directly. No war's course could be predicted with certainty, but the preparations left Bush reasonably confident that he would not preside over a bloody quagmire. Still, his plan had no answer for the question that would come to shadow his legacy and shape the presidency of his son a decade later: What could or should be done about the dictatorship of Saddam Hussein?

TWELVE

"The Situation Is Under Excellent Control"

From the Gulf War's opening hours on January 17, 1991, President George H. W. Bush and his commanders sought to kill Saddam Hussein. Bush had decided against making Saddam's death or removal from power a formal war aim, but he sought this outcome nonetheless, without clarity about what would follow.

After C.I.A. plots to assassinate foreign leaders were revealed during the 1970s, Ronald Reagan had signed an executive order banning the direct assassination of foreign leaders. Yet targeting the commanders of enemy armies in wartime was permitted under American and international law. Saddam wore a military uniform, sported a sidearm, and commanded Iraq's forces with absolute authority. "We don't do assassinations," National Security Adviser Brent Scowcroft explained later. "But yes, we targeted all the places where Saddam might have been." Early drafts of the war plan to liberate Kuwait had recommended an air campaign that would "decapitate" Saddam's regime. The Iraqi leader was a "one-man show" and so "ought to be the focus of our efforts," General Michael Dugan, the U.S. Air Force's chief of staff, told reporters. Defense Secretary Dick Cheney fired Dugan for these candid remarks, even though they accurately reflected White House policy.[1]

But would it work? As the war neared, Bush's generals offered varying forecasts. General H. Norman Schwarzkopf, the top theater commander, believed the odds of success were "high." But Dugan's successor, General Merrill "Tony" McPeak, estimated the chances at no better than 30 percent. The air war's principal planner, Brigadier General Buster Glosson, also told Bush that there was a "high probability" that Saddam would survive. The U.S. had no real-time intelligence on his whereabouts and, in this pre-cell-phone era, no technical means to track him. The Iraqi leader was extremely cautious. He avoided meeting places he had used before. He knew that any use of landline, satellite, or radio telephones could aid enemy targeting. He ordered his comrades and generals to stay off phones altogether and communicate only by letter and courier, a discipline the Iraqi president also maintained. As Saddam advised his comrades early in the 1991 air war, "Whenever the enemy is able to intercept our wire and wireless calls, the correct counter plan is not to buy code machines from the opposition country in the West . . . ; rather, we should stop all our calls."[2]

During the war's first hours, eight Tomahawk cruise missiles slammed into the Republican Palace—the site of multiple meetings between Saddam and American diplomats during the previous decade. The first night's target list also included dozens of bunkers and suspected command centers around the capital. Blue Bird Body Company, the manufacturer of the Wanderlodge recreational vehicles favored by Saddam, informed the Bush administration about its Iraqi customer. When American satellites or aircraft spotted a Wanderlodge, warplanes swooped in to bomb.[3]

Bush hoped that intensive bombing might help depose Saddam, even if it failed to kill him. Led by the U.S. Air Force, they would try to create conditions of such misery for ordinary Iraqis that the people would rid themselves of their president. This was to be accomplished, in part, by bombing Iraq's electric and industrial infrastructure. Some of this targeting had a military purpose—to knock out Iraqi air defenses and prevent Iraqi generals from maneuvering their forces. But the bombing also sought to make Iraqis "feel they were isolated," Glosson explained. "I wanted to play with their psyche."[4]

Before and during the war, the U.S. dropped propaganda leaflets on Iraqi troops to urge them to desert or overthrow Saddam. The C.I.A. organized a network of radio stations in Saudi Arabia that broadcast similar encouragement into Iraq. Coupling such propaganda with attacks on civilian infrastructure, said air-war planner David Deptula, was intended to send a message: "Hey, your lights will come back on as soon as you get rid of Saddam." Of course, many Iraqis were *already* miserable and cowed under Baath Party rule. Despite their suffering, they had not risen up because Iraq's police state had made even passing talk of such rebellion mortally dangerous.[5]

On the war's first morning, Iraqi radio broadcast a statement from Saddam announcing that the "Um Al-Ma'arik," or "Mother of All Battles," was underway. "Satan's great follower Bush committed his treacherous crime, he and the criminal Zionism." Iraq would wage "the great duel . . . between a victorious right and the evil."[6]

It turned out to be one-sided from the first hour. American fighter-bombers knocked out electricity to Baghdad in the first waves of attack. Cruise missiles and F-117 stealth fighters loaded with laser-guided bombs roared into Baghdad and struck Baath Party, Ministry of Defense, and other leadership targets without initially losing a single aircraft. American war planners had been impressed by the number of Iraqi soldiers under arms and the military's "substantial inventory" of "relatively modern instruments of war." But they soon discovered that much of Iraq's military equipment was no match for the latest Western systems. The United States would lose thirty-three aircraft in combat during the forty-two-day war, mainly to antiaircraft fire, but coalition planes maintained mastery of the skies throughout.[7]

Saddam visited a makeshift air defense center in Baghdad on the first morning. He told his officers that staying in the fight was more important than winning every battle. He still believed he could drag the United States into a long war, and that America's aversion to casualties might eventually cause Washington to accommodate his occupation of Kuwait.

He also hoped to arouse the Arab world by striking Israel. That morning, Saddam dispatched a courier to deliver handwritten orders to the commander of Iraq's missile forces. "Begin, with Allah's blessing, striking targets inside the criminal Zionist entity with the heaviest fire possible," he instructed. "The firing must continue until further notice."[8]

It had been a decade since Israeli warplanes surprised and humiliated Saddam by bombing his nuclear reactors at Tuwaitha. Now he would have his revenge. The Scud missiles in his arsenal were each about thirty-seven feet long and weighed about fourteen thousand pounds. He ultimately fired forty-two of them in Israel's direction, although some landed short in Jordan or the occupied West Bank. It was a terrifying and made-for-TV salvo, yet even as Saddam reveled in his attacks, he sought to reduce the chance of an all-out war with Israel. Hussein Kamel had prepared "special warheads" loaded with chemical weapons for seventy-five of Iraq's two hundred and thirty Scud missiles. But when the decision came, Saddam decided not to use gas.

"The strikes must be carried out with 'ordinary' conventional ammunition," he ordered his missile commander. In the end, Saddam would not authorize a single chemical attack on Israel, the United States, or any of the coalition forces arrayed against him. There is no record of his thinking, but it seems clear from his prewar discussions that he was deterred by the threat of massive retaliation, including with nuclear weapons.[9]

In Riyadh, General H. Norman Schwarzkopf established a coordination center where U.S., Saudi Arabian, and other coalition officers could monitor the war. The center housed television screens and military communication equipment and was staffed around the clock. The Saudis were in an especially sensitive position, playing host to hundreds of thousands of infidel soldiers waging war against a brother Arab and Islamic-majority state. The ruling House of Saud relied on America for security but provided financial and political support to Palestinians at war with Israel. These were fault lines Saddam thought he knew how to exploit.

In the early hours of January 18, the night shift in the coordination center, C3IC, watched as five Iraqi Scud missiles smashed into Tel Aviv and Haifa. It was the first strike on Israeli cities with missiles or bombs since the 1973 Arab-Israeli War. "To the shock of the Americans present in the C3IC," recalled Rick Francona, who was present, "virtually every Saudi officer was on his feet applauding and cheering the Iraqi missile strike . . . many shouting 'Allahu Akbar!'"[10]

In Baghdad, Saddam met with his Revolutionary Command Council. He told them about his order to expand the war by sending Scuds at Israel. "We have to be cool and calm," he said. "The battle will be a bit exciting. . . . Let us involve Israel in the fight, let [us] see if they are up to it. . . . Let us break the bone of America's daughter."

He planned to alternate Scud launches against Israel and Saudi Arabia, he explained. "Riyadh, Jeddah, I mean all the cities within our missiles range . . . with the exception of holy Mecca and Medina." He acknowledged that Saudi civilians might die. "If their people want to blame someone, they can blame their rulers," he said. He warned that Israel would likely "reciprocate by attacking us with missiles."[11]

American strategists worried that if Israel did indeed retaliate against Iraq, the U.S.-led coalition would fracture, and Arab and other Muslim allies might withdraw from the fight, or even change sides and join Iraq against Israel. There is no evidence in the available records that Saddam attacked Israel in the specific hope that it would sunder the American-led alliance; his private remarks suggest he sought glory in the Arab world. He also spoke of embarrassing Washington's Arab allies, especially King Fahd of Saudi Arabia and President Hosni Mubarak of Egypt.

Brent Scowcroft telephoned George H. W. Bush with news of the Scud attacks on Tel Aviv and Haifa. Defense Secretary Dick Cheney reported that his Israeli counterpart, Moshe Arens, had called immediately to demand American help in clearing airspace for an Israeli counterattack.

The Bush administration did not enjoy a warm relationship with the taciturn, American-educated Arens, or with his boss, Prime Minister Yitzhak Shamir, a war-hardened leader who, during the 1940s, had served as a member of the underground movement fighting for Israel's creation and had planned lethal attacks on British troops in what was then the Palestine Mandate. Cheney "doubted we could stop" Israel from striking back at Saddam and "could make a bad situation worse by trying," Scowcroft recalled. "He suggested we let them go, go fast, and get it over with."

Scowcroft thought this would be a "serious mistake." Israeli warplanes would have to cross Jordan, Syria, or Saudi Arabia to hit Iraq. If Jordan, for example, reacted to the violation of its airspace by joining Saddam against Israel, it would "change the entire calculus for the coalition" seeking Kuwait's liberation. In an apparent reference to Scowcroft, Cheney recalled that some in Bush's war cabinet wanted to "sort of stiff the Israelis," whereas he advocated for working closely with Tel Aviv, "to let them know that we were doing absolutely everything we could to head off this Scud missile threat . . . that we were sympathetic."[12]

Saddam's Scud attacks ultimately killed four people in Israel and wounded almost two hundred. Shamir warned Bush that he could not sit on his hands. "We have been attacked and are not doing anything," he said. "Our people don't understand."

Yet at Scowcroft's urging, Bush turned down a request from Shamir for data like aircraft transponder codes—the "kind of information" that would allow Israeli planes to "fly their planes with impunity in an area where they were otherwise likely to get shot down by us." At one point, Bush said that if Israel had to strike Iraq, Shamir should order a missile barrage and not employ aircraft. Cheney traveled to Israel and oversaw the transfer of U.S.-made Patriot air-defense missiles for the purpose of trying to knock down incoming Scuds. In the end, Shamir acceded to Bush's pleas for restraint, calculating that Israel's interests would be better served by staying out.[13]

His decision did help solidify the determination of many of Iraq's Arab neighbors to punish Saddam. The shouts and applause of Saudi officers in the Riyadh coordination center reflected one powerful strain of opinion, but many of the region's authoritarian rulers saw no profit in going down with Saddam's burning ship. "You are free to fight the whole world alone," Mustafa Tlass, Syria's minister of defense, told Saddam, but "you are especially not free to call on other people to join you in this folly." Syria had sent troops to Saudi Arabia and remained supportive of the war.

By standing down, Shamir also enabled Bush to quickly finish what he had started. The U.S. air war included extensive strikes on Iraq's known nuclear-, chemical-, and biological-weapons facilities—bombings that would enhance Israel's security even more than that of the United States, at least in the near term, given the limited range of Iraqi missiles. As Bush recalled arguing to Shamir, "Israel couldn't do anything we weren't accomplishing already."[14]

The U.S.-led bombing campaign devastated Iraq. American aircraft dropped more than 150,000 "dumb" gravity bombs, ranging from five hundred to two thousand pounds each, largely on Iraqi conscripts sent to the front lines in and around Kuwait. The bombing killed ten thousand to twelve thousand Iraqi soldiers altogether, according to a later U.S. survey based on prisoner-of-war interviews; other estimates of Iraqi deaths ranged higher. After Iraq's losses endured during the war with Iran, the Gulf War extended the culling of the country's already decimated generation of military-age men.[15]

Before the war, Saddam had sent large, vulnerable Soviet-made transport aircraft to Iran in the hope that they would be safe there and that Iran would return them later. In late January, he also ordered eighteen surviving Mirage fighters, nine Sukhois, and one Falcon 50 business jet to be "evacuated" to Iran. But the Iranians seized the most advanced aircraft and repainted them in their own national colors. Ultimately, more than 130 Iraqi aircraft flew to Iran, but the Iranians only acknowledged 22 and were soon recruiting trainers from abroad to teach their pilots how to fly the impounded planes.

Saddam's state of mind during the initial weeks of intensive bombardment, before the ground war began, was manic, erratic, and cruel. He seemed to have settled upon a war strategy of radical vandalism, in the name of Arab glory and his own. His missile strikes on Israel and Saudi Arabia were frightening and generated heavy news coverage, even if they were of minor military consequence. He also ordered the burning of more than six hundred Kuwaiti oil wells, signaling to his suffering troops that he was destroying the supposed bounty sought by America's oil-thirsty imperialists. The fires sent ghastly plumes of black smoke across the desert, shrouding daylight. The split-screen TV images of raging oil fires and ambulances rushing through Israeli and Saudi cities created an impression that might help Saddam declare victory before his own followers.[16]

Saddam and his sons were merciless toward Kuwaiti detainees, and they threatened the lives of American and British pilots held as prisoners of war. In late January, Qusay, the president's second son, ordered Iraqi Air Vice-Marshal Georges Sada to execute scores of prisoners of war immediately—Americans, British, and other coalition flyers, including one Kuwaiti pilot. Sada refused the orders, he later recounted; the following day, the Mukhabarat arrested him and held him for a week. But his stubbornness apparently delayed the executions, and in the end, Saddam rescinded the order. The president was "capable of diabolical evil, but he was also a very practical man, and he realized that killing the pilots would only have made the situation worse for him," Sada concluded. The Kuwaiti pilot survived, yet Saddam ordered the killing of hundreds of other Kuwaiti prisoners who posed no threat to his regime. According to a Pentagon report, 1,082 Kuwaitis were killed by execution and torture. Sada recounted that the regime executed just over 600 Kuwaitis held as prisoners of war.[17]

Gradually, Saddam realized that his plan to draw the coalition into a long war with grinding casualties that would break America's will was not going to work. "The enemy is planning to shorten the battle, which we planned to prolong," he conceded privately. He could also see that America intended to destroy "Iraq in its entirety, including its willpower." He decided to see if he could save what was left of his country's infrastructure while also saving face before his people and the Arab world.[18]

Mikhail Gorbachev again tried to help. On February 11, 1991, Yevgeny Primakov traveled once more to Baghdad. To reach the Iraqi capital, he had to fly into Tehran and ride overland from there. He was taken at night to a darkened guesthouse. "A power generator suddenly clicked on, and the house was filled with light," he recalled. "Then Saddam Hussein appeared with the entire Iraqi leadership."

Primakov asked for a private audience with Saddam. The bombing Iraq had suffered was just a prelude, he explained. "The Americans are determined to launch a large-scale ground operation to crush Iraqi forces in Kuwait," he said. Politics is the art of the possible, he reminded Saddam. He carried a new proposal from Gorbachev: Iraq should announce the withdrawal of its forces from Kuwait before a ground war began—unconditionally and as soon as possible.

Saddam had questions: Would his departing troops be "shot in the back?" Would the coalition stop the war after he withdrew? Would U.N. sanctions end?[19]

He promised Primakov a written reply from Tariq Aziz, who would then travel to Moscow for further consultations.

That night, American warplanes pounded Baghdad during one of the war's heaviest nights of bombing. At about 4:30 a.m., two stealth jets dropped a pair of two-thousand-pound bombs on a bunker in Amiriyah, a residential neighborhood in west Baghdad. The facility had been built as a civilian air-raid shelter during the Iran-Iraq War and had a roof of concrete and steel ten feet thick. The U.S. Air Force had identified the site as an active Iraqi command center. Whatever its use during the day, at night it served as a shelter where hundreds of Iraqi civilians, including many women and children, tried to sleep. The laser-guided bombs broke through its roof and exploded, killing more than four hundred people and wounding hundreds of others. Entire families perished. Daybreak revealed a scene of devastation and grief as ambulance and rescue workers pored over the rubble, digging for survivors.

The same satellite news channels that had wowed American audiences with Pentagon-released images of precision bombs at the war's opening now broadcast imagery of dead and wounded children as journalists asked how such a massive error could have occurred. Brigadier General Richard Neal, briefing reporters in Riyadh, said the building was targeted because there were "military folks in and around the facility on a routine and continuous basis." He could offer "no explanation at this time really why there were civilians in this bunker." The strike became an indelible tragedy of a war turning uglier by the day.[20]

Following his talk with Primakov, Saddam convened the Revolutionary Command Council to debate how they might find a dignified way forward. On February 15, the Council issued a statement accepting U.N. Resolution 660, which demanded Iraq's unconditional withdrawal from Kuwait. Yet Iraq attached absurd conditions, such as Israel's simultaneous withdrawal from the West Bank and Gaza. Still, Saddam had now signaled that he was searching for a way to terminate the war. His most important aim was his own regime's survival, and to achieve that, he might need to declare victory and pull out of Kuwait sooner than he had forecasted. As he admitted to his colleagues, "It is better to withdraw the troops yourself, instead of the enemy doing it for you!"[21]

George H. W. Bush, too, signaled new thinking: for the first time, the president openly tried to incite an Iraqi military coup or a popular uprising to remove Saddam Hussein from power. He spoke on February 15 as he dismissed Saddam's announced "concessions." He said there was "another way for the bloodshed to stop. And that is for the Iraqi military and the Iraqi people to take matters into their own hands and force Saddam Hussein, the dictator, to step aside and then comply with the United Nations resolution."[22]

The C.I.A. translated Bush's remarks into Arabic and broadcast them into Iraq. The president and the C.I.A. had embarked on an unusually transparent effort to overthrow an enemy dictator. It seemed logical to Bush and Scowcroft that Iraqis would want to rid themselves of Saddam after he had led the country into yet another fiasco so soon after the war with Iran. Yet the C.I.A. had no insider contacts in Baghdad to mobilize. Bush was taking a shot in the dark.[23]

At the Kremlin on February 18, Tariq Aziz met Gorbachev and announced that Iraq would not surrender.

"Your stand seems very inconsistent," Gorbachev noted. He again offered Soviet support if the Iraqis would announce a complete departure from Kuwait with "no strings attached." Moscow would negotiate to make certain that departing troops would not be attacked. "You must act without delay."[24]

Aziz flew back to Baghdad, via Iran, and consulted with Saddam, then returned to Moscow. He reported that Iraq could not complete a withdrawal quickly—a pullout would take many weeks. Gorbachev called Bush, who was on the verge of announcing a final deadline for Iraq's withdrawal—under his ultimatum, if Saddam did not demonstrably withdraw, the ground war would commence.

Although skeptical, Bush carefully allowed Gorbachev room to work. The Soviets negotiated with Aziz through the night. Primakov felt that they "made some progress." Bush's deadline arrived, and the president ordered the U.S.-led ground war to begin. Six hours later, Aziz announced from Moscow that Iraq had agreed to the immediate withdrawal of all its forces from Kuwait, yet he again attached conditions.

Gorbachev called Bush to say that the Iraqi position was new enough to warrant a delay of the ground war. By then, however, United States Marines were already shooting their way into Kuwait City. Bush did not want to lose Gorbachev's support, but "neither could we be dissuaded from our goal."[25]

American commanders worried again about whether Saddam would gas U.S. soldiers and Marines or use germ weapons. They tried to draw blood samples from Iraqi prisoners of war to determine if they had been vaccinated against anthrax, an indication of Iraqi intentions. Through diplomatic channels, the Bush administration passed to Baghdad another round of warnings: if you resort to chemical or biological arms, we will retaliate with everything we have. But the messages were probably unnecessary. The available records suggest that Saddam had decided in January, as the air war began, not to use the chemical and biological arsenal he had deployed. In the available records, he did not return to the possibility of using these weapons as the war went on.

Gorbachev wrote to Saddam. His telegram reached Iraq's Ministry of Foreign Affairs just before dawn on February 24. Saddam gathered that morning with advisers. He had lost hope that the Soviet premier could rescue him, but he asked an aide to read aloud the message. "President Bush keeps pushing . . . and he is not willing to agree to our proposal," Gorbachev reported. "He is doing this because he believes Iraq is planning to burn the Kuwait oil fields. . . . It is very important that you withdraw your forces to the 1990 location before the war, without delay."[26]

Saddam soon sent a message to Moscow saying that he was "very satisfied" with Gorbachev's telegram. Privately, to his comrades, he dismissed Gorbachev as one more conspirator against him. "I knew he would betray us, this liar," Saddam told Aziz.[27]

Iraq had deployed about three hundred thousand troops to occupy Kuwait. But Saddam held the regime's most effective Republican Guard divisions in reserve positions spread across southern Iraq. Saddam clearly did not want to expose his crack troops to entrapment by advancing coalition tanks and infantry. His invasion of Kuwait was a gambit to enlarge his regime's wealth and prestige, but he showed caution to the end about risking key divisions—and therefore his own security—in this piratical adventure.

General H. Norman Schwarzkopf commanded more than seven hundred thousand troops in Saudi Arabia, and his attacking forces included storied names from American, British, and French military history. The U.S. 1st and 2nd Marine Divisions would drive directly into Kuwait and capture Kuwait City. Two corps with elements including Britain's 1st Armored Division, France's Daguet Division, and the U.S. Army's 82nd Airborne Division, 101st Airborne Division, 3rd Armored Division, and 1st Infantry Division would flank Iraqi forces from the west and directly assault the Republican Guard deployed outside Kuwait.

As the campaign unfolded on February 24, Saddam Hussein basked in optimistic reports fed to him by Baath Party advisers. He spent the day offering ad hoc tactical instructions while drafting propaganda messages and musing aloud about his endgame.

"They are going to attack by land," Saddam acknowledged. "Good! They will be defeated."[28]

The enemy was about to launch a counterattack on an Iraqi armored brigade? "Nothing to worry about so far," he commented. The enemy has claimed to have captured an Iraqi-controlled island? "The situation is good and under control." He read out a draft message for broadcast to the Iraqi people: "In general, our troops are in the best possible shape given the current situation. . . . The situation is under excellent control."

At one point, Tariq Aziz popped into the meeting, having arrived in Baghdad after another arduous trip from Moscow, this time via Jordan.

"What a pleasant surprise!" Saddam exclaimed. "Are you up to surprises like Bush?"

Aziz sounded unusually bitter about the failure of his diplomatic efforts. He blamed Soviet appeasement of Washington and Bush's intransigence. Iraq needed to create leverage now on the battlefield. "If we do not cause them to bleed, we will not get any results."

"Yes," Saddam agreed.

"They have been striking us for thirty-eight days and they have not suffered any losses," Aziz continued. "We suffered a lot of material losses, so let them loose and let them get slaughtered. . . . This is what is going to help us get results."

Gorbachev had "tricked us," Saddam complained. The French had gone over to the dark side and joined the war fully.

"The French are attacking?" Aziz asked, apparently surprised.

"They are attacking."

"The French?"

"Yes."

"This Mitterrand is a fox," Aziz said.

"Mitterrand is very despicable," Saddam agreed.

"Despicable."[29]

Saddam had an uncanny ability to think positively about the longer run, even in the midst of disaster. About the Americans, he reflected: "Time will sort things out. With time, America will end up with England and a few of the [Gulf kingdom] oil countries. This coalition is not going to last forever." He was already thinking about how, having survived and "won" the war, he might eventually divide Washington from allies such as France.

He was also sanguine, less shrewdly, about the resilience of his own population. "I believe that the people of this country will completely understand our situation," he said.

By the following day, February 25, Saddam had decided that a full withdrawal from Kuwait, accompanied by declarations of victory, was the best of bad choices. Saddam called Lieutenant General Husayn Rashid Muhammad in Basra to deliver the order. "Husayn, I do not want our army to panic," Saddam said. "Our soldiers do not like humiliation; they like to uphold their pride." But they had to withdraw.[30]

The Iraqi retreat quickly became a catastrophe. Torched Kuwaiti oil wells ignited towering, otherworldly fireballs across the desert, blackening the skies with toxic smoke. Dead camels lay splayed on Kuwait's beaches. An oil slick fifty miles long and twelve miles wide spilled across the Persian Gulf. On a ribbon of carnage leading out of Kuwait City toward Basra—the "Highway of Death," as journalists soon labeled it—bombed, charred Iraqi vehicles sprawled across the road and nearby desert, stalled in the midst of desperate escape, like unlucky entrants in a demolition derby from *Mad Max*.

On the night of Tuesday, February 26, the coalition flew 3,159 air sorties, the largest number of any day in the war. The aircraft attacked not only Iraqi armor but also these civilian cars, buses, trucks, and flatbeds, which were hauling as much loot from Kuwait as they could carry: "pianos, toilets, sinks, entire kitchens, light fixtures, furniture, tires, tools, medical supplies, clothing, foodstuffs, construction materials—everything," as an intelligence officer in Schwarzkopf's command center recalled. Of nearly two thousand destroyed Iraqi vehicles on two evacuation roads, only 2 percent were tanks or armored personnel carriers, a later study found. Thousands of surviving Iraqi foot soldiers surrendered to allied troops.[31]

"He is not withdrawing," Bush said at the White House. "His defeated forces are retreating. He is trying to claim victory in the midst of a rout." The president promised to fight on with "undiminished intensity," but in reality, Colin Powell, chairman of the Joint Chiefs, was already prepared to recommend a cease-fire, and he believed that commanding general Schwarzkopf agreed. The grisly aerial images of the highways out of Kuwait provided visceral evidence that Iraq was defeated.[32]

The Iraqi departure from Kuwait fulfilled a principal war aim of the Bush administration, but not the only one. Coalition air strikes had targeted Iraq's known nuclear, chemical, and biological facilities, and had also tried to pulverize the Republican Guard divisions spread across southern Iraq. But while C.I.A. and D.I.A. analysts poring over photos from spy planes and satellites could count a significant number of Iraqi tanks damaged or destroyed, it was difficult to judge from aerial imagery the Republican Guard's prospects for survival to fight another day.

That afternoon, Washington time, Bush held a series of war councils in the Oval Office.

Powell spoke about the dangers of smashing a helpless enemy on exposed roads. "We don't want to be killing for the sake of killing, Mr. President," he said. The chairman spoke to some of Bush's most heartfelt misgivings—the ones that he had admonished himself about, before the war, in a diary entry.

"We do not want to lose anything now with charges of brutalization," Bush said. "We do not want to screw this up with a sloppy, muddled ending."

He proposed to declare victory that night on national television. The president, Powell, and Cheney all felt that the U.S. military's performance had vanquished the ghosts of Vietnam and that they should seize the moment to clarify this achievement for the American people, without getting further bogged down in fighting remnants of the defeated Iraqi Army.

"What's Norm think?" the president asked.

Powell spoke to Schwarzkopf by satellite phone from the Oval Office. "The thinking is that we should end it today," he reported. "Would you have any problem with that?"

"I don't have any problem with it."[33]

They decided that the president would declare a "cessation of hostilities" following a one-hundred-hour ground war—the round number adding a punctuation mark to the impression of a swift, decisive victory. Yet Bush remained unsettled, worried that Saddam's survival in power would indeed muddle the war's ending. He called King Fahd to ask about the chances of Saddam "being thrown out by his disillusioned people." Bush continued, "If there is anything the United States can do to have him pushed out, I'd be very interested to hear it."[34]

The armored flanking maneuver—the "left hook," as it became known—thrown against the Republican Guard proved much less decisive than any of the American commanders understood at the time. The plan had been for coalition armored forces of the VII Corps and the XVIII Corps on the coalition's western flank to charge across the desert and finish the Guard off. Yet the plan did not account for the confusing disarray of Saddam's sudden pullout from Kuwait or his determination to rescue as much of the Republican Guard as possible in the war's closing hours. In the end, as many as a third of the Guard's top-line Soviet-made T-72 tanks deployed to the war escaped destruction. But this was merely an asterisk. Despite the Guard's partial escape, Iraq's military had been pummeled, with much of its air force lost and much of its armor and artillery destroyed.

"Kuwait is liberated," Bush told the American public in a prime-time address on February 27. "Iraq's army is defeated. Our military objectives are met."[35]

A decade later, after 9/11, the question of whether Bush stopped too soon and missed an opportunity to drive on to Baghdad to depose Saddam informed his son's decision to invade Iraq. At the time, however, the matter was not seriously debated, and there was no dissent in Bush's war cabinet, not even from the future Iraq hawk Dick Cheney. Occupying Baghdad would far exceed the war's U.N. mandate and would undermine the realpolitik agreements that undergirded the U.S.-led coalition. It would deprive America of the chance to break free from Vietnam's legacy with a clear, decisive victory. Neither Powell nor Cheney voiced disagreement with Bush's decision at the time, and neither expressed regret in retrospect. Both men acknowledged that perhaps, with the benefit of hindsight, they might have fought the Republican Guard for another day or two before standing down, to inflict greater damage on Saddam's elite force. But as Cheney later put it, "You'd be hard-pressed to argue" that this missed opportunity "fundamentally altered the strategic landscape."[36]

Privately, Bush worried less about Iraq's tanks than about Saddam's shameless claims that he had won the war. Perhaps his propaganda would resonate in the Arab world, Bush feared. Early the next morning, the president dictated to his diary: "Still no feeling of euphoria. I think I know why it is. After my speech last night, Baghdad radio started broadcasting that we've been forced to capitulate. . . . It is such a canard, so little, but it's what concerns me. It hasn't been a clean end."[37]

It was about to get messier still.

THIRTEEN

Iraqi Spring

n Abu Ghraib's cell blocks for political prisoners, the Gulf War was a distant thunder. Hussain Al-Shahristani, the nuclear scientist and former colleague of Jafar Dhia Jafar, found himself transferred to a new area where he could meet other prisoners for the first time in years. After a decade of prolonged isolation, the opportunity to talk with other inmates was uplifting, even if the stories many told of their experiences of torture and cruelty were grim.

One day, the scientist encountered members of the famous family of Shia scholars from Najaf, the Hakims. The men had been arrested in 1983. They had essentially been taken as hostages in an attempt to influence Muhammad Baqir al-Hakim, the exiled leader of the Supreme Council for the Islamic Revolution in Iraq (SCIRI). This was an Iraqi organization founded in Tehran in November 1982 with the blessing of Ayatollah Khomeini. Led by Iraqis, SCIRI promoted Iran's goal of replacing Saddam Hussein's regime with clerical rule. Saddam's security services imprisoned Hakim family members still living in Iraq in an effort to influence Muhammad Baqir. In one instance, several family members had been executed in the presence of a family elder, who was then sent to Iran to inform Muhammad Baqir. The Hakims at Abu Ghraib had somehow survived this bloody brinkmanship, but they were serving long sentences.[1]

Shahristani still thought about escaping. He reconnected with Ali Aryan, the prisoner who had helped him earlier and who continued to clean uniforms and repair vehicles for the prison's intelligence officers. Shahristani and Ali decided that, amidst the chaos of the war outside, the time had come to act. They refined their plan. Ali would arrange to keep a Mukhabarat SUV overnight, on the pretense of needing to work on it. He would then steal an officer's uniform for Shahristani to wear. With the scientist then posing as an intelligence officer, they would drive out of the prison as if they were members of the Mukhabarat.

Shahristani informed his nephew and his wife, Berniece. If he and Ali made it out of Abu Ghraib, they would pick up the family in Baghdad and drive north to Kurdistan, then from there try to escape into Iran. Ali invited a third prisoner who knew the border areas of Kurdistan. Shahristani brought in a member of the Hakim family, Jafar. His presence might help them gain entry into Iran, if they got that far.

On a cold night in mid-February, Shahristani waited for the prisoner count after dinner, then snuck into a storage room to hide and wait for Ali Aryan. The two other members of the escape party joined him. Hours passed. Around ten o'clock, the door swung open. Ali stepped in carrying a single dark-olive uniform shirt and a matching scarf. He had not been able to find uniform pants, so Shahristani kept on his prison pajamas, hoping they would not be noticed.

They walked to the garage and piled into the Mukhabarat's SUV. Ali took the wheel, and Shahristani sat beside him, the other two in back. Ali gunned toward the first gate, flashing his high beams. Shahristani wrapped his face and neck in his scarf to obscure his features. A guard approached to inspect them, but the scientist waved him off, and Ali blinded him with the high beams. The guard backed down and scurried to open the gate. They powered like this through two more barriers. Soon they were on the road to Baghdad, with no one on their tail. They picked up Berniece, the Shahristanis' three children, and the scientist's nephew. They dumped the Mukhabarat SUV, and as dawn broke, they jammed themselves into a civilian car and drove out of Baghdad toward Kurdistan.

Eleven years and two months after secret police drove him away blindfolded from his office at the Tuwaitha Nuclear Research Center, Hussain Al-Shahristani was free—and on the run.[2]

The Bush administration thought hard about the public symbolism that would attend the Gulf War's ending. How could the U.S.-led coalition amplify Saddam Hussein's defeat before the world? Colin Powell and H. Norman Schwarzkopf had discussed holding cease-fire talks with Iraqi counterparts on the deck of the U.S.S. *Missouri*, the battleship where Japan's leaders surrendered to Douglas MacArthur and allied commanders on September 2, 1945. The idea reflected President Bush's desire to endow his battle against Saddam Hussein with the moral and strategic clarity of the Second World War. After years in mothballs, the *Missouri* had been modernized and recommissioned in 1986, so it was available as a theatrical set, but transporting an Iraqi delegation to a warship in the Gulf amidst the disarray in Kuwait looked like a "complicated if not impossible undertaking," Schwarzkopf concluded. He settled on Safwan, an Iraqi airfield just over the border from Kuwait. It was not much to look at—a slab of asphalt on a featureless plain beneath a barren bluff. But Schwarzkopf ordered his subordinates to create a vivid display of American firepower to intimidate the Iraqi generals dispatched by Saddam for negotiations. At the scene, Lieutenant General William Pagonis erected a giant flagpole bearing the Stars and Stripes and deployed dozens of fully armed tanks, Bradley Fighting Vehicles, and Apache helicopters around the olive-green tents where talks would take place.[3]

Lieutenant General Sultan Hashim Ahmad al-Tai led the Iraqi delegation. He was a proud, youthful-looking man with a full face. On

Sunday, March 3, 1991, after assembling with colleagues in Basra, he rode out to meet Schwarzkopf.

The Iraqis wore black berets and uniforms with full insignia. They drove to a junction near Safwan and transferred into American Humvees escorted by armored vehicles and Apache attack helicopters hovering low. "The Americans had prepared a military show to flex their muscle and display [their] arrogance," Sultan Hashim recalled. To provide security, it seemed to him, the enemy had selected soldiers who were "fit with large physiques, as if they were handpicked and brought there to impress us."[4]

Schwarzkopf, too, arrived in a dyspeptic mood. He had embarked from his war room that morning "determined to conduct the cease-fire talks in a calm, levelheaded, professional way." But flying up from Kuwait City in a Black Hawk helicopter, he saw dark plumes and licking flames from oil fires for miles around. The tableau triggered his temper. "By the time we set down at Safwan, I was just plain mad."

"I'm not here to give them anything," the general told reporters dramatically as he walked to receive the Iraqi delegation. "I'm here to tell them exactly what they have to do."[5]

The goal of the talks was to fashion an indefinite military cease-fire and to resolve issues such as the release of prisoners of war. The Bush administration had sent a formal agenda through Moscow to Baghdad, and the Iraqi generals had come prepared with documents.

The commanders took seats around a plain rectangular wooden table set with bottled water and a single Diet Pepsi for Schwarzkopf. He announced that the meeting would be recorded and that an audio file would be provided to the Iraqis. On prisoners, Sultan Hashim was immediately forthcoming. He provided a list of the two to three dozen American and allied servicemen held in Iraqi custody and pledged that the Red Cross would be allowed "immediate access."

Schwarzkopf presented a map with a proposed cease-fire line that would separate U.S. and allied forces from Iraqi troops so that "young men with weapons" on both sides would not be tempted to skirmish.

The line sliced through Iraqi territory north of the Kuwaiti border. Sultan Hashim blanched—it looked as if Washington had decided to annex part of Iraq for Kuwait, perhaps as restitution.

"It is absolutely not a permanent line," Schwarzkopf clarified. "It has nothing to do with borders. It is only a safety measure."[6]

The Iraqis acquiesced, but not before delivering a bitter complaint that the U.S. and its allies had unnecessarily invaded Iraq after Saddam had announced a withdrawal from Kuwait. Schwarzkopf said he didn't want to get into an argument. "I think we will leave it to history."

"I have just mentioned it for history," Sultan Hashim replied.

Finally, Schwarzkopf asked if the Iraqis had any issues they wished to introduce.

"We have one point," Sultan Hashim said. Iraqi lines of transport and communication had been destroyed. "We would like to fly helicopters to carry officials of our government in areas where roads and bridges are out. This has nothing to do with the front line. This is inside Iraq."

Schwarzkopf readily agreed. Sultan Hashim had been cooperative on the American demands, and this seemed a "legitimate" request. Schwarzkopf stipulated that no fixed-wing aircraft could fly, and that the helicopters must stay away from allied lines, but this would otherwise be "absolutely no problem."

"You mean even helicopters that are armed can fly in Iraqi skies, but not the fighters?" Sultan Hashim clarified, referring to Iraqi fighter jets.

Yes, Schwarzkopf said. He conceded later that the reference to armed aircraft "should have given me pause." But he did not understand why the Iraqis might now want to fly armed helicopters within their borders.[7]

Saad Ibn Abi Waqqas Square is a large Basra plaza where major roads join in a cloverleaf. On the morning Schwarzkopf negotiated in Safwan, thousands of Iraqi protestors with fists and voices raised poured into the square to demand the end of Saddam Hussein's rule. Many of them were armed soldiers who had deserted or civilians toting the personal weapons common in Iraqi households. They shot at posters of Saddam. In the crowd, carrying a rifle, was Qasim Albrisem, a young University of Basra lecturer who had a doctoral degree in phonetics from the University of Exeter, in Britain.

Like many Iraqis, he had seethed at the devastation wrought by Saddam's wars with Iran and America. The burden had fallen heavily on the Shia-majority south, where he lived. The death toll from the Gulf War in the Basra Governorate was the highest in Iraq, more than double that in Sunni-majority areas from where Saddam drew much of his support. During the Gulf War, "we revolted in our soul, in our spirit," Albrisem recalled. "The beginning of the uprising started inside ourselves before it was expressed outwardly."[8]

In those first days of March, smoke from Kuwait's oil fires stifled breath, even in Basra. Albrisem heard rumors of protests. He drove around the city in his car, encouraging revolt. The people he encountered did not need much urging. He saw gunfights between armed citizens and Baathist security forces, and he watched the government men retreat. In central Basra, the regime's security forces fired on restive crowds. The rebels soon deployed mortars and shelled the Baath Party's offices. In the broiling streets, there were few leaders and no clear common cause beyond the overthrow of the regime.[9]

The justice they sought was bloody and unforgiving. Crowds lynched, shot, and physically ripped apart Baath Party bureaucrats, police, and suspected intelligence officers. Terrified government officials abandoned their posts by the hundreds. A regime report later tried to make sense of the rebels' violence. First, there were those would-be revolutionaries belonging to the Iran-based Shia opposition, such as the Dawa Party and the Supreme Council for the Islamic Revolution in Iraq. These were "sectarian gangs," who sought political power "violently and by physical force" because they "feel that they are oppressed . . . and that their rights are violated." In addition, there were the spontaneous crowds of citizens who looted and carried out summary justice, "the immoral masses . . . the masses of frenzy, indecency, ill-manners, drinking." The assessment was self-serving but not wholly inaccurate.[10]

"There was urgency, an instinctive direction to the movement of the crowd as they destroyed one building after another," Albrisem recalled. By the second or third day, effectively, Saddam Hussein's government in Iraq's second-largest city ceased to exist.

The 1991 Iraqi uprisings became a broad and popular rebellion, yet there were fractures from the start. Some of the protesters were less observant Muslims, like Albrisem. Others cried out "Allahu Akbar" and the slogans of Shiite political parties. Some held up pictures of Iran's Ayatollah Khomeini. Iraqi exiles from the Badr Brigade—the armed wing of the Tehran-based Supreme Council for the Islamic Revolution in Iraq—immediately saw a chance to return home to jumpstart an Islamic revolution inspired by Iran's example. But the brigade's history as an Iranian proxy force alienated Iraqis in Basra and elsewhere. The visible efforts by Iran-based rebels to hijack the uprising also gave Saddam Hussein a ready propaganda line to rally his troops for a counterattack: the rebellion was an Iranian invasion, he soon trumpeted.[11]

Ali Hassan al-Majid, "Chemical Ali," happened to be in Basra when the revolution broke out. He was returning from his tour as governor of occupied Kuwait. At a military base outside the city center, he took command of the counterrevolution in the south.

Majid drew on the firepower of four loyal Republican Guard divisions and four additional Guard brigades, plus a unit of the Special Republican Guard, according to evidence later presented in Iraqi courts. On about March 5, Majid entered Basra with a phalanx of armor and infantry. Tanks blasted buildings held by rebels. Bulldozers destroyed the homes of families identified as insurgents. Soldiers ordered to expel "foreign" Iranian radicals gunned down lightly armed civilians.[12]

The Republican Guards fired "randomly, destroying electricity posts and houses," Albrisem recalled. At his checkpoint, where he and his comrades held only Kalashnikovs and a few rocket-propelled grenade launchers, they resisted for about ninety minutes and suffered three fatalities before retreating. Albrisem darted through backstreets, hid at a friend's home, and then made his way to his brother's place in another part of the city.

Majid ordered Baath Party members—civilians and security men—to conduct house-to-house searches and to supervise interrogations and detentions. Party security turned up at the home of Albrisem's brother, arrested the linguist, and brought him to Saad Square. Dead bodies littered the streets. He joined several hundred detainees—a mass of cowering men seemingly put on display, like slaves in a Roman triumph, as public evidence of the government's return to authority. "Our group became bigger and bigger as more blindfolded and handcuffed people were thrown to the ground beside us," he recalled. Rumors of arbitrary cruelty now filled the rebels with dread. Baath Party men forced suspected rebels to drink gasoline and then shot them in the stomach to see if they would explode, according to a persistent story that circulated among survivors.[13]

By about March 10, Majid had reestablished control over central Basra. He turned up personally at detention centers, flanked by a leather-jacketed entourage. Majid carried a Kalashnikov on his shoulder and made a display of his warlordism. He later admitted that he personally shot to death "numerous" detainees he judged to be traitors. He shot other victims with a rocket-propelled grenade and dropped a live grenade down one prisoner's shirt to execute him, according to survivor testimony.[14]

Around the time Ali Hassan al-Majid retook Basra, Abbas Kadhim traveled to his home in Najaf, the city in south-central Iraq that houses the Shrine of Imam Ali, a gold-domed mosque and tomb, inlaid with blue mosaics, that rises above low-slung buildings in a dense quarter. The shrine is one of the holiest places in the Shia tradition because

Ali, the Prophet's son-in-law, is said to be buried there. Kadhim was in his midtwenties; he had recently completed military service. He was stunned to find Najaf in the hands of its citizens. "The government and its authorities were dismembered," he recalled. "Weapons were lying on the street, abandoned, all over the place. . . . Iraqi soldiers returning from Kuwait would trade their rifles for a loaf of bread."[15]

By far the most important authority in Najaf outside the Baath Party was the Hawza clergy, or the Shia religious authorities. They were led by Grand Ayatollah Abu al-Qasim al-Khoei, a scholar in his nineties. The Baath Party had infiltrated the Hawza, but the ayatollah had preserved a measure of independence. Grand Ayatollah Khoei now formed a committee of Najaf religious scholars to try to manage the local uprising. His sons participated at the barricades. But the ayatollah did not see himself as a political revolutionary. Knowing that a counterattack was inevitable, he told his followers, "I am their target. If you stay away from me, you will be safe."[16]

The absence of adequate weapons and well-practiced organization proved to be a vulnerability in city after city as the rebellion spread to Amarah, Karbala, and Nasiriyah, as well as scores of suburbs, market towns, and villages. The Communist and Dawa Parties that Saddam had long battled joined the revolution, as did the Supreme Council. Yet if the diverse rebels were to sustain their sudden gains, they would require outside support and military protection. Many of the protesters across the south had heard President Bush's repeated calls for the Iraqi people to take matters into their own hands, to rid their country of Saddam Hussein. Now they had started to do so. Kadhim was among the hopeful: "We thought that America would help."[17]

O you soldier and civilian, young man and old, O you women and men: Let's fill the streets and alleys and bring down Saddam Hussein and his aides." So exhorted a psyops leaflet dropped by U.S. aircraft on Iraq during the campaign to liberate Kuwait. These fluttering messages, along with clandestine broadcasts by the C.I.A.'s radio

stations and the explicit public words of President Bush, helped to incite the popular revolt.[18]

In a preview of the American-led war in Iraq that lay in the future,
the Bush administration had failed to adequately plan for postwar political scenarios, including the very one it actively promoted. American
decision-making in the days following the Safwan cease-fire "was
ragged," conceded Richard Haass, the White House policymaker on
the Middle East. He recalled an "unfortunate loss of focus and letting
up after seven months of nonstop crisis."

Bush administration planners considered an insider coup carried out
by military officers to be most likely and most desirable—a quick change
of regime that would leave Iraq in the hands of a more manageable
strongman. "We made some very overoptimistic assumptions," recalled
David Mack, then at the State Department. "We assumed the chances
were great" that military officers would move against Saddam.[19]

C.I.A. analysts judged the revolt that spread across the south in
early March to be Saddam Hussein's "most serious political challenge
in more than twenty years of power." Yet inside the administration, "it
was a very painful period where all we were doing was reacting," recalled Ellen Laipson, then vice-chair of the National Intelligence Council. "We didn't think this through: 'What if this traumatized population
actually thinks that America is going to come to the rescue?'" The
Bush administration explained its refusal to back the revolt it had in-
cited by saying that it wished to respect Iraq's sovereignty, a risible position. "We don't think that outside powers should be interfering in the
internal affairs of Iraq," said State spokesman Richard Boucher.[20]

They did consider options, such as covert weapons deliveries to the
Iraqi rebels of Basra and other southern cities, or launching American
air strikes to protect rebel-controlled territory. James Baker, Colin Powell, Brent Scowcroft, and ultimately President Bush came down against
such interventions, however. Powell argued that any action would require synchronizing U.S. military power with eclectic, often leaderless
rebel groups. He advised, recalled Haass, that "telling the good guys
from the bad . . . would be all but impossible." The decision-makers

were conditioned, too, by the assumptions of their tilt toward Iraq during the previous decade: Iran had to be contained, and they preferred a
united, militarily capable Iraq to achieve this. The Badr Brigade's presence among the rebels, waving photos of Khomeini, only reinforced this
outlook.[21]

Saddam kept up a calm and confident front in private as the rebellion spread, but gradually, he confronted the truth that not only had
he been humiliated in Kuwait but much of Iraq had suddenly fallen out
of his control. His close relatives were willing this once—with their
necks on the line—to convey the hard facts. "We are supposed to present you with the complete truth," Hussein Kamel declared at a crisis
meeting. As the Iraqi Army had withdrawn from Kuwait, its morale
had plunged to "the lowest level anyone could ever reach."

"What, exactly, are you trying to say?" Saddam asked his son-in-law
sharply. "You are the only one who feels that way about the Army."

Hussein Kamel stood his ground. He recounted what he had witnessed firsthand in cities seized by rebels. At one intelligence office,
the people he met "appeared very depressed. . . . They appeared
hateful—honestly, sir, you know I only tell the truth. I was very anxious, like never before in my life! I felt that our nation with its large
population [is] full of negative feelings towards us. . . . They all turned
into a hateful enemy."[22]

Saddam had not survived so long by ignoring matters relevant to his
personal security. He still explained away the rebellion as an American-
Iranian conspiracy organized by infiltrators from Iran. Yet he recognized "the feeling of defeat" among Iraqi forces in the Gulf War, "which
spread to the government offices. . . . The defeat was psychological."
He despaired over the poor leadership and indiscipline in his armed
forces. "What standards do we have! I don't want this to be written in
history or in any document or to be published. But it's a fact."[23]

For periods of days, first in the south and later in the Kurdish north,
Saddam's regime lost control of all but four of Iraq's provinces.

Crucially, the rebellion did not catch fire in Baghdad. Saddam later acknowledged to comrades that there had indeed "been trouble" in the capital during March, but because the regime acted decisively, "the repression occurred immediately."

Saddam used the breathing space he enjoyed in Baghdad to issue orders authorizing harsh measures against all rebels elsewhere in the country—including summary execution for unarmed looters and curfew violators. He worked the telephone to appoint and motivate on-scene commanders, but he also delegated dictatorial powers to loyalists. He appointed Majid as minister of the interior and Hussein Kamel as minister of defense. On March 9, he endowed members of the Revolutionary Command Council and the Baath Party's regional commands with "the powers of the President of the Republic to punish and reward." His loyalists would have to put down the rebellion by making their own decisions. He soon made explicit by written order that any Iraqi reasonably suspected of participating in the rebellion should be executed.[24]

Hussein Kamel, assigned to lead the counterattack against the holy cities of Najaf and Karbala, ordered preparations for the use of chemical weapons. Helicopter gunships loaded up with R-400 gravity bombs containing sarin and flew missions against rebel groupings. They dropped an estimated one to two dozen gas bombs before commanders concluded that the bombs were ineffective—the weapons had been designed to be dropped from higher altitudes than the helicopters could manage. Instead, Iraqi forces used those helicopters to launch more than two hundred tear-gas bombs on rebels around Najaf and Karbala. The victims had little way to distinguish tear gas from lethal chemical arms, so the attacks sowed panic and helped break the resistance.[25]

Republican Guard tanks—some stenciled with the slogan "No Shiites After Today"—rumbled toward Najaf, Nasiriyah, Karbala, and Hillah. Artillery units softened their targets by shelling indiscriminately from a distance. Helicopter gunships swooped over rooftops and opened fire with heavy-caliber machine guns. As they neared rebel barricades, tank commanders shelled homes and heedlessly pounded the sacred shrines revered across the Shia world. American bombing during the Gulf War had destroyed water and power plants in Basra and elsewhere, leaving the population without electricity or piped water. Now the sacking of government offices by rebels, followed by regime counterstrikes, completed the ruin of Iraqi cities.

The first wave of regime reprisals across the south took place in an atmosphere of uncontrolled rage. In Hillah, a survivor reported, soldiers charged into a hospital where wounded rebels had sought treatment. The soldiers chased patients and family members onto an upper floor and then hurled people—including at least one doctor—out the windows. A similar attack took place in a hospital in Amarah. Carrying a weapon or having a weapon in one's home—a commonplace just weeks earlier—suddenly became a capital offense. Neighbors denounced neighbors for having held up handmade protest signs or for having erected checkpoints. In Najaf and elsewhere, soldiers lined up male rebels in public squares, schoolyards, or fields, tied their hands behind their backs, and forced them to denounce one another. The authorities would ask a prisoner to stand up and would assure him that he would be set free if he named ten traitors, Kadhim recounted. If he complied, they let him go, while sending those denounced to waiting trucks, to be carried away and, in many cases, never seen again. Soldiers executed some detainees in public, imprisoned and interrogated others under torture, and dumped hundreds of corpses into rivers, canals, or mass graves.[26]

Saddam's commanders surveyed the battlefield from helicopters and directed ground operations, according to a regime after-action study. The helicopters were considered "the best means available to the commander to keep informed on the course of the battle, giving directions to his troops," the study found.[27]

In Najaf, Kadhim watched as forces of the Republican Guard's 41st Armored Brigade blasted into the old city on March 13. Police marked the houses that had checkpoints in front of them and bulldozed those homes into rubble. On March 15, "orders were given . . . to attack the Imam Ali shrine and purge it," a regime after-action study recounted.

As tanks rolled in, many in the rebellion fled. Kadhim fell in with multitudes escaping across the border into Saudi Arabia, where they became refugees. In Najaf, the aged Grand Ayatollah Khoei was arrested and taken to Baghdad. The regime executed most of the committee members the ayatollah had appointed to oversee the city's attempted revolution.[28]

By mid-March, a C.I.A. assessment judged that forces loyal to Saddam had "been able to contain much of the fighting" in Iraq's south and that Saddam "is probably secure as long as his intelligence and security services remain intact, the military backs him," and he is seen to retain power.[29]

On March 16, Saddam released a video of himself dressed in battle fatigues. He appeared at ease and blamed the rebellion on "herds of rancorous traitors, falsely bearing Iraqi identity, who infiltrated from inside and outside to . . . carve up Iraq and spread chaos, destruction, and devastation, and subjugate it to the will of the foreigner."[30]

The following day, two Iraqi generals returned to Safwan to meet General Robert Johnston, Schwarzkopf's chief of staff. The American commander had demanded the meeting after the Iraqis had declared an intention to fly some of their fighter planes—a clear violation of the cease-fire accord.

Johnston warned the Iraqi delegation that their planes would be shot down if they flew. But he only expressed "displeasure" about the use of helicopters to fire on Iraqi citizens. He said that the permission to fly them granted by Schwarzkopf "was never meant as a license for Iraqi aerial bombardment of its own population."[31]

The Iraqis replied that the uprising amounted to a covert invasion of Iraq by the Iranian Revolutionary Guard Corps. They offered to provide I.R.G.C. identity cards captured from infiltrators. Johnston let the matter drop. The meeting ended without any American initiative to stop Saddam from strafing or bombing Iraqis from helicopters.

This was how the White House preferred it, as the National Security Council's Richard Haass recalled: "Many of us in Washington viewed reversing the helicopter decision as starting down a slippery and dangerous slope that would have risked a quagmire." If the U.S. banned Iraq from flying helicopters, and the Iraqis then used tanks and artillery to slaughter civilians, "did that get us on the hook to go back in on the ground? . . . Saddam would have found other ways of repressing the opposition, and we were worried that essentially we would have to get involved directly on the ground, and that's what we wanted to avoid."[32]

Hussain Al-Shahristani and his escape party reached the mountain city of Sulaymaniyah, near the Iranian border, without incident. But they knew no one in the area. If they checked into a hotel, the clerks would demand documents that might expose them. They were low on cash and uncertain how to cross into Iran. But a sympathetic Kurdish stranger at a gas station offered them a house to stay in. Soon they moved to a second home owned by a man they knew as "Teacher Nouri." He became their protector. At prayer time, he escorted the group to a mosque where they met other sympathizers. Shahristani had no access to radio or television, but each day, Nouri would catch them up on Iraq's uprisings, on how the fire had spread from Basra to Karbala. At the mosque, people could talk of little else. Perhaps the Kurdish people's tragic history of failed rebellion had reached a new turning point. The town's population was "waiting to play their cards," Shahristani thought.

"Doctor, be ready," Nouri confided after several days.

"For what?"

"The peshmergas are going to come down from the mountains." He expected the armed rebels who had long fought for Kurdistan's independence to enter the town as soon as the following day.

The next morning, Shahristani joined Nouri at the gates of Sulaymaniyah to see what would happen. Sure enough, fighters packed into pickup trucks roared into town and opened fire on government buildings.[33]

A large metal eye decorated the city's secret police headquarters, to remind citizens of the Baath Party's powers of surveillance. Rebels poured through the gates and broke inside. Another frenzy of lynching and kangaroo courts followed. Rebels captured and summarily executed hundreds of Baath officials across Kurdistan, employing "iron saws and knives" as their victims "screamed and sobbed," as one witness described it. Police and intelligence officers switched sides "by force or willingly," to avoid ending up in the dock, a regime message recounted. Shahristani joined some of the rebels as they searched for political prisoners to free. They found only two survivors.[34]

Amidst the chaos, Shahristani decided to make the attempt to reach Iran. One morning, his escape party secured a ride in the back of a merchant's pickup truck. At the Iranian frontier, Jafar al-Hakim, the nephew of the Supreme Council leader in Tehran, proved to be their golden visa—his famous name was enough to get them across. That evening, in a nearby town, "for the first time in years," the Shahristani family enjoyed a "delicious meal, followed by a good rest." The scientist's exile from Iraq, destined to last about as long as his imprisonment, had begun.[35]

As the Iraqi uprisings spread to Kurdistan, the population took up arms anew. Erbil fell to Kurdish rebels and citizens around March 10. The paramilitaries of the two major Kurdish political parties swiftly captured Dohuk and many other towns, in addition to Sulaymaniyah. The battle for the strategic oil city of Kirkuk was fierce, and the Kurdish rebels took heavy losses, but they won control. At the apex, the rebels claimed to hold fifty thousand regime prisoners. "The result of seventy years of struggle" for Kurdish independence "is at hand now," declared Masoud Barzani, the leader of the Kurdistan Democratic Party. Occupying a pink-and-beige former villa of Saddam Hussein's, Barzani granted interviews to the foreign press. Elsewhere, crowds of liberated Kurds pasted the photographs of national heroes on city walls. In Erbil, they packed a movie theater to watch what a journalist described as a "poorly filmed amateur videocassette showing the gassing of Halabja."[36]

Their liberation was vanishingly brief. On March 10, confident of progress in the south, Ali Hassan al-Majid met with generals to plan a pivot to Kurdistan, his old killing field. He ordered a tactical retreat of regime forces, to concentrate fire on Erbil, Kirkuk, and Dohuk. He ordered curfews between 6:00 p.m. and 7:00 a.m. and instructed soldiers to shoot anyone on the streets during those hours who could not present a pass stamped in red ink. He demanded the execution of anyone caught carrying a weapon. The next day, he issued orders to "attack the stores and the fuel stations" in Erbil with helicopters, and to strike with "the maximum use of fire, with emphasis on the artillery, tanks and helicopters."[37]

As Saddam's forces recaptured territory, they took their own deranged vengeance. By the last days of March, tens of thousands of Kurds were in full retreat toward the Iranian and Turkish borders. Regime helicopters randomly strafed columns of civilians fleeing down the road from Erbil. In Tuz Khurmatu, south of Kirkuk, Iraqi soldiers massacred scores of civilians with automatic weapons, according to survivors. At a village east of Sulaymaniyah, regime soldiers reportedly burned to death about forty accused rebels.[38]

In a stunningly short period, about 750,000 Kurds fled Saddam's onslaught for Iran, and another 280,000 entered Turkey. When Ankara blocked the Turkish border, an additional 300,000 huddled in misery on Iraq's side. As many as 400 to 1,000 Kurdish civilians began to die each day because of a dearth of food, water, shelter, or sanitation. *Washington Post* reporter Jonathan Randal and the Australian-born writer Geraldine Brooks, then a reporter for *The Wall Street Journal*, joined the exodus to Turkey on foot. Around them were "retired civil servants in three-piece business suits, engineers, middle-class mothers with babes in arms," all suddenly desperate refugees. When they discovered the reporters' connections to America, they asked, "Why did you not finish Saddam off?"[39]

In Washington, on March 26, stunned by the images from the Turkish border, Bush met with his national security advisers to reconsider whether to intervene. The president decided firmly to take no military action. However, in early April, as the humanitarian crisis deepened, he sent Secretary of State James Baker to the region. The C.I.A.'s Charlie Seidel accompanied him. After evacuating Baghdad late in 1990, Seidel had taken a leading role for the agency in the Gulf War.

"We are not prepared to go down the slippery slope of being sucked into a civil war," Baker told reporters. "We cannot police what goes on inside Iraq, and we cannot be the arbiters of who shall govern Iraq." It was another strained formulation of policy, given the administration's open record of incitement to overthrow Saddam.[40]

Baker visited the sea of suffering along the Turkish frontier. He walked with Seidel and Turkish escorts in business suits through camps in treeless hills where tens of thousands of desperate Kurdish families huddled. Baker recognized that some sort of humanitarian response was required. Among other things, the crisis threatened to mar the political narrative of a clean victory in Kuwait. (The Bush administration was preparing a massive ticker-tape victory parade in Manhattan for early June.) Unlike in Iraq's south, where international journalists could not travel easily, if at all, newspaper and television reporters transmitted vivid daily reports of the hunger and death of helpless Kurds.

The administration soon organized Operation Provide Comfort, an intervention to protect Kurds from further attacks by Saddam's forces and prevent more Kurds from crossing into Turkey, which did not want them. The U.S. would also send food and medical aid. American C-130s and Chinook transport helicopters initially air-dropped military Meals Ready to Eat to refugees. The United Nations blessed the initiative. To provide space for aid delivery, U.S. armed forces ultimately created a "safe haven" in the north that extended sixty miles into Iraq. Bush did not seek Saddam's permission.

Unintentionally, this would become the first footprint of a U.S.-defended autonomous Kurdistan. To protect a much larger area of Kurdistan beyond the initial one, the Bush administration and European allies soon added to the safe haven a no-fly zone patrolled by Western fighter jets. Operation Provide Comfort was a reactive, improvisational policy, driven by the need to respond to a humanitarian emergency in which the United States was complicit. Bush and his advisers could hardly have imagined that the Kurdish no-fly zone would become a costly pillar of an ambiguous, frustrating U.S. commitment in Iraq for many years to come.

The reprisal killings carried out by Saddam's regime after the Iraqi uprisings rivaled the Anfal in scale and cruelty but never achieved the Anfal's global notoriety. The death toll from regime executions and counterattacks numbered in at least the low tens of thousands. Four mass graves containing hundreds of bodies were unearthed in Basra after 2003, but the violence and chaos that followed the U.S.-led invasion of that year prevented more careful and systematic searches. A regime after-action report about the rebellion in the Maysan Governorate—with a population of only about one million—put rebel losses at two thousand dead and one thousand missing. (It reported regime casualties at two hundred dead and as many as six hundred injured.) Add to that deaths under torture or during prolonged detention in hastily erected camps for political prisoners outside Baghdad and elsewhere. The Maysan report estimated that the regime had taken about five thousand prisoners in that governorate alone; Tariq Aziz told colleagues in the autumn of 1991 that regime security forces had detained fifteen thousand accused rebels. All of the available estimates are rough, but the large scale of detentions is clear, as is the evidence of executions of political prisoners—not only the first spasm of summary executions but also those ordered in carrying out sentences imposed during the months and years that followed.[41]

Fixing the nature of the Bush administration's responsibility for this tragedy requires some precision. It seems likely that retreating Iraqi soldiers and furious citizens would have risen up even if President Bush had not called upon them to do so. And it is true that the president's calls to the Iraqi people to take matters into their own hands did not contain an explicit promise that America would intervene to help them. But these caveats are hardly exculpatory. Schwarzkopf's decision to allow the Iraqis to fly armed helicopters after the cease-fire was an avoidable error that materially aided Saddam's counterattack, as the regime's own after-action study makes clear. Of course, Saddam's henchmen almost certainly would have crushed the disorganized rebellion even if the regime's helicopters had been grounded. Only a decision in Washington to establish full air cover for the liberated areas of south and central Iraq could have protected the rebellion's gains. Such an intervention was clearly not in the cards and likely would have empowered Iran. The administration rationalized its passivity at times by pointing out that Iran-based religious radicals had played a part in the uprising. But if a Shiite revolt collided with American interests, why call for an uprising in the first place? Unarguably, the administration had failed to anticipate and plan for the entirely plausible scenario that it confronted, thus contributing to a tragedy that would echo across generations and color darkly the attitudes of many Iraqis toward the intentions and good faith of the United States.

That April, Frank Anderson arrived at the C.I.A.'s headquarters in Langley to take charge of the Near East and South Asia Division of the Directorate of Operations, his stomping ground as a spy for most of his twenty-three years in the agency. In 1968, after a stint in the U.S. Army, he had joined the C.I.A., where he had studied Arabic. His assignments included three tours as station chief. Akin to Tom Twetten, the overall C.I.A. operations chief who had appointed him, Anderson worked more like a relationship-building diplomat than an adrenaline-fueled James Bond imitator. He was a white-haired man with a boyish face and an open smile. He believed that covert actions by the C.I.A.—attempts to remove foreign leaders from power, or to arm and train rebels, or to influence elections—worked best when they were aligned with a clear foreign policy that was embraced by all sections of the U.S. government.

Some weeks after Anderson had settled into his new job, he found himself at an off-site agency conference with Twetten, in one of those unmarked, blandly decorated centers the C.I.A. maintained across Virginia. At one point, during a meeting, Twetten took out a Top Secret binder and passed it over to Anderson. It contained a covert-action "finding" that President Bush had signed on May 5, 1991, authorizing the C.I.A. to foment conditions that would lead to Saddam's removal from power. (A finding is a legal document that authorizes the C.I.A. to spend taxpayer funds and break laws abroad while in pursuit of a specific foreign-policy objective.) This was a follow-on to the initial order Bush had sent to the C.I.A. just weeks after the invasion of Kuwait. It authorized a more deliberate postwar plan to seek Saddam's ouster.

Anderson flipped through the materials. He hadn't been much involved in the war to liberate Kuwait, or in the C.I.A.'s auxiliary efforts to sow dissent in Iraq. But he knew like everyone else who read the newspapers that Saddam had emerged from the war and the recent rebellions entrenched in power. Now President Bush was asking Anderson, in effect, to finish what the White House and the Pentagon and dozens of international allies had been unable to accomplish—getting Saddam.

Anderson scribbled a note for Twetten on the cover page of the binder—"I don't like this"—and slid it over to his boss.

Twetten wrote his own note: "It's part of your job." He slid the binder back.[42]

The dossier reflected Bush's undiminished conviction that he had to finish Saddam off, at least politically. Bush and Scowcroft had never intended to incite the kind of popular, leaderless rebellion that had taken place in March, both men later insisted. They had tried to target Saddam using lawful means during the bombing of Iraq. Now they hoped to inspire bitter and ambitious Iraqi military officers around him to stage a coup d'état. Iraq's postwar history offered little comfort about what sort of government would follow a successful coup, but the conflict had become highly personalized and the focus was on removing Saddam, backed by a vague hope that the next strongman would be better.

It's the colonel with the brigade patrolling his palace that's going to get him, if somebody gets him, Scowcroft thought.[43]

Reluctantly or not, it was now the C.I.A.'s new mission to find or inspire that colonel.

FOURTEEN

The Liar's Truths

During the war to liberate Kuwait, Jafar Dhia Jafar slept at his Baghdad home near the Republican Palace. American and allied warplanes struck targets around him; they also hit the Tuwaitha Nuclear Research Center. Early on, Jafar and scientists on the secret bomb program drove to the complex to look things over. They found that the two French research reactors—which had never operated after Israel's strike on them in 1981—had suffered new damage. But other facilities were unscathed. To preserve what they could, Jafar and his colleagues decided to remove undamaged equipment to less conspicuous places. This included the irradiated uranium fuel that, under Hussein Kamel's orders, Jafar's team had planned to refine for nuclear-bomb use during the autumn of 1990, before that project was overtaken by the war. They now sealed and packed the fuel and drove it to a nearby farm. The operation protected Baghdad from a possible environmental disaster if further American air strikes hit the cache and caused a release of deadly radiation. It also preserved an asset of Saddam's still-secret atomic-weapons program.[1]

When the war ended, it became clear to Jafar that the United States—backed by a united U.N. Security Council—would closely scrutinize Iraq's nuclear capabilities. He also knew that the C.I.A. and West German intelligence must already have some insights into Iraq's undeclared centrifuge program. Hussein Kamel's aggressive spending of millions of dollars on West German experts had attracted the interest of German criminal investigators, who had likely tipped off Western intelligence services. Jafar also learned that during the chaos of February's ground war and the popular uprisings of March, some Iraqi scientists and technicians had escaped to Saudi Arabia and Turkey. It seemed safe to assume that any scientist who became a refugee would be tempted to trade what they knew to the C.I.A. or Britain's MI6 in exchange for resettling assistance.[2]

On April 3, 1991, the U.N. Security Council adopted Resolution 687, which provided that Iraq would remain under strict economic sanctions until, among other things, it acknowledged and destroyed all of its nuclear, chemical, and biological weapons. Jafar assumed that Saddam would want to come clean about the past in order to gain sanctions relief. He drafted a disclosure paper for the U.N. that narrated the atomic-bomb program's history.

But at a meeting that spring, Hussein Kamel told Jafar that Iraq would not voluntarily confess. "Don't write about anything except the activities that are known already" by the International Atomic Energy Agency, he told the physicist, referring to the U.N.'s nuclear watchdog.

Jafar protested on practical grounds, he recalled. "We can never hide these programs," he said. The effort had grown so large that concealment would be impossible. The U.N. would send inspectors. It clearly possessed clues about where to search: during the Gulf War, U.S. warplanes had bombed Tarmiya, one of the places where Jafar had secretly pursued electromagnetic separation of highly enriched uranium. Moreover, Jafar's work there had required the manufacture of giant iron disks known as calutrons that were fifteen feet across and weighed up to seventy tons each. There were about twenty-five of the disks at Tarmiya and more at Tuwaitha. Offering just one example of why trying to conceal Iraq's secret nuclear infrastructure from inspectors would be impossible, Jafar told Hussein Kamel that his team had no way to hide these iron disks—they were too big and heavy.

"Okay, if you can't do it, hand them over to the Special Republican Guard," Kamel told Jafar, referring to Saddam's elite presidential protection force. He remained determined to pursue a cover-up.[3]

Jafar now set aside his accurate draft report and wrote a false one for the U.N. His narration of lies required quickly inventing alternative stories about secret research sites that inspectors might demand to visit. Meanwhile, they had to clean up their contraband. At Tarmiya, Jafar and his team helped the Special Republican Guard remove the giant calutrons. They also decontaminated the place to erase any traces of radioactive material that inspectors might find. Jafar came up with a story that the facility had manufactured electricity transformers.

Some of the most important concealment work involved documents. Heirs to ancient Babylonia's Code of Hammurabi, an impressive set of laws, and, more recently, the fastidious systems of Britain's imperial civil service, Iraq's government bureaucracy had acquired seemingly unshakable habits of recordkeeping. Jafar was himself "meticulous in documenting all aspects" of the bomb program. He had maintained archives not only at Tuwaitha but also at two other sites that might now be targeted by U.N. inspectors. Jafar collected many of the bomb-related documents he knew about—around one hundred thousand documents in all—and loaded them into a windowless railway wagon. Then he ordered welders to seal the freight car shut. Finally, he placed the wagon into the national railway system, attaching it to a randomly selected train. Within days, the rolling archive was traveling the country inconspicuously.[4]

In May 1991, the first team of U.N. weapons inspectors arrived. They made a beeline for Tarmiya, which lay along the Tigris to the north of Baghdad. For years, Iraq had handled visiting I.A.E.A. inspectors by appointing liaisons and escorts who were technically knowledgeable but entirely unaware of the secret bomb work. In their ignorance, they "could be sincere and say, 'We don't know,'" as Jafar put it later.[5]

This time, the U.N. team encountered Hussein Kamel's menacing security forces, who tailed, blocked, and harassed them. The inspectors managed to take hundreds of pictures at Tamiya and elsewhere. Another team returned in late June with fresh intelligence from a defecting Iraqi scientist and aerial imagery captured by U-2 spy planes operated by the C.I.A. David Kay, an American political scientist, led a renewed search for the calutron disks. Panicked, Hussein Kamel ordered the Special Republican Guard to remove the seventy-ton disks from their hiding place, load them onto tank transporter trucks, and drive them randomly around Iraq until the U.N. inspectors left the country.[6]

The plan devolved into a fiasco for the Iraqis. On June 28, a squad of David Kay's inspectors, racing around in Range Rovers trailed by Special Republican Guards, discovered a line of flatbed trucks rumbling out of Fallujah, apparently loaded with calutrons. The ensuing chase was not high-speed: the iron disks were so heavy that the Iraqi trucks moved no faster than horse carts. Hussein Kamel's men fired over the heads of the U.N. inspectors to deter them, but the team snapped more photos and held on to their film, even when Iraqi gunmen demanded its surrender.

Back at the I.A.E.A.'s headquarters in Vienna, John Googin, a sixty-eight-year-old chemist who had worked on the Manhattan Project, recognized the strange disks in the photographs: "This is definitely an electromagnetic isotope separation process," he declared. The U.N. now had its first hard evidence about the scope and ambitions of Saddam's bomb program.

At the White House and allied capitals, the discovery landed as a shock. How far had Iraq's bomb work progressed? What else had the C.I.A. and other intelligence agencies missed or misinterpreted? By July, it was clear that, at a minimum, Iraq had hidden important scientific work, and the evidence "makes us believe strongly that Iraq has a

IRAQ'S SECRET NUCLEAR PROGRAM, 1981–1991

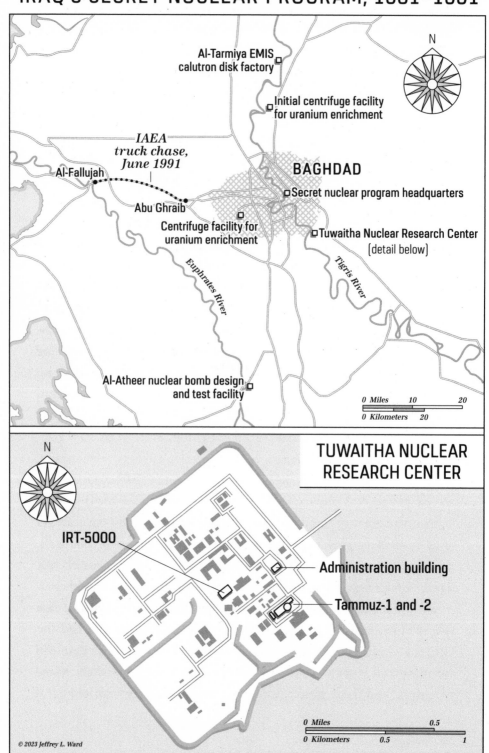

Al-Tarmiya EMIS
calutron disk factory

Initial centrifuge facility
for uranium enrichment

IAEA
truck chase,
June 1991

Al-Fallujah

Abu Ghraib

BAGHDAD

Secret nuclear program headquarters

Centrifuge facility for
uranium enrichment

Tuwaitha Nuclear Research Center
(detail below)

Euphrates River

Tigris River

Al-Atheer nuclear bomb design
and test facility

0 Miles 10 20
0 Kilometers 20

N

TUWAITHA NUCLEAR
RESEARCH CENTER

N

IRT-5000

Administration building

Tammuz-1 and -2

0 Miles 0.5
0 Kilometers 0.5 1

program to develop nuclear weapons," as State Department spokes-
woman Margaret Tutwiler put it. The Bush administration redoubled
the hunt for answers.[7]

The jig was now up, Jafar knew after the truck-chasing episode. A
major portion of his life's work surely "was finished," he thought.
Yet Hussein Kamel still insisted that Iraq should confess nothing. That
June and July, Saddam's son-in-law ordered the rapid destruction of
clandestine nuclear-, chemical-, and biological-weapons facilities before the U.N. could confirm their true purpose. In the case of the calutrons, since it was clear that the iron disks could not be well hidden, he
decided they should be blown to smithereens in the desert. His min-
ions approached Jafar to obtain high explosives. Jafar complied, but he
suspected that even if the Special Republican Guard managed to damage the disks, they would leave behind telltale shards that the U.N.
could identify. Hussein Kamel ordered a centrifuge lab to be plastered
over—a literal whitewash—and directed scientists to dump "designs,
documents, spare parts, and prototypes" into containers for safekeeping, "like convicts handing over their personal belongings at the prison
gates," as the physicist Mahdi Obeidi put it.[8]

He also ordered the destruction of massive amounts of chemical
weapons. In July, a team led by an Iraqi scientist destroyed about a
thousand ready-to-use chemical bombs, as well as twenty concealed
chemical warheads built for missiles that could strike Israel. Other
teams destroyed about two hundred tons of VX precursor chemicals,
ten tons of mustard precursor, and more than a ton of damaged VX
agent. When the frenzied work was completed, Tariq Aziz could credibly say that Iraq had no chemical weapons. But the world had no reason to believe this—and because the destruction had been carried out
without recordkeeping, photography, or other forms of proof, Iraq had
no means to show persuasively what it had done, should it choose
to come clean. Iraq would not admit to its destruction of chemical

weapons until March 1992, and even then, Aziz and other emissaries continued to lie about its historical arsenal.[9]

The decision to secretly destroy large sections of Iraq's WMD stocks and infrastructure without keeping good records would prove to be one of the most fateful events in Saddam's—and America's—march toward disaster. It meant that even when Iraq later sought to be honest about what had been destroyed in the summer of 1991, its officials would struggle to persuade U.N. inspectors. Not even the programs' secret leaders knew fully what had been done. "We didn't know what was destroyed and what was not," Jafar recalled. "It was all a big mess."[10]

There is no simple way to explain Saddam's decision to destroy some of his weapons of mass destruction in such a haphazard and secretive manner during 1991. It seemed to be partly instinctual: defiance of enemies was Saddam's way of life. His pride and his impulse to publicly project strength also played a part. Under pressure, he repeatedly looked for ways to avoid personal and political humiliation. (Defeated in Kuwait, he had declared victory and moved on.) There was also his doctrine of scaring off enemies. He still saw himself as under threat from committed adversaries—Iran, Israel, and now America. He had long believed that Iraq needed nuclear, chemical, and biological weapons to deter or defeat Iran and Israel. After the Gulf War, he judged that by getting rid of prohibited weapons, he might pass U.N. inspection more quickly. Yet if he cooperated with the U.N. and destroyed his inventory as the world watched—if he acquiesced in a public spectacle of defeat, with inspectors from enemy nations recording his humiliation on clipboards—his rule at home might be undermined, and Iran and Israel might feel emboldened to attack him. Finally, Saddam doubted—not without reason—that he would ever be granted relief from sanctions if he admitted the truth about his historical weapons programs. He calculated that honesty would not pay.

The result was that Saddam gave his opponents in Washington, London, and other capitals a welcome reason to prolong economic sanctions. The Bush administration had already made clear that it preferred to maintain sanctions until Saddam was removed from power. But if Iraq had quickly and verifiably surrendered its nuclear, chemical, and biological arms, as well as its longer-range missiles, other U.N. Security Council members might have challenged Washington. The absence of reliable records later made it hard for historical allies of Iraq, such as France and Russia, to credibly argue that Saddam had come clean.

From the calutron truck chase onward, the clear—even cartoonish—evidence that Iraq was cheating and lying conditioned American and European governments to believe that Saddam would never stop trying to deceive. The Baathist state's secrecy, control, and repression made it difficult to imagine a transparent and trustworthy Iraq, even when the regime did start to tell the truth about its prohibited weapons. The result became a self-perpetuating cycle of mutual confusion and misjudgment. But in 1991, at the start of this cycle, Saddam's preemptive destruction of weapons seemed to him to be a clever finesse. He had wriggled out of tighter jams before, and he calculated that with time, he could do so again. He miscalculated how his defiantly unilateral, habitually secret approach to disarming himself of WMD would create levels of confusion that would cost him down the line. Meantime, he saw no advantage in pretending to cooperate.

"One of the mistakes some people make is that when the enemy has decided to hurt you, you believe there is a chance to decrease the harm by acting in a certain way, but . . . The harm won't be less," Saddam told a colleague privately that August.

"What did the Americans show" after the war in Kuwait "as a possible sign for partially decreasing their harm?" he continued. "We didn't see anything. . . . I have given them everything: the missiles, and the chemical, biological, and nuclear weapons. They didn't give us anything in exchange. . . . Well, they have become worse."

"And now an expert is supposed to come and inspect," the colleague remarked.

"Why should we be courteous with him?" Saddam asked. "Nothing in the situation requires us to be courteous."[11]

The top weapons inspectors dispatched by the U.N. Security Council to keep Saddam honest were two Swedish diplomats: Rolf Ekéus and Hans Blix.

Tall, blue-eyed, and with a full head of whitening hair, Ekéus was a talented pianist who had spent years posted to Vienna, where he had participated in disarmament negotiations. The Security Council had just appointed him as chair of a new United Nations Special Commission that would investigate and destroy Iraq's chemical- and biological-weapons programs and certain of its long-range missiles while collaborating with the I.A.E.A. to eliminate its nuclear-weapons program. Ekéus took the assignment believing it was "very clear that this will be an easy job" that would take no more than a year or so. He took it for granted that Saddam "must understand" that his only way out of sanctions was to cooperate with the elimination of his WMD.

At U.N. headquarters in Manhattan, Ekéus found himself assigned to "a small room with one chair and one table, and a telephone that didn't function." His principal deputy, Robert Gallucci, an American diplomat, was professional and careful, but he saw the C.I.A., MI6, and other intelligence services as resources to support muscular inspections. The Special Commission, known by its acronym, UNSCOM, reported directly to the Security Council, bypassing the U.N.'s cumbersome bureaucracy, as well as the office of the secretary-general. As a practical matter, this meant that Ekéus worked directly for the powerful five permanent Security Council members—the U.S., Britain, France, the Soviet Union (soon to dissolve and yield its seat to Russia), and China.[12]

To investigate Iraq's nuclear-weapons capability, Ekéus had to manage his fellow Swede, Blix, the director general of the I.A.E.A., the world's nuclear watchdog. Educated at Columbia and Cambridge, Blix was a balding, precise diplomat and former Swedish politician who sometimes seemed to embody the U.N.'s legalistic, consensus-building principles. Ekéus and Blix belonged to rival Swedish political parties.

They had nonetheless been friendly over the years. They remained correct and polite in public but increasingly became sharp-tongued in private; the tension between them soon complicated the investigation into Iraq's secrets.[13]

Because the I.A.E.A. already had a headquarters full of nuclear experts and formal oversight of Iraq's known program, the Security Council appointed Blix to manage the nuclear file but ordered him to cooperate with Ekéus and conduct inspections in Iraq partially under UNSCOM's authority. After the truck chase, Ekéus and Gallucci prepared for aggressive follow-on UNSCOM inspections. The I.A.E.A. created an Iraq "action team," but Blix's agency was not set up for hostile raids or undercover detective work. Its procedures assumed that inspected governments would cooperate. To UNSCOM, Blix's inspectors "seemed too much like proper civil servants," as Blix summarized it, whereas some of Ekéus's crew "seemed to act Rambo-style." The essence of Blix's resentment was that Ekéus treated his long-established U.N. agency "as a dog on a leash."[14]

On July 14, a Blix action team in Baghdad led by the Greek scientist Dimitri Perricos met with Iraqi representatives in a conference room at the Melia Mansour, the luxury hotel beside the Tigris. Perricos had many questions about the calutrons discovered on fleeing trucks, but the clueless Iraqi minders dispatched to handle the meeting could not answer them. Finally, from the back of the room, where he had been sitting inconspicuously, Jafar spoke up in a "booming voice" and declared, "Well, I will explain."[15]

Jafar had worked in the shadows during the 1980s. Now it was as if he had stepped dramatically into a spotlight. The physicist "projected power and presence, and he gave the impression of one who had not only the technical knowledge to answer questions, but also the authority to decide what to reveal," as Gudrun Harrer, an Austrian journalist who obtained I.A.E.A. records of the session, described it.

In fact, Jafar was freelancing. Hussein Kamel was still pressuring him to keep as much of the bomb program secret as possible, and he knew well the price he might pay if he said too much. He parried Perricos and the other inspectors. He tried to explain "in his own way" what the calutrons and the electromagnetic enrichment program entailed, Perricos recalled, but Jafar held to the line that this work "had nothing to do with any intention to weaponize"—that is, to manufacture a nuclear weapon.[16]

At a second seminar on July 17, Jafar mentioned that Iraq had solicited a "little help from foreign engineers," an oblique reference to the stolen centrifuge designs and engineering expertise provided by West German specialists. The physicist also subtly shifted his argument about Iraq's nuclear intentions. He admitted now that the uranium enrichment work, by its nature, had provided Saddam with a "political option" to become a nuclear-weapons power at some point in the future. But this option had not been exercised, and no weapons work had been carried out. This was a lie, and Perricos saw through the fog. He returned to Vienna nearing a conviction that Jafar's electromagnetic work had "followed exactly the classical recipe learned from the Manhattan Project."[17]

Stunned by the reporting cables now pouring into Washington from the U.N. and the C.I.A., President Bush demanded that Saddam come clean about the history of Iraq's nuclear program. He set a deadline of July 22 and implied that he might attack Iraq again if he was not satisfied. The Iraqis insisted they would cooperate fully. Blix assembled a new action team, led by David Kay.

Kay was a mustachioed, experienced U.N. civil servant who specialized in administration; Blix had hired him years before because he could write well. Blix saw him as smart but "cocky." By virtue of his American citizenship and willingness to cooperate, Kay became a point man for the C.I.A. The agency sought to provide intelligence to the U.N. inspectors and also to place C.I.A. operatives on the inspection teams. Kay clearly found cloak-and-dagger Iraq inspection work more

interesting than his prior career in I.A.E.A. administration. He decided
to adopt Ekéus's aggressive approach and to make active use of intelligence.[18]

The C.I.A. needed Americans like Kay and Gallucci posted at the
U.N. because the agency refused to share its spy photos or human intelligence directly with Ekéus and Blix. The Bush administration had
supported the appointment of the two Swedes, but they were not even
nationals of one of the trusted Cold War–era "Five Eyes" allies—Britain,
Canada, Australia, and New Zealand—with whom the U.S. did share
sensitive eavesdropping and technical intelligence. "If you didn't have a
C.I.A. badge and weren't polygraphed, we didn't trust you with our
information," an agency analyst involved that summer recalled. Moreover, the agency did not see a need to defer to U.N. leadership: "In
typical American fashion, we thought we could run the inspections."
The struggle between the C.I.A. and the U.N. for control of inspection
operations that began in the summer of 1991 would shape and distort
the effort to verifiably disarm Iraq for years to come.[19]

Ekéus and Blix bristled at the C.I.A.'s affront to the integrity of
U.N. procedures, and to their own authority—Blix was especially
prickly on these points. Yet both Swedes wanted the intelligence that
Langley had to offer, to break Iraq's wall of secrecy. No other government could offer near-real-time U-2 photos of mysterious sites or check
out claims by Iraqi defectors.

Blix approved the provision of U.S. intelligence to Kay, who returned to Baghdad on July 27, armed with dossiers covering twenty-
two suspected nuclear sites. As the inspectors rolled out in convoys,
Kay checked in by satellite phone with UNSCOM in New York every
three hours. He had also worked out an old-school codebook arrangement with the C.I.A. If sensitive intelligence had to be transmitted
over an open phone line, Kay and his agency counterpart would recite
references to words on a prearranged page of a book about politics that
Kay carried with him.[20]

Kay resumed interviews with Jafar, who suggested that the U.N.
team could expect to have "all their questions answered and more than

that," as Kay reported to Blix. At a session on August 7, the physicist again shifted his position subtly. He now conceded obliquely that Iraq had done research relevant to weapons-building. He added that he and other physicists had thought about weaponization problems, "some quite deeply," but he continued to insist falsely that there was no specific bomb-building program. Kay cabled Blix to say that he found Jafar "confident and yet chilling. . . . He was clearly playing with us and enjoying it."[21]

Slowly, the inspectors were putting the pieces together. They zeroed in on Al-Atheer, a site just over forty miles southwest of Baghdad. The inspectors were getting warm—Al-Atheer had been the principal location of Iraq's work on a nuclear explosive device.

Three days after the session with Jafar, UNSCOM reported to the Security Council that "Al-Atheer and its companion facilities . . . constitute a complete and sufficient potential nuclear weapons laboratory and production facility." The record that was building up shocked ambassadors and experts on the council. "The horror with which the findings were greeted cannot be overstated," recalled Tim Trevan, a British inspector. Yet the Western public and the press had yet to grasp the full import of the summer's discoveries: that Iraq had run a sophisticated bomb program for at least five years without being caught, and that its current ability to complete a weapon quickly remained unknown.[22]

At the C.I.A., the incipient coup program against Saddam was run out of the Near East Division of the Directorate of Operations, the agency's spying hub for the Middle East. Much of the intelligence supplied to Ekéus and Blix came from another section of the C.I.A. devoted to arms-control intelligence. This staff consisted mainly of analysts, including scientists and missile experts. But as the hunt for Iraq's nuclear secrets acquired fresh urgency that summer, yet another group of spies—operators from the paramilitary division, some with backgrounds in the U.S. Special Forces—got involved.

In September, Kay and Gallucci assembled a new action team in London. This time they mustered forty-five team members, twenty-eight of them Americans, including C.I.A. paramilitary specialists, and an agency expert in penetrating computer systems. The remaining members were from the Five Eyes allies, Germany, and three Arab nations. There were only three I.A.E.A. civil servants on the I.A.E.A. team—nearly all the rest were "special people with special skills," as Gallucci put it. The team was as fully a C.I.A.-led operations unit as was possible to assemble under U.N. auspices.[23]

They met initially in a secure area of the Cabinet Office, the British prime minister's secretariat. This time there would be no chatting with Jafar or chasing hidden equipment in the desert. They intended to search for "smoking gun" documents, based on a fresh defector tip about where an important part of the nuclear archive—copies that Jafar had not collected and put on a wandering freight train—were stored.

The action team flew to a U.S.-U.K. military base in Bahrain, the island nation and former British colonial possession in the Persian Gulf. There they secretly rehearsed their raids. Their trainers included C.I.A. officers "who were used to surreptitious entry and gathering" of documents during break-ins of embassies, offices, and other targets for overseas intelligence collection.[24]

The team flew to Baghdad on September 22 and checked into the Palestine, a concrete tower whose extruding yellow balconies gave it the appearance of an upright honeycomb. Kay's initial target was the conspicuously named Nuclear Design Center, an open civilian facility in the Workers' Union building, close to the inspectors' hotel. Before dawn, and before any Iraqi escorts had arrived, Kay dispatched a reconnaissance team there. Inspectors followed by 6:00 a.m. and fanned out. They opened file cabinets and rifled through Arabic-language documents. After a few hours, Kay's handheld Motorola radio crackled: a colleague in the basement, using a code word, announced that he had found important material.

Kay hustled down. Gallucci was already there: "It didn't take an expert to know what we were looking at," he recalled. The documents contained schematic drawings that were clearly recognizable as nuclear-weapon designs. "Wow!" Gallucci exclaimed, abandoning spy tradecraft.

Kay and his colleagues had assumed during rehearsals that the Iraqis would try to prevent them from taking revelatory documents. Kay now decided to smuggle the incriminating papers out before the Iraqis could act. He was trying to assist an inspector on-site who had become ill and was displaying signs of severe stress. Kay decided to evacuate him. He had the man stuff his clothing with the weapons documents before bundling him off to the airport. It worked; the inspector flew out with the papers on a German transport plane that afternoon.[25]

Kay's team collected hundreds of pages of additional documents and prepared to leave. But the Iraqis refused to allow them to take the papers with them, insisting that they had to leave the originals and take only copies. Jafar arrived and offered two options: Kay could take copies of all the documents he wanted so long as he left the originals, or he could allow the Iraqis to make an inventory of the originals before Kay removed them. But Kay pointed out that U.N. resolutions gave him the sole authority to decide.

"As it became clear that we were finding a very large number of documents stamped SECRET and TOP SECRET relating to fissile material production and weapons development, their concerns deepened," Kay cabled to Vienna, referring to the Iraqis. Ultimately, Jafar stood back while armed Iraqi security officers forcibly seized documents that Kay and Gallucci had loaded into their vehicles. The inspectors returned to the Palestine Hotel. The Iraqis brought "copies" of the seized documents later that night, but it became evident that they had removed papers about bomb design.[26]

The inspectors scoured what they had for clues. Just after six the next morning, they raided a building known as Al-Khairat, which had been mentioned in their papers. It turned out to be the temporary headquarters of Petrochemical Project 3, formerly Department 3000—the bomb-building project. More drama ensued. The inspectors col-

lected hundreds of documents, many marked "Top Secret" and some
dating back to 1981. The scale of what they had exposed was at last
becoming clear: Kay later estimated that Iraq's entire nuclear-weapons
program had involved $5 billion to $10 billion in expenditure and had
employed seven thousand scientists and twenty thousand workers.

Jafar and building security blocked the action team in a parking lot
outside the building. A CNN television crew got wind of the confrontation and began broadcasting what became a ninety-six-hour worldwide news spectacle. Kay and Gallucci cleverly used the attention of
global media as a shield and a lever: They gave interview after interview on their satellite phone to American, British, and European journalists, calling out the Iraqis for trying to stop the world from knowing
the truth about their atomic-bomb program. The inspectors remained
in their vehicles, eating prepared military meals and keeping up morale
by singing and passing around the phone to make calls home to family
members.

Behind the scenes, Saddam sought to avoid a military escalation
while yielding as little as possible. "We should not go to war because of
this, because we are not at a stage to enter a war, but at least let us ha-
rass our enemy," he told his advisers. "America, comrades, America is
not an easy country."[27]

The triumphalism of the inspectors got to Jafar. He was especially
worried that personal information belonging to "thousands" of scientists and other personnel might leak from the inspectors to Israel, to
aid Mossad's periodic assassination campaigns. He took acerbic note,
too, as the U.N. inspectors sang their "patriotic ditties" and called home
to their loved ones, loudly declaring—so that the Iraqi minders could
hear—that they were having a grand time. At one point, Jafar's colleagues managed to sneak into the building through a window, grab
some embarrassing files, and toss them over a fence into the bed of a
waiting truck. "This minor coup provided a fillip to the flagging spirits
of us all," the physicist recalled.[28]

Iraq's position was untenable, and the embarrassment mounted by
the hour as CNN's live coverage streamed. Finally, around dawn on

September 28, after negotiations at the Security Council and with Tariq Aziz, Iraq effectively capitulated and signed a protocol for managing such documents in the future. The inspectors were released from their parking-lot detention and allowed to carry their documents with them. The mission had seized 2,348 separate documents totaling 54,922 pages. The papers smuggled out with the ill inspector on the first day proved to be the most explicit "smoking gun," establishing that Iraq had tackled full-blown nuclear-weapons development, down to the design of specific explosive devices. Overall, the Kay-Gallucci mission with covert C.I.A. assistance had delivered one of the most revelatory, successful inspections in the history of nuclear-arms control, and the overall evidence was irrefutable, as an internal I.A.E.A. document soon summarized:

> The PC-3 employee lists show that Dr. Jafar Dhia Jafar was a senior administrator for the program. Similar documentation shows that Dr. Jafar was intimately linked to the uranium enrichment program. The team accordingly believes that Dr. Jafar had the lead technical and administrative responsibility for the nuclear weapons program as a whole—despite his repeated claims that no such program existed.

Now the headlines in America and Europe blared the big picture: "U.N. Says the Iraqis Could Have Devised A-Bombs in the '90s," *The New York Times* reported on its front page. Another story analyzed the implications: "Iraq's Nuclear Program Shows the Holes in U.S. Intelligence."

Congressmen called for accountability. Hawks demanded Saddam's overthrow. For analysts at the C.I.A. and elsewhere who lived through the summer of 1991, the lesson would echo for years to come: despite possessing the world's best satellite and snooping technology, the United States had failed to detect Iraq's secret bomb program and had badly underestimated Iraqi scientists and Saddam Hussein. They would not let it happen again.[29]

By that autumn, Iraqi intelligence had penetrated the Special Commission, whose multinational membership offered many avenues for recruiting informants. The Iraqis often knew in advance where U.N. inspection teams intended to travel. But the Kay inspection in September had left Hussein Kamel worried that Iraq had its own "security leak," recalled Imad Khadduri, a scientist who had worked for Jafar. Hussein Kamel ordered the arrests of a dozen scientists and administrators who had worked on nuclear archives, including Khadduri.

The secret police detained them at the Fao Establishment Building on Baghdad's Palestine Street. A committee led by one of Hussein Kamel's deputies interrogated the prisoners. Some of the scientists "suffered psychologically, broke down and cried heavily, realizing that our lives were at the whim, ever so fragile, of Hussein Kamel's mood," Khadduri recalled. After eighteen days of questioning, Hussein Kamel grudgingly accepted that there was no evidence of a leak from inside. He ordered the men released but demoted them and kept them under close surveillance.

Jafar's summer of visibility as a liaison to U.N. inspectors had ended with the regime's embarrassment. The fault ultimately lay with Saddam's decisions and Hussein Kamel's implementation. For Saddam, Jafar remained a symbol of Iraq's scientific achievements and potential. Hussein Kamel named the physicist as acting minister of military industrialization, in charge of the rehabilitation of Iraq's electricity sector and other infrastructure smashed by American bombs. All written communication with U.N. nuclear inspectors still passed through Jafar, however. Soon he was given a minister's rank, a rare privilege for a non-Baathist.

On December 16, Saddam summoned Jafar and other technocrats, seeking an update on civilian rebuilding work. He went around the table, and each briefer did his best to assure him that "everything is, God willing, in good shape" and that "all problems have now been resolved," as one colonel put it.

When the problems caused by intrusive U.N. inspectors came up, Saddam told them to be patient; he would wear his enemies out. "They will eventually get tired," he said. "We firmly believe that the siege will gradually erode." He noted that what seemed to concern the United States above all "are our minds," meaning the knowledge of nuclear, biological, and chemical arms that Iraq retained. "What can they do with those people [who] cannot abandon their memory?" he asked.

When Jafar's turn came, the physicist said he wanted to brief the president on a bomb-damaged power station near Basra, as well as on other subjects "which, sir, I seek your permission to address."

Saddam turned to Jafar's former boss at the Tuwaitha nuclear complex. "You were right when you said if Dr. Jafar loves something, he sticks to it," Saddam said, laughing. "Now he loves electricity."[30]

It would prove to be an accurate forecast of much of Jafar's work for the next decade. After the inspection debacles of the summer of 1991, Saddam handled his leading physicist the way he often managed family members and Baathist comrades whom he wanted to reassign, at least temporarily: he changed Jafar's responsibilities but kept him close. Soon Jafar was working from an office tower above the Tigris, still chauffeured as a minister would be, respected and seemingly as secure as it was possible to be in Saddam's Iraq.

Visiting U.N. nuclear inspectors repeatedly asked to see Jafar—he had all but announced himself to them that July as the Oppenheimer of the Iraqi bomb program—but they were now refused permission. For those in Washington, London, New York, and Vienna who would harbor doubts through the 1990s about what had become of Saddam's ambition to acquire an atomic bomb, Jafar's new profile—inaccessible, privileged, and at the highest echelon of Saddam Hussein's regime— hardly seemed reassuring.

FIFTEEN

Mr. Max and the
Mayfair Swindler

For every C.I.A. case officer who glided urbanely under diplomatic cover, there was another who appeared to have just walked off a battlefield. John Maguire, who rotated to the Amman station in 1992, belonged to that subtribe. He was a profane, Spanish-speaking former Baltimore police officer, six foot three and about two hundred pounds, with a whitening walrus mustache. He had joined the agency in the early 1980s as a paramilitary officer. He served initially in Central America, where, among other things, he posed as an outboard motor repairman while helping Nicaragua's anti-Sandinista guerrillas mine three of their country's harbors. Later he enrolled in case officer school at Camp Perry to train in traditional espionage—recruiting agents and running these human sources, or "cases." The Amman station was one of the C.I.A.'s largest in the Middle East, a listening and recruiting post wedged among Baghdad, Jerusalem, and Damascus. The station occupied a section of the U.S. embassy campus, which was centered around a hulking three-story beige building designed like a desert fort.

One of Maguire's tasks was to manage Iraqi "walk-ins"—scientists, generals, spies, diplomats, tribal leaders, businessmen, clerics, farmers, bureaucrats—who made their way to Jordan and sought appointments at the embassy. Some volunteered to cooperate with the U.S. in exchange for money, protection, or resettlement. Hundreds of Iraqis lined up each day. The C.I.A.'s job at the customer-service window was to identify and interview the very small number of potential defectors or agents who really knew something about Saddam Hussein and his regime—particularly his weapons programs or his security services.

Iraq's intelligence services correctly saw the parade at the U.S. embassy as a security threat and infiltrated spies into the long lines to chat up naive countrymen and search for high-ranking personalities who had no good reason to be there. To evade this surveillance, Maguire and his colleagues put out word in Amman's enclave of Iraqi exiles that if you wanted a discreet appointment at the U.S. embassy, you should ask for "Mr. Max." This would speed the applicant to a meeting with Maguire or another case officer, fully made up in an agency-supplied disguise. One after another, they each presented themselves as "Mr. Max," assessed the walk-ins, and recruited new informants or paid agents who might be sent back into Iraq.[1]

Since the Gulf War's end, C.I.A. recruiters had been reaching out to Iraqi military officers, looking for Brent Scowcroft's imagined restive colonel who might strike against Saddam. The message was: "Saddam is our issue, and the inner circle around him," as Maguire put it. "If you were not bloody"—meaning you had not participated in, say, the genocide against Kurds or the torture and murder of Baathist prisoners—"you would be okay in a post-Saddam government," particularly if you could help bring such a government into being.[2]

Sifting walk-in sources for authentic defectors—and vetting each candidate against the possibility that they were a double agent—was time-consuming and treacherous. "It was a wilderness of mirrors," recalled Robert Grenier, who was then working at the Iraq Operations Group in Langley. Early on, some of the best cases out of Amman involved sheikhs from semiautonomous tribes in western Iraq who had social and smuggling ties to Jordan, and who felt no great loyalty to Saddam. The Amman station also ran agents in and out of Baghdad using traditional Cold War–era tradecraft—sewing messages into travelers' clothes before arranging for them to walk across the long desert border to avoid checkpoints and, later, paying couriers to shuttle between Amman and Baghdad, working as traders or drivers. These cases complemented reporting by Iraqi agents in Baghdad that Charlie Seidel had left behind when the U.S. embassy closed late in 1990, as America and Iraq again severed formal diplomatic relations. Yet apart from Kurdish servants working in the households of Saddam's family members, none of the agents had access to Baghdad's inner circle. "It was a very, very difficult environment to operate in," Grenier recalled. "You never really knew exactly who you were dealing with or what they represented."[3]

At headquarters, Frank Anderson, the head of Near East operations and Maguire's ultimate boss, maintained a dutiful but unenthusiastic attitude toward President Bush's instruction to foster a coup. To Grenier, Anderson seemed to have soured on the entire concept of C.I.A. covert action on the grounds that "people get hurt, things go wrong, it's messy. . . . We're here to do intelligence collection—let's just stick with that." Of course, Anderson had good reason to doubt the White House's ambitions. Bush's instructions violated the precept that covert action worked best when it was not used by presidents as a "silver bullet." At the end of the Gulf War, George H. W. Bush had decided not to depose Saddam Hussein by military force. A popular uprising that Bush fomented had also failed. Saddam ran one of the tightest security regimes in the world. There were no C.I.A. career officers stationed permanently inside Iraq. The idea that a covert C.I.A. program mounted from headquarters and regional stations such as Amman would oust Saddam anytime soon seemed implausible to Anderson, and potentially a prescription for embarrassing failure.[4]

Bush's covert-action finding—his official instructions—did not demand that Anderson immediately organize a violent coup attempt in Baghdad. Instead, it authorized attempts to foster such a political

change by organizing opposition to Saddam and by mounting "information operations" to destabilize the regime. This exiles-and-propaganda
effort constituted a kind of Covert Action 101, drawn from a playbook
used repeatedly during the Cold War to pressure dictators and leftist
regimes in the Soviet Union's orbit. The standard elements included
clandestine funding of anti-regime radio broadcasts; perhaps some deception operations designed to confuse the targeted dictator about
whom he could trust; and inevitably, the organization and funding of
exiled political groups, seemingly no matter how fractious or discon-
nected from their home countries these exiles might be. Anderson
soon appointed Robert Mattingly, a former U.S. Marine officer, to run
Iraq operations out of Langley. Near East case officers in London,
where Seidel had now rotated, made contact with Iraqi exiles. By 1992,
the C.I.A. had given a contract to a PR firm, the Rendon Group, to
run a covert information campaign against Saddam. The firm spent
$23 million in one year on such projects as an anti-Baathist comic
book, videos and radio programs, and a photo exhibit that documented
Saddam's atrocities. The effort involved "some silly things," Anderson
conceded later, including, he recalled, once sending a drone to "leaflet-
bomb" Saddam's birthday party.[5]

The only territory inside Iraq's borders where there was a chance
for the C.I.A to set up a base was in Iraqi Kurdistan. The prospects for
a C.I.A.-Kurd alliance were complicated by Kurdish memories of the
C.I.A.'s betrayal of Kurdish rebels during the 1970s. In the skies over
Kurdistan, however, the U.S. and Britain now flew warplanes from
bases in Turkey and Saudi Arabia to enforce the no-fly zone established
in 1991. Under this protection, large swaths of Iraqi Kurdistan had become a de facto autonomous region. Saddam had decided in late 1991
that holding on to the area was too costly. It was ruled now by the two
main Kurdish political parties: the Kurdistan Democratic Party, led by
Masoud Barzani, and the Patriotic Union of Kurdistan, led by Jalal
Talabani. Barzani, a son of the legendary Kurdish guerrilla leader
Mustafa, drew his support from their family's eponymous tribe and

region in Kurdistan's far north. Talabani had been a communist in his youth—he translated Mao's writings into Kurdish—but evolved into a "Falstaffian figure," as one biographer described him, who "enjoyed nothing so much as a bountiful table and Cuban cigars."[6]

Anderson authorized an exploratory mission. From London, Charlie Seidel flew to Turkey and drove into Iraqi territory to meet Barzani and Talabani. The C.I.A.'s initial message was: "We'd like to set up shop here; we'd like your support and assistance," as a colleague of Seidel's described it. The initial idea was to build a platform of agent recruitment and couriers moving back and forth to Baghdad, in cooperation with the two Kurdish parties' security wings. This might lead in time to the identification of Iraqi Army leaders and units willing to move against Saddam. Mattingly, at Langley, wanted to establish a permanent C.I.A. base, protected by the Kurdish parties. Anderson refused, but he allowed rotating teams of C.I.A. career officers, soon dubbed Northern Iraq Liaison Elements, or NILE teams. They visited Kurdistan for about six weeks at a time. As it turned out, Anderson was right to be worried.[7]

The Gulf War and U.N. sanctions had devastated Iraq's economy, yet Saddam and his closest family did not suffer greatly. Barzan Ibrahim al-Tikriti, still in Geneva, now divided his time between diplomacy and sanctions-busting businesses. He financed the import-export company of an Iraqi-born Swiss citizen who specialized in delivering Mercedes-Benzes to Iraq through Jordan. These sorts of rackets kept cash and luxury goods flowing to Hussein Kamel and Uday, as well as to Saddam Hussein's presidential office. (Meanwhile, ordinary Iraqi traders could have their hands cut off if they were convicted of financial crimes.) Yet for all its cross-border smuggling, Saddam's regime, under constant surveillance and hemmed in by sanctions, was looking more and more like a poor sister beside the Swiss-banked kleptocracies of similarly oil-endowed regimes from the Persian Gulf

to post-communist Russia to Africa. Go-go capitalism, resource stripping, and hidden offshore wealth held by political elites were becoming
markers of the post–Cold War order, but Saddam—and the president's
close family members—were missing out on their potential.

Barzan's opaque businesses occasionally carried him to Baghdad.
Early in 1992, he joined Saddam for dinner, he recalled. Barzan noted
that, since 1992 was an election year in the United States, "the Republicans and the Democrats would avoid" talking much about Iraq because each worried that the other might exploit the issue.

"When is this election?" Saddam asked.

Barzan explained that it was in November. Afterward, he marveled
at how the "president of a country in the condition of war with the
United States of America does not know the time of the election there,
who the candidates are, and how the outcome will affect the fight between himself and America."

To Saddam, America's elections looked like phony rituals, window
dressing on a pro-Israeli, neo-imperial deep state relentlessly undermining the Arab world. He believed that America would soon struggle
with the demands of its post–Cold War quasi-empire: "It is incapable
of satisfying its obligations," he told colleagues. "I mean, America has
promised countries of Eastern Europe and has not satisfied its promise. . . . Now Third World countries [say], 'We are now Americans,
make [us] happy.'"[8]

Saddam was right to think that the 1992 U.S. presidential election
would not bring a drastic change in policy toward Iraq. Republicans
and Democrats largely agreed on the need to challenge Saddam's dictatorship. Still, Saddam was becoming unplugged from Washington, a
major change from his position during the previous decade. Between
the opening of the C.I.A. partnership in 1982 and the invasion of Kuwait eight summers later, Saddam's regime had maintained regular
contacts with the C.I.A.; operated a D.C. embassy led by a savvy ambassador, Nizar Hamdoon; and received ranking U.S. envoys in Baghdad, from Donald Rumsfeld to Bob Dole. Now the Iraqi embassy in

Washington and the U.S. embassy in Baghdad were both shuttered. The only Americans eager to visit Iraq—besides U.N. weapons inspectors—seemed to be daredevil businessmen and political gadflies.

In May 1992, Tariq Aziz asked Nizar Hamdoon to return to America, this time as permanent representative to the United Nations in New York—the only senior diplomatic post on American soil that Iraq still maintained. Hamdoon moved with his wife and two daughters to an Iraqi-owned residence at 124 East Eightieth Street, a brick building between Lexington and Park Avenues, near the Metropolitan Museum of Art. The mission itself was just a short walk away, in a townhouse on East Seventy-Ninth. The ambassador remained both a loyal Baathist and a staunch advocate for improved U.S.-Iraq ties.[9]

That summer, Hamdoon watched as George H. W. Bush faltered in his campaign for reelection and Bill Clinton gained momentum. A recession gripped the U.S. economy in 1992, and Bush, a member of what passed for America's aristocracy, seemed out of touch with the concerns of hard-hit citizens. "Message: I care," Bush said at one campaign stop, inadvertently reading out notes intended as prompts. The race drew a strong independent candidate, the businessman Ross Perot, whose candidacy forced Bush to fend off attacks from two sides. By summer, Clinton led opinion polls by more than twenty points.

In August, America and Britain had announced a new no-fly zone to protect civilians in southern Iraq from aerial attack by Saddam's regime. The new zone extended northward from Iraq's borders with Kuwait and Saudi Arabia to the thirty-second parallel, south of Baghdad. Publicly, the Bush administration said the initiative would provide humanitarian protection to Iraq's beleaguered Shia, but the greater purpose, recalled Bruce Riedel, then at the National Security Council, "was to create a buffer zone over southern Iraq so that we would know if he tried to move on Kuwait again." Saddam responded by moving missile batteries into the southern zone to fire at patrolling U.S. and allied planes. America's no-fly zones were becoming permanent low-grade sites of antiaircraft fire from the ground and counterattacks by patrolling planes.[10]

On November 3, Clinton won the presidency. When he learned that Bush had been defeated, Saddam appeared on a balcony in Baghdad and fired a celebratory shot into the air. He soon analyzed Bush's exit with Tariq Aziz and Taha Yassin Ramadan. To avoid further aggravating Washington, Iraq "shouldn't take a formal stand" about Bush's defeat, Aziz cautioned. Still, they gloated in private. Bush lost to Clinton "because he didn't succeed in removing Saddam Hussein," Ramadan declared. "Now he is removed and Saddam Hussein [still] exists."[11]

"Wasn't the Mother of All Battles a basic reason for overthrowing Bush?" Saddam asked. Bush's failure to "save the West from the regime in Iraq" had contributed to his defeat. In a later conversation, Saddam summed up how he thought the 1992 election had enhanced his own influence: "All the world is now saying, 'Man, why are we afraid so much? Bush fell and Iraq lasted!'"

He did not expect that Bill Clinton would—or could—profoundly alter America's conflict with Baghdad, however. "There are proven facts in the American policy that we shouldn't ignore," he said. "Among these facts are interests that meet with—in part—keeping the Zionist entity strong at the expense of the Arabs." Because of this, "we'll find ourselves clashing" with the United States "in one way or another."[12]

Because of the daily skirmishes in the no-fly zones that Saddam provoked, it seemed possible that Bush might attack Iraq before Clinton's inauguration in January. Saddam told the Revolutionary Command Council that an attack was just what he wanted. To fracture the American-led coalition arrayed against him, and to strengthen his position in the Arab world, he had to keep picking fights with the world's sole remaining superpower—as long as they were fights that did not threaten his regime's survival. "We test the enemy and we express ourselves," he explained.[13]

He did not believe the United States would again mount a ground invasion of Iraq. Convinced that he only faced "this method of swift strikes" from the air, Barzan Ibrahim al-Tikriti observed, Saddam "became more stubborn and stuck to his own ways."[14]

During the first days after the U.S. election, Tariq Aziz tried to open a channel to the new administration.

"Saddam has not the slightest idea of distracting Clinton" from his domestic policies, Aziz assured Samir Vincent, an Iraqi-born American scientist and businessman who offered to serve as an intermediary between Baghdad and Washington. "Saddam wants to work with Clinton and reach agreements."[15]

Oscar Wyatt, the Texas oilman, also ferried messages from Saddam to the White House that winter. *Texas Monthly* once described the oilman as Houston's "orneriest, wiliest, most litigious, most feared, most hated, and most beloved son of a bitch." Wyatt flew into Iraq in January 1993, on his private jet, to lobby Saddam's aides for a lucrative concession in Iraqi fields—U.N. resolutions be damned.

"He is going to carry letters to the new administration," an adviser informed Saddam, speaking of Wyatt. The oilman was "not a sneaky person by any means because he is an old man." Another adviser falsely noted that Wyatt had donated $5 million to Clinton's campaign. Such was Saddam's foggy window on Washington at a pivotal moment of political transition. Wyatt did speak to Clinton about Iraq. But Clinton was not about to risk political capital at the outset of his presidency by talking to Saddam.[16]

On Inauguration Day for America's forty-second president, a chilly Wednesday in Washington, Bruce Riedel, the National Security Council's director of Near East and South Asian affairs, huddled in the Situation Room, the secure conference room underneath the West Wing, to monitor firefights in the Iraqi no-fly zones. Just about every day now, "we were shooting at them, they were shooting at us," he recalled. The incidents figured into Clinton's first update briefings as president, as he prepared to celebrate that night at festive balls across Washington.

Early the next morning, Anthony "Tony" Lake, the president's national security adviser, summoned Riedel to the White House and
asked him to explain the "rules of engagement" in the no-fly zones,
meaning the orders and restrictions given to American pilots by the
Pentagon concerning when the pilots could shoot at Iraqi targets. Clinton's aides wanted to know what sort of half war they now had to
manage. Riedel said the engagement rules were "extremely complicated." The basics were: If an Iraqi aircraft flew into a no-fly zone, an
American plane would shoot it down. If an Iraqi aircraft flew into a
zone and then escaped, an American plane would chase it and shoot it
down. And if Iraqi ground forces fired at an American patrol plane, the
U.S. would destroy the offending Iraqi unit or facility. But there were
many subtleties and caveats. Lake and Sandy Berger told Riedel, in essence, "You're leaning pretty far forward here." Conflict could escalate
without warning.

Yes, Riedel acknowledged, but the previous administration was trying to topple Saddam, and the no-fly zones were "part of the process."
He could tell that Clinton's advisers were "very, very uncomfortable." It
soon became evident that Clinton's principal goal in Iraq was making
sure that Saddam didn't become a problem for him. Clinton had been
elected to address the faltering U.S. economy. Iraq was a Bush hang-
over he wished to avoid.[17]

At the C.I.A., Tom Twetten, the former Baghdad liaison and Near
East operations chief, now ran all of the agency's clandestine service as deputy director of central intelligence for operations. As Clinton took power, Twetten arranged to brief Warren Christopher, the
new secretary of state, at his offices in Foggy Bottom. James Woolsey,
whom Clinton had nominated to run the C.I.A., also attended. Woolsey was a smart oddball. Like Clinton, he was a former Rhodes Scholar
and a graduate of Yale Law School. He had served as undersecretary of
the navy during the Carter administration and as an arms control negotiator for President George H. W. Bush. But whereas Clinton was a

remarkably gifted, empathetic politician, Woolsey proved to have a tin ear when he reached Washington's highest echelons.

Woolsey had yet to be confirmed in office, so Twetten ran the briefing. He had heard that Christopher, an attorney who had served in the Carter administration, had serious doubts about the value of the C.I.A.'s covert actions. Twetten gave him a spiel about the agency's qualified utility. Half of the spies in the clandestine service would vote against ever getting involved in covert actions, Twetten said. They preferred to stick with straight intelligence collection. But the C.I.A. was stuck with covert action anyway "because we can do it" under the law and have had successes. As an example, he pointed to the recently concluded C.I.A. program to arm guerrillas fighting the Soviet occupation of Afghanistan. "Covert action is a tool of foreign policy," Twetten said. "It's your tool, you and the president." If you can execute foreign policy without it, that's preferable, but if you think you need an operation "to supplement what your diplomatic efforts are, we're there."[18]

Lake and Berger ran a policy review on Iraq that largely ratified George H. W. Bush's policy, including the covert-action plan to foment a coup against Saddam. Clinton also endorsed the U.N. sanctions regime and the no-fly zones. Colin Powell, still chairman of the Joint Chiefs, described the Iraqi dictator as a "toothache" that could be managed. Proclaimed policy would emphasize tough sanctions to weaken Saddam while secret actions would measure the regime's vulnerabilities. "It was like bending a pencil by putting pressure on both ends— you could not predict exactly when it would snap, but at some point you could be certain it would," a C.I.A. Middle East hand hypothesized.

Martin Indyk, Clinton's senior aide on the Middle East at the National Security Council, soon coined a phrase: "dual containment," meaning simultaneous pressure on Iraq and Iran. Indyk and Clinton had their sights set on other priorities in the region: above all, advancing back-channel peace talks between Israel and the Palestine Liberation Organization—talks that would soon produce the Oslo Accords, an agreement in principle to establish a Palestinian state. Clinton would only consider engaging with Saddam if the dictator opened his own back channel to Israel, following the example of Jordan's King Hussein.[19]

Charles Duelfer, a defense and intelligence specialist who had worked mainly at the State Department, had replaced Robert Gallucci as deputy to Rolf Ekéus at the weapons-hunting U.N. Special Commission. Around this time, Duelfer joined Indyk for lunch at the White House mess, in the basement of the West Wing.

Indyk said that the Clinton administration wanted a new regime in Iraq, but it would have to come from within. To explain their strategy, he "put his two index fingers down on the tablecloth and slowly drew two parallel lines," Duelfer recalled. One line represented international support for Saddam, the other support for the economic sanctions and oil embargo that kept Saddam under tight pressure. "The hope was that support for Saddam would crumble before support for sanctions did," said Duelfer, summarizing Indyk's explanation. Duelfer concluded that Clinton thought Saddam "was a problem that could be managed but not solved. . . . Perhaps we would get lucky and he would simply drop dead."[20]

By early 1993, C.I.A. covert action and the Clinton administration's passivity had produced an unintended result, one little remarked upon in Washington at the time. It had empowered a talented, ambitious, and ruthlessly deceptive figure destined to alter the courses of Iraqi and American history.

Ahmad Chalabi was then in his late forties. He kept a flat in London's Mayfair district and a home in the mountains of Kurdistan. Chalabi had maneuvered his way onto the C.I.A.'s payroll—an organization he controlled received $340,000 a month from the agency—but he was not a controlled C.I.A. agent. He was more of a paid ally and agent of influence. Brilliant and self-regarding, he had "Gaullist aspirations and a nature Machiavellian to its core," as a biographer, Richard Bonin, put it. Rather than acting as an arm of the C.I.A., Chalabi said later, "I saw *them* as an asset that I could use to promote my program."[21]

Chalabi was a scion of one of the wealthiest families of Iraq's royal era. His father was a minister of public works serving King Faisal II. The family acted as a local partner of a British firm that had monopolized Iraq's agricultural exports, and the Chalabis owned tens of thousands of acres in the capital and its environs. They were distinctive in another way, too—they were Shia merchants and social notables in a Baghdad elite otherwise heavily influenced by the Hashemite royal family's Sunni faith.

Born in 1944, Ahmad Chalabi had a boyhood that paralleled that of Jafar Dhia Jafar, who was just a year older, and whose father had also been a royal minister; Chalabi attended the same English boarding school, Seaford College, as young Jafar did. But after the royal family's overthrow, the Chalabis quickly fled Baghdad for London.

While the Chalabis had stashed enough money abroad to live comfortably in exile, they lost much of their Iraqi fortune. Eventually, Chalabi's father moved to Beirut and went into banking. Chalabi attended M.I.T., where he proved to be a precocious mathematician. He went on to earn a doctorate in mathematics at the University of Chicago. The family became actively involved in Iraqi exile politics. In 1969, after completing his doctorate, Chalabi briefly traveled to Iran and Kurdistan, where he served as a courier in an unsuccessful coup attempt against the Baath government by a group of Kurdish rebels, backed by Iranian intelligence. In that adventure, Chalabi acquired a taste for action and intrigue he would never relinquish. In 1975, now a math professor in Beirut, Chalabi watched from a distance as Iran and the C.I.A. abruptly withdrew support for Mustafa Barzani. The lesson Chalabi took from that episode, he said later, was that the C.I.A. "is completely prepared to burn down your house to light a cigarette."[22]

Chalabi moved to Amman to establish Petra Bank, a new outpost of his family's banking business, which now operated from Cairo to Abu Dhabi. Chalabi eased into Amman society—an aristocrat in his early thirties with a taste for Bach and Mozart, but also a backroom operator with a disconcerting habit of playing with knives in his office. In the manner of other unscrupulous bankers in the region, Chalabi used customer deposits to buy favor with powerful Jordanians by lending them millions without expecting repayment. He befriended King Hussein's troubled eldest son and heir apparent, Prince Hassan, and reportedly lent him nearly $30 million. Chalabi himself borrowed millions to build a grandiose home in Amman, with a courtyard full of Greek statues. About 40 percent of Petra's outstanding loans, worth about $175 million, were not being paid back, evidently because this was never expected. Petra was a house of cards awaiting a gust of wind. That came in 1989, when Jordan suffered an economic crisis and King Hussein's government demanded that local banks provide a percentage of their reserves to rescue the country. Chalabi had no cash to give; Petra's insolvency was exposed. On August 9, just after midnight, Chalabi snuck out of Jordan under a half-moon, hiding in a car driven by his brother.[23]

He returned to Mayfair and rented a flat overlooking Green Park. After Saddam invaded Kuwait, Chalabi reinvented himself as a political exile, networking his way into the fractious and ineffective Iraqi opposition. He invented a story that Saddam was responsible for Petra Bank's troubles. In February 1991, under counsel from American friends, he placed an op-ed in *The Wall Street Journal* headlined "A Democratic Future for Iraq" and another, a month later, in *The Washington Post* titled "Democracy for Iraq . . ." The prospect of majority rule in Iraq unsettled some American policymakers, since most Iraqis were Shia, the faith of revolutionary Iran. But Chalabi dressed like a banker, not an aspiring ayatollah. When the C.I.A.'s Iraq Operations Group started to covertly organize opposition-in-exile to Saddam, Chalabi was an obvious recruit—visible, mouthing democratic slogans, connected in America, fluent in English, and with a background in administration. "He has a lot of the skills you would want if you're creating a new political organization," concluded Whitley Bruner, the case officer assigned to bring Chalabi on board.

That Chalabi's tour at Petra Bank was shadowed by allegations of systemic fraud did not deter the C.I.A. The agency's allies and agents were often rogues. A colleague of Bruner's, Linda Flohr, saw a way to turn Chalabi's dodgy escape from Jordan, and the pending charges against him there, into an advantage. His "reputation of corruption . . . is a good cover," as Flohr put it, since Chalabi could funnel C.I.A. funds while creating the impression among fellow Iraqis that he was "financially independent." Of course, another possibility was that the unscrupulous practices that had caused Petra to collapse might foreshadow Chalabi's decision-making as an agency client.[24]

Working with the Rendon Group, the C.I.A.-funded PR firm, Chalabi helped form the Iraqi National Congress, or the I.N.C. In June 1992, with agency funds, he flew about two hundred Iraqis to a conference in Vienna. Some of Chalabi's C.I.A. handlers saw him as merely a conduit and organizer, but Chalabi saw the I.N.C. as a vehicle to advance his own bid for power in a post-Saddam Iraq. Later that year, he set up shop in Salahuddin, Kurdistan, and staged a second conference there. Kurdistan's instability and rivalries seemed to suit him. Rotating C.I.A. and Iranian intelligence officers now both operated there, eyeing one another warily. Chalabi unabashedly played both sides. With more than $4 million in annual funds from the C.I.A., deepening ties to Kurdish guerrillas, and access to Iran's networks, he became a force on the ground.[25]

In Amman, John Maguire watched Chalabi's rise with unease. He was "so loose in the way he ran things, he had all kinds of competing interests," Maguire recalled. A sardonic colleague of Maguire's once made him a metal wall hanging engraved with the C.I.A. seal and dubbed "The Six Phases of a C.I.A. Covert Action Program." These were:

Euphoria.
Confusion.
Disillusionment.
Search for the Guilty.

Punishment of the Innocent.

Distinction for the Uninvolved.

In Chalabi's case, by early 1993, the cycle was underway.[26]

The C.I.A. had little access to one important wing of the opposition to Saddam Hussein: the Shia parties aligned with Iran, including the Supreme Council for the Islamic Revolution in Iraq. Largely hostile to the United States, the Shia religious parties had little interest in collaborating directly with the C.I.A.'s coupmakers—and vice versa. This estrangement would persist for years to come, exacerbating America's blindness to the full contours of Iraqi opposition politics, including how competition for power was likely to unfold if America ever did knock off Saddam.

In the intelligence and national security sections of Saddam's prisons, thousands of accused participants in the 1991 uprisings, mainly Shia, languished still. The secret police advanced prosecutions via memos and appeal letters that outlined specific instances of treason against the state:

"Theft of a car, with hostile slogans written on it."

"Sitting with saboteurs at the mosque."

"Transported saboteurs in his car, and carried a sign."

"Bearing arms and repeated folk songs."[27]

Unlike the regime's Kurdish victims, these mainly Shia prisoners had little visibility in the West. When the nuclear scientist and former political prisoner Hussain Al-Shahristani arrived in Tehran after his prison escape, the Supreme Council invited him to join their cause. With his roots in Karbala, his credentials as a scientist, and his credibility as an Abu Ghraib survivor, Shahristani had become a respected figure in Shia opposition circles. But he was "disappointed" to discover in Tehran that exiled leaders there and elsewhere were "not working together. Their focus was not on bringing down the regime. There was just political rivalry among them."[28]

He decided not to get involved. Ayatollah Ali Akbar Hashemi Rafsanjani, the reformist president of Iran, sought to revive the country's
science and technology sectors. His government provided the Shahristani family with a flat, free of charge. The president's son Yasser offered Shahristani work in Iran's nuclear program. Like Iraq during the
1980s, Iran had a civilian nuclear program as well as the beginnings of
a clandestine bomb effort. Shahristani needed an income. Rafsanjani
said nothing about weapons work; it was all but unthinkable that Iran
would entrust vital state secrets to an Iraqi citizen, no matter his attitude toward Saddam Hussein. Shahristani accepted a part-time position working on the mining of natural uranium, a subject well removed
from bomb development, and delivered occasional lectures in English
on subjects in nuclear chemistry.

Urged on by Hussain's wife, Berniece, the Shahristanis also ran humanitarian relief operations. Tens of thousands of Iraqi refugees still
languished in camps inside Iran, where they had fled in 1991. The wet-
lands that straddled the far southern border between Iraq and Iran had
long provided refuge to dissidents and smugglers, and some anti-
Saddam Shia activists operated from there. Saddam dammed rivers to
dry up the marshes, attacked villages, and created more refugees.

The Shahristanis initially set up a charity, Gulf War Victims, and
later took charge of the Iran office of a British charity, the Iraqi Refugee Aid Council. They staged logistics from Tehran and shuttled to and
from the Iraqi border, delivering food, clothing, and medical supplies.
Hussain also continued a project he had started inside Abu Ghraib:
creating records of political prisoners held by the Iraqi regime.

The Shahristanis worked in a largely hidden subworld of suffering
and defacement caused by Saddam Hussein's rule—the tens of thousands of camp dwellers near the marshes; the long lists of political prisoners and disappeared, as well as the families concerned about them;
and the physical landscape along the Iran-Iraq border, scarred by two
wars and littered with the detritus of combat. Saddam had "destroyed
the good nature of the Iraqi people," a colleague of Shahristani's at the
Aid Council, Abdul Halim, once remarked. "Material losses can be

compensated; destroyed homes can be rebuilt, but what about the goodness of people?"[29]

The words stayed with Shahristani. In the Karbala he had known as a boy in the 1950s, he recalled his neighbors as devout, straightforward, poor but ready to help and protect one another. Now neighbors spied on neighbors, coerced by secret police who could make a person disappear overnight. Then came the wars, "people shoveled into mass graves, bodies mutilated." The unthinkable became commonplace. "Everyone is so viciously for himself."[30]

The cruelty and selfishness played out in ordinary lives but also in the struggle between Saddam and his internal and exiled Iraqi enemies—a dirty war now in its second decade, and soon to intensify.

SIXTEEN

"We Need to Turn This Thing Off, Now!"

On April 14, 1993, George H. W. Bush flew to Kuwait on a chartered jet, to be celebrated for rescuing the emirate from Saddam Hussein. Sword dancers and drummers welcomed him. Kuwaitis waved American flags along the road into the capital. Accompanying the former president were his wife, Barbara; his sons Jeb and Neil; three daughters-in-law; former treasury secretary Nicholas Brady; former White House chief of staff John Sununu; and former secretary of state James Baker. The entourage lodged at the royal Bayan Palace. Jaber al-Ahmad al-Sabah, Kuwait's restored emir, hosted an opulent banquet and put on a "Festival of Gratitude." A beaming Bush proclaimed, "Mere words cannot express how proud I feel to be here." He addressed the Kuwaiti Parliament, accepted an honorary doctorate, and flew out without incident after two days.[1]

Two weeks later, Kuwait's security services announced the arrest of seventeen people for plotting to assassinate Bush during his visit. The accused included eleven Iraqi citizens, led by two whiskey smugglers in their thirties who were said to be agents of Iraqi intelligence. The conspirators allegedly intended to blow up Bush by remotely detonating a Toyota Land Cruiser packed with about 185 pounds of explosives. Kuwaiti authorities told the U.S. ambassador that on the day Bush arrived, they had discovered the vehicle bomb in a warehouse outside Kuwait City. Yet they hadn't informed Bush, the U.S. Secret Service, or anyone else in the U.S. government.[2]

In the long conflict between two Bush presidents and Saddam Hussein, the assassination plot of April 1993 would acquire a special resonance. "You know, he tried to kill my father," Jeb Bush said of Saddam Hussein some thirteen years later. "I was on that trip, too," Jeb continued. "All of us could've been killed." George W. Bush reportedly made similar comments in private and admitted publicly that he was "just as frustrated as many Americans are that Saddam Hussein still lives."[3]

But was this attempt on Bush's life authentic, or was it a concoction of Kuwait's security services to further discredit Saddam Hussein? It is inherently difficult to prove the absence of a secret conspiracy. It is perhaps notable that archives from the Saddam Hussein regime apparently contain no evidence of the plot. Kevin Woods, a military historian who had full access to the files, searched for even an oblique reference and found nothing. Charles Duelfer, who led the C.I.A.'s extensive investigation into Saddam Hussein's weapons programs and regime after 2003, also turned up a blank.[4]

Saddam was certainly reckless enough to order Bush's killing, and there is circumstantial evidence that points to his guilt. There is good evidence that the Land Cruiser vehicle bomb revealed by the Kuwaitis was built by Iraqi intelligence. But whether Saddam Hussein specifically ordered that bomb to be used to kill Bush is another matter.

In late April, the C.I.A. dispatched bomb specialists to Kuwait. They compared the Land Cruiser bomb to two intact vehicle bombs known to have been deployed by Iraqi intelligence in Turkey and the United Arab Emirates during the 1991 war. One bomb-rigged vehicle was discovered parked inside the Iraqi embassy in Abu Dhabi. The C.I.A. experts reported that the blasting caps and the circuit board from the Land Cruiser bomb in Kuwait closely resembled those found in Turkey and the U.A.E. An F.B.I. technician also found that the three vehicle bombs had "signature characteristics" of a single maker.[5]

Yet the fact that Iraqi intelligence built the Kuwait bomb did not prove that it had been deployed to kill Bush. Just as Iraqi operatives had abandoned an undetonated vehicle bomb in the Abu Dhabi embassy, they might also have left one behind in Kuwait when they fled. Perhaps the Kuwaitis discovered the Land Cruiser after the emirate's liberation and kept it around to be used as a prop to discredit Saddam. Such cleverness was not typically associated with Kuwaiti security services, but the emirate's restored regime certainly would have had no qualms about running such a dirty-tricks operation against Baghdad.

In May, F.B.I. agents interviewed the accused suspects. The prisoners had almost certainly been beaten and threatened while incarcerated, so the reliability of their statements is questionable. Two of them, Wali al-Ghazali and Raad al-Assadi, the whiskey smugglers, told the F.B.I. that Iraqi intelligence had recruited them to kill Bush. This recruitment had supposedly taken place at a café, a hotel, and other locations in Basra only several days before Bush arrived. The smugglers' handlers had presented them with the Land Cruiser as well as cash and weapons. The pair were ordered to drive the bomb into Kuwait, along with their usual consignment of liquor. They were told that Bush would give a speech at Kuwait University, but they were left on their own to figure out where that was, when Bush might appear, and how to detonate the bomb so that it would kill him.

Ghazali was given a suicide vest to infiltrate the crowd around Bush if the vehicle bomb plan failed, he said, but he tossed this vest while driving to Kuwait—if the job could not be done by remote control, he was not interested, apparently. On April 13, the day before Bush landed, the conspirators drove the Land Cruiser to a warehouse in Jahra, a suburb of Kuwait City, and parked it inside, they told the F.B.I. When they returned the next day, they saw police swarming around their hiding place. How the police had been tipped off was unclear.

The men said they ran away. They stole a car to return to Iraq, but the vehicle broke down, and they were arrested as they trudged along a road toward the border.[6]

The Day of the Jackal this was not, true or invented. In Washington, Sandy Berger, the deputy national security adviser, "led the doubts" as the evidence reached the White House, recalled Bruce Riedel, the C.I.A. analyst then at the National Security Council. Berger "thought this was all a setup."[7]

Riedel disagreed. For him, the forensics tying the Land Cruiser to a regime-sponsored bombmaker made the case. President Clinton eventually decided that the plot was real, a conclusion backed by analysts at the C.I.A. and the Justice Department, who saw no reason to disbelieve the combination of technical evidence and prisoner testimony. Clinton was "furious" and told Colin Powell that Saddam had "just tried to kill an American president. I think we ought to knock the living hell out of them."

"Mr. President, the question is, 'Do you want to get in another war, or do you want to punish them?'" Powell said. "This was a ham-handed effort with little chance of success. You need a response, but not another war."

Clinton deliberated. There was "agony" inside the administration for "more than a month" about what should be done, Riedel recalled. Finally, on June 26, Clinton ordered a retaliatory strike. Two U.S. warships fired twenty-three Tomahawk cruise missiles at Iraq's intelligence headquarters in downtown Baghdad.

At the last minute, to reduce the risk of loss of life, Clinton ordered that the attack take place at night, Baghdad time, when few people were likely to be at work. Yet a stray missile nonetheless smashed the home of Layla al-Attar, a former director of the Iraqi National Art Museum and one of Iraq's most admired painters. Attar and her husband died. Clinton told the public that he had acted in retaliation for "an elaborate plan devised by the Iraqi government and directed against a former president."[8]

A few days later, Barzan Ibrahim al-Tikriti, who was visiting Baghdad, drove out to Radwaniyah, Saddam's estate. Over lunch, they talked about the U.S. strike. Barzan tried to explain why Clinton felt obliged to hit Iraq even though Bush was no longer President. "When a president in America leaves at the end of his term, he keeps a special status and respect," Barzan said.

Barzan told a long story about how some Sudanese people he'd met defended the honor of their country's retired presidents, too. Saddam interrupted to exclaim, "Look, I swear, I will eliminate them one after the other!" He seemed to be referring to his enemies in general, but perhaps he meant the Bushes. Yet he said nothing to indicate that he had ordered the April hit, or that he had not, in Barzan's account. Whatever the truth, he was plainly satisfied that much of the world believed he was responsible.[9]

By the summer of 1993, three consecutive years of harsh sanctions had left Iraq's population facing severe food and health-care shortages. The U.N. had proposed an "oil for food" compromise to provide relief. The idea was that Iraq could sell at least several billion dollars' worth of oil annually but would have to submit to U.N. supervision to ensure the proceeds were used for humanitarian purposes. Saddam had refused, but he was tempted. "To be honest, even a dollar would help," he told the Revolutionary Command Council that July. Yet he feared that "everything has a price" and that his position as a supplicant of the U.N. was already becoming "a dark tunnel, which I don't see an end to. . . . I have a deep fear of this tunnel." He needed a way to fight the U.N. "Once they are in, they never leave unless they suffer losses. How would we harm them?"[10]

His pessimism was understandable; U.N. weapons inspectors had all but camped out in Iraq, acting much as they pleased. They had the authority of occupiers, even if they were unarmed technocrats. They ordered the demolition of entire Iraqi factories tied to chemical-weapon production or the undeclared nuclear program. They collected the country's remaining stocks of highly enriched uranium and shipped it to Russia to eliminate the risk that Iraq might misuse it for a bomb. The C.I.A.'s U-2 spy planes continued to fly back and forth across Iraq, taking photographs to aid inspection teams on the ground. During 1993, UNSCOM alone would conduct eight missions to Iraq lasting a total of almost two hundred days. Saddam was partly paying the price for his own foolish destruction of illicit weapons and records during the summer of 1991, which had complicated UNSCOM's verification work. Aspects of Saddam's weapons programs "could remain unclear for a long time," Rolf Ekéus would report to the Security Council.[11]

Saddam had to decide whether cooperating with the U.N. would be worthwhile, even if this undermined his image as a Castro-like holdout against the American-led world order. Attempting to come clean might signal weakness to Iran and Israel. He also faced "the cheater's dilemma," as the Norwegian political scientist Målfrid Braut-Hegghammer would later call it. To end sanctions, Saddam needed to satisfy UNSCOM about every last bomb and beaker of his past programs. But each time he authorized fresh disclosures, he invited more questions and seemed to prolong the U.N.'s investigations. His default approach remained deception and defiance—refusing landing rights to UNSCOM, harassing inspectors, and withholding the full story of his biological and nuclear programs, in particular. Three times during 1992 and again in early 1993, a united Security Council had responded to Saddam's intransigence by declaring Iraq to be in breach of its obligations—a veiled way to threaten the renewal of war.[12]

During the second half of 1993, Saddam softened. He allowed the U.N. to set up monitoring cameras at suspect Iraqi facilities, and he turned over information about foreign companies that had supplied Iraq's illicit programs. Tariq Aziz summoned Ekéus to his office and asked the Swede to carry messages of reconciliation to Washington.

In November, Ekéus met Peter Tarnoff, the number-three appointee at the State Department. He explained that Aziz wanted to know "what Iraq could do to get more favorable treatment" from the Clinton administration. Would it help if Iraq were "to make a significant contribution to the Middle East peace process?" How about help in the "struggle" against Islamic fundamentalism?

But Tarnoff only offered a familiar line: the U.S. "wanted only Iraq's full compliance with the U.N.'s resolutions, and it was not prepared to have a dialogue on any other issue." UNSCOM's pressure, Tarnoff continued, "remained the lynchpin of U.S. policy." The inspections were an end in themselves, not a passage to a revival of the cooperation of the Reagan years. The more effective the inspections, "the better the chance of keeping the Iraqis in place," Tarnoff explained. France and Russia were restless about Washington's firm line, Tarnoff admitted. They wanted to do business in Baghdad, and they worried about Iraq's disintegration. But the Clinton administration was not budging and had warned Paris and Moscow against any move to break consensus at the U.N.

At the White House, Ekéus heard the same thing. The U.S. "was in no hurry to see this whole matter completed," Berger told him. "Once sanctions were lifted, there would be no leverage over Saddam Hussein."[13]

Clinton heard from his spy agencies that his punishing approach need not last forever. If inspectors kept up the pressure, Saddam might yet fall from power, according to a National Intelligence Estimate circulated by the C.I.A. that December. "There is a better-than-even chance that Saddam will be ousted during the next three years," the document predicted.[14]

At home, Saddam consolidated his rule around his immediate family. He tried to rehabilitate Uday, his eldest son. In the spring of 1994, Saddam considered appointing him as minister of defense, a huge leap in authority. Uday had given up his hedonistic ways and "is serious, prays, and fasts," Saddam assured family members. He asked aides to canvass army generals. Three high-ranking generals each "noted Uday's total lack of military experience as a potential drawback and suggested that he might be more useful elsewhere," as Ekéus summarized their responses, which he learned about on visits to Iraq. Security officers soon turned up at these generals' homes, told them to bid their families goodbye, and took them away, never to be seen again. Yet Saddam did not go forward with his son's appointment. He might treat honest advice—even advice he had solicited—as a capital crime, yet he remained pragmatic. Marshal Uday was a politically implausible idea.[15]

In the early autumn of 1993, Saddam provoked another crisis with the Clinton administration by rotating tens of thousands of Republican Guard forces toward Kuwait, threatening another invasion. "This crisis might create new horizons where the political environment will be more conducive," he explained to his advisers. Clinton ordered ships and fighter planes to the region. On October 15, the U.N. adopted a fresh resolution demanding that Iraq withdraw its forces. Saddam backed down; he had been testing and bluffing.[16]

At the White House, Martin Indyk received Ekéus, who declared that the U.S. "would not continue to play this cat-and-mouse game." Iraq "should receive absolutely no reward for its recent behavior," and specifically "no movement of sanctions."[17]

The repetitive crises made the C.I.A.'s three-year-old covert action more appealing than ever. Frank Anderson, nearing retirement, had dropped some of his skepticism; he now thought a coup was "unlikely but possible." Cables poured in from the rotating C.I.A. teams in Iraqi Kurdistan about contacts that Ahmad Chalabi and his Iraqi National Congress, working with the Kurdish paramilitaries, had reportedly made with potential coupmakers inside the Iraqi military.

The C.I.A. had "no insight" into Saddam's decision-making, and Iraq outside Kurdistan "was truly a denied area by that time," Anderson recalled, using the intelligence term for an impenetrable black box. Still, Chalabi's ambition and promises were infectious. With White House approval, Anderson ordered the establishment of a permanent C.I.A. base in Iraqi Kurdistan.[18]

For chief of base, Anderson selected Robert Baer, a charismatic troublemaker and nineteen-year agency veteran. Anderson admired

Baer for his "enormous courage, physical courage"—qualities that were, he accepted, "not tempered by a lot of judgment." A passionate down-hill ski racer as a teenager, Baer had enrolled at Georgetown, where he made himself known by riding a Harley motorcycle up the library steps and through the main reading room. Recruited to the Directorate of Operations, he learned Arabic, Farsi, and French and put in hard tours in Beirut during a period of war, hijackings, and kidnappings. Baer himself admitted that it was his way to push things beyond the edge. As C.I.A. veteran Milton Bearden told Anderson, "I used to wake up at five in the morning and start with the question, 'What did I forget to tell Baer not to do today!'"[19]

Baer believed that a coup against Saddam seemed unlikely and cer-tainly would not be bloodless. The fantasy of silver-bullet covert action "helped the big thinkers" in Washington "get to sleep at night, and since we had no human sources inside or even near Saddam's circle—none—there was nothing to bring them back down to earth," Baer recalled. The covert-action program against Saddam had acquired a C.I.A. cryptonym: DB ACHILLES. (The "DB" was cable coding for matters pertaining to Iraq.) Saddam himself had cited the Achilles myth while rallying Arab neighbors in 1990 to his coming war against America. For both the Iraqi dictator and the C.I.A., the example of the Homeric hero with a vulnerable heel offered a call to action, despite long odds. Saddam regarded America as too hubristic and too afraid of taking ca-sualties to defeat a united Arab nation, which he hoped to forge through his own leadership, against all evidence. The C.I.A.'s operatives and leaders embraced hope over experience as they searched for a coup plan that might work. Both sides therefore trapped themselves by imag-ining a fatal flaw in their opponent that did not actually exist.[20]

Early in 1995, Baer and Steve Richter, now the C.I.A.'s chief of Middle East operations, briefed Indyk at the White House. Indyk re-called that he "specifically warned" both the C.I.A. men that "no com-mitments could be made on behalf of the U.S. government to putative coup plotters unless the White House explicitly approved them." If Indyk did issue such instructions, they apparently did not register.

Baer and a fresh team of Northern Iraq Liaison Element colleagues deployed to the C.I.A.'s base in Salahuddin, to the north of Erbil. Ahmad Chalabi had procured a ramshackle house for the operatives; it lacked running water, electricity, and heat. Chalabi was meanwhile peddling a well-worn white paper, "End Game," describing a strategy to get rid of Saddam by fostering an uprising among Kurdish and Shia rebels, who would be aided by defecting military units. It essentially proposed a rerun of the failed 1991 popular uprisings stoked by the Bush administration, but with more generals on the inside to help. Baer dismissed the blueprint as a fantasy. No one at the C.I.A. or the White House believed that Chalabi was in a position to stage an uprising against Saddam, "not even the dreamers," Baer recalled.[21]

Yet there was a new development. An Iraqi general who had been in a high position had recently defected. He wanted to move on Saddam, Chalabi told Baer. And he wanted to meet the C.I.A.

Wafiq al-Samarrai was well known to American intelligence. He had been the number two in the General Military Intelligence Directorate during the era of secret cooperation between Saddam and the Reagan administration. He had met in Baghdad with C.I.A. officers carrying satellite-derived intelligence. Later, he had worked with D.I.A. officers during Druid Leader. He had briefly been promoted into the top job at General Military Intelligence but his career had been sidetracked. In early December 1994, at forty-seven, Samarrai drove to Kirkuk and walked thirty hours into Kurdistan, where he connected with Ahmad Chalabi and Jalal Talabani, the leader of the Patriotic Union of Kurdistan. They set the general up in a mountainside villa near Dohuk. There Samarrai began to receive a succession of intrigued American and U.N. visitors, Robert Baer among them.

"I've been dispatched to the north by a group of military officers who intend to get rid of Saddam," the general told Baer on January 22, 1995. "We need to know whether your country will stand in our way or not." Samarrai also asked for immediate U.S. recognition if the coup were successful.[22]

In the coming days, Samarrai provided specifics. A combat brigade and two divisions commanded by generals with whom he was communicating would strike at Saddam. They expected that such an attack would cause Saddam to take shelter in his home area around Tikrit. There, another military unit in the conspiracy—a tank company attached to a local school for tank operators—would trap Saddam. Neither Baer nor anyone else at the C.I.A. had a way to talk to the Iraqi commanders supposedly involved in the plot. Their plan seemed complex and based on assumptions about how Saddam would behave that were inherently uncertain. Still, Samarrai was the closest thing to a restive senior officer with ties to Saddam that the C.I.A. had encountered up close in years.

Baer cabled the general's statements to Langley. Headquarters replied: "This is not a plan."[23]

Baer did not interpret this sarcasm as an order to stand down. He continued to talk with Samarrai. He collected the names of the conspirators; according to him, their bona fides checked out. And Baer encouraged the general: "Washington wants Saddam out." Baer later acknowledged that he was stretching his authority by making such remarks. He was operating "out where the bright fires burn."[24]

Samarrai also made himself available as an inside source to other agencies. In February, Charles Duelfer flew into Dohuk by helicopter with a U.N. team.

"I'm a soldier and a politician, and I have aspirations for the future," the general told him. Over hours, Samarrai answered questions about Iraq's biological weapons and missile programs, two of the big mysteries that still bedeviled Duelfer and Ekéus. But Samarrai didn't know much about the details. He did offer insights into Saddam's outlook. He said that the president regarded the possession of weapons of mass destruction as essential to his own security.

"We are the number-two country in this region, after Israel, in the biological and atomic fields," he said. "Saddam thinks he's going to be toppled if he doesn't have weapons."[25]

The comment partly explained Saddam's willingness to allow the world to believe that he had weapons when, in fact, he did not. Yet this was a "liar's truth" that the C.I.A. and other intelligence agencies found very difficult to accept.

Ahmad Chalabi had no qualms about lying. He cloaked his personal ambition in a righteous cause that had many passionate backers. He conceded no errors. When things did go wrong, he cast blame in whatever seemed the most convenient direction. He had a sense of theatrical possibility. He understood that a long con requires belief in something grand, entrancing, and just out of reach—in this case, Saddam's overthrow.

As part of Chalabi's "End Game," his I.N.C. had recruited and trained in Kurdistan a small, lightly armed militia. In Chalabi's thinking, this ragtag force would join veteran guerrillas from the two large Kurdish parties in an attack on Saddam's forces, which in turn would ignite armed rebellion in Iraq's southern governorates. Samarrai's defection had allowed Chalabi to weld this plan onto the general's somewhat more plausible-sounding coup d'état.

"For a guy with virtually no internal support in Iraq, Chalabi knew how to get things done and especially how to nudge people where he wanted them to go," Baer recalled. The uprising-cum-coup still looked like a long shot to Baer—among other things, fighters for the two main Kurdish parties, who often skirmished with one another, had escalated their armed rivalry into near civil war.[26]

Yet Baer pushed the plan forward. He filed many cables to C.I.A. headquarters and heard nothing in reply, he recalled. He later said he interpreted this indifference as permission, and he encouraged Chalabi and Samarrai to set a date for an attack. They decided to launch on the night of March 4, 1995.

By now, so many people had been let in on Chalabi-Samarrai-Kurdish plans that leaks flowed in all directions. On March 2, at 7:00 a.m. Washington time, Bruce Riedel, who had returned to the C.I.A. from the White House but still worked on Iraq, telephoned Martin Indyk. He reported that intercepts showed that Saddam was mobilizing elite Republican Guards to attack Kurdistan in order to preempt a coup attempt he expected to be launched from there.

Indyk called Richter, who outlined the plot involving Samarrai; according to Indyk, this was the first time he or anyone else at the White House had heard of such a coup plan or of Samarrai's involvement. The Pentagon reported that Iranian security forces and the Badr Brigade, the Tehran-based Shiite opposition group, were moving into Kurdistan to join the fighting once the coup attempt was launched. "It seemed that everybody—even Saddam—was in on this coup except Clinton, in whose name it was being launched," Indyk reflected.

Indyk and two aides—Ellen Laipson and George Tenet, then the senior White House staffer for intelligence matters—charged into the office of National Security Adviser Tony Lake. He had never heard of Samarrai or the coup plot, either. Laipson showed him a grainy photograph of the tough-looking, overweight Iraqi defector—"direct from central casting"—and they laughed out loud before it occurred to them, as Indyk put it, that "a lot of people were about to get themselves killed for no good purpose."

Lake called Admiral William Studeman, recently appointed as acting director of the C.I.A., following the resignation of James Woolsey. Lake laid into the admiral: "The first time the White House finds out about it is today, not from a report from the C.I.A. but from an intercept!"

Lake turned to his staff: "We need to turn this thing off, now!"

He decided to write personally to Baer so that there would be no confusion. Lake's cable arrived on March 3, Iraq time, at Baer's C.I.A. base in Salahuddin: "The action you have planned for this weekend has been totally compromised. We believe there is a high risk of failure.

Any decision to proceed will be on your own." The message ordered Baer to inform the would-be coupmakers that America would not back them.[27]

A conspiracy months in the making fizzled in days. On March 6, Samarrai told Baer that he was leaving for Damascus to put his children in school there. Saddam had arrested his co-conspirators, he reported. Kurdish guerrillas launched their attack and won a battle against Saddam's forces, but they later had to fall back. No uprising came from the South. And the C.I.A. ordered Baer to leave.

It turned out that days before the March 4 launch date, Chalabi had met with Iranian intelligence officers in Iraqi Kurdistan. He fabricated a story that the White House had dispatched an assassin, "Robert Pope," to get rid of Saddam, and he urged the Iranians to join the action. The Iranians cabled Tehran with this report, and eavesdroppers at America's National Security Agency intercepted it. Lake and C.I.A. officers initially believed that Pope was Baer and that he might have actively plotted Saddam's killing in violation of U.S. law. It took months of investigation to exonerate Baer of this falsehood. There was no Robert Pope.[28]

The episode was such a complete fiasco that it might have disabused Bill Clinton of any hope that C.I.A. covert action could ever solve his Saddam Hussein problem. But Saddam soon proved to be much more vulnerable than he had seemed that March. The twist was that the Iraqi president had no immediate cause to fear his generals. His Brutus was his son-in-law.

SEVENTEEN

"There Would Be
a Bloodbath"

S omething appeared to be wrong with Hussein Kamel, something apart from the violent hubris to which his colleagues had grown accustomed. He suffered seizures. He would black out for a few minutes and then remember nothing of the episode. An Iraqi doctor examined him and detected a brain tumor. The case was operable, but the delicacy of the procedure and the status of the patient called for international expertise. In February 1994, a French specialist operated on Saddam's son-in-law at a military hospital in Jordan. The procedure appeared to be successful, but as he recovered, Hussein Kamel fell into a fresh round of conflict with Uday and Qusay. He had always been frenetic, but by mid-1995, he struck some colleagues as downright un-hinged. They thought his illness might explain his behavior, but it also appeared that the competition among Saddam's princes might be get-ting to him. Jafar Dhia Jafar met him that summer and concluded that he was "experiencing a psychological crisis" caused by his rivalry with Saddam's sons.[1]

At the time of Hussein Kamel's operation in Jordan, the contours of

King Hussein's relations with Iraq were shifting again. The Oslo peace process had led the king to forge a settlement with Israel the previous year. In June 1995, Marwan Kassem, the king's chief of royal court, secretly traveled to see Saddam Hussein. They met in Saddam's hometown of Tikrit. The Jordanian envoy dropped a bombshell: King Hussein wished to visit Baghdad jointly with Yitzhak Rabin, Israel's prime minister, to enlarge the Oslo negotiations.

Kassem argued that Iraq would never rid itself of sanctions without Israel's approval, and he "advised us to change our policy towards Israel in order for the siege to be lifted," as Saddam recalled it. The idea that Saddam would receive Rabin as a guest of Iraq was almost beyond imagination, but these were ambitious times in Middle East peacemaking.

Saddam remembered rejecting the proposal outright; he told Kassem that "he and King Hussein better not mention it again." Saddam also disclosed the proposal to Hussein Kamel, telling him that "defeatists" like Jordan "need people to be defeated with them in order to see that they are not alone in that defeat. For Iraq, this is impossible."

Saddam still trusted his son-in-law and allowed him to travel abroad. In mid-July, Hussein Kamel flew to Moscow. "He told me that he was invited by the Russians and by the Belarusians," Saddam told colleagues later. Hussein Kamel met Kirsan Nikolayevich Ilyumzhinov, a chess enthusiast and the president of the Russian Republic of Kalmykia, an oil-and-gas-endowed enclave by the Caspian Sea. As was typical in the Boris Yeltsin era of Russian government, Ilyumzhinov had prospered as a businessman while he consolidated political power in his region. Hussein Kamel talked with him for hours at a dacha near Moscow. A Russian foreign ministry official and a Kuwaiti businessman joined them. Hussein Kamel's agenda on this journey remains unclear, but it seems most likely that he was engaged in sanctions-evading business of some kind, or was seeking to build ties in the chaotic post-Soviet landscape that might benefit Iraq.[2]

On his way home, he passed through Amman, the crucial gateway for Iraq's illicit trade. Hussein Kamel kept an apartment there, behind the Iraqi Commercial Office. He stayed several days and may have met King Hussein. But Hussein Kamel may have seen the proposal to reset relations with Israel as an opportunity. He had already sent messages to the Clinton administration indicating that he did not necessarily share his father-in-law's unshakable hostility toward Israel. He certainly imagined himself as a next-generation Iraqi leader who could rally America behind him.[3]

By the end of July, Hussein Kamel and his brother, Saddam Kamel, were preparing to leave Iraq with their children and wives—Raghad and Rana, respectively, daughters of Saddam Hussein. On July 27, Hussein Kamel met with an Iraqi brigadier who worked with the U.N. on weapons issues. He grilled the brigadier about what the outside world did and did not know of Iraq's prohibited weapons. They discussed Iraq's aborted atomic-bomb program. Hussein Kamel declared that by 1991, if it weren't for the war over Kuwait, Iraq would have been able to build a bomb within eight to twelve months. The war had deprived Iraq of "a strategic balance with Israel," he said.

That same evening, he summoned Mahdi Obeidi, the physicist who had worked with him, and asked questions about the bomb program's history, as if preparing himself to brief others. These meetings suggested that Hussein Kamel "had already decided" by late July to defect, Saddam later concluded. In final preparation, Hussein Kamel collected at least $9 million in cash, according to later investigations by Saddam's regime.

During his travels in and out of Jordan, Hussein Kamel had indicated to King Hussein's aides that he might break with Saddam. It is difficult to assess how actively the king encouraged him. The Jordanian monarch was working secretly that summer to flip Iraq into the Middle East peace camp, and it is conceivable that, in this context, he recruited Hussein Kamel to defect. Yet it is clear that the exact timing of Hussein Kamel's decision was a surprise in Amman. And there can be no doubt that Hussein Kamel's longstanding rivalry with Uday played a significant part in the events about to unfold. Uday had recently threatened to kill him, Hussein Kamel later told King Hussein's aides.[4]

Hussein Kamel was in a treacherous position. If he betrayed Saddam, he would not only risk his own life but also greatly complicate his wife's position. After marrying Hussein Kamel as a teenager, Raghad had stayed in school and completed a university degree. She had grown into a formidable woman in her own right. "I grew up among giants," Raghad recalled. "Real men. I felt safe amongst them." This was about to change.[5]

Monday, August 7, 1995, was the eve of a national holiday in Saddam's Iraq to commemorate the end of the Iran-Iraq War seven years earlier. Among the celebrants was Watban al-Tikriti, one of Saddam's half brothers. He attended a party on a small farm in south Baghdad. It was a familiar scene—music, female singers, armed men on the prowl, and free-flowing liquor. What could go wrong?

This time, more than usual: Watban was also feuding with Uday, who had publicly questioned his uncle's competence as interior minister—and not without reason. Saddam had then fired Watban back in May. "What was I to do?" the president explained later. "He would drive around Baghdad at night, drunk, and shoot out traffic lights." A Watban-Uday fissure had now been added to the family fault lines.[6]

That August night, Uday hosted his own fete at a former yacht club on the Tigris. It was a suffocating evening; temperatures hung above one hundred degrees long after sunset. Sometime after midnight, after becoming enraged by reports of goings-on at the party Watban was attending, Uday decided to crash his uncle's celebration. The cause of Uday's anger has variously been described as an argument about a woman, a fistfight that escalated, or Watban's indiscreet mocking of Uday. In any event, Uday was drunk, fired up, and armed with a pump-action shotgun.[7]

Uday opened fire when he arrived. He killed several guests and badly wounded Watban in the leg. "Blood spurted everywhere, and Watban was unconscious when Uday stuffed his uncle into the car" and drove him to the exclusive family hospital in Baghdad, according to Ala Bashir, the family physician. Watban survived, but it would require more French surgeons to try to repair his leg, which eventually had to be amputated.

Saddam rushed to the hospital, checked on Watban, and went hunting for Uday, who had wisely gone into hiding. "My father will have to calm down," Uday reportedly told his bodyguard. (This took a while. Some days after the incident, Saddam barged into a garage at the Republican Palace complex where Uday had stored scores of Mercedes-Benzes, BMWs, Porsches, Ferraris, Lamborghinis, and other cars. The president ordered security guards to douse the vehicles with gasoline and strike a match. Years later, hunting for Saddam's illicit weapons, American investigators came across this garage, still filled with charred vehicles.)[8]

Meanwhile, that same fateful night, beneath a waxing desert moon, the Hussein and Saddam Kamel families barreled in Mercedes sedans down the highway toward Jordan to make their dramatic escape. It isn't entirely clear why Uday's shooting spree led Hussein and Saddam Kamel to flee that night. Saddam Kamel may have gotten into a fist-fight with Uday. Raghad Hussein is one of the few surviving witnesses on the inside. She has not gone into details, but she has made clear that they all fled for their lives. "I knew that if we stayed, there would be a bloodbath," she explained. The victims would be close members of her family, she continued. "So in order to prevent this conflict, I supported the decision to leave."[9]

Eid al-Mawlid al-Nabawi, the celebration of the birth of the Prophet Muhammad, as recorded in the Islamic calendar, fell that year on August 9, the day after Hussein Kamel and his family arrived in

Jordan. That morning, Marwan Kassem, King Hussein's chief of royal court, was shaving at his Amman residence when his daughter told him that Hussein Kamel was on the phone.

"I'm Lieutenant General Hussein," Hussein Kamel said when he picked up. "I have a message from the president."

Kassem invited him over. They sat down in the living room. Hussein Kamel seemed ill at ease. He mentioned that he was staying at the Amra Hotel, a comfortable if undistinguished place on the capital's Sixth Circle. He said that he was under "orders from Saddam" to only deliver his message to King Hussein personally.

Later that day, the king invited Hussein Kamel to see him. Only then did Saddam's son-in-law announce that he was seeking political asylum in Jordan. He explained that he was not safe in Baghdad because of Uday. He also sought the king's support in a campaign to succeed Saddam Hussein as Iraq's ruler.[10]

The king transferred Hussein Kamel's family to Hashmiya Palace, a hilltop estate with a view of Jerusalem that had been built during the 1970s. King Hussein had intended to live at Hashmiya with Queen Alia, his Egyptian-born third wife, but in 1977, Alia died in a helicopter crash. Afterward, the palace became a residence for visiting dignitaries, and its staff had hosted Prince Philip of Britain and Jacques Chirac. Now the families of Hussein and Saddam Kamel moved in.

As word spread about Hussein Kamel's defection and ambitions to overthrow Saddam, Amman became a "bee town," as one senior Jordanian official put it, with "all intelligence services, all media—Western, Russian, local, Arab," pouring into the Jordanian capital. The betrayal shook up assumptions about Iraq's future. Prince Turki al-Faisal, the Saudi intelligence chief, flew to Amman to discuss teaming up with Hussein Kamel against Saddam.[11]

The defection had forced King Hussein to abandon the deliberate ambiguity of his relations with Saddam and choose sides. By doing so, he put at risk his fragile kingdom's economic stability, gambling that Washington and London would back him up. Sanctions-busting trade between Jordan and Iraq—tolerated by the United States on the grounds that King Hussein was too important an ally to punish—provided Jordan a crucial source of energy at discounted prices. Saddam could not afford to lose his trade with Jordan, either. But nobody could predict how he would react to the king's decision to shelter Hussein Kamel.

The king's patrons in London and Washington weren't sure what to make of Hussein Kamel's desire to topple his father-in-law, but they welcomed such a dramatic sign that the Baghdad regime might crack up. British prime minister John Major wrote to offer his "very warm support" for Jordan's "brave decision," which had delivered a "serious blow to the Iraqi regime." The king replied that he had acted because Hussein Kamel and his family "sought our help, as a result of total desperation and pressing need to alert the world to the urgent requirement for change in their country."[12]

King Hussein harbored hopes that if he helped engineer a change of regime in Baghdad, he might somehow restore his own extended family's historical royal rule in Iraq. The king's dreams of a Hashemite return in Baghdad were at least as fanciful as his hopes for Saddam's embrace of the Oslo peace process, but the ambitions of monarchs sometimes die hard. "King Hussein is free to dream about anything he wants," Tariq Aziz advised Saddam privately. "King Hussein is controlled by the U.S.; they tell him to do things. . . . There is a deal between King Hussein, Hussein Kamel, and the United States to make a change" in Iraq.[13]

All those hoping that Hussein Kamel's defection might produce Saddam's overthrow still faced the quandary that had bedeviled the C.I.A. for four years now: How would they actually pull this off? And how could they predict confidently that what followed would be any better?

David Manners was the newly arrived C.I.A. station chief in Amman that summer. He was a U.S. Naval Academy graduate in his late thirties who had moved back and forth between the Soviet–East European and Near East Divisions of the Directorate of Operations. He and his family had barely unpacked in Amman when he received a call from Ali Shukri, the director of King Hussein's private office and an influential palace fixer. Shukri said the king wanted to see him.

"I fear that Saddam Hussein may take action against me," the Jordanian monarch told Manners when they were seated in a reception room. He asked to talk to President Clinton, to "get assurances of protection."

Manners delivered a secure phone to the palace and called back to headquarters to see how the C.I.A. might meet the king's request. John Deutch, a chemist and former M.I.T. provost, had recently arrived from the Pentagon to become C.I.A. director. Deutch's good relations with Clinton offered the agency renewed access to the Oval Office. Yet Deutch had little experience with intelligence operations. He had served most recently as deputy defense secretary and had grown accustomed to the reflexive deference shown to superiors at the Pentagon. The C.I.A.'s comparative disdain for hierarchy and its culture of creative insubordination (or indiscipline and lack of accountability, depending on the beholder) seemed to stun Deutch, in the judgment of some of his new colleagues.

Deutch called King Hussein to reassure him while they waited for a slot in Clinton's schedule: "Anything you need, we will provide."[14]

Clinton called later and repeated the assurance that Washington would protect Jordan against Saddam if he retaliated over Hussein Kamel's defection. Clinton followed up with a formal letter restating this commitment. The tight, often secret collaboration between the king and successive American presidents had opened a new chapter.

On Saturday, August 12, Hussein Kamel addressed a press conference in a garden at one of King Hussein's palaces in Amman. He wore a gray suit and spoke calmly from a podium surrounded by yellow roses. He spoke like an aspiring politician: "It was the suffering of our people that prompted us to leave the regime and work for the welfare of our people," he said. He did not denounce his father-in-law by name and pledged not to spill Iraqi state secrets unless this was in the interest of the Iraqi people. But he did not hide his ambition: "We are working to topple the regime."[15]

———————

Saddam wanted his daughters and grandchildren back. Soon after the defection, the Iraqi president dispatched Uday, Ali Hassan al-Majid ("Chemical Ali"), and an intelligence officer to Amman. King Hussein felt he had no choice but to receive the delegation, which would also include Iraq's ambassador in Jordan. The Jordanian Royal Guard, responsible for the king's safety, recommended that they disarm the Iraqi visitors, who typically packed pistols. But the king did not want to insult his guests or seem to be afraid of them. Ali Shukri, the senior palace aide, warned the Iraqi ambassador: "If your people so much as twitch, you are all going to be killed."[16]

Before the meeting, the king summoned Dave Manners. Shukri met him and reported that the king had spoken personally to Saddam's daughters, and that the women had said they wished to stay in Jordan. The king would explain that the daughters could remain under the king's protection for as long as they wished. Manners recalled being ushered into a room adjoining the office where the Iraqis would arrive. He was to sit there during the meeting, out of sight. Before it started, the king came in, pulled out a .45-caliber pistol, chambered a round, and, smiling, handed the gun to Manners. "Who knows what happens?" he said wryly.[17]

When the visitors turned up, three Royal Guard officers with automatic rifles stood by the king. Majid did the talking for the Iraqis. The king heard them out but let them know that Raghad, Rana, and their children would not be leaving his protection unless the women later decided to go home. The discussion was over in less than fifteen minutes. It seemed doubtful, however, that Saddam would let the matter rest.

King Hussein had asked that a high-ranking emissary from the Clinton administration visit with Hussein Kamel to assure him that he had done the right thing by breaking with his father-in-law, and to explore plans to overthrow Saddam.

Manners joined a call with George Tenet, now at the C.I.A. as Deutch's deputy, to discuss who the Clinton administration would send to Amman. Deutch had suggested dispatching J. H. Binford Peay III, the four-star general in charge of Central Command (CENT-COM). But Manners thought that was a terrible idea, he recalled. Hussein Kamel "is a thug in an Armani suit," he said. "You do not send a four-star general or flag-rank officer out to meet this criminal. This is a C.I.A. thing . . . this is dirty stuff."

They settled on David Cohen, a career analyst with a graduate degree in political science who had recently succeeded Ted Price as the head of the C.I.A's global spying operations. Officers at Jordan's Mukhabarat, its General Intelligence Directorate, arranged a dinner at Hashmiya Palace. Hussein Kamel wore a business suit. He was abstemious—he did not smoke and drank only water with lemon. His brother Saddam and a hulking cousin who had come to Jordan with them wore Hawaiian shirts with pistols protruding from their pants. After a meal, they sat down to discuss "how to go forward in terms of cooperation," as Manners put it.[18]

Neither Cohen nor Manners spoke Arabic, so the discussion suffered from the starts and stops of interpretation. Hussein Kamel delivered a rambling monologue about his ambition to rescue Iraq. Some of his remarks were straightforward, yet his ideas about how to seize power were "sprinkled with elements of madness," Manners recalled. At one point, evidently inspired by Saddam Hussein's methods of patronage, he suggested that the United States buy five thousand Mercedes sedans and bring them to the Iraqi-Jordanian border to put on display in a giant parking lot. Then they should announce to Iraqi military officers that if they defected and crossed the border, they would be rewarded with a car. Even more astonishingly, he asked for direct command of the 82nd Airborne Division, according to Manners. "We'll take back Baghdad in a week," he said, speaking of what he could do with those American forces at his disposal.

"I'm not in a position to do that," Cohen said about handing over the 82nd Airborne. He exchanged sideways glances with his colleagues,

and the Americans left abruptly. The C.I.A. soon formed a task force
to work with Jordanian intelligence on debriefing Hussein Kamel about
his potential and about the inner workings of the regime and its weapons programs. But it was already evident that Hussein Kamel was unlikely to be the savior the agency had been seeking.[19]

Hussein Kamel's defection had deprived him of the access and authority that would have made him a danger to Saddam had he remained in Baghdad and tried to seize power there. His years as Saddam's
visible and powerful henchman and his complicity in many of the regime's catastrophic campaigns, such as the brutal occupation of Kuwait
and the murderous repression of the 1991 uprisings, undermined his
ability to attract allies. A British intelligence officer summed up the
situation in a session with King Hussein: "Your majesty, you have a recently cut rose," he said. "It has its own perfume, which will wither
away in no time."[20]

The C.I.A. and MI6 had cultivated opposition to Saddam since the
Gulf War, separately and together. King Hussein maintained close ties
with both spy services. Manners admired his British colleagues but
kept his distance on operational matters. There had long been an air of
sibling rivalry between the two services, and in this case, it played out
in competition for King Hussein's attention. The Americans were
action-oriented and impatient; the British were "more reserved, more
into details," and they knew the region better because of their imperial
experience, recalled Samih Battikhi, then deputy head of the Jordanian Mukhabarat.

After the debacle with Ahmad Chalabi in Kurdistan, the C.I.A. appeared ready to join MI6 in firmly backing another opposition leader
long cultivated by Britain: Ayad Allawi, a physician, businessman, and
former Baathist based in London who had founded the Iraqi National
Accord, a rival opposition group to Chalabi's. Allawi had built a network of former and serving Iraqi military officers, some of whom had
carried out "C.I.A.-inspired" bombings in and around Baghdad in the

year prior to Hussein Kamel's defection, according to Martin Indyk. Unlike Chalabi, Allawi did not have ties to Tehran or lie habitually, and he worked comfortably in the shadows. Yet Allawi made clear that summer that he was not about to share power with Hussein Kamel.

Allawi met with King Hussein and criticized the newcomer: "He doesn't have a plan," Allawi said. He dismissed Hussein Kamel, not inaccurately, as someone with "a very narcissistic streak and a very nasty streak of corruption and hurting people."[21]

For Manners and the C.I.A., the situation was delicate. Hussein Kamel's declarations had made headlines and constituted the most visible fissure in Saddam Hussein's dictatorship since George H. W. Bush had inaugurated covert action four years earlier. King Hussein had openly embraced regime change in Baghdad. The C.I.A. sought to encourage the king's pivot while persuading the monarch that Hussein Kamel was not by himself the answer. "The king needed to learn that the guy's a defector—his utility is in the act he committed," Manners reflected later. "We're not going to get behind him." But King Hussein was understandably skeptical about the C.I.A.'s ability to foment a change of regime by its own methods. And Saddam Hussein had only just begun to fight back.[22]

About two weeks after Hussein Kamel arrived in Amman, Jafar Dhia Jafar received a summons to a meeting in Baghdad. He was taken in a car with thick blackout curtains to a building inside the Republican Palace complex. After being checked for weapons, he entered a small lecture hall filled with colleagues from Iraq's former nuclear program and scientists and administrators from other industrial projects. Saddam entered and took a chair onstage.

"I have gathered you to apologize to you twice: once for appointing Hussein Kamel as your supervisor and once again for his being my son-in-law and being affiliated with my family," Saddam said calmly. During an hour of extemporaneous remarks, he repeated this apology three times. He described Hussein Kamel as "conceited" and "paranoid" and explained that the operation to remove the tumor in his brain had "negatively affected his behavior."[23]

The event was part of an extraordinary secret apology tour Saddam undertook late that summer to minimize the damage of his son-in-law's betrayal and reassert his authority. The president distributed a letter of apology and explanation to ministers and other leaders. He presided over a "lessons learned" session with his Council of Ministers. To an audience at the Military Industrialization Corporation and at a convening of the Revolutionary Command Council, he repeatedly offered the same two-part apology: first, for having saddled the nation with this vile traitor, and second, for having invited Hussein Kamel into his own family. Deftly, Saddam cast the crisis as a shared experience of the Baath Party leadership, a collective trauma.

To the Revolutionary Command Council, Saddam spoke of himself in the third person. He acknowledged Hussein Kamel's abusive actions while in power, but he cleverly absolved his comrades of their own complicity in his son-in-law's misdeeds. "You tolerated the person who insulted you very much and insulted the country," he said, "because it seemed that he has the trust of Saddam Hussein, and because you value Saddam Hussein in your hearts. . . . Therefore, I thank you a lot."

He explained that Hussein Kamel's "treason" was the result of two factors. The first was ambition. As recently as March, his son-in-law had been pressing for a promotion to deputy prime minister, which Saddam had refused to give, knowing that Hussein Kamel's appetite for power was insatiable. "I told him, 'You are sick.'" Hussein Kamel would not be satisfied until he had Saddam's own position. "I told him, 'I am warning you, this is dangerous—dangerous for you, and it is dangerous to have such an imagination.'"

He assured his comrades that he did not believe in family rule. "Saddam Hussein . . . believes in the republican system, and he is not concerned to make the Baath Arab Socialist Party a tool or stairs to his relatives so they [can] sneak into authority one after another."

The possibility that his son-in-law had gone off the rails because of a brain tumor seemed to comfort Saddam. It exonerated him of all responsibility. A doctor had advised Saddam that because of the operation, Hussein Kamel's "brain electricity has changed."[24]

Saddam recounted that he said to himself, "If he is insane and committed suicide, or had he remained insane, it would have been more honorable for me, honorable for him" and for his place in history, "rather than be labeled as a traitor." Saddam maintained that he did not feel threatened. Jordan was "a small and weak country," he told one audience. "King Hussein was raised by the British," he continued. "He was not raised in a rural home in Iraq," as Saddam had been, so he "cannot endure hardships."[25]

King Hussein's own enthusiasm for his guest waned as summer passed. Hussein Kamel "didn't have the charisma," recalled Ali Shukri. "He wasn't properly educated; he didn't speak English or any other language" besides Arabic. Ayad Allawi was not the only opposition leader to shun him. The Shia parties "especially didn't want to have anything to do with" Hussein Kamel because they accurately regarded him as complicit in Saddam's murderous crushing of the 1991 rebellion.[26]

Yet the king was also irritated by the C.I.A. The agency had undermined his secret initiative to bring Iraq into the peace process with Israel, he felt, because the Clinton administration did not trust Saddam enough to explore his political rehabilitation. (So dismayed was King Hussein by the Clinton administration's unwillingness to support Yitzhak Rabin's outreach to Saddam that when a right-wing Israeli gunman assassinated Rabin later that year, the king wondered aloud if Americans were behind the killing.)[27]

Dave Manners worked to persuade the king to back Allawi and the Iraqi National Accord. Yet the Jordanian monarch's top advisers were divided—some favored going all in with Washington, while others preferred maintaining Jordan's business and political ties to Saddam's regime. In September, King Hussein flew to Washington and rode to the

C.I.A.'s wooded campus to hear a pitch about the agency's latest plan to develop an insider coup against Saddam, this time through Allawi.[28]

One of King Hussein's skeptical advisers had warned him "to expect a half-baked presentation" at the C.I.A. The spy agency briefers would cloak their lack of knowledge about the internal situation in Iraq "through the use of elaborate graphs, charts, and presentational aids." Even in these early days of PowerPoint's hegemony over Washington, an overload of colorfully designed but cluttered and questionably relevant information was a common feature of intelligence briefings.

Manners by now sympathized with the skeptics around the king. He was coming to believe that the Clinton administration was not serious about a plan to remove Saddam Hussein from power. The DB ACHILLES covert-action program was very modestly funded, and the White House was clearly ambivalent about taking more risks. A half-assed covert action was worse than none at all, Manners thought.

Saddam was becoming the "new Fidel Castro," entrenched in power and feeding off America's ineffectual enmity, Manners told Deutch and King Hussein in the Langley meeting. King Hussein said he had used the same analogy—if the effort to remove Saddam went as poorly as the effort to remove Fidel, Jordan would pay a steep price.

The king left the session at Langley still undecided about whether to back the C.I.A. Later, on the same visit, however, he met Bill Clinton in the Oval Office. The president pulled him aside, put an arm around his shoulder, and asked him to join the effort to unseat Saddam. The king agreed. The C.I.A.—this time with apparent support at the highest levels—would try again.[29]

EIGHTEEN

Honor among Tyrants

Rolf Ekéus kept an apartment in central Stockholm lined with books and softened by a well-tuned piano. At his club near the capital's waterfront, he could lunch with other notables of Sweden's political elite. As he led UNSCOM's investigations in Iraq, he embodied much of the ethos of Swedish global diplomacy—earnest, balanced, multilingual, and devoted to peacebuilding. Yet he also had to manage some of the tension inherent in Sweden's historical doctrines of neutrality. His wealthy, democratic country was firmly attached to Europe and therefore, by proximity, to the American nuclear and defense umbrella of the Cold War era. Swedes appointed to roles like the one Ekéus held sought credibility as independent fact finders and mediators, but some leaned toward Washington more than others. From his office at the U.N. tower in Manhattan, Ekéus continued to take an aggressive line toward Saddam. His decisions might not fairly be called pro-American, but by 1995, the Clinton administration was certainly satisfied. Ekéus continued to welcome the C.I.A.'s insights into what Saddam might be covering up. He also opened a secret, sensitive intelligence-sharing channel with Israel. Scott Ritter, an American Marine officer posted to the Special Commission, regularly shared U-2 photos with Israeli defense and intelligence analysts so that the Israelis, who watched Iraq closely, might offer suggestions about where Ekéus's inspectors should be hunting.[1]

Tariq Aziz found Ekéus difficult to influence. His standard was "perfection," as Aziz told Saddam. "This is his desire at the behest of the United States, and due to his own cowardice. As a person, he is a coward. He is not one of those international figures that say, 'I am convinced, and this is where I stop.'"[2]

Aziz was on the hook to Saddam for results at the U.N.—sanctions relief, above all. He knew well that his regime was still covering up too many secrets about its past weapons work to expect a passing grade from Ekéus. By 1995, the Special Commission had documented and dismantled much of Iraq's prohibited missile arsenal. Russia had provided serial numbers of Scud missiles the Soviet Union had exported to Iraq, and this data had accelerated accounting work by a specialized U.N. team. Iraq's chemical-arms program had also been well documented. Yet Iraq still harbored important secrets about its missile program and past chemical-weapon use, as well as about its nuclear-bomb program. The regime had still not come clean about its centrifuge work to enrich uranium or its crash program, following the invasion of Kuwait, to use reactor fuel to hurriedly build a bomb.[3]

Yet perhaps the biggest remaining problem, Aziz knew, was Iraq's biological-weapons program. Saddam had approved a robust research and weapons-building effort that dated to the mid-1980s. They had loaded germ agents into about 166 bombs and 25 missile warheads on the eve of the 1991 war. Hussein Kamel ordered those weapons destroyed in May of that year after they weren't used. Yet he again prohibited recordkeeping. Ekéus had been probing this history and hunting for hidden biological stocks since 1991, yet Iraq had admitted next to nothing. The regime had trotted out stone-faced technocrats and scientists who offered one absurd cover story after another about the purposes of suspect facilities. On biological weapons, Ekéus "has solid ground against us, actually," Amer Mohammad Rashid, one of Saddam's weapons advisers, told him. "I regret to say that we are responsible."

Saddam had refused to tell the truth in part because he feared that if he admitted his lies about the germ weapons, Ekéus would "use it as an excuse" to revitalize and prolong other investigations. During the first half of 1995, Aziz advised that this risk was now worth taking because France and Russia were ready to help Iraq achieve sanctions relief—but only if "the existence of a big gap in the biological file" could be addressed. Saddam remained skeptical that Ekéus would ever come around, and he had doubts that France and Russia could be trusted, but he appears to have given Aziz permission to see what might be done.[4]

That April, in Baghdad, Aziz told Ekéus a story about a friend in the city who had been accused of political murder. His friend was innocent, but he confessed nonetheless, after being tortured. Aziz suggested that Iraq might be prepared to make a similar admission about its history of biological-weapons work.

Ekéus flew to Washington and met Tony Lake, the national security adviser. He reported what he had heard. "Tariq Aziz must have gone to the Arthur Koestler school of philosophy," Lake said, referring to the author of the novel *Darkness at Noon*, in which the protagonist, caught up in Stalinist show trials, confesses to crimes he did not commit.

The dance between Ekéus and Aziz continued into the summer. Iraq admitted that it had developed an offensive germ-warfare program but still falsely claimed that it had never assembled weapons. Aziz kept demanding sanctions relief. Ekéus could only say that telling the truth would help at the Security Council.

"Do they want to come clean or not?" Peter Tarnoff, Clinton's undersecretary of state for political affairs, asked Ekéus that June. "Their behavior seems to indicate that they have something to hide."

"Their mindset is one of paranoia," Ekéus said. "Saddam Hussein has a very limited point of view. He deals largely with a small set of people, virtually all Iraqis." His thinking, Ekéus continued, was "limited and maybe bizarre and screwed up."

Tarnoff noted that if "Saddam had made a decision to come clean and the Iraqis followed through, the U.S. alone would not be able to resist."

"We have growing confidence in most areas" of the weapons inspections, Ekéus acknowledged. The open issues about chemical arms and missiles were "not important." Yet it was "crystal clear" that Iraq was hiding "both weapons and documents" from its work on germ warfare. It was also unclear whether they would ever tell the full story. Ominously, Aziz had coupled the disclosure of half-truths that summer with a threat: unless the U.N. ended sanctions, Iraq would cease all cooperation.[5]

This was the state of play when Hussein Kamel's defection rocked Baghdad in August. It was immediately clear to Saddam and Tariq Aziz that if Hussein Kamel turned state's witness for Ekéus—if he started spilling secrets—Iraq's position at the Security Council would spiral from bad to worse. Yet only Hussein Kamel knew the full story of what he had ordered destroyed or hidden. They were flying blind.[6]

Aziz telephoned Ekéus and asked him to visit Baghdad. At twilight on August 17, Ekéus and nine colleagues filed into the cavernous conference room at the Ministry of Foreign Affairs. Aziz brought his own delegation.

Aziz began by saying that after Hussein Kamel's flight to Jordan, he had learned of secrets that had been kept from the U.N. "on Hussein Kamel's instructions." Aziz himself had never "known the truth." They intended to correct the record now. After they did, Aziz continued, he was sure that Ekéus and his colleagues "would conclude that Iraq had no weapons of mass destruction—no weapons and no materials."

Rihab Rashid Taha al-Azawi, a mild-mannered scientist educated in Britain, proceeded to read out a stunning confession of Iraq's development of biological weapons. She recited dates, facilities, equipment used, and approximate production volumes. She described how Iraq had produced botulinum toxin and anthrax, agents so deadly that a drop might kill a person. She explained how germ bombs and warheads had been assembled and deployed. It had all been Hussein Kamel's doing. Ekéus and his team scribbled notes furiously.[7]

Two nights later, the Swede returned alone to the Ministry of Foreign Affairs and met Aziz. Ekéus complained that while Rihab Taha's admissions had been remarkable, he "had not received one single document" to back up her story.

But Aziz wanted to talk about the bigger picture. He knew Ekéus would soon find a way to meet Hussein Kamel, "the American agent," as he called him. Ekéus should be wary. Hussein Kamel would lie, and the Swede must be able to "see the difference between lies and facts." Iraq had no weapons of mass destruction—none. Aziz was "absolutely sure." All its work lay in the past.

If Ekéus would just do the right thing, Aziz continued, Iraq would be appreciative. He looked out the window and exhaled cigar smoke. "We could open an account in Switzerland for you—for instance, five hundred thousand dollars."

Stunned, Ekéus managed to reply, "That's not the way we make business in Sweden."[8]

When Ekéus complained that Iraq had provided no records, he may have sparked an idea in Aziz's brain trust. Days later, an Iraqi minder told Ekéus that he had important news: the regime had just discovered that Hussein Kamel had secretly stored documents about illicit weapons at his farm outside Baghdad.

Ekéus and some of his team members drove straight there. They made their way to a "traditional shotgun-shaped henhouse," Ekéus recalled. Inside they found 170 boxes of documents, microfilm, photographs, and videotapes—the documents alone would total about 680,000 pages when inventoried. It was obvious that the materials had recently been moved to Hussein Kamel's shed—the crates were dust-free. But the treasure was genuine. One inspector quickly found a historical memo updating authorities about Iraq's germ weapons.[9]

Ekéus flew on that day to Amman for an appointment with Hussein Kamel. Riding into the Hashmiya Palace grounds, he saw children's toys and bicycles scattered on the lawns. Inside, he found a large reception room alive with activity—ringing telephones, televisions tuned to the BBC and CNN, aides typing at computers.

Hussein Kamel joined him on a long sofa. For the next two hours, he spoke mainly about how his alienation from the Baathist regime had evolved.

"My departure from Iraq was not a personal matter," he insisted. "It is the country that matters." Iraq was now in bad shape, suffering "executions every day, people in jail, and confiscation of money." Kamel described his conflicts with others on Saddam's team. When he became minister of defense after the war in Kuwait, he had "criticized the wrongdoings of members of the leadership." The backlash had been harsh, and he had resigned. He stayed home for four months. When he returned, he continued to point out incompetence, and there was "a lot of shouting."

"Iraq just continues with policy that leads nowhere," he complained. Saddam had prepared an "enormous shopping list" of conventional arms—tanks, fighter planes, artillery—that he planned to buy from Russia as soon as he was free from sanctions. Iraq's foreign policy, he argued, "should focus on improving relations with the West, reject the militaristic policy of the past, focus upon economic reconstruction and growth, establish cordial relations with all neighbors," and support the Israeli-Palestinian peace process. To achieve this, his father-in-law had to go.

At dusk, Ekéus and Hussein Kamel stepped out onto a patio. To the west, they could see the lights of Jerusalem. Speaking "almost dreamily," Ekéus recalled, Hussein Kamel said that he "saw a future of peace between Israel and its Arab neighbors."[10]

Hussein Kamel's defection made Nizar Hamdoon introspective. Hamdoon had no desire to break with Saddam. Yet he saw himself as a reformer, a truth-teller in a system that he, too, increasingly recognized as broken. After several years of unenviable work defending Iraq before the U.N. Security Council, Hamdoon decided to deliver some realism to Saddam. The ambassador "had credibility" with Saddam, recalled his friend Odeh Aburdene. He dared to tell Saddam that "people are hungry" in Iraq, because of sanctions, provoking Saddam to retort: "Don't worry. Everything is under control." As Aburdene put it, "Nobody else could have that conversation" because Saddam "didn't think that Nizar would conspire against him."[11]

During the first days of September 1995, the ambassador typed on his office computer an extraordinary letter to Saddam, exceeding eight thousand words. He told Saddam "what was on his mind," as he later explained to the scholar Daniel Pipes. He asked, as a colleague who worked with Hamdoon at the time later summarized it, "Where have we gone wrong?" When Saddam staged public referendums endorsing his rule, why did the results always have to be 99.2 percent in favor of the president's continuing reign? "Why not say sixty-five percent?" Hamdoon asked, as this colleague recalled. "Why not make it more realistic?"[12]

Hamdoon had come to think that Iraq was a "good candidate for democracy, from the perspective of its size, history, culture, natural resources and human resources," as he once put it. In recent years, countries across Africa, Asia, and Latin America had staged elections and implemented democratic constitutions. He urged Saddam to embrace this wave of political pluralism. "He wanted Iraq to be like Spain," Aburdene said.[13]

Hamdoon dispatched his letter by diplomatic pouch. He knew he was pushing the edges of what was tolerable. Some weeks later, he was summoned home to Baghdad, the colleague who worked with him at the time recalled. Hamdoon left instructions for the care of his wife and daughters should he fail to return.[14]

Saddam did recognize the letter as a threat—perhaps less for what it said than because it had been written down at all and, worse, typed on a computer that might be penetrated by the C.I.A. or other hostile intelligence services. If Hamdoon's critique leaked, it could be used by Iraq's enemies as evidence of serious dissent within the Baghdad regime. According to Pipes, Saddam directly accused Hamdoon of sending a copy of his letter to the C.I.A., perhaps as a prelude to defecting. Yet Saddam did not punish Hamdoon or execute him. He shared Hamdoon's letter with Baath Party leaders and then wrote a seventy-five-page reply that rebutted Hamdoon's advocacy, the ambassador later told Pipes. As with his confessional tour after Hussein Kamel's departure, Saddam made a display of his own confidence and normalized what might otherwise have been a destabilizing episode.[15]

For all the drama, by the arrival of autumn in 1995, Saddam and Ekéus were in some respects back where they had been before Hussein Kamel's flight to Jordan. The main issue remained Iraq's germ weapons, and the regime's systematic lying about them, which Aziz and his colleagues now sought to undo. Even the truth could sound ludicrous. One part of the biological-weapons program had origins in a poisons unit that sought to protect Saddam against doctored food. "You know as well as I do that every government in the world has a section of their state security organization devoted to the testing of the food of the leadership," Aziz once remarked to an incredulous U.N. inspector.[16]

Amir al-Saadi, a friend of Jafar Dhia Jafar's, sought to persuade Ekéus's team that the germ weapons had been deployed as a deterrent, not as an offensive arsenal. Saadi had been educated in London and was married to a German citizen; he understood the rationales of deterrence. "Nobody would use weapons of mass destruction against us because then we would retaliate—that's the whole idea," he told Ekéus's team. "It was to prevent a war from starting."[17]

He and other sophisticated scientists might have wished to believe this, but the argument did not add up. Saddam had hidden his biological weapons, suggesting that he might be more interested in keeping his options open than in classical deterrence. In any event, it is difficult to deter enemies by developing a terrible weapon if your adversaries do not know for certain that you possess such a weapon. As Dr. Strangelove tells the Soviet ambassador in the filmmaker Stanley Kubrick's classic satire about nuclear deterrence, "Of course, the whole point of a Doomsday Machine is *lost* if you keep it a secret!"

The circularity of Iraq's deception had become a whirlpool, spinning Ekéus and his team around and around, forcing them to consider at an almost metaphysical level what could be known and not known in Saddam Hussein's Iraq. "I didn't lie to you," Aziz assured Ekéus when the Swede returned to Baghdad after his meeting with Hussein Kamel. Since it was obvious that Aziz had, in fact, been deceptive about the germ-weapons program, the Iraqi deputy prime minister added that diplomacy, "according to an English definition," means that "the employee lies for the sake of his government. The concealment of previous information was not my responsibility."

He offered Ekéus updated assurances that September: "We confirm that Iraq is empty of any material, warheads, or anything that contradicts" U.N. resolutions about banned weapons. Yet there was one more caveat: "And if there *is* anything, then it is not in the hands of the Iraqi leadership but in the hands of the American spy," Hussein Kamel.[18]

On October 2, 1995, Ekéus flew back to Amman to meet again with Hussein Kamel. When he arrived at Hashmiya Palace, there were no longer children' s bicycles and toys strewn on the grounds. The televisions and computers in the makeshift command center had gone dark. Hussein Kamel sat alone on a sofa nursing a glass of water. A Jordanian civil servant with imperfect English had been assigned to translate. Ekéus struggled to make himself understood. He and a colleague had come with a list of questions about Iraqi missiles, but Hussein Kamel was not interested.

"I will return to Iraq!" he declared suddenly.

"When?" Ekéus asked, stunned.

"Soon."

Ekéus said he thought this was a bad idea, but Hussein Kamel seemed determined. He had been appointed and fired from powerful positions more than once by the president, he explained. He knew that if he returned, he would face a period of political exile, but this would not last long.

Ekéus concluded that there was little he could do but offer his best wishes and advice. "Don't go to Baghdad yet," he said as he departed.[19]

Hussein Kamel's operations room had gone dark because the exiled Iraqi opposition to Saddam shunned him. His repeated calls to the main Kurdish political parties had produced little, according to the reports of the Amman office of Iraqi intelligence. Ahmad Chalabi, who tolerated few rivals, had no time for him. He explored moving to France or Germany but got no traction. Britain refused to admit him when he sought to attend an opposition conference in London, as Iraqi intelligence found.[20]

David Manners, the C.I.A. station chief, assigned a case officer in his midthirties to stay on top of Hussein Kamel. But "General Hussein" was insulted by the officer's youth. Unhappily, Manners made periodic trips himself to Hashmiya. His message remained that the United States was not going to back the defector—certainly not unless Hussein Kamel did more to prove himself. "The way you can highlight your own importance to people back in Washington is to tell us things that only you know that will help us remove Saddam," Manners told him.[21]

Hussein Kamel did reveal useful information, but the problem, according to Samih Battikhi, the deputy director of Jordanian intelligence, was that the C.I.A. "wanted information from him without promises to support him," and Hussein Kamel therefore resisted full cooperation. The reality was that both Manners and Battikhi thought he was "as bad as Saddam," if not worse. Hussein Kamel and his brother Saddam boasted openly of their cruelty. They recounted a story about an employee in Iraq who had failed at a task Hussein Kamel assigned him. Hussein Kamel supposedly made the man drink gasoline and then shot him in the stomach to try to make him explode—another rendition, whether true or merely twisted bravado, of the savage experiments described by survivors of the 1991 uprisings. Jordanian intelligence was no paragon of human rights—investigators documented widespread abuse of detainees in Jordanian prisons—but this sort of casual bragging about torture and execution seemed beyond the pale.[22]

When King Hussein restricted his ability to talk to the press, Hussein Kamel raised the possibility of moving to Syria. He was free to leave, King Hussein told his aides, but Saddam's daughters must remain. By Iraqi intelligence accounts, Hussein Kamel passed a letter to Syrian president Hafez al-Assad, asking to visit Damascus, but Assad denied the request. The Syrians regarded Hussein Kamel's defection "as an American plot," the spy service wrote, designed to "overthrow the regime in Iraq" and replace it with one that would move closer to Israel. This was something the Syrians "consider[ed] a danger to their position."[23]

Sajida, Saddam's wife, got in touch with Hussein Kamel and told him that he would be protected if he brought her daughters and her grandchildren home. Saddam also called him, according to Ali Shukri, the aide to Jordan's King Hussein, and he, too, offered assurances: "Do you think I could harm the father of my grandchildren?"[24]

On the night of November 4, 1995, Yitzhak Rabin addressed one hundred thousand Israelis at a peace rally in Tel Aviv's municipal square. He joined the folk singer Miri Aloni in a rendition of "A Song for Peace." As he departed the stage, he urged the crowd, "Let's not just sing about peace—let's make peace!" Backstage, Yigal Amir, a twenty-five-year-old Israeli Jew, drew a pistol and shot Rabin twice. He died less than two hours later. Yigal was a right-wing activist who opposed Rabin's support for returning parts of the West Bank to the Palestinians. "I acted alone on God's orders, and I have no regrets," he told the police.

Bill Clinton, King Hussein, and Hosni Mubarak of Egypt attended Rabin's funeral two days later. Clinton and Hussein delivered eulogies. "We belong to the camp of peace," the king declared. The assassination had ripped a hole in the Oslo negotiations, but by their presence in Jerusalem, King Hussein and Mubarak sought to show that they would stay the course.[25]

In Baghdad, Saddam and his comrades watched the funeral on television and then gathered to denounce what it showed about Arab resolve against Israel. King Hussein "now believes deep down that the only thing that will keep his throne is Zionism, not the people of Jordan," Saddam said. He mocked Clinton for wearing a yarmulke at the funeral when he led a nation of Christians.

"Is Clinton waiting to be paid money by the Zionist so he can balance his budget?" Saddam asked. "He needs the support of the Zionist lobby so they will agree to renew his presidency for four more years. So this is liberal democracy." More than thirty years after his education as a pan-Arab nationalist in Cairo cafés, he hewed to the hackneyed antisemitic assumptions of Zionist conspiracy. The revolution in satellite television news that allowed Saddam to watch Rabin's funeral live in Baghdad only reaffirmed his worldview.[26]

That month, Aziz informed Saddam that "Ekéus and his influence on the Council has become stronger than before." Hussein Kamel's information and the document dump Aziz had orchestrated had helped Washington's case that Saddam was chronically unreliable. The French were forecasting that Iraq might require another year or eighteen months to win relief. The news infuriated Saddam.

Yet Iraq continued to cover up small matters about its weapons history. Aziz recounted for Saddam the case of some Iraqi scientists who had recently tossed a batch of imported missile gyroscopes into the Tigris because they feared the consequences of discovery.

"Sir," Aziz said, "as far as cheating, we are cheating and we continue to cheat. But when cheating is not—"

"We need to know how to cheat," Saddam interrupted. "God damn them, they come out with something against us every day." The U.N. inspectors, he insisted, were "the biggest liars!"[27]

In February, convinced that he had a future in Baghdad, Hussein Kamel at last made a firm plan to leave Jordan. He told the journalist Robert Fisk that Saddam "was my uncle before he was my father-in-law. We are one family." Fisk thought Hussein Kamel sounded "excited, expectant, constantly expressing his admiration for Iraq and its president, at times bursting into laughter."

On February 17, 1996, Hussein Kamel wrote to Saddam:

> I would like to extend my complete apology for what has happened despite its dangerous nature. And I hope that you accept my apology for this, and I know how compassionate you are. . . . Mr. Commander, I never intended at any given day to leave my country and stay far away from it, and it never crossed my mind to hurt Your Excellency.

Indirectly, he blamed his defection on his mortal conflict with Uday, perhaps hoping that Saddam would forgive a family feud more readily than he would accept outright treason. He referred to the shooting of Watban and Uday's threats of more violence: "This unfortunate event has forced me to leave quickly against my will." Hussein Kamel also said he was "frustrated" by allegations that he was "an agent for American intelligence. And this is insane. . . . We were raised hating the Americans."

He concluded by appealing to Saddam's sentiments as a grandfather:

> Our children . . . always recall Papa Saddam and Mama Sa-
> jida, also their [uncles] Uday and Qusay and their aunty and
> maternal cousins. This is their daily topic. They keep remind-
> ing us. They keep dreaming their vision, their dreams of
> viewing Your Excellency and the kind family. . . . I repeat my
> sincere apology to Mr. President for what I have done, and the
> rest is reserved for Your Excellency.[28]

Saddam shared Hussein Kamel's pleading with the Baath Party's leadership. On February 19, he convened a meeting of the Revolutionary Command Council and other high-ranking leaders. After lengthy discussion, according to a Council bulletin soon issued to party members: "There is no dispute that Hussein Kamel has betrayed the trust and betrayed the Party and the nation." Still, because of his "total failure and the failure of the deluded enemies who collaborated with him," the party approved Hussein Kamel's plea to return home.

He would be pardoned, but he would have to return "all state and citizens' money he had control over both before and after his escape." He would also be expelled from the Baath Party, the armed forces, and the government. He would only be permitted home "as an ordinary citizen."[29]

It was as much as Hussein Kamel could reasonably hope to hear, and the decision to merely banish him from office was consistent with what he had been expecting.

Hussein Kamel seems to have been alone in his conviction that Saddam's pardon was reliable. His wife, Raghad, pleaded with him to "calm down, let some time pass" before making such a rash decision. She predicted that her father "will divorce us the moment we arrive there." But her husband "could not bear being away from Iraq," she recalled.[30]

The party piled into a convoy of Mercedes-Benzes and drove to the border, trailed by Jordanian intelligence officers. They crossed into Iraq, where Uday awaited them. The Jordanians filmed the encounter and shared it with the C.I.A. According to Manners, Uday embraced his sisters before hugging Hussein Kamel and Saddam Kamel, too. Then Uday separated his sisters for the onward journey to Baghdad.

Watching from the Jordanian side, an officer told Samih Battikhi by telephone, "Khallas," or "He's finished."[31]

The next day, Saddam asked to see his daughters and grandchildren. "We had a long discussion," Raghad recalled. "My father was very hurt. For the first time, I saw him unable to talk." Uday and Qusay were there. Qusay announced to his sisters that they would be divorcing their husbands. Raghad said nothing. She was upset but also regretful, believing that "we should have been more careful in both leaving Iraq and returning to Iraq."[32]

Iraqi television soon announced the divorces. But rather than use judicial or Baath Party authority to further punish the Kamel brothers, Saddam asked the Majid family, led by Ali Hassan, "Chemical Ali," to take responsibility for Hussein Kamel's fate, on the grounds that the Majid family had been dishonored.

At a meeting of family leaders, Ali Hassan and his brethren formally petitioned the president, who was present. They declined to seek the death penalty "because these men are your sons-in-law and fathers to nine grandchildren." However, they continued, "we as a clan do not forfeit our right to take the death penalty." They would carry out the executions themselves, as a matter of family honor.[33]

The Kamel brothers had made their way to their sister's house in the Saidiya neighborhood of Baghdad: "Subdivision 925, Lane 25, House 5," as a subsequent Iraqi intelligence investigation identified it.[34]

In the early hours of February 23, an alarm was raised across Baghdad that Hussein and Saddam Kamel might be attempting an escape. Capture-or-kill orders went out, and plainclothes intelligence police soon flooded the streets. Most likely, Iraqi intelligence had intercepted calls in which Hussein Kamel or other family members had talked about trying to flee.

Meanwhile, the Majids mustered a posse of Special Security Organization officers and armed volunteers to surround the Saidiya house. According to the journalists Andrew and Patrick Cockburn, "in bizarre deference to the proprieties of tribal feuding, the assault party sent ahead a Honda filled with automatic weapons and ammunition for the Kamel family to defend themselves with." By 9:00 a.m., there were reports of gunfire in Saidiya. When a security officer approached, he "saw a house surrounded by civilians exchanging fire [with] people inside the house." He noticed "the presence of Ali Hassan al-Majid, and Uday and Qusay, sons of the president." A commander of Saddam Hussein's bodyguard informed him that the shootout was "a tribal matter involving the traitor Hussein Kamel," and nobody should interfere.[35]

The gun battle lasted until sunset. Finally, an ambulance arrived, and the Majid clan pulled back. The attackers suffered at least several deaths, but they had finished the job. Hussein Kamel, Saddam Kamel, their sister, their sister's children, and their father all lay dead amidst shards of glass, smashed furniture, and broken concrete. Barzan Ibrahim al-Tikriti reported that more than twenty Majid family members died on both sides. They had done their duty, but according to Barzan, the Majids fumed for years afterward at Uday and Saddam, blaming them for Hussein Kamel's defection and the shootout deaths in their branch of the family.[36]

Raghad, who was now twenty-five, was "very hurt, very much, perhaps more than you can imagine" by her father's decision to sanction her husband's killing. "I was angry." Yet she did not blame Saddam, because he took "the decision he deemed appropriate. And those who err will be punished. . . . Everyone in the family knew that, supposedly."[37]

Hussein Kamel's defection was the most significant crack in the Baghdad regime since Saddam had taken full power. Yet the president had vanquished his son-in-law with ease. He had publicly humiliated and then murdered Hussein Kamel while absolving himself of direct responsibility and making one of his henchmen take charge of the execution, dressing it up as clan justice. The episode's dramatic demonstration of Saddam's cunning and resilience in the face of insider threats might have cautioned the C.I.A.'s coupmakers.

It did not.

NINETEEN

Spy vs. Spy

On February 18, 1996, five days before Hussein Kamel's death, Ayad Allawi, the leader of the Iraqi National Accord, held a press conference in Amman, where he vowed to end Saddam Hussein's rule. By then, Saddam and his security services could be in no doubt about what they had to defend against. As Allawi would say later that year, "We think that any uprising should have as its very center the armed forces."

The chapter of C.I.A. covert action that followed Hussein Kamel's demise was modestly resourced. In January 1996, the Clinton administration allocated a budget of about $6 million, largely funneled through the National Accord. Even if, as seems likely, Saudi Arabia and Kuwait chipped in additional funds, this was a tiny sum relative to the scale of the challenge—about the size of the operating budget of a small American town. Also, the program was not very secret. Successful conspiracies to carry out coups d'état don't typically have an address for their targets to zero in on, but the National Accord set up shop openly in Amman, where it broadcast on a C.I.A.-funded station and published newspapers.[1]

Clinton clearly had mixed feelings about any direct C.I.A. attempt to use Iraqi partners to capture or kill the Iraqi president, yet after Kamel's defection, he decided to lean forward with the C.I.A. Rather than a direct assault on Saddam, however, Clinton seems to have authorized plans to back the I.N.A. to "exploit" a coup attempt by someone in the Iraqi military. This "prepare, wait, and exploit" concept stopped well short of real-time C.I.A. involvement in paramilitary operations or the provision of U.S. air support.

"If the administration had said something like, 'Get rid of him and do it in six months,' then okay," David Manners, the Amman station chief, said later. But the Amman station and the Iraq Operations Group at headquarters did not have such instructions, according to Manners and John Maguire, the case officer posted to Amman until 1994 and later deputy head of Iraq operations. "The job was to collect telephone numbers for key Iraqis in the event there was a coup against Saddam" so that the C.I.A. could "contact them and say, 'Hey, we'll support you,'" a third former senior C.I.A. operations officer recalled. This effort had a newly visible leader in Ayad Allawi. His National Accord allies would be largely responsible for their own counterintelligence—the detection of Saddam's efforts to penetrate their ranks. And they were vulnerable. The Jordanian intelligence field officers assigned to provide safe houses and security to the National Accord had longstanding ties to Saddam's regime.[2]

The reporting sources inside Iraq recruited by Charlie Seidel, the last Baghdad station chief before the U.S. embassy's closure in late 1990, had by now largely gone off the air—without resupply, some of the agents had run out of the encryption materials used to send secret messages. But the agency did have a new means to support potential coupmakers. During 1996, at the request of Rolf Ekéus, C.I.A. and British intelligence moved personnel and equipment into Baghdad, under cover of Special Commission operations, to eavesdrop on Iraqi security forces protecting Saddam Hussein.[3]

This operation was part of a Special Commission program to discover hidden WMD by agitating the bodyguards close to Saddam. Weapons inspectors would make surprise visits to sensitive buildings, such as presidential offices. As the Special Security Organization, or the S.S.O., scrambled to hide materials or block the inspectors, the eavesdroppers would intercept their encrypted radio communications and try to discern where illicit weapons might be hidden. The idea was that insights from S.S.O. chatter might reveal how Saddam's "concealment mechanism," as the inspectors called it, actually worked.

The work of clandestine eavesdroppers was coordinated with C.I.A.-managed U-2 spy plane overflights to capture photographic evidence of Iraqi guards scrambling to hide things during surprise inspections. "More sophisticated equipment" deployed in Baghdad allowed the U.N. "to collect more rapidly and be able to immediately adjust our inspections in response to observed Iraqi actions," recalled Charles Duelfer, the deputy to Ekéus who ran the U.N.'s liaison with the C.I.A. The White House approved the operation, but John Deutch warned Duelfer that "it was my ass if it blew up" and the eavesdroppers got caught—in which case Saddam might imprison them as spies or hold them as hostages.[4]

The operation did eventually blow up, but not in the way Deutch feared.

I f there was a reason for optimism among the Americans that spring, it lay in the person of Ayad Allawi. He struck his American allies as the sort of opposition leader who might deliver on his promises. He was a tall, balding, thick-set man with a dignified bearing; he was also prone to displays of temper. He "understood the Mukhabarat culture of intimidation," as a cousin put it, yet he was at home in Western institutions.[5]

"I came from a family that had enjoyed power and had been part of power," Allawi said years later. Like Chalabi and Jafar Dhia Jafar, he was the scion of an elite family from Iraq's Shia majority that had served the royal governments of the Hashemite era. He, too, had attended Baghdad College, the Jesuit high school. After the royal family's overthrow in 1958, his family remained in Baghdad, and as a teenager, Allawi was attracted to Baathism. At the time, politically active and secular-leaning students like himself had to choose between "two conflicting forces": the communists and the Baathists. (The Dawa Party was another path available for devout Shia activists.) Allawi joined the Baath Party, and when the party was repressed during the early 1960s, he was arrested alongside Saddam, whom he got to know. "I was financially well off through my family," Allawi recalled, yet "I enjoyed a very good relationship with most of the Baathists."[6]

He studied medicine and completed his initial degree in Iraq in 1970. He said he turned against the Baathists after they meddled in that year's Black September conflict between Jordan and the Palestine Liberation Organization, a mess that disillusioned him about the Baath Party's devotion to the Arab cause. He moved to London for postgraduate studies and to work at the National Health Service. Later, Allawi would be accused of spying on Iraqis for the Baath Party in Britain, a charge he would adamantly deny. On the contrary, he said, he organized "secret cells" to overthrow Saddam. By the late 1970s, clearly, his opposition to Saddam had attracted the regime's attention.[7]

One night in February 1978, after a long day in London, Allawi returned to his home in Epsom, Surrey, in the suburbs. He chatted with his wife briefly and went to bed. At about three in the morning, he came half-awake and saw "a shadow . . . a flickering reflection" by his bed. He thought he was probably dreaming. Then he was on the floor, blood pouring from his head. A tall man wielding an axe loomed over him, swinging blow after blow. His wife jumped on the intruder, who turned his axe on her and almost severed her hand. Finally, the assailant left the couple for dead. Allawi crawled to a telephone and called for help. Miraculously, he and his wife survived.

During the assault, Allawi recalled warning his attacker: "If I survive, I will gouge your eyes out—and Saddam's." Whether or not this is a reliable memory, it certainly reflected Allawi's attitude toward the

Baathist regime after he recovered. During the 1980s, however, when the Thatcher government joined the Reagan administration in partnership with Saddam, his circumstances changed. "We were forbidden from working in politics here in London," Allawi said. He moved abroad. At some point, Allawi worked clandestinely with MI6, presumably collecting intelligence about Saddam's Iraq, according to Warren Marik, a C.I.A. operations officer in the agency's Near East Division.[8]

After the invasion of Kuwait, Allawi emerged as a semi-public opposition figure. He launched the Iraqi National Accord, or the I.N.A., at a conference in Erbil, in 1992. He traveled to Washington and met influential figures in Congress, such as the Republican senators Lindsey Graham and John McCain. In London, Julian Walker, a legendary Arabist at the Foreign Office, assured Allawi that Britain, like America, had by now officially given up on Saddam. "You can do whatever you like against Saddam Hussein," Walker said, excepting "military action or assassinations" organized from London. The I.N.A. opened offices in Riyadh and Dubai. After King Hussein broke with Saddam in 1995, Allawi set up in Amman, "a dream for us" because of the steady flow of Iraqi travelers, including regime figures.[9]

Allawi developed a concept that he called "defect and defend." The I.N.A. would secretly recruit Iraqi military officers who would revolt against Saddam but then hold their positions at military bases or other secure areas. Saddam would almost certainly order a counterattack, but when he did, the military dissidents' outside allies—the Americans, British, Egyptians, Jordanians—would intervene to shut down Iraqi airspace and help the rebels seize power in Baghdad.

Allawi's ace card was the willingness of outside governments to intervene militarily, in contrast to the White House's refusal to do so when Chalabi and Robert Baer improvised a similar action in the spring of 1995. "We had a very strong commitment from all these countries that once this starts, we will support you," Allawi recalled of the lay of the land by that year's end—or so he had been led to believe. The I.N.A.'s allies in the Iraqi military would "trigger an event," and then

Saddam would "overreact, and then you can force a fissure in the system," as the C.I.A.'s John Maguire described it.[10]

Allawi thought the revolting Iraqi units "would have to hold out for one month, to flip the government" in Baghdad. But during 1996, the C.I.A. and MI6 told him that he would have to tighten that timeline— Washington and London were not going to fight a month-long air war to remove Saddam. The records remain classified, but it seems unlikely that Clinton made a specific promise of air support, à la the Bay of Pigs, but the president seems to have indicated that if an initial revolt looked promising, this time he would consider ordering a military intervention, as long as it would be quick and decisive.

Allawi had reason to be confident. The National Accord leader had become "the preferred choice of the C.I.A.–State Department career people," recalled David Mack, the longtime Middle East hand. In Amman, Rick Francona "thought Allawi was the savior. . . . I really thought he had the leadership, the organization, the education, and the understanding of the West." As a senior C.I.A. analyst then at Langley headquarters summed it up: "We were in love with him because he was our guy." Yet the agency's Iraq watchers also circulated reports that Allawi "has no constituency" among the Iraqi population and was "petulant" and "tended toward grudges . . . too similar to Saddam," the analyst recalled.[11]

One of Allawi's clandestine radio studios created a broadcast directed specifically at the Iraqi Army. The intention was to build a "very compartmented approach to the officers who are working with us—no one should know their names," Allawi recalled. All communication should use only "pseudonyms and code names." Yet Allawi and his allies were challenging Saddam at spy games he had been playing for decades, to the point of obsession.[12]

On April 21, 1996, Dzhokhar Dudayev, the leader of the breakaway Chechen Republic of Ichkeria and an enemy of Moscow, stood by a jeep inside his republic, talking on a satellite telephone. A Russian missile incinerated him. It had targeted him because of his phone signal. This was a mistake Saddam Hussein would never make. Aware of the vulnerability, he had used a telephone only "twice" after 1990, by his own account. Dudayev's assassination that spring set off another season of "acute spying disease," as an aide to Saddam called the president's obsession with counterintelligence.[13]

By 1996, Saddam rarely worked at the Republican Palace. He spent much of his time at Radwaniyah, with its many buildings and tunnels. He had also built many smaller palaces. These were mocked in the West as symbols of Saddam's indulgence in garish luxury. In fact, nobody in the regime actually lived in many of these places, and Saddam rarely slept at them—they functioned as places to hold short-notice meetings. "He got to the point where no one in the government or the party could meet with him without much hassle and weeks of waiting," Barzan Ibrahim al-Tikriti recalled. Ministers only saw him in secure cabinet meetings. Newly arrived ambassadors never presented their credentials to him. Every foreigner in Iraq was considered a potential spy. "It is hard to get in touch with the president, especially in the last few years for security reasons," Tariq Aziz observed after Hussein Kamel's defection.[14]

Saddam rarely let go of his pistol, a Browning 9-millimeter. He brought an armed bodyguard to his regular one-on-one meetings with the leaders of his own security agencies, even though many of these leaders were his relatives. Following Hussein Kamel's defection, Saddam prohibited all high-ranking officials and their wives from traveling abroad, even after they retired, with only rare exceptions. Low-level palace laborers who retired could not leave the country for a year, and then only after a security review.[15]

A unit known as the Group of 40, drawn from Saddam's family, constituted his innermost bodyguard. They were the only individuals permitted to approach him while armed. The Special Security Organization provided the next ring of protection. This was a large and well-paid force drawn from more diverse social networks, a police state's version of the U.S. Secret Service. The Special Republican Guard protected the S.S.O.

Saddam's regime continually investigated potential traitors and spies. The security agencies published doctrines, trained cadets, conducted lessons-learned studies, and collected and analyzed information about potential threats from all over the world. Their assessments dealt in facts, not the usual distortions that attended Saddam's cult of personality. The main agencies all spied on one another, which certainly led to false accusations and wild-goose chases. Yet overall, the Baath Party's work on counterintelligence was the part of governing Iraq that it did best.

In 1993, the Special Security Organization produced a Top Secret training study that asked: "How does the enemy think? What are their ways and means?" It outlined Iraq's policies to thwart the C.I.A., Mossad, and other hostile services. The study's essential point was that Iraq's adversaries would inevitably "think about penetrating into the Presidential Special Security units," including the S.S.O. A later study produced at a training academy for intelligence officers described how enemy spies prioritized "collecting information about the President and his family, and locating and working on penetrating the President's outer perimeter." It accurately summarized C.I.A. and MI6 support for opposition figures; the role of neighbors such as Jordan and Saudi Arabia; C.I.A.-funded propaganda radio and Voice of America broadcasts; and the attempted recruitment of Iraqis who traveled.[16]

No detail was too small. The Special Security Organization used its poisons lab to test ingredients that would be used in Saddam's birthday cakes. Routine surveillance included "installing secret listening devices in the homes of employees, telephone tapping at work and home, personal monitoring of after-work activities, and continual gathering of information about those in the inner circles and their families," as the scholar Joseph Sassoon's detailed study of security service files describes. By design, many of the more than 1,300 employees of Saddam's palaces were Christians, on the theory that this tiny Iraqi minority lacked the ability to threaten Saddam. S.S.O. officers themselves faced intense scrutiny. Saddam built a prison expressly for members of his bodyguard suspected of unreliability. Senior officers carried out interrogations of their own colleagues, sometimes harshly. S.S.O. officers, like Iraqi Army generals, had to apply for permission to marry. The questionnaire they filled out asked what brand of cigarette the individual smoked and how he spent his leisure time: "Do you attend nightclubs? Do you have enemies?"[17]

A study noted that enemy spies employed as couriers "the Arab and Iraqi drivers who are working on the road" between Baghdad and Amman or Baghdad and Damascus. These drivers had been recruited at times as "contact tools with their agents inside the country." This was another accurate insight. It would soon upend the C.I.A.'s latest coup plan, with tragic consequences.[18]

In addition to Allawi, the C.I.A. had another favored partner in Amman, a decorated former Iraqi Special Operations Forces commander named Mohammed Abdullah Shawani, "the General" to his followers or "General Mo" to some of the agency officers who worked with him. Shawani belonged to a notable family in Mosul from Iraq's Turkmen ethnic minority. He rose in the Baathist military after 1968. A stocky, muscled athlete in his youth, Shawani had undergone elite military training in the United States at Fort Benning and Fort Bragg. He became a pilot, provided helicopter instruction to King Hussein of Jordan, and won fame during the Iran-Iraq War by leading an airborne assault on a fortified Iranian position to free up trapped Iraqi forces.

A celebrated pilot-commander with American and Jordanian connections and the proven ability to conduct an air assault was never likely to enjoy a long career in service of Saddam Hussein. To the president, Shawani must have looked like a coup leader in waiting. His patron was the long-serving minister of defense, Adnan Khairallah, Saddam's brother-in-law and a powerful figure in the regime during the 1970s and 1980s. In May 1989, Khairallah died in a helicopter crash that many Iraqis assumed was an assassination ordered by Saddam. Whatever the case, by 1991, Shawani believed that he had himself become a target and was under surveillance, he later told Allawi.

He made his way to Jordan, where King Hussein granted him asylum and introduced him to the C.I.A.

During the early 1990s, Shawani worked with case officers at the Amman station and ran an intelligence network inside Iraq. Three of his sons—two of them retired army officers—remained in Iraq and helped him surreptitiously. "You couldn't help but like him," said Francona. "He was a tough guy . . . but rigid." Manners, the station chief, marveled at Shawani's courage and piloting skills. George Tenet, then the C.I.A.'s deputy director, described him as "a born leader with a significant following" who "quickly became key to developing a strong network inside Iraq for the Agency."[19]

Shawani ran his own intelligence-collection operations, but by 1996 he was "working independently" with the Iraqi National Accord, according to Allawi. Yet the overlapping C.I.A.-backed networks were not tightly organized. "There were too many cutouts," or intermediaries passing messages, Francona recalled. It is an inherently risky practice because "the longer you make your chain [of contacts], the more susceptible it is to being interdicted somewhere." The C.I.A. provided tradecraft training—codes, message security, and the like—but never commanded its allies directly. As Francona put it, "You can tell them not to do things, but assets are assets, and they'll do what they want to do."[20]

Shawani's network became an important part of the 1996 operations. He seems to have been advancing a plan to launch a helicopter raid against Saddam or a similar operation based on Allawi's "defect and defend" model. Such plans were certainly bandied about in Amman. Yet it isn't clear how plausible any specific effort became during 1996. Some C.I.A. officers who worked with Shawani said that his operation still had more to do with collecting intelligence to identify Saddam's vulnerabilities.

In any event, it was far from clear to some C.I.A. officers who worked with Shawani whether the Clinton White House ever intended to take on the breathtaking political and military risks that would be

involved in backing an attack on Baghdad in the way Allawi had designed. According to John Maguire, the C.I.A. repeatedly sent the
Clinton White House draft memoranda of notification—specific covert-
ops proposals—about a defect-and-defend-type operation to rattle and
perhaps topple Saddam. But the agency received no response. "You'd
craft it, send it in—'We're ready, we've got everything in place,'" but
then the White House would not answer, he recalled. "Crickets." As
Maguire saw it, Clinton "set up a system that protected him politically
from claims that he wasn't serious about deposing Saddam, but he set
up a fail-safe system to prevent anything from actually happening."[21]

Ellen Laipson, the senior intelligence analyst then working at the
White House, could sense the C.I.A.'s frustration. "I'm not sure Clinton
or Tony Lake expected Saddam to fall or particularly cared," Laipson
said. The reality was that for Clinton, in 1996, merely containing Saddam "was quite satisfactory" because it meant that the president, who
had many other priorities, including his reelection campaign, "didn't
have to deal with the aftermath of Saddam falling." Containment was
an entirely defensible—even wise—foreign policy for the United States
in the mid-1990s, but it begged the question of why, then, Clinton gave
an impression to the C.I.A. and King Hussein, among others, that he
was actively seeking Saddam's violent overthrow.[22]

Meanwhile, into the first half of 1996, the U.N. teams hunting for
WMD in Iraq now included C.I.A. and British special forces officers
who continued to conduct an eavesdropping program aimed at Saddam's bodyguards. Scott Ritter, a former U.S. Marine intelligence officer, ran the most sensitive Special Commission inspections, but even
he was not privy to the technical details of this work. One of Ritter's
inspections began in Baghdad on June 10. He later concluded that the
C.I.A.-U.K. eavesdroppers were actually there to enable a coup attempt by Shawani or another group of dissident Iraqi officers.

The evidence Ritter discovered was circumstantial but striking. He
quoted British intelligence officers he worked with as confirming that
the C.I.A. had installed a "black box" inside the Special Commission's

office in Baghdad to sweep up encrypted communications by Saddam's security forces and automatically "burst" the data to U-2 spy planes when they passed overhead. In other words, American and British intelligence had hijacked the U.N. inspections—and particularly the one in June—to pursue "the real U.S. objective for Iraq—regime change." Ritter's account is credible, but he concedes that there was no "indisputable proof" that the C.I.A. was using its eavesdropping to run a coup operation against Saddam.

Still, it would be inexplicable—and very bad tradecraft—if the C.I.A.'s eavesdropping on Saddam's bodyguards was not coordinated with the coup plans the agency was developing simultaneously with the I.N.A. Worried that the U.N. was being badly used by the C.I.A., Ritter later presented his analysis to Duelfer, the U.N. liaison to Langley, and Duelfer waved him off. "All I would say is that you probably would do very well not to ever mention it again," Duelfer said.[23]

Once more, it all ended in tears. Early in 1996, Iraqi intelligence obtained a contraband satellite communications device used by Shawani's network. According to Allawi, Saddam's men seized the device from an Iraqi national who worked inside the Egyptian embassy in Baghdad and also as a courier for Shawani's people. Allawi later blamed Shawani for loose tradecraft, but in early 1996, the Iraqi breakthrough was unknown. Iraqi nationals working in foreign embassies were under intense surveillance and effectively had no choice but to report on what they did to Saddam's secret police—the alternative to cooperation was torture. Once the Iraqis captured the device, they bided their time. They listened, watched, and mapped out Shawani's network, including the activities of the general's sons.[24]

In late June, *The Washington Post* quoted Allawi declaring that "the end is near" as he described his plans for a "controlled, coordinated military uprising"—a public statement that did not appear to be recommended covert-action tradecraft, either. The Iraqis pounced within days of that story's release. They arrested Shawani's sons and many dozens of other suspects, "far in excess of the number that we actually had working for us," according to Francona. The detainees were, of course, severely tortured, and some inevitably made false confessions, causing more people not actually involved to be rounded up and marked for execution.[25]

As the crackdown unfolded, an Iraqi intelligence officer contacted Shawani and told him that he could save his sons if he agreed to return to Iraq to exchange himself for his boys. Shawani asked for time to think about it. If the offer were genuine, he would accept it, he told American colleagues, but they told him what he surely also knew: the offer was a mirage, and if Shawani accepted it, he would only add his own demise to that of his doomed sons. He stayed put in Jordan.

The next month, one of Saddam's enforcers telephoned the Shawanis at their home in Amman. Francona and Shawani's wife happened to be there when the phone rang. They were watching the 1996 Summer Olympics in Atlanta on television. The Iraqi caller put the Shawani boys on the phone so that they could say goodbye to their parents before they were executed. The general was stoic. His wife, however, "was really just devastated," Francona remembered. "Took it out on me. My fault."

The death of the Shawani sons and the collapse of the wider coup enterprise was a devastating fiasco that would haunt and anger C.I.A. officers involved for years to come. The Americans to blame were mainly the decision-makers at the top, however. "The whole thing was compromised from day one," recalled Bruce Riedel, the C.I.A. analyst. "And this was Deutch's baby." The C.I.A. director knew that the incipient coup operation "was what the White House wanted to hear, and he overpromised."

"Let me say something to you about operations," Deutch later told the journalist Peter Jennings when challenged about that summer's deaths and failures. "In the Central Intelligence Agency, like everywhere else in the world, they always have risk. They aren't always successful. These were responsible risks carried out by dedicated individuals, coordinated with an overall government policy." But had the sacrifices been made in pursuit of a realistic plan? "I would say we had very careful and very modest expectations about how easily any coup effort could be successful," Deutch said.[26]

King Hussein eventually dismissed the ministers who had urged working with the C.I.A., but he did not wallow in regret. He still ruled a precarious realm in the shadow of Saddam. "That was exciting," he remarked privately, referring to his year of living dangerously with Hussein Kamel and the C.I.A. "What are we going to do now?"[27]

Saddam Hussein spent considerably more hours of his working week thinking about intelligence operations than Bill Clinton did. He did not consider the C.I.A. to be his most formidable adversary. "The best technically able intelligence outfits in the world are the British, the ex-Soviet, and the Israeli," he advised colleagues late in 1996, following his latest triumph. "The Israelis, they use Jews from all around the world for intelligence matters," he continued. "The Soviets use all the communist movements and what you would call the international peace movements, all the names you can think of, for the sake of their intelligence services. But technologically, the British intelligence service is more advanced than any of them."

In late August 1996, Saddam cut a deal with Masoud Barzani, the leader of the opposition Kurdistan Democratic Party in Northern Iraq, to eviscerate Barzani's principal Kurdish rival, Jalal Talabani. The two Kurdish leaders were struggling over control of customs revenues at the Turkish border. Barzani's double cross reflected the role of profiteering in the region's tangled conflicts. With Barzani's cooperation, Saddam sent thirty thousand troops to retake Erbil. His forces also swept up the nearby headquarters of Ahmad Chalabi's Iraqi National Congress, still operating despite its previous failures.

Chalabi was in London. Saddam's conquerors executed dozens of his operatives. A small contingent of C.I.A. officers posted in the region fled. The Clinton administration evacuated about six hundred survivors from Chalabi's network, as well as more than six thousand

THE C.I.A. AND IRAQ'S OPPOSITION, 1994–1996

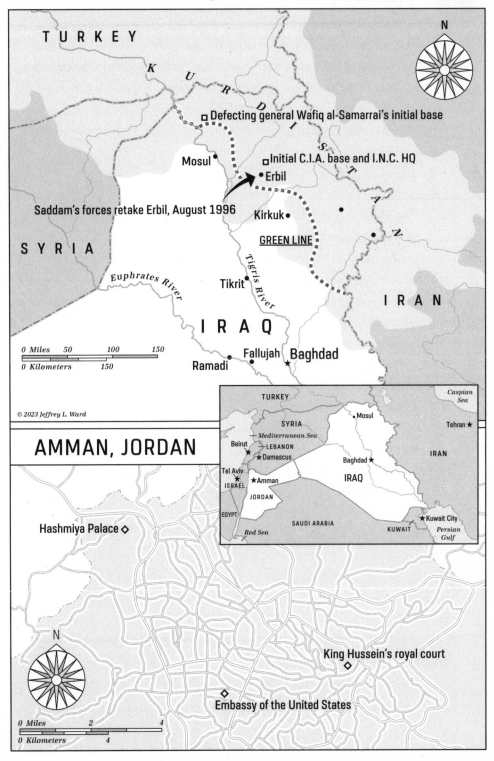

TURKEY

K U R D I S T A N

□ Defecting general Wafiq al-Samarrai's initial base

Mosul

□ Initial C.I.A. base and I.N.C. HQ

• Erbil

Saddam's forces retake Erbil, August 1996

Kirkuk •

GREEN LINE

SYRIA

Euphrates River

Tigris River

Tikrit

IRAN

IRAQ

0 Miles 50 100 150
0 Kilometers 150

Fallujah ★ Baghdad

Ramadi

© 2023 Jeffrey L. Ward

N

Caspian Sea

TURKEY

SYRIA
Mediterranean Sea
Beirut
LEBANON
★ Damascus

• Mosul

Tehran ★

Tel Aviv
★
ISRAEL ★ Amman
JORDAN

Baghdad ★

IRAQ

IRAN

EGYPT

SAUDI ARABIA

Red Sea

KUWAIT

★ Kuwait City
Persian Gulf

AMMAN, JORDAN

Hashmiya Palace ◇

King Hussein's royal court
◇

N

◇
Embassy of the United States

0 Miles 2 4
0 Kilometers 4

Kurdish affiliates of U.S. agencies or U.S.-funded charities. They were airlifted to Guam, from where many were eventually resettled in the U.S. Among the evacuees were Wahid Kochani, the survivor of a mass execution during the Anfal, and his family, aided by Human Rights Watch. Because of Saddam's military incursion, Operation Provide Comfort, the program to aid Kurds in northern Iraq, collapsed, although the U.S.-led no-fly zone, renamed Operation Northern Watch, would continue.[28]

In response to this setback, Clinton ordered an expansion of the no-fly zone over southern Iraq, many miles away from the scenes of Saddam's latest aggression. Tony Lake explained the White House's thinking: "Had Saddam been allowed to use force with impunity," by way of his assault on Kurdistan, "he would have been emboldened to act again. . . . Rather than play Saddam's game by responding in the North, we acted in the South. . . . Saddam's strategic straitjacket has been tightened."[29]

The reality was less impressive. "We didn't know where Saddam was most of the time, we couldn't identify any Iraqi generals who wanted to overthrow him, and the Kurds and the others were pathetically incapable of doing anything," Riedel recalled.

"This system is here to stay," Saddam crowed to his comrades. He had achieved "a big and great national gain" that "not only made people clap" but would make it easier for neighboring Arab states and "international friends" to "change their position" and help Iraq find sanctions relief.[30]

On the evening of December 12, 1996, Uday Hussein, now thirty-two, cruised Baghdad's wealthy Mansour neighborhood in a Porsche Carrera. He and his posse were apparently casing an ice cream shop in the area that attracted young female customers. As his car slowed, two gunmen on the street raised Kalashnikov assault rifles and sprayed his Porsche with bullets, striking Uday in the left side and in his legs.

He was near death when a friend carried him into the presidential hospital. By the time the physician Ala Bashir arrived, surgeons had stabilized him. Saddam arrived at the operating theater later. On a table, Uday lay covered in bloody bandages, unconscious under an anesthetic. His father gripped his hand. "My son, men must allow for such setbacks as these," he said, as Bashir recalled. "But we are right and they are wrong." Three enemies of Saddam—the Dulaimi tribe in western Iraq, which sometimes cooperated with the C.I.A.; the Dawa Party; and a previously unknown Baghdad opposition group of young urban reformers called "the Awakening"—all claimed responsibility for the assassination attempt.[31]

At the end of 1996, following the evacuation of the I.N.C. from Kurdistan, the C.I.A. cut all ties with Ahmad Chalabi, on the grounds that he was fatally unreliable. He had collaborated with Iran, deceived the agency, and led his followers and supporters into catastrophe. "There was a breakdown in trust," George Tenet reflected. "We never wanted to have anything to do with him anymore." Following Bill Clinton's reelection in November, John Deutch resigned—or was pushed out—the following month. In the summer of 1997, Dave Manners also resigned from the C.I.A., disgusted by the Clinton administration's unwillingness to live up to its promises to Iraqi agents and allies in the field.[32]

Allawi and Shawani continued to operate with C.I.A. support, but they, too, were disillusioned. "We found out that there is no seriousness in the position of the United States," Allawi recalled. "A depressed attitude" settled over the Americans. Tenet succeeded Deutch as C.I.A. director. Chastened by the events of 1995 and 1996, he preached realism about the agency's prospects against Saddam.[33]

Uday's bullet wounds turned out to be serious, and his suffering perhaps offered some measure of rough justice to his myriad victims. It required six months of treatment before he could leave the hospital. A German surgeon operated, but even then, Uday "was barely able to walk," Bashir recalled. His speech could be difficult to understand. He seemed even more irascible and aggressive. Blood loss after he was shot might have damaged his brain, but Bashir felt it was difficult to judge, since "he was already insane."

Saddam had long ago accepted assassination plots as the price of power. "You and your brother have to be aware of the possibility of incidents like this," he told Qusay that spring, referring to the hit on Uday. "Be prepared for the worst."[34]

TWENTY

Crime and Punishment

The MGM Grand Hotel and Casino in Las Vegas is a glass-walled, three-winged resort featuring a stair-step design, fronted by a forty-five-foot-tall statue of a bronze lion. Just after 1:00 a.m. on the morning of December 22, 1996, Tongsun Park, a sixty-one-year-old South Korean, deposited $500,000 in cash there, on account at the casino. Park was a charismatic businessman who had turned his attention to the United Nations' efforts to help ordinary Iraqis suffering under economic sanctions. Saddam Hussein had authorized several cash payments to him, and recently, an intermediary in Northern Virginia had presented Park with a shopping bag stuffed with old bills.[1]

Saddam had decided to gamble on an initiative he had previously resisted: the U.N.'s Oil-for-Food program. It would allow Iraq to sell oil under U.N. restrictions—up to $4 billion per year, in its initial formulation—and use about two-thirds of those proceeds to import food, medicine, and other civilian goods. (The rest of the money would provide compensation to Kuwait and pay for the U.N.'s expenditures in Iraq.) Iraq used bags and suitcases of cash to buy powerful friends and alter geopolitics, a project that ran through New York, Washington, Moscow, and Paris, in addition to the MGM Grand Hotel and Casino. Tongsun Park was one player in Saddam's effort to make Oil-for-Food work to his advantage. For its sheer audacity, Saddam's manipulation of the program and his parallel illicit oil sales and kickback schemes must be acknowledged as one of his masterworks of asymmetric foreign policy.

Tongsun was the scion of an influential business family. He enrolled at Georgetown University in 1956, when South Korea was regarded by the Eisenhower administration as a vital anti-communist ally. Park was elected class president his freshman year, and after graduating, he founded the George Town Club on Wisconsin Avenue, where he enlisted Washington socialites and prominent congressmen as members. Back in Seoul, he connected with the Korean Central Intelligence Agency, South Korea's principal spy agency. With the help of $3 million in funds from the K.C.I.A., he decorated his club with suits of armor, Arabian swords, and Asian carpets. He met President Lyndon Johnson and hosted a wedding rehearsal dinner at the club for one of Johnson's daughters.[2]

Park grew into a baby-faced man with thick black hair swept above his forehead; his tortoise-shell glasses gave him a purposeful look. With the help of Richard Hanna, a congressman from California, Park became an exclusive agent for the sale of American rice to South Korea under Food for Peace, an initiative to strengthen anti-communist allies and aid American farmers. Park earned about $9 million in commissions and ultimately plowed about $850,000 of that into gifts and campaign contributions to members of Congress, including Hanna. In 1977, the Justice Department indicted Park on thirty-six felony counts related to bribery and influence buying, charges that inspired banner headlines trumpeting "Koreagate." The hysterical press coverage played up anti-Asian tropes and depicted Park as a conniving man of mystery and subversion. By then, the accused had returned to South Korea; he eventually cut a deal with prosecutors in exchange for his testimony. In the end, his influence peddling in Washington proved to be less sensational than the headlines had promised—many of the congressmen who received his campaign contributions said credibly that they barely knew him. Park escaped jail time.[3]

By the 1990s, Park remained a border-hopping connector seeking lucrative deals. Saddam's regime took an interest in him because of his relationship with Boutros Boutros-Ghali, the cosmopolitan Egyptian diplomat elected secretary-general of the U.N. in late 1991. A Coptic Christian who had earned a doctoral degree in Paris, Boutros-Ghali had played a leading role in Egyptian president Anwar Sadat's historic reconciliation with Israel in 1978. Park cultivated a relationship with him. The South Korean created the impression that he remained well connected in Washington, the source of much of the U.N.'s budget. Boutros-Ghali explained later that the U.N. did not have its own intelligence service, so he had decided to collect intelligence privately, and Park offered "first-class information" because he "knew everybody" and was "an integral part of the Washington nomenclatura."[4]

It had always been obvious that U.N. economic sanctions against Iraq would exacerbate the hardships of Iraqi civilians. The idea of an oil-for-food program attracted support not only on humanitarian grounds but also for reasons of commerce and realpolitik. It would allow America and Britain, the most ardent backers of harsh sanctions, to deflect criticism that their policies punished innocents. It would increase global oil supplies and offer business opportunities to American, European, and other exporters. The U.N. could use proceeds from managed oil sales to address its chronic budget problems. For their part, Iraqi diplomats such as Tariq Aziz and Nizar Hamdoon—who had survived his impertinent correspondence with Saddam and remained Iraq's envoy to the U.N.—saw the proposal as a way to strengthen their battered nation and rescue its people from deepening social and public health crises.

For years, the only major player opposed to the idea was Saddam Hussein. He feared that Oil for Food, by providing a palliative amount of humanitarian relief, might actually delay the end of all international sanctions, the "blockade," as the Baathist government preferred to call it. Saddam held to his refusal, even as he watched the size of Iraq's economy shrink from $180 billion in 1990 to about $13 billion at the end of 1995, crushed by sanctions and weak oil prices.[5]

Nonetheless, Aziz persisted in exploring Oil-for-Food, and Saddam did not stop him. The opportunity to profit from Iraqi oil remained a powerful calling card. Samir Vincent, the Iraqi-born scientist and consultant working for Texas wildcatter Oscar Wyatt, got involved. In 1993, Tongsun Park introduced him to Boutros-Ghali. Park emphasized the need for payments by Iraq to influential friends, to smooth the process. "Some of these people need to be taken care of," Park said, according to Vincent.[6]

Saddam wanted a deal that would maximize Iraq's control over who profited from Iraqi oil sales and humanitarian imports while minimizing U.N. oversight of the program's administration inside Iraq. To achieve that, as an investigation led by former U.S. Federal Reserve chairman Paul Volcker later found, Saddam "decided to smooth the way to an agreement by making payments to Vincent and Park," via Nizar Hamdoon in New York, "with the intent that some of the money be used as a bribe for Boutros-Ghali." Amer Rashid, then Iraq's oil minister, recalled that the Iraqis hoped the payments would make the U.N. secretary-general "more flexible" in negotiations on a final memorandum of understanding.[7]

Park visited Boutros-Ghali's Manhattan residence at least ten times, including on May 21, 1996, the day a final deal was signed. Days later, Iraq dispatched $1 million in cash by diplomatic pouch to Hamdoon's office in New York, and Vincent soon delivered a cache of between $150,000 and $250,000 to Park. The payments continued until the end of the year, climaxing with Park's deposit at the MGM Grand in Las Vegas.[8]

Yet the appearance of straightforward bribery of the secretary-general is almost certainly wrong. There is no evidence that Boutros-Ghali received any of the money.

Saddam vacillated between optimism that his secret agents could help him win a good deal and skepticism that Boutros-Ghali would ever defy the designs of America and Israel. Boutros-Ghali's connections to Judaism and peacemaking with Israel attracted Saddam's attention, and he discussed with advisers whether the secretary-general's mother was Jewish, in which case, the secretary-general "must be a Jew." (She was not Jewish, as it happened, although the secretary-general's wife was.) "Who is Boutros, anyway?" Saddam asked his advisers on another occasion. "He is one of the leaders of the Egyptian government, and the whole of the Egyptian government is a conspirator."

Saddam's wheel-greasing and bullheadedness paid off. The Clinton administration accepted a system in which Iraq alone—meaning Saddam personally—would decide who could sell its oil exports. Saddam saw the deal as a political lever. Clinton saw it as a way to make a global public-relations problem go away. As Saddam said in explaining to colleagues his decision to compromise, "The political situation in the world is changing—I mean, to our advantage. There is confusion in the political situation in America."[9]

Republicans now in control of Congress withheld American dues to the U.N., on the grounds that its bureaucracy was bloated and its agenda was too often hostile to the United States. Bill Clinton and Madeleine Albright grew frustrated that Boutros-Ghali would not act on U.N. administrative reform proposals that might help unblock U.S. funding. During 1996, Albright spearheaded a strong-arming campaign to prevent Boutros-Ghali's reelection as secretary-general.

In a surreal episode, Boutros-Ghali turned to Saddam for help. Samir Vincent passed a message to Baghdad from the secretary-general on September 16, 1996: "I am Iraq's most loyal friend," Boutros-Ghali pleaded. "If there had been another Secretary-General under this tremendous pressure from the United States, he would not have been able to do what I did" to bring Oil-for-Food to life. "And this is the main reason that makes the United States oppose my reelection. I want to repeat my loyalty to my Arab friends in Iraq. . . . I call on my friends in Iraq to assist in my reelection campaign."[10]

It didn't work. Albright's lobbying defeated Boutros-Ghali, clearing the way for the election of Kofi Annan, a Ghanaian diplomat, as his successor. In December, following delays, Oscar Wyatt became the first U.S. oilman to receive an allocation of Iraqi crude under the U.N. program that Boutros-Ghali left as a legacy—eight million barrels.

The role played by wildcatters and influence peddlers in the negotiation of Oil-for-Food partly reflected the prolonged absence of professional diplomacy between Iraq and America. Halfway through his presidency, Bill Clinton still held the opinion that high-level meetings with Iraqi officials might signal a lack of American resolve and undermine the fragile consensus on sanctions at the U.N. Security Council.

Nizar Hamdoon had a line to Nat Kern, a C.I.A.-connected newsletter publisher and oil analyst. They probed whether Kern could introduce C.I.A. officers to high-ranking counterparts at the Mukhabarat in order to hold discreet talks about topics such as the oil markets, terrorism, and Iran. Kern tried, he recalled, but he reported back that the White House had refused to authorize such contacts. The agency did encourage Kern to take Hamdoon to lunch regularly, on the C.I.A.'s tab. Each time Kern returned from a trip to New York, the C.I.A. was there to receive and debrief him.

Clinton feared blowback from the American press and Republicans in Congress if he was discovered engaging with Saddam. He once asked British prime minister Tony Blair, "What's the most direct contact you have had with Iraq since 1991? For instance, has the British foreign minister talked to Tariq Aziz?"

"I honestly don't know," Blair said.

"If I weren't constrained by the press, I would pick up the phone and call the son of a bitch," Clinton went on. "But that is such a heavy-laden decision in America. I can't do that."[11]

Success was improbable, yet in an arena of only bad choices, it was self-defeating to foreclose even secret diplomacy. It deprived the administration of a chance to probe Saddam's motivations and claims about WMD up close, ultimately contributing to America's blindness to the truth.

In May 1996, the *60 Minutes* journalist Lesley Stahl asked Madeleine Albright, then the Clinton administration's ambassador to the U.N., a provocative question. "We have heard that half a million children have died" in Iraq because of U.S.-backed economic sanctions. "I mean, that's more children than died in Hiroshima. And, you know, is the price worth it?"

"I think this is a very hard choice," Albright said. "We think the price is worth it."

Albright would repudiate her remark, calling it "a terrible mistake, hasty, clumsy, and wrong." It was all of those things, but it was also one of those comments by political leaders that give offense by seeming to speak the truth too bluntly. The specific number of child deaths that Stahl cited—a Harvard team's estimate of "excess mortality" over the expected number of Iraqi child deaths since the enactment of economic sanctions—would become an enduring subject of dispute among public health scientists. Yet the big picture was unarguable: Iraqi civilians, including children, were dying because of sanctions, and the U.S. regarded these deaths as a necessary price to pay for its policy of coercive disarmament and containment.

The humanitarian aid that did get through disproportionately benefited semiautonomous Kurdistan. About two-thirds of humanitarian and infrastructure repair funds went to Kurdistan, where about 3.5 million people lived, while only one-third reached the rest of Iraq, where the population was about 17.5 million. This meant that water and electric systems in cities like Basra could not be rehabilitated adequately after the devastating blows of American-led bombing during the Gulf War and Saddam's razing of neighborhoods after the 1991 uprisings.[12]

Clinton and his aides regularly described the humanitarian crisis in Iraq as one of public relations—a problem caused by Saddam's propaganda machine, amplified by credulous sympathizers and cynical, self-interested members of the U.N. Security Council, led by Russia and France. However one apportioned blame, there could be no doubt that the crisis undermined America's credibility. Denis Halliday, an Irishman who became the U.N.'s humanitarian coordinator in Baghdad during 1997, openly called the sanctions policy "genocide." He resigned his position in protest over the moral complicity of the U.N. Halliday and other U.N. civil servants posted to Iraq found themselves continually under pressure from U.N. headquarters, where overlapping and self-contradicting Iraq programs were carried out through a "management structure that must be unique for its incompetence," in the words of Hans-Christof von Sponeck, a German diplomat who followed Halliday in Baghdad and resigned for the same reasons the Irishman had given. Yet the typical messaging out of Washington and London remained that Saddam exaggerated Iraqi public health and nutrition problems—or, to the extent such suffering was indeed severe, it was entirely Saddam's responsibility. "Whenever you tried to come up with figures, observations, analyses that were not supportive of the policies in Washington and in London, you were cut to pieces," von Sponeck recalled.[13]

Although it could be difficult to collect public health and mortality statistics in Saddam's Iraq, there can be no serious doubt that the sanctions regime contributed to the deaths of at least tens of thousands of Iraqis during the 1990s by increasing food insecurity and reducing medical care. The destruction of Iraq's electric power systems degraded the country's water purification plants, contributing to the revival of previously vanquished diseases. Iraq had no recorded cholera cases in 1989, but by 1994, it had 1,344 cases per one hundred thousand people. The prevalence of typhoid grew by more than tenfold. As Oil-for-Food started, Kofi Annan reported that nearly a third of children under five suffered from malnutrition and that clean water and medical supplies were "grossly inadequate."[14]

In a post-1997 study too sensitive for public release, the Baath Party documented its own examination of the country's economic collapse. Per capita Iraqi incomes had fallen from about $4,200 dollars in 1979 to just $485 in 1993, it reported. During the four years after 1989, rates of infant mortality rose from twenty-five deaths per thousand births to ninety-three per thousand. Surgeries in Iraqi hospitals and clinics fell by two-thirds during the same period due to "the lack of anesthetic supplies and medical equipment as well as the clear shortage of hospitals and health centers," the study reported.

These sudden reversals of national health devastated all Iraqis but hit the urban middle classes especially hard, since they had further to fall after Iraq's industrialization drives during the 1970s. And the economy's collapse had led to social breakdown, the unpublished Baath Party study found: there was a nationwide rise in murder, kidnapping, forgery, divorce, unemployment, children begging on the streets, and, for many people, "feelings of fear and stress." The study carefully avoided any criticism of Saddam Hussein, but it described the rise of an Iraqi class of profiteers—"we can call them 'warmongers'"—who enjoyed "speedy wealth without great or real effort." It did not, of course, name Uday Hussein or Saddam's other self-enriching relatives, but readers would have easily recognized the indirect references.[15]

In public, the regime once again discredited itself with crude propaganda, aiding Clinton's efforts to hold a hard line. Saddam oversaw publicity campaigns about child mortality that were so transparently designed to manipulate international opinion that they hurt campaigners' efforts to challenge the morality of sanctions. In a typical example, an Iraqi official urged the Ministry of Health to hoard the bodies of dead children for a mass procession in which the corpses would be paraded in child-size coffins draped with Iraqi flags.[16]

Von Sponeck regarded the "systematic disinformation campaigns" by the U.S. and its allies, which sowed doubt about the true humanitarian picture in Iraq, to be just as appalling. U.N. headquarters, too, he recalled, sometimes downplayed or questioned reliable evidence of hunger and disease. The Iraqis attempted "to dramatize, to exaggerate, and to misrepresent," the German diplomat remembered. "We would argue and say, 'Look, the Iraqi regime cannot in any way be defended. That's a brutal regime. But brutal as it may be, what we are doing here—what the U.N. Security Council does—is as brutal as the other side."[17]

S addam was purposeful in using his reckless defiance of the international order to gain concessions. He once cited for advisers the "political literature" about how a statesman who threatens a crisis gains
leverage and forces "give and take" that results in a more favorable compromise than would otherwise be attainable. Some of Saddam's attempts along these lines were impossible to mistake, such as his
mobilization of Republican Guard divisions to again threaten Kuwait.
Other methods, such as bribery, were subtler.

Once Oil-for-Food began, Saddam alone decided who received the
Ministry of Oil vouchers that authorized the holder to sell a particular
amount of Iraqi crude. In the portrait later pieced together by investigators, Saddam appears as a kind of accountant in chief, hunched over
ledgers containing lists of names, adding voucher recipients and crossing others off the list. The vouchers were tradeable, like stocks—a re-
cipient with no capacity to load or ship physical oil could sell his
vouchers to an oil company at a profit of ten cents to thirty-five cents
per barrel.[18]

Saddam used his favor-granting to advance his campaign to encourage Russia and France to withdraw their support for sanctions and weapons inspections. Russian individuals—typically politicians—received
30 percent of Oil-for-Food vouchers. French recipients took 15 percent; Chinese recipients, another 10 percent. Much of the rest went to
friends of the regime, including interlocutors with the Clinton administration, such as Oscar Wyatt and Samir Vincent, and even a senior
U.N. civil servant who helped supervise Oil-for-Food, Benon Sevan.
The sums these individuals could earn from their vouchers were not
always life-altering—a few hundred thousand dollars here, a million
there—but they were enough to pay off a mortgage or buy a vacation
home, and so more than tempting enough.[19]

After the Soviet Union's collapse, Russia's policies toward Iraq were
informed almost entirely by Moscow's financial straits. Boris Yeltsin,

president of the Russian Federation, pleaded with Clinton "to reduce the sanctions against Iraq" because Saddam owed his country over $6 billion, and Russia desperately needed the loans repaid. Yeltsin thought he might at least get $3 billion back. Clinton put off Yeltsin, aware that Russia needed American direct investment and other economic support. Saddam, meanwhile, doled out oil vouchers to state-linked Russian firms like Lukoil and to Russian nationalists opposed to Yeltsin's tilt toward the West, including Gennady Zyuganov, the head of the Communist Party. Yeltsin gradually distanced himself from U.S. policy on Iraq, but he never broke with Washington in the U.N. Security Council.[20]

In France, Saddam's list of voucher recipients included Charles Pasqua, a former minister of the interior, who was given eleven million barrels, according to a 2005 U.N. investigative report. (In 2013, a French court acquitted Pasqua and other former French officials of any wrongdoing.) President Jacques Chirac, Saddam's friend from the 1970s, steered clear of such favors but offered himself to Clinton as a Saddam interlocutor and explainer.

"The way Saddam thinks," he told Clinton privately, "is the best way to regain control of the people is to pretend to be a martyr." He urged Washington not to overreach, but Clinton was skeptical of France's maneuvering. Chirac "had come to believe that Saddam could be rehabilitated, an opinion Clinton did not share," recalled Martin Indyk, who had by now moved to the State Department.[21]

On average, by all illicit means—including Oil-for-Food kickbacks, unauthorized oil sales to neighboring countries, and sanctions-busting trade with Jordan, Syria, and Turkey—Saddam's regime cleared nearly $2 billion annually after 1990. This was enough to keep the president and his cronies in renovated palaces and new Mercedes-Benzes. And the cash surely buoyed Saddam as he prepared to once again escalate his confrontation with the U.N. over weapons inspections.[22]

Yet the revenue from the regime's rackets amounted to less than 10 percent of a shrunken Iraqi economy—a dictator's commission, as it were. War and sanctions had caused far more harm. Even if Saddam "built $2 billion worth of palaces over a decade, as the United States often claimed, those were not what caused the magnitude of the humanitarian crisis in Iraq," as Joy Gordon has written. Iraq experienced a "catastrophic collapse of every system needed to sustain human life" as a result of "the massive destruction from bombing . . . the inability of Iraq to import goods . . . the collapse of the economy."[23]

By the time of Oil-for-Food, Bill Clinton and Sandy Berger, promoted in 1997 to national security adviser, had installed a somewhat more hawkish network of Iraq advisers at the White House and in Clinton's cabinet. They favored making Saddam's departure from office an explicit goal of American foreign policy. Berger "was much more sympathetic to the hard-line position" than his predecessor, Tony Lake, had been, recalled Kenneth Pollack, who would work on Iraq at the N.S.C. Madeleine Albright, perhaps the most vocal hawk in this loose group, moved from the U.N. to become secretary of state in January 1997. To reset America's declared policy, she chose to make an early flagship speech at Georgetown University. The speech originated with "administration hard-liners and was intended to focus on the need for regime change in Iraq," according to Pollack.[24]

Albright all but announced that even if U.N. disarmament inspectors certified that Iraq had no chemical, biological, or nuclear arms or programs, the U.S. would maintain harsh sanctions until Saddam left office. "We do not agree with the nations who argue that if Iraq complies with its obligations concerning weapons of mass destruction, sanctions should be lifted," Albright declared. "Our view—which is unshakable—is that Iraq must prove its peaceful intentions." Yet she made clear that Saddam could not meet these new requirements: "The evidence is overwhelming that Saddam Hussein's intentions will never be peaceful." As to the humanitarian crisis, she blamed Saddam and said only, "We will do what we responsibly can to minimize the suffering of Iraqi civilians."[25]

here is no record of Saddam discussing Albright's address with advisers, but her main point—that no matter how much Iraq cooperated with the U.N., it could not expect sanctions relief—would hardly have surprised him. In his own councils, Saddam had long been the pessimist in chief, arguing that the U.S. had the U.N. under its thumb and that weapons inspectors would never relent. Iraq had endured "six years, not six weeks," he told his aides. "They destroyed our chemical weapons, all our chances to raise our heads. . . . Their dogs are slandering us"—to the point of even searching his palaces—"while we are silent," enduring humiliation.[26]

To the White House, Albright's speech "was just recognizing reality," as Bruce Riedel, at the National Security Council, put it. Even if Clinton wanted to end economic sanctions, the Republican-led Congress was unlikely to go along. Moreover, Albright's speech reflected an emerging consensus in Washington and London, according to Charles Duelfer, UNSCOM's deputy director. "The United States and the United Kingdom saw Saddam as an irredeemable security risk who could never be trusted," Duelfer recalled, so "sanctions were essential as long as he was in power." Otherwise, Saddam would "inevitably instigate regional conflicts that would require U.S. intervention." Saddam's unchanging outlook seemed increasingly out of step with a world being transformed and connected by the World Wide Web and personal computing; his record of aggression threatened a booming global economy.

Yet by making plain that there was really no way out of sanctions, Albright clarified Saddam's choice and spurred him to act belligerently. As the Iraqi president would put it to his advisers, referring to the disruption and humiliation of U.N. weapons inspections: "Sanctions without all these sacrifices are better than sanctions with them."[27]

The number of disputes Saddam initiated with U.N. weapons inspections rose across 1997, and so did the willingness of France, Russia, and China to plead Iraq's case. The U.S. was losing its grip on the U.N.

Security Council. In a reflective end-of-year memo to Riedel at the White House, Duelfer observed that "a radical change has taken place. . . . In Security Council debates and in relations with many individual countries, the criticism has not been of Iraq but of the Commission" charged with Iraq's disarmament. "There is a belief here that we are fighting a losing battle."

Duelfer described "a concerted effort by France, Russia, and China"—a campaign carried out in coordination with Baghdad—to reduce American and British influence over the inspections. "In sum," he wrote, "my rather pessimistic sense is that [the Special Commission], while an innovative and noble experiment in conflict resolution and nonproliferation enforcement, may not be fully successful and in fact is likely to be a failure."[28]

It was a prescient forecast. A year later, UNSCOM was dead, and international weapons inspectors had been banished from Iraq.

TWENTY-ONE

The Logic of Illusion

n 1997, Rolf Ekéus accepted an offer to become Sweden's ambassador to the United States. Tariq Aziz assured him that the job he was
leaving as the U.N.'s chief weapons hunter "was like a surgical operation without anesthesia: no sane person would want to prolong it."
Ekéus did not feel that way, but he did believe that the Special Commission had largely fulfilled its mandate. Iraq's nuclear-, chemical-, and
biological-weapons programs, as well as its longer-range missiles, had
been discovered and dismantled—not beyond all reasonable doubt but
well enough.

The Swedish embassy in Washington was situated in a modern,
stone-and-glass building on the edge of Georgetown, with striking
views of the Potomac River. In America's access-obsessed capital,
Swedish diplomats found an edge by cultivating relationships with influential Americans who had ancestral ties to Scandinavia. Ekéus inherited a connection to Chief Justice William Rehnquist, whose paternal
grandparents had emigrated from Sweden. Rehnquist had in turn introduced the embassy to Sandra Day O'Connor, the Supreme Court's

first female justice, and in January 1998, O'Connor invited Rolf Ekéus
to a dinner in the court's mahogany-walled, high-ceilinged chambers, a
heavy and traditional space decorated with friezes and busts of past
justices.

Former president George H. W. Bush and his sons George W. and
Jeb were among the guests. The chambers housed a Baldwin piano, and
before dinner, Ekéus performed a few Gershwin pieces. Later, George
H. W. pulled him aside and called over George W., who was then serving his second term as governor of Texas. He already looked like a front-
runner to be the Republican Party's nominee for president in 2000.

The elder Bush asked Ekéus for his analysis of Saddam's threat to
the Middle East. George W. seemed "clearly interested," Ekéus recalled. The Swede said that Iraq's nuclear program was now "under
control" and that its massive chemical-weapons complex "had been destroyed." He described "the great prize," the biological-weapons program, to which Iraq had finally confessed two years before.

"So the weapons are eliminated," the elder Bush said, clarifying the
main point. But George W.'s eyes now darted around the room, and he
appeared visibly skeptical about this conclusion, Ekéus surmised. Of
course, the governor might have just been bored.[1]

The Clinton administration did not believe that the Special Commission's work was finished. Nor did Charles Duelfer or Scott Ritter, the American inspectors at the U.N. They reported now to Ekéus's
successor, Richard Butler, an Australian politician and arms-control
specialist.

Duelfer and Ritter were gung-ho, physically robust characters. Duelfer was lean and long-faced, a skydiving enthusiast with a thick, reddish
mustache. Ritter stood six foot four and weighed more than two hundred pounds, a self-described "alpha dog" who told colleagues that he
conducted inspections with "tail held high." Duelfer was Ritter's supervisor and by far the more polished Washington operator. They were

aligned on the need for inspections conducted like unarmed combat missions, but tensions were growing between them.

"Ritter was a character I found appealing," Duelfer recalled. "But he was high maintenance; key people in Washington thought he was not reliable." For his part, after their dustup over the C.I.A. eavesdropping operation in 1996, Ritter worried that Duelfer was more loyal to Langley than to the U.N. commission on which they served.

The pair had persuaded Ekéus to conduct the investigations that directly targeted Saddam's "concealment mechanism," which referred mainly to the Special Security Organization responsible for Saddam's personal security. This plan had a grounding in logic. Hussein Kamel had revealed in 1995 that Saddam relied on the S.S.O. to hide illicit WMD equipment. By launching surprise inspections of presidential offices and palaces that the S.S.O. protected, and then monitoring how the bodyguards reacted, Duelfer and Ritter believed they might learn how Saddam's bodyguards hid contraband. As Ritter put it, "The entire purpose was to start stressing the system of concealment."[2]

On a visit to Washington, Duelfer tried to explain their approach to Sandy Berger, the national security adviser. He asked Berger to imagine a world where Scott Ritter might "show up at the West Wing gate demanding to search your safe." Berger struggled to see how this escalation would ever end. Either the inspectors would develop full confidence that the Iraqis "really do not have and will not rebuild WMD," Duelfer said, or Saddam would "eventually throw us out," triggering an international crisis. Berger signed off; tough inspections remained a centerpiece of Clinton's policy.[3]

To agitate the regime, Ritter led searches of the Special Security Institute, where Saddam's bodyguards trained, and the Mukhabarat Academy, where prospective spies studied. Those inspections triggered little reaction, but at other sensitive sites, the S.S.O. panicked and scrambled to remove items—or else blocked the inspectors from entering altogether. Ritter concluded that these inspections proved "they were concealing" prohibited weapons or documentation.[4]

They failed to grasp what the S.S.O.'s anxious behavior really meant. Saddam was hiding something from the inspectors, as the arms-control scholar Gregory Koblentz later concluded, but "it wasn't WMD; it was the secret to how he stayed in power." The "concealment mechanism" conceived of by the U.N. team was in fact there to secure the presidential protection system whose overriding purpose was to keep Saddam Hussein safe. As the U.N. inspectors assessed the S.S.O.'s behavior, they fell under the sway of "confirmation bias," the tendency of humans to interpret new evidence in a way that reinforces emotionally charged beliefs they already hold.

Saddam's bodyguards did not lose their cool during the great majority of the U.N.'s inspections. Between April and October 1997, the Special Commission carried out more than 870 visits and were blocked only six times, according to a study by Koblentz. Yet when the inspectors bore down on offices or palaces where Saddam Hussein might be present or where he might choose to visit in the future, the S.S.O. went into fight mode. In those cases, Iraq tried to block access more than four times out of five, the study found.[5]

Ritter believed that the S.S.O. was hiding WMD in presidential compounds. An alternative explanation was that the bodyguards saw the U.N.'s intrusive inspections as a threat to Saddam's safety because the inspectors might collect intelligence to aid future assassination or coup attempts. All U.N. operatives in Iraq should be considered spies, Saddam had long cautioned. "If we had simply recognized at the time that we're getting pretty close to the regime here, and regime survival is the most important thing in a dictatorship, we might have realized what the Iraqi motivation was," Bill McLaughlin, a retired American special-ops soldier who worked with Ritter, said later.[6]

The practices of Saddam's police state compounded the confusion. Saddam did not want U.N. inspectors to find contraband or embarrassing documents, yet he worried about how well his massive weapons bureaucracy of the 1980s had cleaned up its offices, plants, and military bases. He forced Iraqi military officers and scientists to sign pledges that they possessed no material from Iraq's historical programs. "If we violate the rules," declared a "Statement of Commitment" demanded of air force personnel, "we will be responsible for all the legal consequences." That was a euphemism for possible arrest, torture, and execution.

When U.N. inspectors did find stray files touching on WMD, Baathist authorities launched investigations into how the mistake had occurred and who should pay. This heavily incentivized S.S.O. officers to block weapons inspectors from searching buildings for which they were responsible. As Koblentz put it, why allow "foreign spies" into sensitive sites if a successful inspection might result in an S.S.O. officer's arrest and execution?[7]

Tariq Aziz threatened to cease cooperation as Ritter's aggression mounted. "Iraq is not a defeated country," he told Richard Butler. "UNSCOM is not an army of occupation, and you are not General MacArthur!"[8]

By early 1998, another violent confrontation between the United States and Saddam seemed imminent. The U.N.'s secretary-general, Kofi Annan, put himself forward as a negotiator. On February 16, as American warships churned in the Persian Gulf, Bill Clinton called Tony Blair.

"Because of European public opinion and Arab public opinion, we don't want to look bloodthirsty," Clinton said. "Kofi Annan would love to go in and save the day, which is fine with me," as long as any deal he negotiated did not "undermine the integrity of the inspections."[9]

Clinton asked King Hassan II of Morocco, an ally of Washington, to telephone Saddam and assure him that aggressive inspections of presidential palaces were not part of some American assassination plot. "I have no interest in killing him or hunting him down," Clinton told the king. "I'm not fooling with him. I just don't want his chemical and biological program going forward." But given the history of C.I.A.-backed coup plots, including recently, it was hard to see why Saddam would trust this secondhand message.[10]

Annan flew to Baghdad on a private jet provided by France. He negotiated a memorandum of understanding with Tariq Aziz that would create new rules for inspections of presidential sites. Diplomats appointed by Annan would now accompany Scott Ritter and the alpha dogs. Annan met with Saddam to seal the deal. The secretary-general said later that he was impressed with Saddam's "decisiveness" and felt "we did have a good human rapport."[11]

Clinton pored over the draft agreement and concluded that, with a few tweaks, it was good enough. But Charles Duelfer and colleagues at the Special Commission watched Annan's diplomacy with dismay. Saddam had won unacceptable concessions, they felt, such as stripping the Special Commission of the exclusive right to appoint inspectors.

Duelfer drafted a resignation letter. The discovery of Iraq's advancing nuclear-weapons program after the war over Kuwait had shown that "ineffective monitoring may be *worse* than nothing," he wrote. A White House aide warned Duelfer about what his resignation would mean: "You'll never work in this town again." He held off, but his pique reflected a larger reality: the Great Power consensus that had allowed weapons inspectors to box Saddam in since mid-1991 was falling apart.[12]

Jafar Dhia Jafar still worked mainly as a presidential adviser on electricity and other civilian projects. He remained the editor in chief for all written submissions or reports about the history of the nuclear program, however, and he met with I.A.E.A. inspectors periodically. After Hussein Kamel's defection, Saddam asked him to rewrite once more Iraq's formal declaration about the defunct program's past—to admit secrets previously withheld, such as those concerning the "crash program" to build a bomb after the invasion of Kuwait.

Jafar submitted an updated *Full, Final, and Complete Declaration* to the I.A.E.A. in March 1996. The agency's inspectors questioned him extensively about "silly" matters, as Jafar saw it. He rewrote the document three times, handing over what he hoped was a final version in July 1997.[13]

The I.A.E.A. "has for some time been at a point of diminishing returns" in its investigations, Hans Blix told the I.A.E.A. board around this time. Between 1991 and the end of 1998, the I.A.E.A. would conduct 512 inspections in Iraq. Yet there always seemed to be technical matters holding up a clean bill of health. It seemed to Jafar that the endless questions about history amounted to a "scheme" to prolong the sanctions and weaken Iraq in every possible way.

"Isn't it time to tell the Security Council the truth?" he asked Garry Dillon, an I.A.E.A. team leader from Britain.

Dillon complained to Tariq Aziz, who sought out the physicist. "You did well," Aziz assured him.[14]

Saddam kept alive the Iraqi Atomic Energy Commission that had provided cover for the bomb program in the 1980s. Fadhil al-Janabi became its chairman in 1996. He organized commission meetings and occasionally hosted a beaming Saddam for a briefing or a ribbon cutting. As a signatory to the Nonproliferation Treaty, Iraq was still entitled to conduct peaceful nuclear research. But in Washington and London, the Atomic Energy Commission's continued visibility, and the privileges granted to former weapons scientists, looked like evidence that Saddam intended to reconstitute his bomb program at the first opportunity. Who wanted to take that risk again?[15]

Bill Clinton's understanding was that "the inspectors are closer to finishing on the missile and nuclear side than on the biological or chemical side," as he told Boris Yeltsin in late 1997. Yet Clinton did not regard Saddam's all-but-confirmed nuclear disarmament as a turning point. This was partly because he remained deeply worried about Iraq's history with biological and chemical weapons.

"No other country in the world has a major chemical and biological program and has actually used it against others as the Iraqis have used it on Iran and the Kurds," Clinton told Yeltsin. "He could sell it to terrorists or to American, European, Japanese or Russian organized crime networks." Just a tiny amount "can do a lot of damage, as we saw in the

Tokyo subway attack a couple of years ago." He was referring to an attack in 1995 by Aum Shinrikyo, a Japanese cult and terrorist group, which released sarin gas on the metro, killing a dozen people and injuring hundreds. More than three years before the 9/11 attacks, Clinton's fears and his framing of the threat Saddam posed to world peace anticipated the Bush administration's case for invading Iraq.[16]

The president also believed that Saddam's treatment of the U.N. inspectors proved that he was, in fact, hiding chemical and biological arms—he had just not been caught yet. "I've reached the conclusion after eliminating all possible alternatives that Saddam still has the makings of a chemical and biological program he doesn't want to give up," Clinton told Tony Blair.[17]

Clinton had absorbed briefings about how lethal amounts of biological weapons could be made in very small facilities. "Most people, even in our own country, have not thought much about the facts . . . and how little space it takes to produce them," he told Blair. If Saddam was determined to possess such poisons, it would be all but impossible to be certain that Iraq had not secreted away a single tiny lab in a nation of twenty-two million people spread out over 169,000 square miles. The danger of terrorists using chemical and biological agents was credible and terrifying, but Clinton's fears set up a policy toward Iraq with no clear exit, other than Saddam's departure from power. Yet Clinton, like George Tenet at the C.I.A., was by now losing faith in covert action to oust Saddam.

Early in 1998, Clinton and Vice President Al Gore welcomed Tony Blair to the Oval Office.

"We are getting new pressures, especially from Capitol Hill, to go after Saddam's head," Gore reported.

"That approach is nowhere near as simple as it sounds," Clinton said.[18]

Nineteen ninety-eight was shaping up to be a terrible year for the president. The Monica Lewinsky scandal broke in January. Republicans threatened Clinton with impeachment. In Baghdad, Saddam and his advisers—even the America watcher Tariq Aziz—were befuddled by the Lewinsky matter, records of their discussions show. Yet they gathered that Clinton was under serious political assault.

For once, Saddam had a passingly accurate grasp of how domestic American politics might affect him. If Clinton did not strike Iraq militarily, his Republican opposition "will embarrass him," he explained to advisers. "Those in power know very well they are unable to oust" the Iraqi regime, he went on. The Republicans, in particular, knew "that the regime cannot be ousted." They agitated about regime change nonetheless, "to make it difficult for Clinton."

Saddam had concluded that "Zionism is in agreement with the idea of ousting the regime," which was his way of saying that it didn't really matter what Bill Clinton thought—regime change would be America's policy, and therefore, there would be no sanctions relief or clean bill of health on WMD forthcoming.[19]

By the summer of 1998, Scott Ritter had grown disgusted by the Clinton administration. Several grievances animated him. He continued to object to what he regarded as Charles Duelfer's collusion with the C.I.A. He objected to a C.I.A. decision to restrict the sharing of U-2 photographs with Israel. He objected to Richard Butler, his Australian boss at the Special Commission—"more of a car salesman than a diplomat"—because he seemed to Ritter to bend to the will of the Clinton administration.

On August 26, 1998, Ritter resigned and proclaimed in a blistering letter that the U.N. Security Council—and by extension, the Clinton administration—had become a "witting partner" in Saddam's campaign to weaken inspections. Ritter soon shared his detailed critiques of C.I.A. infiltration of the U.N. Special Commission with reporters at *The Washington Post, The New Yorker,* and other major media outlets. His passionate dissent fired up Republicans in Congress. They summoned the square-jawed, straight-talking former U.S. Marine officer— a Washington whistleblower from central casting—to testify at hearings.

This generated yet more headlines about Clinton's alleged fecklessness just as the drive to impeach the president over the Lewinsky matter approached its climax. Saddam Hussein did not require a graduate degree in American politics to understand that the upheavals in Washington meant that an opportunity to expel the U.N. inspectors had at last arrived.[20]

At the end of October, Iraq announced that it would end all cooperation with the Special Commission. Military action again loomed. Clinton spoke with Jacques Chirac. He reported that he had warned Saddam that he was out of line and might be hit. "But in truth I'm afraid we are working here with an unarmed gun," Chirac said. "I think it's in his own interest to be bombed."

"You think even though it wouldn't help him get the sanctions lifted, the people would, in their adversity, be more supportive of him?" Clinton asked.

"Yes, naturally, of course. That explains his attitude. . . . He wants two things today: He wants to regain control of his own people, and look like a martyr in the eyes of Arab public opinion. And secondly, he wants to get rid of UNSCOM once and for all, and the I.A.E.A., and he wants to be able to go about his business as he pleases. And that's why we're in somewhat of a trap here. We have nothing to offer. . . . He's a man who doesn't know anything about the outside world, but he knows his own country very well."[21]

Clinton was out of ideas. During his years in office, the president had changed his policy toward Iraq several times, without calling much attention to his evolution. During his first term, he had clung firmly to containment. On the eve of his reelection campaign, he had turned to the C.I.A., hoping to foster Saddam's removal from power, only to be embarrassed. Finally, while confronting impeachment and a hawkish Congress, Clinton had openly embraced regime change in Baghdad, even though he had no plan to carry it out.

Privately, Clinton seemed to lack conviction about any of his choices. Iraq was "the most difficult of problems because it is devoid of a sensible policy response," he told his advisers. He had expended effort year after year and had little to show. "The constant crises, the weekly Iraq principals meetings, the diversion of attention from more important priorities . . . and the constant carping from the Republican-controlled Congress—all took their toll," recalled Martin Indyk.

The Pentagon and Britain's military nonetheless readied another round of air and missile strikes—a "ritual bloodletting," as Duelfer sardonically called these kinds of strikes. At the last hour, Saddam said he would allow the weapons inspectors back in. Clinton withdrew his attack order while the bombers were in the air. But even Saddam had lost patience with this game. Almost as soon as the inspectors returned, Saddam signaled that he was done—the Special Commission would be expelled, this time for good.[22]

On December 14, Clinton called Blair. By banishing the inspectors, Saddam was all but inviting a military attack again. "I don't see we have any choice but to act," Clinton said.

The timing was inconvenient. Ramadan would begin soon; they did not want to bomb during that time. They could squeeze in an attack beforehand, but the U.S. House of Representatives was about to open Clinton's impeachment trial. If Clinton waged war now, he would be accused of trying to cynically divert the public's attention. "There won't be a single living soul in America who won't believe I did this because of the impeachment," he told his war cabinet. Nonetheless, he went ahead. "My instinct is we gotta go," the president told Blair on December 15. "I will get a world of shit over here, that I jiggered the timing—but I didn't."[23]

Operation Desert Fox launched the next day. U.S. Navy bombers from the aircraft carrier U.S.S. *Enterprise* and U.S. Air Force jets flying from Oman and the island of Diego Garcia struck about one hundred Iraqi targets over four days. The British Royal Air Force also took part. Only thirteen targeted facilities were believed to be involved with

Iraq's WMD programs. Half were regime leadership or military sites. These included Saddam's Radwaniyah estate and Special Security Organization targets. The strikes were more extensive than some past attacks, but the Pentagon noted that they would only "degrade" Saddam's capabilities.[24]

As the bombs fell, Clinton spoke again to Chirac, who asked the essential question: "When the strikes against Iraq are over, what are we going to do?" It seemed doubtful that weapons inspectors would be allowed to return, perhaps not ever.

"I don't know," Clinton said. He thought they should "say we would like to do it," meaning restore a credible U.N. inspection and disarmament program.

Tony Blair, a skilled practitioner of strategic communication, said that they had to persuade the public that Desert Fox had really hurt Saddam's WMD development, that this round of bombing was not just more symbolic violence. "If we were in a position to announce that we put back his military capability by several years, I think people would be supportive," Blair assessed.

"We've got to have our military and intelligence folks as a guide," Clinton cautioned. "It has to be fact driven."

Clinton and his aides had worked up talking points, which the president tested out privately on Blair. They would restate "redlines," promising Saddam more attacks if he threatened his neighbors, developed WMD, or attacked Iraqi Kurdistan. They would advocate for the return of inspectors, but only if Saddam would definitely cooperate. And as a sweetener, Clinton wanted to enlarge Oil-for-Food, which would enrich Saddam's regime but also improve the welfare of the Iraqi population. Blair approved of all these ideas.

The Special Commission would soon yield to a successor organization, the United Nations Monitoring, Verification and Inspection Commission, or UNMOVIC, but this was little more than an office in New York. Saddam did not budge—the inspectors were no longer on the ground in Iraq, and he preferred it that way.[25]

Just as "confirmation bias" misled America, it caused Saddam to misread Washington's claims about his WMD. He assumed that an all-powerful C.I.A. *already knew* that he had no nuclear, chemical, or biological weapons. A C.I.A. capable of getting such a big question dead wrong on the facts was not consistent with Saddam's bedrock assumptions. Since America knew the truth but nonetheless faked claims that he was still hiding illicit arms, he reasoned, what did this imply? It meant that the Zionists and spies lined up against him were using the WMD issue cynically to advance their conspiracy to oust him from power. He saw no reason to play their game or deal with their prying inspectors.

Clinton assured the public that America's "long-term strategy is clear," but in truth it was a muddle. His administration had not thought through the consequences of the Special Commission's demise. Now that the inspectors were banished, the United States would have no eyes on the ground to watch for signs that Iraq might be rebuilding its dangerous weapons. Even while highly trained specialists conducted hundreds of short-notice or no-notice inspections each year, backed by the ability to test samples in laboratories and fly U-2 spy planes overhead, it had proved impossible to confirm to America's satisfaction that Saddam had no WMD. How could they ever have confidence that Iraq had no WMD now?[26]

Ahmad Chalabi sought to revive his place as an indispensable figure in Iraq's exiled opposition. With help from Warren Marik and Linda Flohr, two retired C.I.A. officers, he started a fundraising and publicity campaign in America. Like other flimflammers, Chalabi never apologized; he just kept telling his stories, insisting he had been wronged. Because he was willing to spill secrets about highly classified C.I.A. operations against Saddam, journalists flocked to him, and

Chalabi was able to rewrite the narratives of the Iraqi National Congress's failures in Kurdistan on the front page of *The Washington Post* and during a prime-time documentary broadcast nationally on ABC News, among other outlets. He seized upon the growing interest in ousting Saddam shown by Republicans and hawkish Democrats in Congress.

"When Chalabi showed up, those of us who wanted to see Saddam's regime brought down regarded him as a very important find," recalled Richard Perle, a Pentagon official during the Reagan administration. Perle was a ringleader of Washington's "neoconservatives," as they would become known, often pejoratively. Certainly, they were not conservative, if that implied caution or an inclination to conserve traditions. They were activists, a loose network of like-minded internationalists who advocated for an assertive post–Cold War foreign policy that would advance American power by expanding democracy and by challenging tyranny all around the world. Many were also firm supporters of Israel. They traced their intellectual heritage to figures such as Norman Podhoretz, the longtime editor of *Commentary*, as well as Irving Kristol and Daniel Bell, editors of *The Public Interest*. That generation advocated for human and civil rights as a moral imperative and as a means to undermine the Soviet Union. Their successors during the Clinton years included Perle and other former Reagan administration officials, such as Paul Wolfowitz, Zalmay Khalilzad, and Bill Kristol, Irving's son, then *The Weekly Standard*'s editor in chief. They attracted allies such as Donald Rumsfeld and Dick Cheney—business executives, cabinet-level leaders, and conservative nationalists, but not really men of ideas—on questions such as what to do about Iraq. They signed joint letters and published articles in journals. They formed an impressive-sounding but modestly funded entity called the Project for the New American Century to organize petition drives and develop policy planks for the 2000 presidential campaign.[27]

Saddam brought all sorts of American hawks together and created a unifying cause. He had a record of mass killings and reckless aggression, he had lobbed missiles at Israel, and he was too weak to retaliate dangerously if attacked. Iraq was an easy case relative to WMD-minded dictatorships like North Korea, which, if assaulted, could wreak terrible destruction on South Korea. It was also an easier case than Iran, whose hydra-headed government would be hard to decapitate, among other challenges.

Early in 1998, Perle, Rumsfeld, and such relative moderates as Richard Armitage signed an open letter to Clinton scolding him for not overthrowing Saddam. Eliminating "the possibility" that Iraq might be able to use or threaten to use WMD, they wrote, required "a willingness to undertake military action, as diplomacy is clearly failing."[28]

Here Chalabi stepped in with warmed-over ideas about how to get the job done. Around this time, Wolfowitz and Khalilzad wrote in Kristol's journal that the United States should "arm and train opposition forces" and be "prepared to provide military protection for Iraqi units defecting from Saddam," a suggestion that traced back to Chalabi's proposals from 1995. The generals commanding American forces in the Middle East regarded these ideas as implausible, even crackpot. "It was the siren song of the nineties," as Anthony Zinni, then a U.S. Marine four-star leading CENTCOM, put it later. "No blood. We can do it on the cheap. . . . This wasn't even a viable movie plot, let alone reality."[29]

Chalabi and his wife put about $150,000 a month of their own money into the Iraqi National Congress. Chalabi sought to raise millions more. Through an offshore corporation, he bought a townhouse in Georgetown. Perle invited him to bull sessions in which he impressed with his intelligence and educational achievements; Wolfowitz and Khalilzad, too, had earned doctorates at the University of Chicago. He had a pitch-perfect ear for Washington's hubristic foreign policy discourse. He cast himself as an Iraqi Charles de Gaulle, a principled exile whose sharp elbows and uncompromising insistence on total victory over Saddam might alienate some onlookers, but whose clarity and fortitude would be vindicated by history. In a capital where knowledge of Baathist Iraq ran very thin—only a handful of American officials had even visited the country since 1991—Chalabi got away with his posturing, even though he had no demonstrated following inside Iraq and, unlike de Gaulle, no experience in Iraq's military or government.[30]

The neoconservatives' demand for intervention in Iraq was a talking point for the 2000 presidential election campaign—as much a debate or cable TV zinger as anything else. Just before Desert Fox, Republicans on Capitol Hill advanced the Iraq Liberation Act to enshrine the goal of Saddam's overthrow in federal law and to fund the Iraqi National Congress. Clinton signed the bill into law, less because he believed in it than because he and his party needed its political cover.

Chalabi would later be credited with conning America into war. Yet he was pushing on an open door. To overestimate his importance risks scapegoating a foreigner with an accent and ignoring the responsibility— even eagerness—of Republican and Democratic members of Congress, aspiring cabinet members, and think-tank writers. Chalabi was a prop for ideologues who sought to expand the uses of American military power after the Cold War, as well as for politicians who identified Iraq as a winning campaign issue.

Clinton endorsed regime change on paper but regarded Chalabi as a losing bet. As the president explained in early 1999 to Jordan's King Hussein, "Congress is carried away with the external Iraqi leadership, which we think will fail." The State Department slow-rolled release of Iraq Liberation Act funds. Ultimately, the I.N.C. received about $33 million from twenty-three different contracts. Most of the money was directed toward propaganda operations aimed at Iraq, but some "information collection" programs funded by State during this period helped Chalabi feed false stories about Saddam's WMD programs to American media, Iraq hawks in Congress, and other receptive audiences—a form of "blowback" propaganda that would prove to be astoundingly influential.[31]

The Clinton White House again quietly reviewed whether there was, after all, any practical way to overthrow Saddam. At the National Security Council, the former C.I.A. analyst Kenneth Pollack joined colleagues to explore alternatives, such as having American and British aircraft patrolling the no-fly zones respond to Iraqi attacks on aircraft by "targeting assets of higher value to the regime," to raise pressure on Saddam. After some effort, in Pollack's judgment, "we were able to begin putting together a reasonable, coherent plan" to pursue Saddam's overthrow. But in the end, Sandy Berger and the national security cabinet never even met to consider the possibilities.

By a certain logic, Clinton had two options. He could continue to slow-roll regime change, effectively allowing Saddam to remain in power, pinched by sanctions but no longer subject to weapons inspections. Or he could overthrow him by a full-on, Desert Storm–scale American military invasion. Yet the idea of an invasion was a nonstarter at the time, even among Republican hawks in Congress. Nothing about Saddam seemed to require such a costly, tumultuous project in 1999 or 2000. The American economy was booming; American global military power was unchallenged. The World Wide Web had burst to life, connecting the world, powering productivity growth, and creating vast fortunes overnight. Why would America set all of that aside to mount a neo-imperial tank invasion across the deserts of Iraq?[32]

Arguably, Bill Clinton had achieved the goals that he and Tony Lake, his first national security adviser, had laid out in 1993. They had isolated and contained Saddam, albeit at a high cost in military expenditure, distraction, and human suffering within Iraq. They had avoided a full-scale war, despite Saddam's many provocations. Through ardent support for the Special Commission, they had enabled U.N. inspectors to dismantle Iraq's nuclear, chemical, biological, and missile programs. There was no modern precedent for such large-scale coercive disarmament by unarmed inspectors. Unfortunately, Clinton did not understand how successful the Special Commission had been—and nor did the commission itself.

After parrying Saddam for so long, and after confronting al-Qaeda's mass-casualty terrorism during his second term, Clinton had come to regard WMD as a singular danger of the post–Cold War world. In September 2000, he met Russia's new president, Vladimir Putin, at the Waldorf Astoria in New York. "It may turn out that the biggest threat in the next ten years isn't going to be state-to-state war," Clinton told him. "Rather, it may be terrorists with smaller chemical and biological weapons and even small nuclear weapons, which dogs in airports won't be able to sniff out. . . . We should see Iraq as a precursor of the larger problem we face over the next twenty years."

"I basically agree," Putin answered.[33]

Clinton's remarks were uncannily prescient. He anticipated 9/11, the transformational event of the decade to come, but he did not imagine that simple box cutters might be enough to achieve the impact he feared. In highlighting for Putin the dangers of uncontrolled WMD leaking from Saddam's Iraq, he anticipated how George W. Bush—and also many Democrats and liberal internationalists like Clinton and Tony Blair—would interpret the meaning of the 9/11 attacks.

TWENTY-TWO

The Secret Garden

As he reached his early sixties, Saddam decided to write a novel. He had an elegant hand, his Arabic calligraphy laced with long lines. He might produce ten or thirty or even fifty handwritten pages a day. Starting in the late 1990s, his pages arrived by courier at the office of his press secretary, Ali Abdullah Salman, who worked initially inside the Republican Palace and later in a nearby villa. About half a dozen editors and translators worked with Salman. They rarely saw the president. By this time, Saddam visited the official seat of his presidency infrequently, and his editorial aides had no idea where he drafted his fiction. Before, the press team had produced releases of Saddam's speeches for the Iraqi media or translated foreign news for the president. Once the fiction started coming in, they rallied around a new priority.

Salman did most of the copyediting. It was a delicate task, given the sensitivities of writers generally and the potential penalties for offending this one. He marked up Saddam's manuscripts with proposed corrections of syntax and grammar, then passed them back. Saddam wrote the same way that he spoke: His sentences were long and twisting. He would start out with one line of observation, disrupt himself with a digression, and then strike off in a new direction. "Even when he tackled simple ideas, he couldn't help himself and used a complex style," recalled Saman Abdul Majid, the translator, who was based in the press office. "He would get lost in parenthetical phrases." His asides included Arabic proverbs and, increasingly, Quranic verses. Saddam would accept only some of the changes proposed by his editors. "He did like to have his own personal touch," even if this meant writing in a meandering way, Saman Majid recalled. The president would return a second draft for typing and sometimes asked his editors to check historical facts in the text.[1]

The more he wrote, the more he identified as a man of letters. One evening, at the height of his novel-writing period, Saddam heard a television presenter make a grammatical error while reading a statement. The president telephoned the minister of culture to protest. An investigation ensued; the presenter reread the statement properly on the air and was suspended for six months.[2]

Saddam's first completed work, *Zabiba and the King*, published in 2000, is a polemical allegory set in ancient Babylon. It recounts a love affair between a married king—transparently Saddam—and Zabiba, a young, beautiful, and wise woman who is a stand-in for the Iraqi people. Much of the novel consists of didactic dialogue. Zabiba educates the king on how to rule even more successfully than he already does. The king, as he falls in love with her, takes in her advice respectfully.

The king protects Zabiba from her rapist husband (the United States), and she saves him from an assassination attempt by treasonous relatives. At one point, they discuss the chronic problem of hidden plots. In a recommendation familiar to readers living under Baath Party justice, she proposes a wide crackdown: "I would ask you to arrest all who knew about the preparation of the assassination and did not warn you about it, as well as all those who may have taken part."

Another time, they discuss succession. The passage echoes Saddam's claim that he would only appoint a relative to follow him in power if the individual had merit and won the consent of the Baath Party. "Why do we think that the king's son is any better than a son of a common man?" Zabiba asks. They agree that a son should rule only if he is fully qualified—a tentative, indirect endorsement of Qusay.

At the novel's conclusion, a people's council debates about what sort of ruler should follow the king. "We do not want our children and ourselves to be under the rule of some madman from among the children or grandchildren of this king, do we?" one representative asks, to laughter and applause. As it deliberates inconclusively, the council goes on to banish a Jewish citizen from the country, celebrate the army, and shower curses on "those who had gained their fortunes at the expense of the people."[3]

Writing became a preoccupation as Saddam spent more time in relative isolation following the near-fatal assassination attempt against Uday. In 1998, Saddam ordered a poet who worked in the press office to tutor him for a month on the rules of poetry. Verse had deep roots and visibility in Iraqi and Arab culture, yet while Saddam did compose some poems, he seemed more attracted to the novel, a form suitable for direct propaganda. (Muammar Qaddafi had published a collection of short stories in 1993, so perhaps Saddam thought his lengthy novels would establish his superior credentials.) Crude and awkward as his allegories were, his writing did offer the private joy of composition, as Saddam worked through creative choices about how to render as literary types the dramatis personae of Baathist Iraq—devilish America, the wayward Kurds, despicable landowners. He weaved these allegorical figures into stories of love and war. Saman Majid came to think of his novel writing as "Saddam's secret garden."[4]

Saddam saw the novel—as well as poetry, journalism, and the short story—as instruments of national and Baathist propaganda. During the Iran-Iraq War, his regime produced more than seventy-five novels and ninety book-length collections of short stories authored by writers backed by the Baathist state. (The potboiled plots described Iraqi heroism and noble martyrdom against the Persian enemy.) When Saddam took up his own novel writing, he revived the official propaganda novel.

He did not put his name on his published novels. Each cover states only that the book within was written "by its author." But speculation at the time by at least one C.I.A. analyst that the books were ghostwritten was incorrect. Saddam's decision to keep his name off book jackets was intended to reinforce the self-portrait of a humble ruler in *Zabiba and the King.*

For that novel, he approved cover art depicting a young woman with flowing hair in an idealized setting—an image lifted without license from the work of a Canadian artist. When the book came out in 2000, there was no confusion in Iraq about who had authored it. The Ministry of Culture printed thousands of copies, and Iraqi reviewers showered the novel with praise. Saddam's office ordered that copies be handed out to members of visiting foreign delegations. The Iraqi National Theater staged *Zabiba* as a musical, which Saddam attended, and a twenty-part adaptation eventually aired on Iraqi television.[5]

Saddam soon turned to his second novel, *The Fortified Castle*, an epic of seven hundred pages—twice as long as any of his other novels. It is set during the American-led war to liberate Kuwait from Iraqi occupation. Sabah, a Sunni Arab veteran of Iraq's war with Iran, falls in love with Shatrin, a Kurdish woman from the North. Their union is shadowed by Iran, Israel, America, and Britain. The novel's "long-winded stressing and re-stressing of the unity of Iraq and its people," in the scholar Hawraa Al-Hassan's description, makes for a "particularly boring and repetitive read." More than his other novels, *The Fortified Castle* reads like the mass-produced official novels of the 1980s, with "its extreme zeal and the intensity of its emotions," and especially in its "love of the nation and hatred of its enemies," Hassan writes. Saddam was hardly the first writer to misfire by overindulging himself in his second attempt at a novel, but he was, of course, spared any criticism by domestic reviewers. As with his other releases, every department of government was urged to "order in bulk," Ala Bashir, Saddam's physician, recalled.[6]

Saddam increasingly acted as writer in chief. He oversaw a patronage system of novel writers and poets that assured a steady living for those willing to follow the regime line. The program grouped writers into three tiers and allocated stipends accordingly—more than five million dinars for books written by the top group, according to one internal account. A subsidized program through April 2001 involved commissions to eighty writers of "novels, stories and scripts, who were honored by meeting with the President." A committee of readers evaluated the work for how it "addressed the heroism of the people and the armed forces. . . . Linguistic ability and style were also considered." In addition, Saddam paid between $100 and $500 to poets who adulated him.[7]

Saddam's literary period coincided with changes in his inner political circle. After the expulsion of U.N. weapons inspectors in 1998, the America watchers Tariq Aziz and Nizar Hamdoon lost out. Aziz remained deputy prime minister, but at one point, the regime arrested his son, Zia, a businessman, a signal that his opponents had gained ground. In 1998, Hamdoon was recalled from New York to Baghdad to fill a post running the America desk at the Ministry of Foreign Affairs. Aziz and Hamdoon still searched for ways to establish dialogue with Washington, but in meetings with interlocutors such as Samir Vincent, Aziz could now sound as frustrated and insouciant as his boss. "The U.S. cannot hurt Iraq anymore," he said, echoing a line Saddam sometimes used. "The U.S. has done their best with sanctions and failed." The allegations about Iraq's supposedly ongoing WMD programs were "a big lie," Aziz continued. "The problem with the U.S. is they invent events or facts . . . then turn around and believe their own invention."[8]

The most powerful individual around Saddam now was Abid Hamid Mahmud, a cousin and former bodyguard of Saddam's who was in his forties. He served as secretary of the presidential office, but through his informal power, he had come to occupy a position comparable to the one vacated by Hussein Kamel. Mahmud was a tennis and karate enthusiast, a trusted Tikriti who worked twelve hours a day to enforce Saddam's priorities and execute projects efficiently. He had "a hard and strict appearance," Saman Majid recalled, and he "wouldn't tolerate one mistake. Just a simple letter filed in the wrong place could trigger his ire." Mahmud carried a chrome-plated, Soviet-made Tokarev pistol inscribed to him by Qusay. The trust between the bodyguard and the president "was total."[9]

S addam Hussein barely figured into the 2000 presidential election contest between Al Gore and George W. Bush. The vice president and the Texas governor relied on essentially the same talking points: Saddam was a menace, his departure from power was desirable, and he must comply with U.N. disarmament resolutions. Their positions reflected the premises of the Iraq Liberation Act. Gore's vice presidential running mate, Connecticut senator Joe Lieberman, had coauthored the bill. Bush and Gore both seemed content with abstract tough talk, perhaps because each was politically vulnerable on the issue. Bush's father had left Saddam in power after the Gulf War. The Clinton administration's record since then had little in it for Gore to brag about, beyond the U.N. disarmament regime no longer in place.

The election came down to a few hundred votes in Florida, and in December, after a weeks-long melee of recounts and lawsuits, the United States Supreme Court, in a 5–4 ruling, delivered the White House to Bush. Gore conceded graciously. The new president knew that he would have to review Iraq policy early on, but he had more questions than firm plans. Bush could expect plenty of advice from the heavyweights in his national security cabinet. The president appointed a secretary of state, Colin Powell, who had supervised the war to expel Iraqi forces from Kuwait. He appointed a secretary of defense, Donald Rumsfeld, who had parlayed with Saddam as an envoy of the Reagan administration. Dick Cheney, the vice president, had been defense secretary during the Gulf War and had spent the 1990s as chief executive of Halliburton, an oil-services corporation active in the Middle East. For deputy secretary of defense, Bush appointed Paul Wolfowitz, a visible neoconservative who wanted the U.S. to back a new version of Ahmad Chalabi's "rolling insurgency" plan to overthrow Saddam.

Bush inherited from Clinton the no-fly zone military operations over northern and southern Iraq, as well as a close ally in that endeavor, British prime minister Tony Blair. During the year before Bush arrived at the White House, American and British pilots had entered Iraqi airspace about ten thousand times. They had often been fired upon and had retaliated by firing hundreds of missiles and bombs at Iraqi targets. They had managed to avoid any losses of planes or pilots, but Bush feared that Saddam would get lucky and down a pilot. On February 5, 2001, during Bush's third week in the White House, Condoleezza Rice, the national security adviser, ran a "principals" meeting—a subcabinet group involved in national security—attended by Powell and Rumsfeld. She asked for a thorough review of the no-fly zones, including of how the administration might prepare in advance to rescue a downed aviator.[10]

On February 23, Bush hosted Tony Blair and his wife, Cherie, at Camp David, the wooded presidential retreat in Maryland's foothills. "I wasn't sure what to expect from Tony," Bush recalled. "I knew he was a left-of-center Labour Party prime minister and a close friend of Bill Clinton's. I quickly found he was candid, friendly, and engaging." The prime minister and his wife exuded no "stuffiness," an impression ratified by their willingness one evening to watch *Meet the Parents*, a middlebrow comedy starring Robert De Niro and Ben Stiller.[11]

When they got down to business, Bush told Blair that he wanted to develop "a realistic policy on Iraq." He said he was very concerned that "our Arab friends" thought that "our policy is just not working, but that the sanctions are hurting children."

Bush had invited Colin Powell to the retreat but not Cheney or Rumsfeld. He asked his chief diplomat to sum up. "For the past ten years, our policy has consisted of the sanctions regime, the no-fly zones, and efforts at regime change in Iraq," Powell began. Rather than denounce the Clinton administration's efforts, he praised them: "As a result, Iraq is no longer a danger to the region in the way it was ten years ago," Powell said.

"But there are problems," he continued. "Saddam is still there. And he is using his oil wealth not to benefit his people but to develop weapons of mass destruction." Powell then pitched his main recommendation to Bush: "smart sanctions," meaning a reformed policy to more precisely restrict trade relevant to WMD but one that would not hurt "children and people generally." He added, "We do not regard a military option as the best approach, [but] we reserve the right to act, even unilaterally."

"This seems like a sensible approach," Blair said. Presumably that was because it closely resembled the policies Blair and Clinton had been coordinating since 1998, with the modest wrinkle that Powell wanted to change how sanctions worked.

"We should also try to isolate Saddam, make him less of an actor on the world stage," Bush said. "If we could, the Middle East would be more moderate."[12]

For Saddam Hussein, the headline from the 2000 election was easy to identify: the Bushes were back. "We have to make it clear that a connection exists between the new American president and the interests of the entities—the oil companies," he told advisers. The oil-rich kingdoms neighboring Iraq "lean more toward Bush's family, especially the Saudis," he said.

"The Republican Party and the Bush family are closer to the oil companies," Tariq Aziz agreed.[13]

Yet Saddam saw no reason to change his policies. His spies at the Mukhabarat sent him a detailed analysis that spring of 2001. It suggested that Saddam faced no immediate threat from the new administration. The paper named Paul Wolfowitz as being "very interested" in action to overthrow Saddam but noted that Wolfowitz's ideas had served to highlight "the variance in opinions" within Bush's cabinet. Colin Powell, for example, doubted the Iraqi opposition's ability to unify.

A second analysis prepared at the training academy of the Iraqi spy service advised that the exiled opposition to Saddam had "lost its credibility" in America and Britain and had "troubles between their members." This study's authors took the risky step of listing changes the Baathist regime might consider to strengthen its own legitimacy, such as promoting "political diversity" and a "free press in Iraq."[14]

Saddam showed no interest in these recommendations. His day-to-day life as president had evolved into a familiar routine. In early February, he joined a cabinet meeting to review an eclectic agenda: the possible revival of a cultural agreement with Nigeria; the unknown health effects of depleted uranium used in bombs and shells fired on Iraq during the 1991 war; and changes to the membership of a commission working on air defense.

At one point, Sultan Hashim Ahmad al-Tai, now the minister of defense, mentioned Iraq's Military Language Institute, a place where, he explained, officers learned "languages that are needed by the Army: English, French, Russian, Persian, Turkish, and Hebrew."

Saddam jumped on the minister: "We do not need our army to expand in preparing people who are fluent in the Iranian or the Turkish language. . . . We do not need to teach the officer in the army the English language. . . . If they have extra time, let them . . . read the history of the Arabic Islamic wars." Allowing generals and colonels to learn foreign languages would only lead them to betray their country.

Another minister, failing to read the room, suggested they should graduate "big numbers" of Iraqis who could speak Hebrew.

The president was appalled. "We are hostile to the Jew—we do not want to understand what [they] say," he exclaimed. Iraqis who learned Hebrew would eventually want to "sit down to converse" with a Jewish counterpart, and their shared language would create "a special psychological bridge between them." This was highly undesirable. The only reason Iraq wanted to understand the Jewish people, Saddam advised his ministers, was to "keep [their] evil away" and to learn how to cause them greater harm.[15]

He continued to work on succession, carefully positioning Qusay as an heir who would meet the Baath Party's standards for leadership. On May 17, the day Qusay turned thirty-five, Saddam arranged his ascension to the Revolutionary Command Council. In a packed hall next to the Republican Palace, Barzan Ibrahim al-Tikriti watched the coronation. Qusay entered and walked "cheerfully and proudly, as if the gates of history opened wide for him," Barzan recalled. At a decisive moment, Tariq Aziz rose to say that it was time to give youth a chance. "There was applause and the President did not object," Barzan later wrote. "There is no one better than Tariq Aziz, the man who makes deals and enjoys doing it."[16]

That spring and summer of 2001, Saddam received the sorts of B-list foreign visitors he had long entertained. These included mid-level emissaries from Russia, a parliamentarian from Liberia, and Rodrigo Álvarez Cambras, a Havana-based Cuban physician who had once operated on Saddam (to address a spinal issue). A relaxed Saddam steered most conversations to the vexing problem of American power while displaying no particular sense of urgency.

Cambras had brought a box of cigars from Fidel Castro. "The White House is far away from us," Saddam told him. "What is the nearest city to you?"

"Miami—about one hundred and twenty miles."

"A lot of weapons might come to Miami," Saddam remarked. He mentioned the Scud missile attacks he had ordered against Israel during the 1991 war. "We attacked Tel Aviv because it is America's and Britain's daughter and whatever hurts Tel Aviv will hurt them, too."

"Remember, Your Excellency . . . that in 1962, we pointed nuclear rockets [at America], but the Russians took [them] away," Cambras mentioned.[17]

Emissaries from Moscow carried Saddam a letter from Russian president Vladimir Putin. He sought to rebuild ties with Iraq after Russia's tilt to the West during the Yeltsin years. "Tell President Putin that Baghdad is stable, and the situation is good," Saddam said. "America wants Russia to be weak . . . and what we want is for Russia to be strong. . . . Tell him that we will not surrender to America and that we will keep on fighting them."[18]

Between meetings, Saddam worked on his autobiographical third novel, *Men and a City*, a project of introspection and legacy-building.

In contrast to the progressive, even feminist tropes of *Zabiba*, the rural social setting in *Men and a City* is deeply conservative. "There is a strong element of nostalgia in an old Saddam looking back on his childhood," Hawraa Al-Hassan observes. He seemed conscious now that more of his life lay behind him than ahead.[19]

On July 27, 2001, Donald Rumsfeld sent a memo to Condoleezza Rice, Dick Cheney, and Colin Powell seeking a subcabinet meeting on Iraq. Saddam "appears to believe he is getting stronger," Rumsfeld wrote, and seems to be "riding higher than a year ago." He reviewed options for the no-fly zones, which came down to doing less or becoming more aggressive. But he also wanted to talk again about "the broader subject of Iraq." He laid out three possible courses.

First, the U.S. could "roll up its tents and end the no-fly zones before someone is killed or captured," he wrote. Then the administration could figure out a "way to keep an eye on Saddam Hussein's aggressiveness against his neighbors from a distance." Rumsfeld argued indirectly against this option, asserting that "within a few years" the U.S. would "undoubtedly have to confront a Saddam armed with nuclear weapons."

Another option was to approach "our moderate Arab friends" and see if they might be "willing to engage in a more robust policy." He noted that "the risks of a serious regime-change policy" had to be weighed against the danger of an "increasingly bold and nuclear-armed Saddam in the near future."

Finally, Rumsfeld laid out a third possibility, one that obviously intrigued him: they could talk to Saddam. "He has his own interests," Rumsfeld observed. "It may be that, for whatever reason, at his stage in life, he might prefer to not have the hostility of the United States and the West and might be willing to make some accommodation."

He admitted that such an initiative "would be an astonishing departure" for the U.S., "although I did it for President Reagan [in] the mid-1980s. It would win praise from certain quarters, but might cause friends, especially those in the region, to question our strength, steadiness and judgment." Still, Rumsfeld went on, "there ought to be a way" for the U.S. to avoid simultaneous conflict with Iraq and Iran "when the two of them do not like each other."

Rumsfeld's instinct that Saddam might have reached a "stage in life" when dialogue could be useful was sound. The Iraqi president had not softened about America, but he was clearly interested in talking, and the outlines of a deal—restoration of weapons monitoring, some version of smart sanctions, the resumption of business ties—was not impossible to imagine. "It is possible that Saddam's options will increase with time, while ours could decrease," Rumsfeld wrote.[20]

But the White House was not geared up to make hard decisions about Iraq policy that summer. Four days later, Rumsfeld allowed his deputy, Paul Wolfowitz, to present "A Liberation Strategy" to the White House. Wolfowitz argued for a U.S. military–backed safe haven in southern Iraq where Ahmad Chalabi could organize an insurgency against Saddam. Rumsfeld's management style—allowing a subordinate to advocate for a proposal that could draw the Pentagon into a war while keeping his own distance and privately offering options for diplomacy—did nothing to clarify where the Bush administration was heading. By the end of August 2001, Rumsfeld conceded later, "U.S. policy remained essentially what it had been at the end of the Clinton administration—adrift."[21]

At the C.I.A., the Iraq Operations Group, a.k.a. "the No Operations Group," remained what it had been since the late 1990s, too—a shell of a unit on the sixth floor of the Original Headquarters Building where some officers went to retire on the job. By the late summer of 2001, the I.O.G. comprised just eighteen people, including administrative assistants, name tracers, and report-writing officers. There was but a single fully trained case officer. The C.I.A. had two reporting sources remaining inside Iraq. One could only communicate by mailing letters to an accommodation address in the Arab world, meaning that his information was often two or three months out of date by the time the

C.I.A. absorbed it. Cable traffic through the I.O.G. totaled several hundred cables daily, but the great majority came from the eavesdropping National Security Agency, which swept up and distributed all sorts of raw intercepts that were hard to make much use of without being inside Iraq. There were perhaps twenty cables of varying significance to review each day—by C.I.A. standards, a modest flow. The small agency teams that had earlier rotated into Kurdistan had been shut down after the disasters of 1996. Thereafter, the group's mission, as one of its leaders explained to a job applicant, became to "make sure the words 'C.I.A.,' 'Iraq,' and 'fiasco' don't appear on the front page of *The New York Times*."[22]

That summer, Charles Duelfer, former deputy head of U.N. weapons inspections, attended a closed-door C.I.A. conference about Iraq. During the 1990s, Duelfer had probably spent more time in Baghdad than any other American with official duties. He had never met Saddam, but he had spent countless hours with Tariq Aziz and Iraqi scientists. At the conference, the discussion turned to the subject of Jafar Dhia Jafar. The C.I.A. apparently didn't know where he was working anymore. The talk turned to "lots of very technical ideas" to track Jafar down, including "sensors on satellites, communications-intercept techniques, new widgets on the ground."

Duelfer intervened: "Why not just call him up? His former wife is probably in the U.K., and you could ask for her number." He mentioned Jafar's wealthy brother, Hamid, who ran a trading firm with offices in the United Arab Emirates. "Ask him," Duelfer suggested. "It would be easy to contact him." The discussion left Duelfer reflecting on the apparent "absence of information" at the C.I.A. "about the internal political and social situation in Iraq." How could the United States be so far out of touch?[23]

That summer, the position of Iraq Operations Group chief became vacant, and although he was well aware of the unit's "less than stellar reputation," Luis Rueda decided he was interested. He was serving on the seventh floor as executive assistant to the C.I.A.'s deputy director, John McLaughlin—a position usually given to officers with leadership potential. By informal tradition, executive assistants who finished their rotations could pick their next jobs, within reason. While staffing McLaughlin, Rueda had noted the frequency of meetings about Iraq convened at the White House. The operations group also intrigued because it was a covert-action shop, however moribund. Within the C.I.A., covert action—under which propaganda and paramilitary operations fell—was a distinct specialty. Most case officers spent their careers recruiting and running foreign spies to collect intelligence. But Rueda, who had joined the C.I.A. in 1981, had spent much of his career in the Latin America Division, where covert action had been more commonplace. During the 1990s, Rueda had worked on large-scale covert actions against drug cartels in South America and Mexico, programs that involved multimillion-dollar budgets and "lethal authorities," meaning instructions from the White House that permitted the C.I.A. to equip agents and allies to attack and use lethal force against certain targets.

"I'm an American because of a failed covert action," Rueda explained to colleagues. His father had been a member of the anti-Castro Cuban underground at the time of the Bay of Pigs operation—a "fascist of the first order," as Rueda jokingly called him. At age four, Rueda landed at a refugee camp in Miami. He grew up on Staten Island, endured a strict Catholic education, and joined the C.I.A. as a case officer in 1981. Two decades later, he had grown into a balding man with a gray goatee. He was humorous and "overly opinionated," as he would describe himself, although far more liberal than his father.[24]

He got the position. On August 4, 2001, he moved into a sixth-floor office with windows looking out on other windows. He was senior enough to qualify for a wooden desk, as opposed to the metal ones meted out to junior officers. There was a map of Iraq on one wall. As he read into the files, Rueda learned the situation was at least as bad as he had expected. "We had, for all intents and purposes, lost the Kurds as allies," he recalled, because of the resentments left over from the 1990s. "The only thing that was functioning was Ayad Allawi and his group," the Iraqi National Accord, which received a "pittance."

The C.I.A. no longer enjoyed significant support on Iraq from friendly Arab regimes in the region—Saudi Arabia, Kuwait, Jordan. Generally, they "thought that Saddam was our guy," meaning that the C.I.A. had deliberately left the Iraqi leader in power as a counter to Iran and was perhaps cooperating with him secretly. "They said, 'You didn't kill him, you didn't overthrow him—ergo, he's your man. You slapped him for Kuwait, but he's your man against Iran.'" Like Saddam, Arab leaders had difficulty crediting the possibility of American incompetence.[25]

Rueda called John Maguire, who had worked in Amman during the "Mr. Max" years. He was teaching at "the Farm," the C.I.A.'s Virginia training facility for case officers. Rueda and Maguire had known each other from tours in Central America and had become friends. Maguire had an "obsession" with Iraq operations because of his bitter experiences during the 1990s and the losses endured by Iraqi allies, such as Mohammed Abdullah Shawani, the former Iraqi general whose sons had been executed by Saddam's regime. Maguire knew the files and the personalities. Rueda asked him to serve as his deputy.

"Can you overthrow Saddam?" John McLaughlin, a career analyst known for boiling complicated questions down to their essence, asked Rueda.

"No," he said. "Saddam has killed anybody who is a threat to him, so there's nobody inside that we can tap into. The outside opposition— I mean, nobody knows who they are, they're discredited." The C.I.A. might offer to pay somebody $5 million to overthrow Saddam, but if the operation failed, Saddam would take the coupmaker "and drill through his kneecaps, burn him in acid, slaughter his family, wipe out his village, and throw salt onto the ground so nothing grows. I can't compete with that," Rueda said.[26]

It followed, then, that the U.S. would have to learn how to contain Saddam, perhaps in part by talking to him again and offering financial or other inducements, as Donald Rumsfeld had suggested. Or the U.S. could continue to isolate Baghdad through coercive sanctions and monitoring, as Clinton had done. The alternative—apart from giving up altogether—would be to order the U.S. military to invade Iraq and depose Saddam, an operation that would require at least tens of thousands of troops. It would also entail incalculable geopolitical risks, huge expense, and possibly heavy casualties.

In August 2001, inside the Iraq Operations Group—and in prosperous, peaceful America at large—it was hard to imagine how such an invasion would come about.

PART THREE

BLIND MAN'S BLUFF

September 2001 to March 2003

TWENTY-THREE

The Pundit

On the morning of September 11, Mohammed Aldouri arrived early to the sandstone townhouse on East Seventy-Ninth Street that housed Iraq's Permanent Mission to the United Nations in New York. He had moved to Manhattan earlier that year to succeed Nizar Hamdoon as the highest-ranking Iraqi official posted in America. Aldouri was not a member of the Baath Party and had never met Saddam Hussein. He had earned a doctoral degree at the University of Dijon in France and later joined the law faculty at the University of Baghdad. He was a protégé of Naji Sabri, a former English professor whom Saddam had recently appointed as foreign minister.

Shortly before 9:00 a.m., an Iraqi colleague flipped on the office television to follow a shocking news event. A passenger jet, American Airlines Flight 11, had smashed into the North Tower of the World Trade Center, less than six miles to the south of the Iraqi mission. Aldouri gathered with several employees. Black smoke rose above the city as news anchors speculated about the cause. At 9:03 a.m., United Airlines Flight 175 struck the South Tower and erupted into flames.

"That's not an accident—that is war," Aldouri said. "We are probably going to be blamed."[1]

As the crisis unfolded that day, Aldouri had to manage the symbolism of the Iraqi flag, which billowed above the mission. American rescue workers extinguished fires and dug through wreckage to recover remains at three attack sites—the World Trade Center, the Pentagon, and a field in Pennsylvania where United Airlines Flight 93 had crashed after its passengers revolted against their hijackers. That afternoon, President Bush ordered American flags to be flown at half-staff at federal facilities "as a mark of respect for those killed by the heinous acts of violence perpetrated by faceless cowards." Foreign embassies across Washington and at U.N. missions in New York voluntarily lowered their own flags.[2]

Aldouri hesitated. Spies from Iraq's intelligence services monitored him and reported home about his every move. One of the ambassador's colleagues telephoned Saudi Arabia's U.N. mission to ask what they did with their flag in such circumstances. (Fifteen of the nineteen hijackers responsible for the September 11 attacks came from Saudi Arabia, a U.S. ally. The others were from the United Arab Emirates, Egypt, and Lebanon—also all U.S. allies. No Iraqis were involved.) The Saudi flag—like the Iraqi flag after a 1991 redesign by Saddam Hussein—contained the name of Allah in Arabic script. The Saudis believed it was therefore unacceptable to lower the banner to half-staff. When America was officially in mourning, a diplomat explained, "we just take the flag down and put it in storage, leaving only an empty pole." But when Aldouri contacted the Ministry of Foreign Affairs in Baghdad, he was told, as his colleague later summarized the message, "If that flag goes down, you will go down with it."[3]

The flag waved on. That day, loose bands of protesters gathered on East Seventy-Ninth Street, shouting and denouncing Iraq. By evening, the Bush administration had confirmed that al-Qaeda—the stateless terrorist organization headquartered in Taliban-ruled Afghanistan—had carried out the attacks. Yet the Seventy-Ninth Street protesters seemed to believe that Iraq should be held accountable. They turned up for another day or two, then faded away.

Saddam Hussein's diplomats also had to consider the public ritual of expressing condolences. After any large-scale loss of innocent life, diplomats around the world routinely express condolences on behalf of their governments. On September 11, Saudi Arabia denounced the "regrettable and inhuman bombings and attacks," and the kingdom's council of religious scholars called them "a form of injustice that is not tolerated by Islam." Many other governments of Muslim-majority nations spoke out in kind.[4]

In Baghdad, Saddam's cabinet discussed the matter and recommended a statement "condemning the terrorists and offering condolences to the people of the United States, despite American hostility toward Iraq," according to Abd al-Tawab Mullah Huwaysh, then the deputy prime minister. But Saddam rejected this advice. He later explained to a visitor that if he expressed condolences to President Bush, "it will mean that I do not respect my people, because Bush is the president of the nation declaring war on us and attacking us in a despicable terrorist manner." He did authorize Tariq Aziz to write "personal letters denouncing the attack" to a few American individuals.[5]

Al-Qaeda's strike—the first large-scale surprise attack on American soil since Pearl Harbor—touched off the greatest domestic emergency since at least the 1960s and shaped what would become the most consequential pivot in American foreign policy since the early Cold War. Saddam grasped the event's shock waves and even its transformational impact on the U.S. He watched satellite news and followed the international press. He and his aides thought that al-Qaeda's terrorism might draw the United States closer to Iraq, in common cause against religious radicalism. Yet Saddam had no apparent sense of his vulnerability to false accusations about his own responsibility for the attacks. He took no steps to assuage the Bush administration or American public opinion or to create any record of public statements that might get him off the hook—as he had done quickly and even obsequiously in 1987 after an Iraqi jet struck the U.S.S. *Stark*.

Saddam had never met Osama bin Laden and considered him "no different than the many zealots that came before him." Iraq had nothing to do with the September 11 plot, as the C.I.A. quickly concluded after the attacks, and as subsequent investigations have made indisputable. But Saddam did not explicitly distance himself from al-Qaeda or bin Laden. He initially seemed uncertain about whether to believe America's claim that bin Laden was responsible. More importantly, the September 11 attacks realized a scenario that Saddam had talked about with visitors for years—suicide bombers on American soil, and payback for the humiliation of Iraqis and Palestinians. Saddam identified with the attackers—their strike was like his own bold decision to launch Scud missiles against Israeli cities in 1991.[6]

As America's most persistent enemy, he felt entitled to lecture about what September 11 meant. He became a kind of pundit that autumn, speaking at length to diverse audiences, speculating and arguing like one of those talking heads on satellite-beamed Arabic-language TV channels. He saw the attacks in light of his lifelong critiques of Israel and American "imperialism." He adopted the podium voice familiar to his comrades—rambling and undisciplined, at times shrewd and amusing, at other times ignorant and unhinged, and periodically laced with antisemitism and mind-twisting conspiracy theories. That autumn, not for the first or last time, he would have benefited from a cabinet of advisers who were not afraid to contradict him, or who were at least willing to provide gentle coaching—in this case, to suggest that the president might want to cool his rhetoric while America mourned its dead. Instead, Saddam made a display of his satisfaction over America's suffering and grief.

"The American people should remember that, throughout history, no one crossed the Atlantic to come to them, carrying weapons against them," Saddam said on state television on September 12. "The United States reaps the thorns that its leaders have planted in the world . . . [and] has become a burden on all of us."

"America needs someone to tell her about her mistakes," he told a delegation from Tunisia two days later. "America brought to itself the hatred of the world. . . . The person who does not respect the bloodshed of people makes it difficult for the people to respect his bloodshed."[7]

On September 15, he composed an "open letter from Saddam Hussein to the American people, the people in the West, and their governments," a document of more than 1,500 words. He called the finding that al-Qaeda was responsible a "premise" that was "uncorroborated," but one that he tentatively credited nonetheless. He blamed American and Western policies for "the lack of stability in the world" and asked, "Isn't the evil inflicted on America as a result of the event of September 11, 2001, . . . the result of this?" He urged the U.S. to "avoid an emotional reaction and not pursue the same old methods that America used against the world." He continued:

> If America would only disengage itself from its evil alliance with Zionism, which has been scheming to exploit the world and plunge it in blood and darkness, by using America and some Western countries. What the American people need now is someone who mostly tells the truth bravely . . . so they can experience a real awakening. . . . We say to the American people that what happened on September 11, 2001, should be compared to what their government and their armies are doing in the world.

American missile and aerial attacks on Iraq since 1991 had been launched "from a distance . . . as if they are playing an amusing game," whereas the suicidal hijackers on September 11 "willingly gave their lives." Americans should seek to understand why.[8]

Saddam's comments did not receive much media coverage in the United States. Yet some of these biting words—including his remarks on September 12—were captured by U.S. monitoring and intelligence services and distributed to Bush's cabinet. (Many other of Saddam's remarks apparently went unheard in Washington.) As the Bush administration and its allies in Congress built a case against Baghdad alongside think tanks and the media, they turned Saddam's sound bites against him.

On the day Saddam completed his letter to America, George W. Bush convened his national security cabinet at Camp David.

George Tenet, director of the C.I.A., and General Hugh Shelton, chairman of the Joint Chiefs, laid out plans to attack al-Qaeda and the Taliban in Afghanistan. Nobody at the meeting doubted that al-Qaeda had carried out the hijackings, but Deputy Defense Secretary Paul Wolfowitz insisted, without providing evidence, that there was at least a 10 percent chance, and perhaps a 50 percent chance, that Saddam Hussein had also been involved. The plans proposed by the C.I.A. and the Pentagon to strike al-Qaeda were too narrow: "We really need to think broader," Wolfowitz said. "We've got to make sure we go ahead and get Saddam out at the same time—it's a perfect opportunity."

Bush eventually blew up, according to Shelton. "How many times do I have to tell you we are not going after Iraq right this minute?" the president asked Wolfowitz.

The following day, Vice President Dick Cheney told a television interviewer that the administration was not targeting Saddam: "At this stage, the focus over here is on al-Qaeda. . . . Saddam Hussein's bottled up at this point." He added that there was no evidence linking Iraq to the attacks on New York and Washington.[9]

Yet Bush privately made clear to close allies and his cabinet that he thought Wolfowitz was likely right, just premature. "I believe Iraq was involved," he said at a White House meeting on September 17. "But I'm not going to strike them now. I don't have the evidence at this point." Around the same time, he told Tony Blair, "When we have dealt with Afghanistan, we must come back to Iraq."[10]

On September 26, Bush asked Secretary of Defense Donald Rumsfeld to speak with him alone in the Oval Office. The president "leaned back in the black leather chair behind his desk," as Rumsfeld recalled, and "asked that I take a look at the shape of our military plans on Iraq." Bush wanted something "creative," and he wanted the review kept quiet.

Rumsfeld did not think that Bush had made up his mind to go after

Saddam, but the significance of the request was not lost on him. The secretary of defense was still ambivalent about what to do about Iraq. Even after September 11, he thought that "an aggressive diplomatic effort, coupled by a threat of military force" might persuade Saddam to give up power voluntarily. Rumsfeld wrote a note to himself: "At the right moment, we may want to give Saddam Hussein a way out for his family to live in comfort."[11]

For years, Bush had reflected on his father's presidency. The failure to remove Saddam after the liberation of Kuwait was certainly seen in some Republican Party circles as a blemish on George H. W. Bush's legacy. The realm of Bush father-son psychology is long on easy speculation and short on reliable evidence. Clearly, however, September 11 now offered the son an opportunity to make his own mark.

Bush and many others in his war cabinet—including Cheney and the C.I.A.'s George Tenet—assumed reasonably that al-Qaeda must be planning follow-on attacks. When evidence surfaced that autumn that bin Laden had met with Pakistani nuclear scientists in Afghanistan, they even worried that al-Qaeda might have the capacity to pull off an atomic strike. "I could only imagine the destruction possible if an enemy dictator passed his WMD to terrorists," Bush wrote later.[12]

He assumed that Saddam secretly possessed such dangerous weapons. His logic might also apply to the regimes in North Korea, Libya, Pakistan, and Iran, depending on one's definition of "enemy dictator." But only Iraq was already fighting a low-grade, decade-old war with the United States. Almost viscerally, George W. Bush and Saddam Hussein each seemed to embrace the September 11 attacks as an episode in their ongoing conflict.

During the autumn of 2001, Saddam met with his cabinet as often as twice a week to review such matters as adjustments in pay for college professors, partnerships between business and government, and a self-sufficiency drive in the pharmaceutical industry. He visited military and industrial sites and gave speeches. He received his usual array of visitors from the margins of global politics, such as Vojislav Šešelj, leader of the ultranationalist Serbian Radical Party, and Akhmad Kadyrov, a Chechen politician. He often spoke in these private settings about September 11. Yet he never mentioned Osama bin Laden or al-Qaeda. He spoke approvingly of Palestinian suicide bombing at times, but he never spoke about jihadist terrorism outside the Israeli-Palestinian conflict.

As an advanced student of conspiracies, Saddam was susceptible to emerging internet and Arab media discourse that 9/11 was an inside job, perhaps organized by the C.I.A. or Israel to justify a new American war against the Muslim world. He had considered such scenarios before. In 1993, a loose network of Afghan War veterans inspired by a radical Egyptian cleric detonated a car bomb in a parking garage of the World Trade Center, killing six Americans. Saddam speculated with colleagues at the time about whether the attack had been orchestrated by the C.I.A. Yet even he had doubts about whether the C.I.A. could be *that* cynical and ruthless: "They had losses," he noted, meaning the United States. "So how [could] American intelligence do such a thing even though they knew there would be American human losses?"[13]

Saddam remained an uncompromising rejectionist, committed to Israel's military defeat and destruction. His backing of Palestinian resistance, including its suicide bombers, was often aligned with mainstream Arab opinion, yet he remained fixated on racist caricatures of Jews, and in his private remarks and novels, his grotesque antisemitism was often inseparable from his calls to arms against Israel. At the same time, his critique of America's post-9/11 foreign policy aligned with some mainstream democratic-left opinion in Europe, and similar opinions could be heard that autumn in university coffeehouses across the U.S. as well. His was a common perspective across Arab societies. "No one supports terrorism," he assured Kadyrov, his Chechen visitor. Yet, "there were no Islamic or Arab people that were not happy when they saw the attack, before they knew where it came from," because the killings "let America see fire like the kind it is causing in Palestine and Iraq."

He added, "We consider jihad against the Jews to drive them out of

Palestine is not terrorism, so any other killing or fighting against foreign occupiers is acceptable, as long as they are fighting to free themselves from the occupiers." The Americans were the true terrorists, and
the embargo against Iraq was a form of terrorism, he concluded.

Saddam had been making pronouncements along these lines in
public and private for several decades. He did not think to moderate his
critique just because America was wounded, enraged, and mobilizing
for military retaliation.[14]

On October 7, in a nationally televised address, George W. Bush announced America's war against al-Qaeda and the Taliban. He issued a warning: "Today, we focus on Afghanistan, but the battle is
broader. Every nation has a choice to make. . . . There is no neutral
ground."[15]

The president's speechwriters clearly had Saddam in mind, but the
Iraqi president gave no indication that he understood. Dozens of NATO
and other American allies joined or supported the initial war in Afghanistan, including Muslim-majority nations such as Turkey and Pakistan. For his part, Saddam denounced America's intentions and predicted
failure. "If America established a new government in Kabul according
to its desires, do you think this will end the Afghan people's problems?" Saddam asked at a cabinet meeting. "No. This will add more
causes for so-called terrorism, instead of eliminating it."

The charge that he had not done the honorable thing by offering
public condolences immediately after September 11 clearly grated on
him, but he remained defensive. "I do not believe that your administration deserves to receive condolences from Iraq," he said, addressing
Bush, "unless you first make condolences to the Iraqi people [for] the
1.5 million Iraqis you killed, and apologize to them. . . . Any person
who does not want to see his crops burn should not throw fire on other
people's crops."[16]

"It was not our wish that [America] would become the enemy of
the people," he told Šešelj, his Serbian visitor. "America used to behave

somewhat normally some fifteen years ago," he said, referring to his days of cooperation with the C.I.A. "But now look."[17]

The United States was both reckless and weak: "Americans are living in a pessimistic state, not an optimistic state," he opined at a cabinet meeting. "How can the American citizen live optimistically when he is living in a world that hates him? He can't travel the world [and] they have closed their embassies several times, fearing for the lives of their citizens."[18]

Samir Vincent, the Iraqi-born American who had worked on the Oil-for-Food negotiations, hoped to revive diplomacy between Washington and Baghdad. During 2001, Vincent was in touch with Frank Carlucci, the former Reagan administration secretary of defense now at a private equity firm. He had also gotten to know Jack Kemp, a former Republican congressman who had been Bob Dole's vice presidential running mate in the 1996 campaign.

On September 23, in Baghdad, Vincent met Tariq Aziz and high-ranking Iraqi intelligence officials. He urged his hosts to explore a dialogue with the Bush administration. Aziz encouraged him. Vincent soon asked Carlucci to test "whether a dialogue was possible."

Carlucci spoke with William Burns, the undersecretary of state responsible for the Middle East. Burns relayed a message for Tariq Aziz that Iraq "should stop firing at our planes" in the no-fly zones and "join the battle against terrorism." Burns added that unless Saddam changed his policies, the U.S. would have "no interest in a dialogue."

Aziz sent back an unsigned memo outlining Iraq's "official position." The paper reached Burns on September 27. Aziz wrote that Iraq's position was defensive in nature, and he expressed his "hope" that America would end the no-fly patrols "due to its involvement in other tasks" after 9/11. Such a gesture could "open the door to new opportunities between Iraq and the United States."[19]

The exchange languished, but at Vincent's urging, Kemp picked up the effort. On October 23, he visited Colin Powell at the State

Department. He relayed a suggestion from Vincent that if U.S. war-planes patrolling the no-fly zones refrained from firing on Iraqi targets, this "could be a positive signal" to Saddam.

Powell said that if a dialogue with Iraq could be established, it might help him counter "hawks" and "pundits" who were pushing to attack Iraq, according to contemporaneous notes of what Kemp told Vincent. Yet Powell was nervous. He asked Kemp to tell Vincent "not to speak via the phone to 'friends' over there [in Iraq] and specifically not to mention the Kemp-Powell connection." The implication was that if U.S. or other eavesdroppers picked up such chatter, it might backfire on the secretary of state.[20]

On October 30, Kemp met Powell at the State Department a second time. Powell said that If Iraq "agrees to invite U.N. inspectors back into the country for a limited time and scope, there will be an immediate and positive response from the U.S." If Tariq Aziz indicated that Iraq was ready to do this, he could meet in New York with John Negroponte, the Bush administration's ambassador to the U.N.

Vincent flew again to Baghdad, carrying Powell's messages. He met Tahir Jalil Habbush, Saddam's latest head of intelligence. "It became obvious" to Vincent on this visit that Habbush and Iraqi intelligence had taken charge of Iraq's policy toward Washington.

On November 5, Habbush handed Vincent a letter in Arabic. It was signed by four members of the Revolutionary Command Council—not including Tariq Aziz—and reportedly reflected a discussion with Saddam Hussein. It made unrealistic demands: The U.S. should lift economic sanctions and end the no-fly zones. If this happened, Iraq would be "prepared to deal with all U.S. concerns in a constructive manner." The document was silent on Powell's suggestion that Saddam invite back U.N. weapons inspectors.

Habbush nonetheless told Vincent that Iraq was "very serious about starting a dialogue with the U.S. . . . with no conditions, to resolve all outstanding problems between the two countries." He admitted that Iraq had "misunderstood and misjudged the U.S. in the past." He blamed cultural differences and asked Vincent if he could help the regime understand "the nature and habits of Americans." Speaking of American political leaders, he complained: "The way they talk, we cannot read any subtle messages that might be there. . . . They often come across as blunt and arrogant."[21]

Vincent returned to Washington, where he again hit a wall. If Iraq would not allow the return of inspectors, there was no hope for diplomacy.

On Monday, October 29, Charles Duelfer, who had been the deputy chief of U.N. inspections during much of the 1990s and was now an unpaid consultant at the C.I.A., visited Ahmad Chalabi at an address in Knightsbridge, London. The Iraqi National Congress occupied offices filled with "scruffy" furniture, "a bit like used IKEA," Duelfer recalled. Staffers bathed the rooms in cigarette smoke.

Chalabi had moved decisively after September 11 to fill the void in hard intelligence about Iraq available to the Bush administration. In London that day, he turned to Arras Karim Habib, who trafficked in information from Iraqi defectors. In 1997, during Duelfer's U.N. days, Habib had provided him with an implausible report that Iraq "retained three nuclear weapons," Duelfer recalled. He now claimed that in 1999, Saddam had shipped two tons of precursor chemicals for the nerve agent VX to Osama bin Laden. The idea that Saddam would provide VX precursors to a Saudi radical living in Afghanistan—a fanatic who no doubt regarded Saddam as an apostate—was absurd, Duelfer thought.[22]

Yet this was the sort of "intelligence" that Chalabi brokered to any American official, researcher, or journalist who would listen during the fall of 2001. Chalabi had run C.I.A.-funded propaganda operations against Baghdad. He now turned those techniques on the Bush administration and Congress "by providing false information through defectors," as the Senate Select Committee on Intelligence later concluded. Some of it was deliberately fabricated, as in the case of a supposed colonel who claimed to have trained hijackers on a derelict Boeing 707 plane parked at an Iraqi facility called Salman Pak. (The plane was well known to U.N. inspectors; Iraq said it was used for training commandos to stop hijackings.) The defector's story broke in an October column in *The Washington Post*. It was then retold in *The New York Times*, *The Wall Street Journal*, *Vanity Fair*, and other outlets.

The I.N.C. next produced an Iraqi civil engineer who had documents purporting to describe underground hiding places in Iraq for chemical and biological weapons. He talked to a reporter for *The New York Times*, and the paper published a lengthy story. In December, the I.N.C. successfully promoted the testimony of a third defector named Muhammad Harith. He claimed to know of contacts between Iraq and al-Qaeda and of mobile biological-weapons labs—inventing and planting a tale that would later become a staple of Bush administration indictments of Iraq. Harith told his lies to a prime-time national audience on *60 Minutes*. Two of the I.N.C. defectors who deceived major news organizations—Harith and Adnan Ihsan Saeed al-Haideri—reportedly passed polygraph tests. Credible-seeming Chalabi allies in Washington, such as James Woolsey, President Clinton's first C.I.A. director, also vouched for them.

When it circulated intelligence reports about Iraq in 2001 and 2002, the C.I.A. largely ignored Chalabi's sources because the agency had written off the I.N.C. leader. (The agency endorsed what proved to be false information about Iraq's weapons programs derived from other sources.) Chalabi's false defector stories nonetheless made their way into White House press releases, presidential speeches, and a National Intelligence Estimate.[23]

Chalabi was later candid about his success: "We didn't go to the Bush administration," he recalled. "They came to us." As early as October, John Hannah, an aide to Vice President Dick Cheney, met Chalabi at a Starbucks near the White House. "The administration is looking for people who know about Iraq's weapons of mass destruction," Hannah said. "Can you introduce us to any?"[24]

Hannah's reported solicitation reflected a larger pattern visible by late 2001, according to Paul Pillar, a political scientist and career C.I.A. analyst who was then the national intelligence officer for the Middle

East. The Bush administration used intelligence reports about Iraqi WMD as exhibits in a drive to influence public and congressional opinion. The reliability of any one report mattered less than the overall impact of the publicity campaign. Intelligence "figured prominently in the selling" of the war but played "almost no role" in the eventual decision to invade Iraq, as Pillar put it, because, essentially, that decision was already made, if not by late 2001, then certainly by mid-2002.[25]

In Baghdad, Saddam paid no attention to Chalabi's propaganda. Throughout the 1990s, Saddam had faced accusations that he knew to be lies. He had no WMD, yet America, Britain, and others insisted that he was hiding weapons. Therefore, Saddam could fairly reason, American officials surely *knew* they were making false accusations but did so cynically so as to pursue his overthrow.

Complacent and defiant, Saddam continued to back uprisings and terrorist bombings by Palestinians against Israel, as he had before 9/11. That winter, Wafa Idris, a twenty-six-year-old Palestinian woman wearing a suicide vest, detonated herself in Jerusalem, killing an elderly man and wounding about one hundred others. She was the first known female suicide bomber in the Israeli-Palestinian conflict. Saddam ordered a monument erected in her honor. He soon pledged $25,000 to "the family of any person who performs a suicide mission in Palestine."[26]

Saddam Hussein meant what he so often said: he considered Iraq to be at war with Israel and America; he was not afraid to fight by unconventional means; and he rejected America's definitions of terrorism.

The Taliban regime in Afghanistan collapsed in late November, defeated by American-led bombing and Afghan opposition forces armed and funded by the C.I.A. In early December, Osama bin Laden escaped and disappeared, presumably into Pakistan.

Late in the Afghanistan War, George W. Bush again asked Donald Rumsfeld about plans to invade Iraq. As Michael Morell, the C.I.A. officer who met with Bush every morning to present classified intelligence briefings, later wrote: "The president's thinking on Iraq was motivated by the soul-crushing impact of 9/11 and the legitimate fear that as bad as 9/11 had been, things could be much worse—if Saddam got it into his head to either use his weapons of mass destruction as a terrorist tool against the West, or provide those weapons to an international terrorist group." These dire scenarios were "unlikely," U.S. intelligence analysts believed, yet Bush concluded that they were "risks he could not ignore."[27]

As the Taliban crumbled, Tony Blair's advisers worried about "a real danger that we will part company with the Americans on what comes next," as Jonathan Powell, Blair's chief of staff, wrote to the prime minister. The "real test," cabled Christopher Meyer, the British ambassador in Washington, will be "whether we can . . . stop the Americans doing something self-defeating in Iraq or elsewhere."

Blair spoke with Bush by phone on December 3. The prime minister said that he was open to regime change in Iraq but that this would require "an extremely clever plan." Blair sent the president a paper the next day. "My strategy is to build this over time until we get to the point where military action could be taken if necessary," he wrote. Meanwhile, they should "bring people towards us, undermine Saddam, without so alarming people about the immediacy of action that we frighten the horses, lose Russia and/or half the E.U. and nervous Arab states." The note could be read as recommending secret planning for a war while options were explored and political conditions set. That was the course Bush had already chosen.[28]

A few days after Christmas, at his ranch in Crawford, Texas, the president listened as General Tommy Franks, the commander of U.S. forces in the Middle East, presented the latest secret invasion plan. Franks identified "centers of gravity" in Saddam's regime. These included Saddam and his two sons; the Iraqi leader's intelligence services and bodyguards; and the Iraqi population. The general recommended a stepped-up propaganda campaign: "You've got to create in the minds of the people an overwhelming urge to get rid of Saddam," he said, as if this urge had not already been amply demonstrated in 1991.

Appearing by video, George Tenet, the C.I.A. director, interjected to say that American betrayals had left Iraqis skeptical. "You can build all these thoughts," Tenet continued, "but it's not going to bear fruit unless they see a tangible commitment." By that, he meant American arms supplies, training, or a U.S. military deployment in support of rebellious Iraqi military leaders, Kurdish militia, and Shiite activists in southern Iraq.

"Saddam's a threat," Bush concluded after the discussion. An invasion "is an option."[29]

On January 29, 2002, Bush delivered his first State of the Union address. He celebrated the Taliban's defeat in Afghanistan. He laid out plans to attack al-Qaeda, but also Hamas, Hezbollah, and other designated terrorist groups. Then he turned to the doctrine he had been nurturing for months—preemptive military action against countries that possessed nuclear, chemical, or biological arms and might provide them to terrorists:

> Some of these regimes have been pretty quiet since September the eleventh. But we know their true nature. North Korea is a regime arming with missiles and weapons of mass destruction while starving its citizens. Iran aggressively pursues these weapons and exports terror while an unelected few repress the Iranian people's hope for freedom. Iraq continues to flaunt its hostility toward America and to support terror. . . . This is a regime that has already used poison gas to murder thousands of its own citizens—leaving the bodies of mothers huddled over their dead children. This is a regime that agreed to international inspections—then kicked out the inspectors. This is a regime that has something to hide from the civilized world.

Bush then offered a turn of rhetoric that would become immortal: "States like these, and their terrorist allies, constitute an axis of evil, arming to threaten the peace of the world."[30]

Applause washed through the chamber. A week later, a published poll

revealed that three-quarters of Americans thought Saddam had aided al-
Qaeda. Roughly the same number supported attacking Baghdad.[31]

Bush finally got Saddam's attention. The Iraqi leader discussed the
speech at a Revolutionary Command Council meeting. Tariq Aziz
returned to the idea floated by Colin Powell during the stillborn exchanges of the previous autumn: Iraq should readmit the U.N. weapons inspectors to flummox the Bush administration and to give Russia
and France something to work with as they tried to help Iraq in the
U.N. Security Council. Saddam was rattled enough to allow Aziz to
explore this possibility—but only if Iraq could get sanctions relief in
return. That was implausible and meant that Aziz would again get nowhere.[32]

On February 11, at a cabinet meeting, Saddam opined about Bush's
"axis of evil" formulation. It expressed "the American administration's
viewpoint, which sees all Muslims who don't submit to it as axes of
evil," he said. Bush had only included North Korea in his trio of rogue
regimes to distract from his anti-Muslim bias.

The Iraqi president also analyzed Bush's decision to threaten Iran.
The catastrophic war of the 1980s had yielded an uneasy armistice that
had by now lasted more than a decade. "We are opposed to aggression
against Iran," Saddam explained. Iran was a neighbor, and whatever
"aggression or harm comes upon it—it will eventually come upon us."[33]

Saddam had come full circle since the Reagan years: he believed he
would be better off making common cause with Iran against America
than with America against Iran.

If a certain complacency and literary self-indulgence had crept into
Saddam's outlook by early 2002, it did not extend to his engagement
with the problem of his regime's weak position in Kurdistan. He understood that he remained vulnerable: "The north is the pivoting center for all foreign and regional forces" that seek to "influence Iraq and

harm this country," he told colleagues after the September 11 attacks. "That's for sure."[34]

On March 14, 2002, Saddam sat down with Nechirvan Barzani, a rising figure in Kurdish politics and a nephew of Masoud Barzani, the powerful Kurdistan Democratic Party leader.

Nechirvan reported on a recent visit by an American "delegation" to Kurdistan whose members "did not identify themselves." (This was a C.I.A. team dispatched by Luis Rueda at the Iraq Operations Group.) The Americans had stayed eight days, accompanied by a Turkish escort. They had discussed future cooperation with Kurdish leaders.

"Our conclusions: there is a conspiracy planned against Iraq," Barzani continued. He pledged loyalty in the event of an American attack. The Kuwaitis and Jordanians would likely join any American aggression, as might Turkey, he added.

"We agree with your analysis," Saddam replied. "If we have to face [America] militarily, then we are prepared to do so. The Americans, anyway, as a military force, are trying to avoid coming to Iraq. . . . They were not able to prove that Iraq played a role in what happened [on September 11]—of course, we had no role in what happened.

"In our assessment, the Americans will not strike—or maybe they will only strike military targets," Saddam continued, referring to the sorts of cruise-missile and air attacks that Iraq had endured periodically since 1991. "They will not take action to change the regime at this time, and at least for a while."

A plan to invade Iraq "requires much more time, and there are indications that his [Bush's] popularity is starting to partially diminish," he went on. Without a hint of self-awareness, speaking again of Bush, he concluded: "Narcissism is dangerous and can cost a man the opportunity to be wise."[35]

TWENTY-FOUR

Cold Pitch

On April 26, 2002, Jafar Dhia Jafar rode down the wide, palm-lined highway to Baghdad's Saddam International Airport. He was on his way to New York, and Saddam's inescapable visage gazed down from billboards. Since he had taken charge of Iraq's clandestine nuclear program in 1981, Jafar had been given permission to travel abroad only three times: to the Soviet Union, Jordan, and France. He had not visited the United States since 1976. Saddam's office had approved this trip just two days before, after Jafar was added to an official delegation headed for negotiations at the United Nations—another round in the seemingly quixotic attempt to resolve Iraq's disarmament. At the airport, the physicist passed through immigration and boarded a flight to Amman.

Two days later, Jafar traveled to the U.S. embassy there to attend a visa appointment. Two Iraqi colleagues escorted him.

Jafar cleared security and found a "friendly-looking man in his fifties" waiting for him. The man flipped through the pages of Jafar's diplomatic passport.

"You don't travel much," he remarked.

"I travel from time to time," Jafar said laconically.[1]

Soon he was on his way, visa in hand. The next morning, he boarded a K.L.M. Royal Dutch Airlines jet for Amsterdam, where he would connect to New York. He took a window seat in first class. Just as the doors were shutting, a large, young, clean-shaven American boarded and took the seat next to Jafar. The doors closed, and they had the cabin to themselves.

A few minutes after takeoff, the man introduced himself as "John." He displayed a U.S. government passport. Jafar assumed he was C.I.A.

"I'm here to speak to you in private, as there was no opportunity when you were at the U.S. embassy," John said. "You are the leading Iraqi nuclear scientist, and you are not affiliated with the Baath Party," he continued, as Jafar recalled. "We would like you to cooperate with us."

The man went on with his pitch: "War is going to begin soon between the United States and Iraq," he said. "The American government has already made its decision." Jafar should protect himself while he still could, John said. "The United States is concerned for your personal safety and that of your family."

"Maybe it is true that I was a leader in the Iraqi nuclear program," Jafar eventually replied. "But this program was halted in 1991 and destroyed that same year. I may not be a Baathist, but I am not willing to cooperate with the C.I.A. I have been a government employee in Iraq since 1967 and cannot betray my country."

As they talked, Jafar tried out his own pitch, in the hope he might get through to the Bush administration: "You can rest assured—and inform your government—that Iraq does not possess weapons of mass destruction," he said. The nuclear program had been terminated. "All these weapons that Iraq possessed were destroyed during the year 1991," Jafar continued. Nothing had changed since the inspectors left Iraq in 1998, he emphasized. "If someone tells you otherwise, they are lying," he insisted.

John dropped his recruiting attempt. He handed Jafar a card with a phone number on it. He said the phone was answered around the clock, and he urged the physicist to call.[2]

For the rest of the flight, they talked only about personal and commonplace subjects, as if they were ordinary strangers on a plane. At Schiphol Airport, they parted. Jafar boarded a Northwest Airlines flight to New York. On this leg, he had no solicitous neighbor. But at John F. Kennedy Airport, a uniformed police officer met him and a colleague in the jetway and took them to an area where several men in civilian dress waited. The Americans separated Jafar from his colleague and directed them to interview rooms.

"I have diplomatic immunity," Jafar protested. His mild bemusement about the pitch from John had yielded to anger. "You don't have the right to interrogate me." He assumed these men were C.I.A., too.

Once Jafar was seated, these Americans also sought to recruit him and professed concern for his safety. Their questions included, among others: "How long does Iraq need to produce a nuclear bomb?"

The scientist repeated the answers he had given to "John." The nuclear program had been dead since 1991. Iraq currently had no chemical or biological weapons, either. No illicit weapons programs had been restarted.

After half an hour, he was released into the baggage hall, where he reunited with his colleague. They discovered that their luggage was missing. They filed a complaint with Northwest Airlines. En route to the Carlyle Hotel in Manhattan, Jafar stopped at a drugstore to buy shaving gear and other necessities. Fuming, he made his way to U.N. headquarters in travel clothes unsuitable for a formal diplomatic meeting.[3]

That spring, the C.I.A.'s Iraq Operations Group quietly ramped up for war. The handful of staff Luis Rueda and John Maguire had inherited in August 2001 now swelled week by week toward an eventual roster of several hundred. Among other initiatives, to make up for the C.I.A.'s almost complete lack of reporting agents inside Saddam's regime, the group launched a worldwide "bump" operation, dispatching

case officers to approach Iraqi diplomats, intelligence officers, and scientists wherever they could find them to pitch them on helping the
United States. Jafar had run into this surge of quasi-espionage, although
he would have been a prime target for approach at any time.[4]

Iraq operated about seventy-five embassies worldwide, staffed by
both intelligence officers and diplomats. The embassies offered a lot of
opportunities to "bump"—a technique similar to door-to-door sales, or
what journalists call "doorstepping." A case officer trailed an Iraqi diplomat or spy in Jakarta or Rome or Cairo, approached the subject on
the street, and hurriedly pitched him on cooperating with the C.I.A.,
perhaps handing over a card with a phone number. It was a far cry from
the prolonged process of classical spy recruitment: spotting a potential
agent, assessing them, cultivating the individual, and then pitching
when the chances for success seemed strong. But what bumping lacked
in elegance, it made up for in volume.

It did not take long for Iraqi intelligence to figure out what was happening: "There is the possibility that members of the American administration worldwide will attempt to approach the diplomats of our
embassies overseas to influence them, taking advantage of the vicious
campaign that was launched by the evil administration," warned one
alert sent out that summer. "Take precautionary measures and be wary."[5]

Yet the Americans were all but impossible to avoid. That summer,
Jafar's colleague Fadhil al-Janabi traveled to Amman, on his way to official meetings in Vienna. Soon after checking in with his wife at the
Intercontinental Hotel, he heard a knock on the door. He opened it to
find a young blond man. "I'm from the American embassy," the man
said, "and I'd like to speak with you." He asked to come inside, but
Janabi refused.

"We're going to change the regime in Iraq, and we don't want to
harm you," the man went on. "I can save you." Janabi sent him away.

The hounding, which continued in Austria, only reinforced Janabi's
assumption, widely shared among Iraqi scientists, that the C.I.A. already knew "that we did *not* have weapons of mass destruction." The

Americans weren't looking for the truth; they were looking for scientists to affirm their lies.[6]

Early in 2002, the Bush White House held discussions about what the C.I.A. might do to pressure Saddam, taking into account the many failures of the 1990s. Director George Tenet and his deputy, John McLaughlin, staffed by Luis Rueda, avoided advocating for any policy but said that if a U.S. military invasion occurred, any C.I.A. covert action should complement that effort. If they got lucky, agency influence operations designed to sow doubts among Iraqi elites might spare them a war by triggering a coup d'état or an assassination, but the White House should not consider this very likely.

That winter, Rueda drafted a new "finding" for the White House. As an old hand at covert-action management, he loaded the document with as many permissions as he thought he might need. He asked for authority to conduct sabotage operations inside Iraq—blowing up depots and the like, primarily to spook Saddam and his generals, and to spread distrust among them. Rueda got a lot of what he sought—a covert budget of nearly $200 million a year, vastly more than the C.I.A. had received during the 1990s, as well as authorities for propaganda and operations to disrupt Baghdad's international banking. Rueda also received permission to back opposition groups in preparation for war. But the White House turned down his request to plan for a postwar Iraqi government. (Postwar planning by the State Department was sidelined, too; Donald Rumsfeld's Pentagon took charge.)

After sending the C.I.A. survey team to Kurdistan (the visitors Saddam heard about from a Barzani interlocutor), Rueda invited Kurdistan Democratic Party leader Masoud Barzani and Jalal Talabani of the Patriotic Union of Kurdistan to visit "the Farm" for consultations. From Frankfurt, Barzani and Talabani boarded a "black" C.I.A. flight for Virginia. There, Rueda and other C.I.A. leaders showered the Kurds with promises—money, guns, political support. The overall message was: *This time, we mean it.* Of course, Rueda knew that Bush had not firmly decided on war—the public certainly had no indication that war was inevitable—but he and C.I.A. colleagues felt they had to come on strong. Barzani "was skeptical and very hard to convince," Rueda recalled, because "he didn't believe we were serious, and he'd gotten burned before." Talabani, however, judged that Bush likely intended to invade Iraq, and that it would be in the P.U.K.'s best interests to cooperate. In April, John Maguire flew covertly into Kurdistan to prepare for the full-time return of C.I.A. officers.[7]

Rueda was spared one assignment: the Iraq Operations Group did not get involved with the effort to find Iraq's weapons of mass destruction. That detective work required scientific expertise that lay elsewhere at the C.I.A., in its arms-control and science sections. Rueda assumed that Iraq possessed hidden WMD because everyone did, including the Germans and the British. But the hunt was "tangential" to his covert-action mission. Maguire thought Iraq's weapons were well hidden and that it was a mistake to sell the war on a promise that they would be found quickly. There were plenty of other justifications for overthrowing Saddam, he thought, given the Iraqi leader's record of aggression and atrocities. Yet President Bush repeatedly cited the danger that Saddam might pass WMD to terrorists as the reason why it was no longer acceptable to merely contain him. As the Bush administration's intentions to invade became more visible during the summer of 2002, the White House doubled down on that casus belli.[8]

At U.N. headquarters on the afternoon of May 3, Jafar met Hans Blix, the bespectacled, even-tempered Swedish diplomat. It was a rare encounter between the world's longtime top nuclear watchdog and the physicist whose work during the 1980s had caused the I.A.E.A. such embarrassment. Blix regarded Jafar as a "high-class intellectual" and a "brilliant nuclear scientist." If the Iraqi was an adversary, he was a worthy one.

Jafar explained why he had come to the meeting in casual clothes.

His luggage had been lost; he also mentioned that he had been approached during his journey by "an intelligence agent" who "asked whether he was ready to defect." Blix could see that Jafar was angry.[9]

After leading the I.A.E.A. for sixteen years, Blix had retired in 1997, only to be recruited two years later to become chairman of the United Nations Monitoring, Verification and Inspection Commission, or UN-MOVIC ("un-movick"), the successor to UNSCOM. The unit operated out of offices on the thirty-first floor of U.N. headquarters. This time, there would be no "inspectors at war," as Blix put it, and no two-way cooperation between the U.N. and the C.I.A. or other intelligence agencies. Blix believed that the era of "cowboy" inspectors fostered by his Swedish rival, Rolf Ekéus, had been "counterproductive and discrediting." As one of his first acts, Blix asked Charles Duelfer to resign.[10]

Opinion about Blix within the Bush administration was sharply divided. Paul Wolfowitz and other Iraq hawks feared he was too soft and demanded an investigation of his tenure leading the I.A.E.A. The C.I.A. reported back that Blix had worked honestly within the limits of his agency's mandate. At the White House, National Security Adviser Condoleezza Rice concluded that he was acceptable. He was an expert, and realistically, nobody better was likely to pass muster with France, Russia, and China at the U.N. Security Council. Blix found himself in a familiar position—under not-so-subtle pressure from Washington but condemned as an American lackey in Baghdad.

Around his meeting with the Swede, Jafar listened as Iraqi colleagues declared that they had "nothing new" to offer about their country's weapons programs. It was up to UNMOVIC to explain how a return of inspectors would be helpful. Iraq had already endured hundreds of inspector visits. What more could the U.N. possibly discover?

"Maybe you will find another poultry barn," Blix quipped, referring to the trove of revelatory documents that Iraq had dumped at Hussein Kamel's farm, for the benefit of international inspectors, after Kamel's defection in 1995.[11]

Blix pointed out that in creating UNMOVIC, the Security Council had mandated that if Iraq allowed inspectors to return, they would be given sixty days to look around the country. Only then would Blix recommend what should be done. He needed access, first and foremost.

Jafar understood that it was nearly impossible to prove the absence of weapons or capability beyond all doubt. They had "reached a dead end," he thought.

The nuclear file remained relatively uncontroversial. Mohamed ElBaradei, an Egyptian diplomat who had succeeded Blix as director general of the I.A.E.A., told the meeting that there were only "a few remaining issues" about Jafar's historical program to resolve, and that these could be reviewed even as the U.N. shifted from detective work to long-term monitoring.

Jafar erupted. He had heard this tantalizing promise of a clean bill of health many times before. The I.A.E.A. had been "dishonest," he told Blix and ElBaradei, and the agency's conduct was "two-faced." The meeting broke up. Kofi Annan, the U.N.'s secretary-general, told reporters that the discussions had been "useful and frank."[12]

That evening, Jafar told the head of Iraqi intelligence at the Permanent Mission in New York about his trip from Amman, the cold pitch by "John," and the interview at Kennedy Airport. The officer called him back the next evening. "I want to relay the greetings of President Saddam Hussein, who asks you to be very careful while you are in New York—for your safety," he said. He told Jafar not to leave his hotel without an Iraqi intelligence officer in tow. In fact, he added, there appeared to be American spies sitting right now in the Carlyle Hotel's lobby.

Jafar's phone soon rang: another American. "Good evening, Dr. Jafar. Would you like to come to the hotel lobby and drink tea?"

He declined and hung up. On his last day in New York, Jafar received his missing suitcase. His clothes had been tossed around, and the lining of the case had been shredded. That night, he flew home to Baghdad.[13]

Desperate intelligence collection creates a marketplace, and when the C.I.A. decides to spend $200 million a year on operations against a single regime, hustlers of all kinds can be expected. Amidst the worldwide bump operations, the C.I.A. station in Paris reported to the Iraq Operations Group about an asset of French intelligence who was claiming that he had access to Naji Sabri, the Iraqi foreign minister. The source claimed he could obtain insight from Sabri about ongoing clandestine Iraqi work on WMD. He wanted $1 million dollars and help getting his family out of Iraq.

It's bullshit, Luis Rueda thought. Sabri was a former English professor with only passing access to Saddam; he would not know about WMD programs. But when Rueda dragged his heels on engaging the agent, the Paris station made a call to one of his bosses, and word came down that he should proceed. They settled with the informant on an initial payment of $500,000, and in exchange, the insider was to arrange an encounter between Sabri and the Paris station chief. The meeting did not materialize. They eventually discovered that they had been taken.[14]

Problems with unreliable defectors and sources made the C.I.A.'s liaison with the two major Kurdish parties all the more critical. The Iraqi elite often employed Kurds as household staff. The C.I.A. teams now back inside Kurdistan recruited agents who watered gardens, served dinner, or changed bedsheets. The biggest breakthrough came through the team assigned to Jalal Talabani. They recruited a sheikh named Nahro al-Kasnazan, the leader of a Sufi Muslim religious order whose members included soldiers in Saddam's ringed circles of bodyguards. The network offered the C.I.A. a realistic chance to determine Saddam's daily whereabouts. Tenet authorized Rueda to pay Kasnazan several million dollars—Kasnazan's account suggests his total payments may have exceeded $10 million—to work with the Americans against Saddam. The C.I.A. gave Kasnazan's group a cryptonym for messaging that reflected the agency's optimism: DB ROCKSTARS.[15]

Charles Duelfer had decided to work with the Iraq Operations Group because Rueda was "results-oriented and willing to take risks as long as they were understood," and he grasped "the big picture." Even though the C.I.A. had been formally shut out of planning for a post-Saddam Iraq, Rueda asked Duelfer to develop insights about who might plausibly lead the country after Saddam. Duelfer contacted Iraqis he had known while serving at the Special Commission. He drew up a list of names. These included retired military leaders. He also heard suggestions that Saddam should be succeeded by a council of generals and civilians. He found that although "lots of options" to defect were offered to well-placed Iraqis still working for Saddam, very few were interested: "Senior Iraqis were not particularly loyal to Saddam, but were loyal to their country."[16]

S addam Hussein turned sixty-five that spring. His family and the Baath Party staged an exuberant celebration. About a million people poured into the streets of Baghdad. They sang and danced while holding Saddam's picture aloft. A play based on his novel *Zabiba and the King* opened to appreciative reviews. A delegation presented a gift of a golden statue of Saladin, the conqueror of Jerusalem.

Saddam did not appear among the crowds, in keeping with his regimen of self-protection, but his cousin Ali Hassan al-Majid presided over a public party in Tikrit attended by diplomats and journalists. Majid cut a huge pink cake and fired a gun in the air. Iraqi TV showed Saddam celebrating with children at an unknown location.[17]

On his birthday, *The New York Times* published a front-page story, sourced to "senior officials" in Washington, that began: "The Bush administration, in developing a potential approach for toppling President Saddam Hussein of Iraq, is concentrating its attention on a major air campaign and ground invasion, with initial estimates contemplating the use of 70,000 to 250,000 troops."[18]

Saddam recalled telling his "comrades" around this time that "we ought to get ready for war as if it would happen tomorrow," yet his actions and private comments that spring did not suggest he was especially worried. He analyzed Washington much less often at cabinet meetings and in conversation with visitors than he had in the months after 9/11. He opened meetings with declarations of support for Palestinians battling Israel in the Second Intifada, which had descended into an exceptional crisis that spring when the Israel Defense Forces shelled Yasser Arafat, the P.L.O.'s chairman, in his compound in Ramallah—a running story on satellite TV that had galvanized the Arab world. Meanwhile, Saddam's cabinet discussed loans to farmers, flood prevention, and the management of prizes for literature, art, and science.[19]

During this period, Saddam also delivered secular sermons made up of bromides about self-improvement. ("Do not make your enemy hope for your forgiveness, and do not make your friend lose hope in your forgiveness. . . . Do not let anyone who thinks that you despise him get close to you.") He had offered moral instruction before, but in this reflective season of his life, he devoted notable time to sharing grandfatherly insights, albeit mainly about how to navigate a harsh world teeming with enemies. A compendium of "great lessons provided by the Commanding Comrade" opened with an aphorism that its author might have been advised that summer to reflect on: "Do not aggravate the snake before you get the capability to cut off its head."

He took solace in his belief that America's turn as the dominant world power was passing, a notion he expressed to Ram Naik, India's oil minister, in early July. "The American hand that carries the weapons and the stick while dealing with the world today will weaken in two years, five years, fifteen years, or twenty years," Saddam told Naik. "And it has started to happen now."[20]

TWENTY-FIVE

Cracked Mirrors

I n late July 2002, Sir Richard Dearlove, the chief of MI6, traveled to Washington to learn where Bush administration policy on Iraq stood. He and two other civil servants—David Manning, Tony Blair's top foreign policy adviser, and Kevin Tebbit, the permanent undersecretary of defense—met counterparts and recorded impressions. Manning noted, "Not much doubt here that the Administration is bent on action soon, and convincing itself that it has [a] strong strategic as well as a historical duty to act." Tebbit noted that an American official had forecast an early 2003 invasion. "One is still left with an air of unreality, given the enormity of what is envisaged and the absence of planning detail or policy framework to credibly make it happen," he wrote. Dearlove saw Condoleezza Rice and discerned that a "decision had already been taken" on an invasion, and that the "question was only how and when."

On July 23, at Ten Downing Street, Blair convened a small group of ministers and civil servants privy to secrets about Iraq war discussions with America. Dearlove informed them not only that war seemed inevitable but also that "intelligence and facts were being fixed around the policy." Foreign Minister Jack Straw called the case for war "thin." Among the four countries presenting the greatest threat of WMD use—he listed Iran, North Korea, Libya, and Iraq—Saddam Hussein's regime would rank fourth, he said.[1]

Yet when Straw raised the possibility of breaking with the U.S. if the Bush administration invaded, Blair said that would be "the biggest shift in [British] foreign policy for fifty years," and he was "not sure it's very wise." In reality, as George W. Bush already understood from private conversations with Blair, the prime minister accepted the case for war as a last resort. During five years in office, Blair had led Britain to military interventions in Kosovo and Sierra Leone, partly on humanitarian grounds. In 1999, he had delivered a much-noted speech at the University of Chicago laying out a qualified case for waging war to remove violent dictators and naming Saddam Hussein as an example. During 2002, he repeatedly said in public that the world would be better off without Saddam in power. And he was committed to the American alliance as a pillar of British policy. As Blair admitted to his colleagues that day, referring to plans that could lead Britain to join an invasion of Iraq: "It's worse than you think—I actually believe in doing this."[2]

Blair tried to condition his support to Washington. Antiwar protesters had already taken to London streets over Iraq, and his Labour Party was restive. Politically, it would be implausible for the prime minister to go to war if the Bush administration did not first seek the U.N.'s backing and demand of Saddam that he allow the return of weapons inspectors. Blair also wanted to push the White House to address the Israeli-Palestinian conflict, with the aim of countering predictable outrage in the Middle East should an invasion take place.

The prime minister advocated for a publicity campaign, one that would highlight "all the WMD evidence," including Saddam's "attempts to secure nuclear capability; and, as seems possible, add on the al-Qaeda link," which would be "hugely persuasive over here," as Blair secretly wrote to Bush on July 28. (Both MI6 and the C.I.A. discounted

the significance of historical contacts between Iraqi intelligence officers and al-Qaeda.) Manning hand-carried Blair's letter to Washington
and gave it to Condoleezza Rice on July 29.

"I will be with you, whatever," Blair's note pledged. He proposed a
military buildup that might be accompanied by a Security Council
deadline for Iraq to allow inspectors back. If Saddam did not meet their
demands, as Blair expected, "a strike date could be Jan/Feb next year,"
he wrote.[3]

Bush invited Manning to the Oval Office. A former ambassador to
Washington, Manning understood the emerging divisions in the president's war cabinet. The Iraq "regime changers," such as Dick Cheney
and Paul Wolfowitz, competed against the "multilateralists," led by Colin Powell. As Manning now laid out the case for U.N. diplomacy, he
deftly emphasized that there was no viable alternative in British parliamentary politics. If Blair was not careful, a crisis over Iraq could lead
to his swift overthrow. Bush listened sympathetically but made no
commitments.[4]

On August 8, in Baghdad, Saddam Hussein received George Galloway, a British Labour firebrand on the left of his party's caucus.
The member of Parliament had previously traveled to Iraq and had spoken admiringly of Saddam. Tariq Aziz attended the meeting.

Galloway sought to prevent a war between Britain and Iraq, he told
Saddam. To help make the case, he suggested, Iraq could create an
English-language satellite TV channel to rival the BBC and CNN. Galloway said he could assist with employees and journalists, according to
an Iraqi record of the discussion.[5]

"Whatever happened to British wisdom?" Saddam asked. He and
other Iraqis of his generation had grown up hearing that France and Italy had been brutal colonialists but that Britain ruled its territories "by
using the simplest" of means, he said.

To illustrate, Saddam recounted a jokey fable: Winston Churchill,
Adolf Hitler, Benito Mussolini, and Joseph Stalin are sitting around a

table "where there is a bowl that contains water and a fish." Who can catch the fish? Stalin, Hitler, and Mussolini each grab a fork and attempt to spear it, Saddam said. They fail. Then Churchill takes a spoon and "starts to empty the water out of the bowl one spoonful at a time, until the bowl runs out of water, and he manages to catch the fish."

"Blair is not Churchill," Galloway told Saddam.

Saddam said he liked Galloway's TV channel idea, yet this was just the sort of modern approach to public influence that he seemed incapable of executing. As the pressure on Baghdad mounted, Saddam was content to hand the microphone to old-school comrades such as Vice President Taha Yassin Ramadan. "We are taking the threat seriously," Ramadan told reporters that summer, during a visit to Damascus. George W. Bush leads "a despotic administration; it is an insane, criminal administration." Some weeks later, Ramadan suggested that Bush and Saddam should resolve their conflict in a duel.[6]

During August, the divisions around President Bush over Iraq burst into public view. Brent Scowcroft, who had been the national security adviser to the president's father, published an essay in *The Wall Street Journal* under the headline "Don't Attack Iraq." He argued that an invasion would undermine, "if not destroy," the global effort to defeat al-Qaeda, and that Saddam, if cornered, might unleash WMD against Israel. Perhaps most stinging of all, Scowcroft refuted Bush's judgment about why a preemptive attack on Iraq was necessary. The Iraqi leader "is unlikely to risk his investment in weapons of mass destruction, much less his country, by handing such weapons to terrorists who would use them for their own purposes and leave Baghdad as the return address," he wrote.[7]

The essay appeared to be an indirect intervention by Bush's father. The son was furious and called his dad. "Brent is a friend," the elder Bush said. Scowcroft later denied that George H. W. Bush had encouraged his essay, but as the journalist Peter Baker put it: "There were those who never believed him."[8]

Eleven days later, Vice President Dick Cheney countered with a headline-grabbing speech to the Veterans of Foreign Wars. Cheney argued there was "no assurance whatsoever" that U.N. weapons inspections would work. "We now know that Saddam has resumed his efforts to acquire nuclear weapons," he added, baldly overstating U.S. intelligence reporting. "Many of us are convinced that Saddam will acquire nuclear weapons fairly soon." Cheney skipped the common practice of clearing his speech with the C.I.A. and failed to give White House aides a heads-up, either. Bush was aggravated but declined to confront his vice president directly, instead asking Rice to reel him in.[9]

The president saw himself as a chief executive, "the Decider," but he was losing control of his advisers. He now made a decision. Blair, Powell, and Rice all advocated for the U.N. route, on the grounds that it would isolate Saddam, build the widest possible coalition, and keep Britain viable as a military partner. On August 29, Rice told David Manning that Bush would indeed go to the U.N. To make it work, the two advisers talked about mounting "a really effective public relations campaign" about the dangers Saddam Hussein posed.[10]

At Camp David, on September 7, Bush ratified his decision about the U.N. at a National Security Council meeting. Bush met Blair later that day at the retreat and told him, "I don't want to go to war, but I will do it." Blair "agreed," as Bush recalled it. The president told Alastair Campbell, Blair's communications adviser, "Your man has got cojones."[11]

Bush embraced "coercive diplomacy," a phrase Condoleezza Rice favored. The premise was that a credible threat of war could persuade Saddam to "come clean" about his presumed WMD arsenal. No consideration was given to the possibility that he had nothing to come clean about. That scenario was entirely absent from intelligence reporting and White House debates. They would set the bar very high for Iraqi compliance with a new U.N. resolution. Saddam would have to cooperate unconditionally with inspectors and swallow many of the intrusions on Iraqi sovereignty that he had rejected in 1998. The demands the U.S. and Britain planned to impose on Saddam would be so harsh that "either the regime must change in response," in order to comply, "or it would be changed by military action," as David Manning described the thinking later. That is, if Saddam capitulated, they would have "succeeded in changing the very nature of the regime." Or as Bush put it: "We would have cratered the guy."[12]

Coercive diplomacy had the air of a cynical exercise, a test designed for Saddam to fail. It seemed meant to strengthen international support for an invasion that Bush had already decided on and that Blair had already committed to back. But even if Bush and Blair were prepared to take yes for an answer—to achieve Iraq's disarmament through diplomacy and inspections—the approach they designed was all but guaranteed to provoke Saddam. The only question was how far his resistance would go. The caucus of Iraq "regime changers" in Washington were counting on Saddam's defiance. "No one doubts that inspections will fail," Christopher Meyer, the British ambassador, reported to London. "The argument is how hard to try for international support for the war that will ensue."[13]

On September 12, 2002, Bush addressed the U.N. General Assembly. "We know that Saddam Hussein pursued weapons of mass murder even when inspectors were in his country," he said. "Are we to assume that he stopped when they left? The history, the logic, and the facts lead to one conclusion: Saddam Hussein's regime is a grave and gathering danger." He issued a provocative warning that was already becoming a staple of Bush administration rhetoric: "The first time we may be completely certain" that Saddam possesses nuclear weapons would be when "he uses one."[14]

To gain maneuvering room, Saddam decided at last to make a concession. There is no record of his deliberations, but on September 16, Foreign Minister Naji Sabri wrote U.N. Secretary-General Kofi Annan to report that Iraq would "allow the return of United Nations inspectors without conditions" in order to "remove any doubts that Iraq still possesses weapons of mass destruction."[15]

Three days later, Sabri delivered a speech to the U.N. General Assembly that was written for him by Saddam. He finally offered condolences for the victims of September 11. Sabri also quoted a letter from the Iraqi leader. It decried Bush's speech of a week before as full of "utmost distortions . . . so as to make American citizens believe the deliberate insinuation that Iraq was linked to the American people's tragedy of September 11." Saddam declared that Iraq was "clear of all nuclear, chemical and biological weapons," and he called for an end to "the cyclone of American accusations and fabricated crises against Iraq."[16]

He acted very late. His misjudgments about where his self-interest lay during the first months after 9/11 and his complacency about America's percolating threats during the spring of 2002 had deprived him of precious time. If Saddam had allowed U.N. inspectors back into Iraq the previous autumn or winter, he might have provided Hans Blix and Mohamed ElBaradei with a chance to close out the nuclear file and to establish that many sensitive sites left uninspected since 1998 contained no incriminating evidence. That in turn might have allowed France and other European governments opposed to an invasion of Iraq to persuasively argue that U.N.-led disarmament was working once more. Their campaigning might have strengthened the antiwar lobby in Britain and perhaps even in the United States. Bush might well have ordered an invasion anyway, but Blair's position would have become more difficult. It is impossible to have confidence about this counterfactual scenario, but it can be said that by waiting until September 2002 to permit the return of inspectors, Saddam lost the initiative and allowed Washington and London time to shape how the coming inspections would be judged.

On September 24, Blair published a blockbuster dossier, *Iraq's Weapons of Mass Destruction: The Assessment of the British Government.* It drew on secret intelligence. Britain had no prior practice of releasing intelligence in this form, and Blair took the additional step of writing his own foreword. He explained that the dossier was based on the work of the Joint Intelligence Committee, a sixty-six-year-old Cabinet Office body where the chiefs of Britain's major spy services synthesized intelligence for ministers. Blair wrote that he believed the available information "established beyond doubt . . . that Saddam has continued to produce chemical and biological weapons [and] that he continues in his efforts to develop nuclear weapons." The prime minister's "belief" that Saddam's active production of chemical and biological weapons had been "established beyond doubt" overstated the evidence in his own dossier, according to the later findings of a parliamentary committee. On nuclear weapons, an initial draft had qualified Blair's opinion: "The case I make is not that Saddam could launch a nuclear attack on London or another part of the U.K. (he could not)." The line was cut from the published version.[17]

One claim in the dossier would echo for months and eventually roil American politics: "As a result of the intelligence, we judge that Iraq has . . . sought significant quantities of uranium from Africa, despite having no active civil nuclear power programme that could require it." On its face, the allegation strongly implied that Saddam was again cooking up an atomic bomb. The finding was based on two very recently developed MI6 sources—one with "documentary evidence"— that described attempts by Iraq to buy uranium from Niger.[18]

Even if true, the allegation could mislead audiences unfamiliar with the complicated science of nuclear-bomb manufacturing. Iraq's acquisition of raw uranium or uranium oxide would be an early and relatively uncomplicated aspect of any drive to rebuild a bomb program. (The hard part was separating fissionable uranium isotopes to create "highly enriched" uranium.) Moreover, British and American intelligence agencies judged that Iraq would need years to enrich uranium to bomb grade unless it acquired the stuff from smugglers or another government, an unlikely prospect.

On October 7, in a speech delivered in Cincinnati, Bush repeated his terrifying formulation of the nuclear threat: "We cannot wait for the final proof—the smoking gun that could come in the form of a mushroom cloud." A week later, in Dearborn, Michigan, speaking of Saddam, Bush added an assessment entirely untethered to intelligence reporting: "This is a man who, in my judgment, would like to use al-Qaeda as a forward army."[19]

That month, the C.I.A. published its own unclassified white paper, *Iraq's Weapons of Mass Destruction Programs*. The key judgments declared that Iraq "has continued" its nuclear-, biological-, and chemical-weapons programs and that the regime "has chemical and biological weapons." Since 1998, when Saddam expelled U.N. inspectors, Iraq had "invested more heavily in biological weapons; most analysts assess Iraq is reconstituting its nuclear weapons program." That language echoed findings in a Top Secret National Intelligence Estimate hastily assembled by the C.I.A. and distributed to Congress and cabinet members around this time. Such estimates are designed to be the most authoritative documents issued by U.S. intelligence; they are overseen by the C.I.A. but draw on information from all major spy services. In both the public white paper and the Top Secret NIE, many of the key judgments "either overstated, or were not supported by, the underlying intelligence reporting," according to a later Senate Select Intelligence Committee investigation.[20]

To support the charge that Iraq was rebuilding its atomic-bomb program, the NIE cited the continuing visibility of Iraq's Atomic Energy Commission and the salaries and offices provided by Saddam's regime to top scientists, such as Jafar Dhia Jafar. It also cited an attempt by Iraq, before 9/11, to import high-strength aluminum tubes of a type subject to export restrictions by the Nuclear Suppliers Group—and therefore off limits to Iraq under U.N. resolutions. C.I.A. analysts judged that Iraq wanted the tubes to restart its 1980s-era secret centrifuge program to enrich uranium to bomb grade. Iraq said it had wanted the tubes to build conventional military rockets. Finally, the estimate offered its own take on allegations that Iraq had attempted to buy uranium from Niger, but the C.I.A. had doubts about Britain's Africa reporting, and the matter was not included among the document's "key judgments."

In early October, when the White House tried to include the African uranium claim in public remarks by Bush, the C.I.A.'s director, George Tenet, weighed in personally. He argued that the "president should not be a fact witness on this issue" because C.I.A. analysts believed the "reporting was weak." Yet the allegation would survive zombielike in the archive of speech-ready evidence used by the Bush administration. That autumn, the C.I.A. published a classified handbook of reference material about Iraq that "policymakers, intelligence officers, and military personnel could easily access," as the Senate Select Intelligence Committee's investigation later reported. The handbook contained an alarming adaptation of the British finding: "Iraq may be trying to acquire 500 tons of uranium—enough for 50 nuclear devices after processing—from Niger."[21]

Further, the latest C.I.A. reports alleged that Saddam not only possessed dangerous biological weapons—germs and toxins that could potentially sicken or kill entire populations—but also now manufactured them in secret mobile labs that would be hard to find. Saddam's mobile labs could supposedly produce within three to six months as many deadly agents as Iraq had managed to make in all the years before 1991. One "credible source" of this information was a Germany-based Iraqi defector, the source code-named Curveball, who would turn out to be a notorious fabricator. His true name was Rafid Ahmed Alwan al-Janabi. Seeking asylum, he invented his eyewitness claims about mobile labs, but because he had worked in Iraq's weapons complex for a time, he was able to make himself believable.[22]

All these judgments reflected a "collective presumption" among intelligence analysts and collectors that Iraq had definitely restarted WMD work. The Baghdad regime's deceptions during the 1990s had left the C.I.A. and other agencies with an assumption that the Iraqis continued to lie. This history led analysts to "both interpret ambiguous evidence as conclusively indicative of a WMD program" and to "ignore or minimize" exculpatory information, the Senate Select Intelligence Committee's investigation later found.[23]

George W. Bush suffered regret over going to the U.N. almost as soon as negotiations began with France and Russia on a new Security Council resolution. He told Tony Blair that he was "having trouble holding on to my horse," referring to the flak he was taking from the right. On October 10 and 11, Congress voted overwhelmingly to authorize force against Iraq, by 296–133 in the House and 77–23 in the Senate. Bush was now politically fortified to wage war. For his part, Blair increasingly grasped that the Bush administration was "ruthless about its own power and position," as Alastair Campbell put it.[24]

French president Jacques Chirac and Russian president Vladimir Putin refused to accept initial American and British proposals that would bind the U.N. to endorse war automatically if Iraq cheated or interfered with new inspections. "The French were simply making clear they would not support war at all," Jack Straw recalled. "The Chinese didn't care, the Russians were playing hardball."

Chirac's stance was pivotal. He looked with contempt on Blair's decision to side with Bush's "radical" determination to overthrow Saddam, despite the instability a war would cause in the Middle East. Blair "made no secret to me of the fact that he felt very close to the American point of view," Chirac recalled, and that he believed the best way to forge international peace was "to get rid, one way or another, of leaders like Saddam Hussein." Chirac thought Britain too often "had its eyes riveted on the other side of the Atlantic." He was "saddened and angered" by Blair's failure to "make greater use of the former experience that his country had of the Middle East" during Britain's days of empire, to steer the U.S. away from an invasion based on naive assumptions.

Although he had been charmed by Saddam Hussein in the 1970s, Chirac insisted during an interview with *The New York Times* that "we do obviously want" a new government in Baghdad. But he objected to American unilateralism and preemptive war. Chirac forged an alliance with German chancellor Gerhard Schröder, who ruled out German participation in any invasion. They would use their considerable influence to block Anglo-American plans at the U.N.

For weeks, Blair clung to hopes that the credible threat of war might preclude a need for war. Britain's goal was Iraq's disarmament, not regime change, he insisted, and he declined to assure the Pentagon that British forces would join an invasion. On October 31, after being informed that the U.S. was now preparing for a war without U.K. troops, he finally offered British ground forces "for planning purposes."[25]

In early November, exhausted negotiators tabled U.N. Security Council 1441. The resolution set rules for a tough new round of inspections in Iraq to be led by Hans Blix and Mohamed ElBaradei. But it did not resolve the most important disagreements among Washington, London, Paris, and Moscow about how future Iraqi violations might lead to war. The resolution demanded that Iraq submit a new and truthful declaration about its WMD and missile programs. Paragraph four clarified that false Iraqi statements or omissions in this document would constitute a "material breach" of its obligations to the U.N., which the U.S. might choose to interpret as ample cause for an invasion. Yet the resolution's critical provision, paragraph twelve, stated that if Blix or ElBaradei reported that Iraq had lied or committed other violations, the U.N. Security Council would merely "convene immediately . . . to consider the situation."[26]

On November 8, the Security Council unanimously adopted the resolution. The Bush administration explained its favorable vote: "If the Security Council fails to act decisively . . . this resolution does not constrain any Member State from acting." The upshot was that if the administration could not obtain U.N. backing, it would blame the U.N. for failing to do its job and go to war with a coalition of willing allies, whoever these might be.[27]

In late 1995, during the confessional period that followed Hussein Kamel's defection, when Tariq Aziz had asked Jafar Dhia Jafar to produce

an extensive written history of Iraq's nuclear-weapons program, Jafar
had brought together about thirty veterans of the former bombmaking
enterprise to work on the document. The scientists and engineers
drafted a lengthy declaration for the I.A.E.A., drawn largely from
memory, since U.N. inspectors had seized many of the archival documents. Jafar's one-thousand-page *Full, Final, and Complete Declaration*,
submitted in 1996, lay at the heart of the physicist's disputes with Blix
and ElBaradei over whether Iraq deserved a clean bill of health in the
nuclear arena—arguments that had continued into the summer of
2002.[28]

The latest U.N. resolution gave Saddam thirty days to produce another full, final, and complete declaration about all of its banned weapons and missile programs. Saddam's aides asked Jafar to handle the
section about nuclear weapons. The earlier document was "completely
accurate so far as I am concerned," and no new work on a bomb had
taken place since it was written. So Jafar essentially resubmitted the
earlier declaration, topped by a new "extended summary" of about two
hundred pages. "All facilities, equipment and materials of the former
[Iraqi bomb program] have been destroyed or rendered harmless," he
wrote in the new summary.[29]

He did not initially address the two allegations making headlines in
America during late 2002—that Iraq had sought to buy uranium in
Niger and that it had imported aluminum tubes to restart uranium
enrichment. Jafar knew these charges to be unfounded, and he had not
yet considered how to refute the claims, he said later. The Niger deal
had supposedly been orchestrated by Wissam al-Zahawie, a friend of
Jafar's who had worked on nuclear diplomacy during the 1980s and
'90s. At a time when Saddam was looking to break Iraq out of its political isolation, Zahawie had been sent on a four-country African tour
to invite leaders of those nations to visit his country. He had held meetings in African capitals but had not shopped for uranium. Iraq had six
hundred tons of yellowcake and two hundred tons of pure uranium
dioxide in its stores, so it already had what it required if it were ever to
resort to indigenous enrichment again. Eventually, Jafar detailed all of

this in a letter that refuted the allegations about nuclear material sourced from Niger.[30]

On December 7, in Baghdad, two U.N. staff members loaded nearly twelve thousand pages—the entirety of Iraq's latest declaration—into black, rope-bound suitcases to lug them to New York. (The document would not be made public because it contained "cookbook" information about how to make chemical, biological, and nuclear weapons.) In his office on the thirty-first floor of U.N. headquarters, Blix began reading. He hoped the report would provide "fresh revelations and a fresh start" for his inspectors, who were by now already back in Iraq, digging around.[31]

As the inspectors mobilized, Saddam sat for an interview with an Egyptian journalist. It was his first interview with any foreign media outlet in more than a decade. He called America's designs on Iraq a "prelude" to its conquest of the Middle East. "From Baghdad, which will be under military control," the U.S. would "strike Damascus and Tehran," he predicted. The American plan was to "create small entities" across the Middle East that would be "controlled by safekeepers working for the U.S., so that no country will be larger than Israel. . . . This way the Arab oil will be under its control. . . . The purpose is to make Israel into a large empire in the area."

"Mr. President, do you think that the attack is imminent?"

"We are getting ready as if the war will start in an hour." Iraq was not stronger than America, since the U.S. possessed "long-range missiles and naval forces." Yet Iraq "will not turn the war into a picnic for the American or British soldiers. No way!"

When his interviewer asked if he thought that time was on his side, Saddam said, "We have to buy some more time." It was an admission of what the Bush administration feared. If he could draw things out long enough, he predicted optimistically, the "American-British coalition will disintegrate . . . because of the pressure of public opinion in the American and British street."[32]

On December 9, in Washington, Richard Dearlove, the British intelligence chief, met with George Tenet and Condoleezza Rice. President Bush was being "griddled," Rice said. Republicans had accused the
White House of indulging the U.N. unwisely. She was confident that
Iraq's massive new written declaration, which the administration was
still reviewing, "would be a sham." Rice's "impatience for action was
much more obvious than her commitment to secure international
backing" for war, David Manning reported to London. She "made no
effort to hide the fact that the Administration would now be looking to
build the case for early military action . . . probably mid/late February."
Her mood had "hardened substantially."

Manning told Tony Blair he even feared that the Americans, in their
exasperation, might "overdo the pressure on Blix" and "force him into
resignation," an event that would have "damaging repercussions." He
recommended that Britain undertake "maximum efforts to find a
smoking gun" in Iraq that would prove Saddam's guilt.[33]

Blair was already on the case. He described himself as "cautiously
optimistic" that inspectors would soon make a major breakthrough, or
that some late-arriving defector from Iraq would provide unshakable
evidence about Saddam's weapons stocks or ongoing WMD work.
Dearlove cautioned the prime minister that the odds of this happening
were about 20 percent.[34]

As he made his way through Iraq's latest "Full, Final and Complete
Declaration," Hans Blix found it disappointing. Iraqi technocrats
writing about the country's chemical, biological, and missile programs
had mainly followed Jafar's example: they had recycled documents already provided in 1996 or 1997. "What new information there was—
some of it useful—related mostly to development of missiles and
peaceful developments in the field of biology," Blix recalled, referring
to evolvements since the departure of inspectors in 1998. Iraq had

revealed no "long-hidden truths. It looked rather like a repetition of old, unverified data."[35]

On December 19, 2002, he shared this assessment with the Security Council. After decades at the top of the U.N. system, judicious by training and temperament, Blix had a gift for sailing through gale-force political crosswinds. He rarely gave voice to his own opinions, except when arguing about how inspections should be conducted or about what particular pieces of evidence showed or did not show. David Manning worried needlessly; Blix was not the sort of person who would resign because of American pressure. He would ride Washington out, as he had done many times before during his career at the I.A.E.A.

He and his inspectors were still investigating, he told the Security Council. They had already conducted dozens of inspections across Iraq. They had found nothing of special note. Blix said he was "neither in a position to confirm Iraq's statements, nor in possession of evidence to disprove them." He was merely a steward of the evidence. Washington, London, Paris, and Moscow could make of the facts what they would.[36]

That autumn, Tony Blair asked MI6 to produce a psychological profile of Saddam, "not least for the pointers this may give on splitting off Saddam from his regime." The resulting paper pointed out that "personal survival, survival of the regime, and Iraqi-led Arab unity are the three most powerful factors that motivate Saddam. . . . He is a judicious political calculator." The paper assessed that Saddam would "not wish a conflict in which Iraq will be grievously damaged and his stature as a leader destroyed," but it observed that Saddam's ideas about losing were "far more focused on reputation than on [Iraq's] physical or economic standing. . . . If he feels he is losing control . . . he can become very dogmatic, increasingly impulsive and extremely non-compliant." As long as Saddam believed that he could derail an American-led war, he would play it cool, so there was no immediate danger of "radical or unpredictable action." But that was likely to change if Saddam sensed an invasion was imminent or inevitable.[37]

Even this unusually incisive analysis did not fully account for Saddam's thinking as 2002 ended. He did not possess WMD or operative long-range missiles, so he did not have the options for radical military action that he had available in 1991, the last time U.S. and international troops massed on his borders. And he was not quite the same person he had been then. Age, isolation, and a decade of family struggles had sapped some of his fire. That fall, Saddam published his autobiographical novel, *Men and a City*, a treatise on the Iraqi nation laced with personal nostalgia. As winter arrived, he devoted many hours to a new novel, this one a screed against America. The strategic provocateur of the Iran and Kuwait wars had evolved into a commander in chief as interested in letters and legacy as in victory at arms.

TWENTY-SIX

"Do We Have WMD?"

United Nations weapons inspectors had not tramped around Iraq for four years. The Baghdad regime wanted to avoid inadvertent discoveries of old incriminating documents or stray equipment. Yet this housekeeping effort was hobbled by confusion across the highest levels of the government about whether Iraq really possessed what the inspectors were searching for—hidden WMD stocks, in particular. In the years after 1998, Saddam himself had sometimes appeared uncertain. Once, after a cabinet meeting, apparently referring to biological and chemical weapons, he had asked Abd al-Tawab Mullah Huwaysh, then his deputy prime minister, "Do you have any programs going on that I don't know about?"

"Absolutely not," Huwaysh had answered. Worried that this might be some sort of loyalty test, Huwaysh recited Saddam's policy: such illicit weapons work was permissible only under the president's direct, explicit orders, and he had none.

The matter lingered in Huwaysh's mind. Why had Saddam asked him that question? Was the president overseeing secret work and making sure that even senior civilian leaders like him didn't know about it? Or was he afraid that unauthorized work was continuing? Huwaysh was all the more confused because he had once heard Saddam tell his generals, amidst a round of American bellicosity, that he had "something in his hand," implying that Iraq had a secret weapon available.[1]

"Do we have WMD?" Ali Hassan al-Majid, "Chemical Ali," recalled asking Saddam at another meeting.

"Don't you know?" Saddam replied.

"No."

"No."[2]

Late in 2002, Saddam decided to clear things up once and for all. He now wanted to rally his government to pass U.N. inspections with flying colors, since France and Russia had informed him that this would help them make their case at the Security Council. Saddam may have also wanted to instill some realism in his ranks about Iraq's position in the face of America's threats. In any event, at separate meetings with generals, the Revolutionary Command Council, and his cabinet, Saddam notified them all that Iraq "had no WMD," according to Tariq Aziz and Abid Hamid Mahmud, the presidential secretary.[3]

Some of his commanders and comrades received this news with incredulity. They had assumed that Iraq had special weapons hidden in reserve, not only because of Saddam's elliptical hints but also because this would be in line with a certain kind of military logic. "If you did have a special weapon, you should keep it secret to achieve tactical surprise," said Major General Walid Mohammed Taiee, then chief of army logistics.[4]

To make clear his intent, Saddam issued a fresh round of orders to military officers, bureaucrats, and private-sector importers, demanding that they destroy or turn over any remaining documents or equipment and cease any activity that might run afoul of U.N. review. The orders threatened severe penalties for violators. Republican Guard commanders were ordered to sign declarations that their units possessed no prohibited materials.

Yet as the U.N. scrutinized Iraq anew in December, the problems of the 1990s resurfaced. Once again, Iraq's written declaration was judged to be inadequate. And again, the protocols of Iraqi secret police and presidential bodyguards misled U.N. inspectors. The Special Security Organization still regarded visiting inspectors as foreign spies and even potential assassins who threatened the mission of presidential protection. That mission encompassed not only the safety of Saddam's person but also "anything to do with the President or his family," as well as the concealment of "documents pertaining to human rights violations . . . and photos of senior Regime personnel," according to a former senior S.S.O. officer. As during the 1990s, this all but guaranteed that whenever U.N. inspectors headed for sites regarded as sensitive, Saddam's bodyguards would scramble into defensive action, zipping around in vehicles and chattering over radios as they tried to identify and hide protected places, people, or documents. Their actions made it look like they were hiding something—and they often were, but it was not stocks of WMD.[5]

By the end of 2002, the U.S. had deployed about four hundred military aircraft and at least fifteen thousand troops around Iraq, primarily in Kuwait. That invasion force would grow, but by design, it would remain smaller than the massive force that had assembled to liberate Kuwait nearly twelve years earlier. The Powell Doctrine of overwhelming force that had influenced the 1991 war plan had yielded now to a "hybrid" strategy that would rely on speed, combined arms, and advanced technology. Iraq's military had shrunk in size and atrophied in capability across the 1990s. This time, the American plan—openly described in the Western press—would be to drive hard and fast on Baghdad to depose Saddam.[6]

Even in late 2002, Saddam still seemed to believe that Bush did not intend to mount a conventional land invasion. Around December, he addressed an audience of about 150 military officers. He asked "why the Americans would want to come here," recalled General Zuhayr

Talib Abd al-Sattar al-Naqib, the deputy head of military intelligence, who was present. The Americans had already achieved their goals, Saddam explained: "They wanted to occupy the Gulf States, and look, it has happened," he said.

A decade of American containment policy had conditioned Saddam to doubt the prospect of a land invasion. U.S. presidents repeatedly said that they wished to overthrow him, and they even enshrined this goal as official national policy, yet since 1991, the U.S. had attacked only from the air and only for a few days at a time. This time, too, "Saddam and his inner circle thought that the war would last a few days and then it would be over," recalled Naqib. "They thought there would be a few air strikes and maybe some operations in the south."

Iraqi generals prepared for a full invasion anyway. "We knew the goal was to make the Regime fall," recalled Sultan Hashim Ahmad al-Tai, the minister of defense. "We thought the [American-led] forces would arrive in Baghdad or outside Baghdad in twenty days or a month."[7]

Their baseline defense plan was conventional. Border guards served as sentries and trip wires on Iraq's frontiers. Regular army formations were positioned behind them. Republican Guard corps assembled around Baghdad to defend the capital and mobilize for counterattack. Iraq's generals had also developed contingency plans to better survive heavy air attacks. One such plan, created in 2001, called for the dispersal of troops and weapons away from major cities and likely targets, to ride out a short but intense air campaign.[8]

By the last days of 2002, Saddam finally came to accept that an American and British invasion was at least a realistic enough possibility to warrant planning. On December 18, General Sayf al-Din Fulayyih Hasan Taha al-Rawi, the chief of staff of the Republican Guard, summoned high-ranking commanders to Baghdad to hear about a new plan for the capital's defense. Qusay appeared to make clear that the presentation came straight from the top.

General Rawi stood before a map that depicted Baghdad protected by four defensive rings, each four to six miles apart. Each ring was drawn in a different color. When invading forces reached the outermost perimeter, the general explained, the Iraqi troops deployed there would withdraw inward, to the next ring. This would continue, like a nesting doll repacking itself, until all of Iraq's elite forces were positioned in the capital's innermost districts along the Tigris. Here they would "fight to the death."[9]

The design only made vague sense if the goal of the national military was to keep Saddam Hussein alive and in power for as long as possible. The plan seemed to rest on a hope of trapping American and British forces in urban warfare in Baghdad. American war planners did fear prolonged urban combat. But if Iraq drew all of its most capable soldiers, tanks, and armored vehicles into a small area around the Republican Palace, they would have conceded most of the country and would be relatively easy to destroy. In any event, the plan briefed on December 18 was no more than a light sketch, suggestive of something Saddam had drawn on a napkin. Although the ringed defense of Baghdad was discussed at several subsequent meetings, it never acquired a more specific layout.

In fairness, Saddam did develop that winter a strategic concept for the defense of Iraq, judging by the December 18 plan and other statements he made. He envisioned using Iraq's conventional military to delay and exhaust American and British forces so that a nationwide guerrilla resistance could form to bleed the occupiers. He expected prideful Iraqis to mount a people's war comparable to the ongoing Palestinian intifada that Saddam so often celebrated—but in Iraq's case, the insurgency would mobilize trained soldiers, intelligence officers, security men, and paramilitaries. Such a resistance might not require a clear-cut victory to be successful. If the war bled international forces and disrupted the global economy, Moscow and perhaps Paris might seek to broker a cease-fire that would leave him in power, as Mikhail Gorbachev had attempted to do during the 1991 war.

Saddam's office issued a Top Secret letter that winter providing instructions in the event that his regime did fall to the United States: security and intelligence officers were to "demolish and burn all of the offices in the country," sabotage power and water stations, "cease all internal and external communications," purchase "stolen weapons," and carry out assassinations.

At an Iraqi Naval Forces Command conference during the same period, commanders were told: "Our enemy will fight us using the traditional way." Iraq's response would be to disperse and "work in a non-central form to fight," communicating by "signals, animals, bicycles." At another seminar that winter, a high-ranking Iraqi Army general pointed out that in 1991, the American-led coalition "had specific aims that were clear and limited . . . to get us out of Kuwait." This war would be different. "We are on our land. We fight and sacrifice for its sake."[10]

As the year closed, George W. Bush and his advisers decided that the case for war required another round of public persuasion. The White House asked the C.I.A. to prepare a portfolio of damning evidence about Saddam Hussein's weapons work, terrorism ties, and murderous campaigns against dissent. The administration hoped to fashion an "Adlai Stevenson moment." During the 1962 Cuban missile crisis, John F. Kennedy's ambassador to the U.N. had made a dramatic presentation to the Security Council. Stevenson mounted declassified aerial photos on an easel to show that Moscow had deployed nuclear missiles on the Caribbean island. The photos offered an aesthetic of authenticity, of state secrets revealed. Perhaps a similar closing argument for war could be fashioned against Saddam. On December 21, in the Oval Office, George Tenet and his deputy, John McLaughlin, met Bush, Cheney, Rice, and other advisers to share an initial draft of their best evidence.

McLaughlin walked through the material. He was an amateur magician capable of dazzling audiences, but at this consequential session, his performance was sober and dry. In any event, the case against

Saddam on WMD was entirely circumstantial—there was nothing as direct as Stevenson's photos. Bush was unimpressed. "Nice try," the president said when McLaughlin was done. "It's not something that Joe Public would understand."

The president turned to Tenet. "This is the best we've got?"

The C.I.A. director was embarrassed. He felt that "we had wasted the president's time by giving him an inferior briefing," he recalled. So he reached for an easy phrase from his years of basketball fandom: making a powerful case about Saddam's guilt, he said, was "a slam dunk." He repeated the phrase.

"I believed him," Bush remembered. That Saddam possessed nuclear, chemical, and biological weapons "was nearly a universal consensus." The president admitted later that he should have challenged the intelligence and his own assumptions, but at the time, he asked himself: *If Saddam doesn't actually have WMD, why on earth would he subject himself to a war he will almost certainly lose?*[11]

Over the winter holidays, Condoleezza Rice thought about whether the Bush administration should give up on the U.N. Tony Blair still wanted a second Security Council resolution that would effectively authorize a war against Iraq, on the basis that Saddam had failed to meet the U.N.'s latest demands. Blair had made clear that Britain could not join an invasion if the U.S. did not at least try for a second resolution. Early in January, as a result of her holiday reflections, Rice concluded that "a second resolution was necessary for American interests," too, because the U.S. public was "not necessarily fully on board for an attack on Iraq."

Blair agreed that the public case for war remained inadequate. "People suspect U.S. motives," he wrote to Downing Street colleagues on January 4. They "don't accept Saddam is a threat" and "worry it will make us a target. Yet the truth is, removing Saddam is right; he is a threat, and WMD has to be countered. So there is a big job of persuasion."[12]

Five days later, Blair met Richard Dearlove. He again asked his spy-master about the chances of finding a "silver bullet" in Iraq, meaning irrefutable evidence of Saddam's guilt that would turn international opinion. Dearlove raised his earlier forecast: he now felt the odds of a last-minute breakthrough were about 50 percent.

"Richard, my fate is in your hands," Blair told him.[13]

The Bush administration hoped to crack Saddam's wall of secrecy by interviewing Iraqi scientists outside the country. Bush spoke pub-licly about this effort, and his negotiators had inserted a line in the au-tumn U.N. resolution that permitted (but did not require) Hans Blix and Mohamed ElBaradei to arrange for such meetings. The chief weap-ons inspectors could facilitate "the travel of those interviewed and fam-ily members." Weapons scientists might confess and defect if they believed their families would be safe.

Paul Wolfowitz told Blix that summoning key nuclear- or biological-weapons scientists would be "like issuing a subpoena." Wolfowitz un-derstood Saddam's dictatorship well enough to know that interviews with scientists abroad would rattle Saddam by provoking his chronic fears of spying and uncontrollable dissent. Even if the gambit didn't produce revelatory confessions, it was a test of inspection procedure that Saddam was likely to fail, and that in turn would strengthen Washington's case for war.[14]

As an investigative technique, Blix thought such interviews were unsound. He told Rice that "even if a scientist came out with a family of twelve, he could still have an uncle somewhere in Iraq whose life could be threatened." Blix was right that Iraqi families could not be defined by a single household in a situation like this and that any scien-tist weighing defection would have to consider the dishonor that would befall them if extended family members suffered on their account. Blix also worried that televised images of international inspectors coercing scientists to leave Iraq for interviews would damage the

U.N.'s reputation. But Rice "stressed that this might be the only way to get honest statements," Blix recalled. The matter became his starkest disagreement with the White House.[15]

It also created strains at the highest levels of Saddam's regime, as Wolfowitz and others in Washington had hoped. In January, Saddam appointed a new committee, chaired by Taha Yassin Ramadan, to manage Iraq's relations with the U.N. He named Jafar Dhia Jafar, Tariq Aziz, and Qusay as members. At a session devoted to the matter of scientist interviews, Qusay said that "we could not trust the scientists, especially if they are interviewed outside Iraq with the company of their families." Qusay feared that "some of them could deliver false information" invented to win favor from Iraq's enemies. They decided to refer the question to Saddam personally.[16]

Iraqi scientists well understood that their lives would now depend on how they handled U.N. demands for interviews. Mahdi Obeidi, the nuclear physicist, attended a briefing by Abd al-Tawab Mullah Huwaysh, the deputy prime minister. Huwaysh stared meaningfully at Obeidi as he spoke.

"Let the scientists leave Iraq to meet the inspectors," Huwaysh said.

He drew a finger silently across his throat. "Their families will stay here."[17]

Ramadan soon received an answer from Saddam about interviews abroad. To convey the decision, he called a meeting of about five hundred scientists and engineers. They assembled at the Great Conference Hall in Baghdad. Ramadan "ordered that the meeting be closed," Jafar recalled. He sent administrative and security staff, including his own bodyguards, outside. Ramadan spoke for ninety minutes. His main message—one he repeated several times—was that Saddam was "willing to go to war not to allow any scientist" to be interviewed outside the country.

All scientists were ordered to henceforth refuse such requests. If summoned, they should demand that a colleague join as a witness. If this proved impossible to arrange, the scientist "must record the entire meeting on an electronic recording device and hand it over" to the National Monitoring Directorate, the body charged with managing U.N. inspectors.[18]

In the end, Saddam's qualified acceptance of interviews inside Iraq and Blix's skepticism about Washington's plan to force Iraqis to go abroad eased the pressure on scientists. When Obeidi was summoned, he appeared alone and ran a tape recorder. The inspectors queried him at length about the imported aluminum tubes that had become such a visible part of the evidence Washington cited to argue that Iraq had reactivated its atomic-bomb program. Obeidi "explained the major flaws" in the assumptions of Western intelligence analysts, but his interrogators "were like racehorses wearing blinders."[19]

T he president has made the decision to go after Saddam Hussein," Vice President Dick Cheney told Prince Bandar, the Saudi ambassador to Washington, at a meeting in the West Wing on January 11, 2003. There was no formal announcement, but Bush had firmly decided to invade. Two days later, after a group discussion in the Oval Office, the president asked Colin Powell to stay behind. "I really think I'm going to have to do this," Bush said when they were alone.

"Are you with me on this?" the president asked. "I want you with me."

"I'm with you, Mr. President," Powell assured him.[20]

His decision was no surprise; Powell was a career soldier steeped in the disciplines of command. But it was a consequential choice. No one in Bush's cabinet had more pointedly worried aloud about the potential costs of war with Iraq. No one in the cabinet had greater public credibility. The invasion and occupation plan that Bush had developed violated Powell's storied principles for successful military action: there was no clear exit. If Powell had resigned that winter, as the journalist Robert Draper has written, he might have touched off a chain of political events that could have disrupted the momentum for war and perhaps even stopped it. But "loyalty is a trait that I value," Powell explained later. Moreover, he accepted Bush's judgment that, after

9/11, even though nothing connected Saddam to Bin Laden, Saddam's reign could not be tolerated.[21]

As war appeared inevitable, French president Jacques Chirac kept his options open. He did not rule out committing his troops to a U.S.-led invasion "if military intervention . . . turned out to be legitimate," as he put it later. He was presumably thinking about scenarios such as Tony Blair's "silver bullet," a late-breaking discovery that Saddam was actively building an atomic bomb or germ weapons. That winter, Chirac dispatched aides on a discreet trip to Washington to check in on military planning for Iraq. They received a "courteous and attentive" reception, but the Pentagon made clear that time was running out, and it would soon be impossible to "reserve spaces for French forces." In mid-January, he sent the career diplomat Maurice Gourdault-Montagne to consult with Condoleezza Rice.

A "final phase" of diplomacy was now at hand, Rice said, as they returned to the U.N. for a second resolution. Gourdault-Montagne reported her entreaty to Paris: "The credibility of the United States is at stake. Everyone knows that Saddam Hussein cheats and hides. If we do not act, the countries of the region and of the whole world will note our weakness. . . . We refuse to postpone the inevitable."

At this point, Rice added, the only way to avoid war "would be the immediate departure of Saddam and all his team" from Iraq, followed by the creation of a democratic government. "There has to be a change of government," she said. "After a while, we can lift the sanctions."

At the Pentagon, Gourdault-Montagne met Paul Wolfowitz. The French envoy argued that the U.N. weapons inspectors now back on the job in Iraq could continue to deter Saddam from threatening other nations. They should be afforded more time. Referring to Hans Blix, Wolfowitz asked sarcastically, "Why put your foreign policy in the hands of a Swedish diplomat with fewer men than the police of a provincial French town?"

A few days later, Blix and Mohamed ElBaradei flew to Paris. A

phalanx of police vehicles escorted them to the Élysée. Gourdault-
Montagne's report from Washington only reinforced Chirac's convic-
tion that the Bush administration had adopted "a dominating and
Manichean logic that favored force over law."[22]

Blix briefed Chirac about inspections to date. Though cooperative,
the Iraqis had still failed to resolve the major historical questions. Blix
noted that "a number of intelligence services," including France's, "were
convinced that weapons of mass destruction remained in Iraq." But neither Blix nor ElBaradei had found any evidence.

Chirac distanced himself from his own spies. France did not have
any "serious evidence" that Saddam had retained nuclear, chemical, or
biological weapons, he said. Spy agencies sometimes "intoxicate each
other," he remarked. Personally, Chirac did not believe that Iraq had
retained any WMD. Saddam, however, was "locked up in an intellectual bunker," he continued. If war came, it would inevitably lead to
Saddam's elimination, he predicted.[23]

The political and diplomatic struggle with France offered a rallying cause for U.N. skeptics in Washington. (The cafeterias in the
Republican-controlled House of Representatives would rechristen the
french fries on its menu "freedom fries.") On January 23, British foreign secretary Jack Straw met Dick Cheney in Washington. Cheney
made little effort to hide his frustration that Washington found itself
entangled with Chirac. To have any hope of passing an acceptable second resolution, American diplomats now had to lobby for votes among
the rotating members of the Security Council—Chile, Mexico, Guinea,
Cameroon, and others. Bush "could not let a charade continue," Cheney
declared. He "could not let France and Germany dictate policy."

If France vetoed a second resolution, it "wouldn't hurt one bit in the
States," Cheney said. It was a gratuitous observation, since it was clear
that the political price of failure at the U.N. would be paid by Blair's
government. War would resolve the big questions, the vice president
continued. Once an invasion started, "the Iraqi regime was likely to fall

apart quickly," he predicted, and "Iraqis would reveal all the WMD now hidden away."[24]

By January, Saddam had grown alarmed enough about the prospect of a ground invasion that he called in cabinet-level economic advisers to review how to protect the $1 billion in cash and four tons of gold stored in the vaults of the Central Bank of Iraq, on Rasheed Street in downtown Baghdad.

The bank was headquartered in a modern, cubed building constructed by Saddam during the 1980s. Over the years, because of Iraq's oil bounty and the character of Saddam's dictatorship, a myth had sprung up that Saddam and his family members had many billions of dollars secreted offshore, in Switzerland or other bank secrecy havens, in the manner of the families of other rich oil potentates and dictators around the world. But Saddam was too paranoid and controlling to allow anyone around him to accumulate a billion-dollar personal fortune overseas. The Central Bank and Iraq's major state-owned firms that traded oil and other materials were the principal account holders of Baathist cash, under Saddam's attentive eye.

During the years when Saddam regarded America and Britain as business partners, if not allies, Iraqi firms held several billion dollars in U.S. and British banks. Those governments froze that money after the invasion of Kuwait. During much of the 1990s, as sanctions and embargoes crushed Iraq's export-dependent economy, the Central Bank and other state-owned entities possessed little cash or gold. Once Saddam signed up for the U.N.'s Oil-for-Food scheme, in 1996, the Central Bank reopened accounts overseas to facilitate trading, but it wasn't until 2001, after Saddam imposed a system of illicit kickbacks on Oil-for-Food importers, that the regime began to accumulate serious amounts of cash.

The kickbacks were initially deposited into Lebanese banks. From time to time after 2001, the Mukhabarat secretly trucked pallets of gold and hard currency from Beirut to Baghdad to store them in the

Central Bank's vaults. To cover such expenditures as overseas travel and international medical treatment for favored individuals, Saddam's office drew on this cash by issuing ad hoc withdrawal orders for amounts ranging from a few thousand dollars to $1 million.

At the January meeting, Saddam ordered that $1 billion in cash be taken out of the vaults, "to avoid the risk of all the money being destroyed in one location in the event of an allied attack," according to later investigations by the Iraq Survey Group. It appears that the money—stacks of $100 and $500 notes—was boxed up for removal at this time, but Saddam delayed taking action.[25]

As with so much else about his preparations, Saddam's effort to create a portable treasury for the guerrilla war that he imagined he might soon lead was late and improvised. The president ordered civil servants—including those working in his office—to undergo guerrilla training. Saman Abdul Majid, the French-educated linguist, received instructions to take part. He spent an initial week marching and a second week learning how to strip a Kalashnikov rifle. "You who are so close to the President, you will have to fight to the last," his trainers insisted. They were given only a few boxes of ammunition, however, and by the third week, they had nothing to do.

Saman Majid held out hope that Saddam would find a way to avoid the looming catastrophe. The president was a pragmatic man, in his experience. That winter, Saddam seemed to be going without sleep. He was writing his new novel while dispatching war preparatives to his staff at all hours of the night. The atmosphere was one of peril and confusion. The C.I.A.'s Iraq Operations Group was now relentlessly dialing the phone numbers of Iraqi officials and military officers, running a spam-marketing version of the cold pitches and "bumps" that diplomats and scientists such as Jafar Dhia Jafar had endured the previous year. Civil servants received messages urging them to defect and join the coming order. The message was clear, Saman Majid recalled: "Iraq's defeat is certain. Why stay on the side of the vanquished? Join us. You will make money, and you will have positions in the free Iraq that we will build together."[26]

On February 5, Colin Powell sat at the circular table in the U.N. Security Council chamber and delivered a seventy-five-minute presentation. This was the C.I.A.-informed "Adlai Stevenson moment" the White House had been considering since at least December. C.I.A. director George Tenet and U.N. ambassador John Negroponte flanked Powell. "My colleagues, every statement I make today is backed up by sources, solid sources," Powell said. "These are not assertions. What we're giving you are facts and conclusions based on solid intelligence."

The infamous litany of invented, misinterpreted, and exaggerated intelligence on which Powell relied that day has been exhaustively documented. The worst falsehoods came during his presentation on biological weapons, the first and longest argument Powell made about Iraq's alleged ongoing WMD programs. Based substantially on the testimony of "Curveball," a D.I.A. source who had been previously flagged as a fabricator, Powell described Iraq's active use of "mobile production facilities used to make biological agents." Here he offered one of his Stevenson-inspired flourishes: "Let me take you inside that intelligence file. . . ." He displayed diagrams of the supposed mobile labs based on "what our sources reported." Iraq was making anthrax by the liter, he charged.

Powell also shared audio excerpts of intercepted conversations among Iraqi security officers—evidence, he said, of ongoing deception by Saddam that was making a fool out of the U.N.:

"They are inspecting the ammunition you have—"

"Yes."

"—for the possibility there are forbidden ammo."

"Yes?"

"For the possibility there is, by chance, forbidden ammo."

"Yes."

"And we sent you a message to inspect the scrap areas and the abandoned areas."

"Yes."

"After you have carried out what is contained in the message . . . destroy the message."

"Yes."

"Because I don't want anyone to see this message."

"Okay, okay."

Powell recapitulated this exchange for his audience, embellishing it with sentences that the transcript he had just displayed did not contain: "Clean out all the areas. . . . Make sure there is nothing there." He then asked his audience why the speakers wanted to destroy their own message. He said it was because they were trying "to leave no evidence behind of the presence of weapons of mass destruction."[27]

In reality, Saddam had created an atmosphere of fear among all of the security officers and scientists who were under orders to remove embarrassing historical files. A mistake could result in severe punishments. Most likely, the anonymous speakers Powell cited before the world as conspirators in a cover-up of WMD had acted as they did because they were afraid of their bosses.

By early February, the teams working for Hans Blix in Iraq had conducted more than three hundred inspections inside Iraq at more than 230 sites. Nuclear specialists reporting to ElBaradei had conducted dozens more. As time passed, Blix found it "amazing" that all they had found were some old, empty chemical warheads, some nuclear documents stashed in one scientist's home, and some illegally imported missile engines—hardly enough to seal the case for war. They had found nothing at the places suggested to them by the C.I.A. and other U.S. intelligence agencies. If his inspectors had even come close to hidden contraband, Blix figured that the Iraqis would have denied them access. That hadn't happened. Personally, Blix "tended to think" that Iraq did possess hidden weapons, but the absence of evidence was beginning to seem to him like evidence of absence.[28]

The day after Powell's presentation, Blix and ElBaradei met Tony

Blair at Downing Street. "It would be paradoxical to go to war for something that might turn out to be very little," Blix said.

Blair was unmoved. If Saddam had few banned weapons or none at all, "he should prove it," the prime minister said.[29]

On February 7, Chirac spoke with Bush. He had found Powell's presentation unpersuasive. The conversation was courteous and calm, but it amounted to dialogue between "two men who had used up all their arguments," Chirac recalled.

"We have two analyses, which lead to war or to peace," Chirac said. "It is a moral problem. . . . It involves two different visions of the world, and we have to accept that—but it should not stop us talking to each other."

After hanging up, Bush recalled thinking: *If a dictator who tortures and gasses his people is not immoral, then who is?*[30]

On February 18, Saddam appeared in Baghdad before an audience of officers from the Mukhabarat. He sought to boost morale and prepare his spies for unconventional war. He spoke at first about "principles" of Iraq's glorious history, particularly its emergence as an Arab nation free of Persian domination. He alluded to his plan of resistance. "Our strategy is reducing our losses," he said. "The enemy will try to land here and there, and try to bombard everything." Iraq would evade such tactics. Leaders could resist by working in small groups hidden among a grove of trees or disguised in the shadows of a wall or house.

He addressed the tradecraft of a spy's life. He described the ideal intelligence officer as a person of brains and subtle fighting skills. With his "considerable linguistic and literary repertoire," a spy should not only write well but also be capable of fighting with weapons and without them. He drew on his own life story to explain how his spy force should continually renew skills needed for unconventional warfare. "I trained in a tank," he said, recounting one of his experiences during the 1968 revolution that brought the Baath Party to power. He "learned how to ride a motorcycle" soon afterward. "You need to have skills in everything," he counseled. Apparently forecasting the requirements of the coming war, he urged his officers to "learn how to ride horses." Faith in God and adherence to Iraq's principles would see them through. "The U.S.A. is the strongest state," Saddam said. "But it is not the most capable."[31]

TWENTY-SEVEN

The Edge of the Abyss

After he was reassigned to Baghdad, Nizar Hamdoon received a cancer diagnosis. It was non-Hodgkin's lymphoma. Saddam soon permitted him to undergo chemotherapy at Memorial Sloan Kettering, the well-regarded cancer center in Manhattan. By the time of 9/11, he was back in Iraq, in remission and preparing to retire.

As war with the United States approached, Hamdoon's cancer returned. He was now in his late fifties. Saddam granted him permission to travel to the U.S. alone. He also sent $5,000 in cash as "a personal gift" to pay for medical treatment. Hamdoon remained "part of the group of people in which I had personal trust and knowledge," Saddam recalled. In New York, the envoy moved in with Mohammed Aldouri at the Iraqi mission's Upper East Side and rested there between hospital stays.[1]

Early in March, he met twice with Charles Duelfer. They had lunch at their old haunt, the Peninsula Hotel, on Fifth Avenue and Fifty-Fifth Street. Saddam saw "war as his destiny," Hamdoon observed. The Iraqi president believed that he could survive and rebound, as he had after the 1991 war. Hamdoon was realistic about what lay ahead, however, and he was thinking forward to a post-Saddam Iraq.

"There are many good people who will continue to operate the ministries if they have guidance," he said. "There cannot be a vacuum. . . . They will expect order." President Bush had recently said that the U.S. would deliver food after an invasion. "The Iraqi people will not want to be fed by the United States," Hamdoon said. "It is symbolic of being subservient."

He offered another word of advice: "You must avoid the tone that you are ruling Iraq. There must be a quick shift to a new Iraqi leadership mechanism. If you do not do this, the United States will be blamed for all that follows."

Duelfer knew that Hamdoon was worried about his wife and daughters back in Baghdad. He asked the envoy to identify his family home in an aerial photograph so that Duelfer could try to put the residence on the Pentagon's no-target list—a list that included places protected by international law, such as foreign embassies. Duelfer did not have "particular faith" in this targeting system, but it was "better than nothing." Hamdoon was able to pick out his house, identifiable because it had a white trailer parked outside.

At the Peninsula, the two men parted. Duelfer never saw Hamdoon again.[2]

In successive actions on February 28 and during the first week of March, the Bush administration expelled three Iraqi intelligence officers working at the New York mission—two posing as diplomats and one as a journalist. That left Mohammed Aldouri and about half a dozen other authentic diplomats and administrative personnel in place. They had to navigate uncertain futures. Officially, of course, Baghdad expected the New York team to serve Saddam as he led Iraq to glorious victory in the coming showdown. As a practical matter, Aldouri and each of his colleagues had to decide among difficult options: defect and seek asylum in the U.S.; seek haven in another country; or remain on duty to see what developed.

Aldouri paid the remaining staff six months' wages in advance, in cash. He gathered them together. "We all have our worries," he said, a participant in the meeting recalled. "I have no wife or children, so I have no reason to go back to Baghdad. But each of you will do what you think is best."[3]

As the denouement neared, Barzan Ibrahim al-Tikriti reflected bitterly on Iraq's fate under his half brother's reign. Following his return from Geneva, he was now effectively confined to Baghdad. He had never fully recovered from his break with Saddam in 1983.

Over dinner, he told Ala Bashir, the artist and physician, that Saddam's fatal flaw had turned out to be his inability to recognize that Israel had become a fact of life in the Middle East. Saddam's dated strategy of uncompromising opposition to Zionism was no longer a practical one. "The problem is Israel's security," Barzan said, as Bashir recalled it. "I've tried time and again to get my brother to understand that the world has changed and that we will be internationally completely sidelined if we can't find a solution that we, the Americans, and the Israelis can live with. But I might as well be talking to the wall."

His observations were insightful. Saddam steered Iraq as if the clock had stopped. Through all kinds of post–Cold War political weather—periods of accommodation between Arab states and Israel, as well as the conflagrations of the intifadas—other pro-Palestinian Sunni nations, such as Turkey and the United Arab Emirates, had managed their interests so as to stoke economic growth and avoid isolation.[4]

In his diary, Barzan wrote, "I have said that President Saddam does not care what happens after him. Yes, this is true to a great extent; but what I want to say, for the sake of accuracy, is that the President in his public or private life uses the edge-of-the-abyss policy. The method is similar to playing Russian roulette. . . . This is his mentality and his management style."[5]

S addam continued to deliver rousing speeches. He proclaimed a new
benefit of three million dinars for wounded soldiers and five million
for martyrs. By mid-March he had finalized a plan for Iraq's defense.
He divided the country into four regions and appointed loyalists—not
military professionals—to command each one. His cousin Ali Hassan
al-Majid would take charge of the southern region. The veteran Izzat
Ibrahim al-Douri would command the northern region. Mizban Khadr
al-Hadi, another Revolutionary Command Council stalwart, would
oversee the center of the country. And Qusay would command the
defense of Baghdad. But as with the earlier plan for the ringed defense
of the capital, there was no operational blueprint.[6]

Saddam's distractedness and fatalism may explain some of his conduct. He may have also distrusted his generals. On March 9, Iraqi intelligence sent a "Top Secret and Urgent" note to Saddam's office
reporting from "trusted sources" that America "has intensified both its
intelligence and technical efforts to identify the movements and whereabouts of the President-leader. . . . The aim of such activities is either to
target him or to capture him alive."[7]

Such reporting only confirmed what Saddam already presumed: the
C.I.A. would again be seeking coupmakers among his generals to terminate the war as quickly as possible. Agency operatives did continue
to cold-call military leaders to urge revolt or passive cooperation with
invading forces. (Lieutenant General Raad Majid al-Hamdani, now
commander of the Second Republican Guard Corps, took a robocall at
home: "There is no way to oppose the United States! Stay in your
home, where you will be safe!" The general hung up.) If Saddam engaged with commanders in detailed war planning that provided insights into his own movements, he might unwittingly aid a treasonous
general. The regional command structure he devised ensured that only
trusted Baathists and family members would be inside his day-to-day
communications loop.[8]

Meanwhile, Saddam's aides brainstormed ideas about how to thwart the Americans and suppress internal threats. A circular from the General Military Intelligence Directorate—citing plans of Al-Quds, a paramilitary force—reported that Iraq would shower the American forces with the same kind of psyop leaflets the U.S. had dropped from its planes, except that the Iraqi ones "will contain anthrax." They also planned to dig trenches around the capital and fill them with oil barrels, "for the purpose of burning and causing mayhem." These were fanciful plans but reflected the sorts of things that Al-Quds leaders were expected to boast about in memoranda. The note also described a dispiriting reality: "Diplomats are leaving Iraq," including Russian ones, and "there is a rumor that some of the children of ministers and high-ranking [businessmen] left Iraq for Russia."[9]

At the U.N., the standoff over a second resolution that would effectively authorize war remained bitterly unresolved. By the end of February, José María Aznar, the center-right prime minister of Spain, had emerged as a critical ally of Bush and Blair. The supporting role of Spain's military during any invasion would be marginal, but Aznar's backing added the endorsement of a major European nation to the Anglo-American partnership.

Blair visited Aznar in Madrid and blew off steam in private about Hans Blix. The Swede "was supposed to be a civil servant but had decided to behave like a politician," Blair fumed, as an aide summarized his remarks. "He is just desperate not to be seen as the person who allowed a war to start." Blair also felt that Blix was "being bullied successfully by the French," whose real purpose in opposing the Iraq invasion was to "build Europe as a power rival to the U.S." and to "shaft" him and Britain.[10]

Blair had secretly agreed with Bush that the invasion could begin on March 17, come what may at the U.N., and regardless of whether or not Britain could join the initial hostilities. Politically, Blair had no choice but to present a war-or-no-war motion before the House of Commons. Labour held a comfortable majority, but if enough Labour members of

Parliament opposed the motion, they might then join with the Tory minority in a no-confidence vote to oust Blair from office. The clock was ticking down, and the reports of the U.N.'s chief weapons inspectors were not helping Blair's position.

On March 7, Mohamed ElBaradei of the I.A.E.A. told the Security Council there were no indications that Iraq had restarted its nuclear-weapons program since the departure of inspectors in 1998. Moreover, the much-publicized intelligence reporting about Iraq's attempt to buy uranium from Niger was based on fraudulent documents originating in Italy. He also declared there was no evidence that Iraq's imports of aluminum tubes had been intended for anything "other than . . . rockets," just as Iraq had claimed. ElBaradei's report was as full a confirmation that Iraq had no active atomic-bomb program as the I.A.E.A. had provided since 9/11, and it was a direct repudiation of the Bush administration's warnings.

Two days later, Blair spoke again with Bush. The president was "clearly very irritated" by the negotiations to win over an adequate number of swing votes for a second resolution at the Security Council. And yet he told the prime minister that he would support his backing out if a resolution were unobtainable. "My last choice is for your government to go down," Bush said. "I would rather go it alone than have your government fall."

"I appreciate that," Blair replied.

"I really mean that."

Blair said he wanted Bush to understand that he "really believed in what they were trying to do."

"I know that, but I am not going to see your government fall on this."[11]

Several days later, Blair met with Jack Straw, his foreign secretary, and David Manning, his national security adviser. Straw said that they had become "victims of hopeless bullying and arrogant diplomacy" by the Bush administration, as a colleague summarized his comments. He noted that Bush, on the telephone call, had offered Blair an exit ramp. "Why don't you take it?"

Blair said he did not want a way out. As he explained his thinking later, "If we backed away now, it would have disastrous consequences for a tough stance on WMD and its proliferation, and for our strategic relationship with the U.S., our key ally."[12]

The C.I.A.'s Iraq Operations Group had set up platoon-size bases in Iraqi Kurdistan in the summer of 2002. Their main mission was to work with the intelligence services and militia of the two major Kurdish parties to run agents across the "green line," the informal demarcation between semiautonomous Kurdistan and Saddam-ruled Iraq. The C.I.A. set up an intelligence center in Sulaymaniyah to funnel source reports through one pipeline.

The Operations Group's total personnel had swollen to about three hundred by March 2003. This was still tiny in comparison to the U.S. military ground force of about 140,000 that President Bush had by now dispatched to Iraq's borders. In Afghanistan, after 9/11, small C.I.A. teams had been first on the ground and had played a major role in guerrilla operations that overthrew the Taliban. In Iraq, by March, the agency had taken on a more traditional wartime role of supporting the Pentagon's main effort: gathering intelligence; training, equipping, and advising auxiliary militias; and running propaganda or influence operations to soften up Iraqi resistance when the shooting started.[13]

For a decade, Iraq had been a "denied area" for C.I.A. intelligence collectors. Now the impending war opened the gates. Iraqi Army officers crossed into Kurdistan by the dozen to volunteer as C.I.A. agents—often on condition that they be resettled in America immediately. But the C.I.A. wanted active agents who would continue to report from inside Baathist Iraq, not defectors looking to emigrate. Ultimately, between the Kurdish spy networks and new recruits willing to go back in, the C.I.A. was generating ninety to one hundred intelligence reports a month—as many as the Operations Group had earlier generated in a full year. By March, it "had recruited or debriefed literally hundreds of individuals," according to Charles "Sam" Faddis, a C.I.A. team leader in Kurdistan.[14]

The agency set up other forward teams in Jordan and Kuwait. The unit based in Amman built a clandestine base in the desert near the Iraq frontier. But the best intelligence came out of Iraqi Kurdistan, and most of that was derived from work with Jalal Talabani.

The C.I.A. had endured costly failures in agent communication during the 1990s. Even in the best of circumstances, passing messages through intermediaries—smugglers, truckers, businessmen—often resulted in confusion. Direct communication with agents would avoid that, but first-rate encrypted communication gear was too sensitive to be entrusted to the lightly vetted ad hoc informants that the C.I.A. was now taking on board. The C.I.A.'s Kurdistan teams took to handing out prepaid commercial satellite phones, mainly Thurayas, to Iraqi agents.

"We flooded Iraq with satellite phones, giving us real-time communications from Kurdistan with sources across the length and breadth of Iraq," Faddis recalled. The operational risks were diverse. Some Iraqi agents telephoned relatives in America more often than they called their C.I.A. handlers. Others were "sloppy and got caught by Iraqi security with a phone for which they had no possible legitimate use," according to Faddis. "That ended badly for them." Iraqi forces arrested one C.I.A. asset, tortured him, paraded him on state TV, and warned that anyone caught with a Thuraya would be executed. After that, one C.I.A. team in Kurdistan never heard from about a third of the phones it had distributed. These high-risk wartime "cases," or agent recruitments, were a far cry from the patient, meticulous Cold War espionage tradecraft romanticized in fiction and film.[15]

The C.I.A. did act boldly. The Czech Republic agreed to provide diplomatic cover in its Baghdad embassy for a career C.I.A. operations officer of Czech descent. The officer did not risk trying to recruit Iraqi agents but made observations about Iraqi preparations to defend Baghdad.[16]

The agency's propaganda operations against Saddam's regime—exile radio stations, leaflets, and the like—had never been effective. Saddam's control of Iraqi airwaves, newspapers, public art, and publishing houses overwhelmed outside broadcasts. Nonetheless, the C.I.A. teams again set up radio stations and even loudspeakers that broadcast the Eagles and Sheryl Crow into Baathist territory. The idea, as Faddis put it, was to signal to Iraqi Army officers and civilians alike that "the Americans were here; they weren't afraid, and they weren't leaving until they had Saddam's head on a platter."[17]

The spam dialing of Iraqi phone numbers could seem ineffectual, too, but overall, this aspect of the C.I.A.'s influence operations appears to have worked, at least as a complement to the available public news reporting about the coming war, which on its own may have led many Iraqi officers and civil servants to think twice about dying in another of Saddam's doomed causes. Because CENTCOM did not have enough troops to manage thousands of Iraqi prisoners of war, the C.I.A. pivoted to a leaflet and robocall operation that sought to persuade Iraqi officers and soldiers to "get out of your uniform and go home" rather than surrender. Ultimately, many Iraqi soldiers and civil servants did just that. Whatever their motivations, they could feel relatively safe staying home or visiting relatives in the Iraqi countryside, since this behavior would be consistent with the guerrilla strategy that Saddam had pressed upon Iraq in his orders and speeches that winter.

The Bush administration's plan was riddled with bad assumptions, but one of the largest blind spots involved Iran. Even though Tehran's ayatollahs had been seeking Saddam's overthrow for more than two decades, the president and his advisers failed to think through how Iran would exploit this outcome. For its part, the C.I.A. had never prepared to challenge the ambitious plans of Iran's security services to influence post-Saddam politics and to oppose an American occupation. The agency had been directed away from postwar planning and the focus was on the conventional war that was about to erupt.

The C.I.A. teams trained and equipped Kurdish militia to conduct sabotage operations across the green line once hostilities began. As D-Day neared, responsibility for day-to-day C.I.A. operations shifted from headquarters to Charlie Seidel, the agency Arabist who had been designated as the next chief of station in Baghdad. Seidel embedded with CENTCOM's war command in Kuwait. It would be his second on-the-ground leadership role in a U.S. war against Saddam.[18]

The invasion's approach brought a measure of closure to the C.I.A.'s entanglement in Saddam-era Iraq. It was a mission that had evolved over two decades from stealthy success to well-publicized failure. In 1982, when Tom Twetten landed in Baghdad on King Hussein's jet, hoping to help Saddam avoid losing his war with Iran, the C.I.A.'s mission had been well defined and realistically designed. For years, Twetten and his colleagues, followed by the D.I.A., had used secrecy and America's technological advantages to thwart the expansion of a hostile Iranian revolution. Perhaps the C.I.A. never would have overcome Saddam's mistrust, but if the Reagan White House hadn't conceived the foolhardy and criminal scheme that became known as Iran-Contra, the agency might have helped Washington learn how to contain and perhaps even manage Saddam for the sake of regional stability. That was certainly George H. W. Bush's intention until Saddam invaded Kuwait. Saddam's missile attacks on Saudi Arabia and Israel during that war, and the discovery of his nuclear-weapons program afterward, led Bush to give up on managing Saddam. He turned to the C.I.A. to accomplish what he had decided not to seek by military force—Saddam's death or removal from office. As Twetten noted at the time, the resort to C.I.A. coupmaking in Iraq violated the oft-repeated lesson that covert action rarely worked when it was used as a cheap, deniable substitute for whole-of-government foreign and military policy. Still, the C.I.A.'s tragic and embarrassing failures in Iraq during the Clinton years did not cause the invasion of 2003. After 9/11, the only lesson George W. Bush took from the agency's history in Iraq—a lesson instilled in him by the likes of George Tenet himself—was that there was no easy way to remove Saddam through covert action, and if the president really wanted him gone, he would have to order a full-scale invasion.

The United Nations had failed to prevent war. Renewed inspections, as well as the efforts of Blix and ElBaradei, had not dissuaded the Bush administration. Yet there was one notion about how to avoid or at least shorten armed conflict that refused to die: the hope that Saddam might be induced to voluntarily give up power and perhaps go into exile. The scenario held the same appeal that coup plots had earlier— snap, problem solved.

Early in March, Vladimir Putin wrote a letter to Saddam proposing that he step down as president of Iraq and become chairman of the Baath Party. The formulation was clever—Putin offered Saddam a face-saving outcome that did not require the Iraqi leader to depart his homeland in humiliation. If Saddam accepted, his resignation from the presidency might shake things up enough to delay or complicate a military invasion, expanding Russian influence and undermining the United States. Yevgeny Primakov, Saddam's longtime acquaintance, carried Putin's letter to Baghdad. He told Saddam that Russia's purpose was to persuade the Bush administration not to attack.

Saddam walked out of the room, leaving Primakov to stew, and then returned with Tariq Aziz, Taha Yassin Ramadan, and other Baath Party comrades. He asked Primakov to read Putin's letter aloud, according to Abid Hamid Mahmud, the presidential secretary. The Baathist leaders then dutifully proclaimed their "extreme displeasure" with Putin's ideas and their "strong support" for their president-leader's continuation in office. Primakov left empty-handed.[19]

Apart from Kuwait, Iraq's Arab neighbors did not want America to invade. They feared (with reason) that Saddam's overthrow would destabilize the region and empower Iran, which in turn might inflame Shiite minority populations in Saudi Arabia and elsewhere. Turkey did not want a war, either, fearing (also with reason) that America's intervention would further empower independence-minded Kurds, including violent separatists inside Turkey. Leaders in Ankara, Riyadh, Amman,

Cairo, and elsewhere brainstormed about how to persuade Saddam to go into exile and thus prevent a chaotic rupture in Baghdad.

At one point that winter, Gamal Mubarak, a son of the Egyptian president, visited Bush at the White House. He outlined a plan devised by Saudi Arabia, Jordan, and Turkey to ease Saddam into exile in Egypt. The Iraqi leader would be accompanied by family members and cushioned by a $2 billion nest egg. Bush initially bristled, saying that the U.S. would not offer protection to Saddam or assurances to his prospective hosts. Later, the White House reconsidered. Donald Rumsfeld supported such a plan. "To the very end" of the run-up to war, the secretary of defense "thought, or at least hoped," that Saddam might prefer exile over "the risk of capture and death." Rumsfeld accepted that it "would not be easy to stomach Saddam sipping Campari on the coast of southern France, but if his comfortable exile meant sparing the world—and thousands of American men and women in uniform—a war, I was all for it."[20]

Luis Rueda at the C.I.A. thought that Saddam was unlikely to go. The Iraqi president had announced plans for a guerrilla war against America that reflected his self-identification as a revolutionary hero. He had survived numerous attempts against his life, real and imagined. "He's got a bigger set of balls than most world leaders," as Rueda put it. "He's not going to walk away."

As war approached, a "Middle Eastern government" offered to send Saddam to Belarus with $1 billion to $2 billion, Bush recounted later. The idea "looked like it might gain traction." The details remain obscure, yet it seems all but certain that Saddam never took the proposal seriously.[21]

For Bush, the offer of exile provided a last opportunity to declare publicly that he was willing to forgo war if Saddam gave up power. On March 17, in a national address, the president issued his final ultimatum: "In recent days, some governments in the Middle East have been doing their part. They have delivered public and private messages urging the dictator to leave," Bush said. "Saddam Hussein and his sons must leave Iraq within forty-eight hours. Their refusal to do so will result in military conflict." The invasion now had a definite start date.

The following day, after admitting publicly that a second U.N. resolution had proved impossible to obtain, Tony Blair put his war motion before the House of Commons. It passed comfortably, 412–149. A quarter of Labour M.P.s voted against invasion, well short of the number necessary to threaten Blair's hold on office.

"Landslide!" Bush exclaimed when he spoke with the prime minister. He recalled the "cojones conference" at Camp David a year earlier. "You showed cojones, you never blinked. A leader who leads will win, and you are a real leader."

Blair had what he had expended so much effort to achieve: armed action, if necessary, to disarm Iraq of WMD, cementing under pressure Britain's alliance with America.[22]

At Saddam's last cabinet meeting before the war began, he told his ministers, "Resist one week and after that I will take over." He also instructed his generals "to hold the coalition for eight days and leave the rest to him," recalled Abd al-Tawab Mullah Huwaysh, the deputy prime minister. The clear implication, Huwaysh thought, was that Saddam had a secret weapon that would devastate American-led forces.[23]

Saddam was probably only referring to his plan to go underground and lead a guerrilla war. He had a canny grasp of how to call on national pride to rally his countrymen. Yet he bathed in the delusion that he was beloved. This led him to think that the Iraqi people would now take up arms in his name and hurl themselves into the treads of American tanks. Saddam's expectation of popular Iraqi resistance to American occupation was in some respects prescient, but it was also premature and distorted by his self-regard.

After Bush issued his forty-eight-hour ultimatum, Saddam finally ordered Qusay to move the boxes of money in the Central Bank's vault to various ministries for safekeeping and possible dispersal. Qusay appeared at the bank on the night of March 19 and loaded about $1 billion in dollars and euros into vehicles. The Ministry of Trade received eight boxes. All but about $130 million of the boxed cash was eventually recovered.[24]

The last book Saddam requested from his press office was Ho Chi Minh's *Guerrilla Tactics*. He published a few poems from underground, but his main literary endeavor that March was the completion of his fourth novel, *Get Out, Damned One!*, a work of allegory and propaganda aimed at rallying the nation to insurgency. Two days before the bombs fell, Saddam authorized his press aides to move to "an anonymous house in a bourgeois neighborhood" in Baghdad, as Saman Majid described it. Saddam took refuge in a "large house in Mansour," the upscale enclave he had long frequented. His translator worked during that interval on edits to the new novel. "He was still sending us tens of handwritten pages," Saman Majid recalled.[25]

Set in ancient Babylon, *Get Out, Damned One!* tells of a visionary figure named Ibrahim and his three grandsons, who represent Judaism, Christianity, and Islam. Hasqil, the Jew, is another vehicle for Saddam's crude antisemitism. Hasqil is a cheapskate who attempts rape, prays to a bag of gold coins, and profiteers by inciting wars and then selling weapons to the belligerents. His "desperate tribe" is backed by the imperial Romans (read: America), but righteous Arab resisters ultimately defeat them.

As he prepared to go underground, Saddam raced to the presses against the invasion deadline. *Get Out, Damned One!* might be abysmal fiction, but it was not a publishing or propaganda failure. Saddam's aides managed to print forty thousand copies.[26]

There was something about the lure of killing Saddam Hussein—a clean shot, a silver bullet—that repeatedly attracted American decision-makers. On the day Blair won his go-to-war motion in the House of Commons, sources reporting to C.I.A. teams in Kurdistan offered a fresh opportunity. The network of Sufi clansmen operating under the cryptonym DB ROCKSTARS had placed a source on

Qusay's security detail. A second source monitored S.S.O. communications. That source could tell when the elite bodyguard shut off telecommunications in an area to which Saddam was about to travel. The shutdown was designed to prevent prospective coupmakers from calling one another, or so the source believed. On March 18, the source reported that Saddam appeared to be headed for Dora Farms, a family compound southeast of the capital. The source in Qusay's detail was in touch with a third source at the farm, and this man confirmed that some sort of important gathering seemed to be afoot. The C.I.A. then ordered satellite photography of the farm. The imagery revealed about thirty to forty security vehicles parked amidst palm trees.[27]

George Tenet, Luis Rueda, and two other senior C.I.A. leaders, John McLaughlin and Stephen Kappes, rode to the Pentagon. They briefed Donald Rumsfeld and Richard Myers, a U.S. Air Force general and chairman of the Joint Chiefs. They discussed the uncertainties, Rumsfeld remembered: "Suppose it turned out that Saddam was meeting at the compound to comply with the president's ultimatum to resign and leave Iraq? What if it turned out to be a civilian target? What if our aircraft accidentally killed innocent Iraqis and Saddam got away?"[28]

Rumsfeld and Tenet nonetheless agreed that the intelligence was solid enough to bring to Bush, so they went to the White House. The president, Rice, Cheney, Powell, and Andrew Card, the chief of staff, met them in the dining room off the Oval Office. Tenet bent over a map as he described the C.I.A.'s sourcing. They again discussed the uncertainties but also the rarity of having real-time evidence of Saddam's location.

It seemed clear by now that Saddam would not comply with Bush's ultimatum to leave Iraq. He "had made his choice," Rumsfeld recalled thinking. The invasion was scheduled to begin within hours anyway. The C.I.A.'s source information included a large amount of inference and hearsay, but the appeal of a clean kill and a shortened war that could save American and Iraqi lives cemented the group's consensus.

Bush polled his advisers. They all urged him to strike. They would be improvising a jump start to the war, but the planned invasion would go forward without serious disruption, no matter what happened at Dora Farms.

The president cleared the room and asked Cheney what he thought. "I think we ought to go for it," he said.[29]

Bush gave the order shortly after 7:00 p.m. Washington time, just after 2 a.m. in Iraq. Two American F-117 stealth fighters carrying two-thousand-pound precision-guided bombs lifted off from an airbase in Qatar. General Tommy Franks, the war commander, also launched about forty cruise missiles at the target and Iraqi defenses. He decided not to strike the farm's main building, however, fearing that women and children might be inside.

Air-raid sirens soon sounded in Baghdad as Iraq's air defenses detected the incoming missiles. Antiaircraft guns erupted across the capital.

The attack on Dora Farms killed one of the C.I.A. sources on the ground who had helped bring the strike about. Saddam Hussein was not there.

Bush appeared on national television from the Oval Office soon after the F-117 pilots had safely cleared Iraqi airspace. "America faces an enemy who has no regard for conventions of war or rules of morality," Bush said of Saddam Hussein as he announced the start of America's invasion and occupation of Iraq. "This will not be a campaign of half measures, and we will accept no outcome but victory."

Epilogue

I n the winter of 2003, Jafar Dhia Jafar had felt that war was inevitable. It seemed to him that the Bush administration was using the WMD issue as a pretense to overthrow Saddam. Only a willful desire to ignore all the thousands of pages of declarations and seized documents, as well as the countless inspections and testimonies provided by scientists like himself, could explain the decision to invade, he believed. In any event, war was coming, and Jafar knew from past attacks that once the Americans started bombing, his house near the Republican Palace would sustain damage—shattered windows, at a minimum. He initially decided to shelter with his wife and daughter at an orchard he owned near the Tuwaitha nuclear complex, not far from the Tigris. He started to think seriously about leaving Iraq. They had all heard Saddam's calls for guerrilla resistance, but at sixty, he had no appetite to take up arms.[1]

Jafar had a potential lifeline outside Iraq. His younger brother Hamid was a successful businessman in the United Arab Emirates. He had been educated at Cambridge University and had founded Crescent Petroleum, one of the largest family-owned oil-and-gas companies in the Middle East. A few years earlier, Hamid had sent Jafar a satellite phone for emergencies, but Jafar had never activated it. In late March, he turned it on.

U.S. troops were by now driving through central Iraq toward Baghdad, meeting only sporadic or ineffective opposition. Jafar considered
how he and his family might escape and make their way to the U.A.E.
He discussed his plan with his friend and colleague Amir al-Saadi, the
British-educated chemist. Saadi's German wife was with him in Iraq.

"I'm staying," he told Jafar. "If they take over Baghdad, then I will
give myself up in front of the TV cameras. We have nothing, so what
are we afraid of?"

"Yes, you can say that, but once they grab you, they won't let you
out," Jafar said. "They don't want anybody to know that we have nothing. . . . The people from Afghanistan—they're still in custody, and
they probably had nothing as well."[2]

Saadi said he would stick with his plan. During the 1990s, Saadi
had become a high-profile figure as a liaison between Iraq and U.N.
weapons inspectors. That visibility should offer some measure of protection, along with his wife's German citizenship, he told Jafar. He felt
that surrendering in front of German journalists would be the best
course, if it came to that.

Jafar decided to head for the border. He consulted another friend,
Amer Mohammed Rasheed al-Obeidi, the minister of oil. The ministry had a housing estate near Mosul, not far from Syria. Jafar asked
Obeidi to write a letter that would authorize his family to stay there,
and Obeidi agreed. On April 2, the Jafars and a few bodyguards departed in three cars toward the North.[3]

At the housing estate, Ministry of Oil staff welcomed Jafar, but
after he had settled in, security men came to talk. They feared his presence might endanger the facility. Jafar was not on the infamous American "deck of cards," the portable most-wanted list of fifty-two figures
from Saddam's regime that had been handed out to U.S. soldiers and
others. (Saadi was the seven of diamonds; Obeidi, the minister of oil,
was the six of spades.) Yet the physicist was famous enough to motivate
informers who might be looking for a C.I.A. payday. "They might bomb
this place," the security men warned, explaining why Jafar's presence
was a liability.

"Okay, I'm going to stay only one night," Jafar assured them.

He had a friend near the Syrian border, the sheikh of an influential tribe. During the 1990s, Jafar had helped build an irrigation facility that benefited the sheikh's followers. His friend now received him. The sheikh invited the Iraqi officer in charge of the Syrian border in his area.

The officer listened to Jafar's request to cross out of Iraq but said he could not help without permission from Saddam's regime. American forces were approaching Baghdad, but Saddam and his top aides were still asserting authority from underground. If the officer let Jafar leave without permission and was found out, "I'll be executed," he said.[4]

The gods of war were with Jafar this time. That night, American warplanes struck Iraqi targets near the Syrian border. The telephone lines were cut, Jafar was told, and since the officer could not call to ask permission, he changed his mind. Jafar and his family passed through a border post and made their way to Aleppo. His brother arranged transport to Damascus, where they boarded an Emirates Airlines flight to Dubai. They arrived on Thursday, April 10, as U.S. forces seized Baghdad and the remaining Iraqi Army soldiers and militia fighting in the capital melted away.

Jafar heard from American and British officials soon after he checked into a comfortable hotel booked by his brother. Hamid arranged a suite and sat in on the meeting.

"Do you have an atom bomb?" Jafar's initial visitors asked him. They seemed to be joking—more or less.[5]

His first interrogators weren't experts on Iraq's nuclear program. Back at C.I.A. headquarters, Scott McLaughlin, the former weapons inspector in Iraq who was now a C.I.A. analyst, learned of Jafar's arrival. McLaughlin and the chief nuclear analyst at the C.I.A.'s arms-control unit quickly scrambled onto a flight to Dubai.

The two agency men questioned Jafar in the hotel suite for about five days. They had two big questions: Did you resume enrichment of atomic-bomb fuel? Did you resume work on weapons design? Jafar's answer was an unqualified no.[6]

"He's a very gracious man," McLaughlin recalled of their days together, "but there were times when he would get very annoyed that we
were coming back to the same questions."

Eventually, the C.I.A. analysts asked Jafar if he would submit to a
polygraph examination. Although "lie detector" test results are not ad-
missible in American courts because of their unreliability, the C.I.A.
used them routinely to vet sources and to monitor career employees for
deception that could indicate betrayal. Although it was another affront
to Jafar's dignity, the physicist agreed. He passed—no deception.

The C.I.A. saw no reason to recommend further action against Jafar. The scientist was out of Iraq and a guest of an allied nation. He was
not a war criminal. Hamid would produce him whenever American or
British investigators needed to speak to him, they were assured.

Back in Washington, D.I.A. colleagues initially taunted McLaughlin for crediting Jafar's testimony that Iraq had no bomb program, haz-
ing that continued even after the polygraph results appeared to confirm
the scientist's account. But McLaughlin was in "analyst mode" after the
interviews in Dubai. He knew what Jafar had said. He had the polygraph results. Probably, then, what Jafar had told them was true.

McLaughlin realized what that meant: "We made a terrible mistake."[7]

In assigning responsibility for all that followed the American-led invasion of 2003, it is right to focus first on the decisions taken by George
W. Bush after 9/11, and on the actors and institutions that enabled
those decisions. The president careered toward an unnecessary war
that he and his war cabinet marketed through exaggerations of available evidence and unabashed fearmongering, persuaded as they were
by instinct and flawed intelligence that Saddam's continuation in power
posed an unacceptable threat. As Bush proclaimed repeatedly, it was
his decision alone, as commander in chief, to overthrow Saddam Hussein by military force and to impose a direct occupation of Iraq. America was traumatized and fearful, and the president's actions were

initially popular. Yet it was not public opinion, media cheerleading, or domestic politics that propelled Bush to invade—this was a war of presidential choice.

Could Bush imagine at the time what the invasion might unleash or the human toll it would exact? This seems doubtful. Between 2003 and 2023, about two hundred thousand civilians—nearly all Iraqi—died in the multisided violence and civil conflicts that followed the invasion. More than forty-four hundred American soldiers, Marines, and airmen died in combat in Iraq, along with several thousand contractors, and more than thirty thousand were wounded. Advances in force protection and battlefield medicine meant that many of the American wounded, although fortunate to survive, suffered severe, often lifelong injuries, including traumatic brain injuries and the loss of arms and legs. And the deaths and injuries unleashed by the invasion are only one dimension of the war's impact on Iraq, the Middle East, and America. The invasion and occupation relieved Iraq of Saddam's tyranny and empowered Kurds and the country's long-suppressed Shia majority, but it also further fragmented the Iraqi state, invited Iranian interference, strengthened al-Qaeda for a time, and contributed to the birth of the Islamic State, among other destabilizing consequences that undermined the security of America and its allies. Two decades on, there are many additional and important Iraqi perspectives on the invasion and its aftermath, but in measuring the interests of the United States, Bush's decision still looks like a catastrophe.

Yet the president did not act because of 9/11 alone. His administration inherited a long, unfinished war with Saddam Hussein, certainly as Saddam defined it. The Iraqi leader saw himself resisting an American imperialism motivated by a thirst for oil and manipulated by Zionism's conspiratorial hand. After the Soviet Union's collapse, the Gulf War, and the discovery of Saddam's secret nuclear-bomb program, Bill Clinton embraced the United Nations–endorsed regime of sanctions and disarmament established by his predecessor. Yet the struggle with Saddam proved impossible to stabilize, in part because of the devastating humanitarian impacts of sanctions. Clinton outsourced much of

American policy to the U.N. Led by Rolf Ekéus, the Special Commission disarmed Iraq coercively—a landmark in arms-control history—and yet the commission was unaware of the scope of its achievements and ended in strategic failure.

The recent disclosure of extensive records documenting Saddam's side raises the question of whether Washington might have managed the struggle differently, so that after the 9/11 attacks, Saddam might not have loomed as such an estranged and threatening figure—an enemy so singular that his elimination from office was written into American law, endorsed by Democrats and Republicans alike. That is to ask, why did America fail to contain Saddam Hussein in the way that it managed to contain the rulers of North Korea, Libya, and Syria? The answer cannot be that Saddam was, by comparison with the difficult leaders of those countries, utterly unmanageable. Call it realism or a devil's bargain, but the Iraqi leader rewarded American corporations and found some common ground with the Reagan and George H. W. Bush administrations for nearly a decade, an arrangement rooted in shared interests that likely would have survived if Saddam had not invaded Kuwait.

Perhaps the catastrophic turning point of the Kuwait invasion was unavoidable, given Saddam's secrecy and appetite for the emirate's wealth. Some will argue that the Kuwait invasion and the atomic-bomb program it ultimately revealed offered ample evidence that Iraq posed an unacceptable threat to American interests and global peace so long as Saddam remained in power. Certainly, Saddam's aggression, hostility toward Israel, and suspicion of the United States were unalterable, as the records recently made available from his regime make plain. Yet what if America had stopped Saddam from invading Kuwait in the first place? Speculating about counterfactual history is an exercise in unreliable what-ifs, but it seems clear that Saddam could be deterred from acting on his most dangerous ideas. The George H. W. Bush administration successfully dissuaded him from using WMD during the war over Kuwait. Israel also deterred him from loading his Scud missiles with chemical or biological weapons. It seems likely that if the United States had been able, in the spring and summer of 1990, to clearly describe for Saddam what would happen to his regime if he invaded Kuwait, he would not have done it.

The Clinton administration believed that its enforcement of no-fly zones and its occasional missile strikes kept Saddam penned up. These did constrain him, but the more recently available records show that the Iraqi leader interpreted Clinton's episodic and limited attacks as signs of American weakness. In any event, Saddam was left alone to discern America's intentions because the Clinton administration refused to talk to him about anything significant. Treacherous it may be, but there are benefits to engaging with one's enemies, even if the talks are prolonged, unproductive, emotionally frustrating, politically problematic, or all of these. Clinton told Tony Blair that he could not talk to Saddam because he would be roasted by Republicans. Yet surely this fear did not preclude secret or indirect engagement about Islamist terrorism, Syria, Kurdistan, or other icebreaker topics that might have revived some form of a managed, more stable relationship. As it was, American diplomacy-by-hostile-public-rhetoric persuaded Saddam by 1998 that he would lose little by expelling international weapons inspectors. This action effectively ended the world's on-the-ground investigations about any threat that might still be posed by Iraq's historical WMD programs. The absence of official contacts between Washington and Baghdad clearly contributed to the misjudgment and toxic emotion that, by 9/11, prevailed on both sides, a fog of fury that persisted until war became inevitable in mid-March 2003.

Days after America launched its invasion, Mohammed Aldouri, the Iraqi representative at the U.N., departed the United States, eventually bound for the U.A.E. That left Nizar Hamdoon, still undergoing chemotherapy, alone in the residence on East Eightieth Street. A single local employee looked after the Iraqi mission.

Hamdoon's condition was not improving. He emailed his acquaintance Daniel Pipes, the scholar and publisher of the *Middle East Quarterly*. On May 21, they met at a Starbucks on the Upper East Side.

Hamdoon had shed dozens of pounds and had lost his dark hair and mustache. The pair talked for ninety minutes. The American conquest of Baghdad was by now complete. On May 1, President Bush had appeared on an aircraft carrier near San Diego to declare "Mission Accomplished." The administration had established a government of occupation in Baghdad, the Coalition Provisional Authority. The Baath Party had been dissolved by decree, though Saddam and his sons remained at large.

Pipes asked if Hamdoon had ever been tempted to defect. No, he replied. He liked living in the U.S. but felt rooted in Iraq—"the society, the food, the atmosphere."[8]

Pipes invited him to speak at an event organized by the think tank he ran, the Middle East Forum, and Hamdoon agreed. On June 4, he arrived for an invitation-only lunchtime discussion at the offices of a law firm on Third Avenue. About fifty guests—donors to the forum, policy specialists, and journalists—awaited him. It was the sort of group Hamdoon had addressed hundreds of times during his postings in the U.S.

Looking very sickly but speaking vigorously, Hamdoon offered initial remarks. "Militarily, the war was fought perfectly," he said, referring to the swift U.S. capture of Baghdad. "Now, we are two months into the occupation, and we don't see any real progress."

He worried that America would not complement its military strength with "moral power." In his judgment, Iraq was "a good candidate for democracy. . . . This is an opportunity for America to achieve success in the area of human rights and providing services." But there were already ominous signs, he continued. "Now you find a lot of Iraqis demonstrating in the streets [against the occupation], chanting slogans. You cannot blame them because in principle occupation is not a good thing." A "short occupation" might be accepted, he added. "But do not stay."

The Bush administration's decision to dissolve the Iraqi Army had been a terrible mistake, he went on. Unemployed soldiers were now "in the streets," jobless. "You are disgracing them. You are turning these people into terrorists and criminals, which is not in America's interests."

Hamdoon answered questions about Saddam Hussein's attempt to lead an underground guerrilla movement, Iraq's yet-to-be-discovered WMD, and his country's political future. At one point, the journalist Lally Weymouth asked whether there was "anyone inside the country who can become a leader of Iraq, in your opinion?"

Yes, he answered, but with Saddam at large, the atmosphere of terror and suspicion that Iraqis had lived under was not going to disappear overnight. "If I go back to Baghdad, I will not fear the American soldiers, but don't expect me to be outspoken," Hamdoon said. "No one wants to get his neck chopped."[9]

He did not make it home. He died in New York on July 4, 2003.

When the American-led invasion of Iraq began, Hussain Al-Shahristani, the nuclear scientist and former colleague of Jafar's who had escaped from Abu Ghraib, waited in Kuwait with trucks and stores of humanitarian supplies. In 1998, he had left exile in Iran for Britain, where he now directed the Iraqi Refugee Aid Council.

Shahristani regarded the American-British plan to occupy Iraq as a repeat of Britain's invasion of 1917, when the imperial commanding general, Stanley Maude, had issued a false proclamation of assurance to the Iraqis: "Our armies do not come into your cities and lands as conquerors or enemies but as liberators."

Still, after more than a decade away, he yearned to go home. In April, the border opened to aid groups, and he ferried humanitarian supplies to Basra. He was shocked at how desperate people were for potable water. The water infrastructure shattered by war and sanctions had left Basra's piped supplies almost poisonous.[10]

After setting up aid operations, Shahristani traveled to Karbala and prayed at the Shrine of Imam Hussain. He went on to Baghdad and visited the cell at Abu Ghraib where he had been held in isolation.

Over the months and years to come, Shahristani helped organize the Union of Political Prisoners, to lobby for support and compensation, and moved in and out of government, at one point serving as oil minister.

In August 2005, while attending the International Seminar on Nuclear War and Planetary Emergencies in Sicily, Shahristani reconnected with Jafar Dhia Jafar, who had also been invited to the conference. They had not seen each other since December 1979, when Shahristani had been hauled away by the secret police.

They embraced warmly. Jafar talked about his own incarceration in 1980 and 1981, and about his work on the Iraqi nuclear program after his release. Shahristani recognized that Jafar had risked his own freedom to stand up for him in a moment of crisis. They had made different choices after 1981, but their friendship had survived.[11]

Saddam hid out in Baghdad through the end of March. He issued a flurry of micromanaging orders and exhortations to fight the invaders. "Bury the enemy dead according to the method of their religion," he instructed on March 27. Around the same time, he updated his promises of prize money for successful strikes against the enemy: one hundred million dinars for "one who downs a plane," twenty-five million for killing an enemy soldier, and so on. Also, he pledged, if an Iraqi citizen seized "an enemy vehicle," the citizen "may keep it as a prize" or turn it in to the Baathist regime, which would "pay him the price of the vehicle."[12]

On March 29, through his army headquarters, Saddam distributed an eight-page, handwritten message to generals, fighters, and the public that sought to rally his supporters to "the long war," a campaign that would be decided by "willpower and self-confidence." His directive offered advice about how to form small guerrilla detachments. He diagrammed how to stage a deadly ambush. "The enemy must not feel safe at all, neither at daytime nor at night, and must feel like a stranger . . . unwanted by people, earth, trees, plants, and buildings," he wrote.[13]

Nine days later, American forces seized the Republican Palace and fanned out across Baghdad. On April 9, using ropes and a tank, U.S. Marines helped Iraqi civilians pull down a large statue of Saddam that loomed over Firdos Square. The triumphal image played and replayed on American television networks. The living Saddam appeared that same day about six miles to the north, in the neighborhood of Ad-hamiya. He stood on a pickup truck and received kisses and embraces from a crowd outside the stately Abu Hanifa Mosque. He promised "golden monuments once we defeat the Americans." Qusay was with him, according to witnesses. It was Saddam's last known public appearance in the capital, just shy of twenty-four years after he had become president of Iraq. As an American Special Forces unit, Task Force 20, searched for him, he slipped out of the capital and disappeared.[14]

One by one, family members and retainers close to Saddam surrendered or were betrayed to American forces by informers. As he had planned, on April 12, Jafar's friend Amr al-Saadi held a press conference in Baghdad with the help of a German television network. "I was knowledgeable about these programs," he said of Iraq's WMD. "I never told anything but the truth, and time will bear me out." He then surrendered. As Jafar had predicted, Saadi faced a prolonged period of imprisonment. He was held in U.S. custody and questioned for about eighteen months, then released without charges.[15]

On April 17, a Pentagon spokesman announced the arrest of Barzan Ibrahim al-Tikriti. Tariq Aziz surrendered a week later. Both would be held in U.S. custody and interrogated while a new Iraqi government—initially appointed by the Bush administration but later elected—developed plans to try Baathist leaders for crimes against humanity.[16]

Saddam, Qusay, and Uday initially took refuge in Anbar Province. Saddam soon separated from the boys and sent them toward Syria. Uday remained hobbled by the leg and torso injuries he had suffered in the 1996 assassination attempt. The brothers reached Damascus. Bashar al-Assad, the son and political heir of Saddam's longtime Baathist rival, decided that the potential price of attracting the Bush administration's wrath by granting the boys refuge was too much to bear. His regime forced Qusay and Uday to return to Iraq. They hid in Mosul until the owner of the house where they were staying betrayed them to American forces in return for an advertised $30 million reward. On July 22, 2003, soldiers from the 101st Airborne Division and Task Force 20 assaulted the house. During a five-hour gun battle, they killed both sons, as well as Qusay's son Mustafa, who was fourteen.[17]

A month later, U.S. forces captured Ali Hassan al-Majid, "Chemical Ali." Majid initially joined Aziz, Barzan, and other prominent leaders of the fallen regime at Camp Cropper, a high-security prison and interrogation center built by American specialists near Baghdad International Airport.[18]

Saddam made his way toward Tikrit, to the orchards and palm groves that shrouded the farms along the Tigris—the same area where he had hidden as a young man on his way to exile in Syria and Egypt. That journey had been a pillar of Saddam's myth. It must have appealed to him to return, knowing that if he were hunted down here, at least some of his followers would understand his choice as a political coda. Following the deaths of his sons, he appears to have hidden through the autumn of 2003 at a farm not far from his birthplace, protected by longtime personal bodyguards and fed by his cook. He went to work on a new book. He continued to record messages urging Iraqis to rise up against their occupiers.

More and more did join the opposition to the United States, especially in Sunni areas, such as Anbar Province. As roadside bombs and suicide attacks increased, so did American casualties. These numbered ninety-one in the month of May 2003, when George W. Bush declared "Mission Accomplished." They rose by more than 50 percent the next month, when Donald Rumsfeld dismissed the gathering insurgency as the work of "pockets of dead-enders" who would soon be suppressed. In November, U.S. forces suffered more than four hundred casualties, including eighty-two deaths. By that time, about five hundred Iraqi civilians were being killed monthly as a complex "long war" began to unfold, a war of rebellion against America and its allies, interlaced with a civil war increasingly influenced by sectarian conflict and Iranian involvement.[19]

After a succession of raids, detentions, and interrogations during the spring and summer of 2003, Task Force 20 and supporting troops closed in on a family, the Musslits, who served as Saddam's bodyguards and couriers. In December, American forces arrested Mohammed Ibrahim Omar al-Musslit. He identified the farm where Saddam was hiding. On the evening of December 13, U.S. Special Forces searched the place in vain. Musslit was with them as they stood on a small patio. Finally, the informer slid his foot to subtly point out a mat lying on the floor. Beneath the mat was loose dirt. Beneath the dirt was a hatch. Inside was a disheveled man with matted hair and a full beard, dressed in a robe.

"I am Saddam Hussein, the duly elected president of Iraq," he told the soldiers. "I am willing to negotiate."[20]

As he was placed under arrest, "much cursing and bantering" erupted between Saddam and an Iraqi American translator. When American soldiers tried to inspect Saddam for physical markings, he shoved them, and they struck him, opening a cut above the captive's eye and causing his mouth to bleed. The soldiers stood by as the translator posed for a picture with Saddam. The Bush administration quickly publicized images of the prisoner, selecting ones in which he looked like a bewildered forest hermit. The theory was that Saddam's public humiliation would contribute to the defeat of the incipient Iraqi insurgency.[21]

For the next three years, Saddam was held mainly at or near Camp Cropper, including on a high-security island within his former Radwaniyah complex. With help from his nurse and guards, Saddam managed to obtain a formidable supply of Cohiba cigars, which he smoked with his Lebanese American interpreter. He drank hot Lipton tea with honey and listened to the radio. He read, composed poems, and corresponded with his eldest daughter, Raghad, who had settled in Amman.

At his request, she sent him works by Ibn Khaldun, the fourteenth-century historian and philosopher, as well as poetry and scholarship on Islam.[22]

C.I.A. officers, F.B.I. agents, and Iraq Survey Group investigators were among Saddam's interlocutors during these years. At first, the C.I.A. hoped that Saddam might spill secrets about hidden WMD. Initially, officers considered applying some of the "enhanced interrogation techniques" that the agency had used on al-Qaeda prisoners. The Bush administration instead granted Saddam formal prisoner-of-war status and afforded him the protections of the Geneva Conventions.[23]

Saddam had read enough political and military biography to understand that many conventionally celebrated great men of history—as he certainly considered himself to be—ended their days in prison, sometimes talking to their jailers, as Napoleon had done. The C.I.A. came to refer to its sessions with Saddam as "debriefings." The available transcripts and memoir accounts of Saddam's conversations during this period have a flavor of old wine in new bottles. Saddam often spoke to his captors as he had long spoken to his comrades behind closed doors. About sensitive matters, he lied or snapped angrily at his questioners. On harmless topics, such as geopolitics, "he loved to talk, especially about himself," recalled John Nixon, one of his C.I.A. questioners.

Saddam seemed at ease, Nixon thought: "He showed no signs of anxiety, confusion, paranoia, or delusion. At times, he even displayed a self-deprecating sense of humor. . . . He often answered questions with his own questions or gave answers in the form of parables. . . . He was all about control—not only in the debriefings but also when it came to his guards, meals, medical checkups, and the conditions of his imprisonment."[24]

Around the time Saddam was captured, the U.S.-appointed Iraqi Governing Council established what would become known as the Iraqi High Tribunal to prosecute crimes against humanity during the period of Saddam's rule. (In 2005, following the election of Iraq's Transitional National Assembly, that body replaced the initial law with an amended one.) From Amman, Raghad helped organize her father's defense. The

American patron of unpopular defendants, Ramsey Clark, a Texan who had served as attorney general under President Lyndon Johnson, joined Saddam's team. So did Najeeb al-Nuaimi, a Qatari human-rights activist who had defended prisoners held by the U.S. at Guantanamo Bay.

The civil violence unleashed in Iraq after 2003 dimmed the prospects for fair and orderly trials of Baathist defendants. Shiite victims of state murder carried out by Saddam's regime and Kurdish survivors of the Anfal genocide were impatient over the imported procedural methods of the special tribunal. For his part, Saddam insisted that he had been unlawfully overthrown. "This is all theater," he said. "The real criminal is Bush."[25]

On October 19, 2005, the first trial commenced at the High Tribunal's courthouse, a former Baath Party edifice. The case concerned Baathist executions and reprisals carried out against Iraqi civilians in Dujail after the attempted assassination of Saddam there in 1982. Ultimately, 148 residents of Dujail had been put to death in retaliation; prosecutors charged Saddam, his half brother Barzan, and six others with responsibility.

Saddam was convicted and received a death sentence. Human Rights Watch found "serious administrative, procedural, and substantive legal defects in the trial" and concluded that the High Tribunal lacked the capacity to "fairly and effectively try crimes of this magnitude." Many Iraqis were unconcerned about the court's failure to meet Western standards. A second trial on charges relating to the mass killings during the Anfal opened in August 2006. But the former president's death penalty in the Dujail matter was affirmed before the Anfal case concluded.[26]

During 2006, insurgent violence and sectarian civil war raged across Iraq. More than twenty-nine thousand Iraqi civilians died that year. Iraqi human-rights lawyers and investigators remained committed to the High Tribunal's promise of accountability and record-building for the state crimes of the Saddam era, but Shiite clerics and other politicians called for swift justice. Prime Minister Nouri al-Maliki, of the

Shiite Party that Saddam had violently repressed, declared that there would be "no review or delay" of the former president's death sentence. The High Tribunal's chief judge, Raouf Rasheed Abdel-Rahman, an ethnic Kurd from Halabja, ordered Saddam's hanging.[27]

In the early hours of December 30, 2006, at a government detention facility in northern Baghdad, Iraqi guards in black ski masks led Saddam to the gallows. The well-groomed bearded prisoner wore a black coat and a buttoned white shirt. An unruly audience that included followers of the Shiite cleric Moqtada al-Sadr shouted abuse at him. Saddam stood impassively as masked executioners wrapped his neck in a black cloth and then draped a rope around his neck. As angry voices sounded, a trap door opened, and he dropped to his death.

Acknowledgments

I owe a great debt to my interview sources for their time and trust. Over two days in Dubai in late February 2020, just as the pandemic shuttered global travel, I interviewed Jafar Dhia Jafar, who is among the major surviving Iraqi figures in the book's narrative, and he patiently addressed many additional questions in writing over the next three years. Hussain Al-Shahristani, Ayad Allawi, Wahid Kochani, and other Iraqis who participated in the events described also made time for multiple interviews and detailed correspondence. Rolf Ekéus allowed me access to his archive from his days leading the United Nations Special Commission. Charles Duelfer was similarly generous with his U.N.-era materials. During an early interview, I told Duelfer that I was planning to start my history just after the Gulf War and he argued that I had to go back further. Because he proved to be right, I have only cursed him occasionally over the mountain of additional work. Thomas Twetten, Luis Rueda, John Maguire, and David Manners were among the former C.I.A. operations officers who generously made time to recount and clarify long-ago events.

As noted in the introduction, I also owe a debt to the Reporters Committee for Freedom of the Press, which provided pro bono legal support for my effort to obtain Saddam Hussein regime files from the Pentagon. The Reporters Committee is a distinctive nonprofit that defends the First Amendment but also provides essential help to working journalists. In addition to Adam Marshall, who offered outstanding counsel throughout, the attorneys Katie Townsend, Gunita Singh, and Tiffany Wong also supported my reporting, backed by Bruce Brown, the executive director. I am grateful, too, to the Department of Justice attorneys who facilitated the eventual release of the materials. After I filed my FOIA lawsuit, Michael Brill, a Ph.D. candidate at Princeton, kindly reached out and shared his archive of previously open records. He has been a valued resource in other ways as well. The stalwart press lawyer Stuart Karle offered generous and helpful advice.

Several scholars and experts on Iraq reviewed a draft of my manuscript and provided suggestions and corrections. Joost Hiltermann gave invaluable editorial advice, in addition to his flyspecking of the manuscript. Ibrahim Al-Marashi also improved the book with his suggestions. As noted elsewhere, he consulted the original Arabic recordings and transcripts, where available, and thoughtfully corrected some of the Conflict Records Research Center's original English translations used in the book. Hawraa Al-Hassan's insights about Saddam's novels were exceptional, and her reading of the full draft was very helpful, as were the readings provided by Joseph Sassoon and Charles Tripp. I'm grateful to all of these readers for their time and insights and for directing me to source materials I had overlooked. None of them are responsible, of course, for the errors and problematic interpretations that no doubt remain.

The military historian Kevin Woods, whose outstanding books and papers with multiple collaborators provided a foundational record for my research, has been an excellent steward of the CRRC materials in challenging circumstances. He steered me in the right direction early on. So did Målfrid Braut-Hegghammer, the authoritative scholar of Iraq's nuclear program whose talents include a gift for titles (*Unclear Physics*, "Cheater's Dilemma"). Samuel Helfont, the author of an important new book on Saddam's foreign policy during the 1990s, helpfully directed me to the Clinton Presidential Library's transcripts of presidential calls about Iraq. The archivists at the Ronald Reagan Presidential Library shook off the pandemic, reopened their doors, and provided valuable guidance. For their advice, I owe thanks as well to Omar Sirri of Human Rights Watch and Bill Wiley of the Commission for International Justice and Accountability.

In addition to Sarah Moawad, Amel Brahmi, and David Kortava, several researchers worked hard and carefully to improve the book. Augusta Anthony conducted interviews in Britain. Katherine Proctor patiently culled the Chilcot Report, which yielded fresh details about George W. Bush's decision-making. Sarah Goodman discovered valuable memoirs and documentary sources. Abir and Ahmed Abed Benbuk, Patrick Mulholland, Jonathan Milläng, and Shinhee Kang also made important contributions. I was fortunate to enjoy the support of Columbia University throughout the five years I worked on the book, particularly from Lee Bollinger, Ira Katznelson, Mary Boyce, Jane Booth, Felice Rosan, Donna Fenn, Gerry Rosberg, Janine Jaquet, Paul Schuchert, Winnie O'Kelley, Nick Lemann, Jelani Cobb, Melanie Huff, Kyle Pope, Steve Adler, Ari Goldman, Sam Freedman, Sandro Stille, and my wonderful (almost always) graduate students in journalism. At *The New Yorker*, I benefited again from the support of David Remnick, Dorothy Wickenden, Virginia Cannon, and Mike Luo, and had the good fortune to collaborate with Adam Entous, Tyler Foggatt, Han Zhang, Nina Mesfin, Jamila Wilkinson, and Dan Greene. Thanks as well to Andrew Katzenstein at *The New York Review of Books*.

I have been extraordinarily fortunate to work continuously with the same book editor and literary agent—great friends, too—for the past thirty years. Again, Ann Godoff at Penguin Press backed the highest ambitions for this project, and again, Melanie Jackson provided indispensable advice and support. At Penguin, great thanks to Victoria Lopez, Casey Denis, Amelia Zalcman, and Hal Fessenden. Simon Winder has been my wonderful and inspiring editor in the U.K. for almost two decades. And thanks to Lauren Morgan Whitticom, who provided a meticulous, thoughtful, and error-cleansing line edit.

To survive the pandemic, we all needed help, inside our bubbles and out. I will be forever grateful to the Friedlands, the Fifields, Ellen

Ward, Geoff, Dan, Hannah, Phoebe, and Frank for casting light in the darkness of 2020 and early 2021. I am grateful and humbled by my amazing children—Ally, Emma, Max, and Robert—and my grandson, Charlie. My wife and partner, Eliza Griswold, steered me through the years of this work with her enlivening spirit, hilarity, purpose, and love. I am aware that I am lucky beyond description.

A Note on Sources

This book is based primarily on more than one hundred interviews conducted mainly with surviving participants in the events described, as well as on transcripts of tape-recorded meetings from inside Saddam Hussein's regime; meeting notes and memoranda; oral histories, diaries, and memoirs; and journalism and scholarship.

As noted elsewhere, I filed a FOIA lawsuit against the Pentagon to obtain a collection of materials mainly from Saddam's presidential offices and intelligence ministries, including audio recordings, transcripts, and minutes of meetings at which Saddam was present. These materials were captured by U.S. forces after the 2003 invasion, then collated and translated at a Defense Intelligence Agency facility in Qatar. Starting in 2010, some of the documents were made openly available through an archive—the Conflict Records Research Center, or CRRC—housed at the National Defense University. The CRRC released only about one-tenth of the approximately two thousand hours of Saddam recordings and only a sliver of the millions of pages of other files. The center closed for budgetary reasons in 2015, and the materials it had released were withdrawn. Through a settlement with the Justice Department, I obtained a specific subset of the archive that I had identified from CRRC indexes and requested in FOIA filings.

The CRRC and Defense Department materials, which remain largely unavailable as of this writing, are invaluable in many ways. There are other important archives illuminating the era of Saddam's rule, but the

records that capture Saddam's comments, letters, and memoranda between the late 1970s and 2002 present a rare portrait of a modern dictator's private discourse. They offer extraordinary and vivid insights into
the Iraqi side of Saddam's conflicts and relations with the United States,
as well as into his dealings with the Soviet Union, Iraq's neighbors, the
wider Arab world, and the Global South. Yet the records are also complicated in both ethical and practical respects. After the materials were
seized by U.S. forces, some Iraqi and Western scholars argued that they
rightly belonged to Iraq, had been improperly taken, and should be returned. Iraqi government officials also sought their repatriation. In 2013,
with little publicity, the Obama administration agreed to return millions
of the seized records to the Iraqi government while retaining copies in
Defense Department systems. The records provided to Iraq have not yet
been made available to researchers or the Iraqi public, however. The Iraqi
government has not explained its decision-making, but one general concern is that actors in the country's sectarian and political violence might
exploit information in the records to attack or pressure vulnerable individuals. In settling my FOIA lawsuit and obtaining the CRRC materials,
I agreed to review any excerpts about private Iraqi individuals to be sure
that my writing would not pose such a risk.

Despite the return of the captured records to Iraq, at least a few
international scholars still decline to make use of them on ethical
grounds, because of their provenance as a kind of war booty. I understand this reluctance. Yet in my four-decade career as a journalist, I
have often had to grapple with human sources and documentary files
with problematic histories. Like other American reporters, I work in a
First Amendment tradition that often protects the use of even "stolen"
or illegally leaked information if it is of public interest. Such journalism
can be tricky, but I have found that there are ways to proceed
thoughtfully—by prioritizing accurate information of public importance, minimizing harm, and offering context and transparency to
readers. I have tried to do that here, persuaded as I am that the CRRC
records offer unique and timely insights of lasting significance.

There are also practical issues with the materials. The English translations that were produced at the Defense Department facility in Qatar are sometimes choppy or ungrammatical, raising questions about that project's quality control. I have studied Arabic but am inadequately trained to work in the language, so I collaborated with Ibrahim Al-Marashi, an associate professor and scholar of modern Iraqi politics at California State University, San Marcos. He reviewed the English translations of the excerpts I have quoted in the book, consulting the original Arabic source where available. In some cases, he suggested changes, which I have incorporated, to better capture nuance or a speaker's obvious intention. In a majority of instances, he found that the CRRC translation was acceptable, even if it was not artful. In those cases, I have used the original translations, with only minor grammatical corrections. Here and in my choices of transliteration and recurring Iraqi names (Barzan, Hussein Kamel, etc.), I have accepted some inconsistency while prioritizing the reading experiences of nonspecialists.

Because the U.S. government has declined to make available all of the captured Saddam Hussein regime files, it is impossible to judge whether the materials released through the CRRC and other channels may be misleading or distorted, as excerpts of the entire archive. Subjects such as Iraqi sponsorship of terrorism and the history of Iraq's WMD programs figured heavily in the initial Pentagon-supervised releases, for instance. I have no way to determine whether these files are representative of the whole archive or contradicted by other materials. In my FOIA request, I targeted materials that documented Saddam's meetings and activity after 9/11, because I found this period to be underrepresented in the earlier releases. The records I received turned out to be lively and revealing, but there may be other files of interest from that period that have never seen the light of day. It is long past time for the White House and Defense Department to release the full archive and make it accessible to global researchers, with procedures in place to protect vulnerable individuals.

The chapter-by-chapter notes below offer a full account of the specific CRRC records and the many other sources that I have relied upon in the book.

Notes

Chapter 1: The Physicist and the Dictator

1. Interviews and correspondence with Jafar; that his colleagues thought of him as aristocratic is from interviews with former scientists in the Iraqi program.
2. Tuwaitha's layout is from interviews with former scientists and David Albright, Corey Gay, and Khidhir Hamza, "Development of the Al-Tuwaitha Site: What If the Public or the IAEA Had Overhead Imagery?," Institute for Science and International Security, April 26, 1999, https://www.isis-online.org/publications/iraq/tuwaitha.html.
3. Jafar's visit with Khaliq is described in chapter two of Jafar Dhia Jafar and Numan al-Niaimi, *Al-I'tirāf al-akhīr: Ḥaqīqat al-barnāmaj al-nawawī al-ʿIrāqī* (Beirut: Markaz Dirasat al-Wahdah al-Arabiyah, 2005), hereafter cited as *Last Confession*. Sarah Moawad produced an English translation of this Arabic-language memoir for the author. The memoir's account of Jafar's ordeal from 1979 to 1981 is supported by the recollections and published works of multiple other scientists in the nuclear program, as well as by references in an unpublished manuscript by Barzan Ibrahim al-Tikriti. However, Jafar is the only source of the specific content of some conversations. Hussain Al-Shahristani's activism, family background, sympathy for the Iranian Revolution, and other biographical aspects are from interviews with Shahristani. He has also written two memoirs: *Al-Hurūb ilá al-ḥurrīyah: Awrāq min ayyām al-miḥnah ʿāshahā al-Duktūr Ḥusayn Shahrastānī fī sujūn niẓām Ṣaddām* (hereafter cited by its short English title, *Escape to Freedom*) and, more recently, an English-language memoir, *Free of Fear* (Bloomington, Ind.: AuthorHouse, 2021).
4. Interview with Shahristani; Khomeini's quotations ("that pig," "revolution like ours") from Nigel Ashton and Bryan Gibson, eds., *The Iran-Iraq War: New International Perspectives* (Abingdon, U.K.: Routledge, 2013), 36.
5. Shahristani's arrest is described in Jafar and Niaimi, *Last Confession*, chapter two, and in Shahristani's Arabic-language memoir. Jafar and Shahristani are in agreement about what transpired. The quotations here are from Shahristani.
6. Shahristani's interrogation is from interviews with Shahristani. All quotations are from his two memoirs.
7. Jafar and Niaimi, *Last Confession*, chapter two; Jafar's letters to Saddam are from interviews with Jafar.
8. Interviews with Jafar.
9. Jafar and Niaimi, *Last Confession*, chapter two.
10. Biographical details and "like a shadow" from Barzan Ibrahim al-Tikriti, "The Sweet Years and the Bitter Years" (hereafter "Sweet and Bitter Years"), an unpublished memoir translated by the Conflict Records Research Center, National Defense University, Washington, D.C. (Note: all references to the Conflict Records Research Center are hereafter cited as CRRC followed by the relevant record number). Divided into parts, Barzan's memoir is tagged as SH-MISC-D-001-919 (Part I), SH-MISC-D-000-948 (Part II), or SH-MISC-D-001-204 (Part III). The manuscript partly consists of daily diary entries, often quotidian, made by Barzan during his years as an Iraqi diplomat in Geneva. In some passages, however, he provides autobiographical accounts of his life with Saddam, his meetings, and his family conflicts. The matter of the murders that he and Saddam were involved in as boys comes up late in the manuscript when Barzan describes a "tense and edgy" conversation he had

with Saddam in 2001. At one point during a convoluted discussion about the fatal shooting Saddam committed and other killings, Barzan recounts that he said to Saddam: "I killed four people." He provides a detailed, if difficult to unpack, account of the grievances that led to the killings.

11. "a nitwit": interview with Imad Khadduri; "an asshole": Charles Duelfer, *Hide and Seek: The Search for Truth in Iraq* (New York: PublicAffairs Books, 2009), 402.

12. "Sweet and Bitter Years," CRRC SH-MISC-D-001-919.

13. "Iraqi sitting in a café": Ala Bashir and Lars Sigurd Sunnanå, *The Insider: Trapped in Saddam's Brutal Regime* (London: Abacus, 2005), 87.

14. Jafar and Niaimi, *Last Confession*, chapter two.

15. Shahristani, *Free of Fear*, 67–68; interview with Shahristani.

16. Night dreams at Abu Ghraib from Shahristani, 73–74; Shahristani's meeting with Barzan from an interview with Shahristani.

17. "I want to build an atomic bomb" from Jafar and Niaimi, *Last Confession*, chapter one; Jafar's education and move to CERN from an interview with Jafar.

18. "I shouldn't—I cannot—refuse": interview with Jafar.

19. Iraqi properties in Paris from an interview with a former Iraqi diplomat; medical travel from an interview with Ala Bashir; shopping list from David Styan, *France and Iraq: Oil, Arms and French Policy Making in the Middle East* (London: I. B. Tauris, 2006), 124; oil-revenue figures from Efraim Karsh and Inari Rautsi, *Saddam Hussein: A Political Biography* (New York: The Free Press, 1991), 90.

20. "intelligent . . . rather nice": from Jacques Chirac, *My Life in Politics*, trans. Catherine Spencer (New York: St. Martin's Press, 2012), 55; itinerary from *Le Monde*, September 5, 1975; menu and thousand-franc tips are from an interview with Jean-André Charial, chef at L'Oustau de Baumanierè, by Amel Brahmi.

21. Interview by Amel Brahmi with Jacques Mailhan, who participated in the event.

22. CRRC PDWN-D-000-341.

23. Yahya al-Mashad's murder is from Ronen Bergman, *Rise and Kill First: The Secret History of Israel's Targeted Assassinations* (New York: Random House, 2018), 350–53.

24. Saddam's "mummy" and "rotten man" from Jerry M. Long, *Saddam's War of Words: Politics, Religion, and the Iraqi Invasion of Kuwait* (Austin: University of Texas Press, 2004), 68.

25. "Arabs of corruption": CRRC SH-SHTP-D-000-559; "We will force": CRRC SH-SHTP-A-000-835.

26. Interview with Jafar; Jafar and Niaimi, *Last Confession*, chapter two.

27. May automobile gift from Mahdi Obeidi and Kurt Pitzer, *The Bomb in My Garden: The Secrets of Saddam's Nuclear Mastermind* (Hoboken, N.J.: John Wiley & Sons, 2004), 50; number of Iraqi technicians at Saclay from an interview with Fadhil al-Janabi, scientist then at the Iraqi Atomic Energy Commission; "The alternative is our destruction": "Osiraq/Tammuz-1," Federation of American Scientists, https://fas.org/nuke/guide/iraq/facility/osiraq.htm.

28. CRRC SH-SHTP-A-001-039 and CRRC SH-SHTP-A-001-480. Both transcripts are from around June 1981, following the attack, https://apps.dtic.mil/sti/pdfs/AD1124180.pdf.

29. "Oppenheimer of Iraq": interview with Janabi; Shahristani and Barzan is from an interview with Shahristani.

30. Jafar and Niaimi, *Last Confession*, chapter two.

31. "a feeling of having": interview with Janabi; "vengeance was way up": interview with Khadduri; "a strong conviction": from p. 9 of the *Currently Accurate, Full, and Complete Declaration of the Past Iraqi Nuclear Program*, submitted by Iraq to the U.N. on December 3, 2002. This unpublished document, hereafter cited as the CAFCD, was obtained by the author.

32. Interview with Jafar.

33. Office description from an interview with Mazin Jazrawi by Amel Brahmi; all quotations from Jafar and Niaimi, *Last Confession*, chapter two. Other scientists in the Iraqi nuclear program at this time said in interviews that they soon became aware of Jafar's assignment by Saddam to lead a secret program to develop highly enriched uranium. The scientists are divided on whether Saddam directly ordered a nuclear bomb program in late 1981 or whether the assignment was more ambiguous—that is, to covertly develop fissionable material, which would create a bomb option, while reserving judgment on whether to try to weaponize. Given how far Iraq was in 1981 from being able to construct a finished bomb, this may have been a distinction without much of a practical difference at the time. In any event, the separate accounts of Jafar and Shahristani quoting Barzan in 1980 as stating that Saddam wanted to build a nuclear weapon make clear what Saddam intended, even if he was at times cautious about how to go forward.

Chapter 2: A Spy Bearing Gifts

1. Twetten's tours are from Michael Wines, "After 30 Years in Shadows, a Spymaster Emerges," *New York Times*, November 20, 1990; Twetten profile and mission are from interviews with Twetten; National Security Council quotation (emphasis in original) are from James G. Blight et al., *Becoming Enemies: U.S.-Iran Relations and the Iran-Iraq War, 1979–1988* (Lanham, Md.: Rowman & Littlefield, 2012), 115. *Becoming Enemies* provides an invaluable oral history by participants in U.S. policymaking during the Iran-Iraq War. Twetten's visit in late July may not have been the first made by an American intelligence officer to Baghdad during 1982, but it is the best documented. In February 1982, the United States removed Iraq from the list of countries sanctioned for being state sponsors of terrorism—a factually dubious decision. Wafiq al-Samarrai and a second Iraqi intelligence source describe an initial unsuccessful visit to Baghdad that February or March by men whom they believed to be C.I.A. officers seeking to share satellite-derived battlefield intelligence about Iran. However, Twetten said in an interview that he had no knowledge of such an earlier trip and that if it had been conducted by the C.I.A., he likely would have known. He speculated that perhaps the U.S. Defense Intelligence Agency, or the D.I.A., might have reached Baghdad earlier than he did, if such a visit took place. U.S. intelligence may also have been provided via Jordan initially.

2. "Iraq has essentially lost": Bryan R. Gibson, *Covert Relationship: American Foreign Policy, Intelligence, and the Iran Iraq War, 1980–1988* (Westport, Conn.: Praeger, 2010), 77; "fundamentalist Islamic one": Henry S. Rowen to Geoffrey Kemp, "The Iranian Threat to American Interests in the Persian Gulf," National Intelligence Council study, July 20, 1982, RAC Box 2, Geoffrey Kemp Files, Ronald Reagan Presidential Library (hereafter RRPL); "whatever was necessary and legal": quoting Howard Teicher in Gibson, *Covert Relationship*, 78.

3. Saddam's micromanaging is described in Williamson Murray and Kevin M. Woods, *The Iran-Iraq War: A Military and Strategic History* (Cambridge: Cambridge University Press, 2014); the shrinking of the Iraqi Army from Murray and Woods, *Iran-Iraq War*, 185; "insects": Ofra Bengio, *Saddam's Word: Political Discourse in Iraq* (Oxford: Oxford University Press, 1998), 153; Saddam spoke of the "implementation" of a chemical weapons program in March 1981, CRRC SH-MISC-D-001-334; "keeps our sovereignty": CRRC SH-SHTP-A-000-710.

4. "Discussion Paper for SIG on Policy Options for Dealing with Iran-Iraq War," on policy options for dealing with the Iran-Iraq War, RAC Box 2, Geoffrey Kemp Files, RRPL.

5. Interviews with Twetten. His arrival was smoothed by both King Hussein and Ronald Reagan. In Nigel Ashton, *King Hussein of Jordan: A Political Life* (New Haven, Conn.: Yale University Press, 2010), 218–19, Ashton describes the king's correspondence to persuade Reagan to aid Saddam that spring. On July 17, ten days before Twetten arrived, President Reagan wrote to Saddam Hussein on the occasion of the celebration of the Baath Party's revolution in 1968: "Despite the present difficult circumstances, on this day you and your countrymen can be proud of the strides you have made in the area of economic development." See also RAC Box 2, Geoffrey Kemp Files, RRPL.

6. Interviews with Twetten and Twetten's comments in Blight et al., *Becoming Enemies*, 113–14. Barzan on Saddam's loyalty checks from "Sweet and Bitter Years," CRRC SH-MISC-D-001-204.

7. Interviews with Twetten.

8. Joost R. Hiltermann, *A Poisonous Affair: America, Iraq, and the Gassing of Halabja* (Cambridge: Cambridge University Press, 2007), 42–43; quotation from an interview with Twetten.

9. The executions in Dujail eventually became part of a war crimes case filed against Saddam Hussein following his capture by American forces. Daughter's account: *Al-Sharq al-Aswat*, May 22, 2004.

10. Kissinger's remark appears in Mansour Farhang, "Teheran's Game Plan," editorial, *New York Times*, February 5, 1991; "If the two superpowers wanted": Saddam's interview with *Time* magazine reporters Murray J. Gart and Dean Brelis, July 6, 1982, in Saïd K. Aburish, *Saddam Hussein: The Politics of Revenge* (London: Bloomsbury, 2000), 217.

11. "America has two faces": CRRC SH-SHTP-A-000-561; "You tell me how": Aburish, *Politics of Revenge*, 216; "We are afraid": CRRC SH-SHTP-D-000-846.

12. "We talk about the American": CRRC SH-SHTP-D-000-559; "unnatural": Aburish, *Politics of Revenge*, 216; "I have nothing personal": Aburish, 216.

13. Interviews with several former U.S. officials familiar with the C.I.A. station in Baghdad during the 1980s.

14. Amel Brahmi and I reconstructed this history, which proved to be complex and obscure. We interviewed former U.S. officials who served in the interests section or during the early years of the revived embassy, after 1984: David Mack, James Bullock, William Haugh, Deborah Jones, and Theodore Kattouf, among others. Ryan Crocker, who served there between 1978 and 1980, recalled the sign in the classified area. All quotations, interviews by the author and Brahmi.

15. Interviews with former U.S. diplomats.
16. State Department cable, Baghdad to Washington, March 23, 1983, RAC Box 4, NSC Near East and South Asia Affairs Directorate Collection, RRPL.
17. Aburish, *Politics of Revenge*, 224–25.
18. Interview with Mack.
19. Interview with Twetten. This visit to the C.I.A. occurred after mid-1983, but it is not clear when. It seems likely that the delegation included Hussein Kamel, Saddam's son-in-law, who briefly took charge of the Mukhabarat after Barzan's resignation in late 1983. Qusay, Saddam's second-born son, may have also joined the trip, and he and Kamel may have been the ones who tried to purchase silencers. An Iraqi source familiar with the C.I.A. liaison dated the visit to 1985 and said Kamel and Qusay were in the traveling party. He added that "the visit was a total failure" because "the two men were not qualified in the field." Twetten, speaking almost forty years after the event, said he was "ninety percent" certain that Hussein Kamel was in the delegation. His recollection about the gun incident is clear and in line with other similar incidents.
20. State Department cable, Baghdad to Washington, May 4, 1983, RAC Box 4, NSC Near East and South Asia Affairs Directorate Collection, RRPL. The name of the Iraqi official Eagleton met with is redacted, except on one page, where the subject line reads "Meeting with Barzan al-Tikriti." For these errors in the unnecessary censorship of decades-old meetings with deceased figures in history, we can only be grateful.
21. State Department cable, Paris to Washington, May 11, 1983, Document 18 in Joyce Battle, ed., *Shaking Hands with Saddam Hussein: The U.S. Tilts toward Iraq, 1980–1984*, National Security Archive Electronic Briefing Book No. 82 (hereafter NSA EBB 82), February 25, 2003, https://nsarchive2.gwu.edu/NSAEBB/NSAEBB82/iraq18.pdf.

Chapter 3: A Man and a City

1. Saddam's mother's date of death: "Sweet and Bitter Years," CRRC SH-MISC-D-001-919. Other sources date her death to August 1982, but the date provided by Barzan appears credible. His manuscript also describes Subha's deathbed edicts, issued to Barzan's sister, who attended to her mother in her last days. Photographs of Subha appear in Amir Iskander, *Saddam Hussein: The Fighter, the Thinker and the Man* (Paris: Hachette Réalités, 1980).
2. For many years, Saddam's opponents circulated stories that his biological father abandoned his family and that his mother was a prostitute. Some biographers reported these rumors, but others documented the more prosaic fact of his biological father's early death while acknowledging some gaps in the record. In his autobiographical novel, Saddam describes the sequence of events surrounding his birth; the account here is from a matching one given by Saddam in detention to a C.I.A. interviewer, John Nixon. See John Nixon, *Debriefing the President: The Interrogation of Saddam Hussein* (New York: Blue Rider Press, 2016), 122.
3. All quotations from *Men and a City*, as translated by Hawraa Al-Hassan, in "Propaganda Literature in Ba'thist Cultural Production (1979–2003): The Novels of Saddam Hussein as a Case Study" (hereafter "Propaganda Literature"). This is her invaluable 2014 doctoral thesis at King's College, University of Cambridge. Hassan is also the author of *Women, Writing and the Iraqi Ba'thist State: Contending Discourses of Resistance and Collaboration, 1968–2003* (Edinburgh: Edinburgh University Press, 2020).
4. Saddam's tribal tattoo from Nixon, *Debriefing the President*, 17–18.
5. "bold and brave": Raghad Hussein interview with Al Arabiya, February 17, 2021; all other quotations from "Sweet and Bitter Years," CRRC SH-MISC-D-001-919. Although the luncheon scene and quotations here are from Barzan's self-serving unpublished memoir, the story of the split between Barzan and Saddam in late 1983, and the fact that this falling out coincided with a dispute over Raghad's engagement, is described by other sources, including recent memoirs by Raghad's eldest daughter, Hareer, and those of family retainers, such as Ala Bashir, one of Saddam's personal physicians. See also, for example, Con Coughlin, *Saddam: King of Terror* (New York: Ecco, 2002), 199–200.
6. Arm-for-an-arm—the retributee was Luai Khairallah, Sajida's brother—from Bashir and Sunnanâ, *The Insider*, 157; "trivial person": Tariq Aziz's detention interview with the journalist Ali al-Dabagh, conducted in 2010, broadcast on Al Arabiya in 2013. The English translation was released by the CRRC on July 23, 2013, https://conflictrecords.wordpress.com/2013/07/23/crrc-releases-translation-of-interview-with-tariq-aziz; shot-out traffic light incident is from Saddam while he was detained,

mentioned in, among other accounts, Duelfer, *Hide and Seek*, 105; the kidnapping of two traffic cops from Bashir and Sunnanâ, *The Insider*, 152.

7. Aaron M. Faust, *The Ba'thification of Iraq: Saddam Hussein's Totalitarianism* (Austin: University of Texas Press, 2015), 77.

8. Rising at 5:00 a.m. from an interview with Saman Abdul Majid, a French- and English-language translator in the presidential secretariat; valet from Duelfer, *Hide and Seek*, 388; four cigars a day from Nixon, *Debriefing the President*, 93; "Whoever wants to smoke": CRRC SH-SHTP-A-000-635; satellite TV and poker game details from Saman Abdul Majid, *Les années Saddam: Révélations exclusives* (Paris: Fayard, 2003), 121.

9. "On a personal level": interview with Fadhil al-Janabi; "He looked you straight": Murray and Woods, *Iran-Iraq War*, 24.

10. Saddam's reading from an interview with Majid; his interest in biographies is from Majid, *Les années Saddam*, and Nixon, *Debriefing the President*; his reading of Hemingway is noted in, among other sources, Duelfer, *Hide and Seek*, 405.

11. Publication date of Mualla's *The Long Days* from Hassan, "Propaganda Literature"; for an entertaining account of the filming of *Clash of Loyalties*, see James Montague, "When Saddam Met Oliver Reed," *Esquire Middle East*, July 15, 2014, https://www.esquireme.com/culture/saddam-met-oliver -reed; Terence Young from Aburish, *Politics of Revenge*, 48; "eagle" from Hassan, "Propaganda Literature."

12. "more than one obstacle," description of schools and the Khairallah house, exam grade, and struggles with attendance from CRRC SH-PDWN-D-000-944.

13. "unable to restrain himself" and "immediately opened fire" from Iskander, *Saddam Hussein*, 53. The iconographic episodes in Saddam's political biography recounted here appear in fragments in CRRC records, but they are fully treated in book-length English biographies and journalistic assessments by Aburish, Coughlin, the Cockburns, and Karsh and Rautsi. Iskander's book is informed by distinctive access to Saddam's circle in the late 1970s and contains valuable family photographs.

14. "on such a cold night": Iskander, 67.

15. Saddam's residence in Cairo, the Egyptian branch of the Baath Party, and gatherings at the Qasr al-Nil from CRRC SH-MISC-D-000-860; Saddam's affiliation with the Iraqi Student Association and the Association of Iraqis in Cairo from CRRC SH-BATH-D-000-775; "Cairo for us": Anthony Shadid, *Night Draws Near: Iraq's People in the Shadow of America's War* (New York: Henry Holt and Company, 2005), 55; "this kind of liberal": CRRC SH-SHTP-A-000-723.

16. For an authoritative account of what is known about American involvement in the February 1963 Baathist coup, see Brandon Wolfe-Hunnicutt, "Embracing Regime Change in Iraq: American Foreign Policy and the 1963 Coup d'état in Baghdad," *Diplomatic History* 39, no. 1 (January 2015): 98–125; "some played dominos": Murray and Woods, *Iran-Iraq War*, 136.

17. Iskander, *Saddam Hussein*, 137. Aburish and Barzan, who was in the room with his own gun drawn, confirm the essential details of Iskander's account.

18. Aburish, *Politics of Revenge*, 186.

19. See chapters three and five in Fakhri Qadduri, *Hakadha 'araftu al-Bakr wa-Saddam: rihlah 35 'am fi Hizb al-Ba'th* (*This is how I knew al-Bakr and Saddam, a 35-year journey in the Ba'ath party*) (London: Dar al-Hikmah, 2006). Translation for the author by Amel Brahmi.

20. Karsh and Rautsi, *Saddam Hussein*, 114.

21. Hamdani's memoirs, in Murray and Woods, *Iran-Iraq War*, 287.

22. "Friend of the President" cards and medal benefits from Faust, *Ba'thification of Iraq*, 174–75; artists' salaries from Majid, *Les années Saddam*, 142.

23. Majid, 146.

24. Rolex and Piaget watches from Majid, 150. For a characteristic portfolio of photos from Saddam's public rounds, see CRRC SH-MISC-D-001-963.

25. "The Zionists are greedy": Kevin M. Woods et al., *A Survey of Saddam's Audio Files 1978–2001: Toward an Understanding of Authoritarian Regimes*, Paper P-4548 (Alexandria, Va.: Institute for Defense Analyses, 2010), 80–82, as cited in Hal Brands and David Palkki, "Why Did Saddam Want the Bomb? The Israel Factor and the Iraqi Nuclear Program," *Foreign Policy Research Institute E-Notes*, August 2011; the Iraqi Jewish archive discovered in the Mukhabarat's basement from Sandi Fox, "Who Owns the Jewish Treasures That Were Hidden in Saddam Hussein's Basement?," *PBS NewsHour*, April 29, 2014, https://www.pbs.org/newshour/world/stolen-treasures-iraqi-jewish -community.

26. "One moment he would be": Murray and Woods, *Iran-Iraq War*, 24; Ali Hassan al-Majid's remarks from his F.B.I. detention interview on January 31, 2004.

27. Aziz interview with Dabagh.
28. "Sweet and Bitter Years," CRRC SH-MISC-D-001-919.
29. "Sweet and Bitter Years," CRRC SH-MISC-D-001-919.
30. "Iraq: Foreign Intelligence and Security Services," partially declassified C.I.A. memo, August 1985, Document 5 in Jeffrey Richelson, ed., *Saddam's Iron Grip: Intelligence Reports on Saddam Hussein's Reign*, National Security Archive Electronic Briefing Book 167, October 18, 2005, https://nsar chive2.gwu.edu/NSAEBB/NSAEBB167/05.pdf.
31. "Sweet and Bitter Years," CRRC SH-MISC-D-001-919.

Chapter 4: Ambassadors of Cynicism

1. Saddam International: http://berthetpochy.blogspot.com/p/architecture-interieure.html; *Le Monde*, August 19, 1983; "initiate a dialogue": State Department cable, Baghdad to Amman, December 14, 1983, Document 29, NSA EBB 82; golden spurs from Hiltermann, *A Poisonous Affair*, 49.
2. "despicable act": Reagan remarks on October 23, 1983, RRPL video, https://www.reaganlibrary .gov/archives/speech/remarks-reporters-death-american-and-french-military-personnel-beirut -lebanon; Shultz and Rumsfeld conversation from Donald Rumsfeld, *Known and Unknown: A Memoir* (New York: Sentinel, 2011), 11.
3. "harbored illusions": Rumsfeld, *Known and Unknown*, 4.
4. Tariq Aziz and Rumsfeld from Rumsfeld, 5; "among the four most powerful": memo from Shultz to Reagan, November 20, 1984, Box CFOA 414, Edwin Meese Files, RRPL.
5. Aziz's interview with Ali al-Dabagh.
6. Portrait of Aziz from interviews with Iraqi colleagues and multiple U.S. and European diplomats and officials who negotiated with him, particularly Charles Duelfer and Rolf Ekéus; Baghdad home with car ramp described in Tim Trevan, *Saddam's Secrets: The Hunt for Iraq's Hidden Weapons* (London: HarperCollins UK, 1999), 16.
7. State Department cable, London to Washington, December 21, 1983, Document 32, NSA EBB 82, except "unnatural," which is from a readout cable of Rumsfeld's meeting with Saddam Hussein the next day, also part of Document 32, NSA EBB 82.
8. State Department cable, London to Washington, December 21, 1983, Document 31, NSA EBB 82.
9. Videotape from Rumsfeld, *Known and Unknown*, 9.
10. For a timeline of Iraq's chemical-weapons program from its origins to the 1980s, see Iraq Survey Group, *Comprehensive Report of the Special Advisor to the Director of Central Intelligence on Iraq's WMD*, rev. ed. (Washington, D.C.: Government Printing Office, 2005), 3:1–9. This voluminous report is hereafter cited as the *Duelfer Report*.
11. CRRC SH-MISC-D-001-334.
12. Iraq Survey Group, *Duelfer Report*, 3:6.
13. CRRC SH-AFGC-D-000-094, as quoted in Murray and Woods, *Iran-Iraq War*, 221; July 1983 mustard attack described in Hiltermann, *A Poisonous Affair*, 29.
14. Rashid from Hiltermann, 37; tabun gas use described in Hiltermann, 32–36; "crude sulfur-mustard" and casualty estimate from Murray and Woods, *Iran-Iraq War*, 229.
15. Ricciardone from Hiltermann, *A Poisonous Affair*, 39; for full March 4 statement, see "Press Statement: Iraq's Use of Chemical Weapons," James Placke to James M. Ealum et al., March 4, 1984, Document 43, NSA EBB 82; Bernard Gwertzman, "U.S. Says Iraqis Used Poison Gas against Iranians in Latest Battles," *New York Times*, March 6, 1984, https://www.nytimes.com/1984/03/06 /world/us-says-iraqis-used-poison-gas-against-iranians-in-latest-battles.html.
16. State Department cable, Washington to Khartoum, March 24, 1984, Document 48, NSA EBB 82.
17. State Department cable, Washington to Amman, March 18, 1984, Document 6 in Malcolm Byrne, comp., *Saddam Hussein: More Secret History*, National Security Archive Electronic Briefing Book No. 107 (hereafter NSA EBB 107), December 18, 2003, https://nsarchive2.gwu.edu/NSAEBB /NSAEBB107/.
18. "worsened": State Department cable, Washington to Khartoum, March 24, 1984, Document 48, NSA EBB 82; Rumsfeld's instructions from Document 7, NSA EBB 107, as quoted in Hiltermann, *A Poisonous Affair*, 52.
19. "You got beaten" and habits and attire: Janet Wallach, "The Artful Ambassador," *Washington Post*, December 8, 1985, and author's interview with Samir Vincent; "like a Baath Party thug": David L. Mack, oral history interview by Charles Stuart Kennedy, October 24, 1995, Foreign Affairs Oral History Collection, Association for Diplomatic Studies and Training (hereafter cited as FAOHC, ADST).

20. Hamdoon's education from State Department cable, Baghdad to Washington, undated late 1984, RAC Box 4, RRPL, as well as author's interviews with Samir Vincent, who also attended the Jesuit school, and Odeh Aburdene; Hamdoon on *Cagney & Lacey* and "control the cities . . . control the gangs" from Wallach, "The Artful Ambassador"; gifting of Cuban cigars and champagne from Sarah Moawad interview with Peter Bourne.

21. Moawad interview with Judith Kipper and author's interview with Aburdene.

22. Moawad interview with Mary King.

23. All quotations from interviews with King and Aburdene.

24. Mack's oral history interview, FAOHC, ADST; Daniel Pipes, "'Thank You for Everything. But Do Not Stay': An Exchange with the Late Nizar Hamdoon," *Middle East Quarterly* 10, no. 4 (Fall 2003): 33–44.

25. Pipes, "'Thank You for Everything,'" 33–44; Hamdoon's remarks from his appearance at the Baltimore Council on Foreign Affairs, April 2, 1986, https://www.youtube.com/watch?v=ym_1Z174NbQ.

26. "Iran-Iraq War," C.I.A. memorandum, August 28, 1984, in Matthew M. Aid, ed., *U.S. Intelligence on the Middle East, 1945–2009*, BrillOnline Primary Sources, accessed through the Library of Congress.

27. Memorandum from Robert McFarlane, November 26, 1984, Folder: Iraq 1984 (11/21/1984–12/24/1984), RAC Box 4, Edwin Meese Files, RRPL.

28. Memorandum of Conversation, Oval Office, November 26, 1984, RAC Box 4, NSC Near East and South Asia Affairs Directorate Collection, RRPL.

29. Ronald Reagan, *The Reagan Diaries*, ed. Douglas Brinkley (New York: HarperCollins, 2007), 281.

Chapter 5: Department 3000

1. Dhafir Selbi, Zuhair Al-Chalabi, and Imad Khadduri, *Unrevealed Milestones in the Iraqi National Nuclear Program, 1981–1991*, ed. Imad Khadduri (Scotts Valley, Calif.: CreateSpace Independent Publishing, 2011), 41–42.

2. Saddam's use of Wanderlodges from interviews with Mazin Jazrawi by Amel Brahmi, as well as from Mazin Jazrawi, *'Ashr Sanawat fi qusur Saddam Hussein* (London: Dar al-Hikmah, 2005), hereafter cited in English as *Ten Years in Saddam's Palaces*, translated for the author by Amel Brahmi; see also Patrick J. Sloyan, "Air Force Hunted Motor Home in War's 'Get Saddam' Mission," *Washington Post*, June 23, 1991; luxury Wanderlodges from N. R. Kleinfield, "On the Road in a $350,000 Home," *New York Times*, June 21, 1987.

3. Radwaniyah under construction from *Ten Years in Saddam's Palaces* and interviews with Jazrawi.

4. Jafar and Niaimi, *Last Confession*, chapter three.

5. "fruitful objectives": Selbi, Chalabi, and Khadduri, *Unrevealed Milestones*, 42, and interviews with Selbi and Khadduri; see also Målfrid Braut-Hegghammer, *Unclear Physics: Why Iraq and Libya Failed to Build Nuclear Weapons* (Ithaca, N.Y.: Cornell University Press, 2016), 95–96; Jafar's thinking from correspondence with Jafar; "make a golden statue": Jafar and Niaimi, *Last Confession*, chapter three.

6. Jafar and Niaimi, *Last Confession*, chapter three, and correspondence with Jafar.

7. Interviews and correspondence with Jafar.

8. Interviews and correspondence with Jafar. See also Braut-Hegghammer, *Unclear Physics*, 80.

9. Interviews and correspondence with Jafar, as well as the CAFCD. The chronology in this document is supported by the memoirs of Jafar, Niaimi, Selbi, and Khadduri, as well as by the findings of I.A.E.A. inspectors. See also Jafar and Niaimi, *Last Confession*, chapter four.

10. Interviews with Shahristani; "The hardest part of solitary" and "Dad, open the lid": Shahristani, *Free of Fear*, 86–89.

11. CRRC SH-SHTP-A-000-896 and SH-SHTP-A-001-023.

12. Interviews with Saati and Janabi.

13. C.I.A. Directorate of Intelligence, "The Iraqi Nuclear Program: Progress Despite Setbacks," June 1983, Document 19, NSA EBB 82.

14. C.I.A. Directorate of Intelligence, "Iraq's Nuclear Program: Acquiring a Nuclear Fuel Cycle," partially redacted, February 1985, in Matthew M. Aid, ed., *U.S. Intelligence on the Middle East, 1945–2009*, BrillOnline Primary Sources, accessed through the Library of Congress.

15. "It's time to start" and five-year forecast from an interview with Jafar.

16. Jafar and Niaimi, *Last Confession*, chapter three.

17. CRRC SH-SHTP-D-000-573, as excerpted in Murray and Woods, *Iran-Iraq War*, 19.

18. "Sweet and Bitter Years," CRRC SH-MISC-D-000-948.

19. Interviews with Jafar and Selbi; "could control him": Iraq Survey Group, *Duelfer Report*, 1:45.

20. Obeidi and Pitzer, *Bomb in My Garden*, 57.

21. Obeidi and Pitzer, 59–62.

Chapter 6: A Conspiracy Foretold

1. See "Attorney General Ed Meese Tells Reporters That Between $10–$30 Million Had Been Diverted to the Contras," Meese press conference at the White House, November 25, 1986, AP Archive video, published September 24, 2012, http://www.aparchive.com/metadata/youtube/7615
   e940a0ba4d8baa5cfa976506e949; Bernard Weinraub, "Iran Payment Found Diverted to Contras;
   Reagan Security Adviser and Aide Are Out," *New York Times*, November 26, 1986, https://www
   .nytimes.com/1986/11/26/world/iran-payment-found-diverted-to-contras-reagan-security
   -adviser-and-aide-are-out.html.

2. For an authoritative account of Iran-Contra, see Malcolm Byrne, *Iran-Contra: Reagan's Scandal and
   the Unchecked Abuse of Presidential Power* (Lawrence, Kans.: University Press of Kansas, 2014). The
   details here are from one of the investigative bodies convened to examine the matter, the President's
   Special Review Board, more commonly known as the Tower Commission. It is available as a book:
   John Tower, Edmund Muskie, and Brent Scowcroft, *The Tower Commission Report: The Full Text of
   the President's Special Review Board* (New York: Bantam Books, 1987). The Iranian Jewish population's emigration is from Houman Sarshar, *Esther's Children: A Portrait of Iranian Jews* (Melrose
   Park, Pa.: Jewish Publication Society, 2002), ix, 258.

3. "This is not going": interview with Thomas Twetten; "units, troops, tanks" and "Everyone here at
   headquarters": C.I.A. cable, McMahon to Casey, Eyes Only, "Present Status in Saga Regarding the
   Movement of TOW Missiles," January 25, 1986, NSA, https://nsarchive.gwu.edu/document/16591
   -document-03-cia-cable-deputy-director-john.

4. Interview with Twetten.

5. Murray and Woods, *Iran-Iraq War*, 262.

6. In Ashton, *King Hussein of Jordan*, 224, Ashton describes a November 1986 letter from King Hussein to Ronald Reagan in which the king suggested that C.I.A. advice to Baghdad about Iranian intentions at Faw had been inaccurate, raising questions in Saddam's mind about whether the
   mistaken analysis had been intentional.

7. Interview with Twetten. Cave and other C.I.A. leaders made similar statements. See Malcolm
   Byrne, "Mixed Messages: U.S. Intelligence Support to Both Sides during the Iran-Iraq War" (paper
   prepared for The Iran-Iraq War: The View from Baghdad, a conference held at the Woodrow Wilson
   International Center for Scholars and National Defense University, Washington, D.C., October 25–
   27, 2011); "extensive and encyclopedic": author's correspondence with Lang.

8. Gibson, *Covert Relationship*, 173.

9. "irresponsible press bilge": Ronald Reagan's diary entry for November 12, 1986, White House Diaries, Ronald Reagan Foundation, https://www.reaganfoundation.org/ronald-reagan/white-house
   -diaries/diary-entry-11121986/; Reagan's address: "Address to the Nation on the Iran Arms and
   Contra Aid Controversy," November 13, 1986, RRPL, transcript and video, https://www.reagan
   library.gov/archives/speech/address-nation-iran-arms-and-contra-aid-controversy-november-13
   -1986; "information that must remain classified": Unsigned, Top Secret (declassified), November
   13, 1986, Folder: Iran Policy–Sensitive, RAC Box 2, Howard J. Teicher Files, RRPL.

10. CRRC SH-SHTP-A-000-555.

11. "I am not surprised" and "this level of bad": CRRC SH-SHTP-A-000-555; "Zionism is taking":
    CRRC SH-SHTP-A-000-561; "the real American conspiracy": CRRC SH-SHTP-D-000-609. The
    English translation reflects a change recommended by Ibrahim Al-Marashi as part of his review of
    CRRC materials for the author.

12. Ashton, *King Hussein of Jordan*, 224.

13. State Department cable, Baghdad to Washington, November 16, 1986, RAC Box 2, Howard J. Tei-
    cher Files, RRPL.

14. "somebody took my only son": interview with a former colleague; "about the U.S. being": Hilter-
    mann, *A Poisonous Affair*, 77; "People were out to get": interview with Odeh Aburdene.

15. See full text of official Iraqi translation, Document 6 in Malcolm Byrne, ed., *U.S.-Iran: Lessons from
    an Earlier War*, National Security Archive Electronic Briefing Book No. 394 (hereafter NSA EBB
    394), December 18, 2003, https://nsarchive2.gwu.edu/NSAEBB/NSAEBB394/docs/86-11-18%20S
    addam%20to%20Reagan.pdf.

16. "Sweet and Bitter Years," CRRC SH-MISC-D-001-919; details about Saddam's writings from Bengio, *Saddam's Word*, 78; cake-cutting detail from "Saddam Home Videos Show Private Life," CNN, April 24, 2003, http://edition.cnn.com/2003/WORLD/meast/04/24/sprj.irq.videos/index.html.

17. Gibson, *Covert Relationship*, 199.

18. Blight et al., *Becoming Enemies*, 144. Murphy recounts this exchange during an oral history discussion: "I thought the metaphor showed a keen understanding of the way big powers act," he said. "Tariq Aziz, by the way, nearly fell off his chair laughing at the joke."

Chapter 7: Druid Leader

1. United States Central Command, *Formal Investigation into the Circumstances Surrounding the Attack on the USS Stark (FFG-31) on 17 May 1987* (Washington, D.C.: Department of Defense, 1987), https://www.jag.navy.mil/library/investigations/USS%20STARK%20BASIC.pdf.

2. For Reagan's remarks, see "Statement on the Attack against the U.S.S. *Stark*," May 18, 1987, RRPL, transcript, https://www.reaganlibrary.gov/archives/speech/statement-attack-against-uss-stark; excerpts of Saddam's letter from Blight et al., *Becoming Enemies*, 327–28.

3. Saddam's condolence letter, RAC Box 3, NSC Near East and South Asia Affairs Directorate Collection, RRPL.

4. Murphy to Shultz, "U.S.S. *Stark*: Results of the Joint Investigation Group's Sessions in Baghdad," June 1, 1987, RAC Box 14, NSC Near East and South Asia Directorate Collection, RRPL.

5. Iraq's refusal to allow interview with pilot from interviews and correspondence with Rick Francona and Pat Lang; Saddam's purchase of Dassault Falcons from Ashton and Gibson, *Iran-Iraq War*, 219–20; Falcon in attack on *Stark* from Murray and Woods, *Iran-Iraq War*, 307.

6. Correspondence with Lang.

7. Correspondence with Lang.

8. Francona bio and late-1987 D.I.A. report are from an interview with Francona; Haywood Rankin's quoted recollections from his oral history interview by Charles Stuart Kennedy, July 24, 1998, FAOHC, ADST.

9. Correspondence with Lang and interview with Francona.

10. Correspondence with Lang and interview with Francona. Dialogue from Francona.

11. Details about target packages from correspondence with Lang; "direct, immediate tactical value": interview with Francona.

12. Correspondence with Lang.

13. Correspondence with Lang and interview with Francona. According to Katherine Hennessey, *Shakespeare on the Arabian Peninsula* (London: Palgrave Macmillan, 2018), 14–15, the legend of Sheikh Zubair originated with the nineteenth-century author Ahmad Faris al-Shidyaq, as a joke.

14. Interview with Francona; "chemically dependent": interview with Kenneth Pollack, a C.I.A. analyst during this period; Iraqi Army growth figures from Murray and Woods, *Iran-Iraq War*, 291.

15. Iraq Survey Group, *Duelfer Report*, 3:5–10.

16. Interview with Francona.

17. Correspondence with Lang; Bruce Riedel quotations from Blight et al., *Becoming Enemies*, 180.

Chapter 8: "Who Is Going to Say Anything?"

1. Ali Hassan al-Majid's biography and quotation are from his F.B.I. detention interview, February 4, 2004.

2. "would not prevail" and "Complete destruction hanging over": Bruce W. Jentleson, *With Friends Like These: Reagan, Bush, and Saddam, 1982–1990* (New York: W. W. Norton & Company, 1994), 72.

3. CRRC SH-SHTP-A-000-788.

4. Hiltermann, *A Poisonous Affair*, xx–xxi, 105.

5. Iraqi contemporaneous assessments from Murray and Woods, *Iran-Iraq War*, 315–16; David Hirst from Hiltermann, *A Poisonous Affair*, 6.

6. David B. Ottaway, "U.S. Decries Iraqi Use of Chemical Weapons," *Washington Post*, March 24, 1988.

7. "insisted": Lang's interview with Hiltermann, *A Poisonous Affair*, 203. After a thorough review of the evidence around whether Iran ever used chemical arms during its war with Iraq, Hiltermann concludes that this is "not impossible, but unlikely."

8. Correspondence with Lang and interview with Francona. Dialogue from Francona.

9. Hiltermann, *A Poisonous Affair*, 95.

10. Majid's F.B.I. detention interview, March 20, 2004. The English translation of the directive was read into the interview record by the questioner. Joost R. Hiltermann, *Bureaucracy of Repression: The Iraqi Government in Its Own Words* (New York: Human Rights Watch, 1994), appendix, document 15, https://www.hrw.org/legacy/reports/1994/iraq/APPENDIX.htm.

11. The April 10, 1987, chemical attack on a neighboring village, named Tazashar, is detailed in "Known Chemical Attacks in Iraqi Kurdistan, 1987–1988," an appendix to a Middle East Watch report, *Genocide in Iraq: The Anfal Campaign against the Kurds* (New York: Human Rights Watch, 1993), https://www.hrw.org/reports/1993/iraqanfal/APPENDIXC.htm.

12. Author's interviews with Wahid Kochani, with gratitude to Joost Hiltermann for making the introduction. The narrative in this chapter is largely based on interviews with Kochani. He first provided an account of his experience to Hiltermann for the Middle East Watch / Human Rights Watch July 1993 report (supra note 11). Kochani was given a pseudonym in that document, as he still lived in Iraq at the time. Later he was resettled in the United States. He also provided testimony at a post-2003 trial of Saddam Hussein and gave an extensive interview, in 2013, to the Kurdish researcher Arif Qurbany, translated from Kurdish to English by Abdulkarim Uzeri. His narrative has been consistent across all of these accounts and is corroborated by the investigations of Middle East Watch and others, which identified transit camps that Kochani passed through and collected corroborating testimony from other survivors. There are, inevitably, variations in the language Kochani uses to narrate particular episodes. For Kochani's quotations in this chapter, I have used only my interviews, translated from Kurdish by his son Hemin. Amel Brahmi also conducted supplementary interviews. I relied on Qurbany for some of the Anwar Tayyar narrative.

13. Interviews with Kochani.

14. Murray and Woods, *Iran-Iraq War*, 333.

15. Interviews with Kochani.

16. Interviews with Kochani.

17. Kochani told me that he tried to find the Arab family that saved him but could not identify them.

18. In its initial investigation, Middle East Watch / Human Rights Watch identified at least fifty thousand names of individuals who disappeared during the Anfal, presumed to be executed, and Hiltermann conservatively estimated the toll at about eighty thousand. Kurdish authorities have insisted on a death toll closer to two hundred thousand. The researcher Choman Hardi, who conducted an extensive review of Anfal literature, offered an estimate of one hundred thousand. More recent scholars have credited the higher end of the range. See, for example, Lisa Blaydes, *State of Repression: Iraq under Saddam Hussein* (Princeton, N.J.: Princeton University Press, 2018), 154, which cites estimates of one hundred and fifty thousand to two hundred thousand. That two thousand and six hundred villages were destroyed during the Anfal (more than one thousand had been destroyed in earlier Iraqi campaigns) is noted by Choman Hardi, *Gendered Experiences of Genocide: Anfal Survivors in Kurdistan-Iraq* (Farnham, U.K.: Ashgate, 2011), 13. The account of the bulldozer driver, Abdul-Hassan Muhan Murad, also comes from Hardi, 18. Women, girls, and elderly prisoners who survived detention provided accounts of their experiences as well. After thousands were packed into transit and internment camps, "the majority of the men were killed within days (as well as some of the women), and it was the women who lived through the hunger, illness, loss, and desperation in the camps," writes Hardi, 4.

19. CRRC SH-GMID-D-000-859.

20. Hiltermann, *A Poisonous Affair*, 138.

21. On the quashing of the Prevention of Genocide Act, see, for example, a draft letter, circa September 1988, from Assistant Secretary of State for Legislative Affairs J. Edward Fox to a House committee. "We could not characterize Iraqi actions as 'genocide' based on the evidence available at this time," the draft letter states. Box CFOA 1321, Economic Policy Council Records 1985–1988, RRPL.

22. CCRC SH-SHTP-0000-788.

23. CCRC SH-SHTP-0000-788.

24. Khomeini quotation from Murray and Woods, *Iran-Iraq War*, 337; Saddam's termination of cooperation with the D.I.A from an interview with Francona.

25. Casualties, war expenditures, and initial foreign exchange reserves from Jeffrey A. Engel, ed., *Into the Desert: Reflections on the Gulf War* (Oxford: Oxford University Press, 2013), 28; debt statistics from Glen Rangwala, as cited in Ashton and Gibson, *Iran-Iraq War*, 97; "Victory in the war": Saddam's message to Washington via April Glaspie, July 25, 1990, as cited in Engel, *Into the Desert*, 28.

Chapter 9: The Prodigal Son

1. The basic facts about Uday's killing of Gegeo are well documented, including through remarks Saddam later made about the incident in recorded leadership meetings. Yet exactly what happened that night is less certain. Two published eyewitness accounts are available from Zafer Muhammad Jaber and Latif Yahia. The former was interviewed for Ala Bashir's memoir, *The Insider*, written with Lars Sigurd Sunnanå, a Norwegian journalist. The latter, who has maintained a website, https://www .latifyahia.net, is a former Iraqi Army officer who fled the country in 1993. He claims to have served as Uday's body double. Reporting by the British journalist Ed Caesar ("The Double Dealer," January 23, 2011, *Sunday Times*, https://edcaesar.co.uk/2011/01/23/double-dealer-sunday-times/) raised doubts about Yahia's claims about his relationship with Uday. *The Guardian* also published skeptical reporting (Eoin Butler, "The Tangled Tale behind the Devil's Double," August 13, 2011, https:// www.theguardian.com/global/2011/aug/13/devils-double-tangled-tale). Yahia's account of what led up to Gegeo's killing, cited in Andrew Cockburn and Patrick Cockburn, *Out of the Ashes: The Resurrection of Saddam Hussein* (New York: HarperCollins, 1999), 153–55, overlaps with Jaber's but contains unique details. The Cockburns' book is among the best and most reliable journalistic accounts of Saddam's regime published before 2001, and at the time the book was written, questions about Yahia's reliability had not yet surfaced. I've disregarded Yahia and relied on Jaber's account, as given by Bashir and Sunnanå, *The Insider*, 81–86, as well as on an interview with Bashir. Frank Lloyd Wright's interest in Mother of Pigs is from Michael Kubo, "Genius versus Expertise: Frank Lloyd Wright and the Architects Collaborative at the University of Baghdad," *Histories of Postwar Architecture* 5, no. 8 (2021): 14–42.
2. Bashir and Sunnanå, *The Insider*, 81–86.
3. "His ideas were not clear": interview with Saman Abdul Majid; Tariq Aziz's remarks about Uday from his interview with Ali al-Dabagh.
4. "I did my SATs": Cockburn and Cockburn, *Out of the Ashes*, 151.
5. "watches, jewels and rings": Bashir and Sunnanå, *The Insider*, 83.
6. Bashir and Sunnanå, *The Insider*, 85–86.
7. "Sweet and Bitter Years," CRRC SH-MISC-D-001-919.
8. Bashir and Sunnanå, *The Insider*, 86.
9. "sports attire": "Sweet and Bitter Years," CRRC SH-MISC-D-001-919; Saddam's relationship with Samira Shahbandar has been widely commented upon. She was listed in April 2004 by the United Nations as part of a sanctions regime, and in the Security Council Committee's narrative summary, posted to the United Nations Security Council website on October 29, 2014, she was described as "Saddam's second wife and mother to his third son": https://www.un.org/securitycouncil/sanctions /1518/materials/summaries/individual/samira-shahbandar.
10. "Sweet and Bitter Years," CRRC SH-MISC-D-001-919.
11. CRRC SH-SHTP-A-000-665.
12. "Sweet and Bitter Years," CRRC SH-MISC-D-001-919.
13. "Sweet and Bitter Years," CRRC SH-MISC-D-001-919.
14. Military and economic aid from Engel, *Into the Desert*, 22.
15. "the purging of dozens": Kenneth M. Pollack, *The Threatening Storm: The Case for Invading Iraq* (New York: Random House, 2002), 27.
16. Georges Sada with Jim Nelson Black, *Saddam's Secrets: How an Iraqi General Defied and Survived Saddam Hussein* (Brentwood, Tenn.: Integrity Publishers, 2006), 118–19. Sada was an Iraqi Air Force general whom Saddam commissioned to conduct an investigation into the incident. He concluded that it was an accident. The pilot escaped execution. Sada recounts that after he submitted his report, "much to my surprise," Saddam sent him $10,000 and a gold watch.
17. Karsh and Rautsi, *Saddam Hussein*, 196.
18. Michael S. Schmidt, "Mohammed Ghani Hikmat, Iraqi Sculptor, Dies at 82," September 21, 2011, https://www.nytimes.com/2011/09/21/arts/design/mohammed-ghani-hikmat-iraqi-sculptor -dies-at-82.html.
19. Barzan's September 4 letter (Harmony ISGZ-2004-00172), as quoted in Kevin M. Woods, *The Mother of All Battles: Saddam Hussein's Strategic Plan for the Persian Gulf War* (Annapolis, Md.: Naval Institute Press, 2008), 41–42.
20. Woods, *Mother of All Battles*, 152.
21. Kerr-Bush exchange from Michael R. Gordon and Bernard E. Trainor, *The Generals' War: The Inside Story of the Conflict in the Gulf* (New York: Little, Brown and Company, 1995), 11; "encourage acceptably moderate behavior": George H. W. Bush and Brent Scowcroft, *A World Transformed* (New York: Vintage Books, 1998), loc. 6260 of 11461, Kindle.

22. See declassified National Security Directive 26, "U.S. Policy toward the Persian Gulf," October 2, 1989, National Security Directives, George H. W. Bush Library, https://bush4library.tamu.edu /files/nsd/nsd26.pdf; details about U.S.-Iraq Business Forum members from Jentleson, *With Friends Like These*, 84; Aziz's quip about a refrigerator from Sarah Moawad's interview with Mary King; "consistent with U.S. policy": Jentleson, *With Friends Like These*, 85; "a good-faith effort": Bush and Scowcroft, *World Transformed*, loc. 6285 of 11461, Kindle.

23. Baker and Aziz meeting described by Michael R. Gordon, "The Last War Syndrome," in *Into the Desert*, 118; that the C.I.A. had no significant sources close to Saddam from an interview with Thomas Twetten, then head of Near East operations at the C.I.A.; that the D.I.A.'s access had also dried up after the end of Druid Leader from an interview with Jim Ritchey, defense attaché in Baghdad after January 1989.

Chapter 10: Project 17

1. "finished as a world power" and "free hand": Don Oberdorfer, "Missed Signals in the Middle East," *Washington Post*, March 17, 1991; for Bush's waiver of congressional restrictions, see "Memorandum on Application of Export-Import Bank Restrictions in Connection with Iraq," January 17, 1990, American Presidency Project, University of California, Santa Barbara.

2. Saddam's remarks in Amman from Shibley Telhami, "The Arab Dimension of Saddam Hussein's Calculations," in *Into the Desert*, 154–56, and Long, *Saddam's War of Words*, 16.

3. "He had lost much weight": Donald Trelford, *Shouting in the Street: Adventures and Misadventures of a Fleet Street Survivor* (London: Biteback Publishing, 2017), loc. 4762 of 7459, Kindle; "Saddam is recovering": Augusta Anthony interview with Harold Walker.

4. CRRC SH-SHTP-A-000-910. CRRC logged the conversation as "undated (sometime after 1989)." The discussion makes clear that it took place between Farzad Bazoft's sentencing and execution.

5. Augusta Anthony interview with Robin Kealy.

6. "Thatcher wanted him alive": Salah Nasrawi, "Journalist Hanged for Alleged Spying; Britain Recalls Ambassador," Associated Press, March 15, 1990; "Our competitors would happily step": from declassified British records as quoted by Richard Norton-Taylor and Tracy McVeigh, "'It Would Be Bad for Our Interests': Why Thatcher Ignored the Murder of an *Observer* Journalist," *Guardian*, January 1, 2017.

7. Bull's biography from William Park, "The Tragic Tale of Saddam Hussein's 'Supergun,'" *BBC Future*, March 17, 2016; Mossad's assassination from Bergman, *Rise and Kill First*, 357–58; "We are dealing with": CRRC SH-SHTP-A-000-910.

8. "literally every day": Hamdi A. Hassan, *The Iraqi Invasion of Kuwait: Religion, Identity and Otherness in the Analysis of War and Conflict* (London: Pluto Press, 1999), 47.

9. "I swear to God": as quoted by the Iraqi News Agency and reported in "Saddam Threatens Israel with Chemical Weapons," United Press International, April 2, 1990; 'Everyone must know": from the same speech, as quoted in Long, *Saddam's War of Words*, 17.

10. Bush and Scowcroft, *World Transformed*, locs. 6290–91 of 11461, Kindle.

11. Long, *Saddam's War of Words*, 17.

12. "unambiguous message": Bush and Scowcroft, *World Transformed*, loc. 6307 of 11461, Kindle; Glaspie cable as excerpted by Gordon, "The Last War Syndrome," 121.

13. Cable from Secretary of State Baker to Senator Dole, April 12, 1990, Robert and Elizabeth Dole Archive, Robert J. Dole Institute of Politics, University of Kansas (hereafter cited as Dole Archive); State Department cable, Baghdad to Amman, April 11, 1990, Dole Archive. The letter and a transcript of the discussion were released by Iraq's Ministry of Foreign Affairs under the heading "A Message of Peace." Tariq Aziz almost certainly supervised the English translation, but the Arabic original is also available. The Dole Archive contains a markup of Iraq's English transcript made shortly after the trip that offers only a few amendments. One is the addition of Saddam's answer to Dole, who had just assured him about Bush's benign attentions: "This is sufficient for me." Scowcroft later wrote that the senators emerged from the meeting "basically optimistic" and advised the White House to "stay the course and keep the relationship open."

14. Meeting transcript, Dole Archive.

15. Meeting transcript, Dole Archive.

16. President Bush and King Hussein, "Telephone Conversation with King Hussein of Jordan," April 23, 1990, Memcons and Telcons, George H. W. Bush Presidential Library (hereafter cited as Bush Library), https://bush4library.tamu.edu/files/memcons-telcons/1990-04-23--Hussein%20I.pdf.

17. "Saddam's Message of Friendship to President Bush," State Department cable, Baghdad to Washington, July 25, 1990, Cable 90 BAGHDAD 4237, https://www.margaretthatcher.org/document/110705.

18. Excerpt from a record archived in the Department of Defense's Harmony database (hereafter cited as Harmony). The record, Harmony ISGQ-2003-M0006248, is a twenty-one-minute video file cited in Kevin M. Woods and James Lacey, *Iraqi Perspectives Project: Primary Source Materials for Saddam and Terrorism: Emerging Insights from Captured Iraqi Documents*, Paper P-4287 (Alexandria, Va.: Institute for Defense Analyses, 2007), 4:21.

19. "billions" and "without sweat": CRRC SH-SHTP-A-000-626; "They are afraid": CRRC SH-SHTP-A-000-910.

20. Jaber al-Sabah profile from Youssef M. Ibrahim, "The Exiled Emir," *New York Times*, September 26, 1990; "I know the Kuwaiti society": CRRC SH-SHTP-A-001-232, as excerpted in Kevin M. Woods, David D. Palkki, and Mark E. Stout, eds., *The Saddam Tapes: The Inner Workings of a Tyrant's Regime, 1978–2001* (Cambridge: Cambridge University Press, 2011), 171–72.

21. W. Nathaniel Howell, *Strangers When We Met: A Century of American Community in Kuwait* (Washington, D.C.: New Academia Publishing, 2015), 309.

22. Richard Murphy from Blight et al., *Becoming Enemies*, 222; W. Nathaniel Howell from *Strangers When We Met*, 316–17.

23. Kevin M. Woods et al., *Iraqi Perspectives Project: A View of Operation Iraqi Freedom from Saddam's Senior Leadership* (Norfolk, Va.: Joint Center for Operational Analysis, U.S. Joint Forces Command, 2006), 4.

24. Fred Moore, comp., *Iraq Speaks: Documents on the Gulf Crisis* (Palo Alto: Fred Moore, 1991), 3.

25. Blight et al., *Becoming Enemies*, 222.

26. Directorate of Air Intelligence reconnaissance survey from CRRC SH-AADF-D-000-881; military intelligence analysis from Woods, *Mother of All Battles*, 60–63.

27. Moore, *Iraq Speaks*, 5–8.

28. Bush's July 17 letter from Duelfer, *Hide and Seek*, 64; Revolution Day speech from Long, *Saddam's War of Words*, 20; that C.I.A satellites detected Hammurabi Division elements from Pollack, *Threatening Storm*, xi; "We heard from many quarters": Dick Cheney and Liz Cheney, *In My Time: A Personal and Political Memoir* (New York: Threshold Editions, 2011), 183.

29. State Department press guidance and instructions are from excerpts published in R. Jeffrey Smith, "State Department Cable Traffic on Iraq—Kuwait Tensions, July 1990," *Washington Post*, October 21, 1992. Smith's documents include a cable from Washington to Amman on July 19, 1990, reporting on David Mack's talking points over lunch with Mohammed al-Mashat the previous day, and a July 24, 1990, cable from Washington to Baghdad.

30. Interviews and correspondence with David Mack.

31. Interviews and correspondence with Mack, as well as the cables excerpted in Smith, "State Department Cable Traffic"; Glaspie's handling of statements from correspondence with April Glaspie.

32. Woods, *Mother of All Battles*, 63.

33. John Kelly's oral history interview by Thomas Stern, December 12, 1994, FAOHC, ADST.

34. Interviews and correspondence with Mack.

35. Kelly's oral history interview, FAOHC, ADST.

36. "The sons of Kuwait": Long, *Saddam's War of Words*, 20; Kelly's oral history interview, FAOHC, ADST.

37. "Saddam's Message of Friendship to President Bush," State Department cable, Baghdad to Washington, July 25, 1990, Cable 90 BAGHDAD 4237, https://www.margaretthatcher.org/document/110705. Authored by April Glaspie from her political officer's notes soon after the meeting, this is the cable reporting on her conversation with Saddam. It acknowledges the notification to Baghdad of the U.A.E. exercise.

38. "Iraqi statements suggest": Baker's cable to Baghdad, July 24, 1990; documents Glaspie carried from correspondence with Glaspie.

39. Two written records of the meeting are available in English. One is the full cable authorized by Glaspie (see supra note 37). The second is a long but incomplete transcript originally provided by Tariq Aziz's Ministry of Foreign Affairs to ABC News, which translated it from Arabic to English. This version was published in "Excerpts from Iraqi Document on Meeting with U.S. Envoy," *New York Times*, September 23, 1990. The Iraqi record is the fuller of the two and reads more like a transcript; the American record appears to be paraphrase and summary, with occasional quotations for specificity. The two records track the discussion's evolution from start to finish in the same way and contain some of the same notable exchanges. According to Glaspie, however, the Iraqi transcript contains a number of significant fabrications and omissions. She recalls that the Iraqi transcript omitted her final remarks, wherein she turned aside Saddam's request that she travel to

Washington to deliver his messages personally to President Bush. The quotations in my text in this chapter come from both transcripts, but I have used the Iraqi language only where the two records are in general agreement and the differences in translation choices do not appear to be material. See infra note 45 for an example of one of the fabrications in the Iraqi transcript cited by Glaspie.

40. See supra note 39.

41. Cable 90 BAGHDAD 4237 (supra note 37) and meeting records (supra note 39). If Saddam had asked, what would Glaspie have said? If she had stuck to her professional requirement to not invent U.S. policy, she might have picked up Baker's observation in his July 24 cable that the use of force would violate the principles of the U.N. Charter, a vague way of saying that military action might follow. This would hardly have stopped Saddam in his tracks, and he might not have even noticed the implied threat. In correspondence, Glaspie wrote that, in hindsight, she should have made "even more pointed allusion to the proximity of our fleet in Bahrain," but that this would have required clearance from Washington.

42. Iraqi fabrication, "broke down and wept" remark, and Glaspie's impression of Saddam from correspondence with Glaspie. All other quotations are from the meeting records. See supra notes 37 and 39.

43. Aziz interview with Ali al-Dabagh.

44. Francona, *Ally to Adversary*, 46–47.

45. President Bush and King Hussein, "Telephone Conversation with King Hussein of Jordan."

46. Gordon and Trainor, *The Generals' War*, 23.

47. Richard Haass, "The Gulf War: Its Place in History," in *Into the Desert*, 63.

48. Gordon and Trainor, *The Generals' War*, 26.

49. Bush and Scowcroft, *World Transformed*, locs. 6199 and 6207 of 11461, Kindle.

50. Cogan and Pickering from Blight et al., *Becoming Enemies*, 220.

51. Bush and Scowcroft, *World Transformed*, loc. 6426 of 11461, Kindle; Newton quotation from Blight et al., *Becoming Enemies*, 187.

52. Interview with Charles Duelfer, who led the Iraq Survey Group, a C.I.A.-based investigation into Saddam Hussein's rule, and who supervised some of Saddam's interviews while in custody. The quotation is Duelfer's paraphrase of Saddam's essential point.

Chapter 11: Crash Programs

1. Woods, *Mother of All Battles*, 80–81; Hussein Kamel's orders from Bashir and Sunnanâ, *The Insider*, 103.

2. John Levins, *Days of Fear: The Inside Story of the Iraqi Invasion and Occupation of Kuwait* (Dubai: Motivate Publishing, 1997), 23–27.

3. Brent Scowcroft's remarks from Bush and Scowcroft, *World Transformed*, locs. 6463 and 6507 of 11461, Kindle; Dick Cheney's remarks from minutes of the meeting, Bush Library, Haass, Richard N. files, presidential meeting files subseries.

4. President Bush, King Hussein, and President Mubarak, "Telephone Conversation with King Hussein of Jordan and President Mubarak of Egypt," August 2, 1990, Memcons and Telcons, Bush Library, https://bush41library.tamu.edu/files/memcons-telcons/1990-08-02--Hussein%20I.pdf.

5. "If Iraq wins" and "not helpful": Bush and Scowcroft, *World Transformed*, locs. 6549 and 6554 of 11461, Kindle; all other quotations and Bush's concern about fearing an Israeli nuclear strike from Henry E. Catto Jr., *Ambassadors at Sea: The High and Low Adventures of a Diplomat* (Austin: University of Texas Press, 1998), 3–4.

6. President Bush and King Fahd, "Telcon with King Fahd of Saudi Arabia," August 2, 1990, Memcons and Telcons, Bush Library, https://bush41library.tamu.edu/files/memcons-telcons/1990-08 -02--Fahd.pdf.

7. Cheney and Cheney, *In My Time*, 189–96.

8. Harmony ISGQ-2003-00044897, as excerpted in Woods, *Mother of All Battles*, 95. The transcript was corrected in Saddam's hand in 1993.

9. "spilling of the blood": Joseph Wilson, *The Politics of Truth: Inside the Lies That Led to War and Betrayed My Wife's CIA Identity* (New York: Carroll & Graf Publishers, 2004), 121; "You are a superpower": from Wilson's contemporaneous cable, as excerpted in Bush and Scowcroft, *World Transformed*, loc. 6894 of 11461, Kindle; "the carrot of cheap oil": Wilson, *Politics of Truth*, 121; "The Sabah family is history": Wilson, 121.

10. Saddam's discussions with Majid and Sabawi in Harmony ISGQ-2003-M0005325 and M0003629, as quoted in Woods, *Mother of All Battles*, 96, 99. For a detailed account of Majid's quixotic attempts to manage looting for official purposes rather than for the enrichment of individuals, see Ibrahim

Al-Marashi, "The Nineteenth Province: The Invasion of Kuwait and the 1991 Gulf War from the Iraqi Perspective" (Ph.D. thesis, St. Antony's College, University of Oxford, 2004). Marashi examined tens of thousands of occupation records captured by Kurdish rebels during the 1991 uprising and transferred to the United States. Gold bars from Peter James Spielmann, "Iraq and Kuwait Agree on Return of Stolen Gold," Associated Press, June 14, 1991; $52 billion from "Iraq Makes Final Reparation Payment to Kuwait for 1990 Invasion," UN News, February 9, 2022.

11. Marashi, "Nineteenth Province."

12. Interview and correspondence with Jafar; status and amounts of Iraq's French and Soviet reactor fuel at the time from David Albright, "Iraq's Programs to Make Highly Enriched Uranium and Plutonium for Nuclear Weapons Prior to the Gulf War," Institute for Science and International Security, 1997, revised October 2002.

13. Interview and correspondence with Jafar.

14. Correspondence with A. Q. Khan from CRRC SH-MICN-D-000-741. Khan did sell centrifuge designs and equipment to Iran and Libya, and it seems likely that his outreach to Iraq was not entrapment but a genuine effort to make a sale. Jafar and Obeidi from Obeidi and Pitzer, *Bomb in My Garden*, 131–32.

15. Obeidi and Pitzer, 135.

16. Moore, *Iraq Speaks*, 11, 15.

17. Jon Meacham, *Destiny and Power: The American Odyssey of George Herbert Walker Bush* (New York: Random House, 2015), 440.

18. Bush and Scowcroft, *World Transformed*, locs. 7470–72 of 11461, Kindle.

19. Bush's order to the C.I.A., August 1990, noted in Rick Atkinson, *Crusade: The Untold Story of the Persian Gulf War* (New York: Houghton Mifflin, 1993), 273; Siedel's role is from author's interviews with Dave Manners and Joseph Wilson. For accounts of the evacuation from the U.S. embassy in Kuwait City, see Levins, *Days of Fear*, 184–87, and Howell, *Strangers When We Met*, 335–37.

20. Marashi, "Nineteenth Province."

21. Harmony ISGQ-2003-M0003629 and 10151576, as quoted in Woods, *Mother of All Battles*, 108.

22. "preserve his authority": John Hannah, "The Primakov Mission to Baghdad and Washington: What Happened?," PolicyWatch 24, Washington Institute for Near East Policy, October 24, 1990; quotations from Primakov's meeting in the Oval Office from Bush and Scowcroft, *World Transformed*, locs. 7700–7707 of 11461, Kindle.

23. Atkinson, *Crusade*, 120.

24. Reuters, "Potential War Casualties Put at 100,000," *Los Angeles Times*, September 5, 1990.

25. Bush and Scowcroft, *World Transformed*, locs. 8801–10 of 11461, Kindle.

26. Harmony ISGQ-2003-M0001716, as excerpted in Woods, *Mother of All Battles*, 153.

27. Izzat Ibrahim al-Douri's comments from Harmony ISGQ-2003-M0004608, as excerpted in Woods, 188; "This war was launched": CRRC SH-SHTP-D-000-557, December 15, 1990.

28. Kevin M. Woods et al., "The Revolutionary Command Council Discusses Civil Defense Measures and Iraqi Morale in the Face of Potential Nuclear Strikes on Iraqi Cities (29 December 1990)," in *A Survey of Saddam's Audio Files 1978–2001: Toward an Understanding of Authoritarian Regimes*, Paper P-4548 (Alexandria, Va.: Institute for Defense Analyses, 2010), 288, 289, 291.

29. CRRC SH-SHTP-A-000-670.

30. Peter Baker and Susan Glasser, *The Man Who Ran Washington: The Life and Times of James A. Baker III* (New York: Doubleday, 2020), 418.

31. Baker and Glasser, *Man Who Ran Washington*, 418–20.

32. Iraq Survey Group, *Duelfer Report*, 1:97–100. The report provides a translated transcript of a recording of the meeting.

33. Chemical-arms preparations described in Woods, *Mother of All Battles*, 155–56, citing Harmony CMPC-2003-004325; estimate of biological weapons prepared from Raymond A. Zilinskas, "Iraq's Biological Weapons: The Past as Future?," *Journal of the American Medical Association* 278, no. 5 (1997): 418–24, and Richard L. Russell, "Iraq's Chemical Weapons Legacy: What Others Might Learn from Saddam," *Middle East Journal* 59, no. 2 (Spring 2005): 187–208.

34. Iraq Survey Group, *Duelfer Report*, 1:97–100.

35. Centrifuge preparations from the CACFD; interviews with Selbi and Janabi; Garry B. Dillon, "The IAEA in Iraq: Past Activities and Findings," *IAEA Bulletin* 44, no. 2 (June 2002): 13–16, first published by the Carnegie Endowment for International Peace; C.I.A., "Prewar Status of Iraq's Weapons of Mass Destruction," March 1991 (declassified 2002), Document 4 in Jeffrey Richelson, ed., *Iraq and Weapons of Mass Destruction*, National Security Archive Electronic Briefing Book No. 80, February 11, 2004, https://nsarchive2.gwu.edu/NSAEBB/NSAEBB80/wmd04.pdf.

36. Bush and Scowcroft, *World Transformed*, locs. 9120–23 of 11461, Kindle.

Chapter 12: "The Situation Is Under Excellent Control"

1. "We don't do assassinations": Brent Scowcroft's interview with *ABC News Saturday Night: Peter Jennings Reporting*, season 1, episode 1, "Showdown with Saddam," aired February 7, 1998; "one-man show" and "ought to be": Rick Atkinson, "U.S. to Rely on Air Strikes If War Erupts," *Washington Post*, September 16, 1990. When Cheney fired Dugan, he told reporters that the general's comments about targeting Saddam personally were "potentially a violation" of the executive order banning assassinations of foreign leaders.

2. Schwarzkopf and McPeak estimates from Atkinson, *Crusade*, 273; Glosson estimate from Gordon and Trainor, *The Generals' War*, 137; "Whenever the enemy": Harmony ISGP-2003-00028432, as excerpted in Woods, *Mother of All Battles*, 184.

3. Gordon and Trainor, *The Generals' War*, 216; Wanderlodge targeting from Patrick J. Sloyan, "Air Force Hunted Motor Home in War's 'Get Saddam' Mission," *Washington Post*, June 23, 1991. According to this account, U.S. strikes destroyed two Wanderlodges used by Iraqi generals.

4. "I wanted to play": Gordon and Trainor, *The Generals' War*, 315.

5. Deptula from Gordon and Trainor, 315.

6. Karsh and Rautsi, *Saddam Hussein*, 245.

7. Thomas A. Keaney and Eliot A. Cohen, *Gulf War Air Power Survey: Summary Report*, vol. 4 of 5 (Washington, D.C.: U.S. Government Printing Office, 1993), https://media.defense.gov/2010/Sep/27/2001329817/-1/-1/0/AFD-100927-066.pdf.

8. Woods, *Mother of All Battles*, 182.

9. Woods, 182. On deterrence, see Woods, 156.

10. Francona, *Ally to Adversary*, 113, and an interview with Francona, who was present.

11. CRRC SH-SHTP-A-001-043.

12. Bush and Scowcroft, *World Transformed*, locs. 9206 and 9210 of 11461, Kindle; Cheney's remarks from an interview in *Frontline*, season 14, episode 1, "The Gulf War," written by Eamonn Matthews, narrated by Will Lyman, aired January 9, 1996, on PBS, transcript, https://www.pbs.org/wgbh/pages/frontline/gulf/oral/cheney/1.html.

13. "We have been attacked": Bush and Scowcroft, *World Transformed*, loc. 9264 of 11461, Kindle; Scowcroft on turning down Shamir's request from "Brent Scowcroft Oral History Part II," interview by Philip Zelikow, August 10, 2000, Miller Center, University of Virginia, transcript, https://millercenter.org/the-presidency/presidential-oral-histories/brent-scowcroft-oral-history-part-ii.

14. "You are free to fight": Karsh and Rautsi, *Saddam Hussein*, 250; "Israel couldn't do anything": Bush and Scowcroft, *World Transformed*, loc. 9266 of 11461, Kindle.

15. Gravity bombs from Keaney and Cohen, *Gulf War Air Power Survey*, 4:103; estimated casualties, based on prisoner-of-war interviews, from *Frontline*, "The Gulf War."

16. Aircraft from Woods, *Mother of All Battles*, 193; oil wells from Marashi, "Nineteenth Province."

17. Georges Sada with Jim Nelson Black, *Saddam's Secrets*, 181; Pentagon report from Michael R. Gordon, "Iraqi War Crimes Asserted by U.S.," *New York Times*, March 20, 1993.

18. CRRC SH-SHTP-A-000-931.

19. Yevgeni Primakov, "My Final Visit with Saddam Hussein," *Time*, March 11, 1991; Gordon and Trainor, *The Generals' War*, 333.

20. Strike on civilians from Alessandra Stanley, "Iraq Says U.S. Killed Hundreds of Civilians at Shelter, but Allies Call It a Military Post," *New York Times*, February 14, 1991; additional details and Richard Neal from Robert K. Goldman, *The Bombing of Iraqi Cities* (New York: Human Rights Watch, 1991), https://www.hrw.org/reports/1991/IRAQ291.htm.

21. Woods et al., *Survey of Saddam's Audio Files 1978–2001*, 225.

22. George H. W. Bush, "Remarks to Raytheon Missile Systems Plant Employees," February 15, 1991, Andover, Mass., Government Printing Office transcript, https://www.govinfo.gov/content/pkg/PPP-1991-book1/html/PPP-1991-book1-doc-pg148.htm.

23. Interviews with multiple C.I.A. officers familiar with Iraqi sourcing at the time.

24. Primakov, "My Final Visit with Saddam Hussein."

25. Primakov, "My Final Visit with Saddam Hussein"; "neither could we be dissuaded": Bush and Scowcroft, *World Transformed*, loc. 9621 of 11461, Kindle.

26. CRRC SH-SHTP-A-000-630.

27. "very satisfied": CRRC SH-SHTP-A-000-630; "I knew he would betray": CRRC SH-SHTP-A-000-666.

28. There are three CRRC transcripts of Saddam's discussions with military and civilian advisers on February 24, including one that takes place after Aziz arrives from Moscow. These are SH-SHTP-A-000-630, 666, and 931. All quotations are drawn from these three transcripts.

29. CRRC SH-SHTP-A-000-630, 666, and 931.

30. Harmony ISGQ-2003-10151507, as excerpted in Woods, *Mother of All Battles*, 229.

31. Statistics from Atkinson, *Crusade*, 450–51; "pianos, toilets, sinks": Francona, *Ally to Adversary*, 140.

32. Reuters, "The Bush Statement; Transcript of President's Words on Iraqi Retreat," *New York Times*, February 27, 1991, https://www.nytimes.com/1991/02/27/world/war-gulf-bush-statement-transcript-president-s-words-iraqi-retreat.html; Powell from Atkinson, *Crusade*, 452.

33. Atkinson, 471. See also Robert A. Divine, "The Persian Gulf War Revisited: Tactical Victory, Strategic Failure," *Diplomatic History* 24, no. 1 (Winter 2000): 129–38.

34. Engel, *Into the Desert*, 135.

35. George H. W. Bush, "Address on the End of the Gulf War," February 27, 1991, Miller Center, University of Virginia, transcript and video, https://millercenter.org/the-presidency/presidential-speeches/february-27-1991-address-end-gulf-war.

36. James Mann, *The Great Rift: Dick Cheney, Colin Powell, and the Broken Friendship That Defined an Era* (New York: Henry Holt and Company, 2020), 138.

37. Bush and Scowcroft, *World Transformed*, loc. 9893 of 11461, Kindle.

Chapter 13: Iraqi Spring

1. Interviews with Hussain Al-Shahristani, as well as Shahristani, *Free of Fear*, 89–93; details on the founding of SCIRI from International Crisis Group, *Shiite Politics in Iraq: The Role of the Supreme Council*, Middle East Report No. 70 (Brussels: International Crisis Group, 2007).

2. Interviews with Shahristani, as well as Shahristani, *Free of Fear*, 95–99.

3. "complicated if not impossible": H. Norman Schwarzkopf, *It Doesn't Take a Hero: The Autobiography of General H. Norman Schwarzkopf* (New York: Bantam Books, 1992), loc. 8934 of 9729, Kindle. The author covered the cease-fire talks for *The Washington Post*, flying up to Safwan on a press helicopter. Schwarzkopf describes the landscape and the preparation of the scene (loc. 739 of 9729, Kindle).

4. Woods, *Mother of All Battles*, 244–45, citing a memoir by General Sultan Hashim Ahmad al-Tai.

5. "determined to conduct": Schwarzkopf, *It Doesn't Take a Hero*, loc. 9122 of 9729, Kindle; "I'm not here to give": Philip Shenon, "Cease-Fire Meeting; A Hard-Faced Schwarzkopf Sets Terms at Desert Meeting," *New York Times*, March 4, 1991.

6. Schwarzkopf, *It Doesn't Take a Hero*, loc. 752–57 of 9729, Kindle, and Francona, *Ally to Adversary*, 147–51. The quotations used here are from Schwarzkopf. The two American accounts of the dialogue are essentially the same and are broadly confirmed by the Iraqi side, according to Kevin Woods's translation of Sultan Hashim Ahmad al-Tai's memoir.

7. Schwarzkopf, *It Doesn't Take a Hero*, loc. 752–57 of 9729, Kindle.

8. Interview with Qasim Albrisem.

9. Well-documented open-source accounts of the uprising include: *Endless Torment: The 1991 Uprising in Iraq and Its Aftermath* (New York: Human Rights Watch, 1992), https://www.hrw.org/legacy/reports/1992/Iraq926.htm; Ahlulbayt TV's documentary film *The '91 Uprising: The Story behind the '91 Uprising in Iraq*, https://www.youtube.com/watch?v=8sC38cXiJYw; *Iraq: Human Rights Violations since the Uprising*, MDE 14/05/91 (London: Amnesty International, 1991), https://www.amnesty.org/en/documents/mde14/005/1991/en/; and the opening chapter of Cockburn and Cockburn, *Out of the Ashes*, 3–30. After 2003, the Iraqi High Tribunal and international war crimes investigators attached to the court captured and translated many thousands of pages of contemporaneous regime records, audio recordings, and videos, and they received hundreds of witness statements and complaints from Iraqi survivors of the uprising. Sadly, many of these records remain publicly unavailable. Through journalistic sources, I was able to review a sizable section of records once held by the Regime Crimes Liaison Office, a U.S.-funded unit that assisted the Iraqi High Tribunal. These records are hereafter cited as "RCLO records." The account here is from those and other documentary sources; interviews with Qasim Albrisem and Abbas Kadhim; Albrisem's memoir (with David Hetherington), *Flight from Saddam* (Scotts Valley, Calif.: CreateSpace Independent Publishing, 2013); and Kadhim's study, *The Hawza Under Siege: A Study in the Baath Party Archive*, Occasional Paper No. 1 (Boston: Boston University Institute for Iraqi Studies, 2013).

10. RCLO records.

11. ICG, *Shiite Politics in Iraq*; correspondence with Joost Hiltermann.

12. RCLO records.

13. Interviews with Albrisem, as well as Albrisem and Hetherington, *Flight from Saddam*, 19–21; gasoline rumor from RCLO records.

14. RCLO records.
15. Interviews with Kadhim, as well as his interview for *The '91 Uprising*.
16. Shahristani, *Free of Fear*, 104.
17. Interviews with Kadhim.
18. Leaflet from Pollack, *Threatening Storm*, 48.
19. Richard Haass, "The Gulf War: Its Place in History," in *Into the Desert*, 76; "We made some very overoptimistic": interview with David Mack.
20. Interview with Laipson; Boucher from Human Rights Watch, *Endless Torment*, 94.
21. Gordon and Trainor, *The Generals' War*, 454; "telling the good guys": Haass, "The Gulf War: Its Place in History," 74.
22. CRRC SH-SHTP-A-000-614. Hussein Kamel appears to be reporting back after leading counterstrikes against the rebels in Karbala and Najaf.
23. CRRC SH-SHTP-A-000-739.
24. "been trouble" and "the repression occurred immediately": CRRC SH-SHTP-A-000-739; March 5 announcement of the appointments of Majid and Hussein Kamel from Karsh and Rautsi, *Saddam Hussein*, 272–73; March 9 order and execution order (dated March 27) from RCLO records.
25. That sarin bombs were initially dropped but found ineffective, entailing a resort to tear gas, is from Iraq Survey Group, *Duelfer Report*, 1:25.
26. Amnesty International, *Human Rights Violations since the Uprising*; RCLO records; interview with Kadhim.
27. CRRC SH-RPGD-D-000-581.
28. Interview with Kadhim; specifics about the assault on Najaf and "orders were given" from CRRC SH-RPGD-D-000-581; execution of Najaf committee members from Shahristani, *Free of Fear*, 104. Al-Khoei died of natural causes the following year.
29. Directorate of Intelligence, "Iraq: Implications of Insurrection and Prospects for Saddam's Survival," March 16, 1991, released March 19, 2009, C.I.A. FOIA Collection, FOIA Electronic Reading Room, https://www.cia.gov/readingroom/docs/DOC_0001441917.pdf.
30. Karsh and Rautsi, *Saddam Hussein*, 274.
31. Francona, *Ally to Adversary*, 155–56.
32. Haass, "The Gulf War: Its Place in History," 76; interview with Haass.
33. Interviews with Shahristani.
34. "iron saws and knives" and "screamed and sobbed": Jonathan C. Randal, *After Such Knowledge, What Forgiveness?: My Encounters with Kurdistan* (New York: Farrar, Straus and Giroux, 1997), 49; "by force or willingly": CRRC SH-MISC-D-000-947; search for prisoners recounted by Shahristani in interviews.
35. Interviews with Shahristani.
36. Barzani from Howard Chua-Eoan, "Iraq: Defeat and Flight," *Time*, April 15, 1991; Erbil movie theater from Randal, *After Such Knowledge*, 45.
37. RCLO records.
38. Amnesty International, *Human Rights Violations since the Uprising*.
39. Daily casualty rate of four hundred from Human Rights Watch, "The Prospects for 'Safe Areas' for Internally Displaced Iraqis," backgrounder in *Iraqi Refugees, Asylum Seekers, and Displaced Persons: Current Conditions and Concerns in the Event of War* (New York: Human Rights Watch, 2003); in "U.S. Uncertain of Death Rate at Kurds' Camps," April 25, 1991, *The New York Times* estimated the daily rate in late April at between four hundred and one thousand per day; all quotations from Randal, *After Such Knowledge*, 57.
40. David Hoffman, "Baker Trip to Mideast Has 2 Goals," *Washington Post*, April 8, 1991.
41. Basra graves, Maysan estimates, and Tariq Aziz estimate from RCLO records.
42. Interview with Frank Anderson. Twetten confirmed the thrust of the exchange.
43. Brent Scowcroft's interview with Peter Jennings, "Showdown with Saddam."

Chapter 14: The Liar's Truths

1. Interview with Jafar Dhia Jafar; Gudrun Harrer, *Dismantling the Iraqi Nuclear Programme: The Inspections of the International Atomic Energy Agency, 1991–1998* (Abingdon, U.K.: Routledge, 2014), 53–54.
2. Interview with Jafar.
3. Interviews and correspondence with Jafar, as well as interviews with Dhafir Selbi and Imad Khadduri.

4. Interview with Jafar; "meticulous in documenting": Harrer, *Dismantling the Iraqi Nuclear Programme*, 123; number of documents from Målfrid Braut-Hegghammer, "Cheater's Dilemma: Iraq, Weapons of Mass Destruction, and the Path to War," *International Security* 45, no. 1 (Summer 2020): 51–89. As noted later in this chapter, according to Jafar, after several intrusive U.N. inspections and Iraq's admission of the electromagnetic enrichment program, Jafar tracked down the wandering train car. Many of its materials—along with other crucial documentation of Iraq's WMD programs—remained secret until Hussein Kamel defected in 1995 and Iraq decided to turn over the documents, blaming Hussein Kamel for the deception.

5. Interview with Jafar.

6. Harrer, *Dismantling the Iraqi Nuclear Programme*, 63. Harrer had access to I.A.E.A. files while researching her carefully documented book, which reports on internal records and the I.A.E.A. perspective.

7. John Googin's remark as recalled by Dimitri Perricos in an interview by David Albright, June 14–15, 2001, "Understanding the Lessons of Nuclear Inspections and Monitoring in Iraq: A Ten-Year Review," Institute for Science and International Security, transcript published August 28, 2001, https://isis-online.org/perricos; Margaret Tutwiler from R. Jeffrey Smith, "Reassessing Iraqi Nuclear Capability," *Washington Post*, July 10, 1991.

8. Interview with Jafar; Obeidi and Pitzer, *Bomb in My Garden*, 139.

9. Iraq Survey Group, *Duelfer Report*, 3:32. That Iraq did not admit the destruction until the following March and continued to withhold the full truth about its chemical program is noted in Braut-Hegghammer, "Cheater's Dilemma," 51–89.

10. Interview with Jafar.

11. Dialogue from a "circa 19–21 August 1991" meeting, in Woods et al., *Survey of Saddam's Audio Files 1978–2001*, 306.

12. Interview with Rolf Ekéus.

13. The relationship between Hans Blix and Ekéus is from an interview with Ekéus. Ekéus had recently brought out his Swedish-language memoir when I was in Stockholm in September 2018 to interview both him and Blix. When I arrived at Blix's apartment, I found that the then ninety-year-old retired diplomat had prepared pages on a legal pad—refutations to passages in Ekéus's book, which he proceeded to go through with crisp articulation.

14. Interview with Blix. The quotations here are from Hans Blix, *Disarming Iraq* (New York: Pantheon, 2004), 22–23.

15. Harrer, *Dismantling the Iraqi Nuclear Programme*, 82, and Perricos, interview by Albright.

16. Harrer, 82, and Perricos, interview; correspondence with Jafar.

17. Harrer, *Dismantling the Iraqi Nuclear Programme*, 85, and Perricos, interview by Albright.

18. "cocky": Blix, *Disarming Iraq*, 25; interviews with Blix and David Kay.

19. Interview with the former C.I.A. analyst involved.

20. Interview with Kay; twenty-two inspection sites from Harrer, *Dismantling the Iraqi Nuclear Programme*, 89.

21. Harrer quoting from Kay's contemporaneous cable to Vienna in Harrer, 98.

22. Trevan, *Saddam's Secrets*, 84.

23. Team composition and "special people with special skills" from Harrer, *Dismantling the Iraqi Nuclear Programme*, 106; C.I.A. paramilitary specialists and computer penetration expert from interview with Kay.

24. Interview with Kay.

25. Interview with Kay, as well as Trevan, *Saddam's Secrets*, and Harrer, *Dismantling the Iraqi Nuclear Programme*.

26. Harrer quoting from Kay's cable in Harrer, 111.

27. Kay's estimate of the scale of the Iraqi nuclear program from Jay C. Davis and David A. Kay, "Iraq's Secret Nuclear Weapons Program," *Physics Today* 45, no. 7 (July 1992): 21–27; "We should not go": transcript excerpt circa September–October 1991 from Woods et al., *Survey of Saddam's Audio Files*, 307; "America, comrades, America": CRRC SHSHTP-A-001-210, as excerpted in Woods, Palkki, and Stout, *Saddam Tapes*, 39.

28. Correspondence with Jafar.

29. Harrer, *Dismantling the Iraqi Nuclear Weapons Programme*, 117; I.A.E.A.'s assessment of Jafar from Harrer, 118; *New York Times* headlines: Paul Lewis, "U.N. Says the Iraqis Could Have Devised A-Bombs in the '90s," September 14, 1991, and Elaine Sciolino, "Iraq's Nuclear Program Shows the Holes in U.S. Intelligence," October 20, 1991.

30. CRRC SH-SHTP-A-001-458.

Chapter 15: Mr. Max and the Mayfair Swindler

1. "Mr. Max": interview with Maguire. The account of Amman walk-in recruitment also draws on interviews with other former Near East Division officers.
2. Interview with Maguire.
3. Interview with Robert Grenier.
4. Interviews with Grenier and Frank Anderson. Anderson died in February 2020, at seventy-eight.
5. Interview with Anderson.
6. "Falstaffian figure" and "enjoyed nothing so much": Mark McDonald, "Jalal Talabani, Kurdish Leader and Iraq's First Postwar President, Is Dead at 83," *New York Times*, October 3, 2017.
7. "We'd like to set up": interview with Dave Manners, who served as the C.I.A.'s station chief in Amman during the mid-1990s; no permanent base from an interview with Anderson.
8. Barzan's financing of an import-export company from "Memorandum of Conversation with Ali Shukri, Chief of Staff to King Hussein," November 11, 1995, author's files. Shukri reported that Barzan had been involved in Mercedes imports "for years" and that his partner had recently swindled $5 million from Saddam's half brother. American election discussion from "Sweet and Bitter Years," CRRC SH-MISC-D-000-948; Saddam's comments to comrades about America's empire from Harmony ISGQ-2003-M0004615, as excerpted in Woods, *Mother of All Battles*, 301.
9. Interview with a former Iraqi diplomat.
10. Interview with Riedel.
11. Saddam's celebration from Coughlin, *Saddam*, 288–89; Aziz and Ramadan from Harmony ISGQ-2003-M0007446, as excerpted in Woods, *Mother of All Battles*, 304.
12. "Wasn't the Mother of All Battles" and "save the West": Woods, *Mother of All Battles*, 305; "All the world is now": Woods, *Mother of all Battles*, 299; "There are proven facts": CRRC SH-SHTP-A-000-838, as excerpted in Woods, Palkki, and Stout, *Saddam Tapes*, 41.
13. CRRC SH-SHTP-A-002-065, as excerpted in Kevin M. Woods et al., *Coercion: The United States and Iraq, 1991–2003*, Paper P-5281 (Alexandria, Va.: Institute for Defense Analyses, 2016), 38.
14. "Sweet and Bitter Years," CRRC SH-MISC-D-001-204.
15. Tariq Aziz's comments from contemporaneous notes taken by Vincent.
16. "orneriest, wiliest, most litigious": Mimi Swartz, "The Day Oscar Wyatt Caved," *Texas Monthly*, November 2007; "He is going to carry" and "not a sneaky person": CRRC SH-SHTP-A-000-753, as excerpted in Woods et al., *Saddam Tapes*, 48–49.
17. Interview with Riedel.
18. Interview with Twetten.
19. Interviews with Riedel, Charles Duelfer, and Ellen Laipson, who joined the N.S.C. in 1993. Clinton's February re-endorsement of the Iraq covert action finding from Richard Bonin, *Arrows of the Night: Ahmad Chalabi's Long Journey to Triumph in Iraq* (New York: Doubleday, 2011), 86; "toothache" and "It was like bending a pencil" from Martin Indyk, *Innocent Abroad: An Intimate Account of American Peace Diplomacy in the Middle East* (New York: Simon & Schuster, 2009), locs. 645 and 676 of 8599, Kindle.
20. Duelfer, *Hide and Seek*, 85–86.
21. C.I.A. spending on the I.N.C. from interviews with Anderson and John Maguire; "Gaullist aspirations and a nature": Bonin, *Arrows of the Night*, 84; "I saw *them*": Bonin, 96. Chalabi's biography comes largely from two sources: Bonin's book, which draws on unique interviews with Chalabi, looking back on his rise a few years before his death in 2015, and Aram Roston, *The Man Who Pushed America to War: The Extraordinary Life, Adventures, and Obsessions of Ahmad Chalabi* (New York: Nation Books, 2008), which covers much of the same ground well and is particularly strong on Petra Bank's collapse.
22. Bonin, *Arrows of the Night*, and Roston, *Man Who Pushed America to War*; "is completely prepared to burn": Bonin, 28.
23. Bonin, *Arrows of the Night*, and Roston, *Man Who Pushed America to War*; details about Petra's non-performing loans from Roston, 58, citing an Arthur Andersen audit.
24. Whitley Bruner and Linda Flohr from Bonin, *Arrows of the Night*, 63.
25. Interviews with Riedel, Maguire, and Anderson.
26. Interview with Maguire.
27. RCLO records.
28. Interview with Shahristani.
29. Interview with Shahristani, as well as Shahristani, *Free of Fear*, 111. Abdul Halim made his remarks while being filmed for *Saddam's Killing Fields*, a documentary directed by Christopher Jeans, featuring Michael Woods, and broadcast in 1992.
30. Interview with Shahristani.

Chapter 16: "We Need to Turn This Thing Off, Now!"

1. Associated Press, "Bush, on a Visit to Kuwait, Is Given Hero's Welcome," *New York Times*, April 15, 1993.
2. The details of the investigation in this chapter are drawn from three documents. One is a lengthy, redacted, declassified C.I.A. Counterterrorism Center paper titled "The Attack That Failed: Iraq's Attempt to Assassinate Former President Bush in Kuwait, April 1993," released in 1995. The two others are a report and a lengthy deposition about the case arising from a Justice Department whistleblower's complaint that forensic evidence used to draw comparisons between the Iraqi vehicle bombs and the Kuwait bomb was misinterpreted. These documents are hereafter cited as "C.I.A. and Justice documents."
3. Remarks by Jeb and George W. Bush from Robert Draper, *To Start a War: How the Bush Administration Took America into Iraq* (New York: Penguin Books, 2020), 36–37.
4. Interviews with Woods and Duelfer.
5. C.I.A. and Justice documents.
6. C.I.A. and Justice documents. In the records available, the closest mention of assassination connected to Bush that I could find was in CRRC SH-SHTP-A-001-037, a conversation between Saddam and Yasser Arafat dating to April 1990, before the invasion of Kuwait. Saddam at one point provocatively remarks, "Maybe we cannot reach Washington, but we can send someone who has an explosive belt to reach Washington. . . . For instance, the person with an explosive belt around him would throw himself on Bush's car." That is a strikingly specific image, and one notably similar to Wali al-Ghazali's reported testimony about his backup plan, tainted as his testimony may be by the circumstances in which it was given.
7. Interview with Riedel.
8. Powell from Meacham, *Destiny and Power*, 541–42; interview with Riedel; Clinton from David Von Drehle and R. Jeffrey Smith, "U.S. Strikes Iraq for Plot to Kill Bush," *Washington Post*, June 27, 1993.
9. "Sweet Years and Bitter Years," CRRC SH-MISC-D-001-204.
10. Woods et al., *Coercion*.
11. UNSCOM, *Seventh Report under Resolution 715*, April 10, 1995, https://www.un.org/Depts/unscom/Semiannual/srep95-284.htm.
12. Braut-Hegghammer, "Cheater's Dilemma," 51–89.
13. Ekéus and Tarnoff, Ekéus and Berger from a contemporaneous memorandum of conversation in Ekéus's personal archive.
14. Director of Central Intelligence, *Prospects for Iraq: Saddam and Beyond*, NIE 93-42 (Langley, Va.: Central Intelligence Agency, 1993), 5, C.I.A. FOIA Collection, FOIA Electronic Reading Room, https://www.cia.gov/readingroom/docs/DOC_0001188931.pdf.
15. "serious, prays, and fasts": "Sweet and Bitter Years," CRRC SH-MISC-D-001-204; Uday promotion episode from Ekéus's personal archive.
16. Woods et al., *Survey of Saddam's Audio Files 1978–2001*, 316.
17. Ekéus's personal archive.
18. Interview with Anderson.
19. Interview with Anderson; Baer's biographical details from Robert Baer, *See No Evil: The True Story of a Ground Soldier in the CIA's War on Terrorism* (New York: Crown, 2003), 10–12.
20. "helped the big thinkers" and "get to sleep at night": Baer, *See No Evil*, 175; DB ACHILLES from interviews with C.I.A. officials familiar with the program. The cryptonym has been published in many open sources (e.g., David Ignatius, "The CIA and the Coup That Wasn't," *Washington Post*, May 16, 2003).
21. Indyk, *Innocent Abroad*, loc. 2677 of 8599, Kindle; Bonin, *Arrows of the Night*, 98.
22. Indyk, *Innocent Abroad*, loc. 2682 of 8599, Kindle; Baer, *See No Evil*, 179. Baer does not name the general he met, but Indyk, who was directly involved at the White House at the time, identifies Samarrai as the coup attempt leader who was the focus of C.I.A. attention.
23. Baer, *See No Evil*, 182.
24. Bonin, *Arrows of the Night*, 98.
25. All quotations from a transcript of the meeting in Duelfer's personal archive.
26. Baer, *See No Evil*, 188.
27. Indyk, *Innocent Abroad*, locs. 2695–716 of 8599, Kindle. Cockburn and Cockburn, Baer, and other sources provide overlapping accounts.
28. Bonin's account adds interviews from Ahmad Chalabi to the version of this episode provided in Baer's memoir.

Chapter 17: "There Would Be a Bloodbath"

1. As documented by the CRRC's transcripts, Saddam Hussein and other Iraqi leaders spoke frequently about the history of Hussein Kamel's brain tumor, his surgery in Jordan, and the possible effects of the tumor and surgery on Kamel's health (see below). The specifics here about Kamel's symptoms and the involvement of French surgeons, as well as "experiencing a psychological crisis," come from Jafar and Niaimi, *Last Confession*, chapter seven.

2. CRRC SH-PDWN-D-001-986, a transcript of a 1998 conversation between Saddam and Laith Shubeilat, an Islamist Jordanian political figure. The king's proposal, including the idea of a visit with Rabin, was first reported in Ashton, *King Hussein of Jordan*, 337. Ashton's scoop generated coverage in the Israeli press. His account suggests that Saddam's initial response may not have been as firm and definitive as Saddam later claimed to comrades; "defeatists" and "need people to be defeated": CRRC SH-SHTP-A-001-259, in Woods, Palkki, and Stout, *Saddam Tapes*, 316; "He told me that": CRRC SH-SHTP-A-001-260; Hussein Kamel's travel to Russia from CRRC SH-SHTP-A-001-260 and CRRC SH-IISX-D-000-768, a record of Iraqi intelligence reports from June 1995 to July 1997.

3. Hussein Kamel's apartment in Amman from CRRC SH-IISX-D-001-000.

4. "had already decided": Cockburn and Cockburn, *Out of the Ashes*, 193. Hussein Kamel's meeting with a National Monitoring Directorate brigadier is documented in CRRC SH-INMD-D000-657. This includes an August 1995 memo from the NMD's director, who also reports that Kamel met in the same period with the nuclear scientist Mahdi Obeidi. Obeidi describes such a scene in his memoir (with Kurt Pitzer), *Bomb in My Garden*, 163. He recounts there in detail that Kamel quizzed him about the centrifuge work, apparently in preparation for debriefings after he defected; "at least $9 million": CRRC SH-SHTP-A-000-762. Saddam repeats this figure in another recorded discussion. That Hussein Kamel indicated indirectly he might defect is from Ashton, *King Hussein of Jordan*, 337–38, as well as from an interview with a former senior Jordanian official. It was commonly believed in Iraq that King Hussein had conspired to support Kamel's defection before it took place. The king's secret outreach to Saddam, to propose a visit by Yitzhak Rabin, complicates the picture, as it is not clear whether this sensitive matter had anything to do with the defection or not, except perhaps as an opportunity Kamel saw to reposition Iraq under his leadership. Saddam told aides (SH-SHTP-A-001-260) that he firmly believed Kamel arranged his defection with King Hussein: "I am sure of this, except for the timing." That Uday threatened to kill Hussein Kamel in the spring or summer of 1995, according to Kamel, is from interviews with Dave Manners and Ali Shukri.

5. Raghad Hussein interview with Al Arabiya, February 17, 2021.

6. "What was I to do?" and "He would drive around Baghdad": Duelfer, *Hide and Seek*, 137.

7. The most thorough account of the night of August 7, drawn from contemporary sources, is in Cockburn and Cockburn, *Out of the Ashes*, 193–94. Bashir and Sunnanå, *The Insider*, 162–66, provides another account, citing interviews with a former companion of Uday's and his own experiences at the hospital. Bashir reviewed the evening's events in an interview as well.

8. Interview with Bashir, as well as Bashir and Sunnanå, *The Insider*, 162–66; Duelfer said in an interview that investigators later found the garage full of torched cars.

9. Raghad Hussein, interview with Al Arabiya.

10. Interviews by Sarah Moawad with three former senior officials.

11. Moawad's interviews; Prince Turki contact from Ashton, *King Hussein of Jordan*, 341.

12. Correspondence with Major from Ashton, 338–40.

13. CRRC SH-SHTP-A-001-981.

14. Interview with Manners.

15. See "Jordan—Kamel Presser," Hussein Kamel press conference in Amman, August 12, 1995, AP Archive video, streamed on July 21, 2015, https://www.youtube.com/watch?v=52C8IHreWaY.

16. Moawad interview with Shukri.

17. Interviews with Manners and former senior Jordanian officials.

18. Interview with Manners.

19. Interview with Manners.

20. Interview with a former senior Jordanian official.

21. Interview with Ayad Allawi; "C.I.A.-inspired": Indyk, *Innocent Abroad*, loc. 2537 of 8599, Kindle.

22. Interview with Manners.

23. Jafar and Niaimi, *Last Confession*, chapter seven.

24. CRRC SH-SHTP-A-000-837. Note that "system" was changed from "regime," per Ibrahim Al-Marashi's translation check.

25. "If he is insane": CRRC SH-SHTP-A-001-577; "small and weak country": CRRC SH-SHTP-A-000-828.

26. Moawad interview with Shukri.

27. Ashton, *King Hussein of Jordan*, 349–52.

28. Ashton, 349–52; interview with Manners.

29. "expect a half-baked presentation" and Oval Office scene from Ashton, *King Hussein of Jordan*, 342; "new Fidel Castro": interview with Manners.

Chapter 18: Honor among Tyrants

1. Interviews with Rolf Ekéus; Scott Ritter, *Iraq Confidential: The Untold Story of the Intelligence Conspiracy to Undermine the UN and Overthrow Saddam Hussein* (New York: Nation Books, 2005), 91ff., describes the Israeli liaison in detail.

2. CRRC SH-SHTP-A-001-011.

3. CRRC SH-INMD-D-000-657 contains an August 1995 memo to Saddam's security services summarizing ten major secrets Iraq still harbored about its biological, missile, and nuclear programs.

4. CRRC SH-SHTP-A-001-011; that Hussein Kamel ordered the germ weapons destroyed in May but also ordered records not to be kept is from Braut-Hegghammer, "Cheater's Dilemma," 51–89; preparations for the 1991 war from Russell, "Iraq's Chemical Weapons Legacy," 187–208.

5. All quotations from contemporary memoranda in Ekéus's personal archive.

6. Braut-Hegghammer, "Cheater's Dilemma," 51–89.

7. Ekéus archive.

8. Ekéus archive. The exchange in which Aziz offered Ekéus a bribe is not recorded in these records but comes from an interview with Ekéus. He has recounted this anecdote in several other interviews, noting in those an offer of $1 million. I have used the figure that Ekéus recalled in our interview.

9. Rolf Ekéus, *Between Two Wars: Saddam's Fall and the Birth of ISIS* (Stockholm: Albert Bonniers Förlag, 2018), 225–26, as well as an interview with Ekéus and Trevan, *Saddam's Secrets*, 331–32.

10. Ekéus's archive. The conversation outside about Israel is from Ekéus, *Between Two Wars*, 227–33. Ekéus also reviewed the meeting in an interview.

11. Interview with Odeh Aburdene.

12. "what was on his mind": Pipes, "'Thank You for Everything,'" 33–44; "Where have we gone wrong?": interview with a colleague of Hamdoon's.

13. "good candidate for democracy": Pipes, "'Thank You for Everything,'" 33–44; interview with Aburdene.

14. Interview with a colleague of Hamdoon's.

15. Description of Saddam's reply letter from Pipes, "'Thank You for Everything,'" 33–44.

16. "You know as well": Richard Butler, *The Greatest Threat: Iraq, Weapons of Mass Destruction, and the Growing Crisis of Global Security* (New York: PublicAffairs Books, 2001), 87.

17. CRRC SH-MISC-V-001-426.

18. CRRC SH-MISC-D-000-772.

19. Interview with Ekéus, as well as Ekéus, *Between Two Wars*, 241–42.

20. CRRC SH-IISX-D-001-000. The reporting about Hussein Kamel from Iraqi intelligence's Amman station suggests that the Iraqis had thoroughly penetrated Kamel's communications and inner circle during his exile in Jordan.

21. Interview with Manners.

22. Sarah Moawad interviews with senior Jordanian officials.

23. CRRC SH-IISX-D-001-000.

24. Cockburn and Cockburn, *Out of the Ashes*, 207.

25. *Guardian*, November 6, 1995; for the eulogies delivered by Clinton and Hussein, see "Yitzhak Rabin: Eulogies at Rabin's Funeral," November 6, 1995, Jewish Virtual Library, partial transcripts, https://www.jewishvirtuallibrary.org/eulogies-at-the-funeral-of-yitzhak-rabin.

26. CRRC SH-SHTP-A-000-877, undated but recorded soon after Rabin's funeral. The discussion makes clear that Saddam and his comrades had watched at least some of the funeral on television.

27. All quotations from CRRC SH-SHTP-A-000-789. Describing what transpired after the disclosures of 1995, Braut-Hegghammer writes, "Neither the leadership nor officials down the chain of implementation had reliable information about the other's intentions and actions. The result was disobedience, shirking behaviors, and mistakes by Iraqi scientists and guards interacting with U.N. inspectors on the ground." This is the context for incidents such as the dumping of gyroscopes in the Tigris.

28. The letter is recited in CRRC SH-BATH-D-000-197.
29. CRRC SH-BATH-D-000-197.
30. Raghad Hussein's Al Arabiya interview, February 17, 2021.
31. Interviews with Manners and senior Jordanian officials. Another Tikriti in the brothers' Jordan party, Major Izzadeen al-Majid, who was married to a sister of Hussein and Saddam Kamel's, happened to be visiting Turkey. He escaped the ordeal to follow. Ritter (*Iraq Confidential*, 258) recounted that he led a Special Commission team to debrief Izzadeen in Jordan, in May 1996, and later at a "C.I.A. safe house in Washington." He described Izzadeen's information about Saddam's use of the Special Republican Guard to hide illicit weapons as "invaluable."
32. Raghad, Al Arabiya interview.
33. Raghad, Al Arabiya interview.
34. CRRC SH-IDGS-D-000-383. This file contains interrogation records of intelligence officers who were ordered to search for the Kamel brothers in the early hours of February 23, 1996.
35. CRRC SH-IDGS-D-000-383.
36. CRRC SH-IDGS-D-000-383; "Sweet and Bitter Years," CRRC SH-MISC-D-001-204.
37. Raghad, Al Arabiya interview.

Chapter 19: Spy vs. Spy

1. The February 18 press conference is from Ashton, *King Hussein of Jordan*, 343; covert-action funding of $6 million from, among other media sources from that period, *Peter Jennings Reporting*, "Showdown with Saddam"; "We think that any uprising": John Lancaster and David B. Ottaway, "With CIA's Help, Group in Jordan Targets Saddam," *Washington Post*, June 23, 1996.
2. Interviews with Manners, Maguire, and a third former C.I.A. operations officer. Public release of the chronology of Clinton's revised findings and memoranda of understanding on Iraq would clarify how the "wait and exploit" policy evolved during the 1990s and what specific authorities were in place during the first six months of 1996.
3. Interview with Maguire.
4. Interviews with Charles Duelfer and Scott Ritter; "More sophisticated equipment": Duelfer, *Hide and Seek*, 130; "my ass if it blew": Duelfer, 125. Duelfer's book and Ritter's memoir, *Iraq Confidential*, provide the most authoritative available accounts of the eavesdropping program.
5. "Mukhabarat culture of intimidation": Jon Lee Anderson, "A Man of the Shadows," *New Yorker*, January 16, 2005.
6. Interview with Allawi.
7. Interview with Allawi.
8. Interview with Allawi; interview with Marik.
9. "You can do whatever" and "a dream for us": interview with Allawi. Julian Walker died in 2018 at age eighty-nine.
10. "defect and defend" and "We had a very strong": interview with Allawi; "trigger an event": interview with Maguire.
11. "would have to hold out": interview with Allawi; "the preferred choice": interview with Mack; "thought Allawi was the savior": interview with Francona; "We were in love": interview with the former C.I.A. analyst on Iraq.
12. Interview with Allawi.
13. Twice used telephones from Iraq Survey Group, *Duelfer Report*, 1:11; "acute spying disease": Majid, *Les années Saddam*, 118.
14. "Sweet and Bitter Years," CRRC SH-MISC-D-001-204; Tariq Aziz's quotation from CRRC SH-SHTP-A-000-762.
15. Saddam's mistrust of even his own relatives from Iraq Survey Group, *Duelfer Report*, 1:19; travel restrictions from Joseph Sassoon, *Saddam Hussein's Ba'th Party: Inside an Authoritarian Regime* (Cambridge: Cambridge University Press, 2012), 118.
16. "How does the enemy think?": CRRC SH-SSOX-D-000-869, circa 1993; "collecting information about": CRRC SH-IISX-D-000-360, 2001.
17. Sassoon, *Saddam Hussein's Ba'th Party*, 97–119.
18. CRRC SH-IISX-D-000-360.
19. Interviews with Manners, Maguire, and Francona; George Tenet and Bill Harlow, *At the Center of the Storm: My Years at the CIA* (New York: HarperCollins, 2007), 388.
20. Interview with Allawi and Francona.

21. Interview with Maguire.

22. Interview with Laipson.

23. For Ritter's description of how the C.I.A. and possibly Britain ran the eavesdropping operations during the coup-planning period, see Ritter, *Iraq Confidential*, 213–22; Duelfer's remark from Ritter, 222.

24. Interview with Allawi. Shawani declined to be interviewed.

25. Lancaster and Ottaway, "With CIA's Help, Group in Jordan Targets Saddam"; interview with Francona.

26. Interviews with Francona and Riedel; John Deutch's remarks from *Peter Jennings Reporting*, "Showdown with Saddam," transcript.

27. Ashton, *King Hussein of Jordan*, 346.

28. Randal, *After Such Knowledge*, 312–24; Joost Hiltermann, "The Demise of Operation Provide Comfort," *Middle East Report* no. 203 (Summer 1997), https://merip.org/1997/06/the-demise-of-operation-provide-comfort/. The Iraq Survey Group's report on the Baghdad regime's illicit finance found that total off-the-books oil sales through Kurdistan after 1990 amounted to more than $500 million.

29. Tony Lake, "Building Peace and Security in the Middle East," speech, American Israel Public Affairs Committee Capitol Club Summit, October 15, 1996, Clinton Presidential Library, transcript, https://clinton.presidentiallibraries.us/items/show/9571.

30. Interview with Riedel; "This system is here": CRRC SH-SHTP-A-001-997. Note "regime" changed to "system," per Ibrahim Al-Marashi's translation check.

31. All quotations from Bashir and Sunnanå, *The Insider*, 193–201, and an interview with Bashir. Duelfer, *Hide and Seek*, 191, describes the hit and reports that Uday was driving a Porsche. Cockburn and Cockburn, *Out of the Ashes*, 251–60, describe a tape-recorded bedside rant by Saddam early in 1997. During the diatribe, he denounced his half brothers for their incompetence and asked Uday, "Are you a politician, a trader, a people's leader, or a playboy?" Saddam also declared, "We are not a monarchy, at least not yet." The Cockburns identified the Awakening as a suspect in the hit, based on interviews with participants.

32. Bonin, *Arrows of the Night*, 115.

33. Interview with Allawi.

34. Bashir and Sunnanå, *The Insider*, 193–201.

Chapter 20: Crime and Punishment

1. Jeffrey A. Meyer and Mark G. Califano, *Good Intentions Corrupted: The Oil-for-Food Scandal and the Threat to the U.N.* (New York: PublicAffairs Books, 2006), 12–15. The book draws heavily on an independent investigation of the Oil-for-Food program that was carried out by former Federal Reserve chairman Paul Volcker, who wrote an introduction.

2. Robert B. Boettcher and Gordon L. Freedman, *Gifts of Deceit: Sun Myung Moon, Tongsun Park, and the Korean Scandal* (New York: Holt, Rinehart & Winston, 1980), 56–64. See also Phil McCombs, "Tongsun Park's Club," *Washington Post*, October 16, 1977, https://www.washingtonpost.com/archive/opinions/1977/10/16/tongsun-parks-club/.

3. Commissions, gifts, and Richard Hanna from Freedman, *Gifts of Deceit*, 70–77; Tongsun Park's indictment from Anthony Marro, "Indictment of Park Charges 36 Crimes; Bell Seeking Return," *New York Times*, September 7, 1977.

4. Meyer and Califano, *Good Intentions Corrupted*, 9.

5. Iraq's economy from "Iraq GDP 1960–2023," Macrotrends, https://www.macrotrends.net/countries/IRQ/iraq/gdp-gross-domestic-product. For another estimate, see Joy Gordon, *Invisible War: The United States and the Iraq Sanctions* (Cambridge, Mass.: Harvard University Press, 2010), 21. During the years that Saddam refused to participate in Oil-for-Food, Iraq restricted the operations of U.N. aid agencies. The agencies did manage to contribute, but except in the North, where they benefited from Kurdistan's de facto autonomy, they could not open offices outside Baghdad, and Iraqi minders kept them under surveillance. See Sarah Graham-Brown, *Sanctioning Saddam: The Politics of Intervention in Iraq* (London: I. B. Tauris, 1999), 315–16.

6. Interview with Vincent.

7. Meyer and Califano, *Good Intentions Corrupted*, 10; that Hamdoon was the intermediary comes from an interview with Vincent.

8. Meyer and Califano, 6–20.

9. Saddam's comment about Boutros-Ghali's mother from CRRC SH-SHTP-A-001-010; "Egyptian government is a conspirator": CRRC SH-SHTP-A-000-774; "political situation in the world": CRRC SH-SHTP-A-001-143.

10. Meyer and Califano, *Good Intentions Corrupted*, 14–15.

11. Meyer and Califano, 14–15, as well as an interview with Nat Kern; Clinton and Blair from "Telcon with British Prime Minister Blair," February 16, 1998, Clinton Digital Library, William J. Clinton Presidential Library, https://clinton.presidentiallibraries.us/items/show/48779 (hereafter cited as Clinton Digital Library).

12. For Madeleine Albright's 1996 exchange with Lesley Stahl, see Jon Jackson, "Watch: Madeleine Albright Saying Iraqi Kids' Deaths 'Worth It' Resurfaces," *Newsweek*, March 23, 2022, video clip and article, https://www.newsweek.com/watch-madeleine-albright-saying-iraqi-kids-deaths-worth -it-resurfaces-1691193; "a terrible mistake": Madeleine Albright, *Madam Secretary: A Memoir* (New York: HarperCollins, 2013), 275; for the F.A.O. study from which Stahl's figure was drawn, see Food and Agriculture Organization, "Iraq Sanctions Lead to Half a Million Child Deaths," *BMJ* 311, no. 7019 (December 1995): 1523, https://doi.org/10.1136/bmj.311.7019.1523; proportion of aid to Kurdistan versus the rest of Iraq from Graham-Brown, *Sanctioning Saddam*, 277.

13. Interview with Hans-Christof von Sponeck by Sarah Moawad.

14. Typhoid and cholera statistics from Gordon, *Invisible War*, 34; "grossly inadequate": Gordon, 112.

15. CRRC SH-BATH-D-000-492.

16. Faust, *Ba'thification of Iraq*, 64.

17. Interview with von Sponeck. See also Hans-Christof von Sponeck, "The Politics of the Sanctions on Iraq and the U.N. Humanitarian Exception," in *Land of Blue Helmets: The United Nations and the Arab World*, ed. Karim Makdisi and Vijay Prashad (Berkeley: University of California Press, 2016), 278.

18. "political literature": CRRC SH-SHTP-A-001-253, as excerpted in Woods, Palkki, and Stout, *Saddam Tapes*, 267–68; profit opportunity per barrel from Iraq Survey Group, *Duelfer Report*, 1:31.

19. Iraq Survey Group, 1:31.

20. "President's Dinner with President Yeltsin," cable, January 14, 1994, Clinton Digital Library, https://clinton.presidentiallibraries.us/items/show/58577.

21. "Telcon with President Chirac of France," November 4, 1998, Clinton Digital Library, https://clinton.presidentiallibraries.us/items/show/16192; Indyk, *Innocent Abroad*, loc. 3140 of 8599, Kindle.

22. Just under $11 billion in hard currency from all illicit means between 1990 and 2003 is from Iraq Survey Group, *Duelfer Report*, 1:24.

23. Gordon, *Invisible War*, 101.

24. Pollack, *Threatening Storm*, 86–87.

25. Madeleine Albright, "Policy Speech on Iraq," March 26, 1997, Iowa State University, transcript, https://awpc.cattcenter.iastate.edu/2017/03/21/policy-speech-on-iraq-march-26-1997/.

26. CRRC SH-SHTP-A-001-970.

27. Interview with Riedel; Duelfer, *Hide and Seek*, 135; "Sanctions without all these sacrifices": CRRC SH-SHTP-A-001-298, as excerpted in Woods et al., *Coercion*.

28. All quotations from a memorandum reviewed by the author.

Chapter 21: The Logic of Illusion

1. "was like a surgical operation": Memorandum of conversation reviewed by the author; Supreme Court dinner from an interview with Ekéus and Ekéus, *Between Two Wars*, 400–401.

2. Interviews with Scott Ritter and Charles Duelfer; "alpha dog" and "tail held high" from Peter J. Boyer, "Scott Ritter's Private War," *New Yorker*, November 9, 1998; "Ritter was a character": Duelfer, *Hide and Seek*, 134; "The entire purpose": Ritter, *Iraq Confidential*, 200. In 2011, Ritter was convicted in New York of six counts involving sex with a minor. Ritter served several years in prison.

3. Duelfer, *Hide and Seek*, 142.

4. "they were concealing": Ritter's October 27, 1998, interview with James Sutterlin for the Yale-U.N. Oral History Project, as excerpted in Gregory D. Koblentz, "Saddam versus the Inspectors: The Impact of Regime Security on the Verification of Iraq's WMD Disarmament," *Journal of Strategic Studies* 41, no. 3 (April 2018): 372–409.

5. Koblentz, "Saddam versus the Inspectors," 372–409.

6. Interview with McLaughlin.

7. Statement of commitment from CRRC SH-GMID-D-000-890, records pertaining to an Iraqi Air Force investigation into poorly controlled WMD documents. See also Koblentz, "Saddam versus the Inspectors," 372–409.

8. Butler, *The Greatest Threat*, 114.

9. "Telcon with British Prime Minister Blair," February 16, 1998, Clinton Digital Library, https://clinton.presidentiallibraries.us/items/show/48779.

10. "Telcon with British Prime Minister Blair," Clinton Digital Library.

11. Transcript of press conference by Secretary-General Kofi Annan at U.N. headquarters, February 24, 1998, United Nations Digital Library, https://digitallibrary.un.org/record/250793.

12. Duelfer, *Hide and Seek*, 142–44.

13. Interview with Jafar.

14. "has for some time": Hans Blix, forty-first regular session of the I.A.E.A. General Conference, September 24, 1997, Vienna, Austria, transcript submitted by the Permanent Mission of Iraq to the I.A.E.A., https://www.iaea.org/sites/default/files/gc/gc41inf-20_en.pdf; number of inspections from the CAFCD; Jafar and Niaimi, *Last Confession*, chapter seven.

15. Interview with al-Janabi.

16. "Memorandum of Telephone Conversation with Russian President Yeltsin," November 22, 1997, Clinton Digital Library, https://clinton.presidentiallibraries.us/items/show/57569.

17. "Telcon with British Prime Minister Blair," February 16, 1998, Declassified Documents Concerning Tony Blair, Clinton Digital Library, https://clinton.presidentiallibraries.us/items/show/48779.

18. "little space it takes": "Telcon with British Prime Minister Blair," Clinton Digital Library; exchange with Gore from "Memorandum of Conversation: Meeting with Tony Blair, Prime Minister of the United Kingdom," February 5, 1998, Clinton Digital Library, https://clinton.presidentiallibraries.us/items/show/48779.

19. CRRC SH-SHTP-A-000-756, as excerpted in Woods, Palkki, and Stout, *Saddam Tapes*, 56–57.

20. "more of a car salesman": Ritter, *Iraq Confidential*, 236; "witting partner": Richard Roth and Reuters, "U.N. Weapons Inspector in Iraq Offers Angry Resignation," CNN, August 26, 1998, http://www.cnn.com/WORLD/meast/9808/26/iraq.ritter/index.html.

21. "Telcon with President Chirac of France," November 4, 1998, Clinton Digital Library, https://clinton.presidentiallibraries.us/items/show/16192.

22. Indyk, *Innocent Abroad*, locs. 3229 and 3465 of 8599, Kindle; Duelfer, *Hide and Seek*, 160.

23. "There won't be a single": Indyk, *Innocent Abroad*, loc. 3355 of 8599, Kindle; "Draft Memcon: POTUS–PM Blair," December 15, 1998, Clinton Digital Library, https://clinton.presidentiallibraries.us/items/show/49412.

24. William M. Arkin, "Desert Fox Delivery," *Washington Post*, January 17, 1999.

25. "Telcon with President Chirac of France," December 17, 1998, Clinton Digital Library, https://clinton.presidentiallibraries.us/items/show/16192; Clinton and Blair from "Memorandum of Telephone Conversation," December 18, 1998, Clinton Digital Library.

26. "long-term strategy is clear": Bill Clinton, "Iraq Radio Address 12/19/98," December 19, 1998, Clinton Digital Library, transcript, https://clinton.presidentiallibraries.us/items/show/9946.

27. "When Chalabi showed up": Bonin, *Arrows of the Night*, 142; for a thorough history of the "neoconservatives" who ultimately championed the invasion of Iraq, see Stefan Halper and Jonathan Clarke, *America Alone: The Neo-Conservative and the Global Order* (Cambridge: Cambridge University Press, 2004).

28. ABC, "Were 1998 Memos a Blueprint for War?," ABC News, March 10, 2003, https://abcnews.go.com/Nightline/story?id=128491.

29. Bonin, *Arrows of the Night*, 146; Zinni's quotation from Bonin, 163.

30. Figure of $150,000 a month from Bonin, 126.

31. "Memorandum of Conversation: King Hussein of Jordan," January 5, 1999, Clinton Digital Library, https://clinton.presidentiallibraries.us/items/show/101248; specifics about the I.N.C.'s funding and allocation of funds from General Accounting Office, *Issues Affecting Funding of Iraqi National Congress Support Foundation*, GAO-04-559 (Washington, D.C.: General Accounting Office, 2004), https://www.gao.gov/assets/gao-04-559.pdf.

32. Pollack, *Threatening Storm*, 95–99. Also, interviews with Pollack and Riedel.

33. "Memorandum of Conversation: Meeting with President Vladimir Putin of Russia," September 6, 2000, Clinton Digital Library, https://clinton.presidentiallibraries.us/items/show/100505.

Chapter 22: The Secret Garden

1. Interview with Saman Abdul Majid and Majid, *Les années Saddam*, 134–38.
2. Sassoon, *Saddam Hussein's Ba'th Party*, 68–69. "Saddam Hussein's personal interest in culture and poetry cannot be underestimated," Sassoon writes. "Saddam saw himself as a writer and a poet, and thus he felt a kinship towards artists of all kinds."
3. The translations here are from Saddam Hussein, *Zabiba and the King*, ed. Robert Lawrence (College Station, Tex.: VBW Publishing, 2004).
4. Majid, *Les années Saddam*, 134–38.
5. Hassan, "Propaganda Literature"; description of the role of novels as mass-produced propaganda in Baathist Iraq from an interview with Hassan; for Saddam's attendance at the musical, see Ali Daham al-Nasseri, "Mr. President Commander Saddam Hussein Attends *Zabiba*," streamed on December 10, 2017, https://youtu.be/7F846WMqnK0.
6. Hassan, "Propaganda Literature"; Bashir and Sunnanå, *The Insider*, 283.
7. CRRC SH-PDWN-D-000-499 and CRRC SH-SPCC-D-000-588 contain unintentionally funny accounts of Saddam's bureaucrats trying to manage the output and money demands of the regime's official writers. Poetry fee from Sassoon, *Saddam Hussein's Ba'th Party*, 68.
8. Samir Vincent's contemporaneous notes of the meeting.
9. All quotations from an interview with Majid and from his memoir, *Les années Saddam*, 110; Tokarev pistol from Duelfer, *Hide and Seek*, 149.
10. Ten thousand sorties and February 5 meeting from Bob Woodward, *Plan of Attack: The Definitive Account of the Decision to Invade Iraq* (New York: Simon & Schuster, 2004), 10–13.
11. George W. Bush, *Decision Points* (New York: Crown, 2010), 230.
12. All quotations from "Meeting with British Prime Minister Blair," declassified transcript, *Targeting Iraq, Part 1: Planning, Invasion, and Occupation, 1997–2004*, Digital National Security Archive, https://proquest.libguides.com/dnsa/iraq97 (hereafter cited as NSA Targeting Iraq).
13. CRRC SH-SHTP-A-001-197, as excerpted in Woods, Palkki, and Stout, *Saddam Tapes*, 57–58.
14. Iraqi Intelligence analysis of new administration's ties to Iraqi opposition from CRRC SH-IISX-D-000-488; strategic study from SH-IISX-D-000-360.
15. CRRC SH-SHTP-A-000-874.
16. "Sweet and Bitter Years," CRRC SH-MISC-D-001-204.
17. CRRC SH-MISC-D-000-249.
18. CRRC SH-SPPC-D-000-334.
19. Hassan, "Propaganda Literature," and interview with Hassan.
20. Rumsfeld memo to Rice, July 27, 2001, Document 6 in Joyce Battle, ed., *The Iraq War–Part I: The U.S. Prepares for Conflict, 2001*, National Security Archive Electronic Briefing Book No. 326, September 22, 2010, https://nsarchive2.gwu.edu/NSAEBB/NSAEBB326/doc06.pdf.
21. Wolfowitz's presentation is from Bonin, *Arrows of the Night*, 188; "U.S. policy remained": Rumsfeld, *Known and Unknown*, 419.
22. Interviews with Luis Rueda and John Maguire.
23. Duelfer, *Hide and Seek*, 591–92.
24. Interview with Rueda. Although Rueda is not named, his appointment that summer is described in Tenet and Harlow, *At the Center of the Storm*, 304. Tenet described him as "an articulate, passionate, smart, and savvy Cuban American."
25. Interview with Rueda.
26. Interview with Rueda. Tenet, in his memoir, recalls Rueda's advice similarly. It was very much aligned with what Tenet had been telling the Clinton White House for several years: "Saddam was not going to be removed via covert action alone. As much as some would wish for an 'immaculate deception'—some quick, easy, and cheap solution to regime change in Iraq—it was not going to happen."

Chapter 23: The Pundit

1. Interview with a participant in the discussion. Mohammed Aldouri could not be reached.
2. George W. Bush, "Honoring the Victims of the Incidents on Tuesday, September 11, 2011," Proclamation 7461, September 11, 2001, Government Printing Office transcript, https://www.govinfo.gov/content/pkg/WCPD-2001-09-17/pdf/WCPD-2001-09-17.pdf.
3. Interview with discussion participant.

4. Anthony H. Cordesman, "Saudi Official Statements on Terrorism after the September 11 Attacks," Center for Strategic and International Studies, November 2001, https://www.csis.org/analysis/saudi-official-statements-terrorism-after-september-11th-attacks.

5. "condemning the terrorists": Iraq Survey Group, *Duelfer Report*, 1:33; "it will mean that": CRRC SH-PDWN-D-000-812, which includes Saddam's remarks during a meeting with a visitor from Chechnya, September 26, 2001.

6. "no different than the many": Saddam's F.B.I. detention interview, June 28, 2004, Document 6 in Joyce Battle, ed., *Saddam Hussein Talks to the FBI: Twenty Interviews and Five Conversations with "High Value Detainee # 1" in 2004*, National Security Archive Electronic Briefing Book No. 279, July 1, 2009, https://nsarchive2.gwu.edu/NSAEBB/NSAEBB279/26.pdf.

7. "The American people should remember": Karsh and Rautsi, *Saddam Hussein*, 2. The biographers attribute this oft-cited remark to Baghdad Television. It does not appear in available CRRC records. However, it closely tracks with what Saddam repeatedly said in recorded and minuted remarks during September and October. "America needs someone to tell": CRRC SH-PDWN-D-000-812, which includes a recorded meeting with the "Tunisian president's delegate," September 14, 2001.

8. CRRC SH-PDWN-D-000-806.

9. Peter Baker, *Days of Fire: Bush and Cheney in the White House* (New York: Doubleday, 2013), 144–46.

10. "I believe Iraq was involved": Lewis D. Solomon, *Paul D. Wolfowitz: Visionary Intellectual, Policymaker, and Strategist* (Westport, Conn.: Praeger, 2007), 80; "we must come back to Iraq": Baker, *Days of Fire*, 152.

11. Rumsfeld, *Known and Unknown*, 424–25.

12. Bush, *Decision Points*, 229.

13. Harmony ISGQ-2003-M0007419, as excerpted in Woods and Lacey, *Iraqi Perspectives Project: Primary Source Materials for Saddam and Terrorism*, 4:21. An introductory paragraph to the transcript mistakenly attributes this discussion to the autumn of 2001, but the record makes clear that Saddam is talking about the 1993 attack soon after it took place. The investigation into that bombing was complicated by the involvement of Abdul Rahman Yasin, an Iraqi American who afterward fled to Baghdad. Saddam's regime imprisoned Yasin and could not figure out what to make of him. Seemingly wishing to deflect blame, Saddam suggested privately to colleagues that Iraq could send evidence about Yasin to the U.S. Congress "to aid their investigations."

14. Saddam's comments to Kadyrov recorded in CRRC SH-MISC-D-000-456.

15. George W. Bush, "Presidential Address to the Nation," October 7, 2001, White House press release, George W. Bush White House Archives, National Archives, transcript and RealMedia webcast, https://georgewbush-whitehouse.archives.gov/news/releases/2001/10/20011007-8.html.

16. CRRC SH-PDWN-D-000-812.

17. CRRC SH-PDWN-D-000-145.

18. CRRC SH-PDWN-D-000-409.

19. All quotations from Frank Carlucci's letter to William Burns, September 27, 2001, and Tariq Aziz's reply memo, NSA Targeting Iraq.

20. All quotations from contemporaneous memoranda in Samir Vincent's archive, reviewed by the author.

21. Vincent, contemporaneous memoranda.

22. Duelfer, *Hide and Seek*, 220–22.

23. For an authoritative account of Ahmad Chalabi's use of defectors and their influence on media and official statements, see Roston, *Man Who Pushed America to War*, 184–228.

24. Bonin, *Arrows of the Night*, 193.

25. Paul R. Pillar, *Intelligence and U.S. Foreign Policy: Iraq, 9/11, and Misguided Reform* (New York: Columbia University Press, 2011), 11.

26. CRRC SH-PDWN-D-000-409 and CRRC SH-PDWN-D-000-499.

27. Michael Morell, *The Great War of Our Time: The CIA's Fight against Terrorism—from al Qa'ida to ISIS* (New York: Twelve, 2015), 81.

28. Powell from John Chilcot et al., *The Report of the Iraq Inquiry* (London: Stationery Office, 2016), 1:345. Resulting from seven years of work by a committee chaired by Sir John Chilcot, this British investigative report is hereafter cited as the *Chilcot Report*. See all volumes at https://www.gov.uk/government/publications/the-report-of-the-iraq-inquiry. Meyer from Chilcot et al., *Chilcot Report*, 1:344; Blair with Bush and subsequent memo from Chilcot et al., 1:367–70.

29. Woodward, *Plan of Attack*, 56–66.

30. George W. Bush, "President Delivers State of the Union Address," January 29, 2002, White House press release, George W. Bush White House Archives, National Archives, transcript and RealMedia webcast, https://georgewbush-whitehouse.archives.gov/news/releases/2002/01/20020129-11.html.

31. Baker, *Days of Fire*, 191.

32. Duelfer, *Hide and Seek*, 201; Iraq Survey Group, *Duelfer Report*, 1:61.

33. CRRC SH-PDWN-D-000-409.

34. CRRC SH-SHTP-A-001-441.

35. CRRC SH-SPPC-D-000-304.

Chapter 24: Cold Pitch

1. Jafar and Niaimi, *Last Confession*, chapter nine, as well as an interview and correspondence with Jafar.

2. Jafar and Niaimi, *Last Confession*, chapter nine, and Jafar, interview and correspondence.

3. Jafar and Niaimi, chapter nine, and Jafar, interview and correspondence.

4. Interviews with Rueda and Maguire.

5. CRRC SH-IISX-D-000-088. Note that the qualifying phrase "There is the possibility" added during translation review by Ibrahim Al-Marashi.

6. Interview with Fadhil al-Janabi. After the U.S. invasion, the scientist was detained for eight months.

7. Interviews with Rueda and Maguire. See also Woodward, *Plan of Attack*, 71–73, 107–16.

8. Interviews with Rueda and Maguire.

9. Blix, *Disarming Iraq*, 62.

10. Blix, 44.

11. Jafar and Niaimi, *Last Confession*, chapter nine, and interview with Jafar.

12. Jafar and Niaimi, chapter nine, and an interview with Jafar; Kofi Annan's remark from "'Useful and Frank' U.N.-Iraq Talks End; Next Round Planned within One Month," UN News, May 3, 2002, https://news.un.org/en/story/2002/05/34172-useful-and-frank-un-iraq-talks-end-next-round-planned-within-one-month-annan.

13. Jafar and Niaimi, *Last Confession*, chapter nine, and interview with Jafar.

14. Interview with Rueda. When he led the Iraq Survey Group, Charles Duelfer interviewed Naji Sabri in Qatar in 2004. "He was simply not in a position to have direct access to WMD programs," Duelfer later wrote. "He would not have known about any clandestine, retained WMD." See Duelfer, *Hide and Seek*, 341.

15. Interviews with Maguire and Rueda; DB ROCKSTARS cryptonym from Woodward, *Plan of Attack*, 144. For more on Nahro al-Kasnazan, see Joshua Partlow, David A. Fahrenthold, and Taylor Luck, "A Wealthy Iraqi Sheikh Who Urges a Hard-Line U.S. Approach to Iran Spent 26 Nights at Trump's D.C. Hotel," *Washington Post*, June 6, 2019. Kasnazan acknowledged his work with the C.I.A after 2001.

16. Duelfer, *Hide and Seek*, 235–36, 262.

17. Jane Arraf, "Millions Mark Saddam Hussein's Birthday," CNN, April 28, 2002.

18. Thom Shanker and David E. Sanger, "U.S. Envisions Blueprint on Iraq Including Big Invasion Next Year," *New York Times*, April 28, 2002.

19. "we ought to get ready": CRRC SH-MISC-D-000-780; cabinet meetings from CRRC SH-PDWN-D-000-409.

20. CRRC SH-SPCC-D-000-452.

Chapter 25: Cracked Mirrors

1. Dearlove, Manning, and Tebbit from Chilcot et al., *Chilcot Report*, 2:54–55, 2:60; Straw from Chilcot et al., 2:60–62.

2. "the biggest shift" and "It's worse than you think": Alastair Campbell, *The Burden of Power: Countdown to Iraq*, vol. 4, *The Alastair Campbell Diaries* (London: Hutchinson, 2012), 279.

3. Chilcot et al., *Chilcot Report*, 2:72–75.

4. "regime changers" and "multilateralists": David Manning's testimony to the Iraq Inquiry, November 30, 2009, U.K. National Archives, transcript, http://www.iraqinquiry.org.uk/transcripts/oralevidence-bydate/091130.aspx; Manning's meeting with Bush from Chilcot et al., *Chilcot Report*, 2:82.

5. CRRC SH-MISC-D-000-780. Note that "not Churchill" changed from "no Churchill," in translation review. George Galloway later said that the Iraqi record of the conversation—"Minutes of Galloway's Meeting with the President," not a transcript of a recording—was inaccurate. A parliamentary

committee investigated Galloway's relations with the Iraqi government and the activities of a charity he had created, the Mariam Appeal, which raised money from Iraq and other Arab governments to provide cancer treatment and other aid to the Iraqi population. The parliamentary committee recommended that Galloway be suspended from Parliament for eighteen days. Galloway said that he had never personally benefited from any of the charity's funds. The parliamentary committee, without specifically commenting on Galloway's allegations that the Iraqi record was inaccurate, concluded that the "alleged record of the meeting . . . is authentic." See Select Committee on Standards and Privileges, "Introduction," in *Conduct of Mr. Galloway: Sixth Report of Session 2006–07* (London: House of Commons, 2007), https://publications.parliament.uk/pa/cm200607/cmselect /cmstnprv/909/90903.htm#a7.

6. "insane, criminal": Duelfer, *Hide and Seek*, 206; Taha Yassin Ramadan's duel suggestion from Robert Siegel, "Bush-Hussein Duel Proposed," *All Things Considered*, NPR, October 4, 2002, audio and transcript, https://www.npr.org/templates/story/story.php?storyId=1151149; fishbowl story from CRRC SH-MISC-D-000-780.

7. Brent Scowcroft, "Don't Attack Saddam," *Wall Street Journal*, August 15, 2002, https://www.wsj .com/articles/SB1029371773228069195.

8. Baker, *Days of Fire*, 209.

9. Dick Cheney, "Vice President Speaks at VFW 103rd National Convention," August 26, 2002, White House press release, George W. Bush White House Archives, National Archives, transcript, https:// georgewbush-whitehouse.archives.gov/news/releases/2002/08/20020826.html; Bush asking Rice to handle Cheney from Baker, *Days of Fire*, 211.

10. Chilcot et al., *Chilcot Report*, 2:127–28.

11. Bush, *Decision Points*, 239. Rice's account and other accounts of the National Security Council meeting also quote the president's declaration. Blair from Chilcot et al., *Chilcot Report*, 2:162–68.

12. "coercive diplomacy" and "come clean": Chilcot et al., *Chilcot Report*, 2:160; all other quotations from Manning's testimony to the Iraq Inquiry.

13. Meyer from Chilcot et al., *Chilcot Report*, 2:252.

14. George W. Bush, "President's Remarks at the United Nations General Assembly," September 12, 2002, White House press release, George W. Bush White House Archives, National Archives, transcript and RealMedia webcast, https://georgewbush-whitehouse.archives.gov/news/releases/2002/09 /text/20020912-1.html.

15. Chilcot et al., *Chilcot Report*, 2:209.

16. Chilcot et al., 2:213–15.

17. *Iraq's Weapons of Mass Destruction: The Assessment of the British Government* (London: Stationery Office, 2002), 3; for the excised line in context, see House of Commons Intelligence and Security Committee, *Iraqi Weapons of Mass Destruction—Intelligence and Assessments* (London: Stationery Office, 2003), 26, https://assets.publishing.service.gov.uk/government/uploads/system/uploads/at tachment_data/file/272079/5972.pdf. This report contains the findings of the parliamentary com mittee regarding Blair's misleading dossier.

18. *Iraq's Weapons of Mass Destruction*, 5–6. The reporting about Niger and uranium appears to have originated with an Italian intelligence report passed to the C.I.A. in February 2002. The report included fabricated documents that used stationery stolen from Niger's embassy in Rome. The documents circulated among intelligence agencies until they were revealed as forgeries on the eve of war in 2003. For a well-reported book-length account of the episode, see Peter Eisner and Knut Royce, *The Italian Letter: How the Bush Administration Used a Fake Letter to Build the Case for War in Iraq* (New York: Rodale Books, 2007).

19. George W. Bush, "President Bush Outlines Iraqi Threat," October 7, 2002, Cincinnati, Ohio, White House press release, George W. Bush White House Archives, National Archives, transcript, https:// georgewbush-whitehouse.archives.gov/news/releases/2002/10/20021007-8.html; Bush, "Remarks by the President at Thaddeus McCotter for Congress Dinner," October 14, 2002, Dearborn, Mich., White House press release, George W. Bush White House Archives, National Archives, transcript, https://georgewbush-whitehouse.archives.gov/news/releases/2002/10/20021014-3.html.

20. Director of Central Intelligence, *Iraq's Weapons of Mass Destruction Programs* (Langley, Va.: Central Intelligence Agency, 2002), Document 14 in Jeffrey Richelson, ed., *Iraq and Weapons of Mass Destruction*, National Security Archive Electronic Briefing Book No. 80 (hereafter NSA EBB 80), updated February 11, 2004, https://nsarchive2.gwu.edu/NSAEBB/NSAEBB80/wmd14.pdf; assessment of white paper and NIE from U.S. Senate Select Committee on Intelligence, *Report on the U.S. Intelligence Community's Prewar Intelligence Assessments on Iraq*, S. Rept. 108-301 (Washington, D.C.: Government Printing Office, 2004), 14–15, https://www.intelligence.senate.gov/sites /default/files/publications/108301.pdf (hereafter cited as the *Senate Intelligence Report*).

21. *Senate Intelligence Report*, 55–56.

22. Mobile lab claims from Director of Central Intelligence, "Key Judgments," extract of *Iraq's Continuing Programs for Weapons of Mass Destruction, NIE 2002-16HC* (Langley, Va.: Central Intelligence Agency, 2002), Document 15, NSA EBB 80, https://nsarchive2.gwu.edu/NSAEBB/NSAEBB80/wmd15.pdf; "credible source": *Senate Intelligence Report*, 148; for a thorough and readable book-length account of the Curveball fiasco, see Bob Drogin, *Curveball: Spies, Lies, and the Con Man Who Caused a War* (New York: Random House, 2007).

23. *Senate Intelligence Report*, 18. The report points out that the presumption of Iraqi guilt was "so strong that formalized [intelligence community] mechanisms established to challenge assumptions and 'group think,' such as 'red teams,' 'devil's advocacy,' and other types of alternative or competitive analysis" were not used.

24. "having trouble holding" and "ruthless about its own power": Campbell, *Burden of Power*, 317–18.

25. Straw from Campbell, 316; Chirac, *My Life in Politics*, 265–67; Blair's ground forces offer from Chilcot et al., *Chilcot Report*, 2:329–30.

26. United Nations Security Council Resolution 1441, S/Res/1441, 4644th meeting (2002), https://www.un.org/depts/unmovic/documents/1441.pdf.

27. Chilcot et al., *Chilcot Report*, 2:347.

28. Harrer, *Dismantling the Iraqi Nuclear Programme*, 219, and from an interview with Jafar.

29. CAFCD.

30. Interview and correspondence with Jafar.

31. Blix, *Disarming Iraq*, 101; interview with Blix.

32. Saddam Hussein, "First Interview with Saddam Hussein in 12 Years," interview by Sayyid Nassar, Middle East Media Research Institute, Special Dispatch No. 43, November 4, 2002, https://www.memri.org/reports/first-interview-saddam-hussein-12-years.

33. Chilcot et al., *Chilcot Report*, 3:45–47.

34. Blair and Dearlove remarks from Chilcot et al., 3:52–53. See also 4:311–12.

35. Blix, *Disarming Iraq*, 107; interview with Blix.

36. "neither in a position": Blix, *Disarming Iraq*, 108.

37. Blair and intelligence paper from Chilcot et al., *Chilcot Report*, 3:10–11.

Chapter 26: "Do We Have WMD?"

1. Saddam and Huwaysh from Iraq Survey Group, *Duelfer Report*, 1:59; "something in his hand": Iraq Survey Group, 1:65.

2. Ali Hassan al-Majid's F.B.I. detention interview, January 31, 2004.

3. Iraq Survey Group, *Duelfer Report*, 1:65.

4. Author's interview with Taiee for "Hussein Was Sure of Own Survival," *Washington Post*, November 3, 2003, https://www.washingtonpost.com/archive/politics/2003/11/03/hussein-was-sure-of-own-survival/.

5. Iraq Survey Group, *Duelfer Report*, 1:64.

6. U.S. military deployments by the end of 2002 from Woodward, *Plan of Attack*, 257. See also "Iraq—U.S. Forces Order of Battle, December 2, 2002," GlobalSecurity.org, https://www.globalsecurity.org/military/ops/iraq_orbat_021202.htm. The Pentagon disguised the buildup by embedding forces that would eventually invade within its broader security presence in the region.

7. Iraq Survey Group, *Duelfer Report*, 1:66–67.

8. For a detailed review of professional Iraqi military planning before and after December 2002, see Woods et al., *Iraqi Perspectives Project: A View of Operation Iraqi Freedom*, 75–84.

9. Woods et al., 81–83.

10. "demolish and burn," "cease all internal," and "stolen weapons": CRRC SH-PDWN-D-000-012; "Our enemy will fight," "work in a non-central form," and "signals, animals, bicycles": CRRC SH-BATH-D-000-702; "had specific aims" and "We are on our land": CRRC SH-IZAR-D-000-377.

11. Baker, *Days of Fire*, 239–40; Tenet's recollection from Tenet and Harlow, *At the Center of the Storm*, 360–61; Bush's recollection from Bush, *Decision Points*, 242.

12. Chilcot et al., *Chilcot Report*, 3:75–76.

13. Chilcot et al., 3:88–89.

14. "like issuing a subpoena": Blix, *Disarming Iraq*, 88.

15. Blix, 117.

16. Jafar and Niaimi, *Last Confession*, chapter ten.

17. Obeidi and Pitzer, *Bomb in My Garden*, 10.

18. Jafar and Niaimi, *Last Confession*, chapter ten.
19. Obeidi and Pitzer, *Bomb in My Garden*, 193–94.
20. "The president has made": Rumsfeld, *Known and Unknown*, 450; Bush and Powell from Baker, *Days of Fire*, 241.
21. Draper, *To Start a War*, 272; "loyalty is a trait": ABC, "Colin Powell on Iraq, Race, and Hurricane Relief," ABC News, September 8, 2005.
22. Chirac, *My Life in Politics*, 272–74.
23. Blix, *Disarming Iraq*, 127–28.
24. Chilcot et al., *Chilcot Report*, 3:111–12.
25. Iraq Survey Group, *Duelfer Report*, 1:47–51.
26. Majid, *Les années Saddam*, 14–15.
27. Colin Powell, "Secretary Powell at the U.N.: Iraq's Failure to Disarm," address, February 5, 2003, U.S. Department of State Archive, transcripts, video clips, and presentation slides, https://2001 -2009.state.gov/p/nea/disarm/index.htm. That Powell's remarks reflect embellishments on the material he presented is from Gilbert Cranberg, "Bring Back the Skeptical Press," *Washington Post*, June 29, 2003.
28. February 2003 inspections from Chilcot et al., *Chilcot Report*, 3:124–30; "amazing": Chilcot et al., 3:281; "tended to think": Blix, *Disarming Iraq*, 194.
29. Chilcot et al., *Chilcot Report*, 3:199, 3:201.
30. Chirac, *My Life in Politics*, 276; Bush, *Decision Points*, 245.
31. CRRC SH-IISX-D-001-083.

Chapter 27: The Edge of the Abyss

1. Nizar Hamdoon's cancer diagnosis is from Eric Pace, "Nizar Hamdoon, 59, Former Iraqi Diplomat under Hussein," *New York Times*, August 10, 2003, https://www.nytimes.com/2003/08/10 /world/nizar-hamdoon-59-former-iraqi-diplomat-under-hussein.html; "a personal gift" and "personal trust and knowledge": Nixon, *Debriefing the President*, 152; that Hamdoon moved in with Al-douri from an interview with a former colleague in the New York mission.
2. Interview with Duelfer and Duelfer, *Hide and Seek*, 258, 260.
3. Interview with the participant.
4. Bashir and Sunnanå, *The Insider*, 289.
5. "Sweet and Bitter Years," CRRC SH-MISC-D-001-204.
6. New benefit from CRRC SH-IZAR-D-000-819.
7. CRRC SH-IISX-D-000-442.
8. Robocall from Wendell Steavenson, *The Weight of a Mustard Seed: The Intimate Story of an Iraqi General and His Family during Thirty Years of Tyranny* (New York: Harper Books, 2009), 80.
9. CRRC SH-GMID-D-001-080.
10. Chilcot et al., *Chilcot Report*, 3:332.
11. ElBaradei from Chilcot et al., 3:378; "clearly very irritated" and Bush and Blair from Chilcot et al., 3:409.
12. Campbell, *Burden of Power*, 491–92; Chilcot et al., *Chilcot Report*, 3:446–47, 3:449.
13. Interview with Rueda.
14. Rueda, interview; "had recruited or debriefed": Sam Faddis, *The CIA War in Kurdistan: The Untold Story of the Northern Front in the Iraq War* (Havertown, Pa.: Casemate Publishers, 2020), 81.
15. Faddis, *CIA War in Kurdistan*, 79; phone silence after agent tortured from Woodward, *Plan of Attack*, 337.
16. Interviews with two former C.I.A. officers familiar with the Czech embassy placement.
17. Faddis, *CIA War in Kurdistan*, 143.
18. Faddis, 139, 143; interview with Dave Manners, a former colleague and friend of Charlie Seidel's; "get out of your uniform": interview with Rueda.
19. Duelfer, *Hide and Seek*, 379. The timing of Primakov's visit is confirmed in Chilcot et al., *Chilcot Report*, 3:352–53.
20. Mubarak's visit from Woodward, *Plan of Attack*, 314; Rumsfeld, *Known and Unknown*, 457.
21. Interview with Rueda; Bush, *Decision Points*, 253.
22. George W. Bush, "President Says Saddam Hussein Must Leave Iraq within 48 Hours," March 17, 2003, White House press release, George W. Bush White House Archives, National Archives, transcript and RealMedia webcast, https://georgewbush-whitehouse.archives.gov/infocus/iraq/news/20030317-7 .html; Bush's comments to Blair from Campbell, *Burden of Power*, 510–11.

23. Iraq Survey Group, *Duelfer Report*, 1:66.

24. Money dispersal from Iraq Survey Group, *Duelfer Report*, 1:47; Saddam's verses and reading of Ho Chi Minh's manual from Majid, *Les années Saddam*, 140–41.

25. Majid, 16, 23, 134; interview with Majid.

26. For an analysis of *Get Out, You Damned One!*, see Hassan, "Propaganda Literature." The novel was later translated into Japanese.

27. Tenet and Harlow, *At the Center of the Storm*, 391–92; Woodward, *Plan of Attack*, 373–74; interview with Rueda.

28. Rumsfeld, *Known and Unknown*, 460.

29. Rumsfeld, 460; Cheney from Woodward, *Plan of Attack*, 391. See also Cheney and Cheney, *In My Time*, 399.

Epilogue

1. Interviews and correspondence with Jafar. The physicist had divorced and remarried during the 1980s.

2. Interviews and correspondence with Jafar.

3. Interviews and correspondence with Jafar. The United States soon imprisoned Amer Mohammed Rasheed al-Obeidi. Charles Duelfer had known Rasheed during the 1990s. He considered him a "talented technocrat." By the end of 2004, when it was evident that Rasheed harbored no secrets about Iraq's nonexistent WMD, Duelfer advocated at the White House and before Congress for Rasheed's release from detention. But the U.S. system "was designed to detain people, not release them," Duelfer later wrote, and there was "especially strong resistance from civilian leaders at the Pentagon." So Rasheed "continued to languish in prison on the weakest of rationales." He wasn't released until 2012, after nine years in detention.

4. Interviews and correspondence with Jafar.

5. Interviews and correspondence with Jafar.

6. Interview with Scott McLaughlin.

7. McLaughlin, interview.

8. Pipes, "'Thank You for Everything,'" 33–44.

9. Pipes, 33–44.

10. Interview with Al-Shahristani.

11. Interview with Al-Shahristani, as well as correspondence with Jafar.

12. "Bury the enemy" and war bounties from CRRC SH-MISC-D-000-593; looting order from CRRC SH-IZAR-D-000-819.

13. CRRC SH-IZAR-D-000-368.

14. Agence France-Presse (AFP), "Sunnis Recall Saddam's Parting Words before He Fled Baghdad," Asharq Al-Awsat, December 29, 2007, https://eng-archive.aawsat.com/theaawsat/news-middle-east/sunnis-recall-saddams-parting-words-before-he-fled-baghdad.

15. "I was knowledgeable": "Saddam Adviser Surrenders to US," *Guardian*, April 13, 2003; Saadi's detention and release from an interview with Jafar.

16. Barzan Ibrahim al-Tikriti was convicted of crimes against humanity and hanged on January 15, 2007. Tariq Aziz was convicted of several crimes and sentenced to death in 2010. Diplomats from Europe and elsewhere campaigned for clemency for Aziz. Though he ultimately escaped execution, he was imprisoned for the remainder of his life and often suffered from poor health. In 2015, after having a heart attack and several strokes, he died in an Iraqi hospital at the age of seventy-nine.

17. The movements of Qusay and Uday, including their entry into and expulsion from Syria, come from Michael R. Gordon and Bernard E. Trainor, *Cobra II: The Inside Story of the Invasion and Occupation of Iraq* (New York: Pantheon Books, 2006), 656; the State Department announced the $30 million award payment ($15 million for each of Saddam's sons) on July 31, 2003; Mustafa's death from Julian Borger and Jonathan Steele, "The Last Moments of Saddam's Grandson," *Guardian*, July 23, 2003.

18. Ali Hassan al-Majid was executed for crimes against humanity on January 25, 2010. The charges against him included his role in ordering the gassing deaths at Halabja, Iraq, in 1988.

19. U.S. military casualties through 2009 from "U.S. Casualties in Iraq," GlobalSecurity.org, https://www.globalsecurity.org/military/ops/iraq_casualties.htm.

20. Steve Russell, *We Got Him!: A Memoir of the Hunt and Capture of Saddam Hussein* (New York: Threshold Editions, 2011), 358–65. Russell was a battalion commander in the U.S. Army's 4th Infantry Division who participated in the search for Saddam.

21. Russell, *We Got Him!*, 358–65.
22. Will Bardenwerper, *The Prisoner in His Palace: Saddam Hussein, His American Guards, and What History Leaves Unsaid* (New York: Scribner, 2017), 128. See also Robert Ellis and Marianna Riley, *Caring for Victor: A U.S. Army Nurse and Saddam Hussein* (St. Louis: Reedy Press, 2009), a memoir by a U.S. Army nurse who looked after Saddam during his detention. Other details from Nixon, *Debriefing the President*, 63–64.
23. Nixon, 68–69.
24. Nixon, 64.
25. Quotation from CBS, "Saddam: 'Real Criminal Is Bush,'" CBS News, July 2, 2004.
26. Nehal Bhuta, *Judging Dujail: The First Trial before the Iraqi High Tribunal* (New York: Human Rights Watch, 2006).
27. Iraq Body Count, a nonprofit that tracks the country's civilian casualty toll since the 2003 invasion, reports that 29,526 civilian deaths from violence occurred in 2006; Nouri al-Maliki's quotation is from "No Delay in Saddam Execution, Iraqi PM Says," *Guardian*, December 29, 2006.

Bibliography

Books

Aburish, Saïd K. *Saddam Hussein: The Politics of Revenge*. London: Bloomsbury, 2000.

Albright, Madeleine. *Madam Secretary: A Memoir*. New York: HarperCollins, 2013. First published 2003 by Miramax Books (New York).

Albrisem, Qasim, with David Hetherington. *Flight from Saddam*. Scotts Valley, Calif.: CreateSpace Independent Publishing, 2013.

Ashton, Nigel. *King Hussein of Jordan: A Political Life*. New Haven, Conn.: Yale University Press, 2010.

Ashton, Nigel, and Bryan Gibson, eds. *The Iran-Iraq War: New International Perspectives*. Abingdon, U.K.: Routledge, 2013.

Atkinson, Rick. *Crusade: The Untold Story of the Persian Gulf War*. New York: Houghton Mifflin, 1993.

Baer, Robert. *See No Evil: The True Story of a Ground Soldier in the CIA's War on Terrorism*. New York: Crown, 2003.

Baker, Peter. *Days of Fire: Bush and Cheney in the White House*. New York: Doubleday, 2013.

Baker, Peter, and Susan Glasser. *The Man Who Ran Washington: The Life and Times of James A. Baker III*. New York: Doubleday, 2020.

Bardenwerper, Will. *The Prisoner in His Palace: Saddam Hussein, His American Guards, and What History Leaves Unsaid*. New York: Scribner, 2017.

Bashir, Ala, with Lars Sigurd Sunnanå. *The Insider: Trapped in Saddam's Brutal Regime*. London: Abacus, 2005.

Bengio, Ofra. *Saddam's Word: Political Discourse in Iraq*. Oxford: Oxford University Press, 1998.

Bergman, Ronen. *Rise and Kill First: The Secret History of Israel's Targeted Assassinations*. New York: Random House, 2018.

Blaydes, Lisa. *State of Repression: Iraq under Saddam Hussein*. Princeton, N.J.: Princeton University Press, 2018.

Blight, James G., janet M. Lang, Hussein Banai, Malcolm Byrne, and John Tirman. *Becoming Enemies: U.S.-Iran Relations and the Iran-Iraq War, 1979–1988*. Lanham, Md.: Rowman & Littlefield, 2012.

Blix, Hans. *Disarming Iraq*. New York: Pantheon, 2004.

Boettcher, Robert B., with Gordon L. Freedman. *Gifts of Deceit: Sun Myung Moon, Tongsun Park, and the Korean Scandal*. New York: Holt, Rinehart & Winston, 1980.

Bonin, Richard. *Arrows of the Night: Ahmad Chalabi's Long Journey to Triumph in Iraq*. New York: Doubleday, 2011.

Braut-Hegghammer, Målfrid. *Unclear Physics: Why Iraq and Libya Failed to Build Nuclear Weapons*. Ithaca, N.Y.: Cornell University Press, 2016.

Bush, George H. W., and Brent Scowcroft. *A World Transformed*. New York: Vintage Books, 1998. Kindle.

Bush, George W. *Decision Points*. New York: Crown, 2010.

Butler, Richard. *The Greatest Threat: Iraq, Weapons of Mass Destruction, and the Growing Crisis of Global Security*. New York: PublicAffairs Books, 2001.

Byrne, Malcolm. *Iran-Contra: Reagan's Scandal and the Unchecked Abuse of Presidential Power*. Lawrence, Kans.: University Press of Kansas, 2014.

Campbell, Alastair. *The Burden of Power: Countdown to Iraq*. Vol. 4 of *The Alastair Campbell Diaries*. London: Hutchinson, 2012.

Catto, Henry E., Jr. *Ambassadors at Sea: The High and Low Adventures of a Diplomat*. Austin: University of Texas Press, 1998.

Cheney, Dick, with Liz Cheney. *In My Time: A Personal and Political Memoir*. New York: Threshold Editions, 2011.

Chirac, Jacques. *My Life in Politics*. Translated by Catherine Spencer. New York: St. Martin's Press, 2012.

Cockburn, Andrew, and Patrick Cockburn. *Out of the Ashes: The Resurrection of Saddam Hussein*. New York: HarperCollins, 1999.

Coughlin, Con. *Saddam: King of Terror*. New York: Ecco, 2002.

Draper, Robert. *To Start a War: How the Bush Administration Took America into Iraq*. New York: Penguin Books, 2020.

Drogin, Bob. *Curveball: Spies, Lies, and the Con Man Who Caused a War*. New York: Random House, 2007.

Duelfer, Charles. *Hide and Seek: The Search for Truth in Iraq*. New York: PublicAffairs Books, 2009.

Eisner, Peter, and Knut Royce. *The Italian Letter: How the Bush Administration Used a Fake Letter to Build the Case for War in Iraq*. New York: Rodale Books, 2007.

Ekéus, Rolf. *Between Two Wars: Saddam's Fall and the Birth of ISIS*. Stockholm: Albert Bonniers Förlag, 2018.

Ellis, Robert, with Marianna Riley. *Caring for Victor: A U.S. Army Nurse and Saddam Hussein*. St. Louis: Reedy Press, 2009.

Engel, Jeffrey A., ed. *Into the Desert: Reflections on the Gulf War*. Oxford: Oxford University Press, 2013.

Faddis, Sam. *The CIA War in Kurdistan: The Untold Story of the Northern Front in the Iraq War*. Havertown, Pa.: Casemate Publishers, 2020.

Faust, Aaron M. *The Ba'thification of Iraq: Saddam Hussein's Totalitarianism*. Austin: University of Texas Press, 2015.

Francona, Rick: *Ally to Adversary: An Eyewitness Account of Iraq's Fall from Grace*. Annapolis, Md.: Naval Institute Press, 1999.

Gibson, Bryan R. *Covert Relationship: American Foreign Policy, Intelligence, and the Iran-Iraq War, 1980–1988*. Westport, Conn.: Praeger, 2010.

Gordon, Joy. *Invisible War: The United States and the Iraq Sanctions*. Cambridge, Mass.: Harvard University Press, 2010.

Gordon, Michael R., and Bernard E. Trainor. *Cobra II: The Inside Story of the Invasion and Occupation of Iraq*. New York: Pantheon Books, 2006.

———. *The Generals' War: The Inside Story of the Conflict in the Gulf*. New York: Little, Brown and Company, 1995.

Graham-Brown, Sarah. *Sanctioning Saddam: The Politics of Intervention in Iraq*. London: I. B. Tauris, 1999.

Hardi, Choman. *Gendered Experiences of Genocide: Anfal Survivors in Kurdistan-Iraq*. Farnham, U.K.: Ashgate, 2011.

Halper, Stefan, and Jonathan Clarke. *America Alone: The Neo-Conservatives and the Global Order*. Cambridge: Cambridge University Press, 2004.

Harrer, Gudrun. *Dismantling the Iraqi Nuclear Programme: The Inspections of the International Atomic Energy Agency, 1991–1998*. Abingdon, U.K.: Routledge, 2014.

Hassan, Hamdi A. *The Iraqi Invasion of Kuwait: Religion, Identity and Otherness in the Analysis of War and Conflict*. London: Pluto Press, 1999.

Helfont, Samuel. *Compulsion in Religion: Saddam Hussein, Islam, and the Roots of Insurgencies in Iraq*. Oxford: Oxford University Press, 2018.

———. *Iraq against the World: Saddam, America, and the Post–Cold War Order*. Oxford: Oxford University Press, 2023.

Hiltermann, Joost R. *A Poisonous Affair: America, Iraq, and the Gassing of Halabja*. Cambridge: Cambridge University Press, 2007.

Howell, W. Nathaniel. *Strangers When We Met: A Century of American Community in Kuwait*. Washington, D.C.: New Academia Publishing, 2015.

Hussein, Saddam. *Zabiba and the King*. Edited by Robert Lawrence. College Station, Tex.: VBW Publishing, 2004.

Indyk, Martin. *Innocent Abroad: An Intimate Account of American Peace Diplomacy in the Middle East*. New York: Simon & Schuster, 2009. Kindle.

Iskander, Amir. *Saddam Hussein: The Fighter, the Thinker and the Man.* Paris: Hachette Réalités, 1980.

Jafar, Jafar Dhia, and Numan al-Niaimi. *Al-I'tirāf al-akhīr: Haqīqat al-barnāmaj al-nawawī al-'Irāqī (The Last Confession).* Beirut: Markaz Dirasat al-Wahdah al-Arabiyah, 2005.

Jazrawi, Mazin. *'Ashr Sanawat fi qusur Saddam Hussein (Ten Years in Saddam's Palaces).* London: Dar al-Hikmah, 2005.

Jentleson, Bruce W. *With Friends Like These: Reagan, Bush, and Saddam, 1982–1990.* New York: W. W. Norton & Company, 1994.

Karsh, Efraim, and Inari Rautsi. *Saddam Hussein: A Political Biography.* New York: The Free Press, 1991.

Khadduri, Imad Y. *Iraq's Nuclear Mirage: Memoirs and Delusions.* Toronto: Springhead Publishers, 2003.

Khoury, Dina Rizk. *Iraq in Wartime: Soldiering, Martyrdom, and Remembrance.* Cambridge: Cambridge University Press, 2013.

Levins, John. *Days of Fear: The Inside Story of the Iraqi Invasion and Occupation of Kuwait.* Dubai: Motivate Publishing, 1997.

Long, Jerry M. *Saddam's War of Words: Politics, Religion, and the Iraqi Invasion of Kuwait.* Austin: University of Texas Press, 2004.

Majid, Saman Abdul. *Les années Saddam: Révélations exclusives.* Paris: Fayard, 2003.

Mann, James. *The Great Rift: Dick Cheney, Colin Powell, and the Broken Friendship That Defined an Era.* New York: Henry Holt and Company, 2020.

Al-Marashi, Ibrahim, and Sammy Salama. *Iraq's Armed Forces: An Analytical History.* Abingdon, U.K.: Routledge, 2008.

Marr, Phebe, with Ibrahim Al-Marashi. *The Modern History of Iraq.* 4th ed. Boulder, Colo.: Westview Press, 2017.

Meacham, Jon. *Destiny and Power: The American Odyssey of George Herbert Walker Bush.* New York: Random House, 2015.

Meyer, Jeffrey A., and Mark G. Califano. *Good Intentions Corrupted: The Oil-for-Food Scandal and the Threat to the U.N.* New York: PublicAffairs Books, 2006.

Moore, Fred, comp. *Iraq Speaks: Documents on the Gulf Crisis.* Palo Alto: Fred Moore, 1991.

Morell, Michael. *The Great War of Our Time: The CIA's Fight against Terrorism—from al Qa'ida to ISIS.* New York: Twelve, 2015.

Murray, Williamson, and Kevin M. Woods. *The Iran-Iraq War: A Military and Strategic History.* Cambridge: Cambridge University Press, 2014.

Nixon, John. *Debriefing the President: The Interrogation of Saddam Hussein.* New York: Blue Rider Press, 2016.

Obeidi, Mahdi, and Kurt Pitzer. *The Bomb in My Garden: The Secrets of Saddam's Nuclear Mastermind.* Hoboken, N.J.: John Wiley & Sons, 2004.

Pillar, Paul R. *Intelligence and U.S. Foreign Policy: Iraq, 9/11, and Misguided Reform.* New York: Columbia University Press, 2011.

Pollack, Kenneth M. *The Threatening Storm: The Case for Invading Iraq.* New York: Random House, 2002.

Qadduri, Fakhri. *Hakadha 'araftu al-Bakr wa-Saddam: rihlah 35 'am fi Hizb al-Ba'th (This is how I knew al-Bakr and Saddam, a 35-year journey in the Ba'ath party).* London: Dar al-Hikmah, 2006.

Randal, Jonathan C. *After Such Knowledge, What Forgiveness?: My Encounters with Kurdistan.* New York: Farrar, Straus and Giroux, 1997.

Reagan, Ronald. *The Reagan Diaries.* Edited by Douglas Brinkley. New York: HarperCollins, 2007.

Ritter, Scott. *Iraq Confidential: The Untold Story of the Intelligence Conspiracy to Undermine the UN and Overthrow Saddam Hussein.* New York: Nation Books, 2005.

Roston, Aram. *The Man Who Pushed America to War: The Extraordinary Life, Adventures, and Obsessions of Ahmad Chalabi.* New York: Nation Books, 2008.

Rumsfeld, Donald. *Known and Unknown: A Memoir.* New York: Sentinel, 2011.

Russell, Steve. *We Got Him!: A Memoir of the Hunt and Capture of Saddam Hussein.* New York: Threshold Editions, 2011.

Sada, Georges, with Jim Nelson Black. *Saddam's Secrets: How an Iraqi General Defied and Survived Saddam Hussein.* Brentwood, Tenn.: Integrity Publishers, 2006.

Sarshar, Houman. *Esther's Children: A Portrait of Iranian Jews.* Melrose Park, Pa.: Jewish Publication Society, 2002.

Sassoon, Joseph. *Saddam Hussein's Ba'th Party: Inside an Authoritarian Regime.* Cambridge: Cambridge University Press, 2012.

Schwarzkopf, H. Norman. *It Doesn't Take a Hero: The Autobiography of General H. Norman Schwarzkopf.* New York: Bantam Books, 1992. Kindle.

Selbi, Dhafir, Zuhair Al-Chalabi, and Imad Khadduri. *Unrevealed Milestones in the Iraqi National Nuclear Program, 1981–1991.* Edited by Imad Khadduri. Scotts Valley, Calif.: CreateSpace Independent Publishing, 2011.

Shadid, Anthony. *Night Draws Near: Iraq's People in the Shadow of America's War.* New York: Henry Holt and Company, 2005.

Al-Shahristani, Hussain. *Al-Hurūb ilá al-ḥurrīyah: awrāq min ayyām al-miḥnah 'āshahā al-Duktūr Ḥusayn Shahrastānī fī sujūn niẓām Ṣaddām (Flight to Freedom: Diary of the Ordeal Dr. Hussain Al-Shahristani Suffered in Saddam's Dungeons).* Beirut: Mu'assasat al-Balāgh, 2000.

———. *Free of Fear.* Bloomington, Ind.: AuthorHouse, 2021. Kindle.

Solomon, Lewis D. *Paul D. Wolfowitz: Visionary Intellectual, Policymaker, and Strategist.* Westport, Conn.: Praeger, 2007.

Steavenson, Wendell. *The Weight of a Mustard Seed: The Intimate Story of an Iraqi General and His Family during Thirty Years of Tyranny.* New York: Harper Books, 2009.

Styan, David. *France and Iraq: Oil, Arms and French Policy Making in the Middle East.* London: I. B. Tauris, 2006.

Tenet, George, with Bill Harlow. *At the Center of the Storm: My Years at the CIA.* New York: HarperCollins, 2007.

Trelford, Donald. *Shouting in the Street: Adventures and Misadventures of a Fleet Street Survivor.* London: Biteback Publishing, 2017. Kindle.

Trevan, Tim. *Saddam's Secrets: The Hunt for Iraq's Hidden Weapons.* London: HarperCollins UK, 1999.

Tripp, Charles. *A History of Iraq.* Cambridge: Cambridge University Press, 2007.

———. *The Power and the People: Paths of Resistance in the Middle East.* Cambridge: Cambridge University Press, 2013.

Von Sponeck, Hans-Christof. "The Politics of the Sanctions on Iraq and the U.N. Humanitarian Exception," in *Land of Blue Helmets: The United Nations and the Arab World*, ed. Karim Makdisi and Vijay Prashad. Berkeley: University of California Press, 2016.

Wilson, Joseph. *The Politics of Truth: Inside the Lies That Led to War and Betrayed My Wife's CIA Identity.* New York: Carroll & Graf Publishers, 2004.

Woods, Kevin M. *The Mother of All Battles: Saddam Hussein's Strategic Plan for the Persian Gulf War.* Annapolis, Md.: Naval Institute Press, 2008.

Woods, Kevin M., David D. Palkki, and Mark E. Stout, eds. *The Saddam Tapes: The Inner Workings of a Tyrant's Regime, 1978–2001.* Cambridge: Cambridge University Press, 2011.

Woodward, Bob. *Plan of Attack: The Definitive Account of the Decision to Invade Iraq.* New York: Simon & Schuster, 2004.

Journal Articles, Reports, and Manuscripts

Albright, David. "Iraq's Programs to Make Highly Enriched Uranium and Plutonium for Nuclear Weapons Prior to the Gulf War." Institute for Science and International Security, 1997, revised October 2002. https://www.isis-online.org/publications/iraq/iraqs_fm_history.html.

Albright, David, Corey Gay, and Khidhir Hamza. "Development of the Al-Tuwaitha Site: What If the Public or the IAEA Had Overhead Imagery?" Institute for Science and International Security, April 26, 1999. https://www.isis-online.org/publications/iraq/tuwaitha.html.

Amnesty International. *Iraq: Human Rights Violations since the Uprising.* MDE 14/05/91. London: Amnesty International, 1991. https://www.amnesty.org/en/documents/mde14/005/1991/en/.

Bhuta, Nehal. *Judging Dujail: The First Trial before the Iraqi High Tribunal.* New York: Human Rights Watch, 2006.

Brands, Hal, and David Palkki. "Why Did Saddam Want the Bomb? The Israel Factor and the Iraqi Nuclear Program." *Foreign Policy Research Institute E-Notes*, August 2011.

Braut-Hegghammer, Målfrid. "Cheater's Dilemma: Iraq, Weapons of Mass Destruction, and the Path to War." *International Security* 45, no. 1 (Summer 2020): 51–89.

Chilcot, John, Lawrence Freedman, Roderic Lyne, and Usha Prashar. *The Report of the Iraq Inquiry.* 12 vols. London: Stationery Office, 2016. https://www.gov.uk/government/publications/the-report-of-the-iraq-inquiry.

Davis, Jay C., and David A. Kay. "Iraq's Secret Nuclear Weapons Program." *Physics Today* 45, no. 7 (July 1992): 21–27.

Dillon, Garry B. "The IAEA in Iraq: Past Activities and Findings." *IAEA Bulletin* 44, no. 2 (June 2002): 13–16. First published by the Carnegie Endowment for International Peace.

Divine, Robert A. "The Persian Gulf War Revisited: Tactical Victory, Strategic Failure." Review of *My American Journey*, by Colin L. Powell, with Joseph E. Persico; *It Doesn't Take a Hero*, by H. Norman

Schwarzkopf; *A World Transformed*, by George H. W. Bush and Brent Scowcroft; and *The Generals' War*, by Michael R. Gordon and Bernard E. Trainor. *Diplomatic History* 24, no. 1 (Winter 2000): 129–38.

Goldman, Robert K. *The Bombing of Iraqi Cities*. New York: Human Rights Watch, 1991.

Al-Hassan, Hawraa. "Propaganda Literature in Ba'thist Cultural Production (1979–2003): The Novels of Saddam Hussein as a Case Study." Ph.D. thesis, University of Cambridge, 2014.

Hiltermann, Joost. "The Demise of Operation Provide Comfort." *Middle East Report* no. 203 (Summer 1997).

House of Commons Intelligence and Security Committee. *Iraqi Weapons of Mass Destruction— Intelligence and Assessments*. London: Stationery Office, 2003. https://assets.publishing.service.gov .uk/government/uploads/system/uploads/attachment_data/file/272079/5972.pdf.

Human Rights Watch. *Endless Torment: The 1991 Uprising in Iraq and Its Aftermath*. New York: Human Rights Watch, 1992.

———. *The Iraqi Government Assault on the Marsh Arabs*. Washington, D.C.: Human Rights Watch, 2003.

International Crisis Group. *Shiite Politics in Iraq: The Role of the Supreme Council*. Middle East Report No. 70. Brussels: International Crisis Group, 2007.

Iraq Survey Group. *Comprehensive Report of the Special Advisor to the Director of Central Intelligence on Iraq's WMD*. 3 vols. Rev. ed. Washington, D.C.: Government Printing Office, 2005.

Kadhim, Abbas. *The Hawza Under Siege: A Study in the Baath Party Archive*. Occasional Paper No. 1. Boston: Boston University Institute for Iraqi Studies, 2013.

Keaney, Thomas A., and Eliot A. Cohen. *Gulf War Air Power Survey: Summary Report*. 5 vols. Washington, D.C.: U.S. Government Printing Office, 1993. https://media.defense.gov/2010/Sep/27/20013 29801/-1/-1/0/AFD-100927-061.pdf.

Koblentz, Gregory D. "Saddam versus the Inspectors: The Impact of Regime Security on the Verification of Iraq's WMD Disarmament." *Journal of Strategic Studies* 41, no. 3 (April 2018): 372–409.

Al-Marashi, Ibrahim. "The Nineteenth Province: The Invasion of Kuwait and the 1991 Gulf War from the Iraqi Perspective." Ph.D. thesis, St. Antony's College, University of Oxford, 2004.

Middle East Watch. *Genocide in Iraq: The Anfal Campaign against the Kurds*. New York: Human Rights Watch, 1993.

Pipes, Daniel. "'Thank You for Everything. But Do Not Stay': An Exchange with the Late Nizar Hamdoon." *Middle East Quarterly* 10, no. 4 (Fall 2003): 33–44.

Russell, Richard L. "Iraq's Chemical Weapons Legacy: What Others Might Learn from Saddam." *Middle East Journal* 59, no. 2 (Spring 2005): 187–208.

Tower, John, Edmund Muskie, and Brent Scowcroft. *The Tower Commission Report: The Full Text of the President's Special Review Board*. New York: Bantam Books, 1987.

U.S. Central Command. *Formal Investigation into the Circumstances Surrounding the Attack on the USS Stark (FFG-31) on 17 May 1987*. Washington, D.C.: Department of Defense, 1987.

U.S. Senate Select Committee on Intelligence. *Report on the U.S. Intelligence Community's Prewar Intelligence Assessments on Iraq*. S. Rept. 108-301. Washington, D.C.: Government Printing Office, 2004. https://www.intelligence.senate.gov/sites/default/files/publications/108301.pdf.

Wolfe-Hunnicutt, Brandon. "Embracing Regime Change in Iraq: American Foreign Policy and the 1963 Coup d'état in Baghdad." *Diplomatic History* 39, no. 1 (January 2015): 98–125.

Woods, Kevin M., David D. Palkki, and Mark E. Stout, with Jessica M. Huckabey and Elizabeth A. Nathan. *A Survey of Saddam's Audio Files 1978–2001: Toward an Understanding of Authoritarian Regimes*. Paper P-4548. Alexandria, Va.: Institute for Defense Analyses, 2010.

Woods, Kevin M., with James Lacey. *Iraqi Perspectives Project: Saddam and Terrorism: Emerging Insights from Captured Iraqi Documents*. Paper P-4287. 5 vols. Alexandria, Va.: Institute for Defense Analyses, 2007.

Woods, Kevin M., with Michael R. Pease, Mark E. Stout, Williamson Murray, and James G. Lacey. *Iraqi Perspectives Project: A View of Operation Iraqi Freedom from Saddam's Senior Leadership*. Norfolk, Va.: Joint Center for Operational Analysis, U.S. Joint Forces Command, 2006.

Woods, Kevin M., with Stanley A. Riveles, Ana Venegas, Mary Hawkins, Erica Leinmiller, Will Quinn, and Julie Stabile, *Coercion: The United States and Iraq, 1991–2003*, Paper P-5281. Alexandria, Va.: Institute for Defense Analyses, 2015.

Zilinskas, Raymond A. "Iraq's Biological Weapons: The Past as Future?" *Journal of the American Medical Association* 278, no. 5 (1997): 418–24.

Documents and Oral Histories

Aid, Matthew M., ed. *U.S. Intelligence on the Middle East, 1945–2009*. BrillOnline Primary Sources. Accessed through the Library of Congress, Washington, D.C.

Battle, Joyce, ed. *Shaking Hands with Saddam Hussein: The U.S. Tilts toward Iraq, 1980–1984*. National Security Archive Electronic Briefing Book No. 82. February 25, 2003. https://nsarchive2.gwu.edu/NSAEBB/NSAEBB82/.

Byrne, Malcolm, comp. *Saddam Hussein: More Secret History*. National Security Archive Electronic Briefing Book No. 107. December 18, 2003. https://nsarchive2.gwu.edu/NSAEBB/NSAEBB107/.

Byrne, Malcolm, ed. *U.S.-Iran: Lessons from an Earlier War*. National Security Archive Electronic Briefing Book No. 394. December 18, 2003. https://nsarchive2.gwu.edu/NSAEBB/NSAEBB394/.

Currently Accurate, Full, and Complete Declaration of the Past Iraqi Nuclear Program, submitted by Iraq to the U.N. on December 3, 2002.

F.B.I. detention interview records for Saddam Hussein, Ali Hassan al-Majid, and Tariq Aziz. The Vault, FOIA Library, Federal Bureau of Investigation, Washington, D.C.

Foreign Affairs Oral History Collection of the Association for Diplomatic Studies and Training, Arlington, Va. Accessed through the Library of Congress, Washington, D.C.

George H. W. Bush Presidential Library, Texas A&M University, College Station, Tex.

Harmony database. United States Department of Defense, Arlington, Va. https://ctc.westpoint.edu/harmony-program/.

Presidential Oral Histories. Miller Center, University of Virginia, Charlottesville, Va.

Regime Crimes Liaison Office records (select). United States Department of Justice, Washington, D.C.

Richelson, Jeffrey, ed. *Iraq and Weapons of Mass Destruction*. National Security Archive Electronic Briefing Book No. 80. February 11, 2004. https://nsarchive2.gwu.edu/NSAEBB/NSAEBB80/.

Robert and Elizabeth Dole Archive and Special Collections. Robert J. Dole Institute of Politics, University of Kansas, Lawrence, Kans.

Ronald Reagan Presidential Library, Simi Valley, Calif.

Saddam Hussein Regime Collection. Conflict Records Research Center (CRRC), National Defense University, Washington, D.C.

State Department cables, 2003–2010. WikiLeaks Public Library of U.S. Diplomacy (PlusD). https://wikileaks.org/plusd/.

Targeting Iraq, Part 1: Planning, Invasion, and Occupation, 1997–2004. Digital National Security Archive. https://proquest.libguides.com/dnsa/iraq97.

William J. Clinton Presidential Library, Little Rock, Ark.

Index